INTERGROUP
RELATIONS

Key Readings in Social Psychology

General Editor: ARIE W. KRUGLANSKI, University of Maryland at College Park

The aim of this series is to make available to senior undergraduate and graduate students key articles in each area of social psychology in an attractive, user-friendly format. Many professors want to encourage their students to engage directly with research in their fields, yet this can often be daunting for students coming to detailed study of a topic for the first time. Moreover, declining library budgets mean that articles are not always readily available, and course packs can be expensive and time-consuming to produce. **Key Readings in Social Psychology** aims to address this need by providing comprehensive volumes, each one of which will be edited by a senior and active researcher in the field. Articles will be carefully chosen to illustrate the way the field has developed historically as well as current issues and research directions. Each volume will have a similar structure, which will include:

- an overview chapter, as well as introductions to sections and articles,
- questions for class discussion,
- annotated bibliographies,
- full author and subject indexes.

Published Titles

The Self in Social Psychology	Roy F. Baumeister
Stereotypes and Prejudice	Charles Stangor
Motivational Science	E. Tory Higgins and Arie W. Kruglanski
Emotions in Social Psychology	W. Gerrod Parrott
Social Psychology and Human Sexuality	Roy F. Baumeister

Titles in Preparation

Social Psychology	Arie W. Kruglanski and E. Tory Higgins
Social Cognition	David Hamilton
Close Relationships	Harry Reis and Caryl Rusbult
Group Processes	John Levine and Richard Moreland
Language and Communication	Gün R. Semin
Attitudes and Persuasion	Richard E. Petty, Shelly Chaiken, and Russell Fazio
The Social Psychology of Culture	Hazel Markus and Shinobu Kitayama
The Social Psychology of Health	Peter Salovey and Alexander J. Rothman

INTERGROUP RELATIONS
Essential Readings

Edited by

Michael A. Hogg
University of Queensland,
Brisbane, Australia

Dominic Abrams
University of Kent,
Canterbury, United Kingdom

USA	Publishing Office:	PSYCHOLOGY PRESS
		A member of the Taylor & Francis Group
		325 Chestnut Street
		Philadelphia, PA 19106
		Tel: (215) 625-8900
		Fax: (215) 625-2940
	Distribution Center:	PSYCHOLOGY PRESS
		A member of the Taylor & Francis Group
		7625 Empire Drive
		Florence, KY 41042
		Tel: 1-800-624-7064
		Fax: 1-800-248-4724
UK		PSYCHOLOGY PRESS
		A member of the Taylor & Francis Group
		27 Church Road
		Hove
		E. Sussex, BN3 2FA
		Tel: +44 (0)1273 207411
		Fax: +44 (0)1273 205612

INTERGROUP RELATIONS: Essential Readings

1 2 3 4 5 6 7 8 9 0

Printed by Edwards Brothers, Ann Arbor, MI, 2001.
Cover design by Ellen Seguin.

A CIP catalog record for this book is available from the British Library.
∞ The paper in this publication meets the requirements of the ANSI Standard Z39.48-1984 (Permanence of Paper).

Library of Congress Cataloging-in-Publication Data

Intergroup relations : essential readings / edited by Michael A. Hogg, Dominic Abrams.
    p. cm. — (Key readings in social psychology)
   Includes bibliographical references and index.
   ISBN 0-86377-678-7 (alk. paper) — ISBN 0-86377-679-5 (pbk. : alk. paper)
   1. Intergroup relations. 2. Social groups. 3. Social psychology. I. Hogg, Michael A.,
1954- II. Abrams, Dominic, 1958- III. Series.

HM716 .I58 2001
302.3—dc21

00-065312

ISBN: 0-86377-678-7 (case)
ISBN: 0-86377-679-5 (paper)

Contents

About the Editors   ix
Preface   xi
Acknowledgments   xiii

Intergroup Relations: An Overview   1
Michael A. Hogg and Dominic Abrams

PART 1
Personality and Individual Differences   15

READING 1
Personality and Sociocultural Factors in Intergroup Attitudes:
A Cross-National Comparison   18
Thomas F. Pettigrew

READING 2
Social Dominance Orientation: A Personality Variable
Predicting Social and Political Attitudes   30
Felicia Pratto, Jim Sidanius, Lisa M. Stallworth, and Bertram F. Malle

PART 2
Goal Relations and Interdependence   61

READING 3
Superordinate Goals in the Reduction of Intergroup Conflict   64
Muzafer Sherif

v

READING 4

Perceptions of Racial Group Competition: Extending Blumer's Theory of Group Position to a Multiracial Social Context   71

Lawrence Bobo and Vincent L. Hutchings

P A R T   3

Social Identity and Self-Categorization   91

READING 5

An Integrative Theory of Intergroup Conflict   94

Henri Tajfel and John Turner

READING 6

Intergroup Relations and Group Solidarity: Effects of Group Identification and Social Beliefs on Depersonalized Attraction   110

Michael A. Hogg and Sarah C. Hains

P A R T   4

Intergroup Attitudes and Explanations   129

READING 7

Social Stereotypes and Social Groups   132

Henri Tajfel

READING 8

Affirmative Action, Unintentional Racial Biases, and Intergroup Relations   146

John F. Dovidio and Samuel L. Gaertner

READING 9

The Ultimate Attribution Error: Extending Allport's Cognitive Analysis of Prejudice   162

Thomas F. Pettigrew

P A R T   5

Intergroup Behavior and Discrimination   175

READING 10

Experiments in Intergroup Discrimination   178

Henri Tajfel

READING 11

Intergroup Discrimination in Positive and Negative Outcome Allocations: Impact of Stimulus Valence, Relative Group Status, and Relative Group Size   188

Sabine Otten, Amélie Mummendey, and Mathias Blanz

READING 12

Understanding Why the Justice of Group Procedures Matters: A Test of the Psychological Dynamics of the Group-Value Model   205

Tom Tyler, Peter Degoey, and Heather Smith

PART 6

Motives for Group Membership and Intergroup Behavior   229

READING 13

Comments on the Motivational Status of Self-Esteem in Social Identity and Intergroup Discrimination   232

Dominic Abrams and Michael A. Hogg

READING 14

The Social Self: On Being the Same and Different at the Same Time   245

Marilynn B. Brewer

READING 15

Negotiating Social Identity When Contexts Change: Maintaining Identification and Responding to Threat   254

Kathleen A. Ethier and Kay Deaux

PART 7

Influence in Intergroup Context   267

READING 16

Knowing What to Think by Knowing Who You Are: Self-Categorization and the Nature of Norm Formation, Conformity and Group Polarization   270

Dominic Abrams, Margaret Wetherell, Sandra Cochrane, Michael A. Hogg, and John C. Turner

READING 17

Studies in Social Influence: Minority Influence and Conversion Behavior in a Perceptual Task   289

Serge Moscovici and Bernard Personnaz

PART 8
Disadvantage, Relative Deprivation, and Social Protest   299

READING 18
The St. Pauls' Riot: An Explanation of the Limits of Crowd
Action in Terms of a Social Identity Model   302
Stephen D. Reicher

READING 19
Race and Relative Deprivation in the Urban United States   316
Reeve D. Vanneman and Thomas F. Pettigrew

READING 20
Responding to Membership in a Disadvantaged Group:
From Acceptance to Collective Protest   337
Stephen C. Wright, Donald M. Taylor, and Fathali M. Moghaddam

PART 9
Intergroup Contact and Social Harmony   353

READING 21
Reducing Intergroup Bias: The Benefits of Recategorization   356
Samuel L. Gaertner, Jeffrey Mann, Audrey Murrell, and John F. Dovidio

READING 22
Intergroup Contact: The Typical Member and
the Exception to the Rule   370
David A. Wilder

READING 23
Dimensions of Contact as Predictors of Intergroup Anxiety,
Perceived Out-Group Variability, and Out-Group Attitude:
An Integrative Model   383
Mir Rabiul Islam and Miles Hewstone

References   397

Appendix: How to Read a Journal Article in Social Psychology   403
Christian H. Jordan and Mark P. Zanna

Author Index   413
Subject Index   427

About the Editors

Michael A. Hogg is Professor of Social Psychology and Director of the Centre for Research on Group Processes at the University of Queensland. He is also Director of Research for the Faculty of Social and Behavioural Sciences and is a Fellow of the Academy of the Social Sciences in Australia. His research interests are in group processes, intergroup relations, collective self-conception, and social identity and self-categorization processes. He has published 15 books and over 140 research articles, chapters, and other scholarly works. He is founding editor, with Dominic Abrams, of the journal *Group Processes and Intergroup Relations*.

Dominic Abrams is Professor of Social Psychology and Director of the Centre for the Study of Group Processes at the University of Kent at Canterbury. He is currently Secretary of the European Association of Experimental Social Psychology and Chair of the Committee of Learned Societies in the UK Academy for Learned Societies in the Social Sciences. His research interests are in social identity, intergroup relations, the self-concept, and collective behavior. He has published four books and over 100 articles and chapters. He is founding editor, with Michael Hogg, of the journal *Group Processes and Intergroup Relations*, and also edits the *European Bulletin of Social Psychology*.

Preface

The study of intergroup relations is a critical topic for humanity. It seeks to understand the causes of conflict and hatred between groups, and how this can be transformed into cooperation and harmony. These are the big questions for society. They are also core questions for social psychology, because although group conflict and cooperation have socio-historical origins, it is individual human beings who are prejudiced and discriminate or who interact harmoniously. The social psychological explication of intergroup relations requires a careful articulation of individual and social processes.

Intergroup relations has also been the core focus of our own research for almost 20 years, so we were absolutely delighted to be invited by Arie Kruglanski to prepare this volume. We started surveying the field at the start of 1998, when Michael Hogg was spending a year as visiting professor of social psychology at Princeton University. We were able to meet to flesh out ideas in Lexington in October, 1998 at the annual meeting of the Society of Experimental Social Psychology, and in Oxford, UK in July, 1999 at the meeting of the European Association of Experimental Social Psychology. The outline was shaped up by e-mail between Brisbane, Australia and Canterbury, UK and finalized at a meeting in Canterbury in March, 2000.

Intergroup relations is a huge topic, and so we turned to our colleagues and students to get a feel for what people felt were the main areas and key readings. We pestered people by e-mail, by phone, in corridors, and at conferences. We would like to acknowledge our debt to all those people who gave us advice and suggestions: Richard Bourhis, Nyla Branscombe, Richard Clément, Gerald Clore,

Joseph Forgas, Sam Gaertner, Howard Giles, Steve Hinkle, Brenda Major, Sabine Otten, Felicia Pratto, Anthony Pratkanis, Stephen Reicher, Sheldon Solomon, Peggy Thoits, Daan van Knippenberg, Mark Zanna, and Lucy Zinkiewicz. Particular thanks go to Rupert Brown, Jack Dovidio, Vicki Esses, and Daan van Knippenberg, whose comments on a late outline were influential in our final decisions, to Lucy Zinkiewicz, who gave extraordinarily detailed and very helpful feedback on many versions, and to Kelly Fielding, who did most of the assembly work in Brisbane.

A very special thanks goes to Alison Mudditt, our editor at Psychology Press in Philadelphia. As ever, Alison was a fount of knowledge about social psychology, a paragon of efficiency, and a wise and patient guiding spirit to keep us on track.

Of course, despite all this help and advice, we are ultimately responsible for the final product, which we sincerely hope you enjoy.

Michael A. Hogg and Dominic Abrams
Brisbane and Canterbury
September, 2000

Acknowledgments

The Authors and Publishers are grateful to the following for permission to reproduce the articles in this book:

Reading 1: T. Pettigrew, Personality and sociocultural factors in intergroup attitudes: a cross-national comparison. *Journal of Conflict Resolution, 2,* 29–42. Copyright © 1958 by Sage Publications. Reprinted with permission.

Reading 2: F. Pratto, J. Sidanius, L. Stallworth, & B. Malle, Social dominance orientation: a personality variable predicting social and political attitudes. *Journal of Personality and Social Psychology, 67,* 741–763. Copyright © 1994 by the American Psychological Association. Reprinted with permission.

Reading 3: M. Sherif, Superordinate goals in the reduction of intergroup conflicts. *American Journal of Sociology, 63,* 349–356. Copyright © 1958 by the University of Chicago Press. Reprinted with permission.

Reading 4: L. Bobo and V. Hutchings, Perceptions of racial group competition: extending Blumer's theory of group position to a multiracial social context. *American Sociological Review, 61,* 951–972. Copyright © 1996 by the American Sociological Association. Reprinted with permission.

Reading 5: H. Tajfel and J. Turner, An integrative theory of intergroup conflict. In W. G. Austin & S. Worchel (Eds.), *The Social Psychology of Intergroup Relations,* 33–47. Monterey, CA: Brooks/Cole (1979). Reprinted with permission.

Reading 6: M. Hogg and S. Hains, Intergroup relations and group solidarity: effects of group identification and social beliefs on depersonalized attraction. *Journal of Personality and Social Psychology, 70,* 295–309. Copyright © 1996 by the American Psychological Association. Reprinted with permission.

Reading 7: H. Tajfel, Social stereotypes and social groups. In J. C. Turner & H. Giles (Eds.), *Intergroup Behavior,* 144–167. Oxford, UK: Blackwell. Copyright © 1981 by Blackwell Publishers, Ltd. Reprinted with permission.

Reading 8: J. Dovidio and S. Gaertner, Affirmative action, unintentional racial biases, and intergroup relations. *Journal of Social Issues, 52* (4), 51–75. Copyright © 1996 by Blackwell Publishers, Ltd. Reprinted with permission.

Reading 9: T. Pettigrew, The ultimate attribution error: extending Allport's cognitive analysis of prejudice. *Personality and Social Psychology Bulletin, 5,* 461–476. Copyright © 1979 by Sage Publications. Reprinted with permission.

Reading 10: H. Tajfel, Experiments in intergroup discrimination. *Scientific American, 223,* 96–102. Copyright © 1970 by Scientific American. Reprinted with permission.

Reading 11: S. Otten, A. Mummendey, & M. Blanz, Intergroup discrimination in positive and negative outcome allocations: impact of stimulus valence, relative group status, and relative group size. *Personality and Social Psychology Bulletin, 22,* 568–581. Copyright © 1996 by Sage Publications. Reprinted with permission.

Reading 12: T. Tyler, P. DeGoey, & H. Smith,

Understanding why the justice of group procedures matters: a test of the psychological dynamics of the group-value model. *Journal of Personality and Social Psychology, 70,* 913–930. Copyright © 1996 by the American Psychological Association. Reprinted with permission.

Reading 13: D. Abrams and M. Hogg, Comments on the motivational status of self-esteem in social identity and intergroup discrimination. *European Journal of Social Psychology, 18,* 317–334. Copyright © 1988 by John Wiley & Sons, Inc. Reprinted with permission.

Reading 14: M. Brewer, The social self: on being the same and different at the same time. *Personality and Social Psychology Bulletin, 17,* 475–482. Copyright © 1991 by Sage Publications. Reprinted with permission.

Reading 15: K. Ethier & K. Deaux, Negotiating social identity when contexts change: maintaining identification and responding to threat. *Journal of Personality and Social Psychology, 67,* 243–251. Copyright © 1994 by the American Psychological Association. Reprinted with permission.

Reading 16: D. Abrams, M. Wetherell, S. Cochrane, M. Hogg, & J. Turner, Knowing what to think by knowing who you are: self-categorization and the nature of norm formation, conformity, and group polarization. *British Journal of Social Psychology, 29,* 97–119. Copyright © 1990 by the British Psychological Society. Reprinted with permission.

Reading 17: S. Moscovici and B. Personnaz, Studies in social influence: V. minority influence and conversion behavior in a perceptual task. *Journal of Experimental Social Psychology, 16,* 270–282.

Copyright © 1980 by Academic Press. Reprinted with permission.

Reading 18: S. Reicher, The St. Pauls riot: an explanation of the limits of crowd action in terms of a social identity model. *European Journal of Social Psychology, 14,* 1-21. Copyright © 1984 by John Wiley & Sons, Inc. Reprinted with permission.

Reading 19: R. Vanneman and T. Pettigrew, (1972). Race and relative deprivation in the urban United States. *Race, 13,* 461–486. Reprinted with permission.

Reading 20: S. Wright, D. Taylor, & F. Moghaddam, Responding to membership in a disadvantaged group. *Journal of Personality and Social Psychology, 58,* 994–1003. Copyright © 1990 by the American Psychological Association. Reprinted with permission.

Reading 21: S. Gaertner, J. Mann, A. Murrell, & J. Dovidio, Reducing intergroup bias: the benefits of recategorization. *Journal of Personality and Social Psychology, 57,* 239–249. Copyright © 1989 by the American Psychological Association. Reprinted with permission.

Reading 22: D. Wilder, Intergroup contact: the typical member and the exception to the rule. *Journal of Experimental Social Psychology, 20,* 177–194. Copyright © 1984 by Academic Press. Reprinted with permission.

Reading 23: M. Islam and M. Hewstone, Dimensions of contact as predictors of intergroup anxiety, perceived outgroup variability, and outgroup attitude: an integrative model. *Personality and Social Psychology Bulletin, 19,* 700–710. Copyright © 1993 by Sage Publications. Reprinted with permission.

Intergroup Relations: An Overview

Michael A. Hogg
Dominic Abrams

This book is about the way in which people in groups perceive, think about, feel about, and act towards people in other groups. The sort of groups we have in mind can be small groups such as work teams or divisions in an organization, larger interactive groups such as sports teams or entire departments, large and more dispersed groups such as stamp collectors and train spotters, or very large social categories such as ethnic groups, racial groups, national groups, and religions. The sorts of behaviors that are encompassed range from relatively harmless competition between teams to stereotyping, disadvantage, oppression, war, and genocide. The social psychological study of intergroup relations seeks to understand the psychological dimension of these phenomena.

Because intergroup relations, by definition, require there to be groups that relate to one another, a key issue is how first to define a group in psychological terms. There is no one answer to this fundamental question. Different researchers adopt different perspectives, some focusing on interaction among people and others on collective self-definition. Depending on the perspective adopted, the approach to the explanation of intergroup relations can be vastly different. In addition, because the study of intergroup relations deals with some of the most harmful and distressing aspects of the human condition, the field of research is extensive and wide-ranging, which makes the job of condensing the topic into one volume very challenging.

The aim of this volume is to introduce you to the study of intergroup relations through the eyes of some leading scholars, some key readings, and some intriguing debates and phenomena. Another way to look at this is that we have chosen a set of readings as stepping stones to guide us through an enormous area of research on a central topic of social psychology. As a whole we have tried to select empirical readings, because they not only provide conceptual analyses, but describe the methods used and show the sort of data that are marshaled in support of theory. This introductory chapter gives a short, and by necessity selective, overview of the field of intergroup relations. It is organized so as to correspond to the organization of the readings and structure of the book as a whole.

It is customary to define a topic before embarking on its exploration. However, as noted above, the definition of intergroup relations is problematic because the definition of "group" itself, upon which it rests, is also problematic. Nevertheless, the definition we like is a classic and relatively widely accepted definition provided by Sherif:

> Intergroup relations refer to relations between two or more groups and their respective members. Whenever individuals belonging to one group interact, collectively or individually, with another group or its members in terms of their group identifications we have an instance of intergroup behavior. (Sherif, 1962, p. 5)

1

Early Perspectives on Groups and Intergroup Relations

At the end of the 19th century and early in the 20th century the forebears and progenitors of social psychology (e.g., Durkheim, 1898; LeBon, 1908; Mead, 1934; Wundt, 1916; also see Farr, 1996; Hogg & Williams, 2000) believed that what delineated a distinct scientific role for the new discipline of social psychology was a focus on collective phenomena such as culture, myth, religion, the crowd, society, and the relations among groups and categories in society. The study of individuals was the province of experimental psychology; the study of collective phenomena the province of social psychology. By the early 1920s, however, Watson's (1919) behaviorist agenda for psychology to be a science of behavior rather than mind had prevailed, so that Floyd Allport was able to conclude that "There is no psychology of groups which is not essentially and entirely a psychology of individuals" (Allport, 1924, p. 4).

So, almost right from the outset there were two approaches to the study of intergroup relations—one which focused on the formation and effects of collective representations, and one which reduced intergroup relations into individual processes and interpersonal interaction. The latter has tended to prevail, although, as we shall see, the former has likely made a more significant cumulative contribution to our understanding of intergroup relations, probably because it is better suited to the explanation of large scale social phenomena such as intergroup conflict, social harmony among groups, and so forth.

Individual Personality

Intergroup behavior tends to be competitive and ethnocentric. In intergroup contexts people generally seem to behave in ways that are aimed at gaining or maintaining a relative advantage for their group over other groups in terms of resources, status, prestige, and so forth (e.g., Brewer & Campbell, 1976). Sumner put it beautifully when he described ethnocentrism as:

> a view of things in which one's own group is the center of everything, and all others are scaled and rated with reference to it . . . Each group nourishes its own pride and vanity, boasts itself superior, exalts its own divinities, and looks with contempt on outsiders. Each group thinks its own folkways the only right one . . . Ethnocentrism leads a people to exaggerate and intensify everything in their own folkways which is peculiar and which differentiates them from others. (Sumner, 1906, p. 13)

Taken to an extreme, this constellation of behaviors describes prejudice, discrimination, intolerance, and conflict between groups. Many theories of intergroup relations have, not surprisingly, focused on this extreme form of intergroup behavior. Because the behavior is extreme and destructive, social psychologists have wondered whether there may be something "wrong" with people who behave in this way. Perhaps these people have dysfunctional personalities, perhaps innate or tied to early childhood experiences, that predispose them to be extremely ethnocentric and intolerant. This perspective has spawned one of social psychology's major theories of prejudice and intergroup conflict—Adorno, Frenkel-Brunswik, Levinson, and Sanford's (1950) authoritarian personality syndrome (also see, Titus & Hollander, 1957).

Adorno and colleagues adopted a psychodynamic framework to argue that early childhood rearing practices that are harsh, disciplinarian, and emotionally manipulative produce people who are obsessed by status and authority, intolerant of ambiguity and uncertainty, and hostile and aggressive toward weaker others. These people have an authoritarian personality that predisposes them to extreme forms of intergroup behavior. Research on the authoritarian personality does tend to confirm the existence of such a syndrome, but does not provide good evidence for its origins in early child rearing or for its relationship to prejudice and discrimination (Billig, 1976; Pettigrew, 1958). People who do not have an authoritarian personality can be prejudiced, and people who do have an authoritarian personality can be unprejudiced.

Nevertheless, social psychologists have an enduring tendency to develop explanations of extreme and pathological behaviors, such as prejudice, in terms of extreme individuals who have extreme and perhaps pathological personalities. The notion of authoritarianism continues to be popular, but with an emphasis on people's tendency to submit to ingroup conventions and authority, and to punish ingroup deviants (e.g., Altemeyer, 1994; Duckitt, 1989). Another "individual differences" explanation of prejudice is Rokeach's (1960) idea that some people have a dogmatic and closed-minded personality that predisposes them to ethnocentrism, intergroup intolerance, and prejudice. Recently, Sidanius and Pratto and their associates have described a relatively sophisticated, but nonetheless "individual differences," analysis of exploitative power-based intergroup relations called social dominance theory (e.g., Pratto, 1999; Pratto, Sidanius, Stallworth, & Malle, 1994; Sidanius & Pratto, 1999).

Social dominance theory explains the extent to which people accept or reject societal ideologies or myths that legitimize hierarchy and discrimination, or that legitimize equality and fairness. People who desire their own group to be dominant and superior to outgroups have a high social dominance orientation that encourages them to reject egalitarian ideologies, and to accept myths that legitimize hierarchy and discrimination. These kinds of people are more inclined to be prejudiced than are people who have a low social dominance orientation.

Goal Relations, Interdependence, and Intergroup Behaviors

In contrast to those who emphasize personality and individual differences as an explanation of intergroup behavior—a bottom-up analysis—are those who emphasize the goal relations between groups or individuals—a top down analysis. A champion of this perspective is Sherif, who famously pronounced that "we cannot extrapolate from the properties of individuals to the characteristics of group situations" (Sherif, 1962, p. 5). Sherif proposed a "realistic conflict" or interdependence theory of intergroup relations, which was predicated on the belief that behavior is driven by goals and by people's perceptions of their relationship to one another with respect to achieving goals. If two groups have the same goal (e.g., prosperity) but the goal is such that one group can only gain at the expense of the other (there is a zero-sum goal relationship with mutually exclusive goals and negative interdependence between groups) then intergroup relations will be competitive and disharmonious. If two groups have the same goal and the goal is such that it can only be achieved if both groups work together (there is a non-zero-sum goal relationship with a superordinate goal and positive interdependence between groups) then intergroup relations will be cooperative and harmonious. At the interpersonal level, mutually exclusive goals lead to interpersonal conflict and group dissolution, whereas superordinate goals lead to interpersonal harmony, group formation, and group cohesion.

This idea was initially tested by Sherif and his associates in a series of classic field experiments at boys' camps in the United States (see Sherif, 1958, 1966; Sherif, Harvey, White, Hood, & Sherif, 1961; Sherif & Sherif, 1953). In these studies, Sherif manipulated goal relations between individuals and between groups and was able to create cohesive groups, create extreme intergroup conflict and hostility, and to some extent reinstate intergroup harmony. Variants of the boys' camp paradigm have been used by other researchers (Fisher, 1990). For example, Blake and Mouton (1961) ran two-week studies with more than 1,000 business executives on management training programs (also see Blake, Shepard, & Mouton, 1964), and others have replicated Sherif's studies in different cultures (e.g., Andreyeva, 1984; Diab, 1970). The idea that goal relations determine the complexion of intergroup behavior continues to be a powerful theme—for example, in the work of Morton Deutsch (1949, 1973), in the extensive field research of Brewer and Campbell (1976), in the research of Insko and associates (Insko, Schopler, Kennedy, Dahl, Graetz, & Drigotas, 1992), and perhaps most recently, in the work of Rabbie in his behavioral interdependence model (e.g., Rabbie, Schot, & Visser, 1989; see Turner & Bourhis's, 1996, critique).

Because realistic conflict theory is a top-down analysis of intergroup relations, it is meta-theoretically consistent with more sociological analyses of social behavior. Not surprisingly, it has a substantial legacy in research that traces ethnic and race relations to perceived intergroup threat and to competition over scarce resources (e.g., Bobo, 1999; Bobo & Hutchings, 1996).

Social Categorization and Social Identity

Goals and goal relations undoubtably play a critical role in intergroup behavior, and are an important component of social-psychological explanations of intergroup relations. There is little doubt that groups that can only see themselves as competing over a zero-sum resource are likely to have conflictual intergroup relations, and that this relationship could be improved if those groups could only view themselves as having superordinate goals or non-zero-sum goal relations. However, goal relations may not be the entire story.

One problem is a logical or causal one. How do we understand why people pursue some goals and not others, or in other words why do people internalize some groups' goals and not other groups' goals? The other problem is an empirical one that finds its clearest expression in a series of intriguing "minimal group" experiments originally conducted in the late 1960s and early 1970s (e.g., Tajfel, 1970; Tajfel, Billig, Bundy, & Flament, 1971), but now replicated countless times (see Diehl, 1990). Minimal group studies are laboratory experiments where people are categorized into two groups, ostensibly either randomly or on the basis of some trivial criterion. They then allocate resources (often only points) between anonymous members of their group and anonymous members of the outgroup, and complete various other measures about their feelings about themselves, their group, and the other group. The groups have no prior history and no future, there is no interaction, there is no material gain for individuals from membership, and people do not know who is in their group or in the other group. The remarkable and highly robust finding from these experiments is that relative to people who are not explicitly categorized, people who are categorized discriminate in favor of their group, show evaluative ingroup bias, and indicate that they feel a sense of belonging to their group, and similarity to and liking for their anonymous fellow ingroup members.

From the minimal group studies it seemed that competitive intergroup behavior might be an intrinsic feature of the mere existence of a social categorization into ingroup and outgroup. Competitive goal relations might accentuate the effect or serve as a criterion for the existence of categories, but there was clearly a deeper social-cognitive dynamic at play. This finding and its conceptual implications was a critical catalyst in the development of social identity theory (e.g., Hogg & Abrams, 1988; Tajfel & Turner, 1979; Turner, 1982).

Social Identity and Self-Categorization

Social identity theory argues that people define and evaluate themselves in terms of the groups to which they belong. Groups provide people with a social identity, and people have as many social identities as the groups to which they feel they belong. Because social identities define, prescribe, and evaluate who one is and how one should think, feel, and act, people have a strong desire to establish or maintain the evaluative superiority of their own group over relevant other groups. There is a fierce intergroup struggle for evaluatively positive group distinctiveness. This struggle is, however, tempered by people's understanding of the nature of the relations between their group and relevant outgroups—their social belief systems. In particular, people pay attention to status differences and the stability and legitimacy of such differences, to the permeability of intergroup boundaries and thus the possibility of passing psychologically from one group to the other, and to the existence of achievable alternatives to the status quo. For social identity theory, group behaviors (conformity, stereotyping, ethnocentrism, ingroup favoritism, intergroup discrimination, ingroup cohesion, etc.), as distinct from interpersonal behaviors, occur when social identity is the salient basis of self-conceptualization, and the particular content of group behavior rests on the specific social identity that is salient. Social identity is context specific insofar as different social identities are salient in different social contexts.

Self-categorization theory is a more cognitive elaboration of the role of social categorization in social identity processes (Turner, 1985; Turner, Hogg, Oakes, Reicher, & Wetherell, 1987; also see Hogg, 2001). It describes how people represent groups as prototypes—multidimensional fuzzy sets of attributes that describe and prescribe perceptions, thoughts, feelings, and actions that define the ingroup and distinguish it from relevant outgroups. Social categorization depersonalizes attitudes, feelings, and behaviors such that they conform to the relevant ingroup or outgroup prototype. It is thus self-categorization that is responsible for conformity, normative behavior, and the rest of the edifice of group and intergroup behaviors.

The social identity perspective has made a great impact on the social psychology of intergroup relations, and has also contributed significantly to a revival of research on group processes in general (see Abrams & Hogg, 1998; Hogg & Abrams, 1999; Moreland, Hogg, & Hains, 1994). Some aspects of the research focus on the generative details of group processes (e.g., Oakes, Haslam, & Turner, 1994; Turner, 1991), whereas others focus more directly on intergroup strategies (e.g., Ellemers, 1993; Giles & Johnson, 1987; Taylor & McKirnan, 1984). Recent edited books on social identity research include Abrams and Hogg (1999), Capozza and Brown (2000), Ellemers, Spears and Doosje (1999), and Worchel, Morales, Páez, and Deschamps (1998).

Social Categorization and Intergroup Perception

Social categorization is the foundation of intergroup relations. Relations between groups can only occur if the social world can be categorized into separate groups (see Ehrlich, 1973; Hogg, 2001). Social identity theory is one way in which to understand how social categorizations influence people and cause them to behave in characteristically "groupy" ways that are moderated and guided by beliefs about the nature of intergroup relations. Social cognition research focuses on another effect of social categorization on intergroup behavior.

Social cognition researchers describe how perceptual cues, in particular distinctive visual cues (Zebrowitz, 1996), incline us to categorize people and to imbue them with the properties that are described by our schema of that group (see Fiske & Taylor, 1991). The entire process can be deliberate, but in general it is quite automatic and we are quite unaware that it is happening. Stereotyping of outgroup members may be largely an automatic process that we have little control over (Devine, 1989; Bargh, 1994), although other research suggests that the process may be moderated by a number of factors (Lepore & Brown, 1997). One intriguing line of investigation suggests that if people consciously think about the automatic category-stereotype link, the process paradoxically strengthens the link and increases automatic stereotype activation (Macrae, Bodenhausen, Milne, & Jetten, 1994).

Another effect of social categorization is that it causes us perceptually to accentuate similarities among members of the same category. This appears to be a general consequence of categorization (Tajfel, 1959), but one that is asymmetrical because we tend to see outgroups as more homogenous than ingroups (e.g., Judd & Park, 1988; Quattrone, 1986). A popular explanation for this asymmetry is that we are more familiar with the ingroup and therefore have more individuating information about ingroup than outgroup members (Linville, Fischer & Salovey, 1989). Subsequent research has questioned this explanation (e.g., Jones, Wood, & Quattrone, 1981), with Simon and Brown (1987) showing that relative homogeneity effects may be influenced by strategic considerations. For example, active minorities often consider themselves to be relatively more homogenous than the majority outgroup. This is clearly quite functional as such groups need to be consistent and consensual in order to survive and have a chance at initiating social change (see, Mugny, 1982).

Intergroup Attitudes and Explanations

Intergroup perceptions tend to be stereotypic. However stereotypes, although held by individuals who apply them to outgroups, need to be understood more broadly as widely shared intergroup attitudes (Tajfel, 1981) that act as theories (e.g., von Hippel, Sekaquaptewa, & Vargas, 1995) or social representations (see Farr & Moscovici, 1984) of the attributes of other groups. Tajfel (1981), in particular, makes a strong case for the various social functions that stereotypes serve. For example, he explains how stereotypes may emerge to justify actions that have been committed or planned by one group against another group. If one group exploits another group it may be useful to justify this action by developing a stereotype of the outgroup as unsophisticated and dependent.

Intergroup attitudes are also affected by the wider normative environment in which intergroup relations exist. So, for example, racist attitudes may take different forms depending on whether the normative environment is one that inhibits overt racism or one that permits overt racism. A number of researchers have pursued this idea in order to understand modern forms of racism (e.g., Dovidio & Gaertner, 1996, 1998; McConahay, 1986). In Western societies there is a long history of racism that produces deep-seated racial prejudice, fears, and suspicions. However, there is also a tradition of tolerance and egalitarianism that in recent years has become enshrined in social norms and in legislation that suppress racist behavior. For many people, therefore, there is an uncomfortable psychological conflict between two sets of contrasting beliefs. People tend to resolve the conflict by avoiding the racial outgroup, avoiding the issue of race, denying the existence of disadvantage, opposing preferential treatment, and so forth. Overt forms of racism have, in many sectors of society, been replaced by this "modern" form. Stereotypes are not simply shared intergroup attitudes, but are intergroup attitudes that take their form from the wider sociohistorical context in which a specific intergroup relationship exists.

Stereotyping also has an attributional dimension (Hewstone & Jaspars, 1982). Pettigrew (1979) draws on classic attribution theory, in particular Ross's (1977) fundamental attribution error (people over-attribute others' behavior to dispositions and their own behavior to the situation), to describe what he calls the ultimate attribution error. The ultimate attribution error is a group level attribution in which people behave ethnocentrically. Good acts are attributed dispositionally if performed by an ingroup member and situationally if performed by an outgroup member, and vice versa for bad acts. Research conducted in India (Taylor & Jaggi, 1974) and Malaysia (Hewstone & Ward, 1985) certainly supports this analysis.

A particularly disturbing aspect of intergroup attributions is the tendency to attribute unfavorable outgroup properties to underlying dispositions or essences. This is a process that transforms intergroup attitudes into immutable (perhaps genetic) properties or essences of outgroups and their members (see Medin & Ortony, 1989; Miller & Prentice, 1999). Miller and Prentice (1999) argue that intergroup perceptions resting on such essentialism create insurmountable category division than can make it extremely difficult to improve intergroup relations. They cite examples such as the Balkans, Northern Ireland, and the Middle East.

Discrimination

Intergroup relations are not just about attitudes and perceptions. They are very much about how one group behaves towards another group. The key behavioral feature of intergroup relations is discrimination, which can range from relatively innocuous ingroup favoritism, through prejudiced discourse, name-calling, and verbal abuse, all the way to systematic intergroup violence and ultimately genocide.

A key question is: What is the relationship between intergroup attitudes and intergroup behavior? This question is part of the broader attitude-behavior issue. Attitude-behavior research reveals that people's attitudes and their behavior do not often correspond very closely (see Eagly & Chaiken, 1993). For example, LaPiere's (1934) classic study of attitudes towards Chinese Americans revealed that although a young Chinese American couple were almost never denied service at hotels and restaurants across the United States, almost all those same establishments subsequently expressed the strong anti-Chinese sentiment that they would not serve Chinese people. As we have seen above, unfavorable intergroup attitudes can be well concealed when a normative environment exists that proscribes prejudice or that mutates it into modern forms (Crosby, Bromley & Saxe, 1980)

Because the absence of overt discrimination may not indicate the absence of underlying negative intergroup sentiments, a great challenge for social psychology is to be able to detect prejudice in environments in which the expression of prejudice is normatively (and often legally) prohibited. The key seems to be to use unobtrusive measures. If people do not know they are being observed or measured then they are more likely to behave in accordance with their attitudes (Crosby et al., 1980). Other methods involve the careful analysis of the subtext of what people say in natural conversation (e.g., van Dijk, 1987, 1993) or the analysis of behaviors over which people have little or no conscious control (e.g., Brauer, Wasel, & Neidenthal, 2000; Fazio, Sanbonmatsu, Powell, & Kardes, 1986; Franco & Maass, 1996; Maass, Castelli, & Arcuri, 2000).

Discriminatory behavior is, however, rather easy to obtain in minimal group studies (Tajfel, 1970), probably because the groups have no history and thus no social norms exist to proscribe discrimination against minimal groups. This research has sometimes been interpreted as leading to the rather gloomy prognosis for humanity that, all things being equal, social categorization, per se, leads to discrimination. Fortunately, this inference is not completely accurate. Social categorization may be a necessary condition for intergroup discrimination, but it is not sufficient. A series of minimal group experiments by Hogg (2000) has shown that people need to internalize the social categorization as a context-specific self-definition. People need to self-categorize in order to engage in minimal intergroup discrimination. This research shows that people identify with a minimal categorization if they are in a state of subjective uncertainty. More generally, Hogg (2000; Hogg & Mullin, 1999) argues that subjective uncertainty reduction is an important motivation for self-categorization and social identity processes.

Staying with minimal groups, there is other research showing that whether people discriminate or not is influenced by the available dimension of discrimination. For example, there is a positive-negative asymmetry effect (Otten, Mummendey, & Blanz, 1996; Wenzel & Mummendey, 1996). Although people discriminate against outgroups when they are giving rewards, they do not do so when they are giving punishments, unless their group is under threat by being disadvantaged or being in a minority position.

We should also remind ourselves that "real" groups exist in a socio-historical environment containing wider societal norms that prescribe, proscribe or direct discriminatory behavior. Furthermore, people have social belief systems relating to status stability and legitimacy, intergroup permeability, and realistic alternatives to the status quo (e.g., Tajfel & Turner, 1979). In the pursuit of positive social identity these beliefs influence the form that intergroup behavior takes.

Although discrimination is often viewed unfavorably from the perspective of liberal democratic societies, ingroups generally view it positively. Discrimination indicates ingroup loyalty and commitment. People seem prepared to accept and even praise unfair or unjust practices when they are directed towards outgroups. However, the story is different when such behavior is directed towards the ingroup. Tyler and his colleagues (e.g., Tyler, DeGoey, & Smith, 1996; Tyler, 2001) provide evidence showing that people in groups are not overly concerned about having less than fellow group members (distributive inequality), but they are very concerned about being treated fairly (procedural justice). Ingroup procedural fairness signifies respect, and is an important influence on members' sense of belonging and thus the extent to which they bond with the group.

One implication of Tyler's work is that intergroup discrimination can serve a strategic function. The primary audience for discriminatory behavior may be the ingroup. People may overtly discriminate against an outgroup in order to bolster their own ingroup credentials and standing. For instance, jingoistic rhetoric and overt outgroup discrimination on the part of leaders may serve this function (e.g., Rabbie & Bekkers, 1978; Reicher & Hopkins, 1986), as does the publicly verifiable nature of delinquent behavior (Emler & Reicher, 1995).

Motivational Aspects of Intergroup Relations

Why do people engage in intergroup behavior, and perhaps more fundamentally, why do people identify with groups? What motivates intergroup behavior, and what motivates specific forms of intergroup behavior? One answer is in terms of specific goals that people or groups may want to achieve—goals that can only be achieved by interpersonal or intergroup cooperative interaction (superordinate goals), or goals that are mutually exclusive and can only be achieved by interpersonal or intergroup competition. Functional theories of intergroup relations, such as that proposed by Sherif (e.g., 1958) fall in this camp (see description earlier in this chapter).

Personality approaches like Adorno et al.'s (1950) authoritarian personality, or Rokeach's (1960) dogmatic personality treat people's need to compartmentalize their social world as a core aspect of authoritarianism or dogmatism. Authoritarian or dogmatic personalities are therefore strongly motivated to discriminate starkly between groups, and, in the case of authoritarianism, to displace negative feelings onto lower status outgroups (see description earlier in this chapter). Theories of why people affiliate in the first place have produced a range of motives, of which social reality testing through social comparison is an important one (e.g., Festinger, 1954). According to this theory, people come together with similar others in order to obtain validation from individual others for their perceptions, attitudes, and feelings. Terror management is another motive for affiliation (e.g., Greenberg, Solomon, & Pyszczynski, 1997)—people affiliate with others because they fear death. Finally, there is a plethora of motivational accounts for why people construe themselves in particular ways (see Sedikides & Strube, 1997).

Social categorization research tends to focus on contextual factors that cause us to categorize ourselves and others in particular ways, and on the consequences of categorizing in those ways. One very fundamental motive for social categorization, which also underpins categorization more generally, is a need to structure our subjective environment in contextually meaningful ways that reduce uncertainty and allow us to predict people's behavior and plan our own actions (e.g., Hogg, 2000, 2001). This analysis allows us to understand why disadvantaged groups may acquiesce in their position rather than struggle for change—change may improve status but will also introduce uncertainty (also see Jost & Banaji, 1994). It also allows us to understand why groups whose distinctiveness is threatened may react in ways that are aimed, not so much at improving status, but at raising entitativity and cohesion (e.g., Hamilton & Sherman, 1996), perhaps through rejection of deviates (e.g., Marques & Páez, 1994).

Another powerful intergroup motive is self-enhancement. According to social identity theory, intergroup behavior is motivated by a struggle between groups to promote or protect their positive distinctiveness from one another, and thus secure a relatively favorable social identity. People engage in this struggle because, at the individual level, group membership mediates self-evaluation via social identity, and people tend to be motivated to feel good about themselves—to have a positive sense of self esteem. In intergroup contexts self-esteem may motivate social identity processes, but how this is pursued is significantly impacted by social conventions and social belief systems (see Abrams & Hogg, 1988; Hogg & Abrams, 1990; Long & Spears, 1997; Rubin & Hewstone, 1998).

According to Brewer's (1991) theory of optimal distinctiveness, people simultaneously strive to be the same as other people (assimilation/inclusiveness) and to be different from other people (differentiation/uniqueness). Because these are contrasting human motives, the equilibrium state is one of optimal distinctiveness. Over-satisfaction of one motive engages the contrasting motive to reinstate optimal distinctiveness. Optimal distinctiveness is generally well satisfied by intergroup contexts in which the ingroup is not overly large—there is sufficient intergroup and intragroup distinctiveness to balance ingroup assimilation.

Generally speaking, there is good evidence that threats to group integrity or group valance, and thus to self-conception and self-evaluation, motivate protective reactions that can, depending on available material and psychological resources, manifest themselves as intergroup conflict, "backlash," more subtle forms of intergroup behavior, or as dis-identification (e.g., Ethier & Deaux, 1994). For example, self-affirmation theory (Steele, 1988) describes how people whose identity in one domain is evaluatively threatened engage in practices that publicly affirm a favorable identity in another domain.

Social Influence and Intergroup Relations

Intergroup relations are competitive. Groups and their members compete over scarce resources which can be material (money, land) or psychological (status, prestige). Groups also struggle to have the power to influence one another, and intergroup contexts impact the way in which influence operates within groups. Although social influence phenomena are typically viewed as occurring among individuals within a group (e.g., Asch, 1956; Sherif, 1935), they may be quite distinctly contextualized by intergroup processes and relations and may play themselves out across intergroup boundaries. There is an intergroup dimension to social influence (e.g., Moscovici, 1976; Turner, 1991).

One way in which intergroup relations impact social influence is through their effect on ingroup norms. Within groups, people are influenced by group norms—under appropriate conditions they conform to ingroup norms and express normative attitudes and behaviors. If such group norms prescribe discriminatory intergroup behavior, then conformity will be expressed as intergroup discrimination. Ingroup norms do not emerge and acquire their content in isolation from intergroup relations. Self-categorization and social identity research has shown that where intergroup relations are salient and people are identifying with their respective groups, group norms form and are configured not only to capture ingroup commonalities but also to distinguish the ingroup from the outgroup (e.g., Haslam, Oakes, McGarty, Turner, & Onorato, 1995). In many intergroup contexts ingroup norms are polarized away from the outgroup so that they do not represent the central tendency of ingroup positions, and intragroup influence processes cause the ingroup to become more extreme so that the gulf between ingroup and outgroup widens (e.g., Abrams, Wetherell, Cochrane, Hogg, & Turner, 1990; Mackie, 1986; McGarty, Turner, Hogg, David, & Wetherell, 1992).

Intergroup influence can also happen more directly—groups can try directly to influence one another. However, relations between groups are almost always marked by status and power differences, and so intergroup influence is often a conflict between a powerful majority and a weaker minority (e.g., Wood, Lundgren, Ouellette, Busceme, & Blackstone, 1994). Majority and minority groups have access to different influence resources and may actually influence through different processes (e.g., Moscovici, 1980). Of particular interest here is how active minorities gain influence over majorities and therefore how social change can be possible (e.g., Maass & Clark, 1984; Mugny, 1982).

Active minorities need to adopt a particular behavioral style in order to influence members of a majority group (Mugny, 1982): they need to present a consistent and consensual message, they need to be seen as having made some sacrifice for their cause, they need to be seen as acting out of principle, and they need to be seen by the majority as being ingroup members to some extent. This behavioral style, particularly consistency, creates cognitive conflict in the mind of majority members between majority and minority views. Majority members are not immediately influenced, but experience a sudden conversion to the minority point of view at a later time. Consistent minorities have latent, deep-seated influence over majorities that produces a sudden and enduring conversion effect (Moscovici, 1980; Nemeth, 1986). Minorities that are inconsistent tend to have little impact because their message is easily disregarded. Majorities are taken for granted, and people simply comply with their views without really internalizing them or undergoing any deep-seated cognitive change.

Minority influence research has produced an intriguing paradigm in which minorities are able to change people's chromatic after images (e.g., Moscovici & Personnaz, 1980; but see Martin, 1998). Blue slides, which have yellow/orange after images, were reported by majority members to have red/purple after images (which would have corresponded to having seen a green slide). This occurred after the minority had consistently called blue slides green. This remarkable finding is presented as evidence for the sort of deep-seated cognitive change that minorities can have on the attitudes and perceptions of the majority.

Disadvantage and Social Protest

The power and status inequalities associated with majorities and minorities have far reaching consequences, and are in many ways the essential problem of intergroup relations. If intergroup relations were characterized by groups of equal status and power, disadvantage and all that flows from it would not be present. As it is, intergroup relations are almost always associated with differential status, power, prestige, resources, and so forth. Dominant, majority groups do well out of this arrangement, and their members generally experience a positive sense of identity and esteem. Subordinate, minority groups do not do so well, and their members can sometimes experience status-mediated lowered self-esteem (Allport, 1954; see Crocker & Major, 1989).

Another far-reaching consequence of losing out in the intergroup struggle for power and prestige is material and social disadvantage. Disadvantaged groups can find that their goals and aspirations are continually frustrated relative to other groups, and a sense of reduced efficacy and motivation can eventually set in. Rather than fight for change, groups can sometimes acquiesce to these conditions. For example, groups can deny that they are disadvantaged or members can deny personally being disadvantaged (Crosby, Cordova, & Jaskar, 1993), and some groups can prefer disadvantage to the uncertainties and dangers of fighting for social change (Jost & Banaji, 1994). However, when deprivation is very acute and a recipe for effective social change is available, disadvantaged groups will eagerly challenge the status quo by political means, or through social protest or other collective behaviors including demonstrations, riots, and uprising.

According to theories that focus on frustration and relative deprivation, disadvantaged groups will engage in protest only when they actually experience acute frustration. For example, Berkowitz (1972) offered a detailed analysis of how riots may occur, which he applied to the late-1960s race riots that swept large cities in the United States. He suggested that in addition to a sense of frustration there needed to be three other conditions: (a) aversive environmental circumstances that would amplify chronic frustration (e.g., heat, overcrowding) (b) aggressive environmental cues that would introduce a social learning component (e.g., armed police) and (c) social presence that would engage a social facilitation process (e.g., many people assembled in the streets). Berkowitz emphasizes the automatic, emotional, and impulsive aspects of collective behavior. He is famous for his "long hot summer" analysis of the 1960s urban race riots in the United States which mainly occurred during heatwaves.

Reicher (1984, 2001) provides a quite different analysis of the crowd. He adopts a social identity perspective to argue that crowd behavior is a set of deliberate and logical actions that are directly related to the goals and objectives of the group defining the social identity of the crowd. The apparent volatility of crowd behavior is less extreme than media reports lead one to believe, occurs within limits set by the crowd's identity, and reflects a search for situation-specific behaviors that are consistent with the wider identity of the group.

Although disadvantage, particularly acute disadvantage, can translate into riots and demonstrations, it also, of course, sponsors enduring campaigns for social change—campaigns that can last decades or even centuries. Relative deprivation researchers (e.g., Davis, 1959; also see Walker & Pettigrew, 1984) suggest that disadvantage translates into social action when people suddenly become aware that their expectations and attainments have parted company; in particular, when there is a sudden drop in attainments against a background of rising expectations (Davies, 1969; Gurr, 1970). These conditions have been invoked to explain the rise of anti-Semitism in 1930s Europe, the French and Russian revolutions of 1789 and 1917, the American Civil War of the 1860s, and the Black Power movement of the 1960s.

Runciman (1966) introduced an important distinction between fraternalistic relative deprivation (a feeling that one's own group is deprived relative to relevant other groups), and egoistic relative deprivation (a feeling that oneself is deprived relative to specific other individuals). It is the former that appears to be associated with social protest, whereas the latter is more likely to be associated with acquiescence and depression. For example, racist attitudes in the United States and Britain may be more extreme among skilled blue-collar people than any other group, because this group is most vulnerable to competition from other (e.g., immigrant) groups, and thus feels most threatened and fraternalistically most deprived (Vanneman & Pettigrew, 1972; also see Esses, Jackson & Armstrong, 1998). Walker and Mann (1987) provide a similar analysis of reactions to unemployment among unemployed Australians.

According to social identity theory, disadvantaged groups will engage in direct competition with the dominant group if they perceive intergroup boundaries to be impermeable, if they perceive their lower status to be illegitimate and unstable, and if they can conceive of a new status quo that is achievable (see Ellemers, 1993; Hogg & Abrams, 1988; Tajfel & Turner, 1979). This analysis attributes protest on the part of disadvantaged groups to a conjunction of social-cognitive factors and social belief systems and ideologies. For example, according to research by Wright, Taylor, and Moghaddam (1990), if members of a disadvantaged group believe that entry to an advantaged group is open, even only slightly open (only a token percentage of people can pass), they shun collective action and instead individually try to gain entry to the advantaged group. Collective action is most likely to be taken when entry to the advantaged group is closed, and then it is only taken by those who believe they were closest to entry, because they feel the strongest sense of relative deprivation. Collective action is only likely to be extreme (e.g., riots, terrorism) when socially acceptable normative means (e.g., peaceful protest, lobbying) are unavailable.

Social Harmony Among Groups

The goal of most intergroup relations researchers is to learn enough about these relations to be able to know, and perhaps advise, how to improve intergroup relations and build social harmony. To this end, a prevalent belief is that close and pleasant interpersonal contact between people from different groups is probably the best way to achieve social harmony—the contact hypothesis (Allport, 1954; also see Amir, 1969; Cook, 1985; Hewstone & Brown, 1986; Miller & Brewer, 1984). The idea that appropriate intergroup contact could improve intergroup relations was a central plank in the policy put in place in the United States in 1954 to improve race relations by desegregating the school system. The practice of "busing" children in and out of racially homogenous school districts was partly aimed at increasing inter-racial contact (Schofield, 1991). For contact to be effective it needs to be prolonged and cooperative, it needs to occur within an official and institutional climate that strongly encourages integration, and it needs to be between equal status groups. These conditions are nearly impossible to satisfy, and so contact is notoriously ineffective at changing intergroup attitudes or improving intergroup relations. After all, charged intergroup relations are often associated with groups that are very different and contact simply confirms one's worst fears (Bochner, 1982). In addition, as we have seen earlier in this chapter (e.g., Sherif, 1958), intergroup conflict may rest upon real conflicts of interest over scarce resources. Until perceived or actual goal relations are changed, contact will simply provide a forum for conflict.

One specific problem is that there can be substantial anxiety associated with intergroup contact, which of course renders the interaction somewhat aversive (Stephan & Stephan, 1985). Intergroup anxiety is a state in which people worry about the negative psychological and behavioral consequence for self, and the negative evaluations of self by both ingroup and outgroup, as a consequence of intergroup contact. Intergroup anxiety arises out of past experience of contact, intergroup beliefs (stereotypes), and the degree of normative structure of the contact situation. It affects intergroup behavior. Intergroup anxiety can produce intergroup avoidance and stereotype-confirming perceptions, evaluations, and feelings.

Contact which is not associated with intergroup anxiety can be pleasant; indeed sufficiently pleasant to encourage the development of enduring friendships across group boundaries (Pettigrew, 1998). However, being close friends with people from another group does not guarantee that one has positive attitudes towards that group as a whole (but see Wright, Aron, McLaughlin-Volpe, & Ropp, 1997). Close friendships between members of different groups often do not improve generalized intergroup images. People may like each other as individuals, but they still harbor negative attitudes towards the groups as a whole.

One way to get around this problem is to encourage people in contact situations to de-categorize themselves and treat each other as unique individuals, or to re-categorize themselves as members of a shared superordinate identity. Research by Gaertner and Dovidio and their colleagues (e.g., Gaertner, Dovidio, Anastasio, Bachman, & Rust, 1993; Gaertner, Mann, Murrell, & Dovidio, 1989) shows that both strategies reduce intergroup discrimination, but by different routes: re-categorization improves outgroup attitudes, whereas de-categorization worsens ingroup attitudes. One problem with re-categorization is that it can, particularly in non-laboratory contexts, represent a threat to the distinctiveness of the separate groups and associated social identities that are being encouraged to re-categorize themselves as a single entity. This problem surfaces at the cultural level in the relative ineffectiveness of assimilationist strategies to forge a single harmonious cultural or national identity out of many cultural groups. Social harmony may be better served by a multicultural strategy that avoids the distinctiveness threat raised by assimilationism (see Hornsey & Hogg, 2000; Prentice & Miller, 1999).

Since re-categorization has a tendency to backfire, perhaps improved generalized intergroup attitudes and relations are more likely to emerge from contact that is framed in intergroup terms. But the problem here, as we have already seen, is that intergroup contact is often sufficiently stressful to render it unpleasant or even hostile. It can be very difficult to produce pleasant intergroup contact, which is a prerequisite for improved generalized images. More generally, it is very difficult to create enduring pluralistic contexts where people identify at the subgroup and at the superordinate group level simultaneously, and thus do not experience identity threat and do not interact in a hostile intergroup manner, but do view each other in group terms that permit generalization.

The main aim of contact is for pleasant interaction to change enduring intergroup images—that is, for generalization to occur through the accumulation of favorable outgroup information (bookkeeping), through a sudden encounter with counter-stereotypic information (conversion), or through the development of a more textured outgroup representation (subtyping) (Weber & Crocker, 1983). Research (e.g., Wilder, 1984) shows that people who have pleasant contact with an outgroup member who is clearly viewed as being representative or stereotypical of the outgroup, do develop improved attitudes towards the outgroup as a whole. But generally speaking, the relationship between intergroup contact and enduring social harmony is an enormously complex one which involves a large number of interacting conditions (e.g., Islam & Hewstone, 1993).

The Readings

In this introductory chapter we have given a very broad and by necessity selective overview of the social psychology of intergroup relations. The main aim has been to provide a framework for tackling the body of the book. The book itself is organized to correspond closely to the way that we have structured this introductory chapter.

This is a book of key readings. We have selected readings to give a flavor of the diversity of the field and to present the work of some leading scholars. The readings serve as stepping stones through the field of intergroup relations. Some of the readings are citation classics, others are simply interesting and informative. It was impossible to include everything and everyone we would have liked to include. Consequently, many key publications, leading scholars, and vibrant research teams are missing. This book should be considered one of many possible snapshots of the field of intergroup relations, and should be read in conjunction with other general books and chapters on intergroup relations, for example:

Abrams, D., & Hogg, M. A. (Eds.) (1999). *Social identity and social cognition.* Oxford, UK: Blackwell.

Brewer, M. B., & Brown, R. J. (1998). Intergroup relations. In D. T. Gilbert, S. T. Fiske, & G. Lindzey (Eds.), *The handbook of social psychology: Vol. 2* (4th ed., pp. 554–594). New York: McGraw-Hill.

Brewer, M. B., & Miller, N. (1996). *Intergroup relations.* Buckingham, UK: Open University Press.

Brown, R. J. (2000). *Group processes* (2nd ed.). Oxford, UK: Blackwell.

Brown, R., & Gaertner, S. (Eds.). (2001). *Blackwell handbook of social psychology: Intergroup processes.* Oxford, UK: Blackwell.

Gaertner, S. L. & Dovidio, J. F. (2000). *Reducing intergroup bias: The Common Ingroup Identity model.* Philadelphia: Psychology Press.

Hogg, M. A., & Abrams, D. (1988). *Social identifications: A social psychology of intergroup relations and group processes.* London: Routledge.

Hogg, M. A., & Abrams, D. (in press). Intergroup behavior and social identity. In M. A. Hogg & J. Cooper (Eds.), *Sage handbook of social psychology.* London: Sage.

Mackie, D., & Smith, E. (1998). Intergroup relations: Insights from a theoretically integrative approach. *Psychological Review, 105,* 499–529.

Sedikides, C., Schopler, J., & Insko, C. A. (1998) *Intergroup cognition and intergroup behavior.* Hillsdale, NJ: Erlbaum

Spears, R., Oakes, P. J., Ellemers, N., & Haslam, S. A. (1997). *The social psychology of stereotyping and group life.* Oxford, UK: Blackwell.

Turner, J. C., & Giles, H. (Eds.). (1981). *Intergroup behaviour.* Oxford, UK: Blackwell.

Personality and Individual Differences

Intergroup relations are a major focus of social psychology, probably because they are often characterized by prejudiced attitudes, competitive orientations, discriminatory behavior, and other dark aspects of the human condition. Much of what we hear about intergroup relations focuses on conflict—on how people exploit, humiliate, and oppress people who are not in their group, often engaging in acts of individual aggression or embarking on campaigns of systematic, collective violence.

The extremity of this behavior, its moral unacceptability, and the widespread human tendency to attribute attitudes and behavior to personality conspire to produce scientific social psychological theories of intergroup relations that ground intergroup behavior in personality and individual differences. The idea that prejudice, discrimination, and intolerance stem from dysfunctional personality is a comforting one. It quarantines the behavior among maladjusted individuals and protects the rest of us from "infection." It is also an appealing explanation for the most extreme form of intergroup behavior—genocide.

The revelation to the world in 1945 of the grotesque extremes of the holocaust produced social psychology's best-known personality explanation of prejudice and discrimination—the authoritarian personality theory. Published in 1950 by Adorno, Frenkel-Brunswik, Levinson, and Sanford, this theory, which traced prejudice, through a psychodynamic process, to distorted family dynamics, spawned a prodigious quantity of research. Although there is evidence that some people may be more authoritarian than others, the causal links between family dynamics and authoritarianism and between authoritarianism and prejudice are not at all clear. This is where our first reading comes in.

Thomas Pettigrew, a professor at Harvard at the time, felt that personality alone, or even at all, was not an adequate social psychological explanation of such a widespread collective behavior as prejudice. In 1958, he published a systematic study of racial prejudice and authoritarianism in South Africa and the southern and northern United States to demonstrate that the most parsimonious explanation of racial prejudice is that people who are brought up in a culture of prejudice become socialized into those attitudes and practices—attitudes and practices which become taken-for-granted and second-nature. Pettigrew found little significant relationship between racial prejudice and authoritarianism or the dynamics of family upbringing. Instead, he found that the most prejudiced participants were those who lived in a culture of prejudice, and "who by their roles in the social structure can be anticipated to be conforming to the dictates of the culture" (Pettigrew, 1958, p. 38).

Although Pettigrew's reservations about personality explanations are now widely shared among social psychologists (see Billig, 1976), personality and individual difference explanations are still very appealing. For instance, Milton Rokeach developed an alternative explanation of prejudice and intolerance that traced it to the possession of a dogmatic or closed-minded personality (e.g., Rokeach, 1948, 1960), and even more recently, work on personality and prejudice has been developed by Altemeyer (1994).

Some individual-difference explanations of intergroup behavior are quite sophisticated in that they integrate relatively invariant properties of individuals (e.g., personality) with features of the social context (e.g., social history). A recent example of this approach is the work of Jim Sidanius, at the University of California Los Angeles, and his colleagues. They have developed the notion of social dominance orientation to explain the extent to which individuals accept or reject societal ideologies or myths that legitimize hierarchy and discrimination or that legitimize equality and fairness. People differ in their social dominance orientation (SDO)—the extent to which they desire their own group to be dominant and superior to outgroups. People who have a high SDO are inclined to accept hierarchy-legitimizing myths and reject egalitarian ideologies, whereas the opposite is the case for people with a low SDO. Sidanius has published widely on social dominance. A well-cited example of this work is an article coauthored with Felicia Pratto, Lisa Stallworth, and Bertram Malle (Pratto, Sidanius, Stallworth, & Malle, 1994). Pratto and colleagues develop an internally and temporally reliable scale to measure SDO, and then investigate the relationship between this scale and other personality scales, and the predictive validity of this scale regarding intergroup attitudes and the sorts of (hierarchical or egalitarian) roles that people occupy in society.

Discussion Questions

1. Does prejudice develop and become more entrenched as we get older?
2. Do personality and culture combine additively or interactively to affect prejudice?
3. Is prejudice a general trait or is it restricted to particular targets at particular times?
4. What socialization process could be responsible for individual differences in prejudice?
5. How are individual differences in prejudice manifested and measured?
6. Is prejudice innate?

Suggested Readings

Altemeyer, B. (1994). Reducing prejudice in right-wing authoritarians. In M. P. Zanna & J. M. Olsen (Eds.), *The psychology of prejudice: The Ontario symposium* (pp. 131–148). Hillside, NJ: Erlbaum. Another very recent analysis of the role of personality in prejudice and intergroup discrimination.

Billig, M. G. (1976). *Social psychology and intergroup relations.* London: Academic Press. A scholarly, comprehensive, and meticulous critique of personality and individual differences explanations of intergroup behavior.

Brown, R. J. (1995). *Prejudice: Its social psychology.* Oxford, UK: Blackwell. An up-to-date and comprehensive discussion of the social psychology of prejudice.

Fiske, S. T. (2000). Stereotyping, prejudice and discrimination at the seam between the centuries: Evolution, culture, mind and brain. *European Journal of Social Psychology, 30,* 299–322. A balanced and very recent discussion of the contributions made by evolution, culture, and cognition to prejudice and stereotyping.

Powlishta, K. K., Serbin, L. A., Doyle, A., & White, D. R. (1994). Gender, ethnic and body-type biases: The generality of prejudice in childhood. *Developmental Psychology, 30,* 526–536. An analysis of prejudice in its developmental context.

Pratto, F. (1999). The puzzle of continuing group inequality: Piecing together psychological, social and cultural forces in social dominance theory. In M. P. Zanna (Ed.), *Advances in experimental social psychology* (Vol. 31, pp. 191–263). New York: Academic Press. A more extensive and detailed analysis of social dominance orientation.

Reynolds, K. J., Turner, J. C., Haslam, S. A., & Ryan, M. K. (in press). The role of personality and group factors in explaining prejudice. *Journal of Experimental Social Psychology.* A recent critical analysis of the role played by personality in prejudice and discrimination.

Rokeach, M. (1948). Generalized mental rigidity as a factor in ethnocentrism. *Journal of Abnormal and Social Psychology, 43,* 259–278. The first description of Rokeach's personality/individual differences explanation of prejudice and intergroup attitudes.

Sidanius, J., & Pratto, F. (1999). *Social dominance: An intergroup theory of social hierarchy and oppression.* New York: Cambridge University Press. A book length treatment of social dominance theory.

Personality and Sociocultural Factors in Intergroup Attitudes: A Cross-National Comparison

Thomas F. Pettigrew • Harvard University

Introduction

Along the continuum of prejudice theories, two extreme positions have been popular. One strongly emphasizes the personality of the bigot and neglects his cultural milieu; the other views intolerance as a mere reflection of cultural norms and neglects individual differences. Recent evidence lends little support to either pole. As further data are gathered with more refined research tools, it becomes increasingly apparent that the psychological and sociological correlates of prejudice are elaborately intertwined and that both are essential to provide an adequate theoretical framework for this complex phenomenon.

Carrying this viewpoint further, Smith, Bruner, and White (38, pp. 41–44) have delineated three functions that attitudes may serve for an individual. First, there is the *object-appraisal* function; attitudes aid in the process of understanding "reality" as it is defined by the culture. Second, attitudes can play a *social-adjustment* role by contributing to the individual's identification with, or differentiation from, various reference groups. It should be noted that both these functions—object appraisal and social adjustment—are important reflections on the personality level of sociocultural conditions. But the most studied function of attitudes, *externalization*, is somewhat unique. "Externalization occurs when an individual, often responding unconsciously, senses an analogy between a perceived environmental event and some unresolved inner problem . . . [and] adopts an attitude . . . which is a transformed version of his way of dealing with his inner difficulty." Such a process may serve to reduce anxiety. The principal psychological theories of prejudice–frustration-aggression (9), psychoanalytic (20), and authoritarianism (1)—all deal chiefly with this third process.

External expression of inner conflict is relatively more independent of sociocultural factors than are the other functions of attitudes. Indeed, a heuristic distinction between externalized personality variables and sociological variables contributes to our understanding of much that is known about intergroup conflict.

Minard's observations of race relations in the coal-mining county of McDowell, West Virginia, serve as a direct illustration of the point (26). The general pattern in this region consists of white and Negro miners being integrated below the ground and almost completely segregated above the ground. Minard estimates that roughly 60 percent of the white miners manage to reverse roles almost completely; they can accept Negroes as equals in the mines but cannot accept them as equals elsewhere. Furthermore, he feels that, at one extreme, about 20 percent accept the black miners as equals in both situations, while, at the other extreme, about 20 percent never accept them in either situation. In our terms, the behavior of the majority of these whites studied by Minard can be predicted largely by sociocultural expectations, and the behavior of the consistent minorities can be accounted for largely by externalized personality variables.

The research literature abounds with further examples in which a separation of psychological and sociological factors is helpful. The many papers on interracial contact in housing (7, 40), at work (11), and in the army (39) show the marked effects that can be brought about by certain changes in the social situation between races. But personality factors are still operating. Usually these studies report that some individuals hold favorable attitudes toward minorities even before the contact and that other individuals still hold unfavorable attitudes after the contact. Many of these studies also find that the changes brought about by the contact are quite specific and delimited in nature. That is, the intergroup changes occur only under a narrow range of conditions, since the basic personality orientations of the participants have not changed fundamentally. Thus white department-store employees become more accepting of Negroes in the work situation after equal status contact but not in other situations (11). And the attitudes of white army personnel toward the Negro as a fighting man improve after equal status contact in combat, but their attitudes toward the Negro as a social companion do not change (39).

Desegregation findings furnish further illustrations where the distinction is useful. Social demands for racial desegregation and the irresistible trend of the times are counteracting personality predispositions in many communities. Thus a 1954 public opinion survey in Oklahoma found an overwhelming majority of the residents sternly against desegregation, and yet today mixed schools have become accepted throughout most of the state without incident (17). And in Wilmington, Delaware, two years after successful school integration without apparent public opposition, a poll indicated that only a minority approved of the school desegregation decision of the Supreme Court (17). Indeed, this discrepancy between opinions and demands is a general phenomenon throughout the border states. Hyman and Sheatsley (16) report that only 31 percent of the white population in those border areas that have already inte-

grated their school systems endorse desegregation.

This conflict between authority-supported cultural changes and personal preferences is underscored by another finding that public opinion polls have uncovered in the South. Several investigators have independently shown that respondents themselves make a distinction between what they individually favor and what they expect to happen in their community. Thus the huge majority of southern whites favor racial segregation, but most of them also feel that desegregation is inevitable (16, 28).

Finally, the work originally done by La Piere (19) in 1934 and more recently replicated in different contexts by Saenger and Gilbert (34) and by Kutner, Wilkins, and Yarrow (18) furnishes further justification for a theoretical separation of social and externalization aspects of intergroup conflict. These investigations illustrate the results of conflicting personality predispositions and actual social situations with minority-group members; frequently the face-to-face conditions override previous practices.

Such work has led several authorities in the field to make the sociocultural and personality differentiation. Psychologist G. W. Allport discusses the two classes of factors separately in his definitive volume, *The Nature of Prejudice* (2), and sociologist Arnold Rose makes a similar distinction in a recent theoretical article on intergroup relations (33).

The present paper is a summary report on research conducted chiefly to gain cross-national perspective on these two sets of prejudice factors. The studies were made in two parts of the world where racial conflict today is highlighted and cultural sanctions of intolerance are intense and explicit: the Union of South Africa and the southern United States. First, a more detailed report of previously unpublished data will be presented on the South African study. Following this, a comparison will be made with the southern United States based on a summary of data presented in detail elsewhere (29).

Racial Prejudice in the Union of South Africa[1]

The limited evidence available supports the general belief that white South Africans are unusually prejudiced against Africans (14, 21, 24). This raises the intriguing question as to whether this increased hostility represents (a) more externalizing personality potential for prejudice among South Africans, (b) the effects of different cultural norms and pressures, or (c) both of these.

To provide a tentative answer, a questionnaire study was undertaken of the racial attitudes of students at the English-speaking University of Natal in the Union of South Africa. A non-random sample of 627 undergraduates—approximately one-third of the entire university—completed an anonymous instrument containing three scales and a number of background items.[2] The three scales are a thirteen-item measure of authoritarianism (F scale) whose statements are shown in Table 1.2, a sixteen-item measure of social conformity (C scale) whose statements are shown in Table 1.3, and an eighteen-item measure of anti-African attitudes (A scale) whose statements are shown in Table 1.8.[3] background information includes place of birth, political party preference, father's occupation, and ethnic-group membership.

Taken as a group, these students evidence considerable hostility toward Africans, accepting in large degree the white-supremacy ideology so adamantly propounded by the present government of their country. Thus 72 percent of the sample agree that "there is something inherently primitive and uncivilized in the native, as shown in his music and extreme aggressiveness"; and 69 percent agree that "manual labor seems to fit the native mentality better than more skilled and responsible work." And yet their F-scale responses are roughly comparable to those of American student populations.[4] Thus these South Africans are sharply prejudiced against blacks without possessing any greater externalizing personality potential for intolerance than peoples in more tolerant areas.

In addition, authoritarianism correlates with anti-African attitudes at a level comparable to relationships between authoritarianism and prejudice in other parts of the world. Table 1.1 shows that the A and F scales correlate +0.56 among the Afrikaans-speaking members of the sample and +0.46 among the English-speaking members. Similar scales typically correlate in the fifties in American college samples.[5] The C-scale measure of social conformity—employed for the first time in this investigation—relates to the A-scale scores significantly, too, in both ethnic groups (Table 1.1).

More detailed analyses of the F and C scales'

TABLE 1.1. Correlations Between Anti-African Scale (A) and Authoritarianism (F) and Conformity (C) Scales*

Variables	Ethnic Group †	
	Afrikaners	English
N.........................	50	513
A and F...............	+0.56	+0.46
A and C...............	+0.42	+0.46

* All four of these product-moment correlations are significantly different from zero at better than the 1 percent level of confidence. The scale scores that were correlated vary between 0 and 10. They were calculated on the basis of +4 for agree strongly, +3 for agree, +2 for omitted response, +1 for disagree and 0 for disagree strongly for each item, and then the total scores were collapsed into the 0–10 categories for machine analysis.

† Separate analyses by ethnic group are made necessary by the sharply divergent A-scale means to the two groups (see Table 1.7).

relationships with anti-African attitudes are provided in Tables 1.2 and 1.3. Each of the thirteen authoritarian statements separates the less and more prejudiced halves of the sample in the predicted direction, seven of the differences proving to be significant at better than the 0.001 level of

---

[1] This investigation was conducted during 1956 when the author was an honorary research associate of the University of Natal's Institute for Social Research.

[2] Comparisons between this one-third sample and the total student body of the University of Natal reveal that, in terms of sex, age, and field of concentration, the sample's distributions are quite similar to the student body at large.

[3] All thirteen of the F-scale items are from the original California study on authoritarianism (1, pp. 255–257); the C scale is a new scale composed of both new items and adaptations from the conformity measures of Hoffman (15) and MacCrone (22); and fourteen of the A-scale items are new, while four are adaptations from the E scale (1, items 8, 31, and 34 on p. 105 and item 29 on p. 117).

[4] Comparisons across diverse groups with varying forms of the F scale are difficult and tenuous at best. American college samples generally average slightly below the neutral point on F-scale statements, while the present South African sample averages slightly above the neutral point. This small difference can probably be accounted for by (a) the use of a disproportionate number of high-agreement items in the thirteen-item F scale employed with the South African sample and (b) the inclusion in the South African group of fields of concentration not usually included in tested American college groups (e.g., agriculture) whose members tend to score high on the F scale (due probably to social class factors).

[5] Again, comparisons are difficult. Correlations between long-form F scales and ethnocentrism scales (measuring prejudice against a variety of out-groups) have sometimes reached the sixties and even occasionally the seventies in American college samples (1, 2, 5). But correlations of the magnitude found in this study have been consistently reported when—as in this study—a shortform F scale and a prejudice scale against a single out-group are related.

TABLE 1.2. Anti-African Prejudice and F-Scale Items

| F-Scale Item | Percentage Agreement* | | 2×2 x^2 | p |
	Less Prejudiced Half	More Prejudiced Half		
a) Nowadays when so many different kinds of people move around and mix together so much, a person has to be especially careful not to catch an infection or disease from them	13.6	33.2	33.5	0.001
b) There is hardly anything lower than a person who does not feel a great love and respect for his parents	52.6	70.5	21.2	.001
c) People can be put into two distinct classes: the weak and the strong	23.5	37.8	15.1	.001
d) Most of our social problems would be solved if we could somehow get rid of the immoral, crooked, and feeble-minded people	45.4	60.6	14.8	.001
e) The most important thing a child should learn is obedience to his parents	79.8	90.2	13.2	.001
f) Every person should have faith in some supernatural power whose decisions he obeys without question	46.7	60.9	13.0	.001
g) When a person has a problem or worry, it is best for him not to think about it, but to keep busy with more cheerful things	39.4	53.2	11.8	.001
h) Nowadays more and more people are prying into matters that should remain private and personal	63.5	74.5	8.6	.01
i) If people would talk less and work more, everybody would be better off	67.8	78.2	8.3	.01
j) An insult to our honor should always be punished	31.8	40.3	4.7	.05
k) No sane, normal person would ever think of hurting a close friend or relative	67.9	76.6	4.3	.05
l) Science has its place, but there are many important things that can never possibly be understood by the human mind	80.7	85.8	2.9	0.10
m) Some day it will probably be shown that astrology can explain a lot of things	44.4	48.0	0.9	n.s.

*The respondent was given four categories: agree strongly, agree, disagree, and disagree strongly. Percentage agreement is calculated by combining the first two of these replies.

confidence. The sixteen C-scale items predict almost as well; the more anti-African students in every case agree more often than the less prejudiced. Perhaps the conforming attitude of the bigots is capsuled in the first item of Table 1.3. While only a third of the tolerant members of the group agree with the statement, over half the prejudiced students feel that "it's better to go along with the crowd than to be a martyr."

These personality relationships suggest (a) that personality factors are as important correlates of prejudice in this sample as they are in other, non-South African samples; (b) that social conformity (as measured by the C scale) is a particularly crucial personality variable in this sample's attitudes toward Africans; and (c) that personality compo-

nents do not in themselves account for the heightened intolerance of this sample.

We must turn to sociocultural factors to explain the extreme prejudice of these respondents, and the unusual importance of these variables is made clear by the data. For instance, the 560 students who were born on the African continent are significantly more intolerant of Africans than the remaining 65, but they are *not* more authoritarian. Table 1.4 shows that those not born in Africa are much less likely to fall into the most prejudiced third of the distribution than other sample members. And yet the two groups do not differ significantly in their F-scale scores. More thoroughly influenced throughout their lives by the culture's definition of the white man's situation in Africa,

TABLE 1.3. Anti-African Prejudice and C-Scale Items

C-Scale Item	Percentage Agreement* Less Prejudiced Half	More Prejudiced Half	2×2 x^2	p
a) It's better to go along with the crowd than to be a martyr	34.8	53.2	21.8	0.001
b) When almost everyone agrees on something, there is little reason to oppose it	16.6	31.1	18.5	.001
c) Adherence to convention produces the best kind of citizen	31.8	46.8	14.9	.001
d) To be successful, a group's members must act and think alike	45.7	60.0	12.5	.001
e) It is important for friends to have similar opinions	28.5	42.2	12.1	.001
f) It is more important to be loyal and conform to our own group than to try to co-operate with other groups	25.6	38.5	11.7	.001
g) We should alter our needs to fit society's demands rather than change society to fit our needs	42.4	55.1	11.4	.001
h) A good group member should agree with the other members	21.2	33.2	11.1	.001
i) It is best not to express your views when in the company of friends who disagree with you	23.8	32.9	6.1	.02
j) Before a person does something, he should try to consider how his friends will react to it	54.6	63.1	4.4	.05
k) To become a success these days, a person has to act in the way that others expect him to act	33.2	41.5	4.2	.05
l) A group cannot expect to maintain its identity unless its members all think and feel in very much the same way	59.3	66.8	3.9	.05
m) It is one's duty to conform to the passing demands of the world and to suppress those personal desires that do not fit these demands	43.7	51.1	3.4	.10
n) A person should adapt his ideas and his behavior to the group that happens to be with him at the time	45.7	52.6	3.1	.10
o) It is extremely uncomfortable to go accidentally to a formal party in street clothes	78.5	83.1	2.0	.20
p) To get along well in a group, you have to follow the lead of others	27.2	31.1	1.1	0.30

* Percentage agreement calculated as in Table 1.2

students born on the Dark Continent are more anti-African without the usual personality concomitants of ethnocentrism.

Another such relationship involves students who support the Nationalist party—the pro-*Apartheid* political faction that is presently in power. Table 1.5 indicates that these respondents score significantly higher on the A scale than their fellow undergraduates, but these two groups do not differ on the F scale. Again a prejudice difference is not accompanied by a personality potential difference. These relationships with political party preference and prejudice hold for each of the major ethnic groups—Afrikaners and English—considered separately.

Two other comparisons yield statistically sig-

TABLE 1.4. Place of Birth and Anti-African Prejudice*

Anti-African Attitudes†	N	Place of Birth On African Continent	Not on African Continent
		560	65
Least prejudiced	176	28%	29%
Medium prejudiced	246	38%	54%
Most prejudiced	203	34%	17%

* 2 × 3 chi-square = 9.33; $p < 0.01$.
†The least prejudiced are the students who rated A-scale scores from 0 through 4 by disagreeing with a heavy majority of the items; the medium prejudiced received scores of either 5 or 6 by agreeing with roughly half of the 18 A-scale items; and the most prejudiced obtained scores of 7 through 10 by agreeing with a majority of the statements.

TABLE 1.5. Political Party Preference and Anti-African Prejudice*

Anti-African Attitudes	N	Political Party Preference[†] Nationalist Party	Other Parties
		72	483
Least prejudiced	157	8%	35%
Medium prejudiced	210	26%	36%
Most prejudiced	188	66%	29%

*2 × 3 chi-square = 38.60; $p < 0.001$.
[†]Seventy-two of the 627 students did not indicate any political preference.

nificant differences in both authoritarianism and anti-African prejudice. Table 1.6 indicates that those sample members whose fathers are manually employed are significantly more intolerant of the African than those whose fathers are nonmanually employed. The two groups differ in the same manner in their F-scale scores. But when authoritarianism is controlled for, the groups still differ significantly in their attitudes toward blacks.[6] In other words, the children of manual fathers are more prejudiced and more authoritarian than other students, and they remain more prejudiced even after the difference in authoritarianism is partialed out of the relationship. These upwardly mobile students must be carefully in step with the mores to establish firmly their rise in the social structure, and the mores of South Africa lead to intolerance.

Table 1.7 shows the sharp difference between the Afrikaner and English subjects in the sample. Afrikaners are both more anti-African and more authoritarian, and, when the F-scale differences

TABLE 1.6. Father's Occupational Status and Anti-African Prejudice*

Anti-African Attitudes	N	Father's Occupational Status[†] Manual	Non-manual
		146	417
Less prejudiced half	280	34%	55%
More prejudiced half	283	66%	45%

* 2 × 2 chi-square = 18.90; $p < 0.001$.
[†]Sixty-four of the 627 students did not indicate their fathers' occupations.

are corrected for, they remain significantly more hostile to the African.[7] These 50 students are directly subject to the national ethos and have no conflicting national reference, as many English-speaking South Africans have in Great Britain. Like the upwardly mobile, they are in roles that demand unusual conformity.

Table 1.8 clarifies further the ethnic differences in attitudes toward the African. Sixteen of the A scale's eighteen statements significantly separate the Afrikaners from the English, the former scoring higher in all cases. And, moreover, there is a definite trend in these differences. The five items which discriminate poorest between the ethnic groups (items n through r) are all stereotyped-belief statements; they refer to the standard traits frequently associated with Africans—lazy, primitive, happy-go-lucky, and bad-smelling. Conversely, five of the six best discriminators (items b through f) are all exclusion-discrimination statements; they deny equal rights to Africans in employment, housing, and voting. Afrikaans-speaking and English-speaking students, then, do not differ sharply in the degree to which they harbor the traditional stereotype of the African, but they do possess markedly divergent views on discrimination against the African. A key to these differences may be provided in the lone exception to this trend, item a. Seven out of every ten Afrikaners, as compared with only a third of the English, believe that the "natives will always have a greater tendency toward crimes of violence than Europeans." Strong projection may be operating for those agreeing with this statement, but, in any event, it suggests that physical fear of the black man is especially

[6]Authoritarianism can be controlled out in two ways. First, separate chi-square analyses of father's employment and anti-African attitudes were made for low and high F-scale halves. Second, the A- and F-scale scores were employed in an analysis of covariance that partialed out F scores. Both analyses indicate that father's employment is a significant correlate of anti-African attitudes even after authoritarianism is controlled out of the relationship.

[7]Authoritarianism was controlled out by both of the analyses described in the previous footnote. With their F-scale differences corrected for, Afrikaners in the sample are still significantly more hostile to the African than the English students. The cultural determination of this ethnic-group difference is made apparent when we survey the attitudes of the English students toward the Indians of South Africa. In sharp contrast to their African attitudes, the English members of the sample are considerably more anti-Indian—one-fifth of them "wish someone would kill all of them."

TABLE 1.7. Ethnic Group and Anti-African Prejudice*

Anti-African Attitudes	N	Ethnic Group[†] Afrikaners	English
		50	513
Less prejudiced half	264	14%	50%
More prejudiced half	299	86%	50%

*2 × 2 chi-square = 23.7; $p < 0.001$.
[†]Ethnic group is determined by both the student's own ethnic identification and the principal language spoken in his home. Sixty-four of the students identified with other groups (e.g., Jewish, French, German) and are not included in this analysis.

prevalent among our Afrikaans-speaking respondents and that this may be the fundamental motivation for their emphasis on excluding and discriminating against the African.

All these findings point to the crucial role of the cultural milieu in shaping the attitudes of the white South African toward the blacks in his midst. While externalizing personality factors do not account for the students' unusually prejudiced attitudes concerning Africans, variables which reflect the dominant norms of the white society prove to be important. Students who are especially responsive to these norms—those who were born in Africa, those who identify with the Nationalist party, those who are upwardly mobile, and those who have been molded by the conservative traditions of the Afrikaans-speaking people—tend to be intolerant of Africans to some degree, regardless of their basic personality structure.

Racial Prejudice in the Southern United States

Similar considerations led to an earlier comparative study of anti-Negro prejudice in the southern and northern United States. While considerable evidence indicates that white southerners are typically more intolerant of the Negro than white northerners (16, 27, 30, 35, 36, 39), little work has been focused on the factors underlying this difference. But, like the South African data, the scant data available suggest that sociocultural and not externalization factors may be the crucial determinants of the contrasting regional attitudes toward the Negro.

Thus, if the South did have more externalizing personality potential for prejudice than other American areas, it should also be more anti-Semitic.[8] But Roper (31, 32) has twice found in his national polls that the South is one of the most tolerant regions toward Jews, and Prothro (30) has noted that 40 percent of his adult white Louisiana sample is at the same time favorable in its attitudes toward Jews and highly anti-Negro. Furthermore, there is no evidence that the stern family pattern associated with "prejudiced personalities" (1, 12) is more prevalent in the South than in the North (6, 8). And, finally, the few white southern populations that have been given the F scale have obtained means that fall easily within the range of means reported for non-southern populations (1, 25, 37).

Rose categorically concludes: "There is no evidence that 'authoritarian personality' or frustration-aggression or scapegoating, or any known source of 'prejudice' in the psychological sense, is any more prevalent in the South than in the North" (33). And Prothro adds: "Situational, historical and cultural factors appear to be of considerable, perhaps major, import in addition to personality dynamics" in determining anti-Negro attitudes in the South (30).

In testing these ideas in the two regions, different methods were employed than those used in South Africa. Public opinion polling techniques were utilized with 366 randomly selected white adults in eight roughly matched communities in the North and South. The four small southern towns, located in Georgia and North Carolina, were chosen to have Negro population percentages ranging from 10 to 45 percent, while the small northern towns, all located in New England, have less than 1 percent Negroes each.

The interview schedule contained a ten-item measure of authoritarianism (F scale), an eight-item measure of anti-Semitism (A-S scale), and a twelve-item measure of anti-Negro prejudice (N scale), together with numerous background questions.[9] The poll purported to be concerned with the effects of the mass media upon public opin-

[8]This is true because the prejudiced personality is predisposed to disliking all socially recognized out-groups—Negroes, Jews, Catholics, etc.—and not just one. Being functionally necessary, prejudice generalizes to out-groups of all varieties (1, 2, 13).
[9]There is considerable overlap in items used in the two investigations. Again, all ten of the F items are taken from the work of Adorno et al. (1); seven were used in South Africa (Table 1.2, items a, b, c, f, h, i, and k); and the others are items 1, 13, and 21 of p. 255 in *The Authoritarian Personality*

TABLE 1.8. Ethnic-group Differences on A-Scale Items

A-Scale Items	Percentage Agreement[*]			
	Afrikaners	English	$2 \times 2\ x^2$	p
a) Because of their primitive background, natives will always have a greater tendency toward crimes of violence than Europeans	70.0	34.9	33.6	0.001
b) Native musicians are sometimes as good as Europeans at at swing music and jazz, but it is a mistake to have mixed native-European bands	86.0	54.2	18.8	.001
c) Most of the natives would become officious, overbearing, and disagreeable if not kept in their place	80.0	48.3	18.2	.001
d) Laws which would lone equal employment opportunities for both the natives and Europeans would not be fair to European employers	74.0	44.2	16.2	.001
e) The natives have their rights, but it is best to keep them in their own districts and schools and to prevent too much contact with Europeans	86.0	63.7	9.9	.01
f) The natives do not deserve the right to vote	64.0	41.3	9.5	.01
g) The natives will never have the intelligence and organizing ability to run a modern industrial society	42.0	23.2	8.7	.01
h) As the native will never properly absorb our civilization, the only solution is to let him develop along his own lines	68.0	46.3	8.6	.01
i) Manual labor seems to fit the native mentality better than more skilled and responsible work	88.0	68.9	8.0	.01
j) Seldom, if ever, is a native superior to most Europeans intellectually	72.0	52.2	7.1	.01
k) The natives tend to be overly emotional	66.0	46.5	7.1	.01
l) Because of his immaturity, the South African native is likely to be led into all sorts of mischief and should therefore be strictly controlled in his own best interests	92.0	75.6	6.9	.01
m) The granting of wide educational opportunities to natives is a dangerous thing	36.0	19.9	6.9	.01
n) Most natives are lazy and lack ambition	60.0	44.1	4.6	.05
o) There is something inherently primitive and uncivilized in the native, as shown in his music and extreme aggressiveness	86.0	72.1	4.4	.05
p) Due to the differences in innate endowment, the Bantu race will always be inferior to the white race	54.0	39.6	4.0	.05
q) Most of the natives are happy-go-lucky and irresponsible	70.0	60.0	1.9	0.20
r) In spite of what some claim, the natives do have a different and more pronounced body odor than Europeans	84.0	81.5	0.2	n.s.

[*]Percentage agreement calculated as in Table 1.2.

(1). The A-S items are all from the California investigations, too (1, items 3, 4, 13, 15, 22, and 24 on pp. 68–69 and items 4 and 15 on p. 70). Save for the word substitutions of "white" for "European" and "Negro" for "native," all twelve N-scale items were used in the South African A scale (Table 1.8, items b, c, d, e, f, j, k, m, n, o, q, and r). That virtually the same prejudice and authoritarian statements can be successfully used in the Union of South Africa and in the northern and southern United States suggests that racial prejudice and its personality concomitants take extremely similar forms in many parts of the Western world.

ion, and it seems largely due to this guise that the blatantly phrased prejudice statements caused no interview breakoffs.

Of greatest immediate interest is the striking similarity in these results with those of the South African investigation. First, the southern sample is considerably more anti-Negro than the northern sample but is not more authoritarian. Similar to the Afrikaner-English differences (Table 1.8), the southerners respond in the more prejudiced direction on each of the N-scale statements but are most unique in their extreme attitudes concerning excluding and discriminating against the Negro. That is, southerners and northerners in the samples both share in large degree the lazy, primitive, happy-go-lucky, and bad-smelling stereotype of the Negro, but southerners far more than northerners wish to deny equal rights to the Negro in employment, housing, and voting. And yet there is no difference in the externalization potential for intolerance; the F-scale means of the two samples are almost identical.

Further similarities to the South African data support the contention that personality dynamics, such as authoritarianism, are not responsible for the sharp North-South divergence in attitudes toward the Negro. When age and education are partialed out,[10] the N and F scales correlate to a comparable degree in the two populations. Moreover, with age and education partialed out again, the N and A-S scales relate at equivalent levels in the two regional samples. In other words, the externalizing prejudiced personality as tapped by the F and A-S scales does not account for any more of the anti-Negro variance in the southern sample than it does in the northern sample. This finding, combined with the previously mentioned fact that the two groups do not differ in their F-scale responses, indicates that externalization factors do not explain the heightened bigotry of the southerners. As with the South African results, we must turn to social variables in an effort to account for the regional discrepancy in attitudes toward the Negro.

All six of the sociocultural dimensions tested yield meaningful relationships with Negro prejudice in the southern sample: sex, church attendance, social mobility, political party identification, armed service, and education. These variables reflect southern culture in a manner similar to the social variables tested in the South African study. And as in South Africa, those southerners, who by their roles in the social structure can be anticipated to be conforming to the dictates of the culture, prove to be more prejudiced against Negroes than their counterparts. For example, females, the "carriers of culture," are significantly more anti-Negro than men in the southern sample but *not* in the northern sample.

Two other groups of southerners who manifest conforming behavior in other areas are also more intolerant of Negroes.[11] Respondents who have been to church within the week are significantly more anti-Negro than those who have not been within the month, and there is a tendency (though not statistically significant) for the upwardly mobile to be more anti-Negro than others in the non-manual occupational class. The latter result recalls the finding in the South African study that students whose fathers are manual workers tend to be more anti-African (Table 1.6). In the northern sample, no such trends appear. Protestant churchgoers in the North tend to be more tolerant of the Negro than Protestant non-attenders, and no relationship between upward mobility and attitudes toward Negroes is discernible. Conformity to northern norms—unlike conformity to southern or South African norms—is not associated with hostility for the black man.

In contrast to the conformers, southerners who evidence deviance from the mores in some area of social life tend to be *less* anti-Negro. Non-attenders of church furnish one example. Another example are respondents who explicitly identify themselves as political independents, which also represents a degree of deviance: they tend to be considerably more tolerant of the Negro than are southerners who consider themselves either Democrats or Republicans.[12] Again, no such discrepancy occurs in the northern population.

Downward mobility has been noted by other investigators to be positively related to intolerance in the North (3, 10), and this finding is replicated in the present northern data. But in the southern data a striking reversal occurs. The downwardly mobile in the South are much less anti-Negro than other manually employed respondents, though the two groups do not differ in authoritarianism. Perhaps in a culture that emphasizes status and fam-

---

[10]This was not necessary in the South African data because the college sample is relatively homogeneous in terms of age and education. In heterogeneous, randomly drawn adult samples, however, age and education must be controlled, since both authoritarianism and prejudice are positively related to age and negatively related to education (2, 5, 16, 23).

[11]The church attendance, social mobility, political party identification, and armed service findings reported here were all established with matched-pair analyses. This design made it possible to control the age, education, and sex variables out of these relationships. The detailed results are published elsewhere (29).

[12]It might be thought that Republican party membership in the South constitutes deviance, too. Actually, the "solid South" is not that politically solid; three of the four southern communities polled have favored some Republican candidates in recent elections.

ily background, that makes a sharp distinction between "poor whites" and "respectable whites," and that cherishes its aristocratic traditions (4, 6, 8), the downwardly mobile southerner learns to reject much of his culture. And rejecting the culture's stress on tradition and status makes it easier to reject also the culture's dicta concerning the Negro.

Two groups of southerners—armed service veterans and the highly educated—are potential deviants from southern culture simply because their special experience and study have brought them into contact with other ways of life. And, as we might expect, we find that both veterans and college-educated southerners are considerably more tolerant of the Negro than non-veterans and the poorly educated. Veterans in both regions prove to be more authoritarian than non-veterans,[13] and, consistent with this, northern veterans are less tolerant of Negroes than northerners who had not served. Education is negatively related to N-scale scores in the northern sample, too, but significantly less than in the southern sample. Exposure to non-southern culture leads to deviance from the strict southern norms concerning the Negro; little wonder that southerners who have been out of the region for any considerable length of time are generally viewed as suspect by their neighbors upon return.

These consistent relationships with social factors in the southern data have been interpreted in terms of conformity and deviance from the narrowly prescribed mores of small-town southern life. Evidence for such an analysis comes from a final intra-southern difference. Southern communities with high Negro population ratios (38 and 45 percent) have significantly higher N-scale means than the other communities sampled in the South with low Negro ratios (10 and 18 percent), though they are not different in authoritarianism or anti-Semitism. In southern areas with the most intensely anti-Negro norms, prejudice against the black southerner is greater, even though there is not a greater amount of externalizing personality potential for prejudice.

Though limited by the restricted samples employed, this evidence indicates that sociocultural factors—as in the South African sample—are indeed the key to the regional difference in attitudes toward the Negro. In spite of the marked contrast in samples and method between the two investigations, both the South African and the southern

results underline the unique importance of social variables in prejudice that is sanctioned by the cultural norms.

Summary and Conclusions

Finely interwoven personality and sociocultural variables together form the foundation upon which a broad and satisfactory theory of racial prejudice must be built. Neither set of factors can be neglected, but a heuristic separation between the relatively culture-free externalization factors and social factors aids analysis. The present paper uses this distinction to interpret prejudice data from two parts of the world with tense racial conflict—the Union of South Africa and the southern United States.

Externalization factors such as authoritarianism are associated with prejudice in both the South African and the southern samples at levels roughly comparable with other areas. Data from the South African students hint, however, that susceptibility to conform may be an unusually important psychological component of prejudice in regions where the cultural norms positively sanction intolerance. In addition, there is no indication in either of these samples that there is any more externalizing personality potential for prejudice in these areas than in more tolerant parts of the globe.

The extensive racial prejudice of the South African and southern groups seems directly linked with the antiblack dictates of the two cultures. Sociocultural factors which reflect the mores consistently relate to prejudice—place of birth, political party preference, upward mobility, and ethnic-group membership in the South African data and sex, church attendance, social mobility, political party identification, armed service, and education in the southern data. The pattern is clear: conformity to South African or southern mores is associated with racial intolerance, while deviance from these mores is associated with racial tolerance.

Taken together with other published work, these limited results suggest a broad, cross-national hy-

---

[13]Presumably this increased authoritarianism of veterans is related to their service experience in authoritarian environments, though Christie (5) failed to note an increase in F scores of army recruits after six weeks of infantry basic training.

pothesis:

In areas with historically imbedded traditions of racial intolerance, externalizing personality factors underlying prejudice remain important, but sociocultural factors are unusually crucial and account for the heightened racial hostility.

Should future, more extensive, research support such a hypothesis, its implications for prejudice theory would be considerable. Regions or peoples with heightened prejudice against a particular outgroup would not necessarily be thought of as harboring more authoritarianism; the special conflict may reflect the operation of particular historical, cultural, and social factors. Such a prospect may be encouraging to many action programs—efforts which typically are more successful at changing a person's relation to his culture than they are at changing basic personality structure. Desegregation is a case in point. The success of the movement in the South does not depend—this hypothesis would contend—on changing the deeply ingrained orientations of prejudice-prone personalties; rather, it rests on the effectiveness with which racial integration now going on in the South can restructure the mores to which so many culturally intolerant southerners conform.

A second implication of the hypothesis is that personality factors such as authoritarianism and susceptibility to conform cannot be overlooked in understanding bigotry even in parts of the world like the Union of South Africa, and the southern United States. Most psychological approaches to prejudice, it has been noted, are concerned chiefly with the externalization function of attitudes. Perhaps, as the object-appraisal and social-adjustment functions of attitudes are studied in more detail the direct personality concomitants of cultural pressures will be isolated and better understood.

REFERENCES

1. Adorno, T. W., Frenkel-Brunswick, E., Levinson, D. J., & Sanford, R. N. (1950). *The Authoritarian Personality*. New York: Harper & Bros.
2. Allport, G. W. (1954). *The Nature of Prejudice*. Cambridge, MA: Addison-Wesley Press.
3. Bettelheim, B., & Janowitz, M. (1950). *Dynamics of Prejudice*. New York: Harper & Bros.
4. Cash, W. (1941). *The Mind of the South*. NY: Knopf.
5. Christie, R. (1954). Authoritarianism Re-examined. In R. Christie and M. Jahoda (eds.), *Studies in the Scope and Method of "The Authoritarian Personality,"* pp. 123–196. Glencoe, IL: Free Press.
6. Davis, A., Gardner, B., & Gardner, M. (1941). *Deep South*. Chicago: University of Chicago Press.
7. Deutsch, M., & Collins, M. (1951). *Interracial Housing*. Minneapolis: University of Minnesota Press.
8. Dollard, J. (1937). *Caste and Class in a Southern Town*. New Haven, CT: Yale University Press.
9. Dollard, J., Doob, L., Miller, N., Mowrer, O., & Sears, R. (1939). *Frustration and Aggression*. New Haven, CT: Yale University Press.
10. Greenblum, J., & Pearlin, L. (1953). Vertical Mobility and Prejudice: A Socio-psychological Analysis. In R. Bendix and S. Lipset (eds.), *Class, Status, and Power*, pp. 480–491. Glencoe, IL: Free Press.
11. Harding, J., & Hogrefe, R. (1952). Attitudes of White Department Store Employees toward Negro Co-workers, *Journal of Social Issues*, VIII, No. 1, 18–28.
12. Harris, D. B., Gough, H. G., & Martin, W. E. (1950). Children's Ethnic Attitudes. II. Relationship to Parental Beliefs Concerning Child Training. *Child Development*, XXI, 169–181.
13. Hartley, E. L. (1946). *Problems in Prejudice*. New York: Kings Crown Press.
14. Hellmann, E. (ed.) (1949). *Handbook on Race Relations in South Africa*. Cape Town, South Africa: Oxford University Press.
15. Hoffman, M. L. (1953). Some Psychodynamic Factors in Compulsive Conformity. *Journal of Abnormal and Social Psychology*, XLVIII, pp. 383–393.
16. Hyman, H. H., & Sheatsley, P. B. (1956). Attitudes toward Desegregation. *Scientific American*, CXCV, 35–39.
17. Jones, E. (1957). City Limits. In D. Shoemaker (ed.), *With All Deliberate Speed*, pp. 71–87. New York: Harper & Bros.
18. Kutner, B., Wilkins, C., & Yarrow, P. (1952). Verbal Attitudes and Overt Behavior Involving Racial Prejudice, *Journal of Abnormal and Social Psychology*, XLVII, 649–652.
19. La Piere, R. T. (1934). Attitudes versus Actions, *Social Forces*, XIII 230–237.
20. McLean, H. V. (1946). Psychodynamic Factors in Racial Relations, *Annals of the American Academy of Political and Social Science*, CCXLIV, 159–166.
21. MacCrone, I. D. (1937). *Race Attitudes in South Africa*. London: Oxford University Press.
22. ———. (1953). Ethnocentric Ideology and Ethnocentrism, *Proceedings of the South African Psychological Association*, IV, 21–24.
23. Mackinnon, W. J., & Centers, R. (1958). Authoritarianism and Urban Stratification, *American Journal of Sociology*, XLI, 610–620.
24. Malherbe, E. G. (1948). *Race Attitudes and Education*. Johannesburg, South Africa: Institute of Race Relations.
25. Milton, O. (1952). Presidential Choice and Performance on a Scale of Authoritarianism, *American Psychologist*, VII, 597–598.
26. Minard, R. D. (1952). Race Relations in the Pocahontas Coal Field, *Journal of Social Issues*, VIII, No. 1, 29–44.
27. Myrdal, G. (1944). *An American Dilemma*. New York: Harper & Bros.
28. Pettigrew, T. F. (1957). Desegregation and Its Chances for Success: Northern and Southern Views. *Social Forces*, XXXV, 339–344.
29. ———. Regional Differences in Anti-Negro Prejudice (manuscript presently submitted for publication).
30. Prothro, E. T. (1952), Ethnocentrism and Anti-Negro Attitudes in the Deep South. *Journal of Abnormal and Social*

Psychology, XLVII, 105–108.

31. Roper, E. (1947). United States Anti-Semites, *Fortune*, XXXIII (1946), 257–260.

32. ———. (1947). United States Anti-Semites. *Fortune*, XXXVI, 5–10.

33. Rose, A. M. (1956). Intergroup Relations vs. Prejudice: Pertinent Theory for the Study of Social Change, *Social Problems*, IV, 173–176.

34. Saenger, G., & Gilbert, E. (1950). Customer Reactions to the Integration of Negro Sales Personnel, *International Journal of Opinion and Attitude Research,* IV, 57–78.

35. Samelson, B. (1945). The Patterning of Attitudes and Beliefs Regarding the American Negro: An Analysis of Public Opinion. Unpublished doctoral dissertation, Radcliffe College.

36. Sims, V. M., & Patrick, J. R. (1936). Attitude towards the Negro of Northern and Southern College Students, *Journal of Social Psychology*, VII, 192–204.

37. Smith, C. U., & Prothro, J. W. (1957). Ethnic Differences in Authoritarian Personality, *Social Forces*, XXXV, 334–338.

38. Smith, M. B., Bruner, J. S., & White, R. W. (1956). *Opinions and Personality*. New York: John Wiley & Sons.

39. Stouffer, S. A., Suchman, E. A., DeVinney, L. C., Star, S., A., & Williams, R. M., Jr. (1949). *The American Soldier: Adjustment during Army Life.* (Studies in Social Psychology in World War II, Vol. I.). Princeton, NJ: Princeton University Press.

40. Wilner, D. M., Walkley, R. P., and Cook, S. W. (1952). Residential Proximity and Intergroup Relations in Public Housing Projects. *Journal of Social Issues*, VIII, No. 1, 45–69.

Social Dominance Orientation: A Personality Variable Predicting Social and Political Attitudes

Felicia Pratto, Jim Sidanius, Lisa M. Stallworth, and Bertram F. Malle
• University of California at Los Angeles

Social dominance orientation (SDO), one's degree of preference for inequality among social groups, is introduced. On the basis of social dominance theory, it is shown that (a) men are more social dominance–oriented than women, (b) high-SDO people seek hierarchy-enhancing professional roles and low-SDO people seek hierarchy-attenuating roles, (c) SDO was related to beliefs in a large number of social and political ideologies that support group-based hierarchy (e.g., meritocracy and racism) and to support for policies that have implications for intergroup relations (e.g., war, civil rights, and social programs), including new policies. SDO was distinguished from interpersonal dominance, conservatism, and authoritarianism. SDO was negatively correlated with empathy, tolerance, communality, and altruism. The ramifications of SDO in social context are discussed.

Group conflict and group-based inequality are pervasive in human existence. Currently, every continent is enduring some form of ethnic conflict, from the verbal debate over multiculturalism in the United States and Canada to civil war in Liberia and Bosnia. Other conflicts between groups are ancient: the European persecution of Jews, "Holy Wars" waged by Christians and Muslims around the Mediterranean, imperialism in South America, and anti-Black racism in northern Africa and elsewhere. Regardless of the intensity of the conflict, the participants justify their behavior to others by appealing to historical injustices, previous territorial boundaries, religious prohibitions, genetic and cultural theories of in-group superiority, or other such ideologies.

Prompted by the ubiquitous nature of group-based prejudice and oppression, we developed social dominance theory (see Pratto, 1996; Sidanius, 1993; Sidanius & Pratto, 1993a). The theory pos-

tulates that societies minimize group conflict by creating consensus on ideologies that promote the superiority of one group over others (see also Sidanius, Pratto, Martin, & Stallworth, 1991). Ideologies that promote or maintain group inequality are the tools that legitimize discrimination. To work smoothly, these ideologies must be widely accepted within a society, appearing as self-apparent truths; hence we call them *hierarchy-legitimizing myths*.[1] By contributing to consensual or normalized group-based inequality, legitimizing myths help to stabilize oppression. That is, they minimize conflict among groups by indicating how individuals and social institutions should allocate

---

[1]The term *myth* is meant to imply that everyone in the society perceives these ideologies as explanations for how the world is—not that they are false (or true). Social dominance theory is meant only to describe the social and psychological processes that act on these ideologies, not to ascertain whether these ideologies are true, fair, moral, or reasonable.

things of positive or negative social value, such as jobs, gold, blankets, government appointments, prison terms, and disease. For example, the ideology of anti-Black racism has been instantiated in personal acts of discrimination, but also in institutional discrimination against African-Americans by banks, public transit authorities, schools, churches, marriage laws, and the penal system. Social Darwinism and meritocracy are examples of other ideologies that imply that some people are not as "good" as others and therefore should be allocated less positive social value than others.

Thus far, we have given examples of legitimizing myths that enhance or maintain the degree of social inequality. Other ideologies may serve to attenuate the amount of inequality. For example, the "universal rights of man" and the view summarized by "all humans are God's children" are inclusive, egalitarian ideologies that explicitly do not divide persons into categories or groups. To the extent that such ideologies are widely shared, there should be less group inequality. There are, then, two varieties of legitimizing myths: hierarchy-enhancing legitimizing myths, which promote greater degrees of social inequality, and hierarchy-attenuating legitimizing myths, which promote greater social equality.

Social Dominance Orientation

Given our theoretical postulate that acceptance of legitimizing myths has significant influence on the degree of inequality in societies, it is quite important to understand the factors that lead to the acceptance or rejection of ideologies that promote or attenuate inequality. Social dominance theory postulates that a significant factor is an individual-difference variable called *social dominance orientation* (SDO), or the extent to which one desires that one's in-group dominate and be superior to outgroups. We consider SDO to be a general attitudinal orientation toward intergroup relations, reflecting whether one generally prefers such relations to be equal, versus hierarchical, that is, ordered along a superior-inferior dimension. The theory postulates that people who are more social-dominance oriented will tend to favor hierarchy-enhancing ideologies and policies, whereas those lower on SDO will tend to favor hierarchy-attenuating ideologies and policies.

SDO is thus the central individual-difference variable that predicts a person's acceptance or rejection of numerous ideologies and policies relevant to group relations.

Another way that individuals' levels of SDO may influence their contribution to social equality or inequality is in the kinds of social roles they take on, particularly, roles that either enhance or attenuate inequality. We thus predict that those who are higher on SDO will become members of institutions and choose roles that maintain or increase social inequality, whereas those who are lower on SDO will belong to institutions and choose roles that reduce inequality.

The purpose of the present research was to demonstrate that individual variation in SDO exists and to show that this construct behaves according to the theory outlined above. Specifically, our goals were (a) to develop a measure of SDO that is internally and temporally reliable, (b) to show that SDO is related to the attitudinal and social role variables specified by social dominance theory (predictive validity), (c) to show that the measure is not redundant with other attitude predictors and standard personality variables (discriminant validity), and (d) to show that SDO serves as an orientation in shaping new attitudes.

Hypotheses

The first set of hypotheses we tested was derived from social dominance theory and concerned those variables to which SDO should strongly relate, termed *predictive validity*. The second set of hypotheses, termed *discriminant validity*, states either that SDO should be independent of other variables or that SDO should have predictive value in addition to the effects of these other variables. We also hypothesized that SDO should relate moderately to certain other personality variables, from which SDO is conceptually distinct. The third set of hypotheses we tested concerns SDO's power to predict new social attitudes.

Predictive Validity

GENDER

The world over, men and women hold different roles with regard to the maintenance of hierarchy.

Ubiquitously, men serve as military leaders and hold leadership roles in religious, social, political, and cultural spheres (e.g., Brown, 1991, pp. 110, 137). Moreover, men hold more hierarchy-enhancing attitudes, such as support for ethnic prejudice, racism, capitalism, and rightwing political parties, than do women (e.g., Avery, 1988; Eisler & Loye, 1983; Ekehammar & Sidanius, 1982; Shapiro & Mahajan, 1986; Sidanius & Ekehammar, 1980; see review by Sidanius, Cling, & Pratto, 1991). On the basis of these general societal patterns, we have predicted and shown that, on average, men are more social dominance–oriented than women (see Pratto, Sidanius, & Stallworth, 1993; Sidanius, Pratto, & Bobo, 1995). We tested this hypothesis with the measure of SDO developed in the present research.

LEGITIMIZING MYTHS

Ethnic Prejudice. One of the major kinds of ideology concerning relative group status is ethnic prejudice. In the United States, the most longstanding and widely disseminated version of ethnic prejudice is anti-Black racism. Therefore, we predicted that SDO would be strongly related to anti-Black racism in the present U.S. samples. In the United States, a theoretical and empirical debate about how best to measure anti-Black racism has been conducted for some time (e.g., see Bobo, 1983; McConahay, 1986; Sears, 1988; Sniderman & Tetlock, 1986a, 1986b). Social dominance theory merely postulates that SDO should predict whatever ideologies are potent within the culture at the time of measurement. From our theoretical viewpoint, it does not matter whether the basis for racism is fairness (e.g., Kluegel & Smith, 1986), genetic or biblical racial inferiority theories, symbolic racism (e.g., Sears, 1988), or family pathology (e.g., Moynihan, 1965). Any potent ideology that describes groups as unequal and has policy implications is a legitimizing myth and should, therefore, correlate with SDO. During the period the present research was conducted, our subjects' country was engaged in a war against Iraq, so we also measured anti-Arab racism and expected it to correlate with SDO.

Nationalism. A more general kind of in-group prejudice that can occur in nation-states is nationalism, chauvinism, or patriotism. Kosterman and Feshbach (1989) suggested that procountry feel-

ings (patriotism) can be distinguished from comparative prejudice, that is, that one's country is better than other countries (nationalism), and as such should dominate other countries (chauvinism). Even so, all three reflect attitudinal bias in favor of the national in-group, and thus we postulated that patriotism, nationalism, and chauvinism would all be significantly related to SDO.

Cultural Elitism. All societies share the idea that one of the defining features of those who belong to their society (are part of the in-group, or are considered by them to be human) is that they are "cultured." In some societies, including English and American society, an elitist ideology built on the cultured–not cultured distinction postulates that the elite class has "culture" not shared by middle- and working-class people and is therefore more deserving of the "finer things in life." We term this legitimizing myth *cultural elitism,* and we expected it to correlate with SDO as well.

Sexism. We believe that antifemale sexism is a ubiquitous legitimizing myth, although, as with ethnic prejudice, the content basis of sexist ideology varies widely with religion, cultural history, and technology. In the present U.S. samples, we used scales that assess sexism as the extent to which people believe men and women are "naturally" different and should have different work roles outside and inside the home (Benson & Vincent, 1980; Rombough & Ventimiglia, 1981) and the extent to which people believe that women rather than men can be blamed for unwanted sexual advances such as rape and sexual harassment (Burt, 1980). We predicted that all of these would be positively correlated with SDO, even controlling for subject sex.

Political-Economic Conservatism. Political-economic conservatism is associated with support for capitalism versus socialism (e.g., Eysenck, 1971). Given that capitalism implies that some people and businesses should thrive, while those who are less "competitive" should not, we consider political-economic conservatism to be a hierarchy-enhancing legitimizing myth that should positively correlate with SDO (see also Sidanius & Pratto, 1993b). Other policies supported by conservatives, such as that women should stay home with children and that the USSR must be kept in its place, divide people into groups "deserving" different treatment, so we feel conservatism generally can be viewed as a legitimizing myth. In fact, Wilson's extensive work on the body of attitudes that make up conservatism shows that a preference for hierarchical social relationships is one of conservatism's many dimensions (Wilson, 1973, p. 22).

Noblesse Oblige. A hierarchy-attenuating ideology that exists in many cultures is that those with more resources should share them with those who have fewer resources (e.g., the Marxist maxim, "From each according to his [sic] ability, to each according to his need," and the potlatch custom of the Kwakiutl). The English-American version is, called *noblesse oblige*, which we expected to be negatively correlated with SDO.

Meritocracy. Another hierarchy-enhancing ideology is that wealth and other social values are already distributed appropriately, based on the deservingness of the recipients. The Protestant work ethic and just world theory are examples of meritocratic ideologies, so we administered standard measures of belief in the Protestant work ethic and belief in a just world and predicted that they would be positively correlated with SDO. In the United States, attributions for poverty due to laziness or to some other inherent fault in the poor are predicated on the idea that equal opportunity is available to all (Kluegel & Smith, 1986), so we wrote an equal opportunity scale and predicted that it would correlate positively with SDO.

SOCIAL POLICY ATTITUDES

According to social dominance theory, individuals who are social dominance oriented will favor social practices that maintain or exacerbate inequality among groups and will oppose social practices that reduce group inequality. The particular social policies that correlate with SDO may vary from society to society, but we predicted that SDO would relate to support for, or opposition to, the following policies in U.S. samples.

Social Welfare, Civil Rights, and Environmental Policies. We expected SDO to correlate with opposition to social policies that would reduce inequality between U.S. nationals and foreigners or immigrants, rich and middle class or poor, men and women, ethnic groups, heterosexuals and

homosexuals and humans versus other species. As such, we measured our subjects' attitudes toward a variety of government social programs, racial and sexual discrimination laws, gay and lesbian rights, domination of foreigners, and environmental policies. In several samples we also assessed attitudes toward "interracial dating" and "interracial marriage," because miscegenation has been central to the U.S. racial policy debate.

Military Policy. Because the military is a symbol of nationalism and can be one of the chief means of domination of one nation over others, we expected SDO to correlate positively with expressed support for military programs and actions.

Punitive Policies. Despite its stated creed to enact equality before the law, the U.S. criminal justice system shows class and ethnic bias at all levels from arrest to plea bargaining to sentencing (e.g., Bienen, Alan, Denno, Allison, & Mills, 1988; General Accounting Office, 1990; Kleck, 1981; Nickerson, Mayo, & Smith, 1986; Paternoster, 1983; Radelet & Pierce, 1985; Reiman, 1990; Sidanius, 1988). As one example, in a review of 1,804 homicide cases in South Carolina, Paternoster (1983) found that in cases where Blacks killed Whites, rather than other Blacks, prosecutors were 40 times more likely to request the death penalty. For this reason, we expected support for "law and order" or punitive policies, particularly the death penalty, to be positively related to SDO (see also Mitchell, 1993; Sidanius, Liu, Pratto, & Shaw 1994).

Discriminant Validity

INTERPERSONAL DOMINANCE

SDO, or preference for unequal relationships among categories of people, is conceptually distinguishable from the common personality conception of interpersonal dominance, which concerns the extent to which individuals like to be in charge and are efficacious. For example, people who score high on the California Personality Inventory (CPI) Dominance scale are confident, assertive, dominant, and task oriented, whereas people who score low are unassuming and nonforceful (Gough, 1987, p. 6). People who score high on the Jackson Personality Research Form (JPRF) Dominance scale attempt to control their environments and influence or direct other people; they are forceful, decisive, authoritative, and domineering (Jackson, 1965). We tested this theoretical distinction between social and task or interpersonal dominance by using the CPI and JPRF Dominance subscales in several samples reported here. We predicted that SDO would not correlate with these two measures.

AUTHORITARIANISM

There is clearly some theoretical similarity in the effects of social dominance theory's SDO construct and authoritarian personality theory's authoritarian construct (see Adorno, Frenkel-Brunswik, Levinson, & Sanford, 1950). High-SDO people and authoritarian personalities are theorized to be relatively conservative, racist, ethnocentric, and prejudiced, and they should show little empathy for lower status others. Our conception of SDO, however, differs from classical authoritarianism in several respects. First, classical authoritarian theorists viewed authoritarianism as an aberrant and pathological condition and as a form of ego-defense against feelings of inadequacy and vulnerability (see also Frenkel-Brunswik, 1948, 1949). SDO, however, is not conceived of in clinical terms, as an aberrant personality type, or as a form of ego-defense. Rather, SDO is conceived of as a "normal" human propensity on which people vary. Second, authoritarian personality theory emphasized the sources of authoritarianism as springing from psychodynamic processes. Specifically, Adorno et al. (1950) postulated that strict and harsh parental styles would provoke conflicts between the child and parents that would be "unresolved." As a way of resolving these, the child as an adult would submit to authorities and be intolerant of those who would not. In contrast, we theorize that such a personal history is unnecessary to developing a relatively high SDO tendency. Rather, both temperament and socialization probably influence one's level of SDO. Third and most important, whereas authoritarianism is primarily conceived as a desire for individual dominance resulting from experiences with authority figures, SDO is regarded as the desire that some categories of people dominate others. Because the two constructs are defined differently, measurements of each should not be highly correlated.

Given that authoritarianism should predict many of the same variables we postulate SDO should predict, it is important for us to show that SDO has explanatory value in addition to authoritarianism. We tested the "marginal utility" of the SDO construct by testing whether correlations between SDO and support for legitimizing myths and policies are significant after partialing out authoritarianism.

CONSERVATISM

Political-economic conservatism serves as a legitimizing myth in our theory, and thus we expect it to correlate positively with SDO. Conservatism is also a well-known robust predictor of social and political attitudes (e.g., Eysenck & Wilson, 1978; Wilson, 1973). To show that SDO has utility in addition to political-economic conservatism, we tested whether SDO substantially correlated with social attitudes after partialing out conservatism.

STANDARD PERSONALITY VARIABLES

Because we think our concept of SDO is a yet unstudied personality dimension, we expected it to be independent of other standard personality variables such as self-esteem and the Big Five personality dimensions: Extraversion, Agreeableness, Openness, Neuroticism, and Conscientiousness (see Costa & MacRae, 1985; John, 1990, for reviews).

EMPATHY, ALTRUISM, COMMUNALITY, AND TOLERANCE

People who are highly empathic with others would seem to be less prejudiced and discriminatory against out-groups. Thus, it is reasonable to expect a general concern for other people to be negatively correlated with SDO. Similarly, any general prosocial orientation might mitigate prejudiced feelings and behaviors toward out-group members, so altruism should be negatively correlated with SDO. Furthermore, people who are quite inclusive in their definitions of what constitutes an in-group should be less able to discriminate against out-groups, so we expected communality to be negatively correlated with SDO. And finally, because tolerance is the antithesis of prejudice, we might expect that a general measure of tolerance would be negatively correlated with a general desire for in-group superiority. We used Davis' (1983) multidimensional empathy scale,

Super and Nevill's (1985) altruism subscale, the Personal Attribute Questionnaire (PAQ) Communality scale (Spence, Helmreich, & Stapp, 1974), and the Jackson Personality Inventory (JPI) Tolerance scale (Jackson, 1976) to test these hypotheses. If SDO has merit as a new personality variable, none of these correlations should be very high.

Present Research

Overview

We examined data from 13 samples to test the predictive and discriminant validity and reliability of our measure of SDO. Our logic in using this large number of samples is to examine statistically significant results that are reliable across samples. We organized the results by topic, but we report the results in each sample so that the reader can see the magnitude of effects in each sample and the stability of the results across samples. At the end of the Results section, we provide a summary of the results in the form of meta-analyses.

DATA COLLECTION

Generally, subjects were college students who participated in a study called "Social Attitudes" for partial course credit. All of their responses were anonymous and confidential, and they completed batteries of self-administered questionnaires. Subjects in Samples 2, 3b, 5, 6, 8, 9, and 13 spent about 1 hr in our laboratory completing the questionnaires. The experimenter described the study as designed to measure students' social attitudes and personal preferences. Subjects in Samples 1 and 13 completed the SDO scale after participating in unrelated experiments, and subjects in the remaining samples completed the SDO scale and follow-up scales in two consecutive mass-testing sessions normally conducted on subject pool participants. All subjects completed a demographic background sheet and our 14-item SDO scale intermixed with related items, a Nationalism scale based on Kosterman and Feshbach's (1989) measure, along with other attitude or experience measures, each having their own instructions and response scales. We also administered some standard personality or attitude scales according to the instructions of their authors. In several samples we also administered ideological (legitimizing myths) or policy attitude items on a questionnaire entitled "Policy Issues Questionnaire."

MEASURES

SDO. In previous archival studies, we measured proxies for SDO using items dealing with equality from the National Election Study or the S6 Conservatism scale (see Sidanius, 1976). In developing the present measure of SDO, we tested over 70 items whose content we felt related to SDO or to constructs one can define as separate but that might be considered adjacent to SDO (e.g., nationalism and prestige-striving), following Loevinger's (1957) suggestion about scale construction. However, on the basis of our desire to develop a simple, unidimensional scale that is balanced, we selected 14 items from this extensive questionnaire as the SDO scale. The selected items concerned the belief that some people are inherently superior or inferior to others and approval of unequal group relationships (see items in Appendix A). The 14-item SDO scale was balanced in that half the items indicated approval of inequality and half indicated approval of equality (see items in Appendix A). We assume that these items tap a latent construct and so we are interested in the relationships between the scale mean and other measures rather than relationships between individual SDO items and other measures.

SDO is an attitudinal orientation, so instructions read, "Which of the following objects or statements do you have a positive or negative feeling towards? Beside each object or statement, place a number from '1' to '7' which represents the degree of your positive or negative feeling." The scale was labeled *very positive* (7), *positive* (6), *slightly positive* (5), *neither positive nor negative* (4), *slightly negative* (3), *negative* (2), and *very negative* (1).

The order of the SDO items and the filler items differed among Form A, completed by Samples 1, 2, 3, and 4; Form B, completed by Samples 5, 6, 7, 8, and 12; and Form C, completed by Samples 9, 10, and 11. The format and instructions for the three forms were identical, and we saw no evidence that results pertinent to reliability or validity issues differed across the questionnaire form. Subsequent to the present research, we have used just the 14 items on a questionnaire and found reliability coefficients of .90 and predictive validity results similar to those reported below.

Political-Economic Conservatism. Some of the standard scales assessing political-economic conservatism actually measure individuals' support for particular social policies (e.g., the C-scale, Wilson & Patterson, 1968). Because we wished to measure political-economic conservatism separately from policy attitudes, and because we wanted to use a measure that should not vary with time and place, we used a self-identified liberal–conservative measure in all samples. On the demographic background sheet, the political-economic conservatism question read, "Use one of the following numbers to indicate your political views in the accompanying categories." Below these instructions was a scale labeled *very liberal* (1), *liberal* (2), *slightly liberal* (3), *middle of the road* (4), *slightly conservative* (5), *conservative* (6), and *very conservative* (7) and a blank next to each type of issue: "foreign policy issues," "economic issues," and "social issues." Political-economic conservatism was the mean of self-ratings on these three items.

Authoritarianism. Authoritarianism research has been fraught with measurement difficulties. After surveying the authoritarianism measurement literature, we decided to administer two rather different measures of authoritarianism, both of which are balanced: the Right Wing Authoritarian (RWA) scale by Altemeyer (1981) and Goertzel's (1987) bipolar personality measure. Goertzel (1987) intended his adjective checklist to measure the personality rather than the ideological aspect of authoritarianism, but did show that it correlates with attitudes toward policies falling along toughness and consistency dimensions. Altemeyer's (1981) scale is the only outer internally reliable measure of authoritarianism that is close to the original conception of authoritarianism, including conventionalism, authoritarian submission, and authoritarian aggression (see Duckitt, 1989, for a review).

Original Legitimizing Myths and Policy Attitudes. The consent form and instructions informed subjects that their opinions and preferences toward a variety of ideas, kinds of people, events, and so forth would be measured. On our "Policy Issues Questionnaire" we included items from various legitimizing myth or policy attitude scales. Items from each scale were interspersed throughout the questionnaire. Next to each item was a

1–7 scale, and the instructions read, "Which of the following objects, events, or statements do you have a positive or negative feeling towards? Please indicate your feelings by circling the appropriate number alongside each item. Use one of the following responses. Remember, your first reaction is best. Work as quickly as you can." The scale points were labeled *very negative* (1), *negative* (2), *slightly negative* (3), *uncertain or neutral* (4), *slightly positive* (5), *positive* (6), and *very positive* (7).

Items from the original legitimizing myths and policy attitude scales were selected for their content and for their internal reliability across samples. These scales are shown in Appendix B. Several personality measures were used as well; these are described in the Method section.

Method

Subjects

Although our 1,952 subjects were college students, they represent some diversity in terms of sex, ethnicity, and income groups, coming from public and private universities in California. Demographic information about the samples is shown in Table 2.1.

SAMPLES AND PROCEDURES

Sample 1 (spring 1990) consisted of 98 University of California at Berkeley undergraduates who completed the CPI Dominance, Flexibility, and Capacity for Status subscales (Gough, 1987), the JPRF Dominance subscale (Jackson, 1965), the JPI Tolerance subscale (Jackson, 1976), and the Rosenberg (1965) Self-Esteem Scale (RSE).

Sample 2 (fall and winter 1990–1991) consisted of 463 San Jose State University (SJSU) undergraduates who completed the CPI and JPRF Dominance subscales; Mirels and Garrett's (1971) Protestant Work Ethic Scale; the Just World Scale (Rubin & Peplau, 1975); the four-factor Interpersonal Reactivity Index (IRI), which measures empathy (Davis, 1983); a number of policy attitude measures; and some demographic descriptors.

Sample 3a (September, 1990) consisted of 81 Stanford University undergraduates who completed the SDO scale as part of a mass-testing session. Sample 3b included 57 subjects from the

TABLE 2.1. Description of Samples

Measure	\multicolumn{14}{c}{Sample}

Measure	1	2	3a	3b	4	5	6	7	8	9	10	11	12	13
	\multicolumn{14}{c}{Age and gender breakdown}
n	98	463	81	57	190	144	49	224	115	97	231	100	135	46
Age range	17–34	15–56	17–21	17–21		17–35	17–23		17–59	17–36				
% men	50	47		51	47	49	69	50	40	33	54		59	100
% women	50	53		49	53	51	31	50	60	67	46		41	0
	\multicolumn{14}{c}{Ethnic breakdown}
% Euro-American	48	38		58	38	53	59	49	29	19	67		50	52
% Asian-American	23	40		16	40	24	24	25	51	45	22		33	33
% Hispanic	13	8		4	8	10	15	10	14	17	4		10	11
% Black	15	5		14	5	8	2	6	2	10	4		4	0
% Arab-American	1	2		6	2	0	0	1	3	8	1		1	4
	\multicolumn{14}{c}{Family income}
Under 20K		12			10	21	6		17	19				
20–30K		9			8	16	6		13	15				
30–40K		11			5	12	8		13	17				
40–55K		17			10	8	10		15	12				
55–70K		20			10	19	10		17	15				
70–100K		14			21	14	19		13	9				
100–150K		8			15	6	19		5	2				
150–200K		5			13	3	11		2	3				
200K+		5			8	1	11		5	6				

Note. Missing numbers indicate that information was not available. Samples 4, 7, 10–13 are probably similar in age distribution and range to Sample 3. Income was self-reported annual family income in thousands of dollars.

same population who participated in a study in our lab in December, 1990, during which they completed the SDO scale again and a number of attitude and personality measures. The overlap of these two samples (*N* = 25 with complete data) was used to assess the cross-time reliability of SDO.

Sample 4 (January, 1991) consisted of 190 Stanford University undergraduates who completed the SDO scale and an attitude scale about the Iraq war assessing environmental concerns in the war, anti-Arab racism, willingness to sacrifice for the war, willingness to restrict civil liberties for the war effort, and support for the use of military force by the United States against Iraq.

Sample 5 (fall 1991) consisted of 144 SJSU undergraduates who completed the RSE (Rosenberg, 1965), the Rombough and Ventimiglia (1981) Tri-Dimensional Sexism Scale, the Sexist Attitudes Toward Women Scale (Benson & Vincent, 1980), the Rape Myths Scale (Burt, 1980), the Altruism subscale from the Values Scale (Super & Nevill, 1985), and the IRI (Davis, 1983). We also measured policy attitudes toward gay rights, women's equality policies, militarism, pu-

nitiveness, racial policies, and environmental policies. In addition, we measured ideologies such as anti-Black racism, elitism, patriotism, belief in equal opportunity, and opposition to miscegenation.

Sample 6 (September, 1991) consisted of 49 Stanford undergraduates who completed the same measures as subjects in Sample 5.

Sample 7 (September, 1991) consisted of 224 Stanford undergraduates who completed a battery of personality questions, including Malle and Horowitz's (1994) bipolar descriptions of Factors I (Extraversion), II (Agreeableness), IV (Neuroticism), and V (Conscientiousness) of the Big-Five personality dimensions (see John, 1990, for a review). A few weeks later, in the three days including and following the day Clarence Thomas was confirmed to the Supreme Court, those subjects who had given their prior permission were telephoned and asked four questions about their opinions regarding this Supreme Court nomination. In all, 149 subjects were reached by telephone, and the response rate was 100%.

Sample 8 (February, 1992) consisted of 115

Stanford undergraduates who completed the PAQ (Spence et al., 1974), CPI Dominance scale (Gough, 1987), JPRF Dominance scale (Jackson, 1965), JPI Tolerance scale (Jackson, 1976), IRI (Davis, 1983), RSE (Rosenberg, 1965), a post-Iraq war attitude survey, a general war attitude survey, and a number of other policy attitude measures similar to those in Sample 5.

Sample 9 (April, 1992) consisted of 97 SJSU undergraduates. They completed the CPI and JPRF Dominance subscales; the JPI Tolerance subscale; the IRI; the Protestant Work Ethic Scale; all 19 of the authoritarian bipolar adjective choices (Goertzel, 1987); Altemeyer's (1981) 30-item RWA Scale; John, Donahue, and Kentle's (1992) Big-Five Personality Inventory; the PAQ; McConahay's (1986) Modern Racism Scale; and Katz and Hass' (1988) Pro-Black, Anti-Black, and Humanitarian-Egalitarian Scales. They also completed a number of policy attitude items similar to those for Sample 5.

Sample 10 (March, 1992) consisted of 231 Stanford undergraduates who completed the SDO scale. Two weeks later, 176 of these subjects completed a comprehensive survey about their ideologies and general attitudes about the death penalty and their attitude about the execution of Robert Alton Harris, who was executed by the state of California the day before the survey was administered.

Sample 11 (March, 1991) consisted of 100 Stanford University undergraduates who completed the SDO scale and a battery of other questionnaires including Snyder's (1974) self-monitoring scales; Fenigstein, Scheier, and Buss' (1975) Self-Consciousness scales; and Malle and Horowitz' (1994) bipolar adjective versions of Factors I and IV of the Big-Five personality dimensions.

Sample 12 (January, 1992) included 139 Stanford undergraduates who completed the SDO scale in a mass-testing session. Of these, 70 also completed Malle and Horowitz' (1994) measures of Factors I and IV

Sample 13 included 46 undergraduate men at Stanford during 1990–1991 who were selected to be in an experiment on the basis of having either extremely high or low SDO scores in Samples 3, 4, and 11. They participated in the experiment between 6 weeks and 8 months after their first testing and completed the SDO scale again.

Results

We first present the internal and temporal reliability of our SDO scale. We then examine whether this measure related to the ideological, policy attitude, and hierarchy role variables predicted by social dominance theory. We show that SDO was either independent of other personality variables with which it might be confused or that it predicted the attitudinal outcomes over and above the effects of these other variables. We also show that it was not redundant with other personality measures. Finally, we show that SDO predicted new social and political attitudes. To summarize the results across samples, we report simple averages of the internal reliability coefficients across samples and averaged correlations across samples using Fisher's z-to-r transformation.

RELIABILITY OF THE SDO MEASURE

Unidimensionality. We conducted two kinds of analyses to confirm that the 14 SDO items assessed a single construct. First, within each sample, principal-components analyses of the 14 SDO items showed that a single dimension captured the bulk of the variance in these items. That is, there was a precipitous drop between the values of the first and second eigenvalues in every sample. Second, we subjected our largest sample, Sample 2 ($N = 446$ with complete data on all SDO items) to confirmatory factor analysis. Using maximum-likelihood estimation, we tested a model in which all 14 items were driven by a single latent construct. Each item had a statistically significant relationship to the latent factor ($ps < .0001$). By freeing only 3 of 91 possible off-diagonal elements of the θ_δ matrix,[2] we obtained a satisfactory χ^2/df ratio of 2.89 (e.g., Carmines & McIver, 1981), suggesting that our data are consistent with a model in which a single dimension underlies responses to all the items. Thus, the 14 items appear to measure a unitary construct.

Internal Reliability. Item statistics showed that the 14-item SDO scale showed good internal reliability across all samples, averaging $\alpha = .83$ (see internal reliability coefficients and item statistics by

---

[2] The freed elements of the matrix corresponded to Items 8 and 9, Items 2 and 4, and Items 10 and 11 in Appendix A.

sample in Table 2.2). Item analyses also showed that all items were highly correlated with the remainder of the scale in every sample. The average lowest item-total correlation across samples was .31 and the average highest item–total correlation across samples was .63. Item 7 had the lowest item–total correlation in 4 of 12 independent samples ($Z = 3.52, p < .001$). Item 9 had the highest item-total correlation in three samples ($Z = 2.40, p < .01$). No other items were either the most or least correlated across samples in numbers that differed from chance using a binomial test.

Stability of SDO Measure Over Time. We measured the stability of scores on our scale over time in two samples. Twenty-five of the subjects in Sample 3 were tested on SDO twice at a 3-month interval. Their SDO scores substantially correlated from Time 1 to Time 2 ($r = .81, p < .01$). The mean difference from Time 1 to Time 2 was 0.09 on a 7-point scale, which did not differ reliably from zero ($t < 1$). In contrast the Time 1–Time 2 correlation for the 10-item RSE was .50.

Sample 13 consisted of 46 of the highest and lowest scoring men on the SDO scale from Samples 3, 4, and 11, who completed that scale again some months later. The correlation in this sample from Time 1 to Time 2 was .84 ($p < .001$), and the mean difference in scores from Time 1 to Time 2 was essentially zero ($M = 0.03, t < 1$; for the high group, $M = -0.03$ and for the low group, $M = 0.09$). All of the subjects first classified as "high" or "low" on SDO met this criterion again in the second testing. The near-zero mean changes within both groups are particularly telling because one could have expected at least some regression toward the mean. Thus, even in different testing contexts, our SDO measure appears highly stable in the short term.

PREDICTIVE MEASURES

Gender Differences. The gender difference we expected showed in all but two samples; men were higher on SDO than women (see point-biserial correlations in Table 2.2).

SDO and Hierarchy Role. A question on the demographic background questionnaire asked subjects in what sector of the economy they intended to work after graduation. There were 20 career choices provided. Theoretically, we define those whose work is primarily aimed at protecting, serving, or benefiting elite members of society more than oppressed members of society "hierarchy-enhancing." Those whose work benefits the oppressed more than elites we define as "hierarchy-attenuating." As such, we classified subjects as (a) hierarchy enhancers (those intending careers in law, law enforcement, politics, and business); (b) "middlers" who would not obviously attenuate or enhance inequality through their professional work, such as science and sales; or (c) hierarchy attenuators (those intending to be in such professions as social work or counseling; see also Sidanius, Pratto, Martin, & Stallworth, 1991). We predicted that hierarchy enhancers would have higher SDO levels than hierarchy attenuators, and that middlers' SDO levels would fall somewhere between the other two. Sample 2 was large enough to test this hypothesis; we also combined Samples 5, 6, 8, and 9 to replicate the test. Because more women tend to go into hierarchy-attenuating careers, and because we know that SDO exhibits a gender difference, we also included subject sex as an independent variable along with hierarchy role. SDO was the outcome variable in simultaneous regression-style analyses of variance (ANOVAs) with planned contrasts. In Sample 2, the results were as expected: Those who intended to work in

TABLE 2.2. Coefficient Alphas, Correlation With Subject Gender, and Average Item Means and Variances by Sample for 14-Item Social Dominance Orientation Scale

Measure	Sample												
	1	2	3a	3b	4	5	6	7	8	9	10	11	12
α	.85	.83	.84	.85	.84	.81	.84	.89	.82	.80	.83	.81	.83
r_{pbi}	.29**	.27**	.32**	.31*	.32**	.11	.36*	.28*	.27**	.03	.30**	—	.26**
M	2.44	2.74	2.55	2.31	2.59	2.97	2.50	2.59	3.02	3.12	3.13	2.91	2.60
Variance	0.14	0.22	0.18	0.17	0.21	0.40	0.24	0.23	0.18	0.36	0.66	0.27	0.23

Note. Positive correlations with gender indicate that men were higher than women.
*$p < .05$. **$p < .01$.

hierarchy-attenuating professions had lower SDO levels ($M = 2.28$) than did middlers ($M = 2.72$), $F(1, 432) = 5.49$, $p < .05$, and also lower levels than those intending to work in hierarchy-enhancing professions ($M = 2.88$), $F(1, 432) = 10.21$, $p < .01$. Men also had higher SDO levels ($M = 3.03$) than women ($M = 2.51$), $F(1, 432) = 36.86$, $p < .001$. In the merged sample, hierarchy attenuators again had lower SDO levels ($M = 2.64$) than hierarchy enhancers ($M = 3.09$), $F(1, 378) = 5.01$, $p < .05$. Middlers' SDO levels were in the middle ($M = 2.94$) and were not distinguishable from those of either enhancers or attenuators. Again, men ($M = 3.07$) had higher SDO levels than women ($M = 2.90$), $F(1, 378) = 3.72$, $p = .05$. Results from both these large samples indicate that intended hierarchy attenuators did indeed have lower SDO levels than intended hierarchy enhancers, even after controlling for subjects' sex.

SDO and Hierarchy-Legitimizing Myths. We hypothesized that SDO should be related to any so-cial or political ideology that helps legitimize group-based inequality.

Ideologies. The three-item index of self-described political ideology had good internal reliability, averaging $\alpha = .78$ across samples (see Table 2.3). SDO correlated positively and significantly with political–economic conservatism in 7 of 8 samples, averaging $r = .38$; conservatives were higher on SDO than liberals (see Table 2.3). The scales measuring meritocratic ideologies, the Protestant Work Ethic and Just World Scales, had fairly low internal reliabilities in all samples, considering that they are 19- and 20-item scales, respectively (see Table 2.3). In a Stanford sample (Sample 3b), but not in two samples from SJSU (Samples 2 and 9), the Protestant Work Ethic Scale and Just World Scale had significant positive correlations with SDO (see Table 2.3). This suggested to us that variations in the cultural background of these samples may affect the ideologies known to and accepted by them. Results from our demographic questionnaire showed that compared with

Table 2.3. Coefficient Alphas of Legitimizing Myth Scales and Correlations With Social Dominance Orientation Sample

Measure	No. of items	Sample 2 ($n = 408$)	Sample 3b ($n = 57$)	Sample 4	Sample 5 ($n = 144$)	Sample 6 ($n = 49$)	Sample 8 ($n = 115$)	Sample 9 ($n = 95$)	Sample 10 ($n = 156$)
				Coefficient α					
Political-economic conservatism	3	.69	.83	.89[a]	.80	.71	.80	.72	.78
Protestant Work Ethic	19	.68	.75					.73	
Just World	20	.55	.42						
Nationalism	6	.75	.88	.80[a]	.68	.86	.78	.66	.62
Patriotism	12				.83	.89		.80	
Cultural elitism	7				.67	.78		.59	
Equal opportunity	6				.65	.76		.49	
Noblesse oblige	6	.58	.80	.69[a]	.68	.73	.56	.72	.54
Anti-Black racism	5	.68	.77		.70	.74	.60	.77	
				Correlations					
Political-economic conservatism		.26**	.28*	.44**[b]	.11	.72**	.24*	.17*	.55
Protestant Work Ethic		−.03	.33*					.03	
Just World		.09	.43**						
Nationalism		.52**	.41**	.53**[b]	.43**	.67**	.51**	.47**	.72**
Patriotism					.43**	.65**		.22*	
Cultural elitism					.51**	.23		.44**	
Equal opportunity					.51**	.51**		.34**	
Noblesse oblige		−.39**	−.54**	−.43**[b]	−.60**		−.69**	−.50**	−.72**
Anti-Black racism		.57**	.42**		.49**	.61**	.65**	.52**	

[a]$n = .180$.   [b]$n = 90$.
*$p < .05$.   **$p < .01$.

TABLE 2.4. Coefficient Alphas of Sexism Scales and Correlations With Social Dominance Orientation Within Samples

Measure	No. of items	Coefficient α		Correlations	
		Sample 5	Sample 6	Sample 5	Sample 6
Rombough & Ventimiglia sexism	20	.90	.94	.44**	.54**
Sex differences	5	.68	.65	.38**	.56**
Internal (household) labor	10	.89	.94	.34**	.63**
External (paid) labor	6	.78	.85	.45**	.36*
Sexist Attitudes Toward Women	40	.91	.94	.46**	.55**
Rape Myths	10	.84	.75	.46**	.40**

*$p < .05$. **$p < .01$.

Stanford, SJSU tends to have more first-generation American, more Catholic, and fewer Euro-American students.

The other legitimizing myth scales that we constructed fared better (see items for all other scales, Appendix B). The nationalism, patriotism, cultural elitism, and equal opportunity measures all had good internal reliability and were positively correlated with SDO (rs ranged from .22 to .67), with only one exception (see Table 2.3). These correlations showed that the more subjects tended to prefer group dominance in general, the more nationalistic and patriotic they were (average $rs = .51$ and .45, respectively) and the more they subscribed to cultural elitism (average $r = .40$) and equal opportunity ideologies (average $r = .46$). As predicted, the noblesse oblige scale was strongly negatively correlated with SDO in every sample, ranging from −.39 to −.69 (see Table 2.3). In Samples 1, 3a, and 7 (not shown in Table 2.3), SDO correlated −.47, −.56, and −.67 with noblesse oblige ($ps < .01$), for an overall average correlation of −.54.

Ethnic prejudice. SDO was strongly correlated with our anti-Black racism measure in every sample, ranging from .42 to .65 and averaging .55 (see Table 2.3). In Sample 4, we also measured anti-Arab racism ($\alpha = .73$), which correlated with SDO ($r = .22, p < .05$). In Sample 9, we administered McConahay's (1986) seven-item Modern Racism Scale ($\alpha = .79$), which correlated .53 with SDO. Katz and Hass' (1988) 10-item Pro-Black Scale ($\alpha = .68$) was negatively correlated with SDO ($r = −.38, p < .01$), and their 10-item Anti-Black Scale ($\alpha = .62$) was positively correlated with SDO ($r = .30, p < .01$). These results, using rather different racism measures, are consistent with the idea that generalized preference for group dominance drives belief in culturally specific forms of ethnic prejudice.

Sexism. We assessed antifemale sexism in Samples 5 and 6 with several measures, all of which proved to be internally reliable. These measures were highly correlated with SDO (rs ranging from .34 to .63; see Table 2.4). Across both samples and all sexism measures, the average correlation was .47. Partial correlations controlling for gender with SDO were also reliable and of about the same magnitude. For this reason, the large correlations between SDO and sexism cannot be attributed to gender differences on SDO or sexism measures.

In summary, all of the measured ideologies (hierarchy-legitimizing myths) except the Protestant Work Ethic Scale and Belief in a Just World Scale were reliably correlated with SDO in the expected directions across virtually all samples. SDO was most strongly related with ideologies concerning group prejudice against other nations, ethnic groups, and women.

SDO and Policy Attitudes. We hypothesized that SDO would predict support for social policies with implications for the distribution of social value among groups. We assessed attitudes toward chauvinist policies (United States dominating other national groups), law and order policies, military programs, gay rights, women's rights, social programs generally, racial policies, and environmental policies in most of our samples (see coefficient alphas in Table 2.5).

Support for chauvinist policies and law and order policies were positively correlated with SDO in almost all samples, averaging .34 and .28, respectively. Support for military programs was positively correlated with SDO in all samples, averag-

TABLE 2.5. Coefficient Alphas of Policy Scales, Correlations With Social Dominance Orientation, and Partial Correlations Controlling for Conservatism, Across Samples

Policy scale	No of items	2 (n = 455)	3b (n = 50)	4	5 (n = 129)	6 (n = 37)	8 (n = 100)	9 (n = 89)
		Sample						
Coefficient α								
Chauvinism	8			.73	.73			.58
Law and order	4	.64	.71		.59	.77[a]	.67	.77[b]
Military programs	3	.67[a]	.75		.73	.67		.59
Gay & lesbian rights	2	.82	.91		.85	.86		.83
Women's rights	4	.63	.72		.69	.63	.80[c]	.74
Social programs	10	.78	.77		.79	.86	.66[c]	.81[d]
Racial policy	7	.71	.81		.68	.72	.60[c]	.77
Miscegeny	2	.96	.97		.93	.94	.91	.87
Environmental policies	5				.71	.80		.76
Correlations of social dominance orientation and policy items								
Chauvinism					.37**	.49**		.14
Law and order		.08	.23*		.30**	.59**	.24*	.19
Military programs		.33**	.27*		.33**	.70**		.47**
Gay & lesbian rights		−.32**	−.50**		−.29**	−.55**		−.17
Women's rights		−.42**	−.32**		−.39**	−.34*	−.52**	−.42**
Social programs		−.50**	−.31**		−.29**	−.70**	−.55**	−.39**
Racial policy		−.42**	−.46**		−.23**	−.62**	−.54**	−.34**
Miscegeny		−.31**	−.15		−.30**	−.31*	−.25*	−.18
Environmental policies					−.27**	−.40**		−.47**
Republican party preference		.15**	.25*		.24**	.45**	.33**	.27*
Partial correlations removing political-economic conservatism								
Chauvinism					.40**	.16		.06
Law and order		−.02	.15		.29**	.31*	.25***	.15
Military programs		.16***	.18		.31***	.40**		.46***
Gay & lesbian rights		−.28***	−.32**		−.29***	−.14		−.15
Women's rights		−.38**	−.31**		−.35***	−.27*	−.46***	−.40***
Social programs		−.30***	−.27*		−.30***	−.49**	−.50***	−.37***
Racial policy		−.33***	−.30**		−.22***	−.38**	−.49***	−.31***
Miscegeny		−.28***	−.19		−.31***	−.08	−.23**	−.17*
Environmental policies					−.27***	−.31*		−.46***

[a]Three items. [b]Two items. [c]Six items. [d]Seven items.
*p < .05. **p < .01. ***p < .001.

ing .44. Support for gay rights, women's rights, social welfare programs, ameliorative racial policy, miscegenation, and environmental policy were significantly negatively related to SDO in all but three cases (see Table 2.5). These relationships were of about the same magnitudes as the policy attitudes described above. We assessed political party preference by having subjects rate themselves from *strong Democrat* (1) through *independent* (4) to *strong Republican* (7) and *others*. Excluding "others," Republican political party preference correlated positively and significantly with SDO in six out of six samples, averaging .28 (see Table 2.5).

In addition to support for military programs, we expected support for military action including war to be positively related to SDO. We tested this hypothesis by surveying attitudes toward war in general and specific attitudes toward the war against Iraq fought by the United States and other nations at the time of data collection. In fall 1990, while Iraq was occupying Kuwait and the United States was amassing troops near Iraq, data from Sample 2 were collected, including a single war policy item, "Going to war to maintain low oil prices." This item correlated .30 with SDO (p < .01). In January, 1991, when the United States and allies had just begun bombing Iraq, we administered a balanced scale concerning war and related attitudes to Sample 4. A reliable ($\alpha = .85$) eight-item pro-war scale correlated .51 with SDO ($p < .01$). One year later, we asked Sample 8 about their attitudes toward the Iraq war. The resulting Iraq War Attitudes scale was reliable ($\alpha = .85$) and correlated .29 with SDO ($p < .01$).

Does SDO, then, unconditionally predict support for war, or only war for certain purposes? We attempted to answer this question by designing a General War Attitudes scale including two kinds of items, namely, Wars of Dominance, which we expected to relate positively to SDO, and Wars for Humanitarian Reasons, which we did not expect to relate positively to SDO. This scale was administered to Sample 8 in January, 1992. Factor analysis confirmed that these were two independent dimensions. The Wars of Dominance scale (eight items) was reliable ($\alpha = .82$) and correlated positively with SDO ($r = .31$, $p < .01$). The Humanitarian Wars scale (six items)[3] was also reliable ($\alpha = .73$) and correlated negatively with SDO ($r = -.41$, $p < .01$), so SDO is not merely antipacifism. The Wars of Dominance scale was positively correlated with support for the Iraq war ($r = .63$, $p < .001$), but the Humanitarian Wars scale was uncorrelated with support for the Iraq war ($r = .07$). These results suggest that SDO does not predict support for war unconditionally; rather, SDO predisposes people to endorse group dominance ideologies, thus facilitating support for wars of dominance.

DISCRIMINANT VALIDITY

We expected SDO to correlate with political-economic conservatism, and indeed it did. However, to show that SDO has utility as a predictor of policy attitudes over and above political-economic conservatism, we computed the correlations between SDO and the policy attitudes reported above after partialing out political-economic conservatism. Of the 41 significant zero-order correlations between SDO and policy attitudes in Table 2.5, only five become nonsignificant when political-economic conservatism is partialed out.[4] A few of the very high zero-order correlations were reduced substantially, but many more partial correlations were almost the same as the zero-order correlations (see Table 2.5). Across all the samples, then, there was no consistent evidence that political-economic con-

servatism could replace SDO as a predictor of the policy attitudes we assessed.

In Sample 9, we assessed another rival predictor of policy attitudes, namely authoritarianism, using two measures. Altemeyer's 30-item RWA scale had good internal reliability ($\alpha = .78$); Goertzel's measure was adequate for a bipolar scale ($\alpha = .53$). Both measures of authoritarianism correlated with political-economic conservatism ($r = .31$ for RWA, $r = .29$ for the Goertzel measure, both $ps < .01$), confirming their validity. Neither, however, correlated strongly with SDO. RWA correlated .14 (ns) with SDO, and the Goertzel measure correlated .18 with SDO ($p < .10$). Correcting these correlations for attenuation yielded slightly higher correlations ($r^* = .18$, $p < .05$ for RWA; $r^* = .28$, $p < .01$ for the Goertzel measure).

We also computed partial correlations between SDO and the policy attitudes, partialing the two authoritarianism measures and political-economic conservatism. In Sample 9, all the policies that showed significant zero-order correlations with SDO also had significant correlations with SDO, partialing out the effects of political-economic conservatism, RWA, and the Goertzel measure. Both authoritarianism measures showed substantial zero-order correlations with attitudes that were not as highly correlated with SDO in this sample: gay rights ($r = -.51$ for RWA, $r = -.31$ for the Goertzel measure, $ps < .01$) and chauvinistic policies ($r = .38$ for RWA, $p < .01$, $r = .25$ for the Goertzel measure, $p < .05$). As Peterson, Doty, and Winter (1993) showed recently, authoritarianism still predicts social attitudes, particularly those relevant to untraditional sexual practices and prejudice against foreigners.

Because authoritarian personality theory (Adorno et al., 1950) also postulates that authoritarianism should predict ethnocentrism, racism, nationalism, and conservatism, we tested whether SDO would still predict belief in these legitimizing myths, controlling for authoritarianism. All the reliable zero-order correlations between SDO and ideological measures were reliable after controlling for RWA and the Goertzel measure, except for the correlation with political-economic conservatism. The correlation between SDO and

---

[3]Two unreliable items were eliminated from the scale.

[4]One other correlation actually became significant because partial correlations use one-tailed tests.

political-economic conservatism, partialing RWA, was .13 ($p = .11$). Partialing the Goertzel measure, the correlation between SDO and political-economic conservatism was .16 ($p = .07$), and partialing both measures, the correlation was .13 ($p = .11$). Although the relationship between SDO and conservatism may be explained by their joint relationship to authoritarianism, the relationships between SDO and racism and nationalism cannot.

Dominance and Self-Esteem. Conservatism and authoritarianism were the only rival variables we identified as predictors of social and political attitudes, and the analyses above show that SDO substantially related to such attitudes, even when controlling for political-economic conservatism and for authoritarianism. To show a different kind of discriminant validity, we tested whether SDO correlated with other personality measures. If any of these were large, we would then be obliged to test the partial correlations with the social and political attitudes discussed above.

Only once did SDO correlate with the CPI and JPRF Dominance subscales across five samples (see Table 2.6). On average, CPI Dominance correlated .03 with SDO, and JPRF Dominance correlated −.006. These results clearly indicate that SDO is independent of interpersonal dominance. In Sample 1, SDO was also unrelated to CPI Flexibility ($r = .06$) and Capacity for Status ($r = .05$). For the most part, SDO was also uncorrelated with self-esteem in Samples 1 through 9, averaging −.08 (see Table 2.6).

Other Personality Measures. We used data collected by other researchers at Stanford during mass testing sessions to further investigate the discriminant validity of SDO. SDO was uncorrelated with all the self-monitoring and self-consciousness scales in Sample 11. In Samples 7, 9, 11, and 12, SDO correlated −.06, −.11, .08, and −.19, respectively, with Extraversion; none of these correlations differed reliably from zero. SDO correlated −.02, .13, −.08, and .21 in those samples, respectively, with Neuroticism; none of these differed reliably from zero. SDO correlated −.03 with Agreeableness in Sample 7 and −.41 ($p < .01$) in Sample 9. SDO correlated −.04 and −.14 with Conscientiousness in Samples 7 and 9, neither of which differed reliably from zero. SDO correlated −.28 with Openness ($p < .01$) in Sample 9. These data do not suggest that SDO is redundant with any of the Big-Five dimensions and strongly imply that SDO is independent of Extraversion and Neuroticism. Across this set of correlations, there was also no evidence that SDO is related to the positively valued personality dimensions (e.g., Extraversion and Calmness) as opposed to the negative dimensions (e.g., Introversion and Neuroticism).

CONVERGENT VALIDITY

Empathy, Altruism, and Communality. We expected that feelings of closeness and kindness toward others should mitigate desire to dominate other groups, so empathy, altruism, and commu-

TABLE 2.6. Coefficient Alphas of Interpersonal Dominance and Self-Esteem and Correlations With Social Dominance Orientation Within Samples

Measure	No. of items	Sample								
		1 ($n = 98$)	2 ($n = 403$)	3a ($n = 80$)	3b ($n = 57$)	4 ($n = 90$)	5 ($n = 144$)	6 ($n = 56$)	8 ($n = 115$)	9 ($n = 95$)
		Coefficient α								
CPI Dominance	35	.82	.79		.79				.71	.71
JPRF Dominance	19	.81	.81		.74				.73	.69
Rosenberg Self-Esteem	10	.87	.87	.88	.88	.90	.87	.85	.84	.83
		Correlations								
CPI Dominance		−.11	−.03		−.17				.24**	.20
JPRF Dominance		−.04	.13**		−.17				.01	.04
Rosenberg Self-Esteem		−.09	−.18	.09	.01	.16	−.23**	−.01	−.29**	−.14*

Note. CPI =California Psychological Inventory; JPRF =Jackson Personality Research Form.
*$p < .05$. **$p < .01$.

nality should correlate negatively with SDO. We first tested whether different varieties of empathy were negatively related to SDO using Davis' (1983) IRI. The Concern for Others subscale was significantly negatively correlated with SDO in every sample (rs ranged from −.40 to −.53 and averaged −.46; see Table 2.7). High dominance-oriented people expressed less concern for others than did low dominance-oriented people. The patterns of correlations between SDO and the other subscales were not as consistent across samples, but when they were significant, all correlations were negative (see Table 2.7). The total Empathy scale was negatively correlated with SDO in 5 of 6 samples (averaging r = −.31), but not as highly as the Concern for Others subscale. We conclude that concern for others is the form of empathy that precludes the desire to dominate other groups.

As one might expect, altruism was correlated with the Concern for Others subscale in Samples 5 and 6 (ps < .001) and was negatively correlated with SDO (see Table 2.7). Communality was also negatively correlated with SDO in Samples 8 and 9 (see Table 2.7). In addition, Katz and Hass' (1988) 10-item Humanitarian-Egalitarian Scale correlated negatively with SDO (α = .80, r = −.34, p < .01) in Sample 9; this scale includes altruistic, inclusive, and egalitarian items.

The constellation of qualities including communality, emotional empathy, and altruism has been termed "linking" and is stereotypically associated with the female sex (e.g., Eisler & Loye, 1983). However, it is important to note that SDO's correlations with communality, altruism, and concern for others were significant even after controlling for sex. Thus, gender differences alone are not responsible for the correlations between SDO and communality, altruism, and concern for others. Lest high levels of dominance orientation be confused with agency, it is important to emphasize that there was no correlation between SDO and the PAQ Agency scale in Samples 8 and 9 (see Table 2.7).

Tolerance. SDO was negatively related to the JPI Tolerance subscale (rs = −.27, −.36, and −.27, all ps < .01 in Samples 1, 8, and 9, respectively), despite the low reliabilities of the Tolerance subscale, which has a true–false response format (.53,[5] .59, and .18, respectively). When corrected for attenu-

ation, the correlations were −.40, −.52, and −.71, respectively (ps < .001), but these may be considered "overcorrected" because of the low reliability coefficients of the Tolerance scale. The average correlation between SDO and Tolerance was −.30.

SDO AS AN ORIENTATION: PREDICTING NEW ATTITUDES

According to social dominance theory, one of SDO's most significant functions is orienting people toward or away from new social attitudes. Therefore, we tested whether SDO predicted beliefs in new legitimizing myths and support for new policies. Unfolding public events provided three opportunities to test attitudes toward "new" policies, some of which had rather novel legitimizations provided for them.

Iraq War. War making is an extreme act of discrimination against an out-group; enemy out-group members are routinely starved, raped, killed, maimed, or made ill during war. Given that, we expect that arguments given in support of war would serve as legitimizing myths and thus should relate to SDO. We tested this hypothesis looking at U.S. policy in the aftermath of the Iraqi invasion of Kuwait in 1990. Pundits seemed to feel the White House gave several different reasons for U.S. policy at the time, so this was an opportune occasion to examine the operation of new legitimizing myths. National random-sample opinion polls showed significant fluidity of attitudes about appropriate policy up until the United States began bombing Iraq on January 16, 1991. For example, the *Los Angeles Times* poll showed that merely 38% of the public favored going to war against Iraq on November 14, 1990, but that once U.S. troops had begun bombing, 81% of the public on January 17–18, 1991, and on February 15–17, 1991, approved of the war. Even just before and after the bombing began, there were dramatic shifts in opinion; from January 8–12, 1991, 39% felt that economic sanctions against Iraq should be used without resorting to war, but on January 17–18, 1991, 72% of the public believed President Bush had given enough time for economic

---

[5]By accident, only the 10 false-coded items in the scale were administered to Sample 1.

TABLE 2.7. Coefficient Alphas of Empathy. Altruism, and PAQ Subscales and Correlations With Social Dominance Orientation

Measure	No. of items	Sample 2 (*n* = 403)	Sample 3b (*n* = 57)	Sample 5 (*n* = 144)	Sample 6 (*n* = 56)	Sample 8 (*n* = 115)	Sample 9 (*n* = 95)
		Coefficient α					
Empathy	28	.76	.72	.77	.75	.75	.73
Concern	7	.73	.77	.66	.75	.69	.68
Distress	7	.71	.70	.67	.74	.61	.52
Perspective-taking	7	.64	.78	.74	.84	.71	.58
Fantasy	7	.71	.79	.70	.72	.70	.64
Altruism	5			.87	.87		
PAQ Communality	23					.76	.78
PAQ Agency	28					.80	.80
		Correlations					
Empathy		−.40**	−.21	−.26**	−.36*	−.38**	−.24*
Concern		−.45**	−.51**	−.47**	−.41**	−.53**	−.40**
Distress		−.03	−.11	.10	−.16	.22**	.21*
Perspective-taking		−.30**	.05	−.20*	−.16	−.39**	−.15
Fantasy		−.23**	.01	−.06	−.25*	−.21*	−.23*
Altruism				−.32**	−.24*		
PAQ Communality						−.42**	−.24*
PAQ Agency						−.10	−.08

Note. PAQ = Personal Attributes Questionnaire.
*$p < .05$.   **$p < .01$

sanctions to work. The outcome of the present study was, then, by no means certain.

During the third week of January, 1991, subjects in Sample 4 completed an Iraq War Attitudes survey. We asked subjects how willing they would be to make sacrifices for war (as opposed to making sacrifices to prevent wars), whether they favored suspending certain civil liberties and invoking the draft during war, and whether they favored military action against Iraq. We also measured a new "legitimizing myth," namely, that Iraq should be stopped because of the environmental damage that it was inflicting on the Gulf. This idea was brought up because the Iraqi leader, Saddam Hussein, had threatened to burn all of Kuwait's oil if Iraq was bombed, and the recent 20th anniversary of Earth Day had put environmental concerns on the public's mind. SDO was positively and significantly correlated with each of these attitude dimensions (see Table 2.8). Higher SDO levels were associated with favoring military action against Iraq, favoring suspension of civil liberties for the war, a willingness to make sacrifices for the war effort, and a nationalistic view of environmental problems associated with the war.

Clarence Thomas' Nomination to the Supreme Court. Political appointments can also be considered policies that have implications for intergroup relations, and also can be legitimized; therefore, their relationship to SDO is of theoretical concern. The second new attitude that we assessed was support for Clarence Thomas' appointment to the Supreme Court. This appointment was related to a number of long-standing legitimizing myths, including conservatism, meritocracy, racism, and sexism, shown above to relate to SDO. Thomas, widely considered a Black conservative, was nominated to replace Thurgood Marshall, a Black former civil rights lawyer, who announced his intention to retire. President Bush nominated Thomas to the Supreme Court in the spring of 1991, and the Senate Judiciary Committee held hearings on this nomination in the spring and fall. Just before the vote to confirm Thomas was scheduled, a news story broke that two of Thomas' former subordinates had accused him of sexual harassment. One of these persons, Anita Hill, was called to testify before the Judiciary Committee, and the proceedings received much publicity, including gavel-to-gavel television and radio coverage. Af-

Table 2.8. Coefficient Alphas and Correlations of Social Dominance Orientation With New Attitudes

Scale or item	No. of items	Coefficient α	Correlation with social dominance orientation
	Sample 4		
Favors military action by U.S.	5	.78	.48**
Willing to make sacrifices for war	4	.56	.45**
Favors suspending liberties for war	4	.51	.45**
Concerned about environment in war	4	.57	.28**
	Sample 7		
Favors appointing a Black person			−.20*
Favors appointing a conservative			.32***
Favored Clarence Thomas' confirmation			.22**
Believed Anita Hill's testimony			−.26***
	Sample 10		
Specific deterrence	3	.70	.35**
Favored executing Harris	2	.96	.36**
Painful executions	8	.86	.42**
Belief in retribution	5	.74	.51**

*$p < .05$.   **$p < .01$.   ***$p < .001$.

ter an entire weekend of testimony solely about the sexual harassment charge, the Judiciary Committee voted to confirm Thomas on October 15, 1991.[6]

We telephoned 149 of the 173 (86%) subjects in Sample 7 (who had completed the SDO scale in late September) on that day or on the following 2 days and asked them four attitudinal questions about Thomas and Hill. They responded to statements on 7-point scales where 1 meant *strongly disagree* and 7 meant *strongly agree*. The statements were (a) "after Thurgood Marshall's retirement from the Supreme Court, it was good that George Bush appointed a Black person to the Court," (b) "after Thurgood Marshall's retirement from the Supreme Court, it was good that George Bush appointed a conservative to the Court," (c) "If I were in the Senate, I would have voted in favor of Clarence Thomas' confirmation to the Supreme Court," and (d) "Anita Hill was telling the truth in claiming that Clarence Thomas sexually harassed her." We found that SDO significantly predicted opposition to nominating a Black to the Supreme Court, support for nominating a conservative to the court, support for Clarence Thomas, and disbelief of Anita Hill's testimony (see correlations in Table 2.8).

Death Penalty. Elsewhere, we have argued that SDO should also be related to support of legal institutions that are discriminatory or inegalitarian in their effects (Sidanius, 1993; Sidanius, Liu, Pratto, & Shaw, 1994). Mitchell (1993) showed that SDO is related to ideologies that legitimize the use of the death penalty, such as the belief in legal retribution or the belief that the death penalty has a deterrent effect on crime. We assessed SDO in March, 1992, in Sample 10; 2 weeks later, we administered an extensive survey about death penalty ideologies and about the execution of Robert Alton Harris, who was executed by the state of California the day before the subjects were surveyed. Belief that executions have a specific deterrent effect, support for Harris' execution, support of painful executions, and belief in retribution were positively correlated with SDO (see Table 2.8).

Summary

To provide a summary of the correlations with SDO, we used Fisher's *z*-to-*r* formula to average

[6]Because of the time delay between Washington, DC, and California, Californians heard this news as they awoke.

the correlations across samples (e.g., Rosenthal, 1986, p. 27). To test the average statistical significance of the correlation coefficients, we computed standard normal (Z) scores corresponding to each correlation coefficient using the large-sample formula $Z = r \times (N)^{\frac{1}{2}}$. The total of the Z scores across samples divided by the square root of the number of samples can be compared with the standard normal distribution to test the null hypothesis that the pattern of correlations obtained over samples occurred because of chance associations between SDO and the variable in question.[7]

On average, subject sex correlated .26 with SDO ($Z = 9.92$, $p < .001$). Thus, the data were consistent with our prediction that men will be higher on SDO than women.

In terms of discriminant validity, over five samples, the average correlation between SDO and CPI Dominance was .03 and the average correlation between SDO and JPRF Dominance was −.01. Over nine samples, the average correlation between SDO and RSE was −.08. Averaged over four samples, SDO correlated −.03 with Extraversion and .10 with Neuroticism. Clearly SDO is independent of all of these constructs. As expected, SDO had moderate negative correlations with concern for others, communality, tolerance, and altruism (see average correlations in Table 2.9). The averaged correlations were clearly different from zero, but they were not high enough that they indicate redundancy between these measures and SDO either, given that they ranged from −.28 for altruism to −.46 for concern for others.

SDO strongly and consistently related to belief in a number of hierarchy-legitimizing myths, most strongly to anti-Black racism and nationalism. SDO also was strongly negatively related to a hierarchy-attenuating ideology, noblesse oblige. SDO correlated consistently positively with beliefs in sexism, equal opportunities, patriotism, cultural elitism, conservatism, and a Just World. The Protestant Work Ethic was the only legitimizing ideology that we did not find to relate to SDO reliably over samples (see Table 2.9).

Finally SDO showed strong consistent correlations with scales assessing opposition to social programs, racial policies, and women's rights, and with support for military programs. SDO was also consistently correlated with opposition to gay and lesbian rights, environmental programs, and miscegeny and was consistently correlated with support for U.S. chauvinism, law-and-order poli-

TABLE 2.9. Average Correlations and Significance Tests Across Samples Between Social Dominance Orientation and Personality Variables, Ideologies, and Policy Attitudes

Measure	Mean r	n	Z
Personality variables			
Concern for others	−.46	6	−8.92
Communality	−.33	2	−4.84
Tolerance	−.30	3	−5.31
Altruism	−.28	2	−3.98
Ideologies			
Anti-Black racism	.55	6	15.05
Noblesse oblige	−.57	10	20.30
Nationalism	.54	8	15.96
Sexism	.47	12	14.91
Equal opportunities	.46	3	7.51
Patriotism	.45	3	6.84
Cultural elitism	.40	3	6.94
Political-economic conservatism	.38	8	10.26
Just World	.27	2	3.58
Protestant Work Ethic	.11	3	1.25
Policy attitudes			
Social programs	−.47	6	−12.74
Racial policy	−.44	6	−11.74
Women's rights	−.40	6	−11.52
Military programs	.44	5	−10.12
Gay & lesbian rights	−.37	5	−8.79
Environmental programs	−.38	3	−6.16
Chauvinism	.34	3	5.34
Miscegeny	−.25	6	−7.36
Republican party preference	.28	6	7.08
Law and order	.28	6	6.38

Note. All Zs were significant at $p < .0001$ except for Just World ($p = .0002$) and Protestant Work Ethic ($p = .10$). The mean r was computed using Fisher's z; n denotes number of samples.

cies, and Republican party identification (see Table 2.9). SDO also predicted attitudes toward new political events, including the 1991 war against Iraq, Clarence Thomas as a Supreme Court Justice, and a state execution. Those aspiring to hierarchy-enhancing careers had higher SDO scores than those aspiring to hierarchy-attenuating careers. Thus, we have provided substantial evidence that SDO (a) can be measured reliably, (b) is stable over time, (c) is higher among men than among women, (d) is higher among those who support

---

[7]A Z statistic with smaller variance could also have been computed by using the sample variance to weight the Z from each sample, which would cause all the p values given below to be smaller.

hierarchy-enhancing ideologies and is lower among those who support hierarchy-attenuating ideologies, (e) is higher among those who support hierarchy-enhancing policies and lower among those who support hierarchy-attenuating policies, (f) is higher among those who choose hierarchy-enhancing social roles and lower among those who choose hierarchy-attenuating social roles, and (g) serves to orient new social and political attitudes.

Discussion

On the basis of social dominance theory, we postulated that there is an important individual difference in general preference for group domination, which we call *social dominance orientation.* As its definition and name implies, SDO may best be considered a general social-attitudinal orientation or implicit value relevant to intergroup relations. Some of our data inform us that there may be a significant relationship between one's orientation toward other persons in general and one's orientation toward other groups. People who are highly empathic (specifically, concerned with others' well-being) and to a lesser extent those who feel interdependent or communal with others, tend to prefer egalitarian relationships among groups. Given that SDO predisposes people to believe in legitimizing myths and discriminatory policies, this would seem to make them less likely to believe in ideologies that relegate certain persons to "inferior" categories and to policies that disadvantage certain groups systematically. The recent work being done on interdependence (e.g., Depret & Fiske, 1993; Markus & Kitayama, 1991) may end up being quite informative about how to mitigate intergroup discrimination.

We might note that we came to postulate the existence of SDO not by thinking about "personality" in the traditional, individualistic sense, but by thinking about how group-based human social life is and the considerable data generated by researchers of political attitudes. We consider individual differences on SDO to be important not for showing the uniqueness of each person, nor for enabling us to classify persons into taxonomies. Rather, our finding of individual variation on SDO central to our postulation of a dynamic model of human oppression in which different kinds of people (e.g., with high or low SDO) play different roles (e.g., enhance or attenuate in equality) and

have different effects on each other (e.g., in how much they discriminate in the allocation of resources).

Despite significant variations in the degree of oppression from one society to another, it seems to us that many societies share the basic social-psychological elements that contribute to inequality: socially shared myths that define "superior group" and "inferior group" and that attempt to justify this distinction and the policies that "should" follow from it. As such, we postulate that individual variation on SDO could be reliably measured in many other societies and would show the same patterns of relationships to ideologies, policy attitudes, and hierarchy role as those shown here. Some of our previous research showed that group-dominance orientation significantly correlated with support for military programs, capitalism (Sidanius & Pratto, 1993b), racism, and sexism (Sidanius, Devereux, & Pratto, 1992; Sidanius & Pratto, 1993a) in Sweden, a much more egalitarian country than the United States, and showed the same gender difference in Australia, Sweden, Russia, and the United States (see Sidanius, Pratto, & Brief, 1995). In the future, we hope to examine whether SDO relates to rather different kinds of legitimizing myths that exist in very different cultural contexts, such as anti-Semitism in Poland, xenophobia in Japan, or fatalism in China.

Another kind of research endeavor that could further show the dynamic link between SDO and societal oppression would use SDO to predict attitudes toward new ideologies or policies. We expect that even when societies undergo substantial change as with mass migration, technological innovation, or dramatic changes in borders or political leadership, such changes will be accepted only to the extent that they are satisfactorily legitimized and meet the public's level of desire for social dominance. Hence, the operation of SDO in the invention of new legitimizations and processes that assort persons into hierarchy roles may inform studies of political and social change.

SDO and Social Class

Several political psychologists and sociologists have postulated or investigated the relationship between social class and conservatism, racism, or authoritarianism, with Lipset (1960) postulating that the working class is more authoritarian, and

Stacey and Green (1968, 1971) and many others presenting evidence to the contrary. We have made no predictions concerning whether SDO should be correlated with social class in either direction; instead we suspect that SDO's relationship to these variables may vary as a function of hierarchy-group membership, which in some societies would be designated by class and in others by racial group, caste, and so forth. We tested for correlations between SDO and class in the present samples, and we found no statistically significant relationships between SDO and respondents' social class or family income category. Although there was substantial heterogeneity in these samples on these variables for the respondents' families of origin, the education level in these samples is clearly restricted. In contrast, in a random survey of the Los Angeles area, Sidanius et al. (1995) found statistically significant and monotonic decreases in scores from an abbreviated SDO scale with increasing family income level and increasing respondent's education level. With the data now in hand, we cannot say whether social classes differ on SDO.

Authoritarianism Reconsidered

In the sample in which we assessed SDO and authoritarianism, the correlations between two measures of authoritarianism and SDO were weak. However, because SDO predicts many of the social attitudes conceptually associated with authoritarianism (e.g., ethnocentrism, punitiveness, and conservatism), a more thorough comparison of these constructs is warranted. To begin with, there is little theoretical consensus on the construct of authoritarianism. The original and some contemporary researchers have described authoritarianism as a multifaceted construct; for example, Heaven (1985) suggested that authoritarianism is part achievement motivation, part dominance, part conventionalism, part militarism, part punitiveness, and part ethnocentrism. Although we think that the tendency for these constructs to covary is extremely important, calling this compendium *authoritarianism* is conceptually unsatisfying. It is neither a clear definition of a unitary construct nor a theory of why the separate constructs covary. In our view, punitiveness, ethnocentrism, conservatism, and sometimes conventionalism can function as legitimizing myths. Because legitimizing myths tend to be correlated with

SDO, they are often spuriously correlated with one another. Thus, it is entirely possible that SDO underlies these correlations. By separately defining the presumably causative value orientation (SDO) and ideological stances (legitimizing myths and policy attitudes) and using distinct measures of the constructs, we have avoided the conceptual problem of describing an individual tendency as a set of correlations (see also Duckitt, 1989).

Other definitions of *authoritarianism* have avoided the compendium problem by radically restricting the meaning of the term. Ray (1976) postulated that part of authoritarianism is leadership desire or directiveness. That SDO did not significantly correlate with two robust measures of interpersonal dominance or with CPI Capacity for Status or PAQ Agency suggests that SDO cannot be interpreted as leadership desire. On this dimension, SDO and authoritarianism are distinct.

There is a new view of authoritarianism that we see as complementary to SDO, namely Duckitt's (1989) description of authoritarianism as the desire for individuals to submit to authority figures within the in-group. The three classical dimensions of authoritarianism that covary empirically—submitting to in-group conventions, submitting to in-group authorities, and desiring to punish members who do not submit to in-group norms and authorities (Altemeyer, 1981)—all concern the relation of the individual to the group. Thus, in Duckitt's view, authoritarianism is primarily an intragroup phenomenon concerning individuals' or groups' attitudes about what the relationship between individuals and their in-groups should be. By comparison, SDO concerns individuals' attitudes about what kind of relationship should exist between in-groups and out-groups, which is an intergroup phenomenon.

SDO Versus Political-Economic Conservatism

The other well-known individual predictor of social and political attitudes is political-economic conservatism. The power of political-economic conservatism to predict social and political attitudes and candidate preference is far too robust to refute. In fact, we postulate that political-economic conservatism is a prototypic legitimizing myth: an ideology that separates people into groups and suggests that some groups should be accorded more positive social value (e.g., tax breaks, funds for schools, and access to health care), whereas other groups should be allocated more negative social value (e.g., prison terms, censorship, and layoffs).

Our analysis of conservatism as a legitimizing myth can explain why, in many previous studies, conservatism was correlated with racism (e.g., Dator, 1969; Levinson, 1950; Sidanius & Ekehammar, 1979; Stone & Russ, 1976). We believe political-economic conservatism and racism are spuriously correlated and that both are "driven" by SDO. In fact, recent studies have shown that there was no significant residual correlation between political-economic conservatism and racism once SDO was controlled (see Sidanius & Pratto, 1993a, 1993b; Sidanius et al., 1992).

We believe SDO has significant power to predict policy attitudes over and above political-economic conservatism. In the present study, virtually all partial correlations between policy attitudes and SDO, controlling for political-economic conservatism, were reliable. Part of the advantage SDO may have over political-economic conservatism is that SDO is an attitudinal orientation rather than a policy doctrine and therefore does not require expertise or deliberate application. That is, to formulate a policy attitude consistent with one's political ideology, one must have a thorough understanding of that ideology and think through or know how it "should" apply to the acceptance of new policy initiatives. In contrast, one's SDO level will provide a gut reaction to new policy initiatives that imply changes in intergroup relations, essentially "I like it" or "I don't like it." In other words, we expect SDO to be a better predictor of group-relevant social and political attitudes than political-economic conservatism among non-ideologues, whenever thoughtful ideological reasoning is not engaged, and for new social attitudes.

The present results can be compared with Wilson's (e.g., 1973) extensive work on conservatism as an attitudinal orientation, rather than as an ideology. Wilson found that conservatism was a convenient label for describing the dimension underlying a similar constellation of ideological beliefs and policy attitudes to those we have shown to relate to SDO: racism, nationalism, ethnocentrism, militarism, law and order, and proestablishment politics. Conceptually, our definition of SDO differs from Wilson's conservatism in that we have not included fundamentalist religiosity, antihedonism, or strict morality as part of

SDO. Our supposition is that those beliefs are particularly Western legitimizing myths that happen to be held by people who make distinctions between superior and inferior or deserving and undeserving people in a Calvinist vein, but that they would not necessarily be related to SDO in all cultural contexts. Likewise, it seems that forms of ethnic prejudice other than anti-Black racism would be more powerfully related to SDO in certain other cultural contexts. The comparison between SDO and attitudinal conservatism highlights that our measure of SDO is relatively independent of particular cultural beliefs or policies. That is, our items do not specify which groups of people are referred to (with the exception of nations) because we felt that a general orientation toward groups could predict attitudes toward specific groups or specific group-relevant policies.

We modified our SDO scale so that it related to our conceptual definition more strongly by making each item refer only to the generic concept *group*. We compared the 14-item scale in Appendix A with this new scale in a sample of 199 Stanford students. We administered the 14-item SDO scale ($\alpha = .88$) and a brief policy attitude survey with a 1 (*very negative*) to 7 (*very positive*) response format. Four weeks later, we administered the balanced 16-item SDO scale shown in Appendix C ($\alpha = .91$). The two scales correlated .75 with one another ($p < .01$), comparable with the cross-time reliability correlation of the 14-item SDO scale. Both SDO scales correlated significantly with the policy attitudes in the directions expected and to very similar degrees. The 14- and 16-item SDO scales correlated, respectively, with attitudes toward affirmative action ($rs = -.34$, $-.44$), civil rights ($-.51$, $-.59$), gay rights ($-.36$, $-.32$), the military (.40, .39), decreased immigration (.37, .41), equal pay for women ($-.38$, $-.29$), and the death penalty (.40, .34), all $ps < .01$. We also tested an abbreviated scale consisting of Items 1, 3, 4, 7, 10, 12, 13, and 14 in Appendix C ($\alpha = .86$), which correlated in nearly the same magnitudes with the policy items above. We administered the 16-item SDO scale to another sample of 245 Stanford students along with the Rombough and Ventimiglia (1981) sexism scale. In this second sample, the 16-item scale was internally reliable ($\alpha = .91$) and correlated .51 ($p < .01$) with the sexism scale and .26 with subject sex ($p < .01$). The abbreviated (8-item) version of this scale was internally reliable ($\alpha = .86$) and correlated .47 with sexism ($p < .01$) and .26 with subject sex ($p < .01$). The 16-item scale (and its 8-item abbreviated form) has slightly more face validity than the 14-item SDO scale, and it seems to have similar properties.

SDO and the Dynamics of Oppression

Our present focus on SDO is not meant to imply that all phenomena related to prejudice and group conflict can be solely understood or reduced to individual differences. In fact, social dominance theory implies that SDO and other individual variables must be considered within their social context, because individual variables and social-structural variables have a dynamic relationship.

For example, our data suggest that empathy with other persons may be a significant attenuator of SDO. However, concern for others (particularly out-group members) is not just a fixed individual propensity, but instead seems likely to be influenced by social structures and policies. Social structures and policies that prevent the formation of close relationships and empathy between high- and low-status persons (e.g., economically or legally enforced segregation, language barriers, publishing biases), would seem to discourage empathy between groups and the formation of a common identity. These factors, along with the desire for group-based status and the presumption of status or privilege, may also give rise to SDO. An important enterprise for future research is to investigate the social contextual factors that contribute to SDO and to inequality in general.

As a causal variable, we believe SDO is pertinent to the dynamics of group conflict and institutional discrimination. In the remainder of our discussion, we focus on these ramifications.

SDO and Group Discrimination

Social dominance theory states that SDO should predict prejudice and discrimination against out-groups; social identity theory (e.g., Tajfel & Turner, 1986) implies that emotional affiliation or identification with one's in-group should do the same. Social identity theory posits out-group denigration as a device for maintaining positive social identity; social dominance theory posits it as a device to maintain superior group status. In a minimal groups experiment, SDO and in-group identification each predicted degree of out-group discrimination (Sidanius, Pratto, & Mitchell, 1994). However, these effects were not independent— those who were high on SDO and on in-group identification were even more discriminatory against a minimal out-group. Crocker and Luhtanen (1990) found a parallel interaction in another experiment: People who strongly affiliated with their in-groups and whose group status was threatened especially denigrated out-groups. We consider their results to be consistent with both theories in that both group identification and group status needs motivated greater discrimination. Levin and Sidanius (1993) found a similar interaction between SDO and group status; high-SDO subjects who belonged to artificially high-status groups, especially denigrated out-group members. High group status and group-status threat may work similarly in these studies because high-status groups, having the most status to lose, may experience the most threat when confronted by possible loss of status. Understanding the circumstances under which people have high levels of in-group identification, high group status, and high SDO, then, appears to be important for understanding when discrimination is likely to be especially severe. Some of our other research has addressed the question of when these three predictors of discrimination will co-occur.

Because SDO is the desire for one's group to dominate others, SDO should have a differential relationship to in-group identification depending on the group's level of social status. Sidanius, Pratto, and Rabinowitz (1994) documented that SDO and in-group identification were more positively correlated in higher status than in lower status groups. Using various ethnic identification measures, we showed that the covariance between ethnic identification and SDO was statistically significant and positive within a high-status group (i.e., Euro-Americans), whereas this relationship was statistically significant and negative within a low-status group (Hispanics and African-Americans).

These experimental and correlational findings suggest that high-status groups will be the most discriminatory against out-groups because their members are most likely to have both high SDO levels and high levels of in-group identification. It is important to remember that these two variables, in experimental studies, interact to cause extremely severe out-group discrimination. In total, these results support social dominance theory's contention that higher status groups will tend to be more in-group serving than lower status groups. That is, higher status groups are more discriminatory against out-groups than lower status groups, and the aggregate affect of this asymmetry is not equal groups in conflict, but the maintenance of hierarchical group relations (see Sidanius & Pratto, 1993a).

SDO and Social Role

By performing organizational roles, individuals greatly expand their capacity for group discrimination because collective institutions can often allocate resources or costs on a far larger scale than individuals can. Therefore, institutional discrimination is one of the major contributors to the creation and maintenance of social inequalities and social hierarchy (e.g., Feagin & Feagin, 1978). The individual organizational member, however, is not insignificant. An organization's members help an institution perform its hierarchy role by endorsing legitimizing myths and adapting their SDO levels to the institution's norms. Several processes may contribute to a match between individuals and institutions. There is mounting evidence that people seek roles in an institution compatible with their SDO levels and ideological beliefs. The present research showed two replications of this relationship between SDO and aspired hierarchy role. A previous study showed the same relationship between aspired hierarchy role and belief in legitimizing myths (Sidanius, Pratto, Martin, & Stallworth, 1991). In another study, police recruits were found to have significantly higher SDO levels and related attitudes than public defenders (Sidanius, Liu, Pratto, & Shaw, 1994). Self-selection into roles based on hierarchy-relevant ideologies may be a contributing factor to institutional discrimination.

An institution also reinforces and contributes to the match between individuals' attitudes and institutional hierarchy role. For example, White police academy recruits became increasingly more negative toward Blacks during their first 18 months as police (Teahan, 1975). Also, the initial racial attitudes of intended hierarchy enhancers resisted the usual liberalizing influence of college the longer they stayed in college (Sidanius, Pratto, Martin, & Stallworth, 1991). Any number of socialization or social influence processes may have caused such effects. Hierarchy-enhancing behaviors or attitudes may even be rewarded by

hierarchy-enhancing institutions. One study of campus police officers showed that those who were most successful in their careers, as evidenced by several measures such as superior's evaluations and salary increases, tended to score higher on measures of racism and ethnocentrism (Leitner & Sedlacek, 1976). More recently, in a study of the Los Angeles Police Department, the Christopher Commission (1991) found that those police officers with the highest number of civilian complaints for brutality and excessive force received unusually positive performance evaluations from their supervising officers. In addition, these supervisor evaluations "were uniformly optimistic about the officers' progress and prospects on the force" (Christopher et al., 1991, p. 41).

Apparently, individuals and institutions reinforce each other's hierarchy-enhancing tendencies, which we believe makes their discriminatory behaviors powerful and difficult to change. More research on the detailed processes by which individuals and institutions reinforce one another's prejudices may be useful to those seeking to reduce institutional discrimination.

To summarize, the present research indicates that SDO, the desire for group dominance, is a significant predictor of social and political attitudes pertaining to intergroup relations and also of hierarchy roles. Social dominance theory suggests that the confluence of this individual-difference variable and a number of social factors including lack of common identity, high in-group status, and social role, contributes to the oppression of social groups.

REFERENCES

Adorno, T. W., Frenkel-Brunswik, E., Levinson, D. J., & Sanford, R. N. (1950). *The authoritarian personality.* New York: Norton.

Altemeyer, B. (1981). *Right-wing authoritarianism.* Manitoba: University of Manitoba Press.

Avery, P. G. (1988). Political tolerance among adolescents. *Theory and Research in Social Education, 16,* 183–201.

Benson, P. L., & Vincent, S. (1980). Development and validation of the sexist attitudes toward women scale. *Psychology of Women Quarterly, 5,* 276–291.

Bienen, L., Alan, N., Denno, D. W., Allison, P. D., & Mills, D. L. (1988). The reimposition of capital punishment in New Jersey: The role of prosecutorial discretion. *Rutgers Law Review* (Fall).

Bobo, L. (1983). Whites' opposition to busing: Symbolic racism or realistic group conflict? *Journal of Personality and Social Psychology, 45,* 1196–1210.

Brown, D. E. (1991). *Human universals.* New York: McGraw-Hill.

Burt, M. R. (1980). Cultural myths and supports for rape. *Journal of Personality and Social Psychology, 38,* 217–230.

Carmines, E. G., & McIver, J. D. (1981). Analyzing models with unobserved variables: Analysis of covariance structures. In G. W. Bohinstedt & E. F. Borgatta (Eds.), *Social measurement: Current issues* (pp. 65–115). Beverly Hills, CA: Sage.

Christopher, W., Arguellas, J. A., Anderson, R. A., Barnes, W. R., Estrada, L. F., Kantor, M., Mosk, R. M., Ordin, A. S., Slaughter, J. B., & Tranquada, R. E. (1991). *Report of the Independent Commission on the Los Angeles Police Department.* Suite 1910, 400 South Hope Street, Los Angeles, CA 90071-2899.

Costa, P. T., & MacRae, R. R. (1985). *The NEO Personality Inventory Manual.* Odessa, FL: Psychological Assessment Resources.

Crocker, J., & Luhtanen, R. (1990). Collective self-esteem and in-group bias. *Journal of Personality and Social Psychology, 58,* 60–67.

Dator, J. A. (1969). What's left of the economic theory of discrimination? In S. Shulman & W. Darity, Jr. (Eds.), *The question of discrimination: Racial inequality in the U.S. labor market* (pp. 335–374). Middletown, CT: Wesleyan University Press.

Davis, M. H. (1983). Measuring individual differences in empathy: Evidence for a multidimensional approach. *Journal of Personality and Social Psychology, 44,* 113–126.

Depret, E. F., & Fiske, S. T. (1993). Social cognition and power: Some cognitive consequences of social structure as a source of control deprivation. In G. Weary, F. Gleicher, & K. L. Marsh (Eds.), *Control motivation and social cognition* (pp. 176–202). New York: Springer Verlag.

Duckitt, J. (1989). Authoritarianism and group identification: A new view of an old construct. *Political Psychology, 10,* 63–84.

Eisler, R., & Loye, D. (1983). The "failure" of liberalism: A reassessment of ideology from a feminine-masculine perspective. *Political Psychology, 4,* 375–391.

Ekehammar, B., & Sidanius, J. (1982). Sex differences in socio-political ideology: A replication and extension. *British Journal of Social Psychology, 21,* 249–257.

Eysenck, H. J. (1971). Social attitudes and social class. *British Journal of Social and Clinical Psychology, 10,* 210–212.

Eysenck, H. J., & Wilson, O. D. (1978). *The psychological basis of ideology.* Baltimore, MD: University Park Press.

Feagin, J. R., & Feagin, C. B. (1978). *Discrimination American style: Institutional racism and sexism.* Malabar, FL: Krieger.

Fenigstein, A., Scheier, M. F., & Buss, A. H. (1975). Public and private self-consciousness: Assessment and theory. *Journal of Consulting and Clinical Psychology, 43,* 522–527.

Frenkel-Brunswik, E. (1948). A study of prejudice in children. *Human Relations, 1,* 295–306.

Frenkel-Brunswik, E. (1949). Intolerance of ambiguity as an emotional and perceptual variable. *Journal of Personality, 18,* 108–143.

General Accounting Office. (1990). *Death penalty sentencing: Research indicates pattern of racial disparities.* United States General Accounting Office, Report to Senate and House Committees on the Judiciary (GAO/GGD-90-57). Washington, DC: Government Printing Office.

Goertzel, T. G. (1987). Authoritarianism of personality and political attitudes. *Journal of Social Psychology, 127,* 7–18.

Gough, H. (1987). *California Psychological Inventory: Administrator's guide.* Palo Alto, CA: Consulting Psychologists Press.

Heaven, P. C. L. (1985). Construction and validation of a measure of authoritarian personality. *Journal of Personality Assessment, 49,* 545–551.

Jackson, D. N. (1965). *Personality Research Form.* Goshen, NY: Research Psychologists Press.

Jackson, D. N. (1976). *Jackson Personality Inventory.* Goshen, NY: Research Psychologists Press.

John, O. P. (1990). The Big Five factor taxonomy: Dimensions of personality in the natural language and in questionnaires. In L. A. Pervin (Ed.), *Handbook of personality psychology: Theory and research* (pp. 66–100). Hillsdale, NJ: Erlbaum.

John, O. P., Donahue, E., & Kentle, R. L. (1992). *The Big Five Inventory: Versions 4a and 54.* Technical Report, Institute of Personality Assessment and Research.

Katz, I., & Hass, R. G. (1988). Racial ambivalence and American value conflict: Correlational and priming studies of dual cognitive structures. *Journal of Personality and Social Psychology, 55,* 893–905.

Kleck, G. (1981). Racial discrimination in criminal sentencing: A critical evaluation of the evidence with additional evidence on the death penalty. *American Sociological Review, 46,* 783–805.

Kluegel, J. R., & Smith, P. M. (1986). *Beliefs about inequality: Americans' views of what is and what ought to be.* Hawthorne, NY: Aldine de Gruyter.

Kosterman, R., & Feshbach, S. (1989). Toward a measure of patriotic and nationalistic attitudes. *Political Psychology, 10,* 257–274.

Leitner, D. W., & Sedlacek, W. E. (1976). Characteristics of successful campus police officers. *Journal of College Student Personnel, 17,* 304–308.

Levin, S. L., & Sidanius, J. (1993). *Intergroup biases as a function of social dominance orientation and in-group status.* Unpublished manuscript, University of California at Los Angeles.

Levinson, D. J. (1950). Politico-economic ideology and group memberships in relation to ethnocentrism. In T. Adorno, E. Frenkel-Brunswik, D. J. Levinson, & R. N. Sanford (Eds.), *The authoritarian personality* (pp. 151–207). New York: Norton.

Lipset, S. M. (1960). *Political man.* London: Heinemann.

Loevinger, J. (1957). Objective tests as instrument of psychological theory. *Psychological Reports,* Monograph Supplement 9.

Malle, B. F., & Horowitz, L. M. (1994). *The puzzle of negative self-views: An explanation using the schema concept.* Unpublished manuscript, Stanford University.

Markus, H. R., & Kitayama, S. (1991). Culture and the self. Implications for cognition, emotion, and motivation. *Psychological Review, 98,* 224–253.

McConahay, J. B. (1986). Modern racism, ambivalence, and the modern racism scale. In J. F. Dovidio & S. L. Gaertner (Eds.), *Prejudice, discrimination, and racism* (pp. 91–125). San Diego, CA: Academic Press.

Mirels, H. L., & Garrett, J. B. (1971). The Protestant ethic as a personality variable. *Journal of Consulting and Clinical Psychology, 36,* 40–44.

Mitchell, M. (1993). *Attitudes towards the death penalty and use of executions: A social dominance perspective.* Unpublished dissertation, Department of Psychology, University of California at Los Angeles.

Moynihan, D. P. (1965). *The Negro family: The case for national action.* Washington, DC: Office of Policy Planning and Research, U.S. Department of Labor.

Nickerson, S., Mayo, C., & Smith, A. (1986). Racism in the courtroom. In J. F. Dovidio & S. L. Gaertner (Eds.), *Prejudice, discrimination, and racism* (pp. 255–278). San Diego, CA: Academic Press.

Paternoster, R. (1983). Race of victim and location of crime: The decision to seek the death penalty in South Carolina. *Journal of Criminal Law and Criminology, 74,* 754–785.

Peterson, B. E., Doty, R. M., & Winter, D. G. (1993). Authoritarianism and attitudes towards contemporary social issues. *Personality and Social Psychology Bulletin, 19,* 174–184.

Pratto, F. (1996). Sexual politics: The gender gap in the bedroom, the cupboard, and the cabinet. In D. M. Buss & N. Malamuth (Eds.), *Sex, power, and conflict: Evolutionary and feminist perspectives* (pp. 179–230). New York: Oxford University Press.

Pratto, F., Sidanius, J., & Stallworth, L. M. (1993). Sexual selection and the sexual and ethnic basis of social hierarchy. In L. Ellis (Ed.), *Social stratification and socioeconomic inequality: A comparative biosocial analysis* (pp. 111–137). New York: Praeger.

Radelet, M. L., & Pierce, G. L. (1985). Race and prosecutorial discretion in homicide cases. *Law and Society Review, 19,* 587–621.

Ray, J. (1976). Do authoritarians hold authoritarian attitudes? *Human Relations, 29,* 307–325.

Reiman, J. (1990). *The rich get richer and the poor get prison: Ideology, class, and criminal justice.* New York: Macmillan.

Rombough, S., & Ventimiglia, J. C. (1981). Sexism: A tri-dimensional phenomenon. *Sex Roles, 7,* 747–755.

Rosenberg, M. (1965). *Society and the adolescent self image.* Princeton, NJ: Princeton University Press.

Rosenthal, R. (1986). *Meta-analytic procedures for social research.* Beverly Hills, CA: Sage.

Rubin, Z., & Peplau, L. A. (1975). Who believes in a just world? *Journal of Social Issues, 31,* 265–289.

Sears, D. O. (1988). Symbolic racism. In P. A. Kau & D. A. Taylor (Eds.), *Eliminating racism: Profiles in controversy* (pp. 53–84). New York: Plenum.

Shapiro, R. Y., & Mahajan, H. (1986). Gender differences in policy preferences: A summary of trends from the 1960s to the 1980s. *Public Opinion Quarterly, 50,* 42–61.

Sidanius, J. (1976). *Further tests of a Swedish Scale of Conservatism.* Reports from the Department of Psychology, University of Stockholm, Supplement 36.

Sidanius, J. (1988). Race and sentence severity: The case of American justice. *Journal of Black Studies, 18,* 273–281.

Sidanius, J. (1993). The psychology of group conflict and the dynamics of oppression: A social dominance perspective. In W. McGuire & S. Iyengar (Eds.), *Current approaches to political psychology* (pp. 183–219). Durham, NC: Duke University Press.

Sidanius, J., Cling, B. J., & Pratto, F. (1991). Ranking and linking behavior as a function of sex and gender. An exploration of alternative explanations. *Journal of Social Issues, 47,* 131–149.

Sidanius, J., Devereux, E., & Pratto, F. (1992). A comparison of symbolic racism theory and social dominance theory as explanations for racial policy attitudes. *Journal of Social Psychology, 131,* 377–395.

Sidanius, J., & Ekehammar, B. (1979). Political socialization: A multivariate analysis of Swedish political attitude and preference data. *European Journal of Social Psychology, 9,* 265–279.

Sidanius, J., & Ekehammar, B. (1980). Sex-related differences in sociopolitical ideology. *Scandinavian Journal of Psychology, 21,* 17–26.

Sidanius, J., Liu, J., Pratto, F., & Shaw, J. (1994). Social dominance orientation, hierarchy-attenuators and hierarchy-enhancers: Social dominance theory and the criminal justice system. *Journal of Applied Social Psychology, 24,* 338–366.

Sidanius, J., & Pratto, F. (1993a). The dynamics of social dominance and the inevitability of oppression. In P. Sniderman & P. E. Tetlock (Eds.), *Prejudice, politics, and race in America today* (pp. 173–21 1). Stanford, CA: Stanford University Press.

Sidanius, J., & Pratto, F. (1993b). Racism and support of free-market capitalism: A cross-cultural analysis. *Political Psychology, 14,* 383–403.

Sidanius, J., Pratto, F., & Bobo, L. (1995). Social dominance orientation and the political psychology of gender. A case of invariance? *Journal of Personality and Social Psychology, 67,* 998–1011.

Sidanius, J., Pratto, F., & Brief, D. (1995). Group dominance and the political psychology of gender: A cross-cultural comparison. *Political Psychology, 16,* 381–396.

Sidanius, J., Pratto, F., Martin, M., & Stallworth, L. M. (1991). Consensual racism and career track: Some implications of social dominance theory. *Political Psychology, 12,* 691–720.

Sidanius, J., Pratto, R., & Mitchell, M. (1994). In-group identification, social dominance orientation, and differential intergroup social allocation. *Journal of Social Psychology, 134,* 151–167.

Sidanius, J., Pratto, F., & Rabinowitz, J. (1994). Gender, ethnic status, and ideological asymmetry: Social dominance interpretation. *Journal of Cross-Cultural Psychology, 25,* 194–216.

Sniderman, P. M., & Tetlock, P. E. (1986a). Symbolic racism: Problems of motive attribution in political analysis. *Journal of Social Issues, 42,* 129–150.

Sniderman, P. M., & Tetlock, P. E. (1986b). Reflections on American racism. *Journal of Social Issues, 42,* 173–188.

Snyder, M. (1974). The self-monitoring of expressive behavior. *Journal of Personality and Social Psychology, 30,* 526–537.

Spence, J. T., Helmreich, R., & Stapp, J. (1974). The personal attributes questionnaire: A measure of sex role stereotypes and masculinity-femininity. *JSAS Catalog of Selected Documents in Psychology, 4,* 1–42.

Stacey, B. G., & Green, R. T. (1968). The psychological bases of political allegiance among white-collar males. *British Journal of Social and Clinical Psychology, 7,* 45–60.

Stacey, B. G., & Green, R. T. (1971). Working-class conservatism: A review and an empirical study. *British Journal of Social and Clinical Psychology, 10,* 10–26.

Stone, W. F., & Russ, R. C. (1976). Machiavellianism as tough-mindedness. *Journal of Social Psychology, 98,* 213–220.

Super, D. E., & Nevill, D. D. (1985). *The values scale.* Palo Alto, CA: Consulting Psychologists Press.

Tajfel, H., & Turner, J. C. C. (1986). The social identity theory of intergroup behavior. In S. Worchel & W. G. Austin (Eds.), *Psychology of intergroup relations* (pp. 7–24). Chicago: Nelson-Hall.

Teahan, J. E. (1975). A longitudinal study of attitude shifts among Black and White police officers. *Journal of Social Issues, 31,* 47–56.

Wilson, G. D. (Ed.). (1973). *The psychology of conservatism.* San Diego, CA: Academic Press.

Wilson, G. D., & Patterson, J. R. (1968). A new measure of conservatism. *British Journal of Social and Clinical Psychology, 1,* 264–269.

Appendix A

Items on the Social Dominance Orientation Scale

1. Some groups of people are simply not the equals of others.
2. Some people are just more worthy than others.
3. This country would be better off if we cared less about how equal all people were.
4. Some people are just more deserving than others.
5. It is not a problem if some people have more of a chance in life than others.
6. Some people are just inferior to others.
7. To get ahead in life, it is sometimes necessary to step on others.
8. Increased economic equality.
9. Increased social equality.
10. Equality.
11. If people were treated more equally we would have fewer problems in this country.
12. In an ideal world, all nations would be equal.
13. We should try to treat one another as equals as much as possible. (All humans should be treated equally.)
14. It is important that we treat other countries as equals.

All items were measured on a *very negative* (1) to *very positive* (7) scale. Items 8–14 were reverse-coded. The version of Item 13 in parentheses was used in Samples 5–12. The order of items differed from above and across samples.

Appendix B

Items Used on Scales

Samples 2, 3b, 4, 5, 6, 8, 9: Items Comprising the Original Legitimizing Myths Scales

Anti-Black Racism Scale
A Black president.[a]
Racial integration.[a]
White superiority.
Blacks are inherently inferior.
Civil rights activists.[a]

Anti-Arab Racism Scale
Most of the terrorists in the world today are Arabs.
Historically, Arabs have made important contributions to world culture.[a]
Iraqis have little appreciation for democratic values.
People of the Muslim religion tend to be fanatical.
Muslims value peace and love.[a]

Cultural Elitism Scale
The poor cannot appreciate fine art and music.
No amount of education can make up for the wrong breeding.

Qualifications and not personality should determine whether a candidate gets votes.
The ideal world is run by those who are most capable.
Western civilization has brought more progress than all other cultural traditions.
Someone who treats other people poorly but is very good at his job should be promoted.
Great art is not meant for the common folk.

Equal Opportunity Scale
In America, every person has an equal chance to rise up and prosper.
Lower wages for women and ethnic minorities simply reflect lower skill and education levels.
America is the "land of opportunity."
Salaries are usually reflective of education, which in turn is reflective of intelligence and ambition.
Affirmative Action prevents the more-qualified from attaining positions.
Potential to do well should not be sufficient for admission to any program. Only those with proven competence in that field should be allowed.

Patriotism Scale

Flag burning should be illegal.

In American public schools, every day should begin with the *Pledge of Allegiance*.

I supported the United States' actions in Iraq.

Patriotism is the most important qualification for a politician.

I believe in mandatory military service by all citizens of the United States in the armed forces.

It was disloyal for people to question the President during the Iraq War.

With few exceptions, the American government does a good and honest job.

Other countries should be happy to have American intervention and influence.

I am proud to be an American.

Congressman who voted against the war should be removed from office.

The United States suffers when patriotism wanes.

Patriots are the ones who have made this country great.

Nationalism Scale

In view of America's moral and material superiority, it is only right that we should have the biggest say in deciding United Nations policy.

This country must continue to lead the "Free World."

We should do anything necessary to increase the power of our country, even if it means war.

Sometimes it is necessary for our country to make war on other countries for their own good.

The important thing for the U.S. foreign aid program is to see to it that the U.S. gains a political advantage.

Generally, the more influence America has on other nations, the better off they are.

Noblesse Oblige Scale—Form A

As a country's wealth increases, more of its resources should be channeled to the poor.

The more money one makes, the greater proportion of that money should be paid in taxes.

Those with more resources have more obligations toward their fellow human beings.

Giving to others usually benefits the givers as well.

The man with two coats in his closet should give one away.

Extra food on the table belongs to those who are hungry.

Noblesse Oblige Scale—Form B

As a country's wealth increases, more of its resources should be channeled to the poor.

Giving to others usually benefits the givers as well.

Those with more resources have more obligations toward their fellow human beings.

It is beneficial to all to spend money on the public sector such as education, housing, and health care.

Those who are well off can't be expected to take care of everyone else.[a]

Social charities just create dependency.[a]

Samples 2, 3b, 5, 6, 8, 9: Items on the Policy Scales

Law and Order Policies

Death penalty for drug kingpins.

Death penalty.[a]

Prisoner's rights.[a,b,c]

Longer prison sentences.[d]

Gay Rights

Gay or lesbian marriage.

Gay and lesbian rights.

Women's Rights

Guaranteed job security after maternity leave.

Stiffer penalties for wife beating.[c]

Equal pay for women.

More women judges.

Social Programs

Government sponsored health care.

Better support for the homeless.

More support for early education. [c,d]

Free school lunches.[c,d]

Low income housing.[c,d]

Arresting the homeless.[a,c]

Guaranteed jobs for all.

Reduced benefits for the unemployed.[a]

Greater aid to poor kids.

Increased taxation of the rich.

Racial Policy

Racial quotas.

Affirmative action.

School busing.[c]

Civil rights.

Helping minorities get a better education.

Government helping minorities get better housing.

Government has no business helping any particular ethnic group in the job market.[a]

Military Programs

Decreased defense spending.[a]

Strategic Defense Initiative.

B-2 (Stealth) bomber.

Going to war.[c]

Environmental Policies

Drilling for oil off the California coast.[a]

Government-mandated recycling programs.

Taxing environmental polluters to pay for superfund clean ups.

More government involvement on clean air and water.

Drilling for oil under the Arctic National Wildlife Refuge.[a]

Chauvinism Scale

Central Intelligence Agency (CIA).

English as the official language.

Decreased immigration to the U.S.
National security.
American way of life.
No welfare for new immigrants.
America first.
America as world's policeman.

Sample 4: Iraq War Scales (January, 1991)

Favors Military Action by U.S.
The U.S. really had no choice but to use military force against Iraq.
The U.S. should not be using military force against Iraq.[a]
Saddam Hussein must be stopped by any means necessary–including nuclear weapons.
The U.N. coalition should not participate in any military action that will kill civilians no matter how few.[a]
The U.N. coalition should cease bombing Iraq and offer to negotiate.[a]

Willing to Make Sacrifices for War
It would be worth our country's having a lower standard of living to maintain world peace.[a]
I would be willing to pay double the current prices of gasoline to avoid similar conflicts over oil in the future.[a]
I am willing to risk my life to help with the war effort in the Persian Gulf.
I'd be willing to pay higher taxes to finance the war in the Gulf.

Favors Suspending Liberties for War
President Bush should be given whatever power he needs to conduct war.
Sometimes political leaders must be unencumbered by legislatures so that they can govern effectively.
It is appropriate to reinstitute the military draft to help with the conflict with Iraq.
Military censorship of the press is appropriate in times of war.

Concerned About Environment in War
Iraq should be held entirely responsible for cleaning up the oil spills in the Persian Gulf.
The U.S. is partly to blame for the environmental damage to the Persian Gulf region.[a]
Potential environmental damage should have been considered in the decision to go to war.[a]

Sample 8: Post-War Pro-Iraq War Items (February, 1992)

The U.S. had no choice but to begin bombing Iraq on January 16, 1991.
The U.S. should have tried political and economic pressure for a longer time before bombing Iraq.[a]
Bombing the cities of Iraq was justified.
The President went to war to increase his popularity.[a]

The U.S. could have prevented more civilian casualties in Iraq.[a]
The Gulf War wasn't worth the human cost.[a]
The U.N. Coalition really taught Hussein a lesson.
We should spend as much money and effort on solving domestic problems as we did on the Iraq war.[a]
Once there was 250,000 U.S. troops in the Persian Gulf region, it would have been embarrassing not to "use" them in war.
President Bush should not have set a date for Iraqi withdrawal from Kuwait.[a]
Strict control of the press coverage of the Iraq war was necessary.
If we understood the Iraqis better, we might have been able to avoid the war.[a]
In all, the press reports we received about the war were fair and impartial.
The military response to Iraq's invasion of Kuwait will probably discourage others from invading countries.
The Gulf War wasn't worth the environmental cost.[a]

Wars of Dominance
To insure our influence is felt in that nation.
To protect our economic interests.
To protect our citizens being held hostage.
For U.S. national security purposes.
To restore a freely elected government which had been overthrown by a military coup.
To keep an enemy from acquiring chemical or nuclear weapons.
If we started disarming, it would only lead to more war.
A U.S. Military presence helps maintain peace.

Humanitarian Wars
To ensure that human rights were respected in that country.
To ensure that emergency food supplies could reach civilians.
To protect unarmed civilians from battles.
Ultimatums usually lead to war, rather than diplomatic solutions.
By selling arms to other countries, we increase the likelihood of war.
War should always be considered a last resort.

Sample 10: Items on Death Penalty Survey

Favored Executing Harris
I felt that Robert Alton Harris' death sentence should have been commuted to life in prison without possibility of parole.[a]
I felt that Robert Alton Harris should have been executed.

Believes in Specific Deterrence
If not executed, murderers will commit more crimes in the future.
We don't need the death penalty to insure that a murderer never repeats his crime.[a]

If not executed, a murderer will be on the street in a few years.

Support for Painful Executions

Murderers should suffer when they are executed.

I might support the use of burning alive to execute those who commit the most heinous crimes.

If people have to be executed, they should be executed in the most painless way possible.[a]

The electric chair should be quick and painless.[a]

Executions should be as bloodless as possible.[a]

The crime problem has gotten so bad that maybe we should bring back public hangings.

We should use more graphic forms of executions (such as a firing squad).

When using the electric chair for executions, the voltage should be applied slowly so the criminal suffers before dying.

Belief in Retribution

Society does not have the right to get revenge for murder.[a]

For a terrible crime, there should be a terrible punishment.

Even the worst criminal should be considered for mercy.[a]

Those who hurt others deserve to be hurt in return.

Punishment should fit the crime.

Note. Response scale for all items was *strongly disagree* (1) to *strongly agree* (7) except for the nationalism, anti-Black racism, and chauvinism items, which were *very negative* (1) to *very positive* (7). The instructions for the Wars scales were to indicate how much the subject agreed or disagreed that his or her country would be justified in using military force (for the items beginning with "to" or "for") or agreement or disagreement with support for military use of force in general (for items that are complete sentences). [a]Item was reverse-coded. [b]Item was omitted in Sample 6. [c]Item was omitted in Sample 8. [d] Item was omitted in Sample 9. [e]Item was omitted in Sample 2.

Appendix C

Items on the 16-Item Social Dominance Orientation Scale

1. Some groups of people are simply inferior to other groups.
2. In getting what you want, it is sometimes necessary to use force against other groups.
3. It's OK if some groups have more of a chance in life than others.
4. To get ahead in life, it is sometimes necessary to step on other groups.
5. If certain groups stayed in their place, we would have fewer problems.
6. It's probably a good thing that certain groups are at the top and other groups are at the bottom.
7. Inferior groups should stay in their place.
8. Sometimes other groups must be kept in their place.
9. It would be good if groups could be equal.
10. Group equality should be our ideal.
11. All groups should be given an equal chance in life.
12. We should do what we can to equalize conditions for different groups.
13. Increased social equality.
14. We would have fewer problems if we treated people more equally.
15. We should strive to make incomes as equal as possible.
16. No one group should dominate in society.

Items 9–16 should be reverse-coded. The response scale was *very negative* (1) to *very positive* (7).

Goal Relations and Interdependence

In the previous section we explored ways in which intergroup relations, particularly the more extreme and harmful forms, might be explained in terms of individual differences in enduring personality types. It is fair to say that current thinking in social psychology places little emphasis on personality alone. At the very least, the role of personality is heavily moderated by social contextual factors. Personality and individual difference explanations are "bottom-up"—they construct large-scale intergroup relations from the aggregation of individual predispositions.

A quite different perspective on intergroup relations is one that suggests that the nature of goal relations between social groups determines group members' orientations and their consequent behavior towards members of other groups. Where groups have, or believe they have, a zero-sum relationship (i.e., the more one group gets, the less the other group gets) relative to a scarce resource (e.g., status, money), group members develop negative goal interdependence and competitive behavior that tends to produce intergroup conflict. Where groups have, or believe they have, a non-zero-sum relationship (the more one group gets, the more the other group may get) relative to a resource, group members develop promotive goal interdependence and cooperative behavior that tends to produce intergroup harmony. This is a "top-down" social analysis that traces individual behavior to the socio-historical context of intergroup relations.

The classic work on this is by Muzafer Sherif (1958, 1966; Sherif, Harvey, White, Hood, & Sherif, 1961; Sherif & Sherif, 1953) who developed a functional, or realistic conflict, theory of intergroup behavior. Our first reading (Sherif, 1958) describes Sherif's approach to intergroup relations, his theory, and the intriguing research paradigm he devised. His famous "boys' camp" studies were conducted to demonstrate that how individuals in one group perceive and treat individuals in another group are overwhelmingly influenced by the nature of the goal relations between the groups. These studies represent a benchmark for research in social psychology. They are highly naturalistic and engaging, and yet they contain within them a range of experimental manipulations. A major goal of this research was to understand the conditions needed to reduce intergroup conflict. Sherif placed his money on superordinate goals— "goals which are compelling and highly appealing to members of two or more groups in conflict but which cannot be attained by the resources and energies of the groups separately. In effect, they are goals attained only when groups pull together." (Sherif, 1958, pp. 349–350). Sherif's approach to intergroup relations, although originally elaborated in the 1940s, is strikingly modern.

Sherif's research casts a long shadow over social psychology. Variants of his "boys' camp" paradigm have been used by other researchers, for example in organizational contexts (e.g., Blake, Shepard, & Mouton, 1964), and the idea that goal relations determine the complexion of intergroup behavior continues to be a powerful theme—

for example in the work of Morton Deutsch (1949, 1973) and perhaps most recently in the work of Jaap Rabbie on his behavioral interdependence model (e.g., Rabbie, Schot, & Visser, 1989; see Turner & Bourhis's 1996 critique).

Because this is a top-down perspective, it is meta-theoretically quite consistent with sociological analyses of social behavior. Not surprisingly, many sociological social psychologists continue to approach intergroup behavior in this way. Our second reading in this section, by Lawrence Bobo and Vincent Hutchings (1996), is a recent example of this genre. This is a study of intergroup attitudes among Whites, African Americans, Latinos, and Asian Americans, as a function of their feelings of threat based on perception of competition for scarce resources. The theoretical background is Blumer's (1958) theory of prejudice as a sense of group position derived from feelings of threat from other groups. Bobo and Hutchings argue that Blumer's theory has not been properly tested, and set out to rectify that problem. Unlike much psychological social psychology research that uses small, often undergraduate, samples, experimental settings, and so forth, Bobo and Hutchings draw a sample ($N = 1,869$) from the enormous 1992 Los Angeles County Social Survey.

Discussion Questions

1. Why does competitive interdependence cause more conflict between groups than between individuals?
2. Is cooperative interdependence sufficient to generate positive intergroup attitudes?
3. Can superordinate goals eliminate prejudice between groups?
4. How do groups select their goals?
5. Is there such a thing as "healthy" competition between groups?

Suggested Readings

Bettencourt, B. A., Brewer, M. B., Croak, M. R., & Miller, N. (1992). Co-operation and the reduction of intergroup bias: The role of reward structure and social orientation. *Journal of Experimental Social Psychology, 28*, 301–309. An experimental test of the way the effects of cooperation are moderated by whether people are focused on the task or on relationships between the groups.

Deutsch, M. (1973). *The resolution of conflict*. New Haven, CT: Yale University Press. Another well-known analysis of intergroup relations that focuses on goal relations and cooperation and competition between groups.

Insko, C. A., Schopler, J., Kennedy, J. F., Dahl, K. R., Graetz, K. A., & Drigotas, S. M. (1992). Individual-group discontinuity from the differing perspectives of Campbell's realistic group conflict theory and Tajfel and Turner's social identity theory. *Social Psychology Quarterly, 55*, 272–291. An analysis of the extent to which intergroup behavior is a reflection of real conflict between groups or the operation of social-cognitive processes associated with social identity and collective self-construal.

Rabbie, J. M., Schot, J. C., & Visser, L. (1989). Social identity theory: A conceptual and empirical critique from the perspective of a behavioural interaction model. *European Journal of Social Psychology, 19*, 171–202. A rather long and detailed theoretical and empirical critique, promoting interdependence approaches over social identity approaches in the explanation of intergroup behavior.

Sherif, M., & Sherif, C. W. (1953). *Groups in harmony and tension*. New York: Harper & Bros. The complete statement of Sherif's realistic conflict theory, and description of the "boys' camp" paradigm.

Turner, J. C. (1981). The experimental social psychology of intergroup behaviour. In J. C. Turner & H. Giles (Eds.), *Intergroup behaviour* (pp. 66–101). Oxford, UK: Blackwell. A critical and scholarly overview of interdependence and realistic conflict analyses of intergroup relations.

Superordinate Goals in the Reduction of Intergroup Conflict

Muzafer Sherif • University of Oklahoma

This paper summarizes an experimental study on intergroup relations, with emphasis on the reduction of conflict between groups. In the first phase, two groups were established independently by introducing specified conditions for interaction; in the second phase, the groups were brought into functional contact in conditions perceived by the members of the respective groups as competitive and frustrating. Members developed unfavorable attitudes and derogatory stereotypes of the other group; social distance developed to the point of mutual avoidance, even in pleasant activities. In the final phase of the experiment the measure that proved effective in reducing tension between groups was the introduction of goals which were compellingly shared by members of the groups and which required the collaborative efforts of all.

In the past, measures to combat the problems of intergroup conflicts, proposed by social scientists as well as by such people as administrators, policy-makers, municipal officials, and educators, have included the following: introduction of legal sanctions; creation of opportunities for social and other contacts among members of conflicting groups; dissemination of correct information to break down false prejudices and unfavorable stereotypes; appeals to the moral ideals of fair play and brotherhood; and even the introduction of rigorous physical activity to produce catharsis by releasing pent-up frustrations and aggressive complexes in the unconscious. Other measures proposed include the encouragement of co-operative habits in one's own community, and bringing together in the cozy atmosphere of a meeting room the leaders of antagonistic groups.

Many of these measures may have some value in the reduction of intergroup conflicts, but, to date, very few generalizations have been established concerning the circumstances and kinds of inter-group conflict in which these measures are effective. Today measures are applied in a somewhat trial-and-error fashion. Finding measures that have wide validity in practice can come only through clarification of the nature of intergroup conflict and analysis of the factors conducive to harmony and conflict between groups under given conditions.

The task of defining and analyzing the nature of the problem was undertaken in a previous publication.[1] One of our major statements was the effectiveness of superordinate goals for the reduction of intergroup conflict. "Superordinate goals" we defined as goals which are compelling and highly appealing to members of two or more groups in conflict but which cannot be attained by the resources and energies of the groups separately. In effect, they are goals attained only when groups pull together.

---

[1]Muzafer Sherif and Carolyn W. Sherif, *Groups in Harmony and Tension* (New York: Harper & Bros., 1953).

Intergroup Relations and the Behavior of Group Members

Not every friendly or unfriendly act toward another person is related to the group membership of the individuals involved. Accordingly, we must select those actions relevant to relations between groups.

Let us start by defining the main concepts involved. Obviously, we must begin with an adequate conception of the key term—"group." A group is a social unit (1) which consists of a number of individuals who, at a given time, stand in more or less definite interdependent status and role relationships with one another and (2) which explicitly or implicitly possesses a set of values or norms regulating the behavior of individual members, at least in matters of consequence to the group. Thus, shared attitudes, sentiments, aspirations, and goals are related to and implicit in the common values or norms of the group.

The term "intergroup relations" refers to the relations between two or more groups and their respective members. In the present context we are interested in the acts that occur when individuals belonging to one group interact, collectively or individually, with members of another in terms of their group identification. The appropriate frame of reference for studying such behavior includes the functional relations between the groups. Intergroup situations are not voids. Though not independent of relationships within the groups in question, *the characteristics of relations between groups cannot be deduced or extrapolated from the properties of in-group relations.*

Prevalent modes of behavior within a group, in the way of co-operativeness and solidarity or competitiveness and rivalry among members, need not be typical of actions involving members of an out-group. At times, hostility toward out-groups may be proportional to the degree of solidarity within the group. In this connection, results presented by the British statistician L. F. Richardson are instructive. His analysis of the number of wars conducted by the major nations of the world from 1850 to 1941 reveals that Great Britain heads the list with twenty wars—more than the Japanese (nine wars), the Germans (eight wars), or the United States (seven wars). We think that this significantly larger number of wars engaged in by a leading European democracy has more to do with the intergroup relations involved in perpetuating a far-flung empire than with dominant practices at home or with personal frustrations of individual Britishers who participated in these wars.[2]

In recent years relationships between groups have sometimes been explained through analysis of individuals who have endured unusual degrees of frustration or extensive authoritarian treatment in their life-histories. There is good reason to believe that some people growing up in unfortunate life-circumstances may become more intense in their prejudices and hostilities. But at best these cases explain the intensity of behavior in a given dimension.[3] In a conflict between two groups—a strike or a war—opinion within the groups is crystallized, slogans are formulated, and effective measures are organized by members recognized as the most responsible in their respective groups. The prejudice scale and the slogans are not usually imposed on the others by the deviate or neurotic members. Such individuals ordinarily exhibit their intense reactions within the reference scales of prejudice, hostility, or sacrifice established in their respective settings.

The behavior by members of any group toward another group is not primarily a problem of deviate behavior. If it were, intergroup behavior would not be the issue of vital consequence that it is today. The crux of the problem is the participation by group members in established practices and social-distance norms of their group and their response to new trends developing in relationships between their own group and other groups.

On the basis of his UNESCO studies in India, Gardner Murphy concludes that to be a good Hindu or a good Moslem implies belief in all the nasty qualities and practices attributed by one's own group—Hindu or Moslem—to the other. Good members remain deaf and dumb to favorable information concerning the adversary. Social contacts and avenues of communication serve, on the whole, as vehicles for further conflicts not merely

---

[2]T. H. Pear, *Psychological Factors of Peace and War* (New York: Philosophical Library, 1950), p. 126.

[3]William R. Hood and Muzafer Sherif, "Personality Oriented Approaches to Prejudice," *Sociology and Social Research,* XL (1955), 79–85.

for neurotic individuals but for the bulk of the membership.[4]

In the process of interaction among members, an in-group is endowed with positive qualities which tend to be praiseworthy, self-justifying, and even self-glorifying. Individual members tend to develop these qualities through internalizing group norms and through example by high-status members, verbal dicta, and a set of correctives standardized to deal with cases of deviation. Hence, possession of these qualities, which reflect their particular brand of ethnocentrism, is not essentially a problem of deviation or personal frustration. It is a question of participation in in-group values and trends by good members, who constitute the majority of membership as long as group solidarity and morale are maintained.

To out-groups and their respective members are attributed positive or negative qualities, depending on the nature of functional relations between the groups in question. The character of functional relations between groups may result from actual harmony and interdependence or from actual incompatibility between the aspirations and directions of the groups. A number of field studies and experiments indicate that, if the functional relations between groups are positive, favorable attitudes are formed toward the out-group. If the functional relations between groups are negative, they give rise to hostile attitudes and unfavorable stereotypes in relation to the out-group. Of course, in large group units the picture of the out-group and relations with it depend very heavily on communication, particularly from the mass media.

Examples of these processes are recurrent in studies of small groups. For example, when a gang "appropriates" certain blocks in a city, it is considered "indecent" and a violation of its "rights" for another group to carry on its feats in that area. Intrusion by another group is conducive to conflict, at times with grim consequences, as Thrasher showed over three decades ago.[5]

When a workers' group declares a strike, existing group lines are drawn more sharply. Those who are not actually for the strike are regarded as against it. There is no creature more lowly than the man who works while the strike is on.[6] The same type of behavior is found in management groups under similar circumstances.

In time, the adjectives attributed to out-groups take their places in the repertory of group norms. The lasting, derogatory stereotypes attributed to

groups low on the social-distance scale are particular cases of group norms pertaining to out-groups.

As studies by Bogardus show, the social-distance scale of a group, once established, continues over generations, despite changes of constituent individuals, who can hardly be said to have prejudices because of the same severe personal frustrations or authoritarian treatment.[7]

Literature on the formation of prejudice by growing children shows that it is not even necessary for the individual to have actual unfavorable experiences with outgroups to form attitudes of prejudice toward them. In the very process of becoming an in-group member, the intergroup delineations and corresponding norms prevailing in the group are internalized by the individual.[8]

A Research Program

A program of research has been under way since 1948 to test experimentally some hypotheses derived from the literature of intergroup relations. The first large-scale intergroup experiment was carried out in 1949, the second in 1953, and the third in 1954.[9] The conclusions reported here brief-

---

[4]Gardner Murphy, *In the Minds of Men* (New York: Basic Books, 1953).

[5]F. M. Thrasher, *The Gang* (Chicago: University of Chicago Press, 1927).

[6]E. T. Hiller, *The Strike* (Chicago: University of Chicago Press, 1928).

[7]E. S. Bogardus, "Changes in Racial Distances," *International Journal of Opinion and Altitude Research,* I (1947), 55–62.

[8]E. L. Horowitz, "Race Attitudes," in Otto Klineberg (ed.), *Characteristics of the American Negro,* Part IV (New York: Harper & Bros., 1944).

[9]The experimental work in 1949 was jointly supported by the Yale Attitude Change Project and the American Jewish Committee. It is summarized in Sherif and Sherif, *op. cit.,* chaps. ix and x. Both the writing of that book and the experiments in 1953–54 were made possible by a grant from the Rockefeller Foundation. The 1953 research is summarized in Muzafer Sherif, B. Jack White, and O. J. Harvey, "Status in Experimentally Produced Groups," *American Journal of Sociology,* LX (1955), 370–79, The 1954 experiment was summarized in Muzafer Sherif, O. J. Harvey, B. Jack White, William R. Hood, and Carolyn W. Sherif, "Experimental Study of Positive and Negative Intergroup Attitudes between Experimentally Produced Groups: Robbers Cave Study" (Norman, Okla.: University of Oklahoma, 1954). (Multilithed.) For a summary of the three experiments see chaps. vi and ix in Muzafer Sherif and Carolyn W. Sherif, *An Outline of Social Psychology* (rev. ed.; New York: Harper & Bros., 1956).

ly are based on the 1949 and 1954 experiments and on a series of laboratory studies carried out as co-ordinate parts of the program.[10]

The methodology, techniques, and criteria for subject selection in the experiments must be summarized here very briefly. The experiments were carried out in successive stages: (1) groups were formed experimentally; (2) tension and conflict were produced between these groups by introducing conditions conducive to competitive and reciprocally frustrating relations between them; and (3) the attempt was made toward reduction of the intergroup conflict. This stage of reducing tension through introduction of superordinate goals was attempted in the 1954 study on the basis of lessons learned in the two previous studies.

At every stage the subjects interacted in activities which appeared natural to them at a specially arranged camp site completely under our experimental control. They were not aware of the fact that their behavior was under observation. No observation or recording was made in the subjects' presence in a way likely to arouse the suspicion that they were being observed. There is empirical and experimental evidence contrary to the contention that individuals cease to be mindful when they know they are being observed and that their words are being recorded.[11]

In order to insure validity of conclusions, results obtained through observational methods were cross-checked with results obtained through sociometric technique, stereotype ratings of in-groups and outgroups, and through data obtained by techniques adapted from the laboratory. Unfortunately, these procedures cannot be elaborated here. The conclusions summarized briefly are based on results crosschecked by two or more techniques.

The production of groups, the production of conflict between them, and the reduction of conflict in successive stages were brought about through the introduction of problem situations that were real and could not be ignored by individuals in the situation. Special "lecture methods" or "discussion methods" were not used. For example, the problem of getting a meal through their own initiative and planning was introduced when participating individuals were hungry.

Facing a problem situation which is immediate and compelling and which embodies a goal that cannot be ignored, group members *do* initiate discussion and *do* plan and carry through these plans

until the objective is achieved. In this process the discussion becomes *their* discussion, the plan *their* plan, the action *their* action. In this process discussion, planning, and action have their place, and, when occasion arises, lecture or information has its place, too. The sequence of these related activities need not be the same in all cases.

The subjects were selected by rigorous criteria. They were healthy, normal boys around the age of eleven and twelve, socially well adjusted in school and neighborhood, and academically successful. They came from a homogeneous sociocultural background and from settled, well-adjusted families of middle or lower-middle class and Protestant affiliations. No subject came from a broken home. The mean I.Q. was above average. The subjects were not personally acquainted with one another prior to the experiment. Thus, explanation of results on the basis of background differences, social maladjustment, undue childhood frustrations, or previous interpersonal relations was ruled out at the beginning by the criteria for selecting subjects.

The first stage of the experiments was designed to produce groups with distinct structure (organization) and a set of norms which could be confronted with intergroup problems. The method for producing groups from unacquainted individuals with similar background was to introduce problem situations in which the attainment of the goal depended on the co-ordinated activity of all individuals. After a series of such activities, definite group structures or organizations developed.

The results warrant the following conclusions for the stage of group formation: When individuals interact in a series of situations toward goals which appeal to all and which require that they co-ordinate their activities, group structures arise having hierarchical status arrangements and a set of norms regulating behavior in matters of consequence to the activities of the group.

Once we had groups that satisfied our definition of "group," relations between groups could

---

[10]For an overview of this program see Muzafer Sherif, "Integrating Field Work and Laboratory in Small Group Research," *American Sociological Review,* XIX (1954), 759–71.

[11]E.g., see F. B. Miller, " 'Resistentialism' in Applied Social Research," *Human Organization,* XII (1954), 5–8; S. Wapner and T. G. Alper, "The Effect of an Audience on Behavior in a Choice Situation," *Journal of Abnormal and Social Psychology,* XLVII (1952), 222–29.

be studied. Specified conditions conducive to friction or conflict between groups were introduced. This negative aspect was deliberately undertaken because the major problem in intergroup relations today is the reduction of existing intergroup frictions. (Increasingly, friendly relations between groups is not nearly so great an issue.) The factors conducive to intergroup conflict give us realistic leads for reducing conflict.

A series of situations was introduced in which one group could achieve its goal only at the expense of the other group—through a tournament of competitive events with desirable prizes for the winning group. The results of the stage of intergroup conflict supported our main hypotheses. During interaction between groups in experimentally introduced activities which were competitive and mutually frustrating, members of each group developed hostile attitudes and highly unfavorable stereotypes toward the other group and its members. In fact, attitudes of social distance between the groups became so definite that they wanted to have nothing further to do with each other. This we take as a case of experimentally produced "social distance" in miniature. Conflict was manifested in derogatory name-calling and invectives, flare-ups of physical conflict, and raids on each other's cabins and territory. Over a period of time, negative stereotypes and unfavorable attitudes developed.

At the same time there was an increase in in-group solidarity and co-operativeness. This finding indicates that co-operation and democracy within groups do not necessarily lead to democracy and co-operation with out-groups, if the directions and interests of the groups are conflicting.

Increased solidarity forged in hostile encounters, in rallies from defeat, and in victories over the out-group is one instance of a more general finding: Intergroup relations, both conflicting and harmonious, *affected the nature of relations within the groups involved.* Altered relations between groups produced significant changes in the status arrangements *within* groups, in some instances resulting in shifts at the upper status levels or even a change in leadership. Always, consequential intergroup relations were reflected in new group values or norms which signified changes in practice, word, and deed within the group. Counterparts of this finding are not difficult to see in actual and consequential human relations. Probably many of our major preoccupations, anxieties, and

activities in the past decade are incomprehensible without reference to the problems created by the prevailing "cold war" on an international scale.

Reduction of Intergroup Friction

A number of the measures proposed today for reducing intergroup friction could have been tried in this third stage. A few will be mentioned here, with a brief explanation of why they were discarded or were included in our experimental design.

1. Disseminating favorable information in regard to the out-group was not included. Information that is not related to the goals currently in focus in the activities of groups is relatively ineffective, as many studies on attitude change have shown.[12]
2. In small groups it is possible to devise sufficiently attractive rewards to make individual achievement supreme. This may reduce tension between groups by splitting the membership on an "every-man-for-himself" basis. However, this measure has little relevance for actual intergroup tensions, which are in terms of group membership and group alignments.
3. The resolution of conflict through leaders alone was not utilized. Even when group leaders meet apart from their groups around a conference table, they cannot be considered independent of the dominant trends and prevailing attitudes of their membership. If a leader is too much out of step in his negotiations and agreements with out-groups, he will cease to be followed. It seemed more realistic, therefore, to study the influence of leadership within the framework of prevailing trends in the groups involved. Such results will give us leads concerning the conditions under which leadership can be effective in reducing intergroup tensions.
4. The "common-enemy" approach is effective in pulling two or more groups together against another group. This approach was utilized in the 1949 experiment as an expedient measure and yielded effective results. But bringing some groups together against others means larger and more devastating conflicts in the long run. For

---

[12]E.g., see R. M. Williams, *The Reduction of Intergroup Tensions* (Social Science Research Council Bull. 57 [New York, 1947]).

this reason, the measure was not used in the 1954 experiment.

5. Another measure, advanced both in theoretical and in practical work, centers around social contacts among members of antagonistic groups in activities which are pleasant in themselves. This measure was tried out in 1954 in the first phase of the integration stage.

6. As the second phase of the integration stage, we introduced a series of superordinate goals which necessitated co-operative interaction between groups.

The social contact situations consisted of activities which were satisfying in themselves—eating together in the same dining room, watching a movie in the same hall, or engaging in an entertainment in close physical proximity. These activities, which were satisfying to each group, but which did not involve a state of interdependence and co-operation for the attainment of goals, were not effective in reducing intergroup tension. On the contrary, such occasions of contact were utilized as oportunities to engage in name-calling and in abuse of each other to the point of physical manifestations of hostility.

The ineffective, even deleterious, results of intergroup contact without superordinate goals have implications for certain contemporary learning theories and for practice in intergroup relations. Contiguity in pleasant activities with members of an out-group does not necessarily lead to a pleasurable image of the out-group if relations between the groups are unfriendly. Intergroup contact without superordinate goals is not likely to produce lasting reduction of intergroup hostility. John Gunther, for instance, in his survey of contemporary Africa, concluded that, when the intergroup relationship is exploitation of one group by a "superior" group, intergroup contact inevitably breeds hostility and conflict.[13]

Introduction of Superordinate Goals

After establishing the ineffectiveness, even the harm, in intergroup contacts which did not involve superordinate goals, we introduced a series of superordinate goals. Since the characteristics of the problem situations used as superordinate goals are implicit in the two main hypotheses for this stage, we shall present these hypotheses:

1. When groups in a state of conflict are brought into contact under conditions embodying superordinate goals, which are compelling but cannot be achieved by the efforts of one group alone, they will tend to co-operate toward the common goals.

2. Co-operation between groups, necessitated by a series of situations embodying superordinate goals, will have a cumulative effect in the direction of reducing existing conflict between groups.

The problem situations were varied in nature, but all had an essential feature in common—they involved goals that could not be attained by the efforts and energies of one group alone and thus created a state of interdependence between groups: combating a water shortage that affected all and could not help being "compelling"; securing a much-desired film, which could not be obtained by either group alone but required putting their resources together; putting into working shape, when everyone was hungry and the food was some distance away, the only means of transportation available to carry food.

The introduction of a series of such superordinate goals was indeed effective in reducing intergroup conflict: (1) when the groups in a state of friction interacted in conditions involving superordinate goals, they did co-operate in activities leading toward the common goal and (2) a series of joint activities leading toward superordinate goals had the cumulative effect of reducing the prevailing friction between groups and unfavorable stereotypes toward the out-group.

These major conclusions were reached on the basis of observational data and were confirmed by sociometric choices and stereotype ratings administered first during intergroup conflict and again after the introduction of a series of superordinate goals. Comparison of the sociometric choices during intergroup conflict and following the series of superordinate goals shows clearly the changed attitudes toward members of the out-group. Friendship preferences shifted from almost exclusive preference for in-group members toward increased inclusion of members from the "antagonists." Since the groups were still intact following co-operative efforts to gain superordinate goals, friends were

---

[13]John Gunther, *Inside Africa* (New York: Harper & Bros., 1955).

found largely within one's group. However, choices of out-group members grew, in one group, from practically none during intergroup conflict to 23 percent. Using chi square, this difference is significant ($P < .05$). In the other group, choices of the out-group increased to 36 percent, and the difference is significant ($P < .001$). The findings confirm observations that the series of superordinate goals produced increasingly friendly associations and attitudes pertaining to out-group members.

Observations made after several superordinate goals were introduced showed a sharp decrease in the name-calling and derogation of the out-group common during intergroup friction and in the contact situations without superordinate goals. At the same time the blatant glorification and bragging about the in-group, observed during the period of conflict, diminished. These observations were confirmed by comparison of ratings of stereotypes (adjectives) the subjects had actually used in referring to their own group and the out-group during conflict with ratings made after the series of superordinate goals. Ratings of the out-group changed significantly from largely unfavorable ratings to largely favorable ratings. The proportions of the most unfavorable ratings found appropriate for the out-group—that is, the categorical verdicts that "all of them are stinkers" or ". . . smart alecks" or " . . . sneaky"—fell, in one group, from 21 percent at the end of the friction stage to 1.5 percent after interaction oriented toward superordinate goals. The corresponding reduction in these highly unfavorable verdicts by the other group was from 36.5 to 6 percent. The over-all differences between the frequencies of stereotype ratings made in relation to the out-group during intergroup conflict and following the series of superordinate goals are significant for both groups at the .001 level (using chi-square test).

Ratings of the in-group were not so exclusively favorable, in line with observed decreases in self-glorification. But the differences in ratings of the in-group were not statistically significant, as were the differences in ratings of the out-group.

Our findings demonstrate the effectiveness of a series of superordinate goals in the reduction of intergroup conflict, hostility, and their by-products. They also have implications for other measures proposed for reducing intergroup tensions.

It is true that lines of communication between groups must be opened before prevailing hostility can be reduced. But, if contact between hostile groups takes place without superordinate goals, the communication channels serve as media for further accusations and recriminations. When contact situations involve superordinate goals, communication is utilized in the direction of reducing conflict in order to attain the common goals.

Favorable information about a disliked out-group tends to be ignored, rejected, or reinterpreted to fit prevailing stereotypes. But, when groups are pulling together toward superordinate goals, true and even favorable information about the out-group is seen in a new light. The probability of information being effective in eliminating unfavorable stereotypes is enormously enhanced.

When groups co-operate in the attainment of superordinate goals, leaders are in a position to take bolder steps toward bringing about understanding and harmonious relations. When groups are directed toward incompatible goals, genuine moves by a leader to reduce intergroup tension may be seen by the membership as out of step and ill advised. The leader may be subjected to severe criticism and even loss of faith and status in his own group. When compelling superordinate goals are introduced, the leader can make moves to further co-operative efforts, and his decisions receive support from other group members.

In short, various measures suggested for the reduction of intergroup conflict—disseminating information, increasing social contact, conferences of leaders—acquire new significance and effectiveness when they become part and parcel of interaction processes between groups oriented toward superordinate goals which have real and compelling value for all groups concerned.

Perceptions of Racial Group Competition: Extending Blumer's Theory of Group Position to a Multiracial Social Context

Lawrence Bobo • University of California, Los Angeles
Vincent L. Hutchings • University of Michigan

Perceptions of threat occupy a central place in race relations in Blumer's theory of prejudice but few direct efforts to study such perceptions exist. Extending Blumer's reasoning, we hypothesize that such perceptions are driven by a group's feelings of racial alienation within the larger social order. The more that members of a particular racial group feel collectively oppressed and unfairly treated by society, the more likely they are to perceive members of other groups as potential threats. We also examine whether such perceptions spring from simple self-interest, orthodox prejudice such as negative feelings and stereotyping, or broad beliefs about social stratification and inequality. We use data from the 1992 Los Angeles County Social Survey, a large multiracial sample of the general population, to analyze the distribution and social and psychological underpinnings of perceived group competition. Our results support the racial alienation hypothesis as well as the hypotheses positing effects for self-interest, prejudice, and stratification beliefs. We argue that Blumer's group-position framework offers the most parsimonious integration and interpretation of the social psychological processes involved in the formation of perceptions of group threat and competition.

Ongoing immigration from Asia and Latin America and the earlier internal migration of African Americans out of the rural South have made most large cities in the United States remarkable multiracial conglomerations (Waldinger, 1989). An immediate sociological concern raised by the growing heterogeneity of urban areas is whether members of different groups view one another as direct competitors for scarce economic, political, and social resources (Olzak, 1993). Such perceptions may influence the potential for coalition formation and cooperation among groups as well as the prospects for open antagonism and conflict.

We pose two questions about the nature of interracial tension in modern urban centers: (1) To what extent do Whites, Blacks, Latinos, and Asians view one another as locked in competitive social relations; and (2) what are the social and psychological underpinnings of such outlooks? Although these questions are often the subjects of media attention and speculation, the extant sociological research on interracial attitudes provides limited descriptive or theoretical guidance in answer to these questions.

Most research mapping the basic distribution of racial attitudes focuses almost exclusively on

Whites' views of African Americans (Hyman & Sheatsley, 1956; Taylor, Greeley, & Sheatsley, 1978; Apostle et al., 1983; Schuman, Steeh, & Bobo, 1985; Kluegel & Smith, 1986; Tuch, 1987; Firebaugh & Davis, 1988; Kluegel, 1990; Steeh & Schuman, 1992; Bobo & Kluegel, 1993). To be sure, the classic literatures on social distance (Bogardus, 1928, 1933) and on social stereotypes (Katz & Braly, 1933) have posed questions about many different groups. Yet these important research traditions have two limitations: Typically they rely on samples of college students and they emphasize change over time in relative rankings on a social distance scale (Owen, Eisner, & McFaul, 1981; Smith & Dempsey, 1983; Crull & Burton, 1985) or on a stereotyping scale (Ashmore & Del Boca, 1981; Stephan & Rosenfield, 1982). While informative, such research bears only indirectly on the question of group competition and conflict. In addition, research that draws on multiracial samples of general populations has rarely reached beyond examination of the demographic correlates of attitudes (Dyer, Vedlitz, & Wochel, 1989), tightly focused case studies (Starr & Roberts, 1982), or a concern with beliefs about discrimination (Sigelman & Welch, 1991) and processes of assimilation (Portes, 1984; Portes, Parker, & Cobas, 1988; Uhlaner, 1991).

For these reasons, we undertake research on the issues of perceived group competition and conflict. At a theoretical level, we explore and extend Blumer's (1958) theory of prejudice as a "sense of group position." This view of the social psychology of group relations directs attention to feelings of threat from other social groups, identifying such feelings as dynamic forces in intergroup social and political relations. There are few direct empirical studies, however, of Blumer's concern with perceptions of threat as a core variable in intergroup relations (Jackman, 1994). Some research has inferred feelings of threat based on compositional preferences (Smith, 1981; Schuman et al., 1985) or in-depth interviews (Wellman, 1977). Virtually all studies that attempt direct measurement of feelings of competitive threat are secondary analyses of data designed for other purposes and, again, focus exclusively on Whites' reactions to African Americans (Bobo, 1983, 1988a, 1988b; Giles & Evans, 1986; Fossett & Kiecolt, 1989; Glaser, 1994). Hence, an examination of feelings of competitive threat among Whites, African Americans, Latinos, and Asian Americans provides

a unique chance to test these ideas empirically and to generalize Blumer's model to an increasingly important case: relations within and between racial minority groups.

We bring systematic data to bear on these questions. The 1992 Los Angeles County Social Survey (LACSS) included new multiple item measures of feelings of competitive threat. The sample covers one of the most heterogeneous areas in the nation and includes an oversampling of African American and Asian American respondents. It includes a battery of measures of intergroup attitudes tapping group affect, stereotypes, and feelings of social distance. The LACSS also includes measures of core beliefs about social stratification such as commitment to individualism and inequalitarianism (Kluegel & Smith, 1982; Feldman, 1988). Thus we can determine whether racial prejudice and beliefs about the U.S. opportunity structure shape perceptions of group competition.

Theoretical Background

Previous research offers four theoretical accounts of intergroup hostility that explain why Whites, Blacks, Latinos, and Asians may come to feel competitive threat from one another.[1] These models include simple self-interest models, classical preju-

---

[1] Notions of race and ethnicity, although often ascriptive and based on observable, heritable features like skin color, eye shape, hair texture, and so on, are fundamentally social constructions (Stone, 1985; See & Wilson, 1989). Although racial distinctions often result in sharper and more persistent group barriers compared to ethnic distinctions (Lieberson, 1980; Stone, 1985; Omi & Winant, 1986; Waters 1990), we conceive of race as a special case of an ethnic distinction. Racial and ethnic categories and labels vary over time and place in meaning and salience. We use the labels "White," "Black" or "African American" "Asian" or "Asian American," and "Hispanic" or "Latino." Because our analysis refers to these groups we use the term "race" or "racial" rather than "ethnic." These broad categories may conceal important subgroup differences. Our questionnaire and current usage of these terms reflect our reading of current patterns of discourse. Pretest results suggest that these terms are familiar, understood, and generally noncontroversial. With regard to the questionnaire, it was impractical to distinguish among the several largest Latino (i.e., Mexican, Colombian, Nicaraguan, Salvadorean, Puerto Rican) or Asian groups (i.e., Chinese, Filipino, Korean, and Japanese) in the Los Angeles area. Social interaction and discourse often rely on stereotypes linked to these broad social categories. Blacks, particularly middle-class Blacks, often complain that Whites respond to the category "Black" and ignore social class cues and other individuating factors (Zweigenhaft & Domhoff, 1990; Cose, 1994; Feagin

dice models, stratification beliefs models, and Blumer's theory of group position. These models are not intrinsically opposed to each other, and we consider ways to fruitfully integrate them.

The Simple Self-Interest Model

This familiar explanation of interracial hostility rests on a straightforward pocketbook logic. There is, in short, an objective basis for conflict: Hostility between members of two racial groups reflects an underlying clash of material interests—mainly economic interests, but sometimes political interests as well (Kluegel & Smith, 1986, pp. 18–19, 25–27). Some specifications of this approach ignore notions of group identity, attitudes, and the whole apparatus of subjective interpretation and assignment of meaning to "social facts" (Citrin & Green, 1990; Sears & Funk, 1991). Objective personal vulnerability to economic or political deprivation provides the direct basis for interethnic hostility.

The objective quality of an individual's private life may also be directly affected in noneconomic ways. For instance, the changing racial makeup of one's neighborhood can impose costs or burdens, such as changing availability of services, lessened ability to interact with and draw on neighbors for social support, and the introduction of different

---

& Sikes, 1994). Complaints of blanket stereotyping are increasingly heard from Asian Americans and Latinos as well.

> For many Asian Americans, the Los Angeles riots brought home a sobering truth: The one thing they all have in common is that many other Americans cannot tell them apart. The fear that joined the wealthy fourth-generation Japanese-American in Bel Air to the war-scarred, welfare dependent Cambodian refugee in Long Beach was a wake-up call to anyone with black hair and almond eyes: No one is safe from anti-Asian anger . . . Many Chinese, Japanese, and Vietnamese Americans say their shops were damaged because rioters thought they were Korean. And some have accused Korean immigrants of making trouble for all Asian Americans by treating blacks badly. (Susan Moffat, "Splintered Society: U.S. Asians," *Los Angeles Times*, July 31, 1992, p. A1)

In one of the most shocking hate crimes directed at an Asian American, two unemployed White Detroit auto workers beat Vincent Chin to death, mistaking the Chinese American Chin for someone of Japanese ancestry. Increasing interaction across national subgroup boundaries, state policy use of the category "Asian," and anti-Asian attitudes and violence have contributed to an increase in a "pan-Asian" ethnic identity (Espiritu, 1992). In addition, ethnicity is less "optional" for those groups defined by easily visible physical markers typically understood in "racial" as opposed to ethnic terms (Waters, 1990).

---

cultural patterns (Rieder, 1985). Similarly, the racial composition of work groups and associates may change, potentially altering expected patterns of interaction, performance, and reward in the workplace (Waldinger, 1986). Strict job opportunity, wage competition, and patron-client exchange relations thus are not the only areas in which groups may encounter clashes of "objective" individual interests.

The self-interest model offers relatively clear statements about the determinants of hostility. Individuals who face unemployment, who are concentrated in low-status occupations, who have low incomes, or who face racially changing neighborhoods and workplaces, are most likely to feel threatened by competition from members of other minority groups. Each of these statuses is an objective condition indicating a direct personal vulnerability to displacement, loss, or the imposition of costs of adaptation resulting from racial change in one's social environment.

The Classical Prejudice Model

The classical prejudice approach is almost the polar opposite of the self-interest model. The most widely accepted version of the classical prejudice approach is the sociocultural model (Kinder & Sears, 1981; Pettigrew, 1982; Katz, 1991; Duckitt, 1992).[2] This perspective, associated with Allport (1954), locates interracial hostility in individual psychological dispositions rather than in objective reality. Accordingly, it is the socially learned feelings of dislike and aversion, as well as the stereotypes that undergird such feelings, that occasion racial conflict. Such feelings may, in fact, have little real social or economic basis. Whereas a substantially rational calculus underlies racial conflict in the self-interest model, a psychological and largely irrational calculus underlies the classical prejudice model (Jackman, 1994). The prejudice approach emphasizes the social learning of cul-

---

[2]Other models include the authoritarian personality approach (Adorno et al., 1950), with its emphasis on Freudian psychoanalytic principles and personality structure, and the frustration-aggression model (Dollard et al., 1939), with its emphasis on internal psychological dynamics and processes of scapegoating. Although each model identifies important forms of prejudice, these models do not currently enjoy the wide acceptance of the Allportian or classical sociocultural model of prejudice (Pettigrew, 1982; Katz, 1991; Duckitt, 1992).

tural ideas and affective responses to particular groups, whereas the self-interest approach points to the material conditions of the individual's current social existence that are claimed to drive the level of hostility.

The classical prejudice model does not expect expressed feelings of competitive threat to differ sharply from other expressions of prejudice (Sears & Kinder, 1985). That is, measures of perceived threat should correlate highly with other dimensions of prejudice, such as negative affective responses to groups, stereotypes, and other aversive reactions. In short, perceived threat is only one of several forms of prejudice toward outgroups learned on an individual psychological basis. As such, threat should be closely linked to the familiar indicators of prejudice, like negative affect, stereotypes, and desires for social distance from members of an outgroup.[3]

Allport's model of prejudice emphasizes the irrational component of group hostility (Schuman & Harding, 1964; Jackman & Muha, 1984; Katz, 1991). One factor in this irrationality is ignorance about members of an out-group (Stephan & Stephan, 1984). The learning of feelings and stereotypes takes the place of direct experience and knowledge. Accordingly, any factor that imparts information and knowledge, such as higher education, should reduce levels of prejudice and hostility.

The Stratification Beliefs Model

Individuals' beliefs about social inequality may affect whether they perceive members of other groups as competitive threats. The dominant stratification ideology in the United States holds that opportunities are plentiful and that individuals succeed or fail largely on the basis of their own efforts and talents. As a result, inequality of valued social outcomes is seen as not only fair, but necessary because of differential effort and ability (Huber & Form, 1973; Kluegel & Smith, 1986;

Feldman, 1988). The core of this ideology is captured in the term "individualism," which has both descriptive or existential dimensions and prescriptive or normative dimensions. Accordingly, individuals obtain valued social outcomes by dint of their individual qualities. By implication, the more one adheres to existential and normative individualistic beliefs, the less inclined one is to view members of other racial groups as competitive threats. Indeed, this reasoning from individualistic value and belief premises informs criticism of group-based social policies like affirmative action (Glazer, 1975; Sowell, 1984).

As Kluegel and Smith (1986) emphasize, however, the dominant ideology may encounter challenging beliefs. Some individuals may reject individualistic views of inequality and adopt more structural views (Huber & Form, 1973; Bobo, 1991). The structural outlook recognizes systematic social constraints on opportunity based on social class, racial or gender discrimination, or other institutional barriers. Some maintain that structural thinking encourages a perception of members of other racial and ethnic groups as potential competitive threats. Cheng and Espiritu (1989) use this line of reasoning in attempting to explain the appearance of greater overt social conflict between African Americans and Korean Americans in Los Angeles than between Korean Americans and Latinos in that same city. They argue that the Latino and Asian American populations, which are more often foreign-born, should view opportunities as plentiful in the United States and as less constrained than in their countries of origin. Correspondingly, recent immigrant groups should be less likely to see other such groups as competitive threats compared to groups that arrived earlier.

Blumer's Group Position Model

Under the group-position model, intergroup hostility does not spring simply from material conditions, or simply from individual learning of negative feelings, beliefs, and orientations toward out-group members. *Feelings of competition and hostility emerge from historically and collectively developed judgments about the positions in the social order that in-group members should rightfully occupy relative to members of an out-group.* The core factor in Blumer's model is the subjective image of where the in-group *ought* to stand

---

[3]Early research on prejudice saw little need to distinguish attitude components or dimensions (Harding et al., 1954). Critics of the unidimensional view of prejudice argue that racial attitudes are multidimensional (Brigham, Woodmansee, & Cook, 1976; Jackman, 1977; Bobo, 1983). Nonetheless, some prominent analyses still assume a strong underlying prejudice-tolerance dimension that organizes most, if not all, racial attitudes (Sears, Hensler, & Speer, 1979; Weigel & Howes, 1985; Kleinpenning & Hagendoorn, 1993).

vis-à-vis the out-group (Blumer 1958).[4] Although this model initially referred to a dominant social group's view of a subordinate group, we suggest that the framework is more general. To extend the framework, we focus on the individual-level dynamics of perceived threat and theorize about the attitudes of both dominant and minority racial group members.

Blumer's model explicitly incorporates negative feelings and beliefs as well as a concern with the material conditions of group life. As such, the model provides the frame for a coherent sociological *synthesis* of the self-interest approach, the classical prejudice approach, and the stratification belief approach. Individual psychology, cultural values, and self-interest are situated in a more complete vision of a "sense of group position" and the larger social processes that define such shared images of appropriate group status (Bobo & Tuan, 1995).

Blumer identifies four elements as important in establishing the sense of group position: (1) A *belief about in-group superiority* or in-group preference exists, which in a traditional social science vocabulary could be termed "ethnocentrism." (2) In-group members view members of *out-groups as "alien and different,"* which invokes the notion of out-group stereotyping. These first two elements incorporate the core variables of group identity-affective attachment and stereotyping found in the classical prejudice model. For Blumer, however, two additional elements are necessary to make prejudice a dynamic social force: (3) The sense of group position involves assumptions of *proper or proprietary claim over certain rights,* resources, statuses and privileges—those things that in-group members are duly entitled to. (4) Out-group members desire a greater share of those rights, resources, statuses, or privileges that are "understood" to "belong" to the in-group.

The interweaving of these factors—group identity, out-group stereotyping, preferred group status, and perceived threat—thus constitute the fully developed "sense of group position." Blumer held that such ideas emerge as leaders or significant segments of social groups contend with one another through public discourse and political struggle. Thus, the sense of group position is not reducible to learned individual feelings of group identity, affect, and stereotyping as emphasized by the classical prejudice model. Instead, a long-term social and historical process is shaped by the ex-change of ideas among organized leadership segments of racial groups. This exchange sparks, hones, disseminates, and thereby creates shared ideas about where the in-group ought to stand in the social order relative to other groups (Blumer & Duster, 1980; Lal, 1995).

For our purposes, this theoretical model has two implications. First, it directs our attention to perceived group competition or a group's zero-sum access to important social resources. This focus moves beyond the attitudes considered by the classical prejudice model (affect, stereotyping, social distance preferences). Critically, the group-position model assesses the degree to which individuals feel their group is threatened with the loss of significant resources to other social groups (LeVine & Campbell, 1972). A focus on perceptions of zero-sum competition for social resources flows from Blumer's emphasis on the relational or positional character of racial prejudice and the sense of threat posed by an out-group to a preferred group position.

Second, we maintain that such perceptions are rooted in *race-specific* beliefs about the society's opportunity structure. Blumer's emphasis on the dominant group's beliefs about its status and entitlements resembles but differs from the stratification beliefs model. Because we want to extend Blumer's framework to include racial minority group members, we focus on the closely allied concept of *racial alienation.* Racial alienation ranges along a continuum from the profound sense of group enfranchisement and entitlement typical of members of the dominant racial group to a profound sense of group disenfranchisement and grievance typical of members of subordinate racial groups. Members of a racial group who feel alienated and oppressed are more likely to regard other racial groups as competitive threats to their own group's social position.

---

[4]In fact, Blumer (1958) stressed the subjective and normative thrust of the sense of group position:

> Sociologically it is not a mere reflection of the objective relations between racial groups. Rather it stands for "what ought to be" rather than for "what is." It is a sense of where the two racial groups *belong* . . . In its own way, the sense of group position is a norm and imperative—indeed a very powerful one. It guides, incites, cows, and coerces. It should be borne in mind that this sense of group position stands for and involves a fundamental kind of group affiliation." (P. 5).

(See Bobo & Tuan [1995] for a fuller elaboration of the group position model.)

Feelings of *racial alienation* have a collective dimension and become culturally shared. They emerge from historical experience and the current social, political, and economic niches *typically* occupied by members of a racial group. To understand why members of one group feel threatened by members of another group, individuals' feelings about the treatment, conditions, and opportunities that have historically faced members of their own group must be measured.

The degree of racial alienation is assumed to correspond to a group's historical position in the social structure. With their institutionalized privileges, members of the dominant racial group rarely feel alienated in this sense. Indeed, the more secure the relative power, economic, and status advantages of the dominant group, the less alienated and threatened they will feel. Members of subordinate racial groups, with their institutionalized disadvantages, will often feel such alienation. Among subordinate racial groups, the level of alienation will vary based on group differences in the persistence, pervasiveness across domains of life (i.e., economics, politics, education, etc.), and degree of inequality of life chances. This argument implies that members of more recent (and voluntarily incorporated) subordinate groups will feel less alienated than will members of long-term (and involuntarily incorporated) subordinate groups. In short, the greater the degree of racial subordination, the greater the feeling of racial alienation. By implication, the overall tendency to perceive members of other groups as competitive threats will correspond to the overall degree of racial alienation.[5]

This is an important point because it differentiates the group-position model from the simple self-interest model. We do not expect objective personal vulnerability to racial change to strongly drive feelings of threat or to drive judgments about the degree of racial alienation. *Feelings of alienation and threat are the product of social and collective processes that derive from the long-term experiences and conditions that members of a racial group have faced. These feelings are shaped, as Blumer argued, by an on-going process of collective social definition that cannot be reduced to the current status of individuals.* This suggests that the longer the history of relations between dominant and subordinate group members, the more fully crystallized is the sense of relative group position; the shorter the history of group contact and interaction, the less well crystallized the sense of group position is likely to be.

Race-specific beliefs about opportunity differ from general values and beliefs about opportunity. To feel, for instance, that Latinos historically have not been treated fairly in the United States is different from (even if related to) general societal ideas of the work ethic, reward based on merit, and the necessity for unequal reward as an incentive to achievement (Kluegel & Smith, 1986).

Although they point to different mechanisms and dynamics and sometimes differ in expectations, the self-interest, prejudice, stratification beliefs, and group-position models are not mutually exclusive approaches to intergroup attitudes and relations (Bobo 1988a, 1988b). Indeed, we argue that the group-position model provides an intellectually coherent reconciliation of perspectives often treated as competing.

Hypotheses

H_1: *Simple Self-Interest.* Individuals with low socioeconomic status or who experience changes in the racial composition of their neighborhoods or workplaces are more likely to regard out-group members as significant competitors for scarce social resources.

H_2: *Racial Prejudice.* Individuals who hold more aversive attitudes (i.e., negative affect and social distance feelings) and negative stereotypes are more likely to regard out-group

---

[5]Racial alienation is a dimension of collective memory (Schuman & Scott, 1989), with reference to racial and ethnic stratification. It is part of how the macro-level and historical dimensions of group experience are felt, perceived and understood at the microlevel (Schuman & Hatchett, 1974). "Particular instances of discrimination may seem minor to outside white observers when considered in isolation. But when blatant acts of avoidance, verbal harassment, and physical attack combine with subtle and covert slights, and these accumulate over months, years, and life times, the impact on a black person is far more than the sum of individual instances. . . . The micro-level events of public accommodations and public streets are not just rare and isolated encounters by individuals; they are recurring events reflecting an invasion of the microworld by the macroworld of historical racial subordination" (Feagin, 1991, pp. 114–115). Feelings of racial alienation reflect the accumulated personal, familial, community, and collective experiences of racial differentiation, inequality, and discrimination.

members as significant competitors for scarce social resources.

H$_3$: *Stratification Beliefs*. Individuals who view the U.S. opportunity structure as fair and open are less likely to perceive out-group members as significant competitors for scarce social resources.

H$_4$: *Group Position*. Individuals who feel that their group is racially alienated are more likely to perceive out-group members as significant competitors for scarce social resources.

Data and Measures

The data come from the 1992 Los Angeles County Social Survey (LACSS), a countywide, random-digit dialed, computer-assisted telephone survey of adults living in households. The survey over-sampled telephone numbers in zip code areas with high concentrations of Blacks (65 percent or more) or Asians (30 percent or more) to generate larger numbers of Black and Asian respondents. To capture Los Angeles' large Latino population, a Spanish version of the questionnaire was developed. Spanish-speakers and those who preferred to respond to questions in Spanish were interviewed in Spanish.

A total of 1,869 respondents were interviewed: 625 Whites, 483 Blacks, 477 Latinos, and 284 Asians. Owing to a split-ballot design for some measures, some portions of the analysis are based on fewer cases.

Interviews were conducted by trained student interviewers enrolled in a course on survey methods and by the professional interviewing staff of the UCLA Survey Research Center. The student interviewers received 12 hours of training. The LACSS employs a 12-call callback procedure, systematically varying the day of the week and time of day, before dropping any numbers from the sample. The study had an overall cooperation rate of 55 percent. Interviews averaged 38 minutes in length. The distributions of sample characteristics on key social background variables closely resemble data from the 1990 Census for each group (Bobo et al. 1994).[6] Following the procedure developed by O'Neil (1979), we assessed possible nonresponse bias across a wide range of questionnaire items including measures of racial attitudes and found no signs of such bias (Greenwell, Strohm, and Bobo 1994).

Results

Levels of Perceived Threat

Four items gauge respondents' perceptions of threat or zero-sum competition for scarce social resources. These items spanned the life domains of jobs and economics, politics, and residential space. The items on group competition were asked as part of a split-ballot design in which group-targeted questions were asked of a randomly selected one-third of respondents. The items, which involved a strongly agree to strongly disagree response format and referred either to Blacks, Asians, or Hispanics, were:

Job competition: More good jobs for (Asians/Blacks/Hispanics) means fewer good jobs for members of other groups.

Political competition: The more influence (Asians/Blacks/Hispanics) have in local politics the less influence members of other groups will have in local politics.

Housing competition: As more good housing and neighborhoods go to (Asians/Blacks/Hispanics), the fewer good houses and neighborhoods there will be for members of other groups.

Economic competition: Many (Asians/Blacks/Hispanics) have been trying to get ahead economically at the expense of other groups.

We determine whether feelings of zero-sum competition differed according to the racial group targeted in the question (e.g., are Blacks more likely to be seen as zero-sum competitors by oth-

---

[6]We compared the LACSS data to 1990 Census distributions for nativity, sex, education, age, family income, and occupation: The only noteworthy differences emerged for the education variable, which is typical for telephone surveys. Our sample, particularly the Black and Latino samples, is better educated than the population at large. Not all households have telephones, and telephone coverage varies by social class and race: Affluent households and White households more often have telephones than do poor or Black and Latino households (Groves & Kahn, 1979; Thornberry & Massey, 1988). In particular, individuals lacking a high school diploma are underrepresented in the LACSS data. In addition, because of the many Asian nationality groups and languages—19 different countries of origin were represented among Asians—it was impractical to develop additional foreign language translations of the questionnaire. Thus, although 70 percent of our Asian respondents were foreign-born, this figure is substantially below the 1990 Census figures for Los Angeles County (88 percent).

ers than are Asians or Latinos), by the domain at issue (i.e., jobs versus housing), or by the race of the respondent. Table 4.1 shows the mean scores for each of the items—the higher the score the greater the feeling of zero-sum competition. Information on two types of tests are reported. The final column shows F-test results for overall between-group differences. Within group F-test results for differences in reaction to each targeted group are shown in the body of the table (e.g., do Latinos feel a greater threat from Asians than they do from Blacks, or do Asians feel greater threat from Blacks than they do from Latinos).

Several patterns emerge. At the broadest level, the mean scores reveal only moderate levels of perceived zero-sum competition. This moderate threat of competition holds across race, targeted group, and life domain. Although scores can range from a low 1.0 to a high of 5.0, most mean scores are between 2.0 and 3.0. The highest mean score

of 3.29 occurs for Black respondents' perceptions of job competition with Asians. The lowest mean score (2.43) occurs for White respondents' perceived competition for residential space with Blacks. In sum, significant numbers of people of all racial backgrounds see group relations in zero-sum terms: 28 percent of White respondents gave "agree" or "strongly agree" responses on average to the four zero-sum competition items, compared to 40 percent for African Americans, 39 percent of Latinos, and 24 percent for Asian Americans. Yet the tendency to see group relations in zero-sum terms is not the majority view of any racial group. Indeed, most individuals deny that interracial relations are structured in a zero-sum fashion.

Groups differ in their rreactions to the three targeted minority groups. Depending upon the respondent's race some groups are seen as more threatening than others. Black respondents tend

Table 4.1. Mean Scores on the Zero-Sum Competition Scale by Respondents' Race and Race of Targeted Group: Los Angeles County Social Survey, 1992

Domain and Race of Target Group	Respondents' Race				
	White	Black	Latino	Asian	F-Statistic
Job Competition					
Blacks	2.58	—	2.76	2.82	$(2.55)^{ns}$
Latinos	2.85	3.15	—	2.55	$(8.76)^{***}$
Asians	2.87	3.29	3.05	—	$(6.06)^{**}$
Political Competition					
Blacks	2.60	—	2.88	2.96	$(6.17)^{**}$
Latinos	2.93	2.68	—	2.76	$(2.67)^{ns}$
Asians	2.98	2.90	3.08	—	$(1.02)^{ns}$
Housing Competition					
Blacks	2.43	—	2.77	2.68	$(6.23)^{***}$
Latinos	2.58	2.82	—	2.63	$(2.43)^{ns}$
Asians	2.82	3.00	3.01	—	$(1.78)^{ns}$
Economic Competition					
Blacks	2.55	—	2.98	2.86	$(9.57)^{***}$
Latinos	2.63	2.82	—	2.62	$(1.88)^{ns}$
Asians	2.84	3.24	3.15	—	$(6.76)^{***}$
Zero-Sum Competition Summary					
Blacks	2.53	—	2.85	2.83	$(10.18)^{***}$
Latinos	2.75	2.87	—	2.64	$(2.66)^{ns}$
Asians	2.87	3.10	3.08	—	$(4.13)^{*}$

Note: Brackets and asterisks indicate significance levels for within-group comparisons and F-statistics.
$^{*}p < .05$ $^{**}p < .01$ $^{***}p < .001$ (two-tailed tests) ^{ns} difference not significant at $p < .05$

to perceive greater zero-sum competition with Asians than with Latinos in all four domains. The summary scale scores for Blacks reveals significantly greater threat from Asians than from Latinos ($F = 4.10, p < .05$). Likewise, Latino respondents tend to perceive greater zero-sum competition with Asians than with Blacks. Latinos' score on the summary scale is significantly higher for Asians than for Blacks.[7] A similar pattern emerges among Whites, who consistently feel least threatened by Blacks, and most threatened by Asians, with Latinos typically falling in between. Asian Americans tend to perceive a greater threat from Blacks than from Latinos, but this difference does not meet conventional criteria of significance for any of the individual items or for the summary scale ($F = 3.11, p = 0.7$).[8]

The items measuring competition appear to tap a well-defined attitude. Within each racial group, the perceptions of zero-sum competition measures yield reliable scales. Among all respondents Cronbach's alpha for the summary scale scores for each target group is above .70.[9] Hence, the remaining analyses rely on average scores across the four items for a given target group.

Social Location of Perceived Threat

The self-interest model (Hypothesis 1) contends that individuals in economically vulnerable positions or who face other burdens as a result of ethnic change perceive greater competition from members of other groups. Table 4.2 shows mean scores on the competition summary scale by race of respondent, race of target group, and each of the social background and self-interest measures. We find no consistent or strong effects of the social background and self-interest measures: only 16 significant effects emerge from the 81 tests (9 tests for each of 9 variables). No background or self-interest variable consistently influences perceptions of zero-sum competition across respondent's race and target-group's race.

Nonetheless, a few patterns are worthy of note. Among White respondents, perceptions of threat from each targeted group are influenced by level of education, but in a nonmonotonic fashion. The most highly educated Whites (16 or more years) usually express the least sense of competitive threat, while generally those with a high school degree (12 years of education), not the most poorly educated, express the strongest competitive threat.

Whites with high incomes tend to perceive less threat than their low-income counterparts. Asian American and Latino respondents who are foreign-born tend to perceive greater competition with Blacks than do their native-born co-ethnics. Equally interesting is the comparative lack of consistent effects for employment status and exposure to a changing neighborhood or workplace.

Having found at best only weak support for the self-interest model, we turn to a multivariate examination of the influence of prejudice, stratification beliefs, and sense of group position on perceptions of zero-sum competition. We use three indicators of prejudice: a measure of negative affect, a measure of negative stereotyping, and a social distance measure. Each measure refers to a

[7]The Latino sample is largely of Mexican ancestry (66.2 percent); the remainder is divided among Central American (20.5 percent), South American (5.0 percent), or other Hispanic ancestries (Puerto Rican, Caribbean). No significant differences were found on the competition summary scale scores for Latinos of Mexican ancestry versus Latinos of other Hispanic ancestries. Latinos' significant perception of greater threat from Asians than from Blacks was confirmed within the Mexican ancestry group ($F = 4.26, p < .05$), and was in the same direction but of borderline significance among Latinos with non-Mexican ancestry ($F = 3.52, p = .08$). That Blacks and Latinos both express feeling a significantly greater threat from Asians than from one another contradicts the expectations of Cheng and Espiritu (1989). However, it is consistent with impressions derived from media reports (Dunn, 1992), focus group research (Bobo et al., 1994), and the high level of Latino involvement in the violence against Korean merchants during the 1992 Los Angeles uprisings (Johnson, Farrell, & Oliver, 1993).

[8]The Asian American sample is very heterogeneous and includes Chinese (30.7 percent), Japanese (26.0 percent), Filipino (17.0 percent), Vietnamese (7.4 percent), Korean (4.9 percent), Indonesian (4.6 percent), and other Asian ancestries (9.5 percent). We compared mead scores on the summary scales targeting Blacks and Latinos for four Asian groups: Chinese, Japanese, Filipino, and all other Asians. Within each ancestry group, the pattern of differences mirrors those shown in Table 4.1: A nonsignificant but consistent tendency to perceive greater competition. with Blacks than with Latinos. Japanese Americans, the Asian ancestry group with the highest proportion native-born, tend to consistently express the lowest levels of threat. The statistical power of these comparisons is constrained, however, by the small number of cases for specific national-origin categories.

[9]Within each racial category alphas are well above .60. Among White respondents, alpha for Blacks as the targeted group is .77, for Latinos it is .67, and for Asians it is .81. Among Black respondents, the alpha for Latinos as the targeted group is .73 and for Asians it is .78. Among Latino respondents, the alpha for Blacks as the targeted group is .71 and for Asians it is .68. Among Asian respondents, the alpha when the targeted group is Blacks is .72, and it is .76 when the targeted group is Latinos.

TABLE 4.2. Mean Score on the Competition Summary Scale by Respondents' Race, Race of Targeted Group, and Social Background Variables: Los Angeles County Social Survey, 1992

	Targeted Group								
	Blacks			Asians			Latinos		
Background Variable	White Respondents	Asian Respondents	Latino Respondents	White Respondents	Latino Respondents	Black Respondents	White Respondents	Black Respondents	Asian Respondents
Nativity									
Born in U.S.	2.52	2.56 *	2.65 *	2.85	2.95	3.11	2.78	2.89	2.40 *
Foreign-born	2.68	2.93	2.96	2.97	3.13	2.83	2.59	2.64	2.75
Age									
18–27	2.37	2.83	2.97	2.96	3.04	3.10	2.82	3.05	2.82
28–37	2.52	2.93	2.91	2.77	3.05	2.97	2.82	2.76	2.50
38–51	2.43	2.76	2.60	2.87	3.31	3.16	2.65	2.74	2.70
52–92	2.70	2.83	2.80	2.90	2.87	3.09	2.79	2.92	2.34
Sex									
Male	2.49	2.81	2.88	2.80	3.02	3.06	2.77	2.81	2.47 *
Female	2.58	2.88	2.82	2.93	3.12	3.12	2.74	2.91	2.82
Years of Education									
0–11	2.75 **	3.50	3.01	2.90 ***	3.18	3.21	3.27 ***	3.20 *	2.87
12	2.88	3.10	2.86	3.49	3.03	3.21	2.65	2.92	2.92
13–15	2.57	2.73	2.71	2.88	3.01	3.07	2.93	2.96	2.80
16 or more	2.34	2.79	2.67	2.60	2.86	3.01	2.55	2.48	2.49
Employment Status									
Not in labor force	2.41 **	2.76	2.90	3.15 **	3.20	3.11	2.81	2.88	2.64
Unemployed	2.77	2.67	3.20	2.25	3.21	3.19	2.70	2.79	3.00
Employed	2.81	2.85	2.79	2.78	2.99	3.09	2.72	2.85	2.63
Occupation									
Lower blue-collar	2.63	3.54	2.71	2.93 *	2.96	3.75 **	3.00	3.14	2.87
Upper blue-collar	2.71	2.83	2.94	3.14	2.97	3.37	2.81	3.08	2.67
Lower white-collar	2.33	2.87	2.71	2.88	2.96	2.95	2.73	2.65	2.72
Upper white-collar	2.31	2.62	2.72	2.59	3.14	2.66	2.61	2.79	2.49
Family Income									
Less than $10,000	2.77	2.81	2.96	3.19 **	3.15	3.32	2.43 *	3.21 *	2.75
$10,001–20,000	2.62	3.00	2.93	3.42	3.15	3.11	3.19	3.08	3.08
$20,001–30,000	2.12	2.75	2.70	2.99	3.06	3.19	2.84	2.74	2.61
$30,001–40,000	2.58	3.09	2.82	2.85	3.13	3.02	2.73	2.74	2.39
$40,001–50,000	2.33	2.82	2.41	2.62	2.69	2.98	2.79	2.64	2.56
$50,001–60,000	2.87	2.45	2.53	2.40	2.55	2.64	2.51	2.37	2.54
$60,001 or more	2.48	2.74	2.75	2.78	2.87	3.00	2.58	2.51	2.46
Neighborhood Changing									
Yes	2.61	2.84	2.87	2.77	3.10	3.11	2.78	2.77	2.64
No	2.45	2.83	2.82	2.93	3.05	3.09	2.72	2.94	2.63
Workplace Changing									
Yes	2.65 ***	3.00	2.83	2.59	3.12	3.18	2.81	2.67	2.40
No	2.36	2.83	2.77	2.81	2.96	3.06	2.70	2.90	2.68
Not in labor force	2.77	2.80	2.94	3.02	3.20	3.12	2.83	2.90	2.66

*p < .05   ** p < .01   ***p < .001 (two-tailed tests)

Note: Boxes indicate significant differences in mean scores for each variable within racial group categories.

specific target group (Blacks, Asians, or Latinos). We use four measures of stratification beliefs: a belief in an individualistic explanation of poverty, a belief in a structural explanation of poverty, a belief in the necessity of unequal economic outcomes (inequalitarianism), and a belief in the efficacy of individual hard work and effort (individualism). Each of these measures has been used in other research and is discussed more fully in the Appendix. To tap the concern with racial alienation, it was necessary to develop new measures. We use responses to four Likert-type response items to gauge racial alienation (see Appendix).

Perceptions of the Dominant Racial Group

Whites' perceptions of zero-sum competition appear to involve a blend of racial alienation (at least in relation to Blacks), prejudice, and beliefs about inequality. The results shown in Table 4.3 thus provide some support for the group-position model (Hypothesis 4) and the prejudice model (Hypothesis 2). However, we find no effects of background variables on Whites' perceptions of minorities as zero-sum threats (Hypothesis 1). Also, the pattern of effects for stratification beliefs is the opposite from that predicted by Hypothesis 3.

Whites' perceptions of Blacks as zero-sum competitors increase with increasing racial alienation, with negative stereotyping, social distance, and ironically, increasing income. The positive net effect of income may have a basis in self interest in that many Whites perceive the beneficiaries of affirmative action to have been middle-class Blacks (Wilson, 1978, 1987). Highly educated Whites and Whites who attribute poverty to structural causes

TABLE 4.3. OLS Coefficients for Regression of Mean Score on the Competition Summary Scale on Selected Independent Variables: White Respondents in the Los Angeles County Social Survey, 1992

Independent Variables	Targeted Group					
	Blacks	(S.E.)	Latinos	(S.E.)	Asians	(S.E.)
Constant	1.36	(.81)	.11	(1.03)	1.67	(1.12)
Background						
Native-born	−.00	(.14)	.28	(.16)	−.07	(.18)
Education	−.11*	(.05)	.01	(.05)	−.06	(.05)
Income	.05*	(.03)	-.07	(.03)	−.04	(.04)
Male	.15	(.10)	.11	(.12)	.01	(.14)
Age	.00	(.00)	.00	(.00)	−.00	(.00)
Neighborhood changing	−.04	(.10)	.05	(.11)	.02	(.14)
Workplace changing	.10	(.14)	.14	(.17)	−.09	(.22)
Not in labor force	.15	(.25)	−.27	(.32)	.23	(.37)
Unemployed	.25	(.31)	−.48	(.41)	.06	(.44)
Upper blue-collar	.15	(.23)	−.38	(.28)	.17	(.35)
Lower white-collar	−.13	(.20)	-.40	(.26)	.22	(.34)
Upper white-collar	−.05	(.20)	-.44	(.26)	.13	(.33)
Prejudice						
Negative stereotypes	.12*	(.05)	.15**	(.06)	.02	(.06)
Social distance	.23***	(.06)	.08	(.06)	.34***	(.07)
Negative affect	.00	(.00)	.01*	(.00)	.00	(.00)
Stratification Beliefs						
Individual poverty	.06	(.05)	.17*	(.07)	−.04	(.07)
Structural poverty	−.12*	(.05)	.00	(.06)	.04	(.07)
Individualism	.02	(.05)	.08	(.06)	.05	(.07)
Inequalitarianism	.06	(.06)	.08	(.06)	.20***	(.06)
Group Position						
Racial alienation	.28**	(.08)	.13	(.11)	.09	(.60)
Adjusted R^2	.45		.31		.35	
Number of cases	168		164		170	

*$p < .05$ **$p < .01$ ***$p < .001$ (two-tailed tests)

are less likely to see Blacks as competitive threats. These patterns suggest that Whites who adopt a conventional liberal interpretation (i.e., structural) of the status of Blacks are less likely to see Blacks as a collective threat.

Racial alienation is significant only for Whites' reactions to Blacks. However, feelings of social distance do increase Whites' perceptions of zero-sum competition from Asians—the other *racially* distinct group. The lack of an effect for feelings of social distance in response to Latinos may suggest that racial distinctions differ from ethnic distinctions (Lieberson, 1980; Stone, 1985; Waters, 1990). Nonetheless, negative stereotyping, another important aspect of prejudice, increases Whites' perceptions of Latinos as zero-sum competitors as it does for Blacks.

Stratification beliefs influence Whites' perceptions of Latinos and Asians as zero-sum competitors for social resources. The specific variable with a significant effect differs depending on whether Whites are reacting to Latinos or Asians, but the logical basis of the effects seems similar. Attributing poverty to individual failings increases Whites' perceptions of threat from Latinos, while a commitment to notions of unequal reward (inequalitarianism) increases Whites' perceptions of threat from Asians. In effect, Whites who see relative socioeconomic success or failure in individualistic terms are more likely to perceive Latinos and Asians as competitive threats.

Taken as a whole, these patterns have two implications. First, Whites' perceptions of threat from minority groups have complex determinants and do not seem strongly rooted in a simple self-interest calculus. Second, there are meaningful similarities and differences in the underlying bases of response to the specific target groups. Whites' responses to African Americans and to Asian Americans appear to be based on a perceived racial distinctiveness as indicated by the influence of feelings of social distance on perceived threat.[10] Whites' responses to Latinos and African Americans share a basis in negative stereotypes of these groups, perhaps because of the relative economic disadvantage of both groups. Otherwise, Whites' response to African Americans differs in important respects from their reactions to Latinos and Asian Americans. For Whites' views of African Americans, the model explains more of the variance, the racial alienation measure has a strong effect, and a belief in a structural explanation for

economic inequality is important. For the model explaining Whites' reactions to Latinos and Asian Americans, racial alienation has no effect, and it is individualistic thinking about inequality that is important for perceptions of threat. A large proportion of the Latino and Asian populations are recent immigrants who were admitted to the United States under conditions largely controlled by members of the dominant racial group. The differential responses of Whites to Blacks as contrasted to Latinos and Asians thus seem linked to the historical experiences of these minority groups and to their current relative position in the U.S. economy and polity.

Racial Minority Group Perceptions

Table 4.4 shows models predicting perceptions of zero-sum competition among minority respondents. To simplify the presentation, we pooled the data for the relevant pair of outgroups (e.g., Asians and Latinos) when predicting competition summary scale scores for a particular target group (e.g., Blacks), and included interaction terms where necessary. In general, racial alienation is the most consistently influential factor, but measures of prejudice (negative affect and social distance), one of the background measures (low income), and individualistic beliefs about the nature of inequality (i.e., individualism and individual poverty) sometimes contribute to perceptions of zero-sum competition.

Specifically, perceptions of competition with Blacks increases with increasing racial alienation, particularly so among Asian respondents as compared to Latinos as shown by the large and significant interaction effect. In addition, the greater the social distance Asians and Latinos prefer to maintain from Blacks, the more likely they are to see Blacks as competitors. The background variables and the stratification belief variables do not directly influence whether Asians and Latinos perceive a threat from Blacks.

For Blacks and Asians, rising racial alienation increases the perception of competition with Latinos. (The test for an interaction was not significant.) Negative affect increases perceptions of threat from Latinos among Blacks and Asians as

---

[10]In an analysis of views on racial residential integration, Bobo and Zubrinsky (1996) find a similar pattern among White respondents.

TABLE 4.4. OLS Coefficients for Regression of Mean Score on the Competition Summary Scale on Selected Independent Variables: Black, Asian, and Latino Respondents in the Los Angeles County Social Survey, 1992

Independent Variables	Targeted Group					
	Blacks[a]	(S.E.)	Latinos[b]	(S.E.)	Asians[c]	(S.E.)
Constant	3.63***	(.80)	2.67**	(.94)	.39	(.87)
Background						
Asian	−.92	(.64)	−.92*	(.46)	—	
Latino	—		—		.42	(.52)
Native-born	−.19	(.11)	−.23	(.15)	−.07	(.16)
Education	−.07	(.04)	−.00	(.05)	−.02	(.04)
Income	−.06	(.03)	−.11***	(.03)	−.07*	(.03)
Male	−.03	(.10)	.11	(.11)	.13	(.10)
Age	−.00	(.00)	−.00	(.00)	−.00	(.00)
Neighborhood changing	.09	(.10)	.20	(.10)	.21	(.11)
Workplace changing	−.12	(.14)	−.06	(.16)	.21	(.16)
Not in labor force	−.25	(.22)	−.27	(.26)	.09	(.23)
Unemployed	.00	(.30)	.01	(.39)	.23	(.37)
Upper blue-collar	−.06	(.17)	−.15	(.26)	.06	(.18)
Lower white-collar	−.09	(.18)	−.21	(.25)	−.19	(.20)
Upper white-collar	.06	(.20)	.02	(.26)	−.17	(.22)
Prejudice						
Negative stereotypes	.02	(.04)	−.01	(.04)	.04	(.04)
Social distance	.17*	(.07)	−.09	(.06)	.03	(.05)
Negative affect	.00	(.00)	.01***	(.00)	.01***	(.00)
Stratification Beliefs						
Individual poverty	.03	(.06)	.04	(.06)	.19**	(.06)
Structural poverty	.03	(.06)	−.03	(.06)	.05	(.06)
Individualism	.03	(.06)	−.07	(.07)	.01	(.06)
Inequalitarianism	.04	(.06)	.11	(.06)	.11	(.06)
Group Position						
Racial alienation	−.10	(.10)	.19*	(.08)	.21*	(.10)
Interactions						
Asian × racial alienation	.60**	(.19)	—		—	
Asian × individualism	—		−.34**	(.12)	—	
Latino × negative affect	—		—		−.01***	(.00)
Adjusted R²	.20		.28		.24	
Number of cases	203		205		245	

[a] Predicting whether Latinos and Asians (pooled) perceive competition with Blacks.
[b] Predicting whether Blacks and Asians (pooled) perceive competition with Latinos.
[c] Predicting whether Blacks and Latinos (pooled) perceive competition with Asians.
*$p < .05$ **$p < .01$ ***$p < .001$ (two-tailed tests)

well. However, there is an interaction between individualism and race, with individualism playing a much larger role among Asians than among Blacks. Asian American respondents who accept the idea that hard work yields positive rewards are more likely to view Latinos as a competitive threat. We also find a significant negative net effect of income: Blacks and Asians with low incomes perceive a greater threat from Latinos than do Blacks and Asians with high incomes.

For Black and Latino respondents, we find that as racial alienation rises so does the perception of Asians as competitors. Blacks and Latinos who attribute poverty to individual failings are more likely to regard Asians as competitive threats. But prejudice also influences perceptions of threat from Asians, at least among Black respondents as shown by the significant interaction term for the negative affect measure. Self-interest also matters: Blacks and Latinos with low incomes are more likely than those with high incomes to regard Asians as competitive threats.

Racial Alienation

The effects found for the racial alienation measure and its central place in our extension of Blunter's group-position theory require us to clarify the nature of racial alienation. We wanted to measure shared beliefs about the treatment received by and opportunity offered to one's racial group in the larger social order. The working theory leads us to expect that such beliefs are strongly anchored in group membership per se, and are less powerfully shaped by individual background and status characteristics. The results of OLS regression models predicting racial alienation scores strongly support this hypothesis.

Model 1 in Table 4.5 shows the impact of racial background on racial alienation, with dummy variables for Black, Latino, and Asian respondents compared to White respondents (the omitted category). Members of each racial minority group score significantly higher on racial alienation than do Whites. The Black-White gap is particularly large ($b = 1.18$; $p < .001$), nearly twice the size of the Latino-White ($b = .65$; $p < .001$) or Asian-White difference ($b = .49$; $p < .001$), and the gap is more than a full standard deviation unit in magnitude. Furthermore, the racial background variables alone account for 34 percent of the variance in racial alienation scores! Model 2 reports coefficients for a model that adds the social background and self-interest variables to Model 1. Each of the three race variables continues to show large differences from Whites in degree of racial alienation net of these controls.

Model 3 adds interaction terms for the most plausible sources of differential effects across racial background to Model 2—namely nativity, education, and income. Only one interaction is significant. As income rises, feelings of racial alienation decline among Whites, but the opposite effect occurs among African Americans—increasing income tends to increase Blacks' feelings of racial alienation.[11] Feelings of racial alienation tend to decrease with age among all races. In the presence of numerous interaction terms, the main effect coefficients for the race dummy variables are, of course, not meaningful when viewed in isolation.

Overall, these results point to a relatively clear-cut, largely race-based, but also partly class-based continuum of racial alienation. White Americans unequivocally have the least sense of racial alienation. At the other end of the continuum are African Americans, who express the greatest sense of racial alienation. Between these two are Asian Americans and Latinos, who do not differ significantly from one another in their feelings of alienation.

Conclusions

Feelings of competitive threat from members of other racial groups have complex determinants. The patterns depend on the racial background of who is doing the looking as well as on the background of who is being looked at. The full set of results confirm aspects of the group-position, classical prejudice, stratification beliefs, and self-interest models. Perceptions of competitive group threat thus involve genuinely *social*-psychological processes that are not reducible to a single cause nor to purely individual-level psychological dynamics.

We find that perceptions of competition and threat from other racial groups can be reliably measured. Such perceptions, while not acute in our data, are fairly common. Substantial percentages (though typically less than 50 percent), of Whites, Blacks, Latinos, and Asians perceive members of other groups as zero-sum competitive threats for social resources. African Americans, closely followed by Latinos, are most likely to see other groups as competitive threats, and non-Hispanic Whites tend to be the least likely to hold such views. These patterns reflect the historical and contemporary forms of racial subordination these groups have faced (Blauner, 1972; Almagauer, 1994).

---

[11]We also examined models of racial alienation separately for each racial group. Among Whites we found significant negative effects of education, income, and native-born status. These effects suggest that increasing privilege in the class hierarchy tends to reduce feelings of racial alienation among Whites. For Blacks, we found a significant *positive* effect for income, which confirms Feagin and Sikes's (1994) contention that movement into the middle class often deepens African Americans' sense of never being fully in cluded in the "American mainstream." Although the signs of the coefficients were in the same direction and were roughly comparable in magnitude to those observed among White respondents, none of the individual variables had significant effects on racial alienation among Asian or Latino respondents. These patterns for racial minority respondents are ,consistent with our main contention that feelings of racial alienation are not significantly shaped by individual-level status characteristics.

TABLE 4.5. OLS Coefficients for Regression of Racial Alienation Score on Selected Independent Variables: Los Angeles County Social Survey, 1992

Independent Variables	Model 1		Model 2		Model 3	
	Coefficient	(S.E.)	Coefficient	(S.E.)	Coefficient	(S.E.)
Constant	2.20***	(.03)	2.87***	(.28)	3.22***	(.29)
Race						
Asian	.49***	(.05)	.42***	(.06)	−.36	(.49)
Black	1.18***	(.05)	1.16***	(.05)	.31	(.51)
Latino	.65***	(.06)	.54***	(.07)	.07	(.68)
Background						
Native-born	—		−.07	(.05)	−.16*	(.08)
Education	—		−.02	(.02)	−.02	(.02)
Income	—		−.02	(.01)	−.07***	(.01)
Male	—		−.01	(.00)	−.01	(.04)
Age	—		−.00***	(.00)	−.00***	(.00)
Neighborhood changing	—		−.01	(.04)	−.01	(.04)
Workplace changing	—		.03	(.06)	.02	(.06)
Not in labor force	—		.07	(.10)	.02	(.10)
Unemployed	—		.10	(.14)	.04	(.13)
Upper blue-collar	—		−.08	(.09)	−.09	(.09)
Lower white-collar	—		−.03	(.08)	−.04	(.08)
Upper white-collar	—		−.09	(.09)	−.11	(.08)
Interactions						
Native-born × Asian	—		—		.12	(.13)
Native-born × Black	—		—		−.30	(.46)
Native-born × Latino	—		—		.12	(.14)
Education × Asian	—		—		.53	(.46)
Education × Black	—		—		−.30	(.46)
Education × Latino	—		—		.13	(.66)
Income × Asian	—		—		.03	(.03)
Income × Black	—		—		.15***	(.02)
Income × Latino	—		—		.05	(.03)
Adjusted R^2	.34		.35		.38	
Number of cases	1,190		1,190		1,190	

*$p < .05$ **$p < .01$ ***$p < .001$ (two-tailed tests)

Perceptions of group competition tend to be based on a mix of racial alienation, prejudice, stratification beliefs, and self-interest. As expected under the group-position model (Hypothesis 4), individuals who perceive members of their own group as generally facing unfair treatment in the larger social order tend to be more likely to regard members of other groups as competitive threats. Straightforward self-interest effects (Hypothesis 1) tend to emerge among minority respondents, but not among Whites. African American and Latino respondents with low incomes are more likely to perceive other groups as zero-sum competitors. Prejudice contributes to perceptions of threat as well, but the salient dimension of prejudice hinges on both the target group and the back-

ground of the respondent (Hypothesis 2) and education was not a consistent factor. Most important for our larger argument, however, perceptions of threat involve more than classical racial prejudice.

Stratification ideology also matters (Hypothesis 3), but the relevant aspects of stratification ideology is contingent. More important, the patterns are unexpected. Structural thinking, rather than increasing perceptions of threat, decreases Whites' tendency to view Blacks as competitive threats. Individualistic thinking is more consistently important than is structural thinking. However, rather than decreasing perceptions of threat, individualistic thinking tends to encourage Whites to view Asian Americans and Latinos as competitive threats, to encourage Asians to view Latinos as competitive threats, and to encourage Blacks and Latinos to view Asians as competitive threats. We speculate that these differential patterns are the legacy of the civil rights movement and antidiscrimination struggles led by African Americans that may increase sensitivity to structural constraints when focusing on Blacks. Also, the recent and often economically motivated immigration of many Asian Americans and Latinos may make striving for individual achievement salient when focusing on these groups.

Two patterns are particularly intriguing: the gaping disparity in feelings of racial alienation in the U.S. social order that separate Blacks and Whites, and the strong impact of racial alienation on Whites' perceptions of threat from Blacks given the absence of any impact of racial alienation on Whites' perceptions of threat from Asians or Latinos. Given our conceptualization of racial alienation as a collective and historically developed sense of group position in the social order, it is telling that Whites and Blacks occupy the extremes of the continuum, and that among Whites racial alienation is distinctly linked to perceptions of African Americans. A narrow framing of this result holds that those Whites who have feelings of racial alienation probably have Blacks in mind as the comparison group toward whom they feel a special sense of grievance. A broader framing, and one that we think comports well with the remarkable depth and tenacity of anti-Black racism in the United States (Lieberson, 1980; Massey & Denton, 1993, Feagin & Sikes, 1994; Oliver & Shapiro, 1995), is that African Americans currently constitute a unique cultural reference point for many White Americans—African Americans are the proverbial "faces at the bottom of the well" (Bell, 1992; also see Feagin & Sikes, 1994).

Under either frame, Whites perceive African Americans as competitors in a fashion that differs from their perceptions of Asians and Latinos. That difference appears to involve assumptions about the racial order as a whole. Among Whites, to be sure, aspects of prejudice and stratification ideology increase the chances of perceiving members of *any* racial minority group as competitors. However, White responses to African Americans also suggest a connection to ideas about appropriate status relations among racial groups. We hasten to emphasize, first, that Whites in our Los Angeles sample perceive a low absolute level of threat from Blacks relative to the threat they perceive from Latinos and Asians. Second, the recency of Latino and Asian immigration may leave many Whites with a less well-crystallized sense of group position relative to these groups, hence the weak effects for the racial alienation measure.

Blumer's group-position theory, we believe, provides the most parsimonious framework for integrating the full set of results. Like Jackman's (1994) intergroup ideology approach, Blumer's model views interracial hostility as the product of the historical forging of group identities and attachments, intergroup images (i.e., stereotypes), and assessments of collective interests and challenges to those interests. This perspective recognizes the factors specified in the self-interest, classical prejudice, and stratification beliefs models. None of these models, however, can account for the complexity of our results. Blumer's group-position model provides the most comprehensive theoretical leverage and goes further to emphasize that identity, stereotypes, values, and assessments of interests are shaped historically and involve a collective and relational dimension between groups that powerfully engages emergent normative ideas about appropriate group statuses and entitlements.

Blumer places perceptions of group competition and threat at the core of his sociological analysis of prejudice. We have shown that such perceptions can be reliably measured and that they have meaningful social and psychological underpinnings. Future research on perceptions of group competition needs to move in several directions. Such perceptions should be regularly monitored in a variety of social settings. Large multiracial samples from different communities will make it possible to assess the effects on perceptions of threat of such power resources as relative group size, degree of political organization and leadership, skill levels, and relative group economic inequality (Blalock 1965; Fossett and Kiecolt 1989).

As part of this effort, coverage of the items tapping perceived threat should be expanded to assess whether and why racial minorities perceive White Americans as competitive threats. In hindsight, this was a serious omission in our survey design and should be a high priority in future research. Greater attention should be devoted to disentangling the microlevel processes of within-group interaction and socialization that pass on distinctive group perspectives on the social order, such as feelings of racial alienation. Furthermore, it is essential to examine the part played by perceptions of threat in debates on racially relevant social policies such as affirmative action and immigration.

REFERENCES

Adorno, T., Frenkel-Brunswik, E., Levinson, D. J., & Sanford, R. N. (1950). *The authoritarian personality*. New York: Norton.

Allport, G. W. (1954). *The nature of prejudice*. Garden City, NJ: Doubleday.

Almaguer, T. (1994). *Racial fault lines: The historical origins of white supremacy in California*. Berkeley and Los Angeles: University of California Press.

Apostle, R. A., Glock, C. Y., Piazza, T., & Suelzle, M. (1983). *The anatomy of racial attitudes*. Berkeley and Los Angeles: University of California Press.

Ashmore, R. D., & Del Boca, F. K. (1981). Conceptual approaches to stereotypes and stereotyping. In D. L. Hamilton (Ed.), *Cognitive processes in stereotyping and human behavior* (pp. 1–35). Hillsdale, NJ: Erlbaum.

Bell, D. (1992). *Faces at the bottom of the well*. New York: Basic Books.

Blalock, H. M. (1965). *Toward a theory of minority group relations*. New York: Capricorn Books.

Blauner, R. A. (1972). *Racial oppression in America*. New York: Harper and Row.

Blumer, H. (1958). Race prejudice as a sense of group position. *Pacific Sociological Review, 1,* 3–7.

Blumer, H., & Duster, T. (1980). Theories of race and social action. In *UNESCO, sociological theories: Race and colonialism* (pp. 211–238). Paris, France: UNESCO.

Bobo, L. (1983). Whites' opposition to busing: Symbolic racism or realistic group conflict? *Journal of Personality and Social Psychology, 45,* 1196–1210.

Bobo, L. (1988a). Attitudes toward the Black political movement: Trends, meaning and effects on racial policy preferences. *Social Psychology Quarterly, 51,* 287–302.

Bobo, L. (1988b). Group conflict, prejudice, and the paradox of contemporary racial attitudes. In P. A. Katz & D. A. Taylor (Eds.), *Eliminating racism: Profiles in controversy* (pp. 85–114). New York: Plenum.

Bobo, L. (1991). Social responsibility, individualism, and redistributive policies. *Sociological Forum, 6,* 71–92.

Bobo, L., & Kluegel, J. R. (1993). Opposition to race-targeting: Self-interest, stratification ideology, or racial attitudes? *American Sociological Review, 58,* 443–464.

Bobo, L., & Tuan, M. (1995). *Prejudice in politics: The sense of group position and the Wisconsin Indian Treaty Rights Controversy*. Department of Sociology, University of California, Los Angeles, CA.

Bobo, L., & Zubrinsky, C. L. (1996). Attitudes toward residential integration: Perceived status differences, mere in-group preference, or racial prejudice? *Social Forces, 74,* 883–909.

Bobo, L., Johnson, J. H., Jr., Oliver, M. L., & Zubrinsky, C. (1994). Public opinion before and after a spring of discontent: A social psychological portrait of Los Angeles in 1992. In M. Baldassare (Ed.), *Los Angeles riots: Lessons for the urban future* (pp. 103–134). New York: Westview.

Bogardus, E. S. (1928). Measuring social distances. *Journal of Applied Sociology, 9,* 299–308.

Bogardus, E. S. (1933). A social distance scale. *Sociology and Social Research, 17,* 265–271.

Brigham, J. C., Woodmansee, J., & Cook, S. W. (1976). Dimensions of verbal racial attitudes: Interracial marriage and approaches to racial equality. *Journal of Social Issues, 32,* 9–21.

Cheng, L., & Espiritu, Y. (1989). Korean businesses in Black and Hispanic neighborhoods: A study of intergroup relations. *Sociological Perspectives, 32,* 521–534.

Citrin, J., & Green, D. P. (1990). The self-interest motive in American public opinion. *Research in Micropolitics, 3,* 1–28.

Cose, E. (1994). *The rage of a privileged clan*. New York: Harper Collins.

Crull, S. R., & Burton, B. T. (1985). Possible decline in tolerance toward minorities: Social distance on a midwest campus. *Social Science Research, 70,* 57–62.

Dollard, J., Doob, L. W., Miller, N. E., Mowrer, O. H., & Sears, R. R. (1939). *Frustration and aggression*. Westport, CT: Greenwood Press.

Duckitt, J. (1992). *The social psychology of prejudice*. New York: Praeger.

Dunn, A. (1992). Years of '2-cent' insults added up to rampage. *Los Angeles Times,* May 7, pp. A1, A14.

Dyer, J, Velditz, W., & Worchel, S. (1989). Social distance among ethnic groups in Texas: Some demographic correlates. *Social Science Quarterly, 70,* 607–616.

Espiritu, Y. L. (1992). *Asian American panethnicity: Bridging institutions and identities*. Philadelphia, PA: Temple University Press.

Farley, R., Steeh, C., Krysan, M., Jackson, T., & Reeves, K. (1994). Stereotypes and segregation: Neighborhoods in the Detroit area. *American Journal of Sociology, 100,* 750–780.

Feagin, J. R. (1975). *Subordinating the poor*. Englewood Cliffs, NJ: Prentice Hall.

Feagin, J. R. (1991). The continuing significance of race: Antiblack discrimination in public places. *American Sociological Review, 56,* 101–116.

Feagin, J. R., & Sikes, M. P. (1994). *Living with racism: The black middle class experience*. Boston, MA: Beacon Press.

Feldman, S. (1988). Structure and consistency in public opinion: The role of core beliefs and values. *American Journal of Political Science, 82,* 773–778.

Firebaugh, G., & Davis, K. E. (1988). Trends in anti-black prejudice, 1972–1984: Region and cohort effects. *American Journal of Sociology, 94,* 251–272.

Fossett, M. A., & Kiecolt, K. J. (1989). The relative size of minority populations and white racial attitudes. *Social Science Quarterly, 70,* 820–835.

Giles, M. W., & Evans, A. (1986). The power approach to intergroup hostility. *Journal of Conflict Resolution, 30,* 469–486.

Glaser, J. M. (1994). Back to the black belt: Racial environment and white racial attitudes in the south. *Journal of Politics, 56,* 21–41.

Glazer, N. (1975). *Affirmative discrimination*. New York: Basic Books.

Greenwell, M., Strohm, M. A., & Bobo, L. (1994). Project memoranda: Nonresponse bias evaluation. Department of Sociology, University of California, Los Angeles.

Groves, R. M., & Kahn, R. L. (1979). *Surveys by telephone: A national comparison with personal interviews.* New York: Academic Press.

Harding, J., Proshansky, H., Kutner, B., & Chein, I. (1954). Prejudice and ethnic relations. In G. Lindzey (Ed.), *Handbook of social psychology,* Vol 2 (pp. 1021–1061). Reading, MA: Addison-Wesley.

Huber, J., & Form, W. H. (1973). *Income and ideology: An analysis of the American political formula.* New York: Free Press.

Hyman, H. H., & Sheatsley, P. B. (1956). Attitudes toward desegregation. *Scientific American, 195,* 35–39.

Jackman, M. R. (1977). Prejudice, tolerance, and attitudes toward ethnic groups. *Social Science Research, 6,* 145–169.

Jackman, M. R. (1994). *The velvet glove: Paternalism and conflict in gender, class, and race relations.* Los Angeles: University of California Press.

Jackman, M. R., & Muha, M. J. (1984). Education and intergroup attitudes: Moral enlightenment, superficial democratic commitment, or ideological refinement? *American Sociological Review, 49,* 751–769.

Johnson, J. H., Jr., Farrell, W. C., Jr., & Oliver, M. L. (1993). Seeds of the Los Angeles rebellion of 1992. *International Journal of Urban and Regional Research, 17,* 115–119.

Katz, D., & Braly, K. (1933). Racial stereotypes in one hundred college students. *Journal of Abnormal and Social Psychology, 28,* 280–290.

Katz, I. (1991). Gordon Allport's the nature of prejudice. *Political Psychology, 12,* 25–57.

Kinder, D. R., & Sears, D. O. (1981). Prejudice and politics: Symbolic racism versus racial threats to the good life. *Journal of Personality and Social Psychology, 40,* 414–431.

Kleinpenning, G., & Hagendoorn, L. (1993). Forms of racism and the cumulative dimension of ethnic attitudes. *Social Psychology Quarterly, 56,* 21–36.

Kluegel, J. R. (1990). Trends in whites' explanations of the gap in Black-White socioeconomic status, 1977–1989. *American Sociological Review, 55,* 512–525.

Kluegel, J. R., & Smith, E. R. (1982). Whites' beliefs about Blacks' opportunity. *American Sociological Review, 47,* 518–532.

Kluegel, J. R., & Smith, E. R. (1986). *Beliefs about inequality: Americans' views of what is and what ought to be.* New York: Aldine de Gruyter.

Lal, B. B. (1995). Symbolic interaction theories. *American Behavioral Scientist, 38,* 421–441.

LeVine, R. A., & Campbell, D. T. (1972). *Ethnocentrism: Theories of conflict, ethnic attitudes, and group behavior.* New York: John Wiley.

Lieberson, S. (1980). *A piece of the pie: Blacks and White immigrants since 1880.* Berkeley and Los Angeles: University of California Press.

Massey, D., & Denton, N. A. (1993). *American apartheid: Segregation and the making of the underclass.* Cambridge, MA: Harvard University Press.

Moffat, S. (1992). Splintered society: U.S. Asians. *Los Angeles Times,* July 13, pp. A1, A20–21.

Oliver, M. L., & Shapiro, T. (1995). *Black wealth, white wealth: A new perspective on inequality.* New York: Routledge.

Olzak, S. (1993). *The dynamics of ethnic competition and conflict.* Stanford, CA: Stanford University Press.

Omi, M., & Winant, H. (1986). *Racial formation in the United States: From the 1960s to the 1980s.* New York: Routledge.

O'Neil, M. J. (1979). Estimating nonresponse bias due to refusals in telephone surveys. *Public Opinion Quarterly, 43,* 219–232.

Owen, C. A., Eisner, H. C., & McFaul, T. R. (1981). A half-century of social distance research: National replication of the Bogardus Studies. *Social Science Research, 66,* 80–98.

Pettigrew, T. F. (1982). Prejudice. In S. Thernstrom, A. Orlov, & O. Handlin (Eds.), *Dimensions of Ethnicity* (pp. 1–29). Cambridge, MA: Harvard University Press.

Portes, A. (1984). The rise of ethnicity: Determinants of ethnic perceptions among Cuban cxiles in Miami. *American Sociological Review, 49,* 383–397.

Portes, A., Parker, R. N., & Cobas, J. A. (1988). Assimilation or consciousness: Perceptions of U.S. society among recent Latin American immigrants to the United States. *Social Forces, 59,* 200–224.

Rieder, J. (1985). *Canarsie: The Jews and Italians of Brooklyn against liberalism.* Cambridge, MA: Harvard University Press.

Schuman, H., & Harding, J. (1964). Prejudice and the norm of rationality. *Sociometry, 27,* 353–371.

Schuman, H., & Hatchett, S. (1974). *Black racial attitudes: Trends and complexities.* Ann Arbor, MI: Institute for Social Research, University of Michigan.

Schuman, H., & Scott, J. (1989). Generations and collective memories. *American Sociological Review, 30,* 843–861.

Schuman, H., Steeh, C. G., & Bobo, L. (1985). *Racial attitudes in America: Trends and interpretations.* Cambridge, MA: Harvard University Press.

Sears, D. O., & Funk, C. L. (1991). The role of self-interest in social and political attitudes. *Advances in Experimental Social Psychology, 24,* 1–91.

Sears, D. O., & Kinder, D. R. (1985). Whites' opposition to busing: On conceptualizing and operationalizing 'Group Conflict.' *Journal of Personality and Social Psychology, 48,* 1141–1147.

Sears, D. O., Hensler, C. P., & Speer, L. K. (1979). Whites' opposition to busing: Self-interest or symbolic politics? *American Political Science Review, 73,* 369–384.

See, K. O'S., & Wilson, W. J. (1989). Race and ethnicity. In N. J. Smelser (Ed.), *Handbook of Sociology* (pp. 223–242). Beverly Hills, CA: Sage.

Sigelman, L., & Welch, S. (1991). *Black Americans' views of racial inequality: The dream deferred.* New York: Cambridge University Press.

Smith, A. W. (1981). Racial tolerance as a function of group position. *American Sociological Review, 46,* 558–573.

Smith, T. W., & Dempsey, G. R. (1983). The polls: Ethnic social distance and prejudice. *Public Opinion Quarterly, 47,* 585–600.

Sowell, T. (1984). *Civil rights: Rhetoric or reality.* New York: Morrow.

Starr, P. D., & Roberts, A. E. (1982). Attitudes toward New Americans: Perceptions of Indo-Chinese in nine cities. *Research in Race and Ethnic Relations, 3,* 165–186.

Steeh, C., & Schuman, H. (1992). Young white adults: Did racial attitudes change in the 1980s? *American Journal of Sociology, 98,* 340–367.

Stephan, W. G., & Rosenfield, D. (1982). Racial and ethnic stereotypes. In A. G. Miller (Ed.), *In the eye of the beholder: Contemporary issues in stereotyping* (pp. 92–136). New York: Praeger.

Stephan, W. G., & Stephan, C. W. (1984). The role of ignorance in intergroup relations. In M. Brewer & N. Miller (Eds.), *Groups in contact: The psychology of desegregation* (pp. 229–255). New York: Academic Press.

Stone, J. (1985). *Racial conflict in contemporary society.* Cambridge, MA: Harvard University Press.

Taylor, D. G., Greeley, A. M., & Sheatsley, P. B. (1978). Attitudes toward racial integration. *Scientific American, 238,* 42–50.

Thornberry, O. T. , & Massey, J. T. (1988). Trends in United States telephone coverage across time and subgroups. In R. M. Groves et al. (Eds.), *Telephone Survey Methodology* (pp. 25–49). New York: Wiley.

Tuch, S. A. (1987). Urbanism, region, and tolerance revisited: The case of racial prejudice. *American Sociological Review, 52,* 504–510.

Uhlaner, C. (1991). Perceived discrimination and prejudice and the Coalition Prospects of Blacks, Latinos, and Asian Americans. In B. O. Jackson & M. B. Preston (Eds.), *Racial and ethnic politics in California* (pp. 339–370). Berkeley, CA: IGS Press.

Waldinger, R. (1986). Changing ladders and musical chairs: Ethnicity and opportunity in post-industrial New York. *Politics and Society, 15,* 369–401.

Waldinger, R. (1989). Immigration and urban change. *Annual Review of Sociology, 15,* 211–232.

Waters, M. C. (1990). *Ethnic options: Choosing identities in America.* Berkeley: University of California Press.

Weigel, R., & Howes, P. W. (1985). Conceptions of racial prejudice: Symbolic racism reconsidered. *Journal of Social Issues, 41,* 117–138.

Wellman, D. T. (1977). *Portraits of white racism.* New York: Cambridge University Press.

Wilson, W. J. (1978). *The declining significance of race.* Chicago: University of Chicago Press.

Wilson, W. J. (1987). *The truly disadvantaged: The inner city, the underclass, and public policy.* Chicago: University of Chicago Press.

Zweigenhaft, R. L., & Domhoff, G. W. (1990). *Blacks in the white establishment?: A study of race and class in America.* New Haven, CT: Yale University Press.

Appendix

Methods of Index Construction

PREJUDICE

Negative affect was measured using three 0- to 100-degree "feeling thermometers": one for "Blacks," one for "Asians," and one for "Hispanics." Respondents were told that a score of 0 meant unfavorable or cold feelings toward a group, that a 100 score meant favorable or warm feelings, and that scores of 50 meant neutral feelings. "Don't know" responses were few (less than 5 percent) and were scored at the neutral point of 50. For our analyses scores were *reversed* so that high scores indicate negative affect.

Stereotyping was measured using race-group specific seven-point ratings for three bipolar traits: (1) intelligent—unintelligent, (2) prefer to be self-supporting—prefer to live off of welfare, and (3) easy to get along with—hard to get along with. The items share small to moderate positive intercorrelations across each racial target group for all respondents. "Don't know" responses were few and were scored as neutral. The scores on the three items were averaged to create a target-group-specific (e.g., anti-Asian stereotype) index of negative stereotyping. Similarly formated and constructed items and indices were used by Bobo and Kluegel (1993), by Farley et al. (1994), and by Bobo and Zubrinsky (1996).

Social distance feelings were measured with responses to two questions—one concerning residential integration and one concerning interracial marriage. Respondents were asked: "How about living in a neighborhood where half of your neighbors would be (Asian American/Black/Hispanic American)?" and "What about having a close relative or family member marry an (Asian American/Black/Hispanic American)?" The response format allowed respondents to indicate that they would be "very much in favor of it happening," "somewhat in favor of it happening," "neither in favor nor opposed to it happening," "somewhat opposed," or "very much opposed to it happening." "Don't know" responses were few and were scored at the mid-point. The items share moderate correlations across target groups among all respondents. The scores for the two items were summed and then averaged with high scores indicating greater social distance.

STRATIFICATION BELIEFS

Individualism was measured using responses to two Likert-type items: "If people work hard they almost always get what they want," and "Most people who don't get ahead should not blame the system; they really have only themselves to blame." *Inequalitarianism* was measured using responses to two Likert-type items: "Some people are just better cut out than others for important positions in society," and "Some people are better at running things and should be allowed to do so." "Don't know" responses were few (less than 5 percent) and were scored at the mid-point. Each pair of items shared moderate positive intercorrelations and were more highly correlated internally than across constructs. The items were taken from the National Election Study and the measurement properties and correlates of the items have been analyzed in detail by Feldman (1988).

Individual poverty was measured using responses to two Likert-type items concerning poverty. One item blames poverty on "loose morals and drunkenness" and the other item blames poverty on "lack of effort by the poor themselves." *Structural poverty* was measured using responses to two Likert-type items. One item blamed poverty on the "failure of society to provide good schools for many Americans," and the other item blamed the "failure of industry to provide enough jobs." "Don't know" responses were few (less than 2 percent) and were scored at the mid-point. Each pair of items shared positive intercorrelations and were more highly intercorrelated internally than across constructs. The items originated with Feagin's (1975) 1969 national survey and were repeated in a 1982 national survey (Kluegel & Smith, 1986) and in the 1990 General Social Survey (Bobo & Kluegel, 1993).

GROUP POSITION

The items tapping *racial alienation*, which used Likert-type response formats, were: "American society owes people of my ethnic group a better chance in life than we currently have"; "American society has provided people of my ethnic group a fair opportunity to get ahead in life"; "I am grateful for all of the special opportunities people of my ethnic group have found in America"; and "American society just hasn't dealt fairly with people from my ethnic background." The items have strong face validity as measures of alienation. Each item speaks to the condition of the respondent's group as a whole, and calls for judgments of broad historical sweep rather than of immediate or short-term circumstances. There were few "don't know" responses to these items— 2 percent or less among White, Black, Latino, and Asian respondents. The overall reliability of the scale was acceptable (alpha = .65). The items shared moderate intercorrelations across all groups, and the individual items correlated well with the summary *racial alienation scale,* which is an average score across the four items. The group-specific alphas, however, were less than ideal (alpha = .58 for Whites, .53 for Blacks, .52 for Latinos, and .42 for Asians). There was no single unequivocally weak item in the set. Although the "grateful for special opportunities" item generally had a low correlation with the "fair opportunity" item, it also had the strongest correlation with the "hasn't dealt fairly" item. Hence, we used a scale based on all four items.

Social Identity and Self-Categorization

It is undoubtable that intergroup goal relations impact intergroup behavior. If history places two groups in competition over, for example, power, it is very likely that members of opposing groups will interact competitively. Some social psychologists feel, however, that it is necessary to specify in more detail the social-cognitive processes that mediate the impact of social history on individual behavior. In particular, it has been suggested that self-definition as a group member may be the key mechanism. Group memberships define people's collective self-concept, and prescribe membership-contingent thoughts, feelings, and behaviors. Processes and motivations that are responsible for and associated with collective self-definition produce behaviors that are characteristic of groups. However, the specific nature of these behaviors depends on the specific nature of the group, and on people's perceptions of intergroup relations—how their group relates to other groups. This perspective has been championed by social identity theory, which is now one of the most popular contemporary frameworks in which social psychologists theorize intergroup relations (Tajfel, 1972; Tajfel & Turner, 1979; Turner, 1982; also see Hogg & Abrams, 1988).

Research adopting the minimal group paradigm (e.g., Tajfel, 1970; Tajfel, Billig, Bundy, & Flament, 1971; also see Bourhis, Sachdev & Gagnon, 1994; Diehl, 1990; and Part 5 of this volume), suggests that merely being categorized, under certain conditions, is sufficient to produce characteristic group behaviors—interdependent goals are not necessary. People define themselves in terms of the attributes of a self-inclusive social category (a prototype) that describe and prescribe context-specific perceptions, feelings, attitudes, and behaviors. Social identity theory describes how a self-enhancement motive, the categorization process, and social beliefs about intergroup relations work together to produce characteristic group behaviors that have specific context-dependent forms.

Our first reading, by Henri Tajfel and John Turner (1979), then at Bristol University, is probably the most extensively cited statement of social identity theory, although it is actually presented as an analysis of intergroup conflict. It describes how people have beliefs about the relative status of groups, the legitimacy and stability of such relations, and the permeability of intergroup boundaries. These beliefs determine the specific behaviors that group members adopt in order to address the evaluative social identity implications of intergroup status. These behaviors can include disidentification and attempting to pass into a higher status group, creative ways of reevaluating ones own group, and direct intergroup competition to establish a new status structure. These outcomes flow from the fact that group membership, and all its evaluative, attitudinal, and behavioral correlates, is internalized by individuals as the collective self-concept, or social identity (also see Part 6, this volume).

Our second reading, by Michael Hogg and Sarah Hains (1996) at the University of Queensland, is an empirical article which incorporates the motivational and macrosocial emphasis of social identity theory with a more recent exploration of the cognitive underpinning of social identity processes—self-categorization theory (Turner, 1985; Turner, Hogg, Oakes, Reicher, & Wetherell, 1987). Social identity theory and self-categorization theory are complementary and compatible parts of the social identity perspective. Self-categorization theory focuses on how categorization of self depersonalizes self-perception (in terms of an ingroup prototype) and actually produces group behaviors. People represent groups as prototypes that describe and prescribe group defining attributes. When people categorize themselves and other people as group members, they are perceptually assimilated to the relevant prototype. Self-categorization transforms self-conception, perception, attitudes, feelings, and behavior. Hogg and Hains study intra- and intergroup relations in Australian Netball Teams playing in an amateur league, in order to show that patterns of interindividual attitudes (e.g., liking) are a function of intergroup beliefs and self-categorization processes.

Discussion Questions

1. To what extent is intergroup conflict a result of cognitive processes alone?
2. What is the relationship between intergroup and intragroup processes?
3. Are social and personal identity different parts of the self?
4. How many social identifications can a person have?
5. Under what conditions do people identify more or less strongly with a group?

Suggested Readings

Abrams, D., & Hogg, M. A. (Eds.) (1999). *Social identity and social cognition.* Oxford, UK: Blackwell. A collection of chapters from leading social identity and leading social cognition researchers that explores the developing integration of these historically very separate perspectives.

Abrams, D., & Hogg, M. A. (2001). Collective identity, group membership and self-conception. In R. S. Tindale & M. A. Hogg (Eds.), *Blackwell handbook of social psychology: Group processes* (pp. 425–460). Oxford, UK: Blackwell. Completely up-to-date review of the social identity perspective, with an emphasis on the role of the self-concept.

Deaux, K., Reid, A., Mizrahi, K., & Ethier, K. A. (1995). Parameters of social identity. *Journal of Personality and Social Psychology, 68,* 280–291. Analysis of the different general types of social identities that might exist.

Ellemers, N., Spears, R., & Doosje, B. (Eds.). (1999). *Social identity.* Oxford, UK: Blackwell. A focused and up-to-date collection of chapters on social identity processes with a particular emphasis on intergroup relations.

Gaertner, L., Sedikides, C., & Graetz, K. (1999). In search of self-definition: motivational primacy of the individual self, motivational primacy of the collective self, or contextual primacy. *Journal of Personality and Social Psychology, 76,* 5–18. A forceful but contentious argument in support of the idea that the individual self has primacy over the collective self.

Hogg, M. A. (2001). Social categorization, depersonalization, and group behavior. In M. A. Hogg & R. S. Tindale, (Eds.), *Blackwell handbook of social psychology: Group processes* (pp. 56–85). Oxford, UK: Blackwell. Completely up-to-date review of the social identity perspective, with an emphasis on the role of social categorization in group behavior and self-conception.

Hogg, M. A., & Abrams, D. (1988). *Social identifications: A social psychology of intergroup relations and group processes.* London: Routledge. Still the first and only integrative text describing the social identity approach in social psychology.

Turner, J. C. (1982). Towards a cognitive redefinition of the social group. In H. Tajfel (Ed.), *Social identity and intergroup relations* (pp. 15–40). Cambridge, UK: Cambridge University Press. A classic description of social identity as it relates to the self-concept, self-enhancement motivation, social influence and intergroup relations and behavior.

Turner, J. C, Hogg, M. A., Oakes, P. J., Reicher, S. D., & Wetherell, M. S. (1987). *Rediscovering the social group: A self-categorization theory.* Oxford, UK: Blackwell. A very widely cited book that presents self-categorization theory and shows how it operates in a wide range of contexts including social influence, group solidarity, and collective behavior.

Worchel, S., Morales, J. F., Paez, D., & Deschamps, J-C. (Eds.). (1998). *Social identity: International perspectives.* London: Sage. A recent and quite diverse collection of chapters on social identity processes.

An Integrative Theory of Intergroup Conflict

Henri Tajfel and John Turner • University of Bristol, England

Introduction

The aim of this chapter is to present an outline of a theory of intergroup conflict and some preliminary data relating to the theory. First, however, this approach to intergroup behavior and intergroup conflict must be set in context, in relation to other approaches to the same problems.

Much of the work on the social psychology of intergroup relations has focused on patterns of individual prejudice and discrimination and on the motivational sequences of interpersonal interaction. Outstanding examples of these approaches can be found respectively, in the theory of authoritarian personality (Adorno, Frenkel-Brunswik, Levinson, & Sanford, 1950) and in the various versions and modifications of the theory of frustration, aggression, and displacement (such as Berkowitz, 1962, 1969, 1974). The common denominator of most of this work has been the stress on the intraindividual or interpersonal psychological processes leading to prejudiced attitudes or discriminatory behavior. The complex interweaving of individual or interpersonal behavior with the contextual social processes of intergroup conflict and their psychological effects has not been in the focus of the social psychologists' preoccupations. (For a more detailed discussion, see Tajfel, 1972a, 1975.)

The alternative to these approaches is represented in the work of Muzafer Sherif and his associates, and has been referred to by D. T. Campbell (1965) as the "realistic group conflict theory" (R.C.T.). Its point of departure for the explanation of intergroup behavior is in what Sherif (1966) has called the functional relations between social groups. Its central hypothesis—"real conflict of group interests causes intergroup conflict" (Campbell, 1965, p. 287)—is deceptively simple, intuitively convincing, and has received strong empirical support (including Sherif & Sherif, 1953; Avigdor, 1953; Harvey, 1956; Sherif, Harvey, White, Hood, & Sherif, 1961; Blake & Mouton, 1961a, 1962c; Bass & Dunteman, 1963; D. W. Johnson, 1967; Diab, 1970).

R.C.T. was pioneered in social psychology by the Sherifs, who provided both an etiology of intergroup hostility and a theory of competition as realistic and instrumental in character, motivated by rewards which, in principle, are extrinsic to the intergroup situation (see Deutsch, 1949b; Julian, 1968). Opposed group interests in obtaining scarce resources promote competition, and positively interdependent (superordinate) goals facilitate cooperation. Conflicting interests develop through competition into overt social conflict. It appears, too, that intergroup competition enhances intragroup morale, cohesiveness, and cooperation (see Vinacke, 1964; Fiedler, 1967; Kalin & Marlowe, 1968). Thus, the real conflicts of group interests not only create antagonistic intergroup relations but also heighten identification with, and positive attachment to, the in-group.

This identification with the in-group, however, has been given relatively little prominence in the R.C.T. as a theoretical problem in its own right. The development of in-group identifications is seen in the R.C.T. almost as an epiphenomenon of intergroup conflict. As treated by the R.C.T., these identifications are *associated* with certain patterns of intergroup relations, but the theory does not focus either upon the processes underlying the development and maintenance of group identity nor upon the possibly autonomous effects upon the in-group and intergroup behavior of these "subjective" aspects of group membership. It is our contention that the relative neglect of these processes in the R.C.T. is responsible for some inconsistencies between the empirical data and the theory in its "classical" form. In this sense, the theoretical orientation to be outlined here is intended not to replace the R.C.T., but to supplement it in some respects that seem to us essential for an adequate social psychology of intergroup confliict—particularly as the understanding of the psychological aspects of social change cannot be achieved without an appropriate analysis of the social psychology of social conflict.

The Social Context of Intergroup Behavior

Our point of departure for the discussion to follow will be an a priori distinction between two extremes of social behavior, corresponding to what we shall call *interpersonal* versus *intergroup* behavior. At one extreme (which most probably cannot be found in its "pure" form in "real life") is the interaction between two or more individuals that is *fully* determined by their interpersonal relationships and individual characteristics, and not at all affected by various social groups or categories to which they respectively belong. The other extreme consists of interactions between two or more individuals (or groups of individuals) which are *fully* determined by their respective memberships in various social groups or categories, and not at all affected by the interindividual personal relationships between the people involved. Here again, it is unlikely that "pure" forms of this extreme can be found in "real" social situations. Examples nearing the interpersonal extreme would be the relations between wife and husband or between old friends. Examples near the intergroup extreme are provided by the behavior of soldiers from opposing armies during a battle, or by the behavior at a negotiating table of members representing two parties in an intense intergroup conflict.

The main empirical questions concern the conditions that determine the adoption of forms of social behavior nearing one or the other extreme. The first—and obvious—answer concerns intergroup conflict. It can be assumed, in accordance with our common experience, that the more intense is an intergroup conflict, the more likely it is that the individuals who are members of the opposing groups will behave toward each other as a function of their respective group memberships, rather than in terms of their individual characteristics or interindividual relationships. This was precisely why Sherif (1966, for example) was able to *abolish* so easily the interindividual friendships formed in the preliminary stages of some of his field studies when, subsequently, the individuals who had become friends were assigned to opposing groups.

An institutionalized or explicit conflict of "objective" interests between groups, however, does not provide a fully adequate basis, either theoretically or empirically, to account for many situations in which the social behavior of individuals belonging to distinct groups can be observed to approach the "group" extreme of our continuum. The conflict in Sherif's studies was "institutionalized," in that it was officially arranged by the holiday camp authorities; it was "explicit" in that it dominated the life of the groups; and it was "objective" in the sense that, by the terms of the competition, one of the groups *had* to be the winner and the other group the loser. And yet, there is evidence from Sherif's own studies and from other research (to which we shall return later) that the institutionalization, explicitness, and "objectivity" of an intergroup conflict are not *necessary* conditions for behavior in terms of the "group" extreme, although they will often prove to be *sufficient* conditions. One clear example is provided by our earlier experiments (Tajfel, 1970; Tajfel, Billig, Bundy, & Flament, 1971), which we shall discuss briefly below, in which it was found that intergroup discrimination existed in conditions of minimal in-group affiliation, anonymity of group membership, absence of conflicts of interest, and absence of previous hostility between the groups.

Other social and behavioral continua are associated with the interpersonal-intergroup continuum. One of them may be considered as having a causal function in relation to the interpersonal—intergroup continuum. We shall characterize it again by its two extremes, to which we shall refer as "social mobility" and "social change." These terms are not used here in their sociological sense. They refer instead to the individuals' belief systems about the nature and the structure of the relations between social groups in their society. The belief system of "social mobility" is based on the general assumption that the society in which the individuals live is a flexible and permeable one, so that if they are not satisfied, for whatever reason, with the conditions imposed upon their lives by membership in social groups or social categories to which they belong, it is *possible* for them (be it through talent, hard work, good luck, or whatever other means) to move individually into another group which suits them better. A good example of this system of beliefs, built into the explicit cultural and ideological traditions of a society, is provided in the following passage from Hirschman (1970):

> The traditional American idea of success confirms the hold which exit has had on the national imagination. Success—or, what amounts to the same thing, upward social mobility—has long been conceived in terms of evolutionary individualism. The successful individual who starts out at a low rung of the social ladder, necessarily leaves his own group as he rises; he "passes" into, or is "accepted" by, the next higher group. He takes his immediate family along, but hardly anyone else [pp. 108–109].

At the other extreme, the belief system of "social change" implies that the nature and structure of the relations between social groups in the society is perceived as characterized by marked stratification, making it impossible or very difficult for individuals, as individuals, to invest themselves of an unsatisfactory, underprivileged, or stigmatized group membership. A caste system, based on race or any other criteria perceived as immutable, is an obvious example, but it need not be the train example. The economic or social realities of a society may be such (as, for example, in the case of the millions of unemployed during the depression of the 1930s) that the impossibility of "getting out" on one's own, as an individual, becomes an everyday reality that determines many forms of intergroup social behavior. But even this example is still relatively extreme. Many social intergroup situations that contain, for whatever reasons, strong elements of stratification *perceived as such* will move social behavior away from the pole of interpersonal patterns toward the pole of intergroup patterns. This is as true of groups that are "superior" in a social system as of those that are "inferior" in it. The major characteristic of social behavior related to this belief system is that, in the *relevant* intergroup situations, individuals will not interact *as* individuals, on the basis of their individual characteristics or interpersonal relationships, but as members of their groups standing in certain defined relationships to members of other groups.

Obviously, one must expect a marked correlation between the degree of objective stratification in a social system (however measured) and the social diffusion and intensity of the belief system of "social change." This, however, cannot be a one-to-one relationship for a number of reasons, some of which will be discussed below, although we cannot in this chapter go into the details of the many social-psychological conditions that may determine the transition in certain social groups from an acceptance of stratification to behavior characteristic of the intergroup pole of our first continuum—that is, to the creation of social movements aiming to change (or to preserve) the status quo (Tajfel, 1978). It may be interesting, however, to point to the close relationship that exists between an explicit intergroup conflict of interests, on the one hand, and the "social change" system of beliefs on the other. One of the main features of this belief system is the perception by the individuals concerned that it is impossible or extremely difficult to move individually from their own group to another group. This is precisely the situation in an intense intergroup conflict of interests, in which it is extremely difficult for an individual to conceive of the possibility of "betraying" his or her own group by moving to the opposing group. Although this does happen on occasion, sanctions for such a move are, on the whole, powerful, and the value systems (at least in our cultures) are in flagrant opposition to it. To use an example from social-psychological research, it seems hardly possible that one of the boys in Sherif's holiday camps would decide to change sides, even though some of his previously contracted friendships overlapped group boundaries.

The intensity of explicit intergroup conflicts of interests is closely related in our cultures to the degree of opprobrium attached to the notion of "renegade" or "traitor." This is why the belief systems corresponding to the "social change" extreme of our continuum are associated with intense intergroup conflicts. These conflicts can be conceived, therefore, as creating a subclass or a subcategory of the subjective intergroup dichotomization characteristic of that extreme of the belief continuum. They share the basic feature of the "social change" system of beliefs, in the sense that the multigroup structure is perceived as characterized by the extreme difficulty or impossibility of an individual's moving from one group to another.

The continuum of systems of beliefs discussed so far has been seen to have a causal function in shifting social behavior toward members of outgroups between the poles of "interpersonal" and "intergoup" behavior. To conclude this part of our preliminary discussion, we must characterize briefly two further and overlapping continua, which can be considered as encompassing the major *consequences* of social behavior that approaches one or the other end of the interpersonal–intergroup continuum. They both have to do with the variability or uniformity within a group of behavior and attitudes concerning the relevent out-groups. The first may be described as follows: the nearer are members of a group to the "social change" extreme belief-systems continuum and the intergroup extreme of the behavioral continuum, the more uniformity they will show in their behavior toward members of the relevant out-group; an approach toward the opposite extremes of both these continua will be correspondingly associated with greater in-group variability of behavior toward members of the out-group. The second statement is closely related to the first: the nearer are members of a group to the "social change" and the "intergroup" extremes, the more they will tend to treat members of the out-group as undifferentiated items in a unified social category, rather an in terms of their individual characteristics. The vast literature in social psychology on the functioning of group stereotypes in situations of intense intergroup tensions is no more than an example of this general statement.

Thus, this preliminary conceptualization represents an approach to the social psychology of intergroup relations that takes into account social realities as well as their reflection in social behavior through the mediation of *socially shared* systems of beliefs. This convergence occurs at both ends of the sequence just discussed: at the beginning, because it can be assumed without much difficulty that the "social change" belief system is likely to reflect either an existing and marked so-

cial stratification or an intense intergroup conflict of interests, or both; at the end, because the consequences of the systems of beliefs arising from the social situations just mentioned are likely to appear in the form of unified group actions—that is, in the form of social movements aiming either to create social change or to preserve the status quo. We shall return later to an elaboration of the kinds of hypotheses that can be put forward concerning the creation of change versus the preservation of status quo. But before this is done, the realistic group conflict theory must be considered against this general background.

The implications of this conceptualization for intergroup relations in stratified societies and institutions are both evident and direct. Whenever social stratification is based upon an unequal division of scarce resources—such as power, prestige, or wealth—between social groups, the social situation should be characterized by pervasive ethnocentrism and out-group antagonism between the over- and underprivileged groups (Oberschall, 1973, p. 33). However, decades of research into ethnic-group relations suggest that ethnocentrism among stratified groups is, or at least it has been, very much a one-way street. Two recent books (Milner, 1975; Giles & Powesland, 1976) summarize a great deal of evidence that minority or subordinate group members—such as the American Blacks, the French Canadians, the New Zealand Maoris, or the South African Bantus—frequently tend to derogate the in-group and display positive attitudes toward the dominant out-group. In other words, deprived groups are not always ethnocentric in the simple meaning of the term; they may, in fact, be positively oriented toward the depriving out-group. Data of this kind are not consistent with a simple application of the R.C.T.

Some writers (including Gregor & McPherson, 1966; Morland, 1969; Milner, 1975, p. 93) have argued that the status relations between dominant and subordinate groups determine the latters' identity problems. (By *social status* we mean a ranking or hierarchy of perceived prestige.) Subordinate groups often seem to internalize a wider social evaluation of themselves as "inferior" or "second class," and this consensual inferiority is reproduced as relative self-derogation on a number of indices that have been used in the various studies. Consensual status itself—where subjective and accorded prestige are identical—is problematic for the R.C.T., which conceptualizes prestige as a scarce resource, like wealth or power. Status differences between groups, like other inequalities, should tend to accentuate the intergroup conflicts of interests. Therefore, according to the R.C.T., the impact of low status upon a subordinate group should be to intensify its antagonism toward the high-status group (Thibaut, 1950). Yet, under some conditions at least, low social status seems to be correlated with an enhancement, rather than a lessening, of positive out-group attitudes.

It could be argued that only conflicts of interest perceived as such create hostility. This requires that groups must compare the irrespective situations. And, according to some views, it is only relatively similar groups that engage in mutual comparisons; therefore, many forms of status differences will reduce perceived similarity (see Festinger, 1954; Kidder & Stewart, 1975). It follows that status systems may reduce social conflict by restricting the range of meaningful comparisons available to any given group. This hypothesis may be a useful tool to account for some of the determinants of social stability; but if it is taken to its logical conclusion, it can account for no more than that. It fails to account for social change (in the sense of changes in the mutual relations, behavior, and attitudes of large-scale human groups that have been distinctly different in status in the past), particularly when the processes of change become very rapid. Status differences between groups often do not *remain* unilaterally associated with low levels of intergroup conflicts. For example, the generalization made above—that certain forms of political, economic, and social subordination of a social group tend to eliminate or even reverse its ethnocentrism—is already dated. Research conducted in the last decade or so reveals a changing pattern in intergroup relations. American Blacks (see N. Friedman, 1969; Hraba & Grant, 1970; Paige, 1970; Brigham, 1971; Harris & Braun, 1971), French Canadians (Berry, Kalin, & Taylor, 1976), New Zealand Maoris (Vaughan, in press), and the Welsh (Bourhis, Giles, & Tajfel, 1973; Giles & Powesland, 1976), for instance, now seem to be rejecting their previously negative in-group evaluations and developing a positive ethnocentric group identity. This construction of positive in-group attitudes is often accompanied by a new militancy over political and economic objectives (see Tomlinson, 1970).

But these developments do not rescue the R.C.T. in its original form. The very suddenness with which the scene has changed effectively rules out objective deprivation and therefore *new* conflicting group interests as sufficient conditions for the "subordinate" group ethnocentrism. On the contrary, there is often less "objective" deprivation than there has been in the past. An active and new search for a positive group identity seems to be one of the critical factors responsible for the reawakening of these groups' claims to scarce resources (Dizard, 1970).

In summary, the R.C.T. states that opposing claims to scarce resources, such as power, prestige, or wealth, generate ethnocentrism and antagonism between groups. Therefore, low status should tend to intensify out-group hostility in groups that are politically, economically, or socially subordinate. The evidence suggests, however, that where social-structural differences in the distribution of resources have been institutionalized, legitimized, and justified through a consensually accepted status system (or at least a status system that is sufficiently firm and pervasive to prevent the creation of cognitive alternatives to it), the result has been less and not more ethnocentrism in the different status groups. The price of this has been the subordinate groups' self-esteem. On the other hand, whenever a subordinate group begins, for whatever reasons, to question or deny its presumed characteristics associated with its low status, this seems to facilitate the reawakening of a previously dormant conflict over objective resources. At the same time, it is likely that one of the counterreactions from the dominant groups in such situations will be to work for the preservation of the previously existing "subjective" and "objective" differentiations.

A tentative hypothesis about intergroup conflict in stratified societies can now be offered: An unequal distribution of objective resources promotes antagonism between dominant and subordinate groups, provided that the latter group rejects its previously accepted and consensually negative self-image, and with it the status quo, and starts working toward the development of a positive group identity. The dominant group may react to these developments either by doing everything possible to maintain and justify the status quo or by attempting to find and create new differentiations in its own favor, or both. A more detailed specification of some of the strategies and "solutions" that can be adopted in this situation can be found in Tajfel (1978); we shall return later to a discussion of some of them. For the present, it will be sufficient to state that, whether valid or not, the hypothesis raises some important theoretical problems that need to be considered. The first question is: what social-psychological processes are involved in the development of positive group identity? The second question concerns the conditions under which the status differences between social groups are likely to enhance or to reduce intergroup conflict. In order to continue the discussion of these questions, we must now abandon speculation and consider some relevant data.

Social Categorization and Intergroup Discrimination

The initial stimulus for the theorizing presented here was provided by certain experimental investigations of intergroup behavior. The laboratory analog of real-world ethnocentrism is in-group bias—that is, the tendency to favor the in-group over the out-group in evaluations and behavior. Not only are incompatible group interests not always sufficient to generate conflict (as concluded in the last section), but there is a good deal of experimental evidence that these conditions are not always *necessary* for the development of competition and discrimination between groups (for example, Ferguson & Kelley, 1964; Rabbie & Wilkens, 1971; Doise & Sinclair, 1973; Doise & Weinberger, 1973). This does not mean, of course, that in-group bias is not influenced by the goal relations between the groups (see Harvey, 1956).

All this evidence implies that in-group bias is a remarkably omnipresent feature of intergroup relations. The phenomenon in its extreme form has been investigated by Tajfel and his associates. There have been a number of studies (Tajfel et al., 1971; Billig & Tajfel, 1973; Tajfel & Billig, 1974; Doise, Csepeli, Dann, Gouge, Larsen, & Ostell, 1972; Turner, 1975), all showing that the mere perception of belonging to two distinct groups—that is, social categorization per se—is sufficient to trigger intergroup discrimination favoring the in-group. In other words, the mere awareness of the presence of an out-group is sufficient to provoke intergroup competitive or discriminatory responses on the part of the in-group.

In the initial experimental paradigm (Tajfel, 1970; Tajfel et al., 1971), the subjects (both children and adults have acted as subjects in the vari-ous studies) are randomly classified as members of two nonoverlapping groups—ostensibly on the basis of some trivial performance criterion. They then make "decisions," awarding amounts of money to pairs of *other* subjects (excluding self) in specially designed booklets. The recipients are anonymous, except for their individual code numbers and their group membership (for example, member number 51 of the X group and member number 33 of the Y group). The subjects, who know their own group membership, award the amounts individually and anonymously. The response format of the booklets does not force the subjects to act in terms of group membership.

In this situation, there is neither a conflict of interests nor previously existing hostility between the "groups." No social interaction takes place between the subjects, nor is there any rational link between economic self-interest and the strategy of in-group favoritism. Thus, these groups are purely cognitive, and can be referred to as *minimal.*

The basic and highly reliable finding is that the trivial, ad hoc intergroup categorization leads to in-group favoritism and discrimination against the out group. Fairness is also an influential strategy. There is also a good deal of evidence that, within the pattern of responding in terms of in-group favoritism, maximum difference (M.D.) is more important to the subjects than maximum in-group profit (M.I.P.). Thus, they seem to be competing with the out-group, rather than following a strategy of simple economic gain for members of the in-group. Other data from several experiments also show that the subjects' decisions were significantly nearer to the maximum joint payoff (M.J.P.) point when these decisions applied to the division of money between two anonymous members of the in-group than when they applied to two members of the out-group; that is, relatively less was given to the out-group, even when giving more would not have affected the amounts for the in-group. Billig & Tajfel (1973) have found the same results even when the assignment to groups was made explicitly random. This eliminated the similarity on the performance criterion within the in-group as an alternative explanation of the results (see Byrne, 1971). An explicitly random classification into groups proved in this study to be a more potent determinant of discrimination than perceived interpersonal similarities and dissimilarities not associated with categorization into groups.

The question that arises is whether in-group bias in these "minimal" situations is produced by some form of the experimenter effect or of the demand characteristics of the experimental situation—in other words, whether explicit references to group membership communicate to the subjects that they are expected to, or ought to, discriminate. The first point to be made about this interpretation of the results is that explicit references to group membership are logically necessary for operationalizing in these minimal situations the major independent variable—that is, social categorization per se. This requires not merely that the subjects perceive themselves as similar to or different from others as *individuals,* but that they are members of discrete and discontinuous categories—that is, "groups." Second, a detailed analysis of the subjects' postsession reports (Billig, 1972; Turner, 1975) shows that they do not share any common conception of the "appropriate" or "obvious" way to behave, that only a tiny minority have some idea of the hypothesis, and that this minority does not always conform to it.

The more general theoretical problem has been referred to elsewhere by one of us as follows:

> Simply and briefly stated, the argument (e.g., Gerard & Hoyt, 1974) amounts to the following: the subjects acted in terms of the intergroup categorization provided or imposed by the experimenters not necessarily because this has been successful in inducing any genuine awareness of membership in separate and distinct groups, but probably because they felt that this kind of behavior was expected of them by the experimenters, and therefore they conformed to this expectation. The first question to ask is why should the subjects be expecting the experimenters to expect of them this kind of behavior? The Gerard and Hoyt answer to this is that the experimental situation was rigged to cause this kind of expectation in the subjects. This answer retains its plausibility only if we assume that what was no more than a hint from the experimenters about the notion of "groups" being relevant to the subjects' behavior had been sufficient to determine, powerfully and consistently, a *particular form* of intergroup behavior. In turn, if we assume this—and the assumption is by no means unreasonable—we must also assume that this particular form of intergroup behavior is one which is capable of being induced by the experimenters much more easily than other forms (such as cooperation between the groups in extorting the maximum total amount of money from the experimenters, or a fair division of the

spoils between the groups, or simply random responding). And this last assumption must be backed up in its turn by another presupposition: namely, that for some reasons (whatever they may be) competitive behavior between groups, at least in our culture, is extraordinarily easy to trigger off—at which point we are back where we started from. The problem then must be restated in terms of the need to specify why a certain *kind* of intergroup behavior can be elicited so much more easily than other kinds; and this specification is certainly not made if we rest content with the explanation that the behavior occurred because it was very easy for the experimenters to make it occur [Tajfel, 1978].

Two points stand out: first, minimal intergroup discrimination is not based on incompatible group interests; second, the baseline conditions for intergroup competition seem indeed so minimal as to cause the suspicion that we are dealing here with some factor or process inherent in the intergroup situation itself. Our theoretical orientation was developed initially in response to these clues from our earlier experiments. We shall not trace the history of its development, however, but shall describe its present form.

Social Identity and Social Comparison

Many orthodox definitions of "social groups" are unduly restrictive when applied to the context of intergroup relations. For example, when members of two national or ethnic categories interact on the basis of their reciprocal beliefs about their respective categories and of the general relations between them, this is clearly intergroup behavior in the everyday sense of the term. The "groups" to which the interactants belong *need not* depend upon the frequency of intermember interaction, systems of role relationships, or interdependent goals. From the social-psychological perspective, the essential criteria for group membership, as they apply to large-scale social categories, are that the individuals concerned define themselves and are defined by others as members of a group.

We can conceptualize a group, in this sense, as a collection of individuals who perceive themselves to be members of the same social category, share some emotional involvement in this common definition of themselves, and achieve some degree of social consensus about the evaluation of their group and of their membership of it. Following from this, our definition of intergroup behavior is basically identical to that of Sherif (1966, p. 62): any behavior displayed by one or more actors toward one or more others that is based on the actors' identification of themselves and the others as belonging to different social categories.

Social categorizations are conceived here as cognitive tools that segment, classify, and order the social environment, and thus enable the individual to undertake many forms of social action. But they do not merely systematize the social world; they also provide a system of orientation for *self*-reference: they create and define the individual's place in society. Social groups, understood in this sense, provide their members with an identification of themselves in social terms. These identifications are to a very large extent relational and comparative: they define the individual as similar to or different from, as "better" or "worse" than, members of other groups. (For a more detailed discussion, see Tajfel, 1972b.) It is in a strictly limited sense, arising from these considerations, that we use the term *social identity*. It consists, for the purposes of the present discussion, of those aspects of an individual's self-image that derive from the social categories to which he perceives himself as belonging. With this limited concept of social identity our argument is based on the following general assumptions:

1. Individuals strive to maintain or enhance their self-esteem: they strive for a positive self-concept.
2. Social groups or categories and the membership of them are associated with positive or negative value connotations. Hence, social identity may be positive or negative according to the evaluations (which tend to be socially consensual, either within or across groups) of those groups that contribute to an individual's social identity.
3. The evaluation of one's own group is determined with reference to specific other groups through social comparisons in terms of value-laden attributes and characteristics. Positively discrepant comparisons between in-group and out-group produce high prestige; negatively discrepant comparisons between ingroup and out-group result in low prestige.

From these assumptions, some related theoretical principles can be derived:

1. Individuals strive to achieve or to maintain positive social identity.
2. Positive social identity is based to a large extent on favorable comparisons that can be made between the in-group and some relevant out-groups: the in-group must be perceived as positively differentiated or distinct from the relevant out-groups.
3. When social identity is unsatisfactory, individuals will strive either to leave their existing group and join some more positively distinct group and/or to make their existing group more positively distinct.

The basic hypothesis, then, is that pressures to evaluate one's own group positively through in-group/out-group comparisons lead social groups to attempt to differentiate themselves from each other (see Tajfel, 1974a, 1974b; Turner, 1975). There are at least three classes of variables that should influence intergroup differentiation in concrete social situations. First, individuals must have internalized their group membership as an aspect of their self-concept: they must be subjectively identified with the relevant in-group. It is not enough that the others define them as a group, although consensual definitions by others can become, in the long run, one of the powerful causal factors for a group's self-definition. Second, the social situation must be such as to allow for intergroup comparisons that enable the selection and evaluation of the relevant relational attributes. Not all between-group differences have evaluative significance (Tajfel, 1959), and those that do vary from group to group. Skin color, for instance, is apparently a more salient attribute in the United States than in Hong Kong (Morland, 1969); whereas language seems to be an especially salient dimension of separate identity in French Canada, Wales, and Belgium (see Giles & Powesland, 1976; Fishman & Giles, in press). Third, in-groups do not compare themselves with every cognitively available out-group: the outgroup must be perceived as a relevant comparison group. Similarity, proximity, and situational salience are among the variables that determine out-group comparability, and pressures toward in-group distinctiveness should increase as a function of this comparability. It is important to state at this point that, in many social situations, comparability reaches a much wider range than a simply conceived "similarity" between the groups.

The aim of differentiation is to maintain or achieve superiority over an out-group on some dimensions. Any such act, therefore, is essentially competitive. This competition requires a situation of mutual comparison and differentiation on a shared value dimension. In these conditions, intergroup competition, which may be unrelated to the "objective" goal relations between the groups, can be predicted to occur. Turner (1975) has distinguished between social and instrumental, or "realistic," competition. The former is motivated by self-evaluation and takes place through social comparison, whereas the latter is based on "realistic" self-interest and represents embryonic conflict. Incompatible group goals are necessary for realistic competition, but mutual intergroup comparisons are necessary, and often sufficient, for social competition. The latter point is consistent with the data from "minimal" group experiments that mere awareness of an out-group is sufficient to stimulate in-group favoritism, and the observations (Ferguson & Kelley, 1964; Rabbie & Wilkens, 1971; Doise & Weinberger, 1973) that the possibility of social comparison generates "spontaneous" intergroup competition.

Social and realistic competition also differ in the predictions that can be made about the consequences for subsequent intergroup behavior of winning or losing. After realistic competition, the losing groups should be hostile to the out-group victors, both because they have been deprived of a reward and because their interaction has been exclusively conflictual. However, when winning and losing establish shared group evaluations concerning comparative superiority and inferiority, then, so long as the terms of the competition are perceived as legitimate and the competition itself as fair according to these legitimate terms, the losing group *may* acquiesce in the superiority of the winning out-group. This acquiescence by a group considering itself as legitimately "inferior" has been shown in a recent study by Caddick (1974). Several other studies report findings that are in line with this interpretation: losing in-groups do not always derogate, but sometimes upgrade, their evaluations of the winning out-groups (for example, Wilson & Miller, 1961; Bass & Dunteman, 1963).

Retrospectively, at least, the social-identity/social-comparison theory is consistent with many of the studies mentioned in the preceding section of this chapter. In particular, in the paradigm of the "minimal group" experiments (such as Tajfel et al., 1971), the intergroup discrimination can be conceived as being due not to conflict over monetary gains, but to differentiations based on comparisons made in terms of monetary rewards. Money functioned as a dimension of comparison (the only one available within experimental design), and the data to suggest that larger absolute gains that did not establish a difference in favor of the in-group were sacrificed for smaller comparative gains, when the two kinds of gains were made to conflict.

There is further evidence (Turner, 1978a) that the social-competitive pattern of intergroup behavior holds even when it conflicts with obvious self-interest. In this study, the distribution of either monetary rewards or "points" was made, within the "minimal" intergroup paradigm, between self and an anonymous "other," who was either in the in-group or in the out-group. As long as minimal conditions existed for in-group identification, the subjects were prepared to give relatively less to themselves when the award (either in points or in money) was to be divided between self and an anonymous member of the in-group, as compared with dividing with an anonymous member of the out-group. These results seem particularly important, since the category of "self," which is by no means "minimal" or ad hoc, was set here against a truly minimal in-group category, identical to those used in the earlier experiments. Despite this stark asymmetry, the minimal group affiliation affected the responses.

The theoretical predictions were taken outside of the minimal categorization paradigm in a further study by Turner (1978b). He used face-to-face groups working on a discussion task. In each session, two three-person groups discussed an identical issue, supposedly to gain an assessment of their verbal intelligence, and then briefly compared their respective performance. The subjects were 144 male undergraduates. The criterion for intergroup differentiation was the magnitude of in-group bias shown in the ratings of the groups' work. Half the triads, composed of Arts students, believed that verbal intelligence was important for them (High Importance, or H.I.); half, composed of Science students, did not (Low Importance, or L.I.). Half the sessions involved two Arts or two Science groups (Similar Outgroup), and half involved one Arts and one Science group (Dissimilar Outgroup). Finally, in the Stable Difference condition, subjects were instructed that Arts students were definitely superior and Science students definitely inferior in verbal intelligence; in the Unstable Difference condition, there was no explicit statement that one category was better than the other. These variables were manipulated in a 2 × 2 × 2 factorial design.

The results showed that the Arts groups (H.I.) were more biased than the Science groups (L.I.); that similar groups differentiated more than dissimilar groups in the Stable condition, but that they were more biased (and sometimes even less so) in the Unstable condition; and that, on some of the measures there was a significant main effect for out-group similarity: in-group bias increased against a similar out-group. Although these data are relatively complex, they do support some of our theoretical expectations and provide an illustration that variations in in-group bias can be systematically predicted from the social-identity/ social-comparison theory.

We have argued that social and realistic competition are conceptually distinct, although most often they are empirically associated in "real life." In an experiment by Turner and Brown (1976), an attempt was made to isolate the effects on intergroup behavior of the postulated autonomous processes attributed to a search for positive social identity. Children were used as subjects, and the manipulations involved decisions by the subjects about the distribution of payments for participation in the experiment, to be shared equally by the in-group, between the in-group and out-groups that were made relevant or irrelevant to comparisons with the in-group's performance. Monetary self-interest (of a magnitude previously ascertained to be of genuine significance to the subjects) would have produced no difference in the distribution decisions involving the two kinds of out-group; it would also have led to decisions tending toward maximum in-group profit (M.I.P.) rather than toward maximum difference (M.D.).

M.D. was the most influential strategy in the choices. Furthermore, when the subjects could choose in-group favoritism (M.D. +M.I.P.) and/or a fairness strategy, they were both more discriminatory and less fair toward the relevant than the irrelevant comparison group. Other measures of in-group favoritism produced an interaction between reward level and type of out-group: more discrimination against the relevant than the irrelevant group with high rewards, and less with low

rewards. Whatever may be other explanations for this interaction, we can at least conclude that when reward levels are more meaningful, in-group favoritism is enhanced against a more comparable out-group, independently of the group members' economic interests. Indeed, insofar as the subjects used the M.D. strategy, they sacrificed "objective" personal and group gain for the sake of positive in-group distinctiveness.

On the whole, these studies provide some confirmation for the basic social-identity/social-comparison hypotheses. We shall now attempt to apply this analysis to some of the problems raised in the earlier sections of this chapter.

Status Hierarchies and Social Change

The reconceptualization of social status attempted earlier in this chapter needs now to be made more explicit. Status is not considered here as a scarce resource or commodity, such as power or wealth; it is the *outcome* of intergroup comparison. It reflects a group's relative position on some evaluative dimensions of comparison. Low subjective status does not promote intergroup competition directly; its effects on intergroup behavior are mediated by social identity processes. The lower is a group's subjective status position in relation to relevant comparison groups, the less is the contribution it can make to positive social identity. The variety of reactions to negative or threatened social identity to be discussed below are an elaboration of the principles outlined earlier in this chapter.

1. *Individual Mobility.* The more an individual approaches the structure of beliefs (most often socially shared) described in the Introduction to this chapter as that of "social mobility," the more it is likely that he will try to leave, or dissociate himself from, his erstwhile group. This usually implies attempts, on an individual basis, to achieve upward social mobility, to pass from a lower- to a higher-status group. In a four-group hierarchy, G. F. Ross (1975) found a direct linear relationship between low status and the desire to pass upwards into another group. Many earlier studies report the existence of strong forces for upward social movement in status hierarchies. Tendencies to dissociate oneself psychologically from fellow

members of low-prestige categories are known to many of us from everyday experience; they have been noted more systematically by Jahoda (1961) and Klineberg and Zavalloni (1969), among others, and indirectly by the whole literature on racial identification and preference. The most important feature of individual mobility is that the low status of one's own group is not thereby changed: it is an individualist approach designed, at least in the short run, to achieve a personal, not a group, solution. Thus, individual mobility implies a disidentification with the erstwhile in-group.

2. *Social Creativity.* The group members may seek positive distinctiveness for the in-group by redefining or altering the elements of the comparative situation. This need not involve any change in the group's actual social position or access to objective resources in relation to the out-group. It is a group rather than an individualistic strategy that may focus upon:

(a) Comparing the in-group to the out-group on some new dimension. Lemaine (1966) found, for example, that children's groups which could not compare themselves favorably with others in terms of constructing a hut—because they had been assigned poorer building materials than the out-group—tended to seek out other dimensions of comparison involving new constructions in the hat's surroundings. The problems that obviously arise here are those of legitimizing the value assigned to the new social products—fast in the in-group and then in the other groups involved. To the extent that this legitimization may threaten the out-group's superior distinctiveness, an increase in intergroup tension can be predicted.

(b) Changing the values assigned to the attributes of the group, so that comparisons which were previously negative are now perceived as positive. The classic example is "Black is beautiful." The salient dimension—skin color—remains the same, but the prevailing value system concerning it is rejected and reversed. The same process may underlie Peabody's (1968) finding that even when various groups agree about their respective characteristic, the trait is evaluated more positively by the group that possesses it.

(c) Changing the out-group (or selecting the out-group) with which the in-group is compared—in particular, ceasing or avoiding to use *the high-status out-group as a comparative frame of reference.* Where comparisons are not made with the high-status out-group, the relevant inferiority should decrease in salience, and self-esteem should recover. Hyman's (1942) classic paper on the psychology of status suggested that discontent among low-status-group members is lessened to the degree that intraclass rather than intergroup comparisons are made. More recently, Rosenberg and Simmons (1972) found that selfesteem was higher among Blacks who made self-comparisons with other Blacks rather than Whites. Other work also suggests (see I. Katz, 1964; Lefcourt & Ladwig, 1965) that, in certain circumstances, Black performance was adversely affected by the low self-esteem induced by the presence of the members of the dominant out-group. It follows that self-esteem can be enhanced by comparing with other lower-status groups rather than with those of higher status. This is consistent with the fact that competition between subordinate groups is sometimes more intense than between subordinate and dominant groups—hence, for example, lower-class or "poor white" racism.

3. *Social Competition.* The group members may seek positive distinctiveness through direct competition with the out-group. They may try to reverse the relative positions of the in-group and the out-group on salient dimensions. To the degree that this may involve comparisons related to the social structure, it implies changes in the groups' objective social locations. We can hypothesize, therefore, following the R.C.T., that this strategy will generate conflict and antagonism between subordinate and dominant groups insofar as it focuses on the distribution of scarce resources. Data relevant to this strategy have been referred to earlier in this chapter.

Let us assume as an ideal case some stratification of social groups in which the social hierarchy is reasonably correlated with an unequal division of objective resources and a corresponding status system (based on the outcomes of comparisons in terms of those resources). Under what conditions will this not lead to intergroup conflict—or, more precisely, to the development of competitive ethnocentrism on the part of the subordinate group?

First, to the extent that the objective and the subjective prohibitions to "passing" are weak (see our earlier discussion of the "social mobility" structure of beliefs), low status may tend, in conditions of unsatisfactory social identity, to promote the widespread adoption of individual mobility strategies, or at least initial attempts to make use of these strategies. Insofar as individual mobility implies disidentification, it will tend to loosen the cohesiveness of the subordinate group. This weakening of subjective attachment to the in-group among its members will tend: (a) to blur the perception of distinct group interests corresponding to the distinct group identity; and (b) to create obstacles to mobilizing group members for collective action over their common interests. Thus, the low morale that follows from negative social identity can set in motion disintegrative processes that, in the long run, may hinder a change in the group status.

Second, assuming that the barriers (objective, moral, and ideological prohibitions) to leaving one's group are strong, unsatisfactory social identity may stimulate social creativity that tends to reduce the salience of the subordinate/dominant group conflict of interest. Strategy 2(c) mentioned above is likely to be crucial here since, in general, access to resources such as housing, jobs, income, or education is sufficiently central to the fate of any group that the relevant comparisons are not easily changed or devalued. Few underprivileged groups would accept poverty as a virtue, but it may appear more tolerable to the degree that comparisons are made with even poorer groups rather than with those that are better off (see Runciman, 1966).

As noted above, some writers (Festinger, 1954; Kidder & Stewart, 1975) imply that strategy 2(c) is a dominant response to status differences between groups. The assumption is that intergroup comparability decreases as a direct function of perceived dissimilarity. If this were the whole story, then, somewhat paradoxically, the creation of a consensual status system would protect social identity from invidious comparisons. The causal sequence would be as follows: similar groups compare with each other; the outcome determines their relative prestige; the perceived status difference reduces their similarity and hence comparability; intergroup comparisons cease to be made; subjective superiority and inferiority decrease in salience; correspondingly, the groups' respective self-esteems return to their original point. There may be occasions when this social-psychological recipe for the maintenance of the status quo can be observed in something like its pure form. However, we shall argue presently that there are many status differences that do not reduce comparability.

For the moment, we can note that both individual mobility and some forms of social creativity can work to reduce intergroup conflict over scarce resources—though with different implications. The former is destructive of subordinate-group solidarity and provides no antidote to negative social identity at group level. The latter may restore or create a positive self-image but, it can be surmised, at the price either of a collective repression of objective deprivation or, perhaps, of spurious rivalry with some other deprived group. It is interesting in this context that the French Canadians, having recently gained a more assertive identity, are now apparently more disparaging of other minority groups than are the English Canadians (see Berry et al., 1976).

By reversing the conditions under which social stratification does not produce intergroup conflict, we can hypothesize that negative social identity promotes subordinate-group competitiveness toward the dominant group to the degree that: (a) subjective identification with the subordinate group is maintained; and (b) the dominant group continues or begins to be perceived as a relevant comparison group. As a great deal of work has been done in social psychology on the determinants of cohesiveness and loyalty within groups, we shall concentrate on the second condition. Let us consider a comparison between two football teams that have come first and second in their league, respectively. There is no argument about which has the higher status, but alternative comparative outcomes were and, in the future, still will be possible. When the new season begins, the teams will be as comparable and competitive as they had been before. In this instance, the status difference does not reduce the meaningfulness of comparisons because *it can be changed*.

This example illustrates Tajfel's (1974a) distinction between *secure* and *insecure* intergroup comparisons. The crucial factor in this distinction is whether *cognitive alternatives* to the actual outcome are available—whether other outcomes are conceivable. Status differences between social groups in social systems showing various degrees of stratification can be distinguished in the same way. Where status relations are perceived as immutable, a part of the fixed order of things, then social identity is secure. It becomes insecure when the existing state of affairs begins to be questioned. An important corollary to this argument is that the dominant or high-status groups, too, can experience insecure social identity. Any threat to the distinctively superior position of a group implies a potential loss of positive comparisons and possible negative comparisons, which must be guarded against. Such a threat may derive from the activity of the low-status group or from a conflict within the high-status group's own value system (for example, the sociopolitical morality) and the actual foundations of its superiority. Like low-status groups, the high-status groups will react to insecure social identity by searching for enhanced group distinctiveness,

In brief, then, it is true that clear-cut status differences may lead to a quiescent social system in which neither the "inferior" nor the "superior" groups will show much ethnocentrism. But this "ideal type" situation must be considered in relation to the perceived stability and legitimacy of the system. Perceived illegitimacy and/or instability provide new dimensions of comparability that are directly relevant to the attitudes and behavior of-the social groups involved, whatever their position in the system. This is the social-psychological counterpart to what is widely known today as "the revolution of rising expectations." Providing that individual mobility is unavailable or undesirable, consensual inferiority will be rejected most rapidly when the situation is perceived as both unstable and illegitimate. This is probably the set of conditions underlying the development of ethnocentrism among Black Americans, French Canadians, and New Zealand Maoris, for instance. Vaughan (1978) reports that the perceived feasibility of social change (probably including, in this instance, the perceived illegitimacy of the present situation) is an important predictor of the developing Maori ethnocentrism; N. Friedman (1969) argues that what we may term the "cognitive alternative" of Black nationalism in the developing countries was influential in enhancing Black American social identity.

On the other hand, when the dominant group or sections of it perceive their superiority as legitimate, they will probably react in an intensely discriminatory fashion to any attempt by the subordinate group to change the intergroup situation. Such perhaps was the post-bellum situation in the Southern United States: the Whites, threatened by those who had been their slaves, rapidly abandoned their paternalistic stereotypes of the Blacks as "childlike" in favor of openly hostile and derogatory ones (see Van der Berghe, 1967). The reactions of illegitimately superior. groups are snore complex (Turner & Brown, 1976). It seems that conflicts of values are reduced by greater discrimination when superiority is assured, but by less discrimination when it is unstable. This calls to mind some Prisoner Dilemma studies in which White discrimination against Black opponents increased the more cooperative was the opponent, but decreased the more competitive he was (Baxter, 1973; Cederblom & Diers, 1970). Baxter suggested in the title of his article ("Prejudiced Liberals?") that a conflict of values may underlie his data.

Many of the points and hypotheses we have advanced in this chapter are not, in themselves, new (see, for instance, M. Sherif, 1966; Runciman, 1966; Milner, 1975; Billig, 1976). What is new, we think, is the integration of the three processes of social categorization, self-evaluation through social identity, and intergroup social comparison, into a coherent and testable framework for contributing to the explanation of various forms of intergroup behavior, social conflict, and social change. This framework contains possibilities of further development, and, to this extent, we hope that it may stimulate theoretically directed research in areas that have not been considered here.

But some cautionary points should be made. The equation of social competition and intergroup conflict made above rests on the assumptions concerning an "ideal type" of social stratification in which the salient dimensions of intergroup differentiation are those involving scarce resources. In this respect, we have simply borrowed the central tenet of the R.C.T. There is no reason, in fact, to assume that intergroup differentiation is inherently conflictual. Some of the experimental work that is proceeding at present at the University of Bristol points to the conclusion that evaluative derogation of an out-group is conceptually and empirically distinct from out-group hostility. On the other hand, social-identity processes may provide a source of intergroup conflict (in addition to the cases outlined above) to the degree that the groups develop conflicting interests with respect to the maintenance of the comparative situation as a whole. It seems plausible to hypothesize that, when a group's action for positive distinctiveness is frustrated, impeded, or in any way actively prevented by an out-group, this will promote overt conflict and hostility between the groups. This prediction, like many others, still remains to be tested.

"Objective" and "Subjective" Conflicts

None of the arguments outlined in this chapter must be understood as implying that the social-psychological or "subjective" type of conflict is being considered here as having priority or a more important causal function in social reality than the "objective" determinants of social conflict of which the basic analysis must be sought in the social, economic, political, and historical structures of a society. The major aim of the present discussion has been to determine what are the points of insertion of social-psychological variables into the causal spiral; and its argument has been that, just as the effects of these variables are powerfully determined by the previous social, economic, and political processes, so they may also acquire, in turn, an *autonomous* function that enables them to deflect in one direction or another the subsequent functioning of these processes.

It is nearly impossible in most natural social situations to distinguish between discriminatory intergroup behavior based on real or perceived conflict of "objective" interests between the groups and discrimination based on attempts to establish a positively-valued distinctiveness for one's own group. However, as we have argued, the two can be distinguished theoretically, since the goals of actions aimed at the achievement of positively-valued in-group distinctiveness often retain no value outside of the context of intergroup comparisons. An example would be a group that does not necessarily wish to increase the level of its own salaries but acts to prevent other groups from getting nearer to this level so that differentials are not eroded. But the difficulty with this example—as with many other similar examples—is that, in this case, the preservation of salary differentials is probably associated with all kinds of "objective" advantages that cannot be defined in terms of money alone. In turn, *some* of these advantages will again make sense only in the comparative framework of intergroup competition. Despite this confusing network of mutual feedbacks and interactions, the distinctions made here are important because they help us to understand some aspects of intergroup behavior which have often been neglected in the past.

A further distinction must be made between "explicit" and "implicit" conflicts—a distinction that has to do with objectivity in a different way. A conflict can be "objective" despite the fact that the goals the groups are aiming for have no value outside of the context of intergroup comparison. This is so when the conflict is institutionalized and legitimized by rules and norms, whatever their origin, that are accepted by the groups involved. This was the case in Sherif's studies in their phase of competition between the groups; and it also is the case in any football match and in countless other social activities. The behavior toward out-groups in this kind of conflict can be classified, in turn, into two categories, one of which can be referred to as *instrumental* and the other as *noninstrumental*. The instrumental category consists of all those actions whose explicit aim can be directly related to causing the group to win the competition. The noninstrumental category, which could be referred to as "gratuitous" discrimination against the out-group, includes the creation of negative stereotypes and all other aspects of the "irrelevant" in-group/out-group differentiations so well described, for example, in Sherif's studies. The first category of actions is both commonsensically and theoretically accounted for by assuming nothing more than the group's desire to win the competition—although this poses all the theoretical "comparison" problems discussed in this chapter; the second category of actions can be directly and parsimoniously accounted for in terms of the social-comparison–social-identity–positive-ingroup-distinctiveness sequence described here.

The "implicit" conflicts are those that can be shown to exist despite the absence of explicit institutionalization or even an informal normative acceptance of their existence by the groups involved. The proof of their existence is to be found in the large number of studies (and also everyday occurrences in "real life") in which differentiations of all kinds are made between groups by their members although, on the face of it, there are no "reasons" for these differentiations to occur. Clear examples of this have been provided in several studies mentioned in this chapter in which the introduction by the subjects of various intergroup differentiations directly *decreased* the "objective" rewards that could otherwise have been gained by the in-group, or even directly by the individual. Findings of this kind, which can be generalized widely to many natural social situations, provide a clear example of the need to introduce into the complex spiral of social causation the social-psychological variables of the "relational" and "comparative" kind discussed in this chapter.

REFERENCES

Adorno, T. W., Frenkel-Brunswick, E., Levinson, D. J., & Sanford, R. N. (1950). *The authoritarian personality.* New York: Harper & Row.

Avigdor, R. (1953). Etude expérimentale de la génèse des stéréotypes. *Cahiers Internationaux de Sociologie, 14,* 154–168.

Bass, B. M., & Dunteman, G. (1963). Biases in the evaluation of one's own group, its allies, and oponents. *Journal of Conflict Resolution, 2,* 67–77.

Baxter, G. W. (1973). Prejudiced liberals? Race and information effects in a two-person game. *Journal of Conflict Resolution, 17,* 131–161.

Berkowitz, L. (1962). *Aggression: A social psychological analysis.* New York: McGraw-Hill.

Berkowitz, L. (1969). The frustration-aggression hypothesis revisited. In L. Berkowitz (Ed.), *Roots of aggression: A re-examination of the frustration-aggression hypothesis.* New York: Atherton Press.

Berkowitz, L. (1974). Some determinants of impulsive aggression: Role of mediated associations with reinforcements for aggression. *Psychological Review, 81,* 165–176.

Berry, J. W., Kalin, R., & Taylor, D. M. (1976). *Multiculturalism and ethnic attitudes in Canada.* Unpublished paper, Queen's University, Kingston, Ontario.

Billig, M. (1972). *Social categorization in intergroup relations.* Unpublished doctoral dissertation. University of Bristol.

Billig, M. (1976). *Social psychology and intergroup relations.* London: Academic Press, European Monographs in Social Psychology.

Billig, M., & Tajfel, H. (1973). Social categorization and similarity in intergroup behavior. *European Journal of Social Psychology, 3,* 27–52.

Blake, R. R., & Mouton, J. S. (1961). Competition, communication and conformity. In I. A. Berg & B. M. Bass (Eds.), *Conformity and deviation.* New York: Harper.

Blake, R. R., & Mouton, J. S. (1962). The intergroup dynamics of win-lose conflict and problem-solving collaboration in union-management relations. In M. Sherif (Ed.), *Intergroup relations and leadership.* New York: Wiley.

Bourhis, R. Y., Giles, H., & Tajfel, H. (1973). Language as a determinant of Welsh identity. *European Journal of Social Psychology, 3,* 447–460.

Brigham, J. C. (1971). *Views of White and Black schoolchildren concerning racial differences.* Paper presented at the meeting of the Midwestern Psychological Association, Detroit.

Byrne, D. (1971). *The attraction paradigm.* New York: Academic Press.

Caddick, B. (1974). *Threat to group distinctiveness and intergroup discrimination.* Unpublished manuscript, University of Bristol.

Campbell, D. T. (1965). Ethnocentric and other altruistic motives. In D. Levine (Ed.), *Nebraska Symposium on Motivation* (Vol. 13). Lincoln: University of Nebraska Press.

Cederblom, D., & Diers, C. J. (1970). Effects of race and strategy in the Prisoner's Dilemma. *Journal of Social Psychology, 81,* 275–276.

Deutsch, M. (1949). A theory of cooperation and competition. *Human Relations, 2,* 129–151.

Diab, L. (1970). A study of intragroup and intergroup relations among experimentally produced small groups. *Genetic Psychology Monographs, 82,* 49–82.

Dizard, J. E. (1970). Black identity, social class and Black power. *Psychiatry, 33,* 195–207.

Doise, W., Csepeli, G., Dann, H. D., Gouge, C., Larsen, K., & Ostell, A. (1972). An experimental investigation into the formation of intergroup representations. *European Journal of Social Psychology, 2,* 202–204.

Doise, W., & Sinclair, A. (1973). The categorisation process in intergroup relations. *European Journal of Social Psychology, 3,* 145–157.

Doise, W., & Weinberger, M. (1973). Représentations masculines dans differentes situations de rencontres mixtes. *Bulletin de Psychologie, 26,* 649–657.

Ferguson, C. K., & Kelley, H. H. (1964). Significant factors in overevaluation of own group's product. *Journal of Abnormal and Social Psychology, 69,* 223–228.

Festinger, L. (1954). A theory of social comparison processes. *Human Relations, 7,* 117–140.

Fiedler, F. E. (1967). The effect of inter-group competition on group member adjustment. *Personnel Psychology, 20*(1), 33–44.

Fishman, J., & Giles, H. (in press). Language in society. In H. Tajfel & C. Fraser (Eds.), *Introducing social psychology.* Harmondsworth, Middlesex: Penguin Books.

Friedman, N. (1969). Africa and the Afro-American: The changing Negro identity. *Psychiatry, 32*(2), 127–136.

Gerard, H. B., & Hoyt, M. F. (1974). Distinctiveness of social categorization and attitude toward ingroup members. *Journal of Personality and Social Psychology, 29,* 836–842.

Giles, H., & Powesland, P. F. (1976). *Speech style and social evaluation.* London: Academic Press, European Monographs in Social Psychology.

Gregor, A. J., & McPherson, D. A. (1966). Racial preference and ego identity among white and Bantu children in the Republic of South Africa. *Genetic Psychology Monographs, 73,* 217–254.

Harris, S., & Braun, J. R. (1971). Self-esteem and racial preference in Black children. *Proceedings of the 79th Annual Convention of the American Psychological Association, 6.*

Harvey, O. J. (1956). An experimental investigation of negative and positive relations between small groups through judgmental indices. *Sociometry, 14,* 201–209.

Hirschman, A. O. (1930). *Exit, voice and loyalty: Responses to decline in firms, organizations and states.* Cambridge, MA: Harvard University Press.

Hraba, J., & Grant, G. (1970). Black is beautiful: A re-examination of racial preference and identification. *Journal of Personality and Social Psychology, 16,* 398–402.

Hyman, H. H. (1942). The psychology of status. *Archives of Psychology, 269.*

Jahoda, G. (1961). *White man.* London: Oxford University Press for Institute of Race Relations.

Johnson, D. W. (1967). Use of role reversal in intergroup competition. *Journal of Personality and Social Psychology, 7,* 135–141.

Julian, J. W. (1968). The study of competition. In W. E. Vinacke (Ed.), *Readings in general psychology.* New York: American Book Co.

Kalin, R., & Marlowe, D. (1968). The effects of intergroup competition, personal drinking habits and frustration in intra-group cooperation. *Proceedings of the 76th Annual Convention of the American Psychological Association, 3,* 405–406.

Katz, I. (1964). Review of evidence relating to the effects of desegregation on the intellectual performance of Negroes. *American Psychologist, 19,* 381–399.

Kidder, L. H., & Stewart, V. M. (1975). *The psychology of intergroup relations.* New York: McGraw-Hill.

Klineberg, O., & Zavalloni, M. (1969). *Nationalism and tribalism among African students.* The Hague and Paris: Mouton.

Lefcourt, H., & Ladwig, G. (1965). The effect of reference group upon Negroes' task persistence in a biracial competitive game. *Journal of Personality and Social Psychology, 1,* 668–671.

Lemaine, G. (1966). Inegalité, comparaison et incomparabilité: esquisse d'une théorie de l'originalité sociale. *Bulletin de Psychologie, 252, 20,* 1–2, 1–9.

Milner, D. (1975). *Children and race.* Harmondsworth, Middlesex: Penguin.

Morland, J. K. (1969). Race awareness among American and Hong Kong Chinese children. *American Journal of Sociology, 75,* 360–374.

Oberschall, A. (1973). *Social conflict and social movements.* New York: Prentice-Hall.

Paige, J. M. (1970). Changing patterns of anti-White attitudes among Blacks. *Journal of Social Issues, 26,* 67–86.

Peabody, D. (1968). Group judgments in the Phillipines: Evaluative and descriptive aspects. *Journal of Personality and Social Psychology, 10,* 290–300.

Rabbie, J., & Wilkens, C. (1971). Intergroup competition and its effect on intra- and intergroup relations. *European Journal of Social Psychology, 1,* 215–234.

Rosenberg, M., & Simmons, R. G. (1972). *Black and White self-esteem: The urban school child.* The A. and C. Rose Monograph Series in Sociology, American Sociological Association.

Ross, G. F. (1975). *An experimental investigation of open and closed groups.* Unpublished manuscript, University of Bristol.

Runciman, W. G. (1966). *Relative deprivation and social justice.* London: Routledge and Kegan Paul.

Sherif, M. (1966). *In common predicament: Social psychology of intergroup conflict and cooperation.* Boston: Houghton Mifflin.

Sherif, M., Harvey, O. J.,White, B. J., Hood, W. R., & Sherif, C. W. (1961). *Intergroup cooperation and competition: The Robbers Cave experiment.* Norman, OK: University Book Exchange.

Sherif, M., & Sherif, C. W. (1953). *Groups in harmony and tension.* New York: Harper Brothers.

Tajfel, H. (1959). Quantitiative judgment in social perception. *British Journal of Psychology, 10,* 16–29.

Tajfel, H. (1970). Experiments in intergroup discrimination. *Scientific American, 223*(5), 96–102.

Tajfel, H. (1972a). Experiments in a vacuum. In J. Israel & H. Tajfel (Eds.), *The context of social psychology: A critical assessment.* London: Academic Press, European Monographs in Social Psychology.

Tajfel, H. (1972b). La catégorisation sociale. In S. Moscovici (Ed.), *Introduction à la psychologie sociale* (Vol. 1). Paris: Larousse.

Tajfel, H. (1974a). *Intergroup behavior, social comparison and social change.* Unpublished Katz-Newcomb Lectures, University of Michigan, Ann Arbor.

Tajfel, H. (1974b). Social identity and intergroup behaviour. *Social Science Information, 13*(2), 65–93.

Tajfel. H. (1975). The exit of social mobility and the voice of social change: Notes on the social psychology of intergroup relations. *Social Science Information, 14*(2), 101–118.

Tajfel, H. (1978). The psychological structure of intergroup relations. In H. Tajfel (Ed.), *Differentiation between social groups: Studies in the social psychology of intergroup relations.* London: Academic Press.

Tajfel, H., & Billig, M. (1974). Familiarity and categorization in intergroup behaviour. *Journal of Experimental Social Psychology, 10,* 159–170.

Tajfel, H., Billig, M. G., Bundy, R. P., & Flament, C. (1971). Social categorization and intergroup behaviour. *European Journal of Social Psychology, 1,* 149–178.

Thibaut, J. (1950). An experimental study of the cohesiveness of underprivileged groups. *Human Relations, 3,* 251–278.

Tomlinson, T. M. (Ed.). (1970). Contributing factors in Black politics. *Psychiatry, 33*(2), 137–281.

Turner, J. C. (1975). Social comparison and social identity: Some prospects for intergroup behaviour. *European Journal of Social Psychology, 5,* 5–34.

Turner, J. C. (1978a). Social categorization and social discrimination in the minimal group paradigm. In H. Tajfel (Ed.), *Differentiation between social groups: Studies in the social psychology of intergroup relations* (pp. 101–140). London: Academic Press.

Turner, J. C. (1978b). Social comparison, similarity and ingroup favouritism. In H. Tajfel (Ed.), *Differentiation between social groups: Studies in the social psychology of intergroup relations* (pp. 235–250). London: Academic Press.

Turner, J. C., & Brown, R. J. (1976). Social status, cognitive alternatives and intergroup relations. In H. Tajfel (Ed.), *Differentiation between social groups: Studies in the social psychology of intergroup relations.* European Monographs in Social Psychology. London: Academic Press.

Van der Berghe, P. C. (1967). *Race and racism.* New York: Wiley.

Vaughan, G. (1978). Social change and intergroup preferences in New Zealand. *European Journal of Social Psychology, 8,* 297–314.

Vinacke, W. E. (1964). Intra-group power differences, strategy, and decisions in inter-triad competition. *Sociometry, 27,* 25–40.

Wilson, W., & Miller, N. (1961). Shifts in evaluations of participants following intergroup competition. *Journal of Abnormal and Social Psychology, 63,* 428–431.

Intergroup Relations and Group Solidarity: Effects of Group Identification and Social Beliefs on Depersonalized Attraction

Michael A. Hogg and Sarah C. Hains • University of Queensland

An intergroup extension of M. A. Hogg's (1992, 1993) social attraction hypothesis is proposed. Netball teams were investigated with measures assessing the relationship between (a) objective status; (b) "social beliefs" about intergroup status, stability, legitimacy, and permeability; (c) group identification, self-categorization, and prototypicality; (d) interpersonal relations and similarity; (e) depersonalized social attraction; and (f) true personal attraction. As predicted, group-membership-based social attraction was directly influenced by self-categorization; indirectly influenced, through self-categorization, by intergroup status and stability beliefs; and uninfluenced by interpersonal relations. Social attraction (related to prototypicality and group identification) was relatively independent of personal attraction (related to similarity and interpersonal variables). Legitimacy, permeability, and the empirical co-occurence of social and personal attraction in cohesive groups are discussed.

Members of the same group generally tend to like one another. Indeed, positive intermember attitude is popularly considered to be a major feature of the solidarity that characterizes cohesive small groups, for example, sports teams, work units, street gangs. This view has its scientific expression in formal social psychological treatments of group cohesiveness and psychological group formation that assign interpersonal attraction a fundamental causal role (e.g., Festinger, Schachter, & Back, 1950; Lott & Lott, 1965; Lott, 1961; Schachter, Ellertson, McBride, & Gregory, 1951). Over the years, however, interpersonal-attraction-based models of cohesiveness such as this have been critically reviewed (e.g., Carron, 1982; Cartwright, 1968; Evans & Jarvis, 1980; Hogg,

1987, 1992, 1993; McGrath & Kravitz, 1982; Mudrack, 1989; Turner, 1984). Although there is little disagreement that positive interindividual attitude is an important feature of cohesive groups, critics have wondered whether the concept of interpersonal attraction alone is adequate to explain cohesiveness as a distinctly *group* phenomenon.

Recent research framed by an intergroup perspective and based on social identity theory (e.g., Hogg & Abrams, 1988; Tajfel & Turner, 1979; Turner, 1982) and self-categorization theory (Turner, 1985; Turner, Hogg, Oakes, Reicher, & Wetherell, 1987) provides an alternative perspective. Interpersonal relations, behaviors, and processes are conceptually distinguished from inter- and intragroup relations, behaviors, and processes.

The latter are associated with social identity: the definition and evaluation of self in terms of a self-inclusive social category. Social identity is constructed and has its effects through a process of self-categorization that accentuates attitudinal, emotional, and behavioral similarity to the group prototype—one's representation of the features that best define the in-group in the salient social comparative context (Oakes, Haslam, & Turner, in press). Self-categorization *depersonalizes* perception and conduct such that members, including oneself, are not processed as complex, multidimensional whole persons but rather as embodiments of the contextually salient perceived group prototype.

From this perspective, a cohesive group is one in which the process of self-categorization has produced, through depersonalization, a constellation of effects that includes intragroup conformity, intergroup differentiation, stereotypic perception, ethnocentrism, and positive intermember attitude. Positive intermember attitude produced thus is *social attraction* in which in-group members are liked not as unique individuals but as embodiments of the group—the more prototypical they are perceived to be, the more they are liked (Hogg, 1987, 1992, 1993). Depersonalized social attraction can be distinguished from *personal attraction* that is based on idiosyncratic preferences grounded in personal relationships. Personal attraction is independent of group-membership-based processes.

Direct tests of the depersonalized attraction hypothesis have revolved around demonstrating that social and personal attraction are relatively independent and that the former is based on perceived prototypicality and is influenced by group identification, whereas the latter is based on interpersonal similarity and is influenced by interpersonal relations, not group identification. For example, Hogg and Hardie (1992) manipulated the salience of group membership for four-person single-sex groups taking part in an autokinetic experiment and assessed self-categorization by means of conformity (i.e., the degree of intragroup convergence of estimates) across trials. They found, overall, that the pattern of attraction was more strongly influenced by perceived group prototypicality in groups that converged more, rather than less, sharply. That is, groups that converged most sharply had the most consensual pat-terns of liking and perceived prototypicality and were least likely to use interpersonal similarity as a basis for liking.

Stepping outside the laboratory, Hogg and Hardie (1991) conducted a questionnaire study of an Australian football team. They found that the perceived team-prototypicality of members was more strongly associated with liking and popularity under conditions in which the team was rendered salient than under conditions in which individuality and interpersonal relationships were rendered salient. Furthermore, members who themselves identified more strongly with the team used prototypicality as a stronger basis for attraction. Through the use of a very similar methodology, two further naturalistic studies, of established organizational groups and ad hoc student discussion groups, replicated these findings and found additional evidence that people who identify more strongly with the group are more favorably evaluated as group members but liked less on an interpersonal basis (Hogg, Cooper-Shaw, & Holzworth, 1993). Interpersonal similarity was found to be more strongly related to interpersonal than to group-based liking, and the relationship between interpersonal similarity and interpersonal liking was independent of group identification. In another study, in which a quasi-minimal group paradigm in the laboratory was adopted, the researchers were able to show that even similarity can be associated with social attraction, but only when it is similarity which is depersonalized in terms of the group prototype (Hogg, Hardie, & Reynolds, 1995).

Although the data from these five studies provide some support for the depersonalized attraction hypothesis (see reviews in Hogg, 1992, 1993), one important dimension is missing—the intergroup dimension. It is this aspect of social attraction which is the focus of the present study. Social identity theory and self-categorization theory are framed by, and were consciously developed within, an intergroup perspective on group membership in which the analysis of groups (of any size or character) is considered incomplete without a proper conceptual recognition of the fact that in-groups cannot exist without out-groups or non-in-groups (Tajfel, 1974, 1978; Tajfel & Turner, 1979; see Hogg & Abrams, 1988). A full analysis of what happens within groups requires consideration of intergroup relations (Hogg, 1996a, b).

One way in which intergroup relations may influence groups is by causing a perceptual polarization of the in-group prototype away from the out-group. From a self-categorization perspective, the prototype is defined as that in-group position which simultaneously minimizes intragroup differences and maximizes intergroup differences (e.g. Hogg, Turner, & Davidson, 1990; Turner, 1991; Turner et al., 1987; Turner & Oakes, 1989). The implication for depersonalized attraction is that as the intergroup context changes, intragroup patterns of social attraction also will change to follow changes in the prototype—a member who was particularly socially attractive in one context may now be less socially attractive because the prototype has shifted. For instance, one of the groups in Sherif's (1966) boys' camp studies changed its leader, and thus its leadership evaluations, as a consequence of discovering that there was a competing out-group (cf. Hains, Hogg, & Duck, 1995).

Another way in which the intergroup context may affect social attraction is through the actual or perceived nature of intergroup relations. Tajfel and Turner (1979) described how "social beliefs" concerning the relative status of the in-group, the stability and legitimacy of its status, and the permeability of intergroup boundaries (i.e., the possibility of "passing" from one group to the other) influence strategies of inter- and intragroup conduct as mediated largely by self-esteem concerns and identification with the in-group (also see Hogg & Abrams, 1988; Taylor & McKirnan, 1984; Taylor & Moghaddam, 1987). The main focus was on strategies that members of low-status groups might adopt to improve the relatively low self-esteem that such group memberships often entail. For instance, the perception of stable low status and permeable intergroup boundaries tends to encourage disidentification and attempts to pass as an individual into the higher status group. The perception of unstable, illegitimate low status with no possibility of passing can encourage strong in-group identification and intergroup conflict.

This aspect of social identity theory has spawned a great deal of research into social beliefs and intergroup strategies (e.g., Ellemers, 1991; van Knippenberg & Ellemers, 1993)—much of it is laboratory based (e.g., Ellemers, Wilke, & van Knippenberg, 1993; Wright, Taylor, & Moghaddam, 1990). Although laboratory experimentation has the advantage of control, it is a method that may be particularly problematic in this specific area of research because it may miss many aspects of real intergroup relations that need to be incorporated (cf. Lalonde, 1992). There is, however, a whole tradition of more naturalistic social-identity-related research into social beliefs and ethnolinguistic intergroup relations (e.g., Giles & Johnson, 1987; Sachdev & Bourhis, 1993) and into relations among smaller interactive groups, such as nurses in a hospital (e.g., Oaker & Brown, 1986; Skevington, 1981) or groups in an organization (e.g., Brown, 1978; Brown, Condor, Mathews, Wade, & Williams, 1986). It should be emphasised that social identity theory, including its treatment of intergroup beliefs and intergroup relations, is a general theory of the social group that is intended to be as relevant to the analysis of large-scale social categories, such as ethnic groups, as to small interactive groups, such as sports teams (cf. Hogg, 1996a, b; Hogg & Abrams. 1988; Turner, 1982, 1985).

This article is a preliminary investigation of how social beliefs concerning the status, stability, and legitimacy of intergroup relations, and the permeability of intergroup boundaries, affect depersonalized social attraction among group members. Although research on intergroup contact—the "contact hypothesis"—focuses on the effect of intergroup relations on intergroup attitudes and stereotypes (e.g., Hewstone & Brown, 1986; Johnston & Hewstone, 1990; Miller & Brewer, 1984; Norvell & Worchel, 1981), there are other studies that focus on the effects of intergroup relations on intragroup attraction—that is, "cohesiveness" as traditionally defined. The major finding is that although intergroup conflict usually enhances cohesion both in small interactive groups (e.g., Dion, 1979; Myers, 1962) and in large-scale social categories (e.g., Brewer & Campbell. 1976; LeVine & Campbell, 1972; cf. Sumner, 1906), it can sometimes produce intragroup disruption (e.g., Fisher, 1990; Stein, 1976). There also is evidence that intergroup conflict focuses affective attention on central group members with concomitant affective rejection of fringe members (e.g., Lauderdale, Smith-Cunnien, Parker, & Inverarity, 1984; Stagner & Efflal, 1982)—what Marques and his associates have called the *black sheep effect* (e.g., Marques, 1990; Marques & Paez, 1994; Marques & Yzerbyt, 1988; Marques, Yzerbyt, & Leyens, 1988).

Although some of these studies explored the

relationship between intergroup relations and intragroup attitude, they do not generally spell out the way in which social beliefs and self-categorization (social identification) mediate the link between intergroup relations and depersonalized attraction. The general hypothesis under examination in the present study is that objective intergroup status relations affect subjective social beliefs, which in turn influence identification (cf. Ellemers, 1991; van Knippenberg & Ellemers, 1993), and that it is identification that directly influences depersonalized social attraction. Interpersonal attraction will be largely independent of processes related specifically to group membership.

To access real intergroup status relations, we investigated female amateur netball teams playing in a competitive league—objective status derived from the teams' performance in the league (cf. Lalonde, 1992). (Netball is a variant of basketball that is played by women and is very popular in Europe and Australia—seven-person teams score goals by throwing a ball into their opponents' net.) Because they are small interactive groups, such teams are relevant to the small-group perspective of traditional group cohesiveness research, and they are appropriate for comparison of social and personal attraction processes. Furthermore, they make comparison with previous studies of social attraction relatively straightforward.

The players completed a questionnaire designed to measure (a) in-group identification, (b) social beliefs (team *status* as a function of team performance in the league, *stability* of the team's status position, *legitimacy* of the basis of the team's status, and *permeability* of the boundaries between own and other teams in the league), (c) interpersonal relations and personal attraction (ratings and sociometric choice measures), and (d) prototypicality and depersonalized social attraction (ratings and sociometric choice measures, cf. Hogg et al., 1993; Hogg & Hardie, 1991). The questionnaire allowed us to investigate the impact of (a) objective intergroup status relations on (b) sociometric choice relations concerning prototypicality, social attraction, personal attraction, and interpersonal similarity, as mediated by (c) subjective perceptions of status, stability, permeability, and legitimacy; (d) self-prototypicality, self-categorization/group identification, prototype clarity; and (e) interpersonal relations.

We predicted that (Hypothesis 1 [H1]) deper-sonalized attraction would be directly related to self-categorization (group identification) and prototypicality, and (Hypothesis 2 [H2]) personal attraction would be relatively unrelated to self-categorization processes but related more to interpersonal similarity. Predictions for the role of intergroup relations in social attraction derive from the application of social identity theory to the specific circumstances of competitive sports teams. Such teams exist to win, and so objective status is of paramount importance and will be directly reflected in subjective status. Furthermore, relative to less successful teams, teams that feel that they are more successful (higher subjective status) may also construct a belief that their status is relatively more stable and more legitimate and that there is no reason to change teams (possibly reflected in lower perceived permeability). The general hypothesis (Hypothesis 3 [H3]) was that (a) higher objective status would be associated with higher subjective status, which (b) is associated with greater perceived stability and legitimacy and lower perceived permeability. However, we did not expect (Hypothesis 4 [H4]) subjective beliefs concerning status, stability, legitimacy and permeability to be directly associated with social attraction, but rather (Hypothesis 5 [H5]) that social beliefs (principally status, but perhaps less strongly the correlated beliefs in stability, legitimacy, and permeability) would (a) directly affect self-categorization/social identification and would (b) indirectly affect social attraction by means of identification.

Method

Participants

Participants were 74 female netball players (aged 14–29 years, $M = 16.5$ years) from 11 teams in amateur netball leagues in Brisbane, Australia (population 1.4 million). The 11 teams had 95 players (from 7 to 16 on each team, $M = 8.6$). Nineteen were absent when the questionnaires were distributed, and 2 declined to participate—hence we sampled 78% of the membership, with only a 3% refusal rate. We obtained between 50% and 100% ($M = 78\%$) of members of each of the 11 teams (samples ranged from 4 to 12 players per team, $M = 6.8$). Participants had been playing with their teams for 1–7 seasons ($M = 1.8$).

Procedure

The study was described to team coaches who granted us permission to administer the questionnaires. Data were collected during evening practice sessions near the end of a 12- to 15-week season (excluding quarterfinals, semifinals, and finals). At this point in the season all teams had played between 11 and 13 games and so had established a more or less stable status based on their pattern of wins or losses in the competition. Furthermore, all teams had 1 or 2 games left to play, and some—those going forward to the quarterfinals, semifinals, and finals—would have 2 or more games to play. All teams were, therefore, able to comment on their past and future performance. Objective measures of the teams' performance were obtained at a later date from the netball league organizers, in the form of a complete record of the number of goals scored by each team in each match played during the season prior to the study.

A female experimenter attended the practice sessions and administered the questionnaires. The study was introduced as an investigation of the behavior of people in groups, in which we would be asking participants a number of questions about their perceptions of their netball team. It was explained that participation was voluntary and that anonymity and confidentiality would be ensured by a secret ballot procedure in which anonymous questionnaires were sealed in an envelope which, together with a signed consent form, was sealed in a second envelope. It was explained that the questionnaire and the consent form would be separated once the data were collated. Participants sat apart from one another to complete the questionnaires in silence, calling the experimenter over to deal with queries. After completing the questionnaires and placing them in the envelopes, the study was declared over. and participants were debriefed and thanked for their participation.

Measures

Participants completed four questionnaires (total of 34 questions), mainly employing a 9-point response format with 9 signifying a great deal of the property being measured. Some questions had slightly different response formats, including open-ended ones. The questionnaires were clipped together in one of two set sequences, which were distributed randomly so that half the participants received each sequence. All participants received the team perceptions questionnaire first and the team prototype questionnaire last, but half completed the personal relations questionnaire second and the group relations questionnaire third and half vice versa.

Team perceptions questionnaire. This questionnaire measured demographic variables, performance variables, and subjective perceptions of intergroup status, stability, legitimacy, and permeability. After asking participants their age and how many seasons they had played with their team, the remaining 12 questions monitored subjective perceptions of status, stability, legitimacy, and permeability. *Status* was measured with two questions that asked participants to place their team relative to the other seven teams in the competition "in terms of playing ability and success" ("1st" through "7th") and to indicate how good they considered their team "to be at playing netball" (1 = *very poor*, 9 = *very good*). There were two questions that measured *stability*: "How consistent has your team's performance been" over the season so far (1 = *very inconsistent*, 9 = *very consistent*) and "How well do you feel your team will do in the remaining games" relative to performance so far (1 = *much worse*, 5 = *same*, 9 = *much better*). *Legitimacy* was measured with two items: One general item asked participants to indicate how much they thought the outcome of the games so far had been a fair reflection of their team's "ability and skill at playing netball" (1 = *not very much*, 9 = *very much*), and the other item had participants rate on 9-point scales how important a contribution they felt each of good/ bad luck, umpire bias, good/poor coaching, own team ability, and other team ability had made to their team's performance over the season. Finally, there were five 9-point scale items that measured *permeability*: Participants indicated how positively changing teams would be viewed by their own team and by players in general, how easy it would be to become accepted by the new team, how easy it would be to change teams for next season, and how likely it was that they would change teams after the season.

Personal relations questionnaire. The four questions in this questionnaire focused on interpersonal relationships. To make interpersonal relationships salient, the questionnaire was preceded by the following directions:

This section measures your feelings about yourself and your personal relationships. . . . Take a minute or so to think about yourself and the other people in your team, not as team members but as separate, unique individuals—think about the people with whom you might be close friends. Also, think about how you, personally, are a unique individual with particular likes and dislikes.

The first question monitored *interpersonal relations* by asking participants to indicate the percentage of their friends who were members of the team, members of a competing team, and not involved with netball. The second question had participants list the five people in the team whom they would choose to join them for "a social activity . . . (such as) going away on holiday, attending a movie or concert—something (they) would like to do with a personal friend." This measured sociometric choice based on *personal attraction*, and the order in which the five names were written down was assumed to reflect a rank ordering in terms of decreasing personal attraction. In the next question participants were asked to indicate on 9-point scales how much they felt they liked each of these five people as friends. The final question monitored sociometric choice based on *interpersonal similarity*—participants listed the five team members who they thought were most similar to themselves "in terms of their general attitudes, likes and dislikes."

Group relations questionnaire. The 10 questions in this questionnaire focused on group-membership-based perceptions and feelings about the team and its members. To make group membership salient, the questionnaire was preceded by the following directions:

This section measures your feelings about your team as a whole. . . . Take a minute or so to think about your team. Think about the things you like (and don't like) about your team. Think about how your team functions. When you have formed an impression of your team as a whole, turn the page and begin.

The first nine questions measured *group identification* on 9-point scales. The first four items were adapted from previous social attraction studies (e.g., Hogg et al., 1993; Hogg & Hardie, 1991, 1992), and the other five questions were adapted from Brown et al.'s (1986) group identification scale. Participants were asked: (1) how similar they felt they were to the team as a whole in terms of general attitudes and beliefs, (2) how much they like the team as a whole, (3) how well they felt they fit into the team, (4) how cohesive they felt the team was, (5) how important the team was to them, (6) how much they identified with the team, (7) how strong their ties were with the team, (8) how glad they were to be members of the team, and (9) how much they saw themselves as belonging to the team. The final question measured sociometric choice based on *social attraction* by asking participants to list five team members they would choose to recruit if they were starting a new team.

Team prototype questionnaire. The seven questions in this questionnaire were designed to monitor perceptions of the team prototype. To make the team salient, the questionnaire was preceded by the following directions:

This section is designed to measure a particular aspect of your team: your team's "identity." Your team's "identity" is a cluster of things about your team which describes how your team operates and how your team is different from other teams. Think about your team in terms of how you play netball, how your team behaves on and off the court, and particular things which are unique to your team and which serve to differentiate your team from other teams in the competition. This picture is what we would call your team's identity.

The first question was open-ended and required participants to write down what they considered to be their team's identity, this served to make their specific perceptions of the team's identity salient by eliciting the subjective prototype. All other questions related to this prototype. Three questions measured *prototype clarity* by asking participants how easy they found it to generate the prototype, how confident they were that it was an accurate description, and what percentage of fellow members would agree with their prototype. One question measured *self-prototypicality* by asking participants how typical they considered themselves to be of the team prototype. One question measured sociometric choice based on prototypicality by having participants list the five members who they felt best embody the team's prototype. The final question asked participants to indicate on 9-point scales how much they liked each of these five people "as team members"—this is a measure of overall social attraction for the five most prototypical members of the team.

Results

Team Prototypes

Responses to the open-ended question that asked participants to describe their team prototypes were inspected by two coders (instructed to reach agreement) to establish (a) the nature of the prototypes, (b) their valence, and (c) the degree of intermember agreement (agreement was scored on a 1–5 scale). Prototypes varied between teams mainly as a function of the unique mix in emphasis of two general dimensions: (a) social functions, reflected in terms relating to sociability, getting along well together, having fun, and being supportive and friendly, and (b) task functions, reflected in terms such as *cooperative, playing as a team, functioning as a cohesive unit, working well together, and taking the game seriously*. Prototypes were generally very positive (six teams) or moderately positive (four teams), but one team had a moderately negative prototype, and they were generally consensual (scores of 4 or 5), except in the case of two teams with a mid-range score of 3 and one with a low 2. These analyses confirm the existence of relatively consensual, positive team prototypes that differentiate to some extent between teams.

Computed Measures

We calculated objective measures of team performance from the teams' performance records. *Objective status* was computed by dividing the number of goals scored by the team by the total number of goals scored by both teams during the match and then dividing this by the total number of matches that the team played—thus 0 indicates that the in-group never scored any of the goals (very low status), 0.5 indicates that the in-group scored half the goals, and 1.0 indicates that the in-group scored all the goals (very high status). *Objective stability* was computed by calculating the standard deviation across the season of the proportion of goals scored by the in-group (low standard deviations indicate a more stable, and high standard deviations a more variable, performance).

Raw sociometric measures comprise sociometric choice of five team members based on (a) personal attraction (PA), (b) interpersonal similarity (SIM), (c) social attraction (SA), and (d) prototypicality (PROT). We computed a number of new variables from these measures. For each

participant on each measure we calculated the average rank received from the other members of the group—if a participant had not been ranked by another member, then she was allocated a rank of 6 for that member. This produced four received rankings per participant to reflect the participant's consensual "popularity" in the group (1 = all team members ranked the participant first, and 6 = no team members nominated the participant at all—these scales were all reflexed so that 1 meant *unpopular* and 6 meant *popular*).

For each participant we calculated all six possible bivariate correlations (Spearman's rho) between responses on the four sociometric choice measures; an appropriate rank was assigned to members not nominated in one or another list in any given bivariate correlation. These correlations measure associations between social attraction and prototypicality (SA.PROT), social attraction and similarity (SA.SIM), personal attraction and prototypicality (PA.PROT), personal attraction and similarity (PA.SIM), social attraction and personal attraction (SA.PA), and similarity and prototypicality (SIM.PROT). Inspection of distributions contraindicated transformation of these variables.

The five liking ratings of the five people chosen as personally attractive were averaged to form a mean personal attraction measure, and the five liking ratings of the five people chosen as most prototypical also were averaged to form a measure of mean prototype-based liking (or social attraction).

Data Reduction to Produce Focal Scales

In addition to these computed scales, we combined a number of other measures in various ways to produce the other focal scales. An initial check for normality of distributions of all variables revealed that none required transformation. The two subjective status measures (placing of the team in the competition [reflexed and rescaled so that 1 indicated low status and 9 indicated high status] and playing ability) were significantly correlated, $r(72) = .71$, $p < .001$: A single measure was computed by taking the mean. The two subjective stability measures (performance consistency and future performance relative to past performance [rescaled so that 1 indicates low consistency and 9 indicates high consistency]) were significantly correlated, $r(73) = .30$, $p < .01$: A single measure was computed by taking the mean.

The two legitimacy measures are actually six items (fairness of the competition, importance to the outcome of good/bad luck, umpire bias, good/poor coaching, own team ability, and other-team ability). Initial factor analyses led to the exclusion of the measures of other-team ability and fairness of the competition as they were split between indistinct factors. A final analysis of the remaining four variables produced two factors (see Table 6.1 for details of factors associated with data reduction). We used means for the two high loading measures in each factor to produce a measure of perceived legitimacy of the status differential based on (a) the importance of external factors and (b) the importance of internal factors.

We factor analyzed the five permeability measures (how positively the changing of teams would be viewed by one's own team and by players in general, how easy it would be to become accepted by the new team, how easy it would be to change teams for the next season, and how likely it was that they would change teams after the season). The measure of general ease of changing teams

was split between indistinct factors and was dropped. A final analysis of the remaining four variables produced two factors. One factor loaded on favorability of in-group and people in general's reactions to changing teams—it measures whether one "*ought* to pass." The other factor loaded on the intention to change teams at the end of the season and the belief that out-group acceptance would be easy—it measures whether one "*can* pass." Means were calculated to produce these two measures of permeability: "ought" and "can."

We factor analyzed the nine questions measuring group identification and used the mean of the nine measures as our measure of group identification. We also factor analyzed the three questions measuring prototype clarity to produce a single factor and took the mean as our measure of prototype clarity. The final two subjective measures were single variables: interpersonal relations (the percentage of their friends that participants indicated were members of their team) and self-prototypicality (how typical participants considered themselves to be of the team prototype).

Table 6.1. Factor Analyses for Focal Scales of Legitimacy, Permeability, Identification, and Prototype Clarity

Dependent measure	Legitimacy		Permeability		Identification	Prototype Clarity
	External	Internal	Ought	Can		
Luck	.84	—				
Bias	.78	—				
Ability	—	.82				
Coach	—	.75				
Favorable			.90	—		
Reactions			.86	—		
Intention			—	.82		
Acceptance			—	.77		
Glad					.90	
Ties					.88	
Important					.87	
Liking					.87	
Similar					.86	
Belong					.85	
Cohesive					.82	
Fit in					.78	
Identify					.77	
Agree						.85
Confident						.83
Ease						.73
Eigen value	1.53	1.18	1.79	1.09	6.42	1.95
Percentage variance accounted for	38	29	45	27	71	65

Note. Orthogonal varimax rotation, rotated factor loading cutoff = .25. See text for full labeling of constituent variables. External and internal legitimacy, and ought and can, were uncorrelated: *r*s = .10 and .21, respectively.

A final check of all new computed variables revealed that none required transformation for subsequent analyses.

Objective Performance Differences Among the 11 Teams

Examination of the objective measures of status and stability revealed that three teams were doing rather badly (.29, .40, and .47: i.e., scoring about 39% of goals)—these can be classified as low-status teams, five teams were doing rather averagely (.50, .51, .51, .52, and .54: scoring about 52% of goals)–these can be classified as medium-status teams, and three teams were doing rather well (.58, .61, and .68: scoring about 62% of goals)—these can be classified as high-status teams. It was difficult to identify clearly more or less objectively stable teams. In any case, objective status and stability were statistically independent: $r(11) = .33$, two-tailed $p = .32$.

In addition, the bivariate correlations (Pearson's r, $N = 11$, two-tailed test, $\alpha = .01$) of objective status and stability with team means for the 6 subjective measures of intergroup relations, the 4 identity type measures, and the 12 sociometric measures revealed no significant correlations for objective stability. However, objective status was positively correlated with subjective status ($r = .94$, $p < .001$) and with the tendency for participants to attribute their performance to internal factors ($r = .80$, $p < .01$).

We performed 2 (order of presentation of the personal relations and group relations questionnaire) × 11(team) analyses of variance (ANOVAs) on all 22 focal dependent variables to reveal no significant main or interaction effects for order of presentation. This factor was excluded for all subsequent analyses.

Comparison of Low-, Medium-, and High-Status Teams

The classification of teams as low, medium, or high status on the basis of their objective performance produced a hierarchically nested design (Winer, 1971) in which participants are nested within teams within levels of status. There is thus potential nonindependence of observations due to grouping of participants in teams (Anderson & Ager, 1978; Kenny & Judd, 1986; Kenny & La Voie,

1985; Koomen, 1982). A typical solution to this problem is to test the significance of the intraclass correlations across all the groups (Kenny & Judd, 1986; Kenny & La Voie, 1985) and, if the correlations are significant, to use a hierarchically nested ANOVA procedure (Anderson & Ager 1978; Hopkins, 1982).

Because we intended there to be differences among low-, medium-, and high-status teams, we were concerned only to establish that observations within each condition were generally independent of team membership. Within each condition, we calculated intraclass correlations for each of the 22 focal measures. Only 3 (of a possible 66) were significant ($\alpha = .01$): There was significantly less variance within than between teams on status in the low-status condition and on identification and social attraction popularity in the medium-status condition. The absence of systematic overall effects of team membership is further evinced by a one-way multivariate analysis of variance (MANOVA) performed on the 22 focal variables to investigate differences among all 11 teams. This revealed no significant overall effect: $F(\text{Pillais})(220, 340) = 1.18$, $p = .086$. Because the classification of teams as low, medium, or high objective status would be expected to produce an apparent effect due to team (but actually due to status condition) on the measure of subjective status, we repeated the MANOVA with subjective status excluded: $F(\text{Pillais})(210, 360) = 1.12$, $p = .181$, adjusted $R^2 = .05$. On the basis of these investigations we decided that it would be possible, though with caution, to treat participants as independent observations for the purpose of comparison among the three levels of status.

A one-way MANOVA on the 22 focal variables revealed a significant effect for status level, $F(\text{Pillais})(44, 68) = 1.77$, $p < .01$, which emerged by one-way ANOVA on 8 of the 18 measures on which effects might be expected—no effects would be expected on the four popularity measures as high popularity for one participant would necessarily be associated with low popularity for another in the same team. (Table 6.2 shows cell means, F statistics, and Newman-Keuls contrasts; popularity measures are not shown.) As predicted under H3 (see beginning of article for statement of hypotheses), the perceived status, stability, and importance of internal factors determining team status increased significantly from low-, to medium-, to high-status teams, and members of

Table 6.2. Means and F Statistics From One-Way (Status) Analysis of Variance (ANOVA) on Focal Measures

| | Cell means (N = 74) | | | |
| | Low (n = 17) | Medium (n = 36) | High (n = 21) | F (df = 2, 71) |
Measure				
Status	4.02$_a$	7.17$_b$	8.45$_c$	87.31***
Stability	4.34$_a$	5.88$_b$	7.21$_c$	14.73***
Legitimacy Internal	6.25$_a$	7.22$_b$	8.05$_c$	7.33**
Legitimacy External	4.50	5.33	4.95	1.30
Permeability Ought	5.19$_b$	3.69$_a$	3.79$_a$	5.17**
Permeability Can	4.56	3.95	3.81	0.97
Identification	6.30$_a$	7.12$_b$	7.38$_b$	4.39*
Clarity	6.56	5.87	6.52	1.40
Interpersonal relations	15.24	24.24	20.00	0.99
Self-prototypicality	6.76	6.67	6.89	0.38
SA.PROT	0.57$_b$***	0.26**	0.19$_{ab}$	3.24*
SA.SIM	0.28	0.44***	0.38$_a$***	1.17
PA.PROT	0.18	0.22*	0.16	0.06
PA.SIM	0.48**	0.61***	0.44***	0.89
SA.PA	0.24$_a$	0.49^b***	0.67^b***	5.66**
SIM.PROT	0.17	0.27*	0.21	0.12
Mean SA	7.04$_a$	7.88$_b$	7.78$_b$	3.73*
Mean PA	6.70	7.46	7.17	2.00

Note. Means can vary between 1 and 9, except for sociometric correlations (−1–+1) and interpersonal relations (0–100). In some cases, because of missing data, n is reduced and df_es are reduced to values in the range 63–70. Means in a significant ANOVA not sharing a superscript differ significantly by Newman–Keuls. One-sample t tests (two-tailed) were performed on cell means for the six intercorrelations of social attraction, personal attraction, similarity, and prototypicality to establish whether the correlations were significantly different to 0. SA = social attraction; PROT = prototypicality; SIM = interpersonal similarity; PA = personal attraction.

*p < .05. **p < .01. ***p < .001.

low-status teams felt it would be more acceptable to change teams ("ought to pass") than did members of medium- or high-status teams. As predicted under H5, these status effects on social beliefs were associated with stronger identification and greater social attraction in medium- and high-status teams than in low-status teams. These last two effects, perhaps in conjunction with the weaker relationship between social and personal attraction (SA.PA) in low- than in medium- or high-status teams provides some support for H1. Finally, social attraction was more strongly associated with prototypicality (SA.PROT) in low- than in medium-status teams—high-status teams did not differ from either.

Overall, aside from the unusual effect on SA.PROT, which was only marginally significant (p = .048), the general pattern of results is that, relative to members of low-status teams, members of high-status teams felt that their team had stable high status that was legitimate, as it was due to internal factors, and that intergroup permeability was low, and they ought not to try to pass. These

people identified with their team, liked prototypical members, and chose similar people as socially and personally attractive. Members of medium-status teams mainly behaved like members of high-status teams but did not behave like members of low-status teams.

To examine H1 and H2, we performed two-way, 3 (status) × 2 (a repeated measure) ANOVAs comparing (a) SA.PROT with SA.SIM, (b) PA.PROT with PA.SIM, (c) SA.PROT with PA.PROT, (d) SA.SIM with PA.SIM, and (e) mean social attraction with mean personal attraction. A number of main and interaction effects for the repeated measure emerged. Social attraction was more strongly based on prototypicality than on similarity in the low-status groups (Ms = .58 and .22), but there was no significant difference in the medium- (Ms = .26 and .42) and high-status groups (.19 and .38), F(2, 66) = 4.89, p < .01. Prototypicality was more strongly associated with social attraction than with personal attraction (Ms = .32 and .19), F(1, 66) = 8.05, p < .01, but the significant interaction with status, F(2, 66) = 4.20, p < .05, reveals that this was the case only in the low-status groups (Ms = .58 and .18)—the relevant means for SA.PROT and PA.PROT were .26 and .21 in medium-status groups and .19 and .16 in high-status groups. These findings are broadly consistent with H1. Personal attraction was significantly more strongly associated with similarity (M = .50) than with prototypicality (M = .19), $F(1, 67)$ = 13.02, $p <$ .01, and similarity was more strongly associated with personal attraction than with social attraction (Ms = .51 and .37), $F(1, 68)$ = 6.30, $p < .05$. These are broadly consistent with H2. Finally, participants liked prototypical members (mean social attraction) more than interpersonal friends (mean personal attraction: (Ms = 7.61 and 7.18), $F(1, 62)$ = 5.91, $p < .05$. They also gave higher liking ratings, irrespective of whether the target was a friend or a prototypical member, in the high- and medium-status groups (Ms = 7.50 and 7.65) than in the low-status group (M = 6.81), $F(2, 62)$ = 4.25, $p < .05$, but, as reported above, this was significant only on the mean social attraction variable.

Correlations Among Subjective Measures

We performed a series of correlations: Pearson's r, N = 65–74 depending on missing data, two-tailed test with α = .01. The six subjective measures of intergroup relations were intercorrelated to reveal three significant correlations: As predicted under H3b, the higher the perceived status of the in-group, the more stable that status was thought to be, $r(71)$ = .47, $p < .001$, the less it was felt that one ought to change teams, $r(70)$ = −.34, $p < .01$, and the greater the internal attribution for performance, $r(72)$ = .45, $p < .001$. The three measures of self-typicality, prototype clarity, and group identification were significantly intercorrelated, $rs(70$ and $71)$ = .44, .60, and .61, $p < .001$. The measure of interpersonal relations correlated only with group identification, $r(73)$ = .32, $p < .01$—the more friends people had on the team, the more they identified with the team, and vice versa.

Various combinations of the 12 sociometric type measures were intercorrelated to reveal that the four popularity measures were strongly correlated (r = .60–.75, $p < .001$), and liking for prototypical members was correlated with liking for interpersonal friends, $r(65)$ = .40, $p < .01$. The correlational measures were generally correlated (r = .31– .63), and so it is notable that, as predicted under

H1 and H2, the similarity and prototypicality bases of social attraction were unrelated (SA.SIM was *not* correlated with SA.PROT, $r[69]$ = .13, $p \geq .28$), and personal attraction based on similarity was unrelated to social attraction based on prototypicality (PA.SIM was *not* correlated with SA.PROT, $r[69]$ = .03, $p \geq .81$).

Table 6.3 displays a 10×12 correlation matrix showing the relationship between each of the 10 intergroup relations and group-membership type variables on the one hand and each of the 12 sociometric type measures on the other. Participants who identified with the team and saw themselves as highly prototypical were overselected by other team members on the basis of social and personal attraction, similarity, and prototypicality. The most socially popular members were also those who had the clearest understanding of the group prototype and who attributed the team's performance externally. External attributors were also the most prototypically popular team members. Participants who had the most friends on the team and who felt the team's status was stable tended to have a strong correlation between their social and their personal sociometric choice of fellow members. High identifiers and those who felt there was a stable status relationship tended to like prototypical members more than those who scored low on these variables. Finally, high identifiers liked personal friends and based social attraction on similarity.

Linear Structural Equation Modeling

We used linear structural equation modeling (using Bentler's [1992] EQS program) to test the hypothesized relationship among social identification, social belief structures, interpersonal relations, social attraction, and personal attraction. This method allows the simultaneous investigation of direct and indirect "causal" pathways among measured and latent variables (cf. Stacy, Newcomb, & Bentler, 1991; Stacy, Widaman, & Marlatt, 1990). The alternative method for simultaneously testing all five experimental hypotheses would have been a large number of cumbersome hierarchical regressions of different combinations of measured variables.

We excluded four cases because of excessive missing data, and other missing data (representing less than 1% of observations) were replaced by the sample mean for that variable. This left 70

Table 6.3. Correlations Between 10 Predictor Variables (Intergroup Relations and Group Membership) and 12 Outcome Variables (Sociometric Type Measures)

Predictor variable	Outcome variable											
	Sim pop	SA pop	PA pop	PROT pop	SA. PROT	SA. SIM	PA. PROT	PA. SIM	SA. PA	SIM. PROT	Mean SA	Mean PA
Status	.00	.01	.00	−.08	−.22	.18	.07	.12	.31	.09	.29	.11
Stability	.19	.12	.10	.09	−.10	.20	.00	.20	.42***	.06	.32**	.24
Legitimacy Internal	.00	.00	.16	−.06	−.28	.01	−.05	.17	.05	−.01	−.03	−.01
Legitimacy External	.24	.34**	.26	.31**	.05	.0l	.19	.00	.05	.18	.02	.28
Permeability Ought	−.15	−.07	−.15	.05	.18	.07	.00	.00	−.01	.11	−.21	−.05
Permeability Can	−.08	.02	.02	−.09	.14	−.04	−.16	.06	−.09	−.23	.07	.08
Identify	.34**	.36**	.39***	.28	−.06	.36**	.00	.16	.28	.02	.54***	.42***
Clarity	.26	.31**	.27	.30	.09	.04	.01	−.09	.04	−.01	.23	.21
Interpersonal relations	.07	.13	.11	.11	.16	.13	.25	.11	.32**	.22	.26	.17
Self-proto-typicality	.34**	.43***	.44***	.39***	.02	.09	.15	.11	.10	.06	.12	.19

Note. Pearson's *r*, two-tailed test, $\alpha = .01$, $N = 65-73$, depending on missing data. SIM = interpersonal similarity; SA = social attraction; PA = personal attraction; PROT = prototypicality; pop = popularity.
**$p < .01$.   ***$p < .001$.

cases for the analyses, which is rather a small sample for structural equation modeling. As such, it was advisable to include as few variables and paths as possible in the structural model. In addition, small sample size constrains the choice of parameter estimation method. The generalized least squares (GLS) method incorporating the Satorra–Bentler scaling correction (i.e., METHOD = GLS,ROBUST in the EQS program) has been shown to be the "most adequate test statistic for evaluating model fit when sample size is small" (Hu & Bentler, 1995, p. 80; also see Chou, Bentler, & Satorra, 1991; Hu, Bentler & Kano, 1992).

The first step was to investigate the measurement model (see Table 6.4 for means, skewness, and kurtosis of variables in reported EQS analyses): This refers to the extent to which the four possible latent variables of group identification, subjective status, permeability, and legitimacy were accurate representations of the measured variables of (a) self-typicality, prototype clarity, and group identification; (b) subjective status and stability; (c) ought and can; and (d) internal and external legitimacy, respectively. The intercorrelation of these variables, reported above, suggests that identification and status may well be latent variables but that permeability and legitimacy are not. Structural analysis of the measure-

ment model confirmed this. The full model had very poor fit to the data, and only after the four measured variables of permeability and legitimacy had been excluded was a satisfactory fit achieved. Using the Satorra–Bentler scaled generalized least squares (GLS,ROBUST) method (normalized multivariate kurtosis = 1.65), we found that the fit of the model ($\chi^2[6] = 12.35$, $p = .055$—for EQS,

Table 6.4. Means, Skewness, and Kurtosis for Variables Reported in EQS Analyses

Variable	*M*	Skewness	Kurtosis
Status	6.80	−1.02	0.64
Stability	5.91	−0.15	−0.58
Self-prototypicality	6.79	−0.35	−0.54
Clarity	6.31	−0.09	−0.46
Identification	7.05	−1.09	1.63
Permeability Ought	4.09	0.32	−0.34
Legitimacy Internal	7.24	−1.19	1.62
Interpersonal relations	20.54	1.25	1.37
Mean SA	7.64	−1.51	4.71
SA.PROT	0.32	−0.48	−0.91
SA popularity	3.21	−0.14	−0.44
PROT popularity	3.11	−0.09	−0.65

Note. Means ($N = 70$) can vary between 1 and 9, except for SA.PROT (−1–+1), interpersonal relations (1–100), and SA and PA popularity (1–6). SA = social attraction; PA = personal attraction; PROT = prototypicality.

the smaller the chi square, the better the fit, with significant fit conventionally being associated with $p > .01$) was superior to the null model (in which all parameters are assumed to equal zero; $\chi^2[10] = 643.37$, $p < .001$): χ^2 difference $[4] = 631.02$, $p < .001$ (see Figure 6.1). Both the non-normed fit index (NNFI) and the comparative fit index (CFI) exceeded the recommended criterion of .90. In this and subsequent structural analyses we were careful to check that parameter estimates were in or-

der and that no special problems were encountered during optimization.

The proposed structural model is one in which social beliefs affect identification, which affects social attraction, but social attraction is not affected directly by social beliefs or at all by interpersonal relations. The focal dependent variable is depersonalized social attraction, which can be represented by (a) a factor incorporating the two measures of social attraction and prototypical

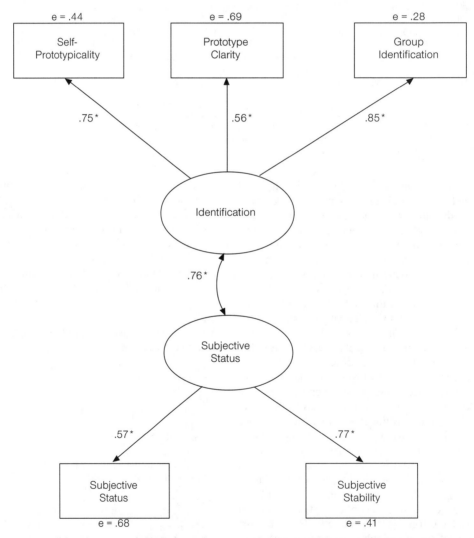

FIGURE 6.1 ▪ Measurement model (EQS) of identification and subjective status factors. Circles indicate latent variables (factors), and boxes indicate measured variables. Arrows indicate paths, and bidirectional curved paths indicate covariation. Standardized path coefficients marked with an asterisk are significant by directional Z test. Standardized residual variances are represented by e: $R^2 = 1 - e$.

popularity, (b) the measure of the correlation of social attraction and prototypicality (SA.PROT), or (c) the measure of mean social attraction. Although the measurement model failed to identify a single permeability or a single legitimacy factor, we included the individual variables of ought and internal attribution in the structural model to see if these aspects of permeability and legitimacy (assumed to covary with one another and with the latent variable of subjective status) had any influence on social attraction.

We used the Satorra–Bender scaled GLS method to test the path model associated with each of the three indexes of depersonalized social attraction in turn. The clearest finding emerged when the popularity factor was the focal measure of depersonalized attraction. The fit of the proposed model, $\chi^2(28) = 41.35$, $p = .050$, was significant and superior to the null model, $\chi^2 (45) = 1,716.33$, $p < .001$: χ^2 difference $(17) = 1,674.98$, $p < .001$. Both the NNFI and the CFI exceeded .90, and normalized multivariate kurtosis was a low 0.39. Figure 6.2 shows the standardized path coefficients and standardized residual variances for the model. Depersonalized attraction was significantly influenced (one-tailed test) by identification alone. Subjective status influenced identification and had a near-significant indirect influence on depersonalized attraction: standardized coefficient = .18, $Z = 1.51$ ($Z = 1.64$ for $p < .05$). Ought and internal attribution had no significant effect on identification or depersonalized attraction. It is notable that both variables that make up the depersonalized attraction factor were indirectly influenced ($p < .05$) by identification: standardized coefficients of .34 and .25 for social attraction popularity and prototypical popularity, respectively.

Structural equations associated with the other two measures of social attraction produced a similar pattern of paths; however, none were significant for the measure of the correlation of social attraction and prototypicality. Where the focal measure was mean social attraction, normalized multivariate kurtosis was 3.30, and the fit of the proposed model, although not statistically significant by conventional criteria, $\chi^2(21) = 41.88$, $p = .005$, was superior to the null model, $\chi^2(36) = 1,371.04$, $p < .001$: χ^2 difference $(15) = 1,329.16$, $p < .001$. Both the NNFI and the CFI exceeded .90. Mean social attraction was significantly influenced by identification. The structural equation with standardized path coefficients is: mean so-

cial attraction (standardized residual variance, e = .67) = identification (.41) + ought (.03) + internal attribution(–.13) + interpersonal relations (.18). Identification was significantly influenced by subjective status only: identification (e = .70) = subjective status (.54) + ought (–.18) + internal attribution (–.21). The indirect effect of subjective status on mean social attraction was significant ($p < .05$): standardized coefficient = .22.

Discussion

Members of higher status, well-performing teams correctly perceived their teams to be of higher status (H3a) but also perceived, incorrectly, that their status was stable. They also felt that their status was legitimate, as it was due to internal factors, and that intergroup permeability was low and they ought not to try to pass (H3b). These people identified with their team, liked prototypical members (social attraction), and chose similar people as socially and personally attractive. Path analyses revealed, as predicted under H1 and H2, that prototype-based social attraction was significantly influenced by group identification variables (identification, self-prototypicality, prototype clarity) but not by interpersonal relations (proportion of friends on the team). Although social beliefs concerning status, stability, permeability, and legitimacy were intercorrelated to some extent, only the latent variable of status/stability had any effect on identification or social attraction—it directly increased identification (replicating findings by Ellemers and colleagues, e.g., van Knippenberg & Ellemers, 1993) and indirectly increased social attraction by means of identification (H4 and H5).

These findings quite clearly implicate social identification, not interpersonal relations, in the production of prototype-based social attraction. Social beliefs have an indirect influence, through their direct effect on identification. Factor analysis revealed that the variable of group identification, based on nine measures, was distinct and clearly defined. As expected, this variable was also clearly linked with perceptions of the clarity of the group prototype and the prototypicality of self—together these represented the latent variable of identification for the path analysis.

The measures of subjective status and stability represented two clear scales, which were closely correlated. However, the measures of legitimacy

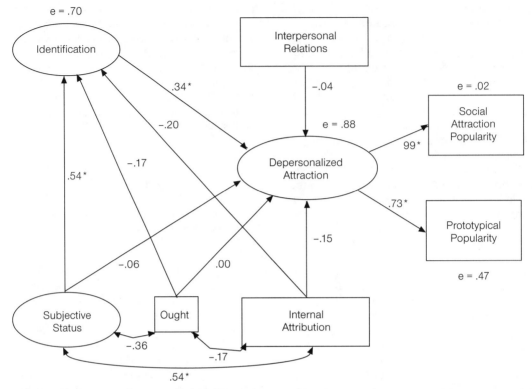

FIGURE 6.2 ■ Structural equation model (EQS) of influences on depersonalized attraction. Circles indicate latent variables (factors), and boxes indicate measured variables. Arrows indicate paths, and bidirectional curved paths indicate covariation. Standardized path coefficients marked with an asterisk are significant by directional Z text. Standardized residual variances (errors and disturbances) are represented by e: $R^2 = 1 - e$.

and permeability were less clear. Only after exclusion of certain measures were we able to obtain clear factors representing these variables, and then two factors emerged for both variables. Legitimacy was reflected in internal attributions and in external attributions; only the former was associated with any other effects. Permeability was reflected in beliefs about whether one "ought" to pass and beliefs about whether one "can" pass; only "ought" was associated with other effects.

As foreshadowed earlier in the article, one reason why these legitimacy and permeability aspects of social beliefs had no significant effect on identification is that the nature of intergroup relations in this particular context (formal, rule-governed competition) might stress status and stability concerns to the detriment of legitimacy and permeability concerns. Although players differed in their perceptions of the degree of legitimacy and *im*permeability of the status hierarchy, they did not

actually perceive the hierarchy to be *il*legitimate or permeable—they generally agreed that status was due to internal, not external, factors; that one should not try to pass; and that in fact one could not pass. Against this background, variation in perceived legitimacy and permeability may have been less important relative to status and stability. Legitimacy and permeability may have a more significant role in less formally regulated intergroup contexts such as relations among professions, classes, ethnic groups, or even ad hoc laboratory groups. It is quite consistent with the original notion of "social beliefs" (Tajfel, 1974) that contextual factors influence the relative importance of different components. Another possibility, which finds support in research by Ellemers and colleagues (e.g. Ellemers, van Knippenberg, de Vries, & Wilke, 1988; Ellemers et al., 1993; van Knippenberg & Ellemers, 1993), is that perceived legitimacy and permeability are not directly linearly related to identification; permeability increases identification in higher status groups but reduces it in lower status groups, and the effects of legitimacy on identification are a function not only of status but also of perceived stability.

An examination of team prototypes revealed that they differed among teams, mainly in the admixture of the two dimensions of social functions (sociability, etc.) and task functions (competition-oriented behavior)—there is robust evidence in social psychology for a distinction between social and task aspects of groups (e.g., Anderson, 1975; Carron, 1982). In addition, team prototypes were generally positive, and they were shared among members within a given team, thus acting as consensual, positively valued, group-membership-based, self-referent standards (cf. norms or stereotypes; Tajfel, 1981; Turner, 1991). Inspection of differences in prototypes as a function of objective team status revealed, not surprisingly, that prototype valence was generally associated with status: Members of higher status teams had more positive prototypes than did members of lower status teams. There also was a tendency for the highest status teams to emphasize task functions more than social functions, whereas the lowest status teams did the opposite. Both the highest and the lowest status teams tended to have the most consensual prototypes, with lower consensus among members of intermediate teams.

There was evidence from the sociometric choice data that, as expected under H1 and H2, social and personal attraction are distinct phenomena, with the former based on prototypicality and the latter on interpersonal similarity: (a) prototypicality was more strongly associated with social than with personal attraction, (b) similarity was more strongly associated with personal than with social attraction, and (c) personal attraction was more strongly associated with similarity than with prototypicality. Furthermore, (a) variation in the strength of the social attraction–prototypicality correlation was independent of variation in the social attraction–similarity correlation, and (b) variation in the personal attraction–similarity correlation was independent of variation in the social attraction–prototypicality attraction (Hogg et al., 1993, 1995; Hogg & Hardie, 1991, 1992).

The four popularity measures were correlated, indicating that people who were consensually chosen by the group as being socially attractive and prototypical also were everyone's friend and were considered similar to self. Ideally, we would have liked social attraction popularity and prototypical popularity to be correlated but to be uncorrelated with personal attraction and similarity. However, the reality of small interactive groups that endure over time is that personal attraction and social attraction, although separately generated, will tend to co-occur—people tend to choose their friends from those with whom they interact and in turn may join groups of which their friends are already members (cf. Berscheid, 1985; Festinger et al., 1950; Lott & Lott, 1965). Against a background of relatively strong entitativity and group identification (i.e., high identification [$M = 7.01$], high prototype clarity [$M = 6.21$], high self-prototypicality [$M = 6.75$], and high social attraction [$M = 7.66$]), social and personal attraction were indeed correlated, and the relationship between social and personal sociometric choice was stronger among people with more friends on the team. Given this fact, it may be all the more remarkable that we were able to find evidence for the proposed distinction between depersonalized social attraction and personalized personal attraction.

Finally, given this general point, it is not surprising that the popularity measures were significantly associated with identification and self-prototypicality and that personal attraction was correlated with identification. What is important is that, despite this empirical linkage between social and personal attraction, there also is an identification dynamic that differentiates between these two forms of interindividual attitude.

It is puzzling, however, that identification was correlated with social attraction based on similarity. One possibility is that in such cohesive groups, perceptions of similarity were depersonalized, at least to some degree. This is certainly consistent with findings from a previous study of ours (Hogg et al., 1995) in which group identification (in highly salient groups) was found to depersonalize perceptions of interindividual similarity (i.e., similarity was assessed in terms of prototypicality). Social attraction was found to be based on this depersonalized similarity rather than true inter*personal* similarity.

The present study extends previous research on cohesiveness as depersonalized social attraction by introducing the role of subjective intergroup relations (social beliefs). It is a study of naturally occurring small groups and so suffers from some of the limitations of such research—for example, small sample size ($N = 74$), interdependence of observations, and reduced experimental control. We have strived to recognize such factors by adopting a conservative significance level ($\alpha = .01$) where relevant and by carefully checking interdependence before deciding to treat individual participants as independent observations. A clear agenda for future research would be to replicate the present study with different naturally occurring groups (in which the relative significance of status, stability, legitimacy, and permeability beliefs may be different) and with a much larger sample (particularly for replication of the structural equation model), or to test the hypotheses in a controlled laboratory experiment. One strength of a laboratory study would be that it might allow a more direct investigation of causal links among focal constructs. However, there is a strong sense in which the study of the impact of social beliefs on identification and social attraction might be weakened by retiring to the laboratory, as the social beliefs of interest reside in enduring intergroup relations among real groups. Some of the practical and scientific limitations of investigating real interacting groups may be outweighed by conceptual advantages (Hogg & Moreland, 1993; Levine & Moreland, 1990; Moreland, Hogg, & Hains, 1994).

In conclusion, the present study consolidates previous findings that social and personal attraction are relatively distinct phenomena: The former is depersonalized liking based on prototypicality and produced by self-categorization, whereas the latter is personalized liking based on interpersonal similarities and idiosyncratic preferences. Intergroup relations influence social attraction, not directly, but by means of subjective perceptions of the nature of intergroup status relations that influence group identification. It is group identification which is the direct influence on group-membership-based intragroup attraction. Interpersonal relations do not directly affect social attraction. These findings support a self-categorization model of group cohesiveness (Hogg, 1987, 1992, 1993) and represent an important incorporation of intergroup relations.

Future research might consider in more detail the complex interrelationship among perceived status, stability, legitimacy, and permeability, and its effect on social attraction and group identification. The present study, however, suggests that such social belief factors are likely to influence social attraction not directly but instead through their impact on self-categorization.

REFERENCES

Anderson, A. B. (1975). Combined effects of interpersonal attraction and goal-path clarity on the cohesiveness of task-oriented groups. *Journal of Personality and Social Psychology, 31,* 68–75.

Anderson, L. R., & Ager, J. W. (1978). Analysis of variance in small groups. *Personality and Social Psychology Bulletin, 4,* 341–345.

Bentler, P. M. (1992). *EQS: Structural equations program manual.* Los Angeles: BMDP Statistical Software.

Berscheid, E. (1985). Interpersonal attraction. In G. Lindzey & E. Aronson (Eds.), *Handbook of social psychology* (3rd ed., Vol. 2, pp. 413–484). New York: Random House.

Brewer, M. B., & Campbell, D. T. (1976). *Ethnocentrism and intergroup attitudes: East African evidence.* New York: Sage.

Brown, R. J. (1978). Divided we fall: An analysis of relations between sections of a factory work-force. In H. Tajfel (Ed.), *Differentiation between social groups* (pp. 395–429). London: Academic Press.

Brown, R. J., Condor, S., Mathews, A., Wade. G., & Williams, J. (1986). Explaining intergroup differentiation in an industrial organization. *Journal of Occupational Psychology, 59,* 273–286.

Carron, A. V. (1982). Cohesiveness in sports groups: Interpretations and considerations. *Journal of Sport Psychology, 4,* 123–138.

Cartwright, D. (1968). The nature of group cohesiveness. In D. Cartwright & A. Zander (Eds.), *Group dynamics: Research and theory* (3rd ed., pp. 91–109). London: Tavistock.

Chou, C. P., Bender, R. M., & Satorra, A. (1991). Scaled test statistics and robust standard errors for nonnormal data in covariance structure analysis: A Monte Carlo study. *British Journal of Mathematical and Statistical Psychology, 44,* 347–357.

Dion, K. L. (1979). Intergroup conflict and intragroup cohesiveness. In W G. Austin & S. Worchel (Eds.), *The social psychology of intergroup relations* (pp. 211–224). Monterey, CA: Brooks/Cole.

Ellemers, N. (1991). *Identity management strategies.* Unpublished doctoral thesis, Rijksuniversiteit Groningen, Germany.

Ellemers, N., Knippenberg, A. van, de Vries, N., & Wilke, H. (1988). Social identification and permeability of group boundaries. *European Journal of Social Psychology, 18,* 497–513.

Ellemers, N., Wilke, H., & Knippenberg, A. van (1993). Effects of the legitimacy of low group or individual status on individual and collective identity enhancement strategies. *Journal of Personality and Social Psychology, 64,* 766–778.

Evans, N. J., & Jarvis, R. A. (1980). Group cohesion: A review and reevaluation. *Small Group Behavior, 11,* 359–370.

Festinger, L., Schachter, S., & Back, K. (1950). *Social pressures in informal groups.* New York: Harper & Row.

Fisher, R. J. (1990). *The social psychology of intergroup and international conflict resolution.* New York: Springer-Verlag.

Giles, H., & Johnson, P. (1987). Ethnolinguistic identity theory: A social psychological approach to language maintenance. *International Journal of the Sociology of Language, 68,* 256–269.

Hains, S. C., Hogg, M. A., & Duck, J. M. (1995). *Self-categorisation theory and leadership: Effects of group prototypicality and leader stereotypes.* Manuscript submitted for publication.

Hewstone, M. R. C., & Brown, R. J. (Eds.). (1986). *Contact and conflict in intergroup encounters.* Oxford, UK: Basil Blackwell.

Hogg, M. A. (1987). Social identity and group cohesiveness. In J. C. Turner, M. A. Hogg, P. J. Oaken, S. D. Reicher, & M. S. Wetherell, *Rediscovering the social group: A self-categorization theory* (pp. 89–116). Oxford, UK: Basil Blackwell.

Hogg, M.A. (1992). T*he social psychology of group cohesiveness: From attraction to social identity.* London: Harvester Wheatsheaf, and New York: New York University Press.

Hogg, M. A. (1993). Group cohesiveness: A critical review and some new directions. *European Review of Social Psychology, 4,* 85–111.

Hogg, M. A. (1996a). Intragroup processes, group structure and social identity. In W. P. Robinson (Ed.), *Social groups and identity: Developing the legacy of Henri Tajfel* (pp. 65–93). Oxford, UK: Butterworth-Heinemann.

Hogg, M. A. (1996b). Social identity, self-categorization and the small group. In E. H. Witte & J. H. Davis (Eds.), *Understanding group behavior (Vol. 2): Small group processes and interpersonal relations* (pp. 227–253). Hillsdale, NJ: Erlbaum.

Hogg, M. A.. & Abrams, D. (1988). *Social identifications: A social psychology of intergroup relations and group processes.* London: Routledge.

Hogg, M. A., Cooper-Shaw, L., & Holzworth, D. W. (1993). Group prototypicality and depersonalized attraction in small interactive groups. *Personality and Social Psychology Bulletin, 19,* 452–465.

Hogg, M. A., & Hardie, E. A. (1991). Social attraction, personal attraction, and self-categorization: A field study. *Personality and Social Psychology Bulletin, 17,* 175–180.

Hogg, M. A., & Hardie, E. A. (1992). Prototypicality, conformity and depersonalized attraction: A self-categorization analysis of group cohesiveness. *British Journal of Social Psychology, 31,* 41–56.

Hogg, M. A., Hardie, E. A., & Reynolds, K. (1995). Prototypical similarity, self-categorization, and depersonalized attraction: A perspective on group cohesiveness. *European Journal of Social Psychology, 25,* 159–177.

Hogg, M. A., & Moreland, R. L. (1993). Studying social processes in small groups. *British Journal of Social Psychology, 31,* 107–110.

Hogg, M. A., Turner, J. C., & Davidson, B. (1990). Polarized norms and social frames of reference: A test of the self-categorization theory of group polarization. *Basic and Applied Social Psychology, 11,* 77–100.

Hopkins, K. D. (1982). The unit of analysis: Group means versus individual observations. *American Educational Research Journal, 19,* 5–18.

Hu, L.-t., & Bentler, P. M. (1995). Evaluating model fit. In R. H. Hoyle (Ed.), *Structural equation modeling: Concepts, issues and applications* (pp. 76–99). Thousand Oaks, CA: Sage.

Hu, L.-t., Bentler, P. M., & Kano, Y. (1992). Can test statistics in covariance structure analysis be trusted? *Psychological Bulletin, 111,* 351–362.

Johnston, L., & Hewstone, M. R. C. (1990). Intergroup contact: Social identity and social cognition. In D. Abrams & M. A. Hogg (Eds.), *Social identity theory: Constructive and critical advances* (pp. 185–210). London: Harvester Wheatsheaf, and New York: Springer-Verlag.

Kenny, D. A., & Judd, C. M. (1986). Consequences of violating the independence assumption in analysis of variance. *Psychological Bulletin, 99,* 422–431.

Kenny, D. A., & La Voie, L. (1985). Separating individual and group effects. *Journal of Personality and Social Psychology, 48,* 339–348.

Knippenberg, A. van., & Ellemers, N. (1993). Strategies in intergroup relations, In M. A. Hogg & D. Abrams (Eds.), *Group motivation: Social psychological perspectives* (pp. 17–32). London: Harvester Wheatsheaf.

Koomen, W. (1982). A note on the analysis of group data. *European Journal of Social Psychology, 12,* 297–300.

Lalonde, R. N. (1992). The dynamics of group differentiation in the face of defeat. *Personality and Social Psychology Bulletin, 18,* 336–342.

Lauderdale, P., Smith-Cunnien, P., Parker, J., & Inverarity, J. (1984). External threat and the definition of deviance. *Journal of Personality and Social Psychology, 46,* 1058–1068.

Levine, J. M., & Moreland, R. L. (1990). Progress in small group research. *Annual Review of Psychology, 41,* 585–634.

Le Vine, R. A., & Campbell, D. T. (1972). *Ethnocentrism: Theories of conflict, ethnic attitudes and group behavior.* New York: Wiley.

Lott, A. J., & Lott, B. E. (1965). Group cohesiveness as interpersonal attraction. *Psychological Bulletin, 64,* 259–309.

Lott, B. E. (1961). Group cohesiveness: A learning phenomenon. *Journal of Social Psychology, 55,* 275–286.

Marques, J. M. (1990). The black-sheep effect: Out-group homogeneity in social comparison settings. In D. Abrams & M. A. Hogg (Eds.), *Social identity theory: Constructive and critical advances* (pp. 131–151). London: Harvester Wheatsheaf, and New York: Springer-Verlag.

Marques, J. M., & Paez, D. (1994). The "black sheep effect": Social categorization, rejection of ingroup deviates and perception of group variability. *European Review of Social Psychology, 5,* 37–68.

Marques, J. M., & Yzerbyt, V. Y. (1988). The black sheep effect: Judgmental extremity towards ingroup members in inter-and infra-group situations. *European Journal of Social Psychology, 18,* 287–292.

Marques, J. M., Yzerbyt, V. Y., & Leyens, J.R. (1988). The black sheep effect: Extremity of judgements towards in-group members as a function of group identification. *European Journal of Social Psychology, 18,* 1–16.

McGrath, J. E., & Kravitz, D. A. (1982). Group research. *Annual Review of Psychology, 33,* 195–230.

Miller, N., & Brewer, M. B. (1984). *Groups in contact: The psychology of desegregation.* New York: Academic Press.

Moreland, R. L., Hogg, M. A., & Hains, S. C. (1994). Back to the future: Social psychological research on groups. *Journal of Experimental Social Psychology, 30,* 527–555.

Mudrack, P. E. (1989). Defining group cohesiveness: A legacy of confusion. *Small Group Behavior, 10,* 37–49.

Myers, A. (1962). Team competition, success, and the adjustment of group members. *Journal of Abnormal and Social*

Psychology, 65, 325–332.

Norvell, N., & Worchel, S. (1981). A reexamination of the relation between equal status contact and intergroup attraction. *Journal of Personality and Social Psychology, 41,* 902–908.

Oaker, G., & Brown, R. J. (1986). Intergroup relations in a hospital setting: A further test of social identity theory. *Human Relations, 39,* 767–778.

Oakes, P. J., Haslam, S. A., & Turner, J. C. (in press). A consideration of prototypicality from the perspective of self-categorization theory. In J. C. Deschamps, J. F. Morales, & H. Paicheler (Eds.), *Current perspectives on social identity and social categorization.* Barcelona: Anthropos.

Sachdev, I., & Bourhis, R. (1993). Ethnolinguistic vitality: Some motivational and cognitive considerations. In M. A. Hogg & D. Abrams (Eds.), *Group motivation: Social psychological perspectives* (pp. 33–51). London: Harvester Wheatsheaf.

Schachter, S., Ellertson, N., McBride, D., & Gregory, D. (1951). An experimental study of cohesiveness and productivity. *Human Relations, 4,* 229–238.

Sherif, M. (1966). *In common predicament: Social psychology of intergroup conflict and cooperation.* Boston: Houghton-Mifflin.

Skevington, S. (1981). Intergroup relations and nursing. *European Journal of Social Psychology, 11,* 43–59.

Stacy, A. W., Newcomb, M. D., & Bentler, P. M. (1991). Personality, problem drinking, and drunk driving: Mediating, moderating, and direct-effect models. *Journal of Personality and Social Psychology, 60,* 795–811.

Stacy, A. W., Widaman, K. R., & Marlatt, G. A. (1990). Expectancy models of alcohol use. *Journal of Personality and Social Psychology, 58,* 918–928.

Stagner, R., & Efflal, B. (1982). Internal union dynamics during a strike: A quasi-experimental study. *Journal of Applied Psychology 67,* 37–44.

Stein, A. A. (1976). Conflict and cohesion: A review of the literature. *Journal of Conflict Resolution, 10,* 143–172.

Sumner, W. G. (1906). *Folkways.* Boston: Ginn.

Tajfel, H. (1974). *Intergroup behaviour: Social comparison and social change.* Unpublished Katz-Newcomb lectures, University of Michigan.

Tajfel, H. (Ed.). (1978). *Differentiation between social groups.* London: Academic Press.

Tajfel, H. (1981). Social stereotypes and social groups. In J. C. Turner & H. Giles (Eds.). *Intergroup behaviour* (pp. 144–167). Oxford, England: Basil Blackwell.

Tajfel, H., & Turner, J. C. (1979). An integrative theory of intergroup conflict. In W. G. Austin & S. Worchel (Eds.), *The social psychology of intergroup relations* (pp. 33–47). Monterey, CA: Brooks/Cole.

Taylor, D. M., & McKirnan, D. J. (1984). A five-stage model of intergroup relations. *British Journal of Social Psychology, 23,* 291–300.

Taylor, D. M., & Moghaddam, F. M. (1987). *Theories of intergroup relations.* New York: Praeger.

Turner, J. C. (1982). Towards a cognitive redefinition of the social group. In H. Tajfel (Ed.), *Social identity and intergroup relations* (pp. 15–40). Cambridge, England: Cambridge University Press.

Turner, J. C. (1984). Social identification and psychological group formation. In H. Tajfel (Ed.), *The social dimension: European developments in social psychology* (Vol. 2, pp. 518–538). Cambridge, England: Cambridge University Press.

Turner, J. C. (1985). Social categorization and the self-concept: A social cognitive theory of group behavior. In E. J. Lawler (Ed.), *Advances in group processes: Theory and research* (Vol. 2, pp. 77–121). Greenwich, CT: JAI Press.

Turner, J. C. (1991). *Social influence.* Milton Keynes, UK: Open University Press.

Turner, J. C., Hogg, M. A., Oakes, P. J., Reicher, S. D., & Wetherell, M. S. (1987). *Rediscovering the social group: A self-categorization theory.* Oxford, UK: Basil Blackwell.

Turner, J. C., & Oakes, P. J. (1989). Self-categorization theory and social influence. In P. B. Paulus (Ed.), *The psychology of group influence* (2nd ed., pp. 233–275). Hillsdale, NJ: Erlbaum.

Winer, B. J. (1971). *Statistical principles in experimental design* (2nd ed.). New York: McGraw-Hill.

Wright, S. C., Taylor, D. M., & Moghaddam, F. M. (1990). Responding to membership in a disadvantaged group: From acceptance to collective protest. *Journal of Personality and Social Psychology, 58,* 994–1003.

Intergroup Attitudes and Explanations

Social categorization is the foundation of intergroup relations. Relations between groups can only occur if the social world can be categorized into separate groups. In the previous section, we discussed the effects of social categorization on self-conception, perception, attitudes, feelings, and behavior. Not only does social categorization, via self-categorization, contextually transform people into group members, but it also causes people to perceive outgroup members stereotypically and homogeneously. The process may be cognitively quite automatic or may be influenced by strategic or social perceptual factors (e.g., Devine, 1989; Simon & Brown, 1987).

Whereas social cognition researchers have tended to focus on the automaticity of stereotyping, intergroup relations researchers have tended to try to integrate automatic processes with characteristics of the social context, in order to gain a more fine-grained analysis of intergroup perceptions and explanations. An important aim has often been to articulate cognitive, social, and societal levels of analysis (Doise, 1986).

One premise of intergroup relations researchers is that intergroup attitudes are shared perceptions that members of one group have of members of another group; and that the key feature of stereotypes is precisely this sharedness. Our first reading is by Henri Tajfel (1981), then at Bristol University, who emphasized the social functions of stereotypes. Tajfel believed that basic cognitive processes like categorization have a clear and important role in stereotyping, for example, in producing a perceptual accentuation of differences between and similarities within groups. However, stereotypes are also social products in the sense that their form and expression are intricately tied to the dynamics of social identity and intergroup relations in a socio-historical context. Stereotypes develop and persist to the extent that they provide an explanation and justification for social discontinuities and social conduct. Tajfel argued that stereotypes are beliefs, or belief systems, that serve social functions. They provide a consensual interpretative and evaluative framework that locates people in intergroup context.

The relationship between internalized attitudes and social life as they impact on intergroup behavior is explored further by John Dovidio, at Colgate University, and Samuel Gaertner, at the University of Delaware. Beginning with the premise that social norms and conventions may impact the form and the expression of shared intergroup attitudes, Dovidio and Gaertner (1996) explore what they call modern forms of prejudice. They argue that the absence of florid "redneck" racism should not be taken as evidence that people are not racist. Social history lays down deep-seated prejudices, but contemporary liberal democratic norms may suppress their expression. Under these "modern" conditions, intergroup prejudices, fears, and suspicions conflict with egalitarian social norms. The resolution of this conflict produces a range of modern forms of prejudice that includes intergroup avoidance, denial of disadvantage, opposition to preferential treatment, and so forth. The article reproduced here discusses modern forms of racial prejudice, primarily in the United States, in the context of people's attitudes towards affirmative action.

Our final reading in this section is by Thomas Pettigrew (1979), then at Harvard University. This is a classic work on what Pettigrew called the "ultimate attribution error." Attribution theory in social psychology argues that people need to construct an explanation of their world, and that in order to do this they attribute causes to people's behavior. In doing this, people are not very scientific. They tend to make a fundamental attribution error in over-attributing people's behavior to underlying dispositions and in underestimating the role of situational constraints. In contrast, people tend to do the opposite for their own behavior. Pettigrew argued that in intergroup contexts this same effect takes a different form, which he called the ultimate attribution error. People tend to attribute negative acts performed by an outgroup member to underlying dispositions, often with genetic correlates; whereas the same act performed by an ingroup member is externally attributed to chance or situational factors. The attribution pattern is reversed for positive acts performed by ingroup and outgroup members. Pettigrew believed that the ultimate attribution error helps maintain ethnocentric attitudes.

Discussion Questions

1. To what extent can we say prejudice exists even if people do not express it?
2. Under what conditions does prejudice result in discrimination?
3. How do people justify their prejudices?
4. Are stereotypes normal?

Suggested Readings

Brauer, M., Wasel, W., & Niedenthal, P. (2000). Implicit and explicit components of prejudice. *Review of General Psychology, 4,* 79–101. Recent discussion and study of the
multifaceted and many-tiered nature of prejudiced attitudes—depending on what you
measure you get evidence for the presence or absence of prejudice.

Dovidio, J. F., & Gaertner, S. L. (1998). On the nature of contemporary prejudice: The
causes, consequences, and challenges of aversive racism. In J. L. Eberhardt & S. T.
Fiske (Eds.), *Confronting prejudice: The problem and the response* (pp. 3–32). Thousand Oaks, CA: Sage. Extensive discussion of modern forms of prejudice.

Glick, P., & Fiske, S. T. (1996). The ambivalent sexism inventory: Differentiating hostile
and benevolent sexism. *Journal of Personality and Social Psychology, 70,* 491–512.
Discussion of modern forms of sexism, and the development of a scale to measure modern sexism.

Hewstone, M., & Ward, C. (1985). Ethnocentrism and causal attribution in Southeast Asia.
Journal of Personality and Social Psychology, 48, 614–623. An empirical study and
extension of the ultimate attribution error.

Monteith, M. (1996). Contemporary forms of prejudice-related conflict: In search of a
nutshell. *Personality and Social Psychology Bulletin, 22,* 461–473. An empirical study
of the relationship among different dimensions of people's racial attitudes and feelings.

Oakes, P. J., Haslam, S. H., & Turner, J. C. (1994). *Stereotyping and social reality.* Blackwell,
UK: Oxford. A detailed analysis, from a social identity perspective, of the relationship
between social cognitive processes and the nature of social reality in stereotyping.

Social Stereotypes and Social Groups

Henri Tajfel • University of Bristol

Introduction: Stereotypes and Social Stereotypes

The *Oxford English Dictionary*, in its definition of "stereotypes," draws a tight circle in admitting only that they "Make {things} unchangeable, impart monotonous regularity . . . fix in all details, formalize. . . ." This static formality of the semi-officially recognized use of the term contrasts nicely with the awareness of its social significance shown by the late Oliver Stallybrass, co-editor of *The Fontana Dictionary of Modern Thought* (1977). He wrote in it that a stereotype is

an over-simplified mental image of (usually) some category of person, institution or event which is *shared*, in essential features, by large numbers of people. The categories may be broad (Jews, gentiles, white men, black men) or narrow (women's libbers, Daughters of the American Revolution). . . . Stereotypes are commonly, but not necessarily, accompanied by prejudice, i.e., by a favourable or unfavourable predisposition towards any member of the category in question. (p. 601, my emphasis)

This definition will do for our purposes. By using the term "shared" as a central part of his statement, Stallybrass went further than many *social* psychologists have done in encompassing the social psychological significance of stereotypes and of the processes on which their functioning is based. He was not unique in doing so. The important social functions of unfavourable stereotypes were at the forefront of the discussions held at the Edinburgh International Television Festival in August 1978. Some extracts of the statements

made at the Festival by various playwrights, producers and executives, and reported in *The Times* (30 August, 1978), are worth quoting:*

> . . . stereotyping should be seen as a part of the comic method by which we tried to diminish what we feared: in the case of contemporary Britain, not only the Irish but also Afro-Asians and Arabs. (John Bowen)

> It was appalling . . . to find programmes like the *Black and White Minstrel Show* or *Mind Your Language* being broadcast in a multiracial society under strain, when what they did was reinforce stereotypes of black and brown people as being lovable but ridiculous. (Brian Winston)

> A socially damaging caricature becomes a stereotype. (Fay Weldon)

> . . . a distinction [needs to be made] between the creation of a dramatic 'type', which meant achieving the subjectivity of another person or group, and the creation of stereotypes, which were essentially weapons in the struggle for power constantly being waged in society. (John McGrath)

It is clear from all this that some of the people whose jobs put them in daily contact with the creation and diffusion of social stereotypes are keenly aware of the variety of social functions served by these stereotypes. After some years of relative neglect, we have also recently seen a revival of interest amongst social psychologists in the study of stereotypes. Their approach stands, however, in

*These statements are not verbatim reproductions of what was said at the Festival, but quotations from the account of the proceedings as published by *The Times*.

stark contrast to the awareness of the social dimension of the problems shown by the practitioners of the media. This will become clear from our second series of quotations:

> Illusory correlation refers to an erroneous inference about the relationship between two categories of events. [The hypothesis] suggested that the differential perception of majority and minority groups would result *solely* from the cognitive mechanisms involved in processing information about stimulus events that differ in their frequencies of co-occurrence. (Hamilton and Gifford, 1976, p. 392, my emphasis)

> . . . there is no theoretical or empirical reason to assume that forming generalizations about ethnic groups is radically different from forming generalizations about other categories of objects. (Taylor et al., 1978, p. 778)

> The present writers believe that stereotypes are not a unique structure or process but exist and operate in the same manner that cognitive processes in general influence an individual when he deals with any aspect of his environment. (Taylor and Aboud, 1973, p. 330)

> . . . the group's impression may depend on the way in which data on individuals are organized in memory. . . . Specifically, the proportion of extreme individuals in a group was retrospectively overestimated; this was true for both physical stimuli (height) and social stimuli (criminal acts). (Rothbart et al., 1978, p. 237)

All this is a consistent echo of earlier views:

> These judgemental effects of categorization {of physical objects} are probable fairly general. . . . It is likely that the same is happening in the use of more abstract social judgements which are implicitly quantitative, such as, for example, those concerning the relative frequency of crimes in various social groups. . . . (Tajfel, 1957, pp. 202–203)

Or:

> One of the aims of the investigations reported here was to show that evidence for the essential unity of judgement phenomena, social or physical, can be slowly accumulated and that . . . it is possible to attempt an understanding of seemingly varied phenomena in terms of the same general judgement principles. (Tajfel and Wilkes, 1963, p. 114)

These quotations do not stress the social functions of stereotypes but consider them as aspects of general cognitive processes, products of the basic ways in which individuals perceive and interpret their environment. An important point must be stressed at this juncture. It is emphatically not the argument of this chapter that general cognitive processes can be neglected in the study of the formation, diffusion and functioning of social stereotypes. On the contrary, as will be seen later, we fully agree with the views expressed in the above quotations that the understanding of the cognitive "mechanics" of stereotypes is essential for their full and adequate analysis. The question that arises is whether such a study is all that is needed—a view which, as we have seen, seems to be adopted in some of the recent (and also earlier) work on the subject.

Two definitions of stereotypes were provided at the beginning of this chapter, the "formal" one from the *Oxford English Dictionary*, and the more "social" one formulated by Stallybrass (1977). The difference between the two illustrates (albeit rather crudely) the difficulties which are bound to arise in an approach to the study of stereotypes which remains exclusively or primarily cognitive. "Stereotypes" are certain generalizations reached by individuals. They derive in large measure from, or are an instance of, the general cognitive process of categorizing. The main function of this process is to simplify or systematize, for purposes of cognitive and behavioural adaptation, the abundance and complexity of the information received from its environment by the human organism (see Bruner, 1957; Bruner and Klein, 1960; Bruner and Potter, 1964; Tajfel, 1959, 1972b, 1978d). But such stereotypes can become *social* only when they are *shared* by large numbers of people within social groups or entities—the sharing implying a process of effective diffusion. There are at least two important questions which cannot be answered if we confine our interest to the cognitive functions alone. The first concerns an analysis of the functions that stereotypes serve for a social group within which they are widely diffused. The second question concerns the nature of the links between these social or group functions of stereotypes and their common adoption by large numbers of people who share a social affiliation. It is the asking of these two questions which defines the difference between the study of stereotypes *tout court* and the study of *social* stereotypes.

The Four Functions of Social Stereotypes

The cognitive emphasis, just discussed, in the recent revival of interest in the study of stereotypes is but one instance of a much more general trend of work and thought in social psychology. This is based on two assumptions, implicitly adopted or explicitly made in some of the highly influential traditional texts in the subject (for example, Berkowitz, 1962; Jones and Gerard, 1967; Kelley and Thibaut, 1969). The first is that the analysis of individual processes, be they cognitive or motivational, is necessary *and* also (very often) sufficient for the understanding of most of social behaviour and interactions. The second assumption follows from the first: such an analysis need not take into account *theoretically* the interaction between social behaviour and its social context. The latter is seen as providing classes of situations in which the general individual laws are displayed. Alternatively, the social context is conceived as providing classes of stimuli which "impinge" upon social interactions, in other words, they selectively activate certain individual "mechanisms" or modes of functioning which are already fully in existence. These "individualistic" views have recently been contested in a number of publications (for example, Doise, 1978; Moscovici, 1972; Perret-Clermont, 1980; Stroebe, 1979; Tajfel, 1972a, 1978a, 1979), so the detail of the arguments will not be rehearsed here once again. It is enough to say that, in the case of social stereotypes, "social context" refers to the fact that stereotypes held in common by large numbers of people are derived from, and structured by, the relations between large-scale social groups or entities. The functioning and use of stereotypes result from an intimate interaction between this contextual structuring and their role in the adaptation of individuals to their social environment.

The remainder of this chapter will be concerned with outlining these individual and social functions of stereotyping and with the nature of the interaction between them. In the case of individual functions, stereotypes will first be discussed (as they have been in the earlier and recent work mentioned in the previous section) in relation to their cognitive aspects; this will be followed by a consideration of stereotypes as tools which help individuals to defend or preserve their systems of values. Two social functions of stereotypes will then be considered: first, their role in contributing to the creation and maintenance of group "ideologies" explaining or justifying a variety of social actions; and, second, their role in helping to preserve or create positively valued differentiations between one's own and other social groups. Finally, we shall attempt to specify the links that possibly relate these two social functions of stereotypes to their individual counterparts.

The Cognitive Functions of Stereotypes

The basic cognitive process in stereotyping is categorization, the structuring of sense data through grouping persons, objects and events (or their selected attributes) as being similar or equivalent to one another in their relevance to an individual's actions, intentions or attitudes. The essential cognitive function of stereotyping is thus to systematize and simplify information from the social environment in order to make sense of a world that would otherwise be too complex and chaotic for effective action. When G. W. Allport discussed the categorization process in his classic (1954) book on prejudice, he assigned to it the following "five important characteristics" (pp. 20–22):

1. It forms large classes and clusters for guiding our daily adjustments.
2. Categorization assimilates as much as it can to the cluster.
3. The category enables us quickly to identify a related object.
4. The category saturates all that it contains with the same ideational and emotional flavour.
5. Categories may be more or less rational.

In his later discussion in the same book of "the cognitive process" in prejudice, Allport assigned to it the characteristics of selecting, accentuating and interpreting the information obtained from the environment. He distinguished, however, between a category and a stereotype (p. 191). The latter was "an exaggerated belief associated with a category. Its function is to justify (rationalize) our conduct in relation to that category." In this way, Allport combined the cognitive and the "value" functions of stereotyping. But his definition of stereotyping located the phenomenon as no more than an adjunct to his fourth "important characteristic" of the process of categorization (see above), as something which itself "is not a category" but an "image" which "often exists as a fixed mark upon the category" (p. 192). Since then, we have gone beyond Allport's static conception of a "fixed mark" or an image.

This section is concerned with the details of the functioning of categories which, as Allport put it, guide "our daily adjustments." As it is not possible to describe in detail the extensive literature on the subject, we shall summarize the issue of "adjustments" by a few statements followed by a lengthy quotation of a general hypothesis. Categorizing any aspect of the environment, physical or social, is based on the adoption of certain criteria for the division into (more or less inclusive) separate groupings of a number of items which differ in terms of these (and associated) criteria and resemble each other on the same (or associated) criteria within each of the groupings. The "differing" and the "resembling" need not necessarily be based on any easily ascertainable concrete similarity or dissimilarity. A common linguistic labelling may be sufficient, as in Wittgenstein's (1953) example of games: "for if you look at them you will not see something that is common to *all,* but . . . we see a complicated network of similarities overlapping and crisscrossing" (see Billig, 1976, for an extensive discussion of this issue as it applies to social categorization). It might be argued that, for example, the social category of "nations" represents some of the characteristics attributed by Wittgenstein to the category of "games."

Whatever these classifying criteria may be, *some* of the attributes of the items separated into, for example, two categories may present varying degrees of bimodal correlation (or subjectively experienced bimodal correlation) with the division into categories. In turn, these correlated attributes, which are associated in an orderly fashion with the categorial division *need not* be the original criteria for the categorization. For example, if oranges were to be classified as being of Spanish or Californian origin, and at the same time it turned out that the Spanish ones tended to be larger than the Californian ones (or vice versa), the size would be an attribute correlated with the categorization, but not a criterion for it.[. . .] Starting from this basis, the following general hypothesis has been formulated:

> When a classification in terms of an attribute other than the physical dimension which is being judged is superimposed on a series of stimuli in such a way that one part of the physical series tends to

fall consistently into one class, and the other into the other class, judgements of physical magnitude of the stimuli falling into the distinct classes will show a shift in the direction determined by the class membership of the stimuli, when compared with judgements of a series identical with respect to this physical dimension, on which such a classification is not superimposed. When a classification in terms of an attribute other than the physical dimension which is being judged is superimposed on a series of stimuli, and the changes in the physical magnitudes of the stimuli bear no consistent relationship to the assignment of the stimuli to the distinct classes, this classification will have no effect on the judged relationships in the physical dimension between the stimuli of the series. (Tajfel, 1959, p. 21–22)

This hypothesis was later elaborated to predict that when a classification is correlated with a continuous dimension, there will be a perceptual tendency to exaggerate the differences on that dimension between items which fall into distinct classes and to minimize these differences within each of the classes (Tajfel, 1969a; Tajfel and Wilkes, 1963). In this form, the same hypothesis and some others related to it were extended to explain cognitive aspects of social stereotyping. These aspects which follow directly from the hypothesis are the perceptual accentuation of differences between people belonging to different social groups or categories (on those personal attributes which are subjectively correlated with their division into categories), and the perceptual accentuation of the corresponding similarities between people belonging to the same social group or category. To create the fullblown stereotype, we need only assume that the physical dimension described above stands for some personal attribute such as "intelligent," "lazy," or "dishonest" which has become subjectively associated with some social group through personal or cultural experiences and that the classification itself is in terms of some racial, ethnic, national or other social criterion. It seems likely that the categorization process, as described in the hypothesis, is responsible at least in part for the biases found in judgements of individuals belonging to various human groups [. . .].

Secondary hypotheses were concerned with the effects of the amount of past experience with the correlation between the classification and the stimulus dimension, the strength of the correlation, and its salience in any particular social situation (see Tajfel, 1959; Tajfel and Wilkes, 1963).

Most of these hypotheses were subsequently confirmed in experiments using both physical stimuli and categorizations of people into social groups (see Billig, 1976; Doise, 1978; Eiser, 1979; Eiser and Stroebe, 1972; Irle, 1975; Lilli, 1975; Tajfel, 1969a, 1972b for general reviews of the earlier work). Some of the same hypotheses have been rediscovered and retested in very recent experiments (for example, S. E. Taylor et al., 1978, pp. 779–780).

In one sense, some of these recent reformulations represent a theoretical retreat from the earlier work. This is so for two reasons. The first concerns the crucial role played in stereotypes by value differentials associated with social categorizations. This "value" aspect of categorizations, to be discussed in the next section, was one of the cornerstones of the earlier theories (see most of the references mentioned above). It has lost its explicitness through the emphasis in the more recent work upon the near-monopoly of "pure" cognitive processes in the functioning of stereotypes. The second reason for the theoretical retreat is a lack of specification in some of the more recent work of the *nature* of the dimensions on which differences between social groups, or similarities within such groups, would or would not be accentuated. As was seen above, clear specifications of this kind were amongst the principal aims of the earlier hypotheses. The understanding of the use of categorizations in simplifying and ordering the social environment clearly depends upon these specifications. They help us to predict when and how various aspects of these categorizations fit or do not fit requirements posed by the need to systematize the information which individuals receive or select from their environment. What is equally important, they provide predictions as to when and how the various social differentiations or accentuations will or will not occur.

Rothbart et al. (1978) point out that: "Research on the nature of group stereotypes has focused far more on the description of social stereotypes than on the mechanisms or processes implicated in their formation . . . " (p. 237), and that: "Traditionally, research and theory on stereotypes have emphasized the motivational functions of group stereotypes, with particular attention paid to the inaccuracy, irrationality and rigidity of such judgements" (p. 254). It can be seen from the work described above that there has also been a long tradition of cognitive research into stereotypes, done and mul-

tiply reported from the late 1950s onwards. At present there seems to be a resurgence of such research (both in stereotyping and in social psychology at large). Unfortunately, some of the more recent work seems to be almost completely unaware of the earlier tradition. There is a danger that the frequent complaints about the non-cumulative character of much social psychological research will find here, once again, their unwelcome vindication. We seem sometimes to be working by a series of successive starts or jerks, separated from each other by a few years during which a topic drops more or less out of sight; each of the new starts then claims in turn to be the harbinger of a fresh and previously neglected approach.

The research of Rothbart et al. (1978) and Hamilton (1976) and Hamilton and Gifford (1976) and their colleagues draws our attention to another cognitive aspect of the functions of social stereotyping. This has to do with the subjective inflation or exaggeration of the significance of social events which either occur or *co*-occur with low frequency in the social environment. Rothbart's research is concerned with the fact that impressions of groups of people are affected by "the way in which data on [some individual members of these groups] are organized in memory" (Rothbart et al., 1978, p. 237). Extreme events or extreme individuals are more accessible to memory retrieval than are more average instances. In turn, following Tversky and Kahneman (1973), Rothbart et al. argue that this affects judgement in the sense that those instances from a class of events which are the most available for retrieval serve as a cue for judging the frequency of their general occurrence in the class as a whole. In this way, *negative* behaviours of members of *minority* groups are likely to be over-represented in memory and judgement. (This is a brief summary of a more complex argument made by Rothbart et al.) The attitudinal aspects of these interactions between social categorizations and memory have recently been studied by Eiser, Van der Pligt, and Gossop (1979).

There is a family resemblance between some of this research and the work on "illusory correlations" reported in Hamilton (1976) and Hamilton and Gifford (1976). As the latter wrote, the concept of "illusory correlation" was introduced by Chapman (1967) who defined it as "the report by observers of a correlation between two classes of events which, in reality, (a) are not correlated, or (b) are correlated to a lesser extent than reported"

(p. 151). Experiments conducted by Hamilton and Gifford show that this kind of processing of information (associating, as in Rothbart's views, "infrequent" events with "infrequent" people) is directly related to the formation of stereotypes about minority groups.

In sum, there exists a long and reputable tradition of work which shows that the formation and use of social stereotypes cannot be properly understood without a detailed and painstaking analysis of the cognitive functions they serve. We must now turn to the second major function of stereotypes: the role they play in the preservation of an individual's system of values.

Social Stereotypes and Individual Values

Much of the argument in the previous section and the studies mentioned in it referred to a general cognitive process which can be briefly restated as follows: once an array of stimuli in the environment has been systematized or ordered through their categorization on the basis of some criteria, this ordering will have certain predictable effects on the judgements of the stimuli. These effects consist of shifts in perceived relationships between the stimuli; these shifts depend upon the class membership and the relative salience of the stimuli in the total array. The resulting polarization of judgements and the special weight given to some of the stimuli serve as guidelines for introducing subjective order and predictability into what would otherwise have been a fairly chaotic environment.

But this is not enough if one is concerned with the issues of social categorization and stereotyping. Many of the categorizations applying to objects in the physical environment are neutral, in the sense that they are not associated with preferences for one category over another, with one category being "bad" and another "good," or one being "better" than another. When, however, this does happen in the physical environment, certain clear-cut effects appear which distinguish between "neutral" and "value-loaded" classifications.

In the heyday of the "New Look" in the study of perceptual processes, some of these effects were considered to consist of an overestimation of the magnitude of the stimuli which had some value relevance to the individual judging them (see particularly Bruner, 1973, Part I). In a pioneering paper Bruner and Rodrigues (1953) drew atten-

tion to the possibility that what appeared to be a simple overestimation may have been in fact a *relative* increase in the judged subjective differences between stimuli (such as coins) which varied simultaneously in their size and value to the subjects. This notion was elaborated and developed a few years later (Tajfel, 1957) and confirmed in a number of subsequent experiments (see, in particular, Eiser and Stroebe, 1972, for a general review and analysis of the theoretical considerations and the earlier empirical work).

Three consequences followed. The first was that there was no reason why what appeared to be true for judgements of physical magnitudes of individual stimuli should not also apply to judgements of differences between individual people on various dimensions of person perception (see Tajfel and Wilkes, 1964). The second was that the model of increased polarization of judgements relating to value differentials between *individual* stimuli should also apply to *classes* of stimuli which differed in their respective value to the people making the judgements. The third consequence was a combination of the first two: the increased accentuation of judged differences, due to value differentials, between classes of stimuli and of judged similarities within each of the classes should apply, once again, to value differentials not only in the physical environment but also (and much more importantly) to social categorizations of people into differing groups (see Doise, 1978; Eiser and Stroebe, 1972; Tajfel, 1959,1963).

It is at this point that it is important to state the clear-cut *functional differences* between the "purely" cognitive processes manifested in the shifts of judgement applying to neutral categories, which were discussed in the previous section of this chapter, and the social value differentials with which we are now concerned. Two of these differences are particularly relevant to the present discussion.

The first concerns the nature of the feedback obtained from the environment when the use of categorizations as a guiding device for judgements leads to shifts or biases which are in accordance with the *assumed* characteristics of the stimuli belonging to the different classes. In the case of judgements applying to the physical environment, it can be expected that shifts leading to erroneous responses which are maladaptive will be quickly eliminated. Exaggerating the differences between two coins of different value is a "good error" as long as it provides an additional guarantee that there will be no confusion between them. But any errors or shifts of judgement which do lead to misidentification or a confusion between objects which should be clearly discriminated will have as a direct consequence the correction of the errors. The speed and accuracy of these corrections will depend upon the degree of clarity of the information received after the response has been made.

In the case of the social environment, it is not only that the information received (about, for example, the personal characteristics of people) is generally much more ambiguous to interpret and lacking in clear-cut criteria for its validity. If we now return to the shared nature of social stereotypes, discussed in the first section of this chapter, the judgements made of people who belong to one or another social groups or categories which are stereotypes in certain ways are likely to receive, by definition, the positive feedback of general social consensus. Less information than is the case for physical categories will be needed to confirm these judgements, and considerably more to disconfirm them in the face of what appears to fit in with what is generally accepted as a social reality.

The second of these two issues is perhaps even more important. It concerns once again a difference between social categorizations which are neutral and those which are value-loaded. A neutral social categorization means that certain stereotyped traits may be applied to certain social groups ("Swedes are tall," for instance) without having a positive or negative value connotation. It is not that the trait "tall" is necessarily value-free; it is the category "Swedes" which may be neither positive nor negative, and therefore meeting a Swede who happens to be short will not present much of a crisis—if there are enough short Swedes around, this may even modify the general stereotype. But the story is very different if and when a social categorization into groups is endowed with a strong value differential. In such cases, encounters with negative or disconfirming instances would not just require a change in the interpretation of the attributes assumed to be characteristic of a social category. Much more importantly, the acceptance of such disconfirming instances threatens or endangers the value system on which is based the differentiation between the groups. As we have seen, for G. W. Allport (1954) the cognitive process in prejudice consisted of "selecting,

accentuating and interpreting" the information obtained from the environment. It is in this way that the process fulfils its function of protecting the value system which underlies the division of the surrounding social world into sheep and goats. There are many and varied daily social situations which enable us to select, accentuate and interpret in accordance with our value differentials information about different "kinds" of people; but we shall select here only two instances of the process since both have been subjected to fairly systematic study by social psychologists.

The first of these can be discussed very briefly, as it is no more than a simple extension of the earlier discussion in this and the previous sections about value differentials magnifying *still further* the accentuation of differences between classes, and similarities within classes, which is characteristic of neutral categorizations. Just as the judged differences in size between individual items in a series of coins tend to be larger than the corresponding differences in a neutral series of stimuli (Tajfel, 1957), so the judged differences on certain dimensions correlated with the classification tend to be larger in the case of social categorizations related to value differentials than they are in neutral categorizations (Tajfel, 1959, p. 21). One way to test this hypothesis has been to compare the ratings of personal attributes of people belonging (or assigned) to two different social categories and made by two groups of subjects; one of these groups of subjects was previously ascertained to be prejudiced against one of the two categories while the other group of subjects was not. The underlying assumption was that the categorization presents a stronger value differential for the former than for the latter group. The results usually showed that the prejudiced group judged the differences on certain dimensions between the members of the two categories to be larger than the non-prejudiced group (Doise, 1978, for a recent review of some of the earlier studies). We shall return later, when discussing the group functions of stereotypes, to this issue of intergroup differentiation. For the present, it will be enough to point to the value-preserving function of differentiations of this kind. The ordering by individuals of their social environment in terms of social groups, some of which are viewed favourably and some unfavourably, becomes more efficient and stable if and when various relevant differences between these groups (and similarities within them) can be conceived to be as constant and clear-cut as possible.

The second line of social psychological evidence concerns the identification in ambiguous conditions of members of disliked social categories. Bruner, Goodnow, and Austin (1956, Chapter 7) presented an early and detailed analysis of the conditions in which individuals will commit errors of overinclusion or overexclusion in their assignment of ambiguous items into one of two categories which are available for such assignments. The first of these errors consists of including into a category an item which, on specified criteria, does not belong to it; the second, of excluding an item which does belong.

In their analysis, Bruner, Goodnow, and Austin related the frequencies of the type of errors to their perceived consequences, that is; to the weighing up of the respective risks entailed by making one or the other kind of mistake. This analysis of risk can be extended to the subjective consequences of misidentifying the group membership of individuals when the social categories to which they belong are related to a strong value differentiation for the person making the category assignments. The risks are that a "bad" person could be assigned to a "good" category or a "good" person to a "bad" one. If this happens too often, it could threaten or even invalidate the value differential. From the empirical evidence we have, it looks as if the former of these two kinds of errors is avoided more persistently than the latter. In other words, there seems to be a preference for not having the wrong person inside an exclusive club over the risk of having the right person out of it. This conclusion can be can be drawn from a group of studies conducted in the 1950s in the United States in which comparisons were made in the accuracy of recognition of Jews by antisemites and non-antisemites. The prejudiced subjects showed greater accuracy in recognizing Jews. This was due to a response bias; they labelled a relatively larger number of photographs as Jewish (for example, Scodel and Austrin, 1957). "The mistakes committed by [this] group . . . tend in the direction of assuming that some non-Jews are Jewish rather than the other way round" (Tajfel, 1969b, p. 331).

Here again, the value differentials guide the use made of ambiguous information. As in the previously discussed case of accentuation of differences and similarities, the maintenance of a system of social categories acquires an importance which goes far beyond the simple function of ordering and systematizing the environment. It represents a powerful protection of the existing system of social values, and any mistakes made are mistakes to the extent that they endanger that system. The scope, frequency and enormous diversity of witch-hunts at various historical periods (including our own) of which the basic principle is not to miss out anyone who might be included in the negative category, bear witness both to the social importance of the phenomenon and to the importance of the psychological processes insuring the protection of the existing value systems or differentials. In this section we discussed a few rather undramatic instances of this process. It must not be thought that the value aspects of the functioning of social stereotypes remain equally undramatic in periods of high stress, social tensions and acute intergroup conflicts.

The Ideologizing of Collective Actions

The witch-hunts just mentioned above bring us to a discussion of the role of collective actions in the functioning of social stereotypes. Tens of thousands of "witches" were tortured and killed in Europe in the sixteenth and seventeenth centuries. As Thomas (1971) wrote:

> It was the popular fear of *maleficium* which provided the normal driving-force behind witch prosecution, not any lawyer-led campaign from above. . . . Even when the courts ceased to entertain witch-trials, popular feeling against witches continued, as the periodic rural lynchings demonstrated. . . . The reason for the new popular demand for witch-prosecution cannot be found in the changing attitude of the legislature and the judiciary. It must be traced to a change in the opinion of the people themselves. (pp. 548, 550, 551, 1973 edition)

Thomas's point about witch-hunting having been a massive and widespread phenomenon in the population at large is important, since it is likely that it applies to many social situations where causes of distressful social events are sought in the characteristics, intentions or behaviour of outgroups. In his early functionalist analysis of witchcraft, Kluckhohn (1944) characterized witches as being generally "outsiders." It is interesting to see that the social psychological parallels to the hotly contested functionalist views in social anthropology have mainly stressed the in-dividual motivational processes rather than their social equivalents. They consisted, in the main, of adopting perspectives on mass violence or mass hatred which extrapolated from individual dis-placement or redirection of aggression to the large-scale instances of social aggression or vio-lence (see Tajfel, 1972a, 1978a, for a discussion of this issue and of the theoretical difficulties pre-sented by extrapolations of this kind).

In contrast, the large-scale diffusion of hostile or derogatory social images of outsiders do not seem to have been the subject of explicit applica-tions of cognitive theories in social psychology, although such theories might have made a useful contribution to our understanding of the large-scale acceptance and resilience of social stereotypes. These theories would include, for example, the "justification of behaviour" aspects of cognitive dissonance, the work within attribution theory on the attribution of responsibility and intentionality, the research on internal versus external locus of control, etc. The traditions of social psychologi-cal research on stereotypes originate primarily from two sources: the descriptive one, consisting of a detailed analysis of the contents of stereo-types; and the cognitive one which emphasizes, as we have seen, the *individual* cognitive processes.

These two traditions have not, however, come together to work towards the construction of a theory of *contents* of stereotypes as shared by so-cial groups. The outer limit of the social psycholo-gists' interests resided in manipulating the salience of social categorizations in natural or laboratory conditions and finding that, as a result, intergroup stereotypes became more "active," intense or ex-treme. As I wrote elsewhere (Tajfel, 1979, p. 188):

. . . there are undoubtedly some social contexts in which these salient social categorizations are gen-erally induced in many individuals, for one rea-son or another; there are other social contexts in which they are not. But all the rest remains a deep mystery to the social psychologist. Thus, social categorization is still conceived as a haphazardly floating 'independent variable' which strikes at random as the spirit moves it. No links are made, or, attempted, between the conditions determin-ing its presence and mode of operation, and its outcomes in widely diffused commonalities of social behaviour. Why, when and how is a social categorization salient or not salient? What kind of shared constructions of social reality, mediated

through social categorizations, lead to a social cli-mate in which large masses of people feel that they are in long-term conflict with other large masses? What, for example, are the *psychological* transi-tions from a stable to an unstable social system?

It is quite obvious that an approach to a social psychological theory of the contents of stereotypes would address itself to no more than a small cor-ner of the large issues raised by the questions above (see Tajfel, 1978a). We have, however, at our dis-posal all the elements needed to make a modest beginning, and we can trace some general direc-tions that could be taken. This will be done in two steps. The first consists of a rough classification of the psychological functions that stereotypes can serve for social groups; and the second, of point-ing to some potential developments which could provide a theoretical and research articulation for these functions.

The classification of functions is not presented here as an a priori or deductive exercise. It is a rough attempt to bring together what is generally known from social psychology, social history, so-cial anthropology and common sense. It appears, from all these sources, that outgroup social ste-reotypes tend to be created and widely diffused in conditions which require: (a) a search for the un-derstanding of complex, and usually distressful, large-scale social events; (b) justification of ac-tions, committed or planned, against outgroups; (c) a positive differentiation of the ingroup from selected outgroups at a time when such differen-tiation is perceived as becoming insecure and eroded; or when it is not positive, and social con-ditions exist which are perceived as providing a possibility for a change in the situation. We shall refer to these three functions, respectively, as those of social causality, justification and differentiation.

No more can be done here than to cite a brief selection of examples in order to illustrate or clarify the nature of each of these categories. To start with causality: something was "needed" in the seven-teenth century to explain the plague, but as Tho-mas (1971) wrote; its incidence "was too indis-criminate to be plausibly explained in personal terms." Thus, "the Scots were accused to have poi-soned the wells of Newcastle in 1639." Catholic sorcery was held responsible for an outbreak of gaol fever in Oxford in 1577, and the local Inde-pendent congregation was blamed for an outbreak of plague in Barnstaple in 1646 (Thomas, 1971

(1973 edition), pp. 667–668). An even clearer example can be found in antisemitism. This is carefully and brilliantly traced in Norman Cohn's (1967) description of the persistence of the myth about the Protocols of the Elders of Zion. As Billig (1978, p. 132) wrote:

> The emotional ferocity of the crudest anti-Semitism makes it easy to forget that anti-Semitism can provide an extensive cognitive interpretation of the world. Above all, crude anti-Semitism is based upon a belief that Jews have immense powers of evil in the world. Modern anti-Semitic dogma asserts that Jews control both communism and capitalism and that they aim to dominate the world in a régime which will destroy Western civilization. All facts are explained in terms of this pervasive and perverse belief.

The "justification" principle is well documented throughout Kiernan's (1972) work. Two examples, taken almost at random, illustrate the principle:

> The idea of Europe's 'mission' dawned early, but was taken up seriously in the nineteenth century. Turkey, China, and the rest would some day be prosperous, wrote Winwood Reade, one of the most sympathetic Westerners. "But those people will never begin to advance . . . until they enjoy the rights of men; and these they will never obtain except by means of European conquest." (p. 24)

> An ex-soldier from Tonking whom W. S. Blunt talked to in Paris exclaimed against his government's folly in sending armchair philosophers to run the colonies, who fancied that all men were brothers—it was the English in India who were realistic—'en agissant avec des brutes il faut être brutal.' (p. 97)

The "differentiation" principle could be considered as a part of the general syndrome of ethnocentrism understood in Sumner's (1906) sense of the term, but this is an oversimplification. It is a dynamic process which can only be understood against the background of *relations* between social groups and the social comparisons they make in the context of these relations. The creation or maintenance of differentiation, or of a "positive distinctiveness" of one's own group from others which are relevant to the group's self-image seems to be, judging from the accounts of social anthropologists, a widespread phenomenon in many cultures. As this intergroup differentiation has been discussed recently and extensively elsewhere (see Tajfel, 1974, 1978a, 1978c, 1979; Tajfel and

Turner, 1979; Turner, 1975a; see also chapter 3) we shall simply note it here as the third of the major group functions served by stereotyping.

Links between the Collective and the Individual Functions

Two points remain to be made, concerning the relationship of this discussion to the potential development of a properly social psychological theory of stereotyping. The first of these two points has to do with the social functions of stereotypes—social causality, justification and differentiation or some combination between them—as they relate to the contents of a stereotype. The analysis of such a relationship cannot be done in psychological terms alone. The competitive and power relations between groups will largely determine the nature of the psychological functions which need to be fulfilled by the groups' reciprocal images. But when this is taken for granted as the indispensable background for any social psychological analysis, such an analysis should then be able to make theoretical sense of the contents of ingroup and outgroup stereotypes. This can be done through identifying one or more of the major group functions that the stereotype may be serving. A perspective of this kind would undoubtedly be a significant advance upon the descriptive tradition of work which often did not go much further than eliciting a cultural consensus about certain traits attributed to certain groups and, at times, monitoring the stability or changes over time of these collective descriptions.

The second and final point concerns the links between the group functions of stereotyping discussed in the previous section of this chapter and the individual functions discussed in the preceding sections. It seems that, if we wish to understand what happens, the analytical sequence should start from the group functions and then relate the individual functions to them. As we argued in sections 2 and 3 of this chapter, an individual uses stereotypes as an aid in the cognitive structuring of his social environment (and thus as a guide for action in appropriate circumstances) and also for the protection of his system of values. In a sense, these are the structural constants of the sociopsychological situation; it is the framework within which the input of the socially derived influence and information must be adapted, modified and recreated. No doubt, individual differences in personality, motivation, previous experiences, etc., will play an important part in the immense variety of ways in which are shaped these adaptations, modifications and recreations. It remains equally true, however, that—as we argued at the beginning of this chapter—a stereotype does not become a *social* stereotype until and unless it is widely shared within a social entity. As long as individuals share a common social affiliation which is important to them (and perceive themselves as sharing it), the selection of the criteria for division between ingroups and outgroups and of the kind of characteristics attributed to each will be directly determined by those cultural traditions, group interests, social upheavals and social differentiations which are perceived as being common to the group as a whole. As Berger and Luckmann (1967) so cogently argued some years ago, social reality is not "out there" to be comprehended or assimilated in some manner which asymptotically approaches to its faithful reflection in individual attitudes and beliefs. It is constructed by individuals from the raw materials provided to them by the social context in which they live. If this were not the case, the selection and contents of social categorizations and social stereotypes would have to be conceived as arbitrary and random occurrences, capriciously varying from one society to another, from one historical period to another. As it is, the restricted variety of the combination and recombination of their common elements can be attributed to the restricted number of the major group functions that they generally seem to be serving; and their common structure to the two major psychological functions they serve for the individual.

As was mentioned earlier, social psychological theories of stereotypes have not been much concerned in the past with establishing the links between these collective and individual functions. This is why no grand theory can be offered in this chapter—or perhaps an all-encompassing theory is not possible, or even desirable. Theories in social psychology have often been characterized by a strong positive correlation between the scope of their ambitions and the bluntness of their predictions or explanations. As Hinde (1979) recently argued in relation to another area of social psychology, we are still at a stage in which a strong dose of theoretical criticism is not only unavoid-

able, but is perhaps the most useful way to proceed.

The suggestion made here is that future research in social psychology could relate the group functions of explanation, justification and differentiation to the individual functions of cognitive structuring and value preservation by using two recent theoretical and research initiatives. These concern the study of social groups conceived as social categories, each immersed in a complex and wider structure of many social categories which are *defined as such* by the individuals involved and are related to each other in a variety of definable patterns (such as those of power, status, prestige, majority–minority, perceived stability or perceived possibility of change, flexibility or rigidity of group boundaries, etc.). The first of these two research initiatives relates an individual's self-respect or self-concept (or his "social identity")—through the process of intergroup social comparison—to the relative position of his group on a number of dimensions in a multigroup social system. This idea helps to account for the ways in which individuals shape the realization of the group functions of differentiation and justification. It is not possible to review here, even briefly, the substantial amount of recent research on this subject (see Tajfel, 1978a, 1982; Tajfel and Turner, 1979)[. . .]. An apt one-sentence summary has been provided by Commins and Lockwood (1979, p. 282): "The social group is seen to function as a provider of positive social identity for its members through comparing itself and distinguishing itself, from other comparison groups, along salient dimensions which have a clear value differential."

There is a clear theoretical continuity here with some of the processes of accentuation of differences occurring when certain criteria of classification are combined for individuals with value differentials between those categories which have been selected as important in systematizing the social environment (sections 2 and 3 of this chapter). Thus, a social psychological theory which relates the group differentiation function to social representations of the macrosocial context has at the same time direct implications for the individual functions of categorization and value-preservation in stereotyping. This continuity is consonant both with the general argument of the chapter and also much empirical research on the role of social categorization in structuring our views of the social environment (see Tajfel, 1978d). The social context of values and requirements for adaptation to the environment helps the individual to seek out, to select for special attention, to exaggerate, and, if necessary, to create, those similarities and differences which fit in with the general consensus about what matters and what does not matter in the potentially infinite number of possible structures of social divisions and social equivalence.

The second of the two initiatives mainly concerns the social or group function of explanation, but it also has important implications for the two other functions of justification and differentiation. It consists of some recent attempts to draw attention to the fact that traditional attribution theory has remained largely individualistic and has neglected both the social determinants and the social functions of the processes of attribution (see Apfelbaum and Herzlich, 1971; Deschamps, 1977, 1978; Duncan, 1976; Hamilton, 1978; Hewstone and Jaspars, 1982; Mann and D. M. Taylor, 1974; Stephan, 1977; D. M. Taylor and Jaggi, 1974).

The remainder of this brief excursion into "social" attribution is a paraphrase of some of the arguments put forward by Hewstone and Jaspars (1982)—to whom I am grateful for first drawing my attention to the synthesis that can be made of some of the ideas outlined in this chapter with their attempts to socialize traditional attribution theory. As they wrote:

> ... the main point is that traditional attribution theory has failed to introduce the fact that *individuals* may belong to different social *groups*. ... In this alternative perspective ... an observer attributes the behaviour of an actor not simply on the basis of individual characteristics, but on the basis of the group or social category to which the actor belongs and to which the observer belongs.

Hewstone and Jaspars provide a number of recent empirical examples of this kind of social attribution, although perhaps the earliest instance can be found in the famous study of rumour by G. W. Allport and Postman (1947). As Hewstone and Jaspars argue, this is a dynamic interaction, in the sense that perceptions of the causes and reasons for the behaviour of members of the ingroup and the outgroup are determined by the existing relations between the groups, they are interdependent, and they contribute in turn to the future course of the intergroup relations. Following Buss (1978), Hewstone and Jaspars define causes as "that which brings about a change" and reasons as "that for which a change is brought about." They also expect that "reasons" would tend to be used to explain the behaviour of ingroup members and "causes" would apply to outgroup members. At the same time, this hypothetical dichotomy would be strongly affected by the positive or negative evaluations of the behaviour to which the explanation is applied. The results, such as those from the study of D. M. Taylor and Jaggi (1974) in which internal attributions were made of socially desirable acts performed by ingroup members and external attributions to the socially undesirable acts performed by them (with the opposite pattern applying to members of the outgroup), are not too far removed from the "reasons–causes" dichotomy. It is obvious that this kind of a model can lead to useful predictions of a number of complex interactions in the perception or attribution of social causality.

To return to the main argument of this section, it is also quite obvious that these "internal" (that is, dispositional) explanations are an instance of the functioning of social stereotypes. But the static, stable consensus implied by the older descriptive studies of stereotypes is replaced here by shifting perspectives closely related to the individuals' evaluation of the equally shifting social situations which are perceived *in terms of the nature of the relations between the groups involved*. It is in this way that the potential development of a *social* attribution theory provides the second of our links between the group and the individual functions of stereotyping. Just as the previously mentioned social identity perspective helps to transpose the differentiation and justification group functions of stereotypes to the level of individual functioning, so the social attribution perspective seems to be a promising tool for a similar link from the group functions of justification and explanation.

Conclusion

In this chapter we moved from the individual to social functions of stereotypes, and then reversed directions in proposing a sequence of analysis which would start from the social functions to reach the individual ones. This is not the usual sequence in social psychological texts. It is, however, justified on two grounds at least. The first is that, in this way, we come closer in our work to a healthy respect for the social realities of intergroup relations, including social conflict, than is often the case in the study of stereotypes focusing exclusively or predominantly upon cognitive or motivational processes inherent in the individual. At the same time, the resulting individual processes of stereotyping are not conceived as some mystical offshoot of a group mind—the theoretical and empirical integrity of moving from one researchable perspective to another and of linking them explicitly seems to be preserved. Much of what has been proposed here is no more than a hazy blueprint for future research. But if we wish our discipline to become more directly and theoretically involved in the study of the tough realities of our social functioning we need to make a start, even if it consists, for the present, of no more than speculations and blueprints. As I recently wrote elsewhere (Tajfel, 1979, p. 189): "The point is that we shall never be able to formulate adequate guidelines for research on collective social behaviour if we do not go beyond constructing sets of independent variables seen as functioning in a social environment which is assumed to be psychologically unstructured in its homogeneous and all embracing 'inter-individuality.'"

REFERENCES

Allport, G. W. (1954). *The nature of prejudice*. Cambridge, MA: Addison-Wesley.

Allport, G. W., & Postman, L. (1947). *The psychology of rumour*. New York: Holt.

Apfelbaum, E., & Herzlich, C. (1971). La théorie de l'attribution en psychologie sociale. *Bulletin de Psychologie, 24,* 961–976.

Berger, P. L., & Luckmann, T. (1967). *The social construction of reality*. London: Allen Lane.

Berkowitz, L. (1962). *Aggression: A social psychological analysis*. New York: McGraw-Hill.

Billig, M. G. (1976). *Social psychology and intergroup relations*. European Monographs in Social Psychology, No. 9. London: Academic Press.

Billig, M. G. (1978). *Fascists: A social psychological view of the National Front*. European Monographs in Social Psychology, No. 15. London: Academic Press.

Bruner, J. S. (1957). On perceptual readiness. *Psychological Review, 64,* 123–152.

Bruner, J. S. (1973). *Beyond the information given: Studies in the psychology of knowing* (ed., J. M. Anglin). New York: Norton.

Bruner, J. S., Goodnow, J. J., & Austin, G. A. (1956). *A study of thinking*. New York: Wiley.

Bruner, J. S., & Klein, G. S. (1960). The functions of perceiving: New look retrospect. In B. Kaplan & S. Wapner (Eds.), *Perspectives in psychological theory: Essays in honour of Heinz Werner*. New York: International Universities Press.

Bruner, J. S., & Potter, M. C. (1964). Interference in visual recognition. *Science, 144,* 424–425.

Bruner, J. S., & Rodrigues, J. S. (1953). Some determinants of apparent size. *Journal of Abnormal and Social Psychology, 48,* 585–592.

Buss, A. R. (1978). Causes and reasons in attribution theory: A conceptual critique. *Journal of Personality and Social Psychology, 36,* 1311–1321.

Chapman, L. J. (1967). Illusory correlations in observational report. *Journal of Verbal Learning and Verbal Behaviour, 6,* 151–155.

Cohn, N. (1967). *Warrant for genocide*. New York: Harper.

Commins, B., & Lockwood, J. (1979) The effects of stress differences, favoured treatment and equity on intergroup comparisons. *European Journal of Social Psychology, 9,* 218–219.

Deschamps, J.-C. (1977). *L'Attribution et la catégorisation sociale*. Bern: Peter Lang.

Deschamps, J.-C. (1978). La perception des causes du comportement. In W. Doise, J.-C. Deschamps, & G. Mugny (Eds.), *Psychologié Sociale Expérimentale*. Paris: Armand Colin.

Doise, W. (1978). *Groups and individuals: Explanations in social psychology*. Cambridge: Cambridge University Press.

Duncan, B. L. (1976). Differential social perception and attribution of intergroup violence: Testing the lower limits of stereotyping of Blacks. *Journal of Personality and Social Psychology, 34,* 590–598.

Eiser, J. R. (1979). *Cognitive social psychology*. London McGraw-Hill.

Eiser, J. R., & Stroebe, W. (1972). *Categorisation and social judgement*. European Monographs in Social Psychology, No. 3. London: Academic Press.

Eiser, J. R., Van der Pligt, J., & Gossop, M. R. (1979). Categorisation, attitude and memory for the source of attitude statements. *European Journal of Social Psychology, 9,* 243–251.

Hamilton, D. L. (1976). Cognitive biases in the perception of social groups. In J. S. Carroll & J. W. Payne (Eds.), *Cognition and social behaviour*. Hillsdale, NJ: Erlbaum.

Hamilton, D. L. (1978). Who is responsible? Towards a social psychology of responsibility attribution. *Social Psychology, 41,* 316–328.

Hamilton, D. L., & Gifford, R. K. (1976). Illusory correlations in inter-personal perception: A cognitive basis of stereotypic judgements. *Journal of Experimental Social Psychology, 12,* 392–407.

Hewstone, M., & Jaspars, J. (1982). Intergroup relations and attribution processes. In H. Tajfel (Ed.), *Social Identity and Intergroup Relations*. Cambridge: Cambridge University Press, and Paris, Editions de la Maison des Sciences de l'Homme.

Hinde, R. A. (1979). *Towards understanding relationships*. European Monographs in Social Psychology. London, Academic Press.

Irle, M. (1975). *Lehrbuch der sozialpsychologie*. Göttingen: Hogrefe.

Jones, E. E., & Gerard, H. B. (1967). *Foundations of social psychology*. New York, Wiley.

Kelley, H. H., & Thibaut, J. W. (1969). Group problem solving. In G. Lindzey & E. Aronson (Eds.). *The Handbook of Social Psychology, Volume IV.* Reading, MA: Addison-Wesley.

Kiernan, V. G. (1972). *The lords of human kind: European attitudes to the outside world in the imperial age.* Harmondsworth, Middlesex: Penguin Books.

Kluckhohn, C. (1944). *Navaho Witchraft.* Harvard University, Peabody Museum Papers, Volume 22, No. 2.

Lilli, W. (1975). *Soziale akzentuievung.* Stuttgart: Kohlhammer.

Mann, J. F., & Taylor, D. M. (1974). Attribution of causality: Role of ethnicity and social class. *Journal of Social Psychology, 94,* 3–13.

Moscovici, S. (1972). Society and theory in social psychology. In J. Israel & H. Tajfel (Eds.), *The context of social psychology: A critical assessment.* European Monographs in Social Psychology, No. 2. London: Academic Press.

Perret-Clermont, A. N. (1980). *Social interaction and cognitive development in children.* European Monographs in Social Psychology. London: Academic Press.

Rothbart, M., Fulero, S., Jensen, C., Howard, J., & Birrell, P. (1978). From individual to group impressions: availability heuristics in stereotype formation. *Journal of Experimental Social Psychology, 14,* 237–255.

Scodel, A., & Austrin, H. (1957). The perception of Jewish photographs by non-Jews and Jews. *Journal of Abnormal and Social Psychology, 54,* 278–280.

Stallybrass, O. (1977). Stereotype. In A. Bullock & O. Stallybrass (Eds.), *The Fontana dictionary of modern thought.* London: Fontana/Collins.

Stephan, I. D. (1977). Stereotyping: Role of ingroup-outgroup differences in causal attribution of behaviour. *Journal of Social Psychology, 101,* 255–266.

Stroebe, W. (1979). The level of social psychological analysis: A plea for a more social social psychology. In L. H. Strickland (Ed.), *Social psychology—A modern perspective: Western and Soviet points of view.* Oxford: Pergamon Press.

Sumner, G. A. (1906). *Folkways.* New York: Ginn.

Tajfel, H. (1957). Value and the perceptual judgement of magnitude. *Psychological Review, 64,* 192–204.

Tajfel, H. (1959). Quantitative judgement in social perception. *British Journal of Psychology, 50,* 16–29.

Tajfel, H. (1963). Stereotype. *Race, V,* 3–14.

Tajfel, H. (1969a). Cognitive aspects of prejudice. *Journal of Social Issues, 25,* 79–97.

Tajfel, H. (1969b). Social and cultural factors in perception. In G. Lindzey & E. Aronson (Eds.), *Handbook of social psychology,* Volume 3. Cambridge, MA: Addison-Wesley.

Tajfel, H. (1972a). Experiments in a vacuum. In J. Israel & H. Tajfel (Eds.), *The Context of Social Psychology: A Critical Assessment.* European Monographs in Social Psychology, No. 2. London: Academic Press.

Tajfel, H. (1972b). Social categorisation. English ms of La catégorisation sociale. In S. Moscovici (Ed.), *Introduction à la Psychologie Sociale, Volume I.* Paris, Larousse, Chapter 8, pp. 272–302.

Tajfel, H. (1974). Social identity and intergroup behaviour. *Social Science Information, 13, 2,* 65–93.

Tajfel, H. (Ed.). (1978a). *Differentiation between social groups: Studies in the social psychology of intergroup relations.* London: Academic Press.

Tajfel, H. (1978c). The social psychology of minorities. Report No. 38, Minority Rights Group, London.

Tajfel, H. (1978d). The structure of our views about society. In H. Tajfel & C. Fraser (Eds.), *Introducing social psychology.* Harmondsworth, Middlesex: Penguin Books.

Tajfel, H. (1979). Individuals and groups in social psychology. *British Journal of Social and Clinical Psychology, 18,* 183–190.

Tajfel, H. (Ed.). (1982). *Social identity and intergroup relations.* Cambridge: Cambridge University Press, and Paris: Editions de la Maison des Sciences de l'Homme.

Tajfel, H., & Turner, J. C. (1979). An integrative theory of intergroup conflict. In W. G. Austin & S. Worchel (Eds.), *The social psychology of intergroup relations.* Monterey, CA: Brooks/Cole.

Tajfel, H., & Wilkes, A. L. (1963). Classification and quantitative judgement. *British Journal of Psychology, 54,* 101–114.

Tajfel, H., & Wilkes, A. L. (1964). Salience of attributes and commitment to extreme judgements in the perception of people. *British Journal of Social and Clinical Psychology, 2,* 40–49.

Taylor, D. M., & Aboud, F. E. (1973). Ethnic stereotypes: Is the concept necessary? *Canadian Psychologist, 14,* 330–338.

Taylor, D. M., & Jaggi, V. (1974). Ethnocentrism and causal attribution in a South Indian context. *Journal of Cross-Cultural Psychology, 5,* 162–171.

Taylor, D. M., Simard, L. M., & Papineau, D. (1978). Perceptions of cultural differences and language use: a field study in a bilingual environment. *Canadian Journal of Behavioural Science, 10,* 181–191.

Taylor, S. E., Fiske, S. T., Etcoff, N. L., & Ruderman, A. (1978). Categorical and contextual bases of person memory and stereotyping. *Journal of Personality and Social Psychology, 36,* 778–793.

Thomas, K. (1971). *Religion and the decline of magic.* London: Weidenfeld and Nicolson, reprinted in 1973, Penguin Books.

Turner, J. C. (1975a). Social comparison and social identity: Some prospects for intergroup behaviour. *European Journal of Social Psychology, 5,* 5–34.

Tversky, A., & Kahneman, D. (1973). Availability: A heuristic for judging frequency and probability. *Cognitive Psychology, 5,* 207–232.

Wittgenstein, L. (1953). *Philosophical investigations.* Oxford, UK: Blackwell.

Affirmative Action, Unintentional Racial Biases, and Intergroup Relations

John F. Dovidio • Colgate University

Samuel L. Gaertner • University of Delaware

This paper examines whether affirmative action is still needed, investigates why it may be needed in terms of contemporary racial attitudes, and considers ways of reducing intergroup conflict and tension surrounding this issue. Although the nature of contemporary bias is more subtle than traditional forms, this unintentional bias can produce barriers to the employment and advancement of well-qualified members of historically disadvantaged groups, as well as resistance to affirmative action. Nevertheless, affirmative action policies may address contemporary biases more effectively than passive equal employment opportunity policies because they emphasize outcomes rather than intentions, provide unambiguous standards of behavior, and establish monitoring systems that insure accountability. Strategies for improving intergroup relations and reducing intergroup conflict associated with this issue are considered.

The United States was founded on principles of social equality, and White Americans, more than ever before, are rejecting negative stereotypes of Blacks and are endorsing the ideal of equal opportunity for all people. For example, adjective checklist studies (Dovidio & Gaertner, 1986; Karlins, Coffman, & Walters, 1969), in which respondents are asked to select traits that are most typical of particular racial and ethnic categories, and other self-report studies and surveys (Devine & Elliot, 1995), indicate that personal negative characterizations of Blacks among Whites are consistently declining. As Table 8.1 indicates, surveys of White college students reveal that, today, fewer Whites than ever before describe Blacks in strongly negative terms. These trends are consistent with nationwide polls that have also demonstrated that Whites are currently articulating negative characterizations of Blacks substantially less frequently

than in the past (see Davis & Smith, 1991; Schuman, Steeh, & Bobo, 1985).

In addition to characterizing the personal qualities of Blacks more positively, White acceptance of Blacks across a range of formal and informal settings is at an unprecedented high. Prointegration sentiments among Whites concerning bringing a Black person home for dinner, allowing Blacks into the neighborhood, and permitting interracial marriage have become generally stronger across time (Dovidio, Brigham, Johnson, & Gaertner, 1996; Schuman et al., 1985). White America is also becoming more accepting of Black leaders. In 1958, the majority of Whites reported that they would *not* be willing to vote for a well-qualified Black presidential candidate; in the 1990s, over 90% said that they would (Davis & Smith, 1991). Thus, a number of questionnaires, surveys, and polls converge on the same result: White people are less

TABLE 8.1. Percent of Subjects Selecting a Trait to Describe Black Americans (Formerly "*Negroes*") in 1933, 1951, 1967, 1982, 1988, 1990, 1993, and 1996

	1933	1951	1967	1982	1988	1990	1993	1996
Superstitious	84	41	13	6	2	3	1	1
Lazy	75	31	26	13	6	4	5	2
Happy-go-lucky	38	17	27	15	4	1	2	1
Ignorant	38	24	11	10	6	5	5	2
Musical	26	33	47	29	13	27	12	18
Ostentatious	26	11	25	5	0	1	1	0
Very religious	24	17	8	23	20	19	17	23
Stupid	22	10	4	1	1	3	0	0
Physically dirty	17	—	3	0	1	0	1	0
Naive	14	—	4	4	2	3	1	0
Slovenly	13	—	5	2	1	1	0	0
Unreliable	12	—	6	2	1	4	1	0
Pleasure loving	—	19	26	20	14	14	14	12
Sensitive	—	—	17	13	15	9	4	5
Gregarious	—	—	17	4	6	2	4	6
Talkative	—	—	14	5	5	8	13	9
Imitative	—	—	13	9	4	3	0	1
Aggressive	—	—	—	19	16	17	24	21
Materialistic	—	—	—	16	10	3	13	6
Loyal to family	—	—	—	39	49	41	39	39
Arrogant	—	—	—	14	7	7	5	3
Ambitious	—	—	—	13	23	16	24	18
Tradition loving	—	—	—	13	22	16	16	18
Individualistic	—	—	—	—	24	17	19	16
Passionate	—	—	—	—	14	17	19	14
Nationalistic	—	—	—	—	13	13	19	6
Straightforward	—	—	—	—	12	15	24	19
Intelligent	—	—	—	—	—	14	5	21
Sportsmanlike	—	—	—	—	—	13	8	17
Quick-tempered	—	—	—	—	—	12	13	13
Artistic	—	—	—	—	—	12	6	9
Argumentative	—	—	—	—	—	—	14	11
Loud	—	—	—	—	—	—	11	24
Progressive	—	—	—	—	—	—	11	14
Radical	—	—	—	—	—	—	10	8
Revengeful	—	—	—	—	—	—	11	5
Suspicious	—	—	—	—	—	—	10	6
Talkative	—	—	—	—	—	—	13	9
Faithful	—	—	—	—	—	—	—	15

likely than ever before to say disparaging things about Blacks.

However, these changes may reflect compliance with increasing egalitarian norms rather than a more complete internalization of nonprejudiced value (Crosby, Bromley, & Saxe, 1980). With respect to racial stereotyping questionnaires (as with other self-report measures), there is evidence that respondents often systematically alter their answers to appear more egalitarian than they actually are (Roese & Jamieson, 1993). Thus, what may have changed acros time in the adjective checklist studies is what people regard as socially desirable rather than racial attitudes per se.

Contemporary Racial Attitudes

The nature of prejudice appears to have changed. Whereas traditional forms of prejudice are direct and overt, contemporary forms are indirect and subtle. Aversive racism (see Dovidio & Gaertner,

1991; Dovidio, Mann, & Gaertner 1989; Gaertner & Dovidio, 1986; Kovel, 1970) has been identified as a modern form of prejudice that characterizes the racial attitudes of many Whites who endorse egalitarian values, who regard themselves as nonprejudiced, but who discriminate in subtle, rationalizable ways. Most of the work on aversive racism that will be discussed here involves Whites' attitudes toward Blacks. Elsewhere we have demonstrated the generalizability of these processes to attitudes toward Latinos (Dovidio, Gaertner, Anastasio, & Sanitioso, 1992) and women (Dovidio & Gaertner, 1983).

According to the aversive racism perspective, many people, who consciously and sincerely support egalitarian principles and believe themselves to be nonprejudiced also unconsciously harbor negative feelings and beliefs about Blacks. These feelings and beliefs, which may be based in part on almost unavoidable cognitive (e.g., informational processing biases that result when people are categorized into ingroups and outgroups; see Hamilton & Trolier, 1986), motivational (e.g, personal or group interest), and sociocultural process (e.g., social learning; see Gaertner & Dovidio, 1986).

The feelings of aversive racists toward Blacks are characterized by mild negative feelings, such as fear, disgust, and uneasiness, that tend to motivate avoidance rather than intentionally destructive or hostile behavior, which is more likely to characterize the traditional, old-fashioned form of racism. Relative to the more overt, traditional racists (see Kovel, 1970), aversive racists do not represent the open flame of racial hatred nor do they usually *intend* to act out of bigoted beliefs or feelings. Instead, that bias is expressed in subtle and indirect ways that do not threaten the aversive racist's nonprejudiced self-image. When a negative response can be rationalized on the basis of some factor other than race, bias against Blacks is likely to occur; when these rationalizations are less available, bias is less likely to be manifested. In addition, whereas aversive racists may be very guarded about behaving in anti-Black ways, their biases may be more likely unintentionally manifested in pro-White behaviors (i.e., ingroup favoritism rather than outgroup derogation).

Consistent with the aversive racism perspective, other theories of contemporary racism and sexism also hypothesize that bias is currently expressed more subtly than in the past. One such approach is symbolic racism theory (Kinder & Sears, 1981; McConahay & Hough, 1976; Sears, 1988; Sears, Citrin, & van Laar, 1995; Sears, Hensler, & Speer, 1979; Sears & Allen, 1984) or modern racism (McConahay, 1986) theory. Work on symbolic (Sears, 1988) and modern (McConahay, 1986) racism evolved from the conceptual and practical problems that arose from the weak relationships between traditional self-report prejudice items and racially relevant behaviors, such as voting intentions, that were being obtained in survey data. According to symbolic racism theory, negative feelings toward Blacks that Whites acquire early in life persist into adulthood but are expressed indirectly and symbolically, in terms of opposition to busing or resistance to preferential treatment, rather than directly or overtly, as in support for segregation. The items and theory that were developed focused on "the expression in terms of abstract ideological symbols and symbolic behaviors of the feeling that blacks are violating cherished values and making illegitimate demands for changes in the *status quo*" (McConahay & Hough, 1976, p. 23). These "cherished values" were those, such as personal freedom, that were associated with a politically conservative ideology.

McConahay's (1986) theory of modern racism accepted the basic tenets of symbolic racism but amplified the definition "to add the belief that discrimination no longer exists and that the cherished values are those associated with 'equality' or 'equality of opportunity'" (pp. 95–96). McConahay (1986) further proposed that because modern racism involves the rejection of traditional racist beliefs and the displacement of anti-Black feelings onto more abstract social and political issues, modern racists, like aversive racists, are relatively unaware of their racist feelings. Swim, Aikin, Hall, and Hunter (1995) have extended these notions to contemporary prejudice toward women.

Whereas symbolic and modern racism are subtle forms of contemporary racism that seem to exist among political conservatives, aversive racism is more strongly associated with liberals. In addition, we have proposed that because of the sensitivity of aversive racists to race-related issues, it may not be possible to assess individual differences in aversive racism using self-report measures of prejudice (Gaertner & Dovidio, 1986). Kleinpenning and Hagendoorn (1993), believing otherwise however, have suggested that aversive racism can be assessed through self-reports of how pleasant or unpleasant social interactions (e.g., as classmates) or intimate relations (e.g., as marriage partners) with members of other groups would be. They conceptualize forms of racism on a continuum, beginning with aversive racism (which they regard as the mildest form), and followed by symbolic racism and then old-fashioned racism. Kleinpenning and Hagendoorn (1993) conclude that prejudice is a cumulative dimension that begins with avoidance of minorities in private contexts (aversive prejudice) and runs through beliefs that minority groups receive more social and economic benefits than they deserve (symbolic prejudice) to full-blown racist ideologies portraying minorities as being genetically inferior (old-fashioned prejudice).

Empirical Evidence

Although contemporary forms of bias may be expressed subtly and often unintentionally, the effects may be profound. Across a number of paradigms, we have found consistent evidence of the impact of aversive racism in Whites' responses to Blacks (see Gaertner & Dovidio, 1986). For example, one of our early studies (Gaertner & Dovidio, 1977) demonstrated its influence in an emergency situation.

Emergency Helping

In one early test of the aversive racism perspective, we investigated whether or not high and low prejudice-scoring White students would help Black or White victims in emergency situations depending upon the clarity of norms regarding intervention (Gaertner & Dovidio, 1977). White subjects were led to believe they were the only bystanders or were among three witnesses (all White) to an emergency involving a Black or White victim. According to Darley and Latané (1968), the normatively appropriate behavior, helping, is clearly defined when a bystander is the only witness to an emergency. In contrast, the appropriate response when other bystanders are believed to be present is less clear and obvious: The presumed presence of other bystanders allows bystanders to diffuse responsibility (Darley & Latané, 1968), to relieve feelings of obligation to help by coming to the conclusion that someone else will act.

Gaertner and Dovidio (1977) found that the

White bystanders who believed they were the only witnesses to the emergency were as likely to help Black victims as White victims. When other White bystanders were present, however, Whites were more likely to diffuse responsibility and less likely to intervene to aid the Black victim than the White victim—here they helped the Black victim *half as often* as they helped the White victim. Thus, in the situation in which socially appropriate behavior was clearly defined, White subjects behaved in accordance with their generally nonprejudiced self-images and did not discriminate against the Black victim; when witnesses could rationalize nonintervention, White bystanders discriminated against Black victims. Whereas the situational context was a strong predictor of bias, traditional measures of racial attitudes were not. Neither self-report of prejudice nor authoritarianism correlated overall with responses to the Black victim when bystanders were alone or in the presence of others.

The impact of aversive racism continues to persist today. Its consequences are evident in more considered, deliberative judgments as well as in spontaneous expression of behavior.

Evaluative Judgments

The principles and processes associated with aversive racism may be manifested in situations involving personnel selection. For instance, in a recent study (Dovidio, 1995), White students were recruited ostensibly to help select resident (dormitory) advisors, highly prestigious and competitive student positions, for the coming semester. When the information provided about candidates was unambiguous (i.e., uniformly positive or uniformly negative), Black and White applicants were treated equivalently. However, when the candidate's record was more ambiguous—involving a combination of positive and negative information—White applicants were endorsed more strongly than Black applicants. As in the emergency helping study, contextual ambiguity, not self-reported racial attitudes, predicted whether or not discrimination against Blacks would occur.

Because self-reported prejudice is susceptible to evaluative concerns and impression management motivations and thus may not be a consistent predictor of manifestations of aversive racism, we have sought alternative ways, using response latency procedures (see Dovidio & Gaertner, 1993), to assess an individual's racial beliefs and attitudes. Response latency techniques can limit the influence of consciously controlled processes and provide more social-desirability free measures of attitudes and indications of less censored and perhaps unconscious racial bias (Dovidio & Fazio, 1992).

Response Latency Measures of Bias

Response latency techniques reflect a range of different paradigms. We have used two in our investigations of racial bias. In one study (Gaertner & McLaughlin, 1983), a lexical decision task was used. Participants were presented simultaneously with two strings of letters and were asked to decide (yes or no) if both strings were words. Meyer and Schvaneveldt (1971) reported that highly associated words (e.g., doctor–nurse) produce faster response times than do unassociated words (e.g., nurse–apple). Gaertner and McLaughlin paired the words "Blacks" and "Whites" with positive and negative attributes. In other response latency experiments (Dovidio & Gaertner, 1993), a priming paradigm has been used. Rosch (1975) found that "priming" by first presenting the name of a category, such as "fruit," facilitates decisions about typical instances (e.g., "orange") more than atypical instances (e.g., "prune"). In our studies, participants were first presented with the category primes "Black" and "White," representing racial groups. These primes were then followed by positive and negative characteristics. The subject's task was to decide if the characteristic could ever describe a member of the primed social category. Faster response times are assumed to reflect greater association.

The results of our two response latency paradigms were consistent. As indicated by response latencies, negative characteristics were not more associated with Blacks than with Whites; in both experiments, positive characteristics were more associated with Whites than with Blacks. As in our previous studies, bias exists but is expressed in an indirect and less overtly anti-Black form—and in ways that would not threaten an aversive racist's liberal and egalitarian self-image.

Furthermore, in subsequent research we demonstrated that response latency measures of prejudice such as these predict (over and above traditional self-report measures) subtle and unconscious expressions of bias, such as negative nonverbal cues (e.g., lower levels of eye contact) by Whites

engaged in interracial interaction (Dovidio et al., 1994). These negative nonverbal behaviors, in turn, can produce a self-fulfilling prophecy by contributing to a less trustful and friendly exchange and to more negative reciprocal displays by Black partners (Dovidio & Gaertner, 1995). For example, Fazio, Jackson, Dunton, and Williams (1995) found that a response latency measure of racial attitudes (based on automatic, unintentional associations) predicted perceptions of how friendly White participants behaved toward a Black experimenter, whereas consciously expressed racial attitudes did not. Word, Zanna, and Cooper (1974) demonstrated that subtle negative displays can have significant detrimental effects on Black applicants in interview situations; these recent studies extend this finding by directly documenting the role of contemporary forms of prejudice. Thus, because of these unintentional biases, providing equal opportunity may not be sufficient to insure fair and equal outcomes.

When Is Equal Opportunity Unequal?

Even when equal access for employment is provided in principle, subtle, perhaps unconscious, expressions of bias related to aversive racism, like more blatant forms, may limit opportunities for Blacks and other minorities in practice. We have hypothesized that aversive racism is more intensely manifested in situations in which Whites may be directly or symbolically threatened by the advancement of Blacks to positions of status and control.

Acceptance of Competence

In one study, for instance, we investigated the relationship between status and bias in the context of a decision with implications for participants–making admissions decisions for their university (Kline & Dovidio, 1982). Applicant qualifications were systematically varied: Participants evaluated a poorly qualified applicant, a moderately qualified candidate, or a highly qualified applicant. In addition, the race of the applicant was manipulated by a photograph attached to the file. The central question concerned how this picture would affect participants' admissions decisions.

Discrimination against the Black applicant occurred, but, as expected, it did not occur equally in all conditions. Students rated the poorly qualified Black and White applicants equally low. They showed some bias when they evaluated the moderately qualified White applicant slightly higher than the comparable African-American candidate. Discrimination against the Black applicant was most apparent, however, when the applicants were *highly* qualified. This bias can also be interpreted as a pro-White manifestation of aversive racism (Gaertner et al., 1996). Although White students evaluated the highly qualified African-American applicant very positively, they judged the highly qualified White applicant—with exactly the same credentials—as even better. Thus, a situation that appears to offer equal opportunity to very well-qualified applicants still favors Whites over Blacks because of subtle and pervasive biases.

This study also included individual items that contributed to the overall evaluative score—scaled according to how directly they related to the information presented in the applicant's transcript. The less directly related the item was to the transcript information, the greater the bias ($r = .69$). These results are consistent with the finding that Whites tend to evaluate Blacks less favorably than Whites on subjective dimensions of work performance (Kraiger & Ford, 1985) and support Goddard's (1986) observation in applied settings that "vague, ill-defined, subjective criteria lend themselves to all kinds of biased judgments" (p. 34).

Maintaining the Status Quo

Whereas blatant racial and ethnic prejudices relate to support for policies that unconditionally restrict the rights and opportunities of minority groups, subtle racism is associated with support for the *status quo* or for restrictions when other justifications (e.g., lack of credentials) are available (Pettigrew & Meertens, 1995). Thus, in other research we investigated the possibility that the generally articulated issue of relative competence is a rationalization in which a nonracial factor, competence, is used by Whites to object to the advancement of Blacks in ways that increase the likelihood that Whites will be subordinated to minority groups.

This reasoning also has relevance to reactions to affirmative action. Consistent with the aversive racism framework, resistance to affirmative action is not commonly expressed directly, but rather mainly as concerns about individual freedom or about unfair distribution of rewards. Nevertheless, although common protests by Whites regarding affirmative action seem to express mainly the concern that *qualified* Whites will be disadvantaged relative to *less qualified* Blacks, it is possible that the reversal of the traditional role relationship, in which Whites occupied positions of superior status, represents the primary threat to Whites.

The results of two separate studies comparing the reactions of White male and female participants to a Black male partner (Dovidio & Gaertner, 1981) and a White female partner (Dovidio & Gaertner, 1983) relative to a White male partner produced convergent findings. Specifically, relative status, rather than relative ability, was the primary determinant of positive behaviors toward Black male and White female partners. Regardless of their competence, Black male and White female supervisors were responded to *less favorably* than were Black male or White female subordinates. In contrast, in both studies White male supervisors were responded to somewhat *more positively* than were White male subordinates.

How could participants in these experiments rationalize not responding as positively to competent Black and female supervisors? Participants' postexperimental evaluations of their partners revealed that their behaviors may have been mediated by perceptions of *relative* intelligence (competence). Although participants' ratings indicated that they accepted high-ability White male partners as being somewhat more intelligent than themselves, participants described even high-ability Black partners as significantly less intelligent than themselves and high-ability female partners as no more intelligent than themselves. To the extent that majority group members are reluctant to believe Blacks and women are higher or equal in competence compared to themselves, they are likely to perceive programs that foster the advancement of members of these groups over themselves and members of their group as unfair preferential treatment. This biased perception of relative competence also decreases the likelihood that passive equal employment opportunity programs can insure truly equitable treatment of disadvantaged groups by the majority group.

Subtle Bias and the Glass Ceiling

Aversive racism and contemporary forms of sexism are difficult to identify definitively in complex organizations because they are subtle and other explanations are usually possible. In fact, aversive racism is generally manifested *only* when other explanations that can rationalize bias are present. Thus, we cannot say that simply because disparities exist in organizations, racism is the cause. But, where racism exists, disparities will exist (see Murrell & Jones, 1996). These disparities generally reflect the patterns we have discovered in the laboratory. Across organizations as diverse as the armed forces, federal government, and Fortune 1000 companies, greater racial disparities occur at higher status levels. In addition, these patterns have persisted over the past decade.

Across the different branches of the military in 1988, African Americans who were identified as qualified for officer promotions succeeded at significantly lower rates than did White candidates. Consistent with our laboratory demonstrations, disparities in promotion rates tended to increase with higher ranks. Within the Navy, for example, in 1988 African Americans represented 13% of the force, but only 5% of the officers and 1.5% of the admirals. We have also examined patterns of disparities for various segments of federal employees and found similar evidence: Blacks are generally less well represented in higher grades (e.g., GS 16–18) than in lower grades. Furthermore, these disparities have remained relatively stable across time as well.

A recent Department of Labor survey of Fortune 1000 companies provides independent evidence of the "glass ceiling effect" for Blacks and other minorities in industry. Representations of minorities consistently declined with higher occupational status (see Murrell & Jones, 1996). A Department of Commerce survey further confirmed substantial income disparities between African-American and White men. In 1989, African-American men with a high school education earned $6230 less per year than White men with comparable education ($20,280 vs. $26,510). The gap was even larger ($9710) between college-educated African-American and White men ($31,380 vs. $41,090).

Thus, across a range of settings we see consistent patterns of disparities in occupational advancement and income. We acknowledge that the "glass ceiling effect" can occur for a wide range of reasons and that the leap from laboratory to organizations is a large one. Nevertheless, the pattern of disparities that we see in organizations conforms to our predictions.

Contemporary Bias and Affirmative Action

We contend that one important factor in reactions to affirmative action programs is subtle, modern racism. Like Kluegel and Smith (1986), we argue that "opposition to equal opportunity programs stems from the threat these programs present to an economic order that is believed to be just in principle and to work well in fact" (Kluegel & Smith, 1986, p. 212).

Thus, although racist traditions may have initially produced social inequalities, many Whites, truly believing they are nonprejudiced and nondiscriminating, may presently be participating in the continued restriction of opportunities for Blacks and other minorities by opposing programs that threaten their own advantaged status.

Perceived Fairness

One popular criticism of affirmative action centers on negative reactions to specific selection procedures. The protest expressed by many Whites concerning the *Regents of the University of California v. Bakke* (1978) decision illustrates this point. In the Bakke case, many people objected to the admissions procedure of the medical school because it was seen as a form of "reverse discrimination" that violated their fundamental beliefs about procedural fairness or justice (Binion, 1987). That is, the commonly articulated reason for challenging the admissions procedure that involved preferential treatment for Blacks was that this policy was discriminatory and negated individual selection, evaluation, and advancement based on merit. Thus, policy-based explanations, particularly those focusing on preferential treatment, suggest that resistance to affirmative action occurs because individuals believe that category membership (e.g., race or sex) should not be a relevant criterion used in merit-based decisions.

There is indeed theoretical and empirical support for this view. According to the concept of procedural justice (Thibaut & Walker, 1975), the perceived fairness of a procedure influences an individual's evaluations of agents, representatives, and other persons associated with that procedure.

The fairer a procedure is perceived to be, the more positive are the evaluations of those associated with the policy (Lind, Kurtz, Musante, Walker & Thibaut, 1980). With respect to affirmative action, the more weight given to category-based criteria, such as race or sex, the less fair the procedure is perceived to be and the more negative the reaction to the policy and the persons involved (Greenberg, 1987; Lind et al., 1980; Nacoste, 1985, 1986, 1987a, 1987b, 1994). From this perspective, perceived fairness of the specific policy is highly influential in determining a person's evaluation of an affirmative action program.

If perceptions of fairness are a key factor in reactions to affirmative action, then how a specific policy is framed can substantially influence an individual's response (Gamson & Modigliani, 1987). Clayton and Tangri (1989) distinguish between microjustice and macrojustice evaluations of affirmative action. Microjustice includes perceptions of justice and fairness that are relevant to a specific individual (e.g., a specific affirmative action candidate or policy). Macrojustice refers to perceptions of fairness that consider the broader social, historical, legal, and moral contexts. It is possible that what appears to be unfair at the micro level of a particular instance may be seen as very fair at a more macro level.

Whereas many people may initially feel that affirmative action policies violate equity when characteristics such as race or sex are weighed in the decision at the micro level, they may come to see the procedure as fair if, at the macro level, they recognize the value of diversity—"that individuals bring with them into the organization not merely different amounts of the same things, but also different kinds of things that make them valuable to an organization" (Clayton & Tangri, 1989, p. 180). Similarly, whereas preferential action may be seen as unfair in a specific case, the same action may be perceived as more fair if it is presented as a compensatory response to address historical inequities. Thus, Clayton and Tangri (1989) propose that affirmative action is justifiable in terms of equity if the relevant inputs are defined appropriately, that is, at the macro level. In the absence of the aggregated information about disparities that are commonly provided by affirmative action programs, issues of microjustice are frequently more salient than issues of macrojustice in determining reactions to affirmative action.

Racism and Resistance

Racism may also motivate resistance to affirmative action, either directly or indirectly. However, it is important to note that, although racism may motivate resistance to affirmative action, opposition to affirmative action does not *necessarily* imply racially biased motivations. Opposition may be based, for example, on individual beliefs in meritocracy or individualistic values, independent of racial considerations. In fact, automatically and erroneously equating opposition to affirmative action with racism may obfuscate productive policy debate. Nevertheless, it is quite possible that opposition to affirmative action may be motivated to a significant degree by overt and subtle racism.

The connection between opposition to affirmative action, on the one hand, and racism, on the other, has been suggested by several authors (see Benokraitis & Feagin, 1978), and this relationship, in terms of old-fashioned racism, has been empirically verified (Kinder & Sears, 1981; Kravitz, 1995). With respect to contemporary racism, in particular, Jacobson (1985) found that symbolic racism was a stronger predictor of negative attitudes toward affirmative action than old-fashioned racism, stereotyping, or self-interest. In addition, symbolic racism was the best predictor of negative reactions to a concrete instance of the implementation of affirmative action: Respondents were asked to state their approval or disapproval of the Supreme Court's dismissal of a case involving a union's claim that AT&T's affirmative action program constituted reverse discrimination.

Similarly, Sears et al. (1995), using data from four representative surveys, recently found that measures of symbolic racism predicted Whites' opposition not only to policies specifically presented as benefitting Blacks (affirmative action for Blacks; open housing for Blacks) but also to policies designed to benefit all racial and ethnic groups but which are commonly associated with Blacks (e.g., welfare support). Furthermore, for policies designed to support minorities in general (e.g., multiculturalism policies), measures of symbolic racism toward Blacks and Latinos (but not Asians) were significant predictors of opposition. Thus, although there may be a number of predictors of who will oppose affirmative action, symbolic racism appears to be among the strongest.

Aversive Racism and Affirmative Action

Racism may also manifest itself more subtly and indirectly in opposition to affirmative action—when this resistance can be justified on the basis of some factor other than race, such as unfair procedures. The aversive racism framework predicts that negative reactions to affirmative action among Whites will be most pronounced when its benefits to groups associated with negative feelings and beliefs (e.g., Blacks) are emphasized *and* the procedures are framed in ways that can be perceived of as unfair (e.g., preferential treatment). Consistent with this reasoning, Kinder and Sanders (1990) found that framing affirmative action in different ways could influence the extent to which it evoked reactions based on racial sentiments.

Two studies illustrate how aversive racism indirectly influences Whites' reactions to affirmative action. One was a study by Murrell, Dietz-Uhler, Dovidio, Gaertner, and Drout (1994) in which participants were questioned using a full-profile (factorial) survey design (Rossi & Anderson, 1982; Wittink & Cattin, 1989). Specifically, White respondents were questioned about their perceptions of fairness and support of four common ways of presenting affirmative action policies. Two of these policies focused on micro level actions varying in the degree to which the action places emphasis on nonmerit factors to address disparities (preferential treatment and reverse discrimination). The other two policies provided a macro level justification in terms of achieving diversity or remedying historical injustices. Based on Clayton and Tangri's (1989) analysis, we predicted that respondents would show less resistance to policy statements with explicit macro justifications than to policy statements that focus at the micro level of implementation. In addition, to evaluate the possibility that resistance to affirmative action may be an expression of racial bias, we assessed subjects' reactions to affirmative action policies involving three target groups that subjects were not members of: Blacks, elderly persons, and physically handicapped persons. To the extent that racial bias is a key factor in reactions to affirmative action, White subjects would be expected to exhibit more negative responses to policies targeted at Blacks than at other groups, particularly when these reactions could be justified on the basis of some factor other than race, such as violations of macro justice.

The findings supported the predictions. Our results underscore the importance of how a policy is framed: Programs that were framed in terms of macrojustice by remedying historical injustice (past discrimination) or increasing cultural diversity were more acceptable to respondents than those that focused on specific implementation (i.e., preferential treatment and reverse discrimination). In addition, consistent with the hypothesis that racism contributes to resistance to affirmative action, *in general* policies directed at benefitting Blacks were responded to more negatively than were policies for persons with physical handicaps or elderly persons. Moreover, consistent with the specific predictions of the aversive racism framework, Whites' responses to affirmative action were *particularly* negative when the group described as benefitting was Blacks (vs. handicapped or elderly persons) *and* when the goal of the policy was presented as involving "preferential treatment" or "reverse discrimination" (vs. as achieving cultural diversity or compensating for past discrimination). If, as egalitarian values would suggest, race were truly an irrelevant factor, attitudes toward "reverse discrimination" polices would be uniformly negative, regardless of the specific target group involved. However, we found that, whereas giving preference based on nonmerit factors is reacted to negatively, giving such preference to Blacks produces a significantly stronger negative reaction.

A second experiment (Dovidio, Gaertner, & Murrell, 1994) further pursued the potential mediating role of perceived fairness. In particular, it was hypothesized that the effects of policy framing and subtle racism affect perceptions of fairness, and perceptions of fairness in turn influence Whites' acceptance of or resistance to affirmative action policies (see Nacoste, 1996; Kravitz, 1995). In this study, to facilitate a perception of macrojustice, affirmative action was presented as a policy "to correct for past discrimination by re-considering the procedures by which decisions are made" (p. 5). In a second condition, affirmative action was presented as a policy "designed to produce positive actions (outcomes) . . . for members of particular minority groups" (p. 6)—essentially a rephrasing of the term affirmative (positive) action. It was hypothesized that framing affirmative action as a remedy for past discrimination would produce perceptions of greater fairness, which in turn would predict greater support.

Following the Murrell et al. (1994) study, we manipulated the salience of the group associated with affirmative action. Although affirmative action was always presented as a program benefitting a minority group, different question formats focused on African Americans, Native Americans, and handicapped persons. Native Americans were included because pretesting indicated that they represented a minority group that did not evoke significant negative reactions among potential participants. Again, based on the aversive racism framework, we hypothesized that support for affirmative action would be lower when the association with African Americans was made salient than when the association was with Native Americans or handicapped persons. Furthermore, we predicted that this effect would be more pronounced when the affirmative action was not framed in terms of compensating for past injustices. As we noted earlier in this paper, Dovidio and Gaertner (1981) found that Whites may use issues such as procedural unfairness as race-related rationalizations for resistance to affirmative action. Thus, this study also directly examined the extent to which these differential responses are mediated by perceptions of fairness. Attitudes were measured in this study both to affirmative action and colorblind opportunity programs.

Overall, support for affirmative action (Positive Action) and equal opportunity (Colorblind Opportunity) policies were significantly negatively correlated, $r = -.51$, supporting Crosby's (1994) contention that these represent alternative and potentially competing approaches to addressing racial disparities. In general, support was much stronger for colorblind equal opportunity policies than for affirmative action. The results for both policy framing and the group benefiting from the program conceptually replicated the results of Murrell et al. (1994). Providing an explanation of the need for affirmative action (i.e., to remedy past discrimination) uniquely affected attitudes toward these programs. Endorsement for Positive Action was stronger when the description of affirmative action included a justifying explanation than when it did not; no difference was obtained for Colorblind Opportunity. With respect to racial attitudes, Whites' self-reported racial attitudes (Brigham, 1993) directly predicted more negative reactions to affirmative action, $r = -.40$, $p < .03$.

Supportive of the aversive racism framework, which proposes that racism *subtly* influences

policy-related attitudes, when affirmative action was accompanied by an explicit justification, the benefitting group had no impact on attitudes toward affirmative action. However, when no explanation occurred, support for Positive Action tended to be weaker and support for Colorblind Opportunity stronger when the presentation made the benefits to African Americans salient than when the presentation emphasized the benefits to persons with handicaps or Native Americans.

Consistent with the hypothesized role of perceived fairness in policy-related attitudes, perceived fairness was positively correlated with the strength of support for Positive Action, $r = .71$. Respondents who judged affirmative action to be more fair indicated greater support for Positive Action. In contrast, people who viewed affirmative action to be less fair showed stronger support for Colorblind Opportunity, $r = -.27$. Furthermore, as expected, fairness mediated the effects of attitudes toward affirmative action—but only partially and incompletely. The effect of policy framing and Whites' racial attitudes on responses to affirmative action remained statistically significant even after perceptions of fairness were controlled. Thus, even though perceptions of unfairness may be used to justify racially motivated resistance to affirmative action (Dovidio & Gaertner, 1981), the effect of overt racism may also continue to be more direct.

These perceptions and reactions can significantly undermine the effectiveness of the beneficiaries of affirmative action and help to create a self-fulfilling prophecy. Turner and Pratkanis's (1994; see also Pratkanis & Turner, 1996) review of the literature on recipient reactions to preferential selection and affirmative reaction revealed that perceptions of unfairness in the selection process negatively influenced self-evaluations of competence and task performance. For example, with respect to both sex and race, work by Major, Crocker, and their colleagues (e.g., Crocker & Major, 1989; Major & Crocker, 1993; Major, Feinstein, & Crocker, 1994) has demonstrated that ambiguity about personal merit in selection or promotion can be detrimental to the esteem and performance of members of groups whose competence is doubted by themselves or others. Thus, when selection procedures are *perceived* to be unfair in any way, members of the benefitting groups may become stigmatized.

Implications for Policy and Research

In previous sections we have offered evidence that the prejudices of the majority group continue to exist, often in subtle contemporary forms. The basic propositions of the aversive racism framework, which have received empirical support, are summarized in Table 8.2. This type of subtle prejudice contributes along with the traditional form to unequal treatment of traditionally disadvantaged groups and to resistance to programs designed to ameliorate the disadvantaged status of these groups caused by past injustices. The operation of these prejudices demonstrate the *need* for affirmative action.

Three key aspects of aversive racism present particular conceptual and practical challenges to ensuring truly fair treatment and equitable outcomes for traditionally disadvantaged groups. First, discrimination against members of disadvantaged groups occurs in situations in which evaluative criteria are ambiguous. Second, discrimination may occur unintentionally or unconsciously, often involving ostensibly nonrace-related rationalizations. Third, establishing positive egalitarian norms and developing greater awareness of intergroup interdependence and connection may ultimately be needed to address some of the root causes of modern forms of bias.

Evaluative Criteria

Both laboratory and field studies have demonstrated that when criteria for evaluation are am-

biguous, Whites favor other Whites over people of color (see also Gaertner & Dovidio, 1986). Thus discrimination may occur, but in ways that can be defended as nonracially motivated. These biases increase as the criteria for evaluation become more subjective and as members of traditionally disadvantaged groups approach positions of greater status.

This subtle process underlying discrimination can be identified and isolated under the controlled conditions of the laboratory. However, in organizational decision making, in which the controlled conditions of an experiment are rarely possible, this process presents a substantial challenge to the equitable treatment of members of disadvantaged groups. Krieger (1995), in the *Stanford Law Review,* notes that this aspect of contemporary bias poses a particular problem for society and the legal system: "Herein lies the practical problem. . . . Validating subjective decisionmaking systems is neither empirically nor economically feasible, especially for jobs where intangible qualities, such as interpersonal skills, creativity, and ability to make sound judgments under conditions of uncertainty are critical" (p. 1232).

Because the role of aversive racism is difficult to identify definitively (legally or even personally) in an individual case, affirmative action policies are particularly important. As Crosby and Cordova observed (1996), a primary function of affirmative action policies is to maintain accurate records of aggregated outcomes for various groups. Systematic monitoring of disparities along consensually accepted dimensions can therefore reveal cu-

Table 8.2. Propositions of the Aversive Racism Framework: Summary of the Evidence

Aversive racists

- Have a conscious commitment to equality; they
  - —score low on self-report measures of prejudice
  - —do not discriminate when these actions can readily be attributed to racial bias
- But at the same time harbor negative feelings toward Blacks; they
  - —have unconscious negative associations with Blacks
  - —typically express more positive attributions of Whites than of Blacks while avoiding overtly negative attributions of Blacks
- Discriminate unintentionally in subtle and rationalizable ways, such as
  - —when a negative response can be justified on the basis of some factor other than race
  - —when evaluative criteria are ambiguous
  - —in terms of ingroup favoritism rather than outgroup derogation
- Are more likely to manifest subtle discrimination in response to direct or symbolic threats to the *status quo,* such as
  - —by showing less acceptance of and support for high status relative to low status Blacks
  - —by resisting policies designed to change the *status quo* that benefit Whites when these policies can be opposed on nonracial grounds

mulative effects of contemporary forms of bias that are more evident than the impact that can be determined in any particular case. This is an essential contribution of affirmative programs for recognizing and ultimately addressing biases.

Intentionality

As research has indicated, good intentions are not sufficient to guarantee that equal opportunity will insure equal treatment. Contemporary forms of prejudice toward people of color and toward women (Swim et al., 1995) exert their influence subtly and typically unconsciously and unintentionally. Aversive racists, modern racists, and symbolic racists believe they are nonprejudiced and often perceive that, in general, discrimination is no longer a social problem. In addition, negative responses to members of traditionally disadvantaged groups or to policies designed to benefit these groups are typically justified on the basis of nonrace-related rationales. For example, the research demonstrates that although concerns about the fairness of affirmative action programs may be articulated as reasons to oppose these programs, subtle biases may be operating by influencing these perceptions of fairness, which in turn affect the intensity of the negative reactions.

This general process insulates aversive racists from recognizing that their actions might have been racially motivated and permits unintentional bias to persist. It protects people from legal liability as well. Krieger (1995) writes, "What implications derive from . . . the proposition that a broad class of discriminatory employment decisions result not from discriminatory motivation, but from normal cognitive processes and strategies that tend to bias intergroup perception and judgment? The overwhelming conclusion is that there now exists a fundamental 'lack of fit' between jurisprudential construction of discrimination and the actual phenomenon it purports to represent" (p. 1217). For instance, although the Supreme Court has never explicitly labeled intentionality as a mandatory presumption in discrimination cases, it has traditionally been treated as such (Krieger, 1995). Furthermore, until recently (see *Price Waterhouse v. Hopkins,* 1989), the burden of proof in discrimination cases involved demonstrating that intentional discrimination was the *only* cause of unequal treatment.

This aspect of aversive racism also suggests that

affirmative action policies are likely to be more effective than passive equal employment opportunity policies for combatting the effects of contemporary bias. Affirmative action policies are *outcome based*; issues of intentionality are not central. This is important because demonstrating intentionality, which is typically a major issue of concern for equal employment opportunity programs, is problematic because of contemporary forms of bias. For instance, we provided evidence in this paper that people may discriminate against traditionally disadvantaged groups without being aware of it. Complementing these findings, other researchers (see Crosby, 1982, 1984; Taylor, Wright, Moghaddam, & Lalonde, 1990) have found that the *victims* of discrimination may also not recognize that they have been personally discriminated against.

Intergroup Relations

To the extent that subtle forms of bias present invisible but substantial barriers that prevent passive equal employment opportunity programs from achieving equitable outcomes, attention also needs to be given to addressing this bias in a larger context—in the climate of intergroup relations within the organization and society. Affirmative action policies can have an important role at both levels. A key element is the acknowledgement of racial or gender category membership rather than the "color-blind" model that is associated with many passive equal employment opportunity policies.

Affirmative action programs help to establish clear norms about the importance of full equality for groups recognized as different than one's own. Pettigrew (1994) has argued that to address the motivations underlying contemporary forms of bias, it is as important to establish positive norms for pursuing equality actively as it is to strengthen existing norms against discrimination. At the very least, these norms can produce significant compliance. For instance, across a number of years in the U.S. Army, among candidates identified as qualified, the officer promotion rates of minorities were consistently lower than rates for Whites. Concerned about these disparities, the Army set as an explicit goal for promotion boards in 1991 and 1992 that women and minorities be promoted at a rate no lower than the overall service rate. The promotion boards achieved these objectives in a way that was unprecedented in any previous year.

In 1993, however, the promotion boards were not informed explicitly of this goal; in that year, minorities were again promoted at rates consistently below the service average.

The impact of these proactive norms can also have longer term effects. To the extent that administrators and top management strongly and persuasively present affirmative action as an egalitarian policy, aversive racists should embrace it in practice as well as in principle. To resist affirmative action under these circumstances could readily be interpreted as a racially biased reaction. Our research on aversive racism indicates that when norms for appropriate behavior are clearly defined and when a biased response can be recognized, Whites are consistently as positive in their behavior toward Blacks as toward Whites (Gaertner & Dovidio, 1986).

In addition, these norms may be internalized as an important aspect of organizational citizenship. Corporate research has revealed that commitment to affirmative action by top management and higher administration is a key factor for successfully implementing affirmative action and achieving corporate equality (Hitt & Keats, 1984; Marino, 1980). Allstate Insurance, for example, made corporate diversity a high priority in 1976, initiating a voluntary diversity program that exceeded federal affirmative action requirements. From 1975 to 1995, it increased its representation of Black white-collar workers from 9.5% to 14.8%, a rate of increase that is more than double the rate of increase for all other corporations (Annin, 1995).

Using an alternate strategy involving the recognition and recategorization of group memberships, we have attempted to reduce intergroup bias by changing group members' cognitive representations from two groups to one group (Gaertner et al., 1993, 1994). In application, recategorization from different, potentially competing groups to one group can be achieved by increasing the salience of existing common superordinate group memberships or by introducing new factors (e.g., common goals or fate) that are perceived to be shared by members. For instance, the Allstate diversity program was established, in part, to help reach a broader market, which would benefit all members of the Allstate staff. We have varied the spatial arrangement of members of different groups in a room and the presence of symbols that highlight either separate group memberships or a superordinate group identity, and we have found that evaluations of former outgroup members significantly improve as these individuals become identified with the superordinate, more inclusive ingroup (Gaertner et al., 1993).

We view the recategorization of different groups into one group as a particularly powerful and pragmatic strategy for improving reactions to affirmative action. Paralleling Pettigrew's suggestion of facilitating positive behaviors in addition to inhibiting negative discriminatory behaviors, recategorization redirects ingroup biases (Brewer, 1979; Messick & Mackie, 1989) to the direct benefit of people formerly perceived as outgroup members. Creating the perception of a common ingroup promotes the self-sacrificing behaviors that affirmative action apparently requires for an advantaged majority to yield its privileges to a disadvantaged minority (Kramer & Brewer, 1984; Meindl & Lerner, 1983). People also apply different and more generous standards of morality, justice, and fairness to ingroup members than to outgroup members (Opotow, 1990). Moreover, we hypothesize that in assigning jobs or in deciding admissions, people would be more willing to use a need-based rule than an equity-based rule (Deutsch, 1975) when applicants are perceived to be members of a common salient ingroup rather than individual strangers. Furthermore, in general, people tend to be more helpful to ingroup members than to other people (Hornstein, 1976; Piliavin, Dovidio, Gaertner, & Clark, 1981). Directly relevant to affirmative action, Smith and Tyler (1996) found that middle-class Whites who identified more strongly as Americans—a more inclusive group identity—than as Caucasians had more positive attitudes toward affirmative action policies intended to benefit disadvantaged groups. Thus, this strategy cannot only improve general intergroup attitudes, but also it can facilitate the acceptance of policies and the implementation of programs that enhance the employment opportunities for minorities and permit an equitable redistribution of economic resources.

Conclusion

In this paper, we have attempted to identify and document the subtle nature of contemporary forms of bias. In contrast to the direct and easily discernible traditional forms, contemporary biases are expressed, often unintentionally, in indirect and rationalizable ways. Because of the subtle nature of contemporary bias, passive equal opportunity employment policies may not insure the fair and unbiased treatment of traditionally disadvantaged groups. Policies designed to protect disadvantaged individuals and groups from one type of discrimination based on overt antioutgroup actions may be ineffective for addressing biased treatment based on ingroup favoritism that may characterize aversive racism (Gaertner et al., 1996). In contrast, affirmative action, with its focus on documenting and responding to disparities at the aggregate level, addresses some of the particularly problematic aspects of subtle biases that permit disparities to persist despite people's good intentions.

REFERENCES

Annin, P. (1995, April 3). The corporation: Allstate saw the light when it started following the money. *Newsweek,* 32–33.

Benokraitis, N. V., & Feagin, J. R. (1978). *Affirmative action and equal opportunity: Action, inaction, reaction.* Boulder, CO: Westview Press.

Binion, G. (1987). Affirmative action reconsidered: Justifications, objections, myths, and misconceptions. *Women and Politics, 7,* 43–62.

Brewer, M. B. (1979). In-group bias in the minimal intergroup situation: A cognitive-motivational analysis. *Psychological Bulletin, 86,* 307–324.

Brigham, J. C. (1993). College students' racial attitudes. *Journal of Applied Social Psychology, 23,* 1933–1967.

Clayton, S. D., & Tangri, S. S. (1989). The justice of affirmative action. In F. A. Blanchard & F. J. Crosby (Eds.), *Affirmative action in perspective* (pp. 177-192). New York: Springer-Verlag.

Crocker, J., & Major, B. (1989). Social stigma and self-esteem: The self-protective properties of stigma. *Psychological Review, 96,* 608–630.

Crosby, F. J. (1982). *Relative deprivation and working women.* New York: Oxford University Press.

Crosby, F. J. (1984). The denial of personal discrimination. *American Behavioral Scientist, 27,* 371–386.

Crosby, F. J. (1994). Understanding affirmative action. *Basic and Applied Social Psychology, 15,* 13–41.

Crosby, F. J., & Cordova, D. I. (1996). Words worth of wisdom: Toward an understanding of affirmative action. *Journal of Social Issues, 52,* 33–49.

Crosby, F., Bromley, S., & Saxe, L. (1980). Recent unobtrusive studies of Black and White discrimination and prejudice: A literature review. *Psychological Bulletin, 87,* 546–563.

Darley, J. M., & Latané, B. (1968). Bystander intervention in emergencies: Diffusion of responsibility. *Journal of Personality and Social Psychology, 8,* 377–383.

Davis, J. A., & Smith, T. W. (1991). *General social surveys, 1972–1991: Cumulative codebook.* Chicago, IL: National Opinion Research Center.

Deutsch, M. (1975). Equity, equality, and need: What determines which value will be used as a basis for distributive justice? *Journal of Social Issues, 31*(3), 137–149.

Devine, P. G., & Elliot, A. J. (1995). Are racial stereotypes really fading? The Princeton Trilogy revisited. *Personality and Social Psychology Bulletin, 21,* 1139–1150.

Dovidio, J. F. (1995). *Bias in evaluative judgments and personnel selection: The role of ambiguity.* Unpublished manuscript, Department of Psychology, Colgate University, Hamilton, NY.

Dovidio, J. F., Brigham, J. C., Johnson, B. T., & Gaertner, S. L. (1996). Stereotyping, prejudice, and discrimination: Another look. In N. Macrae, M. Hewstone, & C. Stangor (Eds.), *Foundations of stereotypes and stereotyping* (pp. 276–319). New York: Guilford.

Dovidio, J. F., & Fazio, R. H. (1992). New technologies for the direct and indirect assessment of attitudes. In J. Tanur (Ed.), *Questions about survey questions: Meaning, memory, attitudes, and social interaction* (pp. 204–237). New York: Russell Sage Foundation.

Dovidio, J. F., & Gaertner, S. L. (1981). The effects of race, status, and ability on helping behavior. *Social Psychology Quarterly, 44,* 192–203.

Dovidio, J. F., & Gaertner, S. L. (1983). The effects of sex, status, and ability on helping behavior. *Journal of Applied Social Psychology, 13,* 191–205.

Dovidio, J. F., & Gaertner, S. L. (1986). Prejudice, discrimination, and racism: Historical trends and contemporary approaches. In J. F. Dovidio & S. L. Gaertner (Eds.), *Prejudice, discrimination, and racism* (pp. 1–34). Orlando, FL: Academic Press.

Dovidio, J. F., & Gaertner, S. L. (1991). Changes in the nature and expression of racial prejudice. In H. Knopke, J. Norrell, & R. Rogers (Eds.), *Opening doors: An appraisal of race relations in contemporary America* (pp. 201–241). Tuscaloosa, AL: University of Alabama Press.

Dovidio, J. F., & Gaertner, S. L. (1993). Stereotypes and evaluative intergroup bias. In D. M. Mackie & D. L. Hamilton (Eds.), *Affect, cognition, and stereotyping* (pp. 167–193). San Diego, CA: Academic Press.

Dovidio, J. F., & Gaertner, S. L. (1995, September). *Stereotyping, prejudice, and discrimination: Spontaneous and deliberative processes.* Paper presented at the joint meeting of the Society for Experimental Psychology and the European Association of Experimental Social Psychology, Washington, DC.

Dovidio, J. F., Gaertner, S. L., Anastasio, P. A., & Sanitioso, R. (1992). Cognitive and motivational bases of bias: The implications of aversive racism for attitudes toward Hispanics. In S. Knouse, P. Rosenfeld, & A. Culbertson (Eds.), *Hispanics in the workplace* (pp. 75–106). Newbury Park, CA: Sage.

Dovidio, J. F., Gaertner, S. L., & Murrell, A. J. (1994, August). *Why people resist affirmative action.* Paper presented at the annual convention of the American Psychological Association, Los Angeles, CA.

Dovidio, J. F., Johnson, C., Gaertner, S. L., Validzic, A., Howard, A., & Eisinger, N. (1994, April). *Racial bias and the role of implicit and explicit attitudes.* Paper presented at the annual meeting of the Eastern Psychological Association, Providence, RI.

Dovidio, J. F., Mann, J. A., & Gaertner, S. L. (1989). Resistance to affirmative action: The implication of aversive racism. In F. A. Blanchard & F. J. Crosby (Eds.), *Affirmative action in perspective* (pp. 83–102): New York: Springer-Verlag.

Fazio, R. H., Jackson, J. R., Dunton, B. C., & Williams, C. J. (1995). Variability in automatic activation as an unobtrusive measure of racial attitudes: A bona fide pipeline? *Journal of Personality and Social Psychology, 69,* 1013–1027.

Gaertner, S. L., & Dovidio, J. F. (1977). The subtlety of White racism, arousal, and helping behavior. *Journal of Personality and Social Psychology, 35,* 691–707.

Gaertner, S. L., & Dovidio, J. F. (1986). The aversive form of racism. In J. F. Dovidio & S. L. Gaertner (Eds.), *Prejudice, discrimination, and racism* (pp. 61–89). Orlando, FL: Academic Press.

Gaertner, S. L., Dovidio, J. F., Anastasio, P. A., Bachman, B. A., & Rust, M. C. (1993). The common ingroup identity model: Recategorization and the reduction of intergroup bias. In W. Stroebe & M. Hewstone (Eds.), *European review of social psychology* (Vol. 4, pp. 1–26). New York: John Wiley & Sons.

Gaertner, S. L., Dovidio, J. F., Banker, B., Rust, M., Nier, J., Mottola, G., & Ward, C. (1996). Does racism necessarily mean anti-Blackness? Aversive racism and pro-Whiteness. In M. Fine, L. Powell, L. Weis, & M. Wong (Eds.), *Off white* (pp. 167–178). London: Routledge.

Gaertner, S. L., & McLaughlin, J. P. (1983). Racial stereotypes: Associations and ascriptions of positive and negative characteristics. *Social Psychology Quarterly, 46,* 23–30.

Gaertner, S. L., Rust, M. C., Dovidio, J. F., Bachman, B. A., & Anastasio, P. A. (1994). The contact hypothesis: The role of a common ingroup identity on reducing intergroup bias. *Small Groups Research, 25,* 224–249.

Gamson, W. A., & Modigliani, A. (1987). The changing culture of affirmative action. In R. D. Braugart (Ed.), *Research in political sociology* (Vol. 3, pp. 137–177). Greenwich, CT: JAI Press.

Goddard, R. W. (1986, October). Post-employment: The changing current in discrimination charges. *Personnel Journal, 65,* 34–40.

Greenberg, J. (1987). Reactions to procedural injustice in payment distributions: Do the means justify the ends? *Journal of Applied Psychology, 72,* 55–61.

Hamilton, D. L., & Trolier, T. K. (1986). Stereotypes and stereotyping: An overview of the cognitive approach. In J. F. Dovidio & S. L. Gaertner (Eds.), *Prejudice, discrimination, and racism* (pp. 127–163). Orlando, FL: Academic Press.

Hitt, M. A., & Keats, B. W. (1984). Empirical identification of the criteria for effective affirmative action programs. *Journal of Applied Behavioral Science, 20,* 203–222.

Hornstein, H. A. (1976). *Cruelty and kindness: A new look at aggression and altruism.* Englewood Cliffs, NJ: Prentice-Hall.

Jacobson, C. K. (1985). Resistance to affirmative action: Self-interest or racism? *Journal of Conflict Resolution, 29,* 306–329.

Karlins, M., Coffman, T. L., & Walters, G. (1969). On the fading of social stereotypes: Studies in three generations of college students. *Journal of Personality and Social Psychology, 13,* 1–16.

Kinder, D. R., & Sanders, L. M. (1990). Mimicking political debate with survey questions: The case of White opinion on affirmative action for Blacks. *Social Cognition, 8,* 73–103.

Kinder, D. R., & Sears, D. 0. (1981). Prejudice and politics: Symbolic racism versus threats to "the good life." *Journal of Personality and Social Psychology, 40,* 414–431.

Kleinpenning, G., & Hagendoom, L. (1993). Forms of racism and the cumulative dimension of ethnic attitudes. *Social Psychology Quarterly, 56,* 21–36.

Kline, B. B., & Dovidio, J. F. (1982, April). *Effects of race, sex, and qualifications on predictions of a college applicant's performance.* Paper presented at the annual meeting of the Eastern Psychological Association, Baltimore, MD.

Kluegel, J. R., & Smith, E. R. (1986). *Beliefs about inequality: Americans' views of what is and what ought to be.* New York: Aldine deGruyter.

Kovel, J. (1970). *White racism: A psychohistory.* New York: Pantheon.

Kraiger, K., & Ford, J. K. (1985). A meta-analysis of ratee effects in performance ratings. *Journal of Applied Psychology, 70,* 56–65.

Kramer, R. M., & Brewer, M. B. (1984). Effects of group identity on resource use in a simulated commons dilemma. *Journal of Personality and Social Psychology, 46,* 1044–1057.

Kravitz, D. A. (1995). Attitudes toward affirmative action plans directed at Blacks: Effects of plan and individual differences. *Journal of Applied Social Psychology, 25,* 2192–2220.

Krieger, L. H. (1995). The content of our categories: A cognitive bias approach to discrimination and equal employment opportunity. *Stanford Law Review, 47,* 1161–1248.

Lind, E. A., Kurtz, S. Musante, L., Walker, L., & Thibaut, J. W. (1980). Procedure and outcome effects on reactions to adjudicated resolution of conflicts of interest. *Journal of Personality and Social Psychology, 39,* 643–653.

Major, B., & Crocker, J. (1993). Social stigma: The consequences of attributional ambiguity. In D. M. Mackie & D. L. Hamilton (Eds.), *Affect, cognition, and stereotyping* (pp. 345–370). San Diego, CA: Academic Press.

Major, B., Feinstein, J., & Crocker, J. (1994). Attributional ambiguity and affirmative action. *Basic and Applied Social Psychology, 15,* 113–142.

Marino, K. E. (1980). A preliminary investigation into behavioral dimensions of affirmative action compliance. *Journal of Applied Psychology, 65,* 346–350.

McConahay, J. B. (1986). Modem racism, ambivalence, and the modern racism scale. In J. F. Dovidio & S. L. Gaertner (Eds.), *Prejudice, discrimination, and racism* (pp. 91–125). Orlando, FL: Academic Press.

McConahay, J. B., & Hough, J. C. (1976). Symbolic racism. *Journal of Social Issues, 32*(2), 23–45.

Meindl, J. R., & Lerner, M. J. (1983). The heroic motive: Some experimental demonstrations. *Journal of Experimental Social Psychology, 19,* 1–20.

Meyer, D. E., & Schvaneveldt, R. W. (1971). Facilitation in recognizing pairs of words: Evidence of dependence between retrieval operations. *Journal of Experimental Psychology, 90,* 227–234.

Messick, D. M., & Mackie, D. M. (1989). Intergroup relations. *Annual Review of Psychology, 41,* 65–82.

Murrell, A. J., Dietz-Uhler, B. L., Dovidio, J. F., Gaertner, S. L., & Drout, C. (1994). Aversive racism and resistance to affirmative action: Perceptions of justice are not necessarily color blind. *Basic and Applied Social Psychology, 15,* 71–86.

Murrell, A. J., & Jones, R. (1996). Assessing affirmative action: Past, present, and future. *Journal of Social Issues, 52,* 77–92.

Nacoste, R. W. (1985). Selection procedure and responses to affirmative action: The case of favorable treatment. *Law and Human Behavior, 9,* 225–242.

Nacoste, R. W. (1986). The effects of affirmative action on minority persons: Research in the Lewian tradition. In E. Stivers & S. Wheelan (Eds.), *The Lewin legacy: Field, theory and current practice* (pp. 268–281). New York: Springer-Verlag.

Nacoste, R. W. (1987a). But do they care about fairness? The dynamics of preferential and minority influence. *Basic and Applied Social Psychology, 8,* 77–171.

Nacoste, R. W. (1987b). Social psychology and affirmative action: The importance of process in policy analysis. *Journal of Social Issues, 43*(1), 127–132.

Nacoste, R. W. (Barnes) (1994). If empowerment is the goal . . . : Affirmative action and social interaction. *Basic and Applied Social Psychology, 15,* 87–112.

Nacoste, R. W. (1996). Social psychology and the affirmative action debate. *Journal of Social and Clinical Psychology, 15,* 261–282.

Opotow, S. (1990). Moral exclusion and injustice: An introduction. *Journal of Social Issues, 46*(1), 1–20.

Pettigrew, T. F. (1994, October). *Education and policy.* University of Massachusetts Conference on Racism, Amherst, MA.

Pettigrew, T. F., & Meertens, R. W. (1995). Subtle and blatant prejudice in Western Europe. *European Journal of Social Psychology, 25,* 57–76.

Piliavin, J. A., Dovidio, J. F., Gaertner, S. L., & Clark, R. D.,III. (1981). *Emergency intervention.* New York: Academic Press.

Pratkanis, A. R., & Turner, M. E. (1996). The proactive removal of discriminatory barriers: Affirmative action as effective help. *Journal of Social Issues, 52,* 111–132.

Price Waterhouse v. Hopkins (1989). *490 U.S.* 228.

Regents of the University of California v. Bakke (1978). *U.S. Law Weekly, 46,* 4896.

Roese, N. J., & Jamieson, D. W. (1993). Twenty years of bogus pipeline research: A critical review and meta-analysis. *Psychological Bulletin, 114,* 363–375.

Rosch, E. (1975). Cognitive representations of semantic categories. *Journal of Experimental Psychology: General, 104,* 192–233.

Rossi, P. H., & Anderson, A. B. (1982). The factorial survey approach: An introduction. In P. Rossi & S. Nock (Eds.), *Measuring social judgments: The factorial survey approach* (pp. 15–67). Beverly Hills, CA: Sage.

Schuman, H., Steeh, C., & Bobo, L. (1985). *Racial attitudes in America: Trends and interpretations.* Cambridge, MA: Harvard University Press.

Sears, D. O. (1988). Symbolic racism. In P. A. Katz & D. A. Taylor (Eds.), *Eliminating racism: Profiles in controversy* (pp. 53–84). New York: Plenum Press.

Sears, D. O., & Allen, H. M., Jr. (1984). The trajectory of local desegregation controversies and Whites' opposition to busing. In M. B. Brewer & N. Miller (Eds.), *Groups in contact: The psychology of desegregation* (pp. 123–151). New York: Academic Press.

Sears, D. O., Citrin, J., & van Laar, C. (1995, September). *Black exceptionalism in a multicultural society.* Paper presented at the joint meeting of the Society for Experimental Psychology and the European Association of Experimental Social Psychology, Washington, DC.

Sears, D. O., Hensler, C. P., & Speer, L. K. (1979). Whites' opposition to "busing": Self-interest or symbolic politics? *American Political Science Review, 73,* 369–384.

Smith, H. J., & Tyler, T. R. (1996). Justice and power: When will justice concerns encourage the advantaged to support policies which redistribute economic resources and the disadvantaged to willingly obey the law? *European Journal of Social Psychology, 26,* 171–200.

Swim, J. K., Aikin, K. J., Hall, W. S., & Hunter, B. A. (1995). Sexism and racism: Old-fashioned and modern prejudices. *Journal of Personality and Social Psychology, 68,* 199–214.

Taylor, D. M., Wright, S. C., Moghaddam, F. M., & Lalonde, R. N. (1990). The personal/group discrimination discrepancy: Perceiving my group, but not myself, to be a target for discrimination. *Personality and Social Psychology Bulletin, 16,* 254–262.

Thibaut, J., & Walker, L. (1975). *Procedural justice: A psychological analysis.* Hillsdale, NJ: Erlbaum.

Turner, M. E., & Pratkanis, A. R. (1994). Affirmative action as help: A review of recipient reactions to preferential selection and affirmative action. *Basic and Applied Social Psychology, 15,* 43–70.

Wittink, D. R., & Cattin, P. (1989). Commercial use of conjoint analysis: An update. *Journal of Marketing, 53,* 91–96.

Word, C. O., Zanna, M. P., & Cooper, J. (1974). The nonverbal mediation of self-fulfilling prophecies in interracial interaction. *Journal of Experimental Social Psychology, 10,* 109–120.

The Ultimate Attribution Error: Extending Allport's Cognitive Analysis of Prejudice

Thomas F. Pettigrew • Harvard University

Allport's *The Nature of Prejudice* is a social psychological classic. Its delineation of the components and principles of prejudice remains modern, especially its handling of cognitive factors. The volume's cognitive contentions are outlined, and then extended with an application from attribution theory. An "ultimate attribution error" is proposed: (1) when prejudiced people perceive what they regard as a negative act by an outgroup member, they will more than others attribute it dispositionally, often as genetically determined, in comparison to the same act by an ingroup member; (2) when prejudiced people perceive what they regard as a positive act by an outgroup member, they will more than others attribute it in comparison to the same act by an ingroup member to one or more of the following: (a) "the exceptional case," (b) luck or special advantage, (c) high motivation and effort, and (d) manipulable situational context. Predictions are advanced as to which of these responses will be adopted and under which conditions the phenomenon will be magnified. A brief review of relevant research is also provided.

Gordon Allport was a modest man. Yet in his reserved, even shy, manner, he was justly proud of *The Nature of Prejudice* (Allport, 1954). His place in psychology as a personality theorist had long been established with the publication of *Personality: A Psychological Interpretation* (Allport, 1937). But it was his book on intergroup prejudice that most directly expressed his deepest concerns and values, that translated his more abstract work into concrete ideas for reform and social change.

Were he alive today, Allport would undoubtedly be honored and pleased by the *Bulletin*'s joint observance of the silver anniversaries of the "separate is inherently unequal" public school decision

of the U.S. Supreme Court and the publication of *The Nature of Prejudice*. For while the Supreme Court's ruling was widely publicized, the issuance of his book was obscure. The cloth-bound, unabridged version that appeared in 1954 attracted relatively little attention and only modest sales. It was not until the paperback edition appeared four years later, one-fifth shorter and selling in drug stores and airports, that the full impact of the volume began to be felt (Allport, 1958). Sales multiplied and continue brisk to this day, making *The Nature of Prejudice* one of the most widely read social psychological books both inside and outside of the discipline.

Allport would also be pleased by the judgments of the book's intellectual content now being rendered a generation later. He realized that the specific examples tellingly applied throughout the

Brief portions of this paper are drawn from two other publications (Pettigrew, 1978, 1979).

book would become dated. And two of his students, Professor Bernard Kramer, of the University of Massachusetts at Boston, and I, are currently revising and updating it. Like *Gray's Anatomy*, Allport's *The Nature of Prejudice* may continue through multiple editions as the field's standard reference.

Though the examples age quickly, Allport hoped that the volume's basic outline would stand the test of time. "The content will have to change," he often remarked, "but I think the book's contribution is its table of contents." Indeed, its table of contents has organized the scholarly study of prejudice. *The Nature of Prejudice* delineated the area of study, set up its basic categories and problems, and cast it in a broad, eclectic framework that remains today. The book continues to be cited as the definitive theoretical statement of the field; and it remains unchallenged throughout social science as *the* book on prejudice.

Both Brewster Smith (1973) and Elliot Aronson (1978) note that the value perspective of the volume marks its twenty-five years; Smith calls it "something of a period piece," Aronson "a time capsule of what it was like in 1954." But both admire its ageless quality of scholarship. Writes Smith:

Allport's compendious book still invites reading and defies summary. What seemed wise and judicious in 1954 mostly still seems so today . . . His pervasive fairmindedness, his democratic values, and his concern for evidence continues to set a model for humane, problem-focused social science . . . [F]rom Allport, we can still get wise guidance in our attempts to give more human substance to our democratic aspirations. (Smith, 1978, pp. 31–32)

Aronson concurs:

Gordon Allport's book was a harbinger and a reflection of the thinking that went into the Supreme Court decision [*Brown v. Board of Education*, 1954]. *The Nature of Prejudice* is a remarkable mixture of careful scholarship and humane values. Allport marshalled an impressive array of data and organized these data clearly and passionately. The book has influenced an entire generation of social psychologists, and deservedly so . . . What is modern about the book is Allport's perspective; he carefully chose among existing theories and data to come up with a brilliant and accurate statement of the eclectic causes and possible cures of

prejudice . . . This is a tribute to the wisdom, scholarship, and judgment of a graceful mind. Allport avoided the twin pitfalls of championing one position to the exclusion of all others, or of giving each position equal status. (Aronson, 1978 p. 92)

The modern ring of Allport's principles is, perhaps, best illustrated in his sophisticated handling of the cognitive components of prejudice. Allport was a closet Gestaltist. He remained dubious about the Gestalt theorists' nativistic view of perception (Allport & Pettigrew, 1957). But during his year of study in Germany following his Harvard doctorate, he developed a deep respect for and lasting interest in Gestalt theory. And this clearly guided his writing on the cognitive aspects of prejudice three decades later.

In the early 1950s, it was fashionable to think of ethnic stereotypes as aberrant cognitive distortions of "prejudiced personalities." The dominant influence of *The Authoritarian Personality* (Adorno, Frenkel-Brunswik, Levinson, & Sanford, 1950) furthered this conception. Allport broke sharply from this view. He insisted that the cognitive correlates of prejudice were natural extensions of normal processes. Ten of the volume's 31 chapters include a discussion of cognitive factors (Chapters 2, 8, 10, 11, 12, 13, 18, 19, 25, and 27), for cognitive factors are central to his approach. Prejudice for Allport involves both affective and cognitive components; he defined it as "an antipathy based upon a faulty and inflexible generalization." (Allport, 1954, p. 9)

Allport emphasized his fresh view in the title of the second chapter, "The normality of prejudgment." And it begins with a rhetorical question: "Why do human beings slip so easily into ethnic prejudice? They do so because the two essential ingredients . . .—*erroneous generalization* and *hostility*—are natural and common capacities of the human mind" (Allport, 1954, p. 17). Fifteen years prior to Henri Tajfel's (1969, 1970) important research on the point, Allport maintained that the mere "separation of human groups" was enough to trigger the psychological processes that lead to intergroup prejudice. And the primary process was held to be that of categorization, an essential, "least effort" means of handling sensory overload upon which "orderly living depends" (Allport, 1954, p. 20).

The emphasis upon categorization continues throughout *The Nature of Prejudice*. In Chapter 8, visibility and strangeness are shown to be critical in much the same manner that cognitive social psychologists today demonstrate the critical role of perceptual salience. Visible differences, runs the argument, imply real differences. And attitudes symbolically "condense" around visible cues.

In Chapter 10, Allport discusses cognitive processes generally. Here the then "New Look in Perception," centered around such figures as Jerome Bruner and Leo Postman (1948), influenced Allport's treatment. Selection and accentuation receive particular attention. Yet today's emphasis upon attribution theory is anticipated. Citing Fritz Heider's (1944) famous paper on phenomenal causality, Allport (1954, pp. 169–170, 177) maintains that "cause and effect thinking" is especially crucial, and that the human tendency "to regard *causation* as something *people* are responsible for . . . predisposes us to prejudice." It is this recognition of "the fundamental attribution error" (Ross, 1977) to which we shall return in a suggested extension of Allport's cognitive analysis.

So armed, the reader of *The Nature of Prejudice* is then led to see how categorization is centrally involved in a variety of related phenomena: emotionally toned intergroup labels ("nouns that cut slices" was Allport's [1954, p. 178] early statement of labeling theory); stereotypes ("highly *available* . . . exaggerated belief[s] associated with a category"—Allport, 1954, p. 191, italics added); the phenomenological approach to prejudice; the development of prejudice in children and in later life; and the cognitive correlates of prejudiced and tolerant personalities (through "dichotomization," "the need for definiteness," and "tolerance for ambiguity" [Allport, 1954, pp. 400–403, 438]).

To be sure, there are aspects of Allport's cognitive analysis that are dated or confusing. He stresses Zipf's (1949) "principle of least effort" as the primary motivational component underlying human cognition. Though here again, old wine may be returning in new bottles in the recent interest in "mindlessness" (Langer, Blank, & Chanowitz, 1973; Langer & Newman, 1979). But John Harding (1977) points out that three further emphases in *The Nature of Prejudice* are in need of correction. First, Allport is too expansive in his use of the concept of "category." He employs it to describe personal values as well as using it as synonymous with the process of generalization; and

these expansions lead him into making the difficult distinction between rational and irrational categories. Second, the focus on the irreversibility of stereotypes as the key criterion of their rationality now seems misplaced in light of recent advances in research on stereotyping. Finally, Allport's assumption that the intergroup antipathy involved in prejudice is *based upon* a faulty generalization seems unduly restrictive; the causal order can and does flow from hate to stereotype as well.

Yet, taken as a whole, Allport's cognitive analysis of prejudice seems surprisingly current a generation later. And this fact is all the more remarkable given the exciting advances made in this area in recent years by cognitive social psychologists. Certainly, Allport's Gestalt leanings helped him to project the future trends in the field, for it has been Gestalt influence via Fritz Heider that has shaped the field's progress in recent years.

The Ultimate Attribution Error

Building on attribution theory, we can expand Allport's analysis by proposing a systematic patterning of intergroup misattributions shaped in part by prejudice. The proposal is an extension of "the fundamental attribution error" noted by Heider (1958) and explicated by Ross (1977). It refers to observers' consistent underestimations of situational pressures and overestimations of actors' personal dispositions on their behavior. This "error" occurs over a wide range of situations, has extensive social implications, and can be easily demonstrated in the laboratory. Thus, Jones and Harris (1967) showed that listeners inferred a "correspondence" between communicators' private opinions and their anti-Castro remarks, even though the listeners were well aware that the remarks were made only to obey the explicit instructions of the experimenter. In another straightforward study (Ross, Amabile, & Steinmetz, 1977), subjects played a quiz game with the assigned roles of "questioner" and "contestant." Though the game allowed the "questioners" the enormous advantage of generating all of the questions from their own personal store of knowledge, later ratings of general knowledge were higher for the "questioners." This dispositional attribution was made not only by uninvolved observers but by the disadvantaged "contestants" themselves.

Note the three common elements of the fundamental attribution error illustrated in these experiments: (1) powerful situation forces (the experimenter's instructions and the quiz game format) are minimized; (2) internal, dispositional characteristics of the salient person (the communicator and the questioner) are causally magnified; and (3) role requirements (of being an experimental subject or quiz contestant) are not fully adjusted for in the final attribution.

There are systematic exceptions to the phenomenon. Actors often attribute their own behavior to situational causes when there are salient extrinsic rewards (Lepper & Greene, 1975), few choices open, and few similarities with past behavior (Monson & Snyder, 1977). And we shall maintain that observers often employ external, situational attributions to explain "away" positive behavior by members of disliked outgroups. In any event, it should be noted that the typical attribution investigation to date maximizes those conditions likely to elicit situational attributions from actors and dispositional attributions from observers. Yet the "real world" seems more likely to elicit the reverse attributional pattern, correctly or in error, when actors are performing familiar acts in situations under their control.

There are other qualifications. Dispositional and situational causal attributions do not form a neat, unidimensional continuum: that is, a dispositional attribution is not necessarily the opposite of a situational attribution. In addition, there appears to be a positivity bias for intimate others, such that you grant them the benefit of the doubt by attributing positive actions to dispositional causes and negative actions to situational causes (Taylor & Koivumaki, 1976).

Granting members of a disliked outgroup the benefit of the doubt, however, may not be so common. Taylor and Koivumaki (1976, p. 408) suggest that "a person who is disliked or hated may well be viewed as responsible for bad behaviors and not responsible for good ones. In other words, we may find a corresponding 'negativity' effect for disliked others." It is this possibility of a "negativity" effect extended to the intergroup level that forms the basis of the proposed ultimate attribution error.

The proposal follows, too, from Heider's (1958) writings on the attribution process. For example, Heider believed that negative self-attribution might be avoided in order to protect one's self-esteem. Here we propose that a stereotyped view of the outgroup needs to be protected from a positive outgroup evaluation. If the outgroup member is seen as performing a negative act consistent with our negative view, the fundamental error of dispositional attributions will be enhanced. And often when race and ethnicity are involved, these attributions will take the form of believing the actions to be a result of immutable, genetic characteristics of the derogated group in general—the bedrock assumption of racist doctrine.

But the problematic instance arises when we perceive the outgroup member is "out of role"—that is, the outgrouper is performing a positive act inconsistent with our negative view of the group. The most primitive defense, of course, is simply to deny the act altogether or to reevaluate it as potentially negative. An ambitious act becomes "pushy," an intelligent act becomes "cunning." But here we are concerned with the causal attributions made when the outgroup behavior is perceived as unquestionably positive in direct violation of the stereotype held.

Two aspects of this process may trigger what Heider (1958) and Kelley (1967) call "egocentric assumptions." The positive behavior is by definition positive in the terms of the prejudiced perceivers themselves; thus, it fits their conceptions of behavior that they might well expect of themselves. Here a familiar point of attribution theory is relevant. Perceivers possess the historical data about themselves performing similar acts, but little or no such data about outgroup members performing them. They have generally attributed such positive behavior by themselves as dispositionally caused, as further evidence of their being decent, upstanding human beings. Yet it is precisely this mode of explanation that is now in conflict with their established conceptions of the disliked outgroup. Moreover, if the perceivers are themselves the direct beneficiaries of the outgroup member's positive act, the attributional issue is made still more problematic. Phrased more generically, the more personally involving the outgrouper's positive act is, the more difficult it becomes to explain "away" the stereotype-challenging behavior.

Balance theory suggests that one way out of the dilemma is to change our views of the entire outgroup. And the intergroup contact research literature (Pettigrew, 1971), inspired by Allport's (1954, chapter 16) carefully qualified but often misinterpreted contact hypothesis, has established that this possibility does in fact occur under specified situational conditions. But this alternative typically requires the perception of repeated positive acts by the outgroup and is usually strongest among the initially least prejudiced. Here we concentrate our attention upon what happens when one positive act by an outgroup member is perceived by more prejudiced individuals.

In the interaction under discussion, the perceiver does not possess cause-and-effect information over time. And it is precisely this type of attributional situation that invokes Kelley's (1972) discounting effect. Discounting the importance of a particular dispositional cause in the presence of other "plausible" causes arises with greater force when the outgroup member performs a positive rather than negative act. In contrast to the contention of Jones and Davis (1965) that in-role acts are more discounted and therefore less "confident" than out-of-role acts, we are here proposing that intergroup perception may often reverse this pattern. In other words, the same anti-social behavior that would qualify *within* a social group as out-of-role will frequently be seen as in-role *across* social groups if it matches hostile stereotypes and expectations. Likewise, pro-social acts by the disliked outgroup will be regarded as out-of-role and made problematic by a range of plausible causes.

This same reasoning has already been applied and verified for low-status actors in the classical research by Thibaut and Riecken (1955) and its replication by Ring (1964). Negative acts by low-status actors in Ring's work were apparently *less* discounted by subjects than the same acts by high-status actors. And both studies showed that positive acts were *more* dispositionally attributed for high-status actors and *more* discounted and situationally attributed for low-status actors. In a comment pertinent to the present argument, Kelley (1972, p. 9) notes that greater uncertainty would be expected for the positively behaving, low-status actor "inasmuch as both internal and external reasons are plausible"—that is, a lower-status person could have performed the positive act because

of personal qualities and/or because of the greater power of the attributor. We are applying in this paper a similar logic across racial and ethnic groups of varying status differentials, though later research may show that the ultimate attribution error is strongest in the causal conclusions of higher-status groups.

A further suggestion by Kelley (1972) allows us to organize systematically the attributional possibilities. He advances the interesting idea that "attributional processes are closely linked to the effective exercise of control" (Kelley, 1972, p. 23). In ambiguous situations, he predicts that there will be a bias toward attributing cause to factors that are potentially controllable by the perceiver. But in situations with potentially important consequences, there will be a bias toward causes that may be less controllable yet could link to the vital consequences. Crossing the perceived degree and locus of control, Table 9.1 generates four possible attributional directions for resolving the explanatory problem raised by the perception of a positive act by a member of a disliked outgroup.

The abscissa is the familiar, if oversimplified, internal–external locus of control dimension (Rotter, 1966: Phares, 1976). The ordinate follows Kelley's suggestion and specifies two levels of perceived control of the act by the attributor. If Kelley is correct, there will be a bias toward regarding the problematic act as having been or potentially becoming influenced by the attributor. Consequently, alternatives C and D should be more frequently employed than alternatives A and B. But, as Kelley emphasized and both the Thibaut and Riecken and Ring studies demonstrated, there are frequent instances where the attributor still chooses the low-control alternatives. For example, if long-term future involvement with the outgroup member is anticipated (an "important consequence"), a high internal evaluation of the person as quite exceptional might well be preferred. Likewise, the perception of minority group members successfully acquiring a sought-after-goal can easily be regarded as the result of luck or an unfair

TABLE 9.1. Classification Scheme for "Explaining Away" Positive Behavior by a Member of a Disliked Outgroup

		Perceived Locus of Control of Act	
		Internal	External
Perceived Degree of	Low	A. The Exceptional Case	B. Luck or Special Advantage
Controllability of Act	High	C. High Motivation and Effort	D. Manipulable Situational Context

special advantage—external attributions beyond the attributor's control. The furor over and distorted views of affirmative action programs in recent years illustrate cell B. More fundamentally, low-status perceivers who are attributing cause to positive actions of high-status outgroup members are likely to adopt the two low-control alternative explanations. Let us briefly consider each of Table 9.1's four alternatives.

The Exceptional Case

This alternative can be derived from a consideration of cognitive heuristics (Tversky & Kahneman, 1974). Negative intergroup stereotypes offer striking examples of the operation of heuristics. They are readily *available* images that act as displacing *anchors* from which to judge outgroup behavior and with which to match outgroup behavior for its *representativeness*. The anchoring effect underscores once again the initial tendency not to perceive the act as positive, but rather to assimilate it toward the negative stereotype. But if perceived, the pro-social act by an outgroup member appears to be odd, even deviant. Similar instances cannot be called up readily in the bigot's mind. And, as it does not match the stereotype, the actor and the behavior seem *un*representative. This line of analysis suggests that one mode of resolution for the prejudiced perceiver will be to exclude this particular actor from the disliked outgroup. This resolution can even lead to generous, if often patronizing, exaggeration of the positive qualities of this exceptional person in order to differentiate this "good" individual from the "bad" outgroup in a fashion not unlike that found for solo-role minorities in the laboratory (Taylor, in press) and in the field (Kanter, 1977). Popular expressions capture the phenomenon. "She is really the exception that proves the rule." "He's really different; he's bright and hard-working, not like other Chicanos." Allport (1954) observed this common response, and described it as "fence mending" our stereotypes.

Luck or Special Advantage

Table 9.1's classification scheme resembles the scheme proposed by Weiner et al. (1972) for attributions of achievement behavior. They derived their scheme by crossing locus of control with the perceived degree of stability. Their four attribu-

tional modes—ability, effort, task difficulty, and luck—only roughly coincide with those described here, for the goals of the two schemes are different. Weiner and his colleagues sought to understand attributions of achievement behavior viewed across successive points in time. Here we attempt to categorize attributions for a wide range of positive behaviors at one point in time. Thus, rather than the controllability of the cause, Weiner et al. focused upon the time-linked degree of stability of the attributed cause—relatively stable ability and task difficulty attributions versus the more unstable dimensions of effort and luck.

The luck attribution, then, assumes a somewhat different meaning in the present context. The positive outgroup act can be seen as beyond the control of either the attributor or the actor and therefore of little significance. "He's dumb like the rest of his group, but he won anyway out of sheer luck." With no means of inferring luck from any past variable pattern of outcomes (save, perhaps, for occasional perceptions of behavior by *other* members of the outgroup), the use of this attribution is less "rationally" established than in the research reported by Weiner et al. (1972).

More common, then, is the attribution of special advantage. The actor is seen as having behaved positively and achieved a stereotype-breaking result, because the actor had the benefit of a special advantage conferred by virtue of the outgroup status. Typically, the special advantage is regarded as discriminatory and accompanied by a sense of resentment and fraternal deprivation (Runciman, 1966; Vanneman & Pettigrew, 1972). Black Americans have traditionally explained away positive behaviors and outcomes of white Americans in this manner. But the generality of the phenomenon is suggested by the recent vehemance of many whites, including many who label themselves "liberals," against affirmative action programs for minorities.

High Motivation and Effort

Individual members of a disliked outgroup are often seen by more benign bigots as "overcoming" through great personal effort the 'handicaps involved with belonging to an unfortunate people. The traditional phrase for such "compensatory" behavior in American race relations was "a credit to his race." As indicated in Table 9.1, the distinction between this mode and the exceptional case attribution involves the amount of control that is seen as exerted over the cause. Out-group members who work hard at being anti-stereotypical in their behavior are not seen as intrinsically exceptional, since they are nerceived to be responding positively to aspects of the interaction under some control of others. They are not viewed as true exceptions, for they would return to their "true," stereotypical state were it not for their keen motivation. But both exceptional and striving outgroup members are important exemplars for prejudiced individuals to point to as "proof" that discrimination and other situational factors are not responsible for negative behaviors and outcomes of the outgroup. "They made it, didn't they? So there must be something personally wrong with the rest of them."

Manipulable Situational Context

Most, but by no means all, structural factors of interaction are out of our immediate control. Those factors that are within one's power to manipulate are thus highly valued. The symbolic interactionist wing of social psychology, in particular Erving Goffman (1959, 1969, 1971), has vividly demonstrated the many forms such situational manipulations can assume. An outgroup member's positive act can, therefore, be seen not as a function of effort but as a consequence of situational factors at least partly influenced by others. "What could the cheap Scot do but pay the whole check once everybody stopped talking and looked at him?" Here we return to the role point of Jones and Davis (1965). This attribution often arises when the situationally-defined role is regarded as more powerful and salient than the group role.

THREE FURTHER POINTS

Two comparative frames of reference are involved with these predictions. Tajfel's (1970) skillful work suggests that virtually all human beings are subject to patterned differences in their perceptions of ingroup versus outgroup behavior. Thus, the ultimate attribution error is likely to characterize the attributions of most human beings, not just those of prejudiced individuals. So the predictions advanced in this paper are relative in two ways: (1) the perceptions of acts by outgroup members will tend to show the predicted trends relative to perceptions of the same acts by ingroup members:

and (2) prejudiced individuals will tend to show these phenomena more sharply than others.

These predictions also assume reasonably high salience of group membership. Adherence to religious doctrine (Charters & Newcomb, 1958) and even tolerance for pain (Buss & Portnoy, 1967; Lambert et al., 1960) have been enhanced by making group membership salient. Doise and Sinclair (1973) demonstrated how favorability ratings of both ingroups and outgroups can be altered by varying degrees of group salience. And McKillip, DiMiceli, and Luebke (1977) showed that under conditions of high salience of sex roles men made greater use of the male competence stereotype and women of the female warmth stereotype. Similarly, the ultimate attribution error is most likely to occur when perceivers are conscious of both their and the actor's group memberships.

Finally, not all group relations, fortunately, are hostile and marked by negative stereotypes. The fascinating research on East Africa by Brewer and Campbell (1976) underlines this fact and suggests that there is no inexorable strain toward boundary convergence and Sumner's (1906) full-blown version of extreme ethnocentrism. The intensity of the ultimate attribution error should therefore vary considerably across contrasting intergroup situations. As a first approximation, we propose two related hypotheses. The ultimate attribution error will be greatest when the groups involved have histories of intense conflict and possess especially negative stereotypes of each other. It will also be greatest when racial and ethnic differences covary with national and socioeconomic differences; or, more strongly phrased, the more bounded the two groups, the greater the ultimate attribution error is likely to be.

THE FORMAL PREDICTIONS

Based on this discussion we propose that: Across-group perceptions are more likely than within-group perceptions, especially for prejudiced individuals, to include the following:

1. For acts perceived as negative (antisocial or undesirable), behavior will be attributed to personal, dispositional causes. Often these internal causes will be seen as innate characteristics, and role requirements will be overlooked.
2. For acts perceived as positive (prosocial or desirable), behavior will be attributed to any one

or the combination of the following: A. to the exceptional, even exaggerated, special case individual who is contrasted with his/her group; B. to luck or special advantage and often seen as unfair; C. to high motivation and effort; and/ or D. to manipulable situational context. (See Table 9.1)

3. For acts perceived as positive, the most probable causal attributions are:

   a. 2A and 2B when the consequences of the attribution are deemed potentially important.

   b. 2C and 2D when the short-term control of the behavior is valued.

   c. 2A and 2B when the attributor is lower status than the actor.

   d. 2C and 2D when the attributor is higher status than the actor.

   e. 2A and 2C when the behavior is culturally regarded as generally dispositionally determined.

   f. 2B and 2D when the behavior is culturally regarded as generally situationally determined.

   g. 2A when the outgroup member is a solo or token participant and thus separated from the outgroup, highly salient, and less threatening.

   h. 2B when successful and valued outcomes are likely to result from the behavior.

   i. 2C when the behavior is culturally regarded as difficult.

   j. 2D when a situationally defined role is seen as more powerful and salient than the group membership role.

   The attributional tendencies of 1, 2, and 3 above will be enhanced:

4. When there exists high salience for perceivers of both their own and the actor's group memberships.

5. When perceivers are highly involved in the actor's behavior (e.g., when they are the target). Extremely high involvement will often lead to either attitude change toward the entire outgroup and/or to multiple attributions of cause.

6. When the groups represented in the interaction:

   a. have had histories of intense conflict and possess especially negative stereotypes of each other.

   b. have their racial and ethnic differences covary with national and socioeconomic differences; further, the more bounded the groups, the greater the ultimate attribution error.

Initial Evidence

While the ultimate attribution error evolves directly from the theoretical writings of Heider, Kelley, Weiner, Ross, Tversky, Kahneman, Campbell, and others, its direct empirical base is thin. The research on the influence of status upon causal attributions by Thibaut and Riecken (1955) and Ring, (1964) is importantly, even if only indirectly, relevant, and it shaped the predictions. Indirectly relevant, too, is the ingenious work on group discrimination of Tajfel. He and his coworkers have found strong experimental evidence of a "generic norm of outgroup behavior" among English schoolboys "divided into groups defined by flimsy and unimportant criteria" (Tajfel, 1970). Familiarity with the experimental setting only increases the group discrimination (Tajfel & Billig, 1974). The ultimate attribution error attempts to describe part of the cognitive mediating process of this "norm of outgroup behavior."

The few directly relevant studies support the present contentions. Duncan (1976), for example, showed 100 white undergraduates a videotape depicting one person (either black or white) ambiguously shoving another (either black or white). His subjects tended to attribute the shove to personal, dispositional causes when the harm-doer was black, but to situational causes when the harm-doer was white. In addition, the shove was labeled as more violent when it had been administered by a black. These findings support prediction 1 above, though they depend heavily upon Duncan's having developed videotapes that portray truly equivalent degrees of aggression. In any event, Allport and Postman (1947) investigated the operation of this violent stereotype of blacks three decades ago in their famous research on rumor transmission. One of their pictures employed to initiate a rumor chain showed a white man holding a razor while arguing with a black man. In over half of their all-white experimental groups, the final report indicated that the black in the picture (instead of the white) held the razor. The black was sometimes said to be "brandishing it wildly" and "threatening" the white.

Taylor and Jaggi (1974) report the most complete test to date. They conducted their study with 30 Hindu office clerks in southern India. First, the subjects rated the concepts "Muslim" and "Hindu" on twelve evaluative traits. Their responses indicate sharply different stereotypes of their ingroup and the outgroup. Hindus were seen as significantly more generous, hospitable, kind, friendly, sociable, sincere, and honest; while Muslims were regarded as being more rude and more often cheaters.

Taylor and Jaggi next gave their subjects short descriptions of either a Moslim or a Hindu behaving positively or negatively in one of four contexts involving the subject: a shopkeeper being either generous or cheating; a teacher either praising, or scolding the subject as a student; an actor either supplying appropriate help or ignoring the slightly injured subject; and a householder either sheltering or ignoring the subject when caught in the rain. For each of the sixteen descriptions (outgroup or ingroup × positive or negative behavior × four situations), the subjects chose the major reason for the actor's behavior from a list of four or five, one reflecting an internal attribution and the remainder external attributions. The results are summarized in Table 9.2.

These unequivocal results are consistent with the ultimate attribution error predictions of this paper. Dispositional attributions are employed largely for the ingroup's positive behavior and the outgroup's negative behavior. Such attributions for these two types of acts are more frequent in *all* comparisons with negative ingroup and positive outgroup acts. These findings support predictions 1 and 2, and provide at least inferential support for prediction 6. The relatively bounded Muslim and Hindu groups have experienced a history of intense conflict on the Indian sub-continent, including the 1971 Pakistani-Indian war that took place not long before this research was conducted. Consequently, the Taylor and Jaggi investigation focuses upon a situation where the ultimate attribution error would be expected to operate with special force.

The Taylor–Jaggi research design can be faulted, however. By first eliciting ratings on evaluative traits, the study probably made the crossgroup stereotypes especially salient for their subjects; and, consistent with prediction 4, the responses on the second task were thereby heightened. Fortunately, then, this work has been partially replicated in the United States without this design problem. Wang and McKillip (1978) utilized the accident responsibility approach to determine the effects of nationality on judging an automobile accident. Thirty foreign Chinese college students (from Taiwan, Hong Kong, and Singapore), 30 American college students, and 30 adult residents of Carbondale, Illinois read one of three versions of an automobile accident: Chinese driver and American victim, American driver and Chinese victim, and no national identifications at all. All subjects then assigned a fine (from $0 to $50) to either the driver or the victim, rated the driver and victim on seven evaluative traits, and answered a 13-item measure of American and Chinese ethnocentrism.

Wang and McKillip's findings strongly support prediction 1. The three groups did not differ in their assessments of the control accident without national identification; each tended to find the driver culpable and rated the victim more favorably. But the three groups differed in degree of ethnocentrism, with the Chinese students and town residents significantly more ethnocentric than the American students. Accordingly, the Chinese students and the town residents revealed large nationality biases in their judgments, but the American students did not. Thus, the Chinese subjects tended to place responsibility for the accident on either the American victim or driver and rate them negatively in comparison to the Chinese involved in the accidents. Resident subjects yielded precisely the opposite results. And the American college subjects revealed no responsibility differences by nationality and only slight trait differences in favor of the American targets.

A third relevant study by Banks, McQuarter, and

TABLE 9.2. Internal Attributions of Hindu Subjects*

Situation	Hindu Ingroup Actor		Muslim Outgroup Actor	
	Positive Behavior	Negative Behavior	Positive Behavior	Negative Behavior
Shopkeeper	43%	3%	10%	40%
Teacher	43%	3%	10%	23%
Help to Injured	67%	3%	10%	33%
Householder	80%	0%	20%	33%

*Adapted from Taylor and Jaggi (1974).

Pryor (1977) had black and white high school students evaluate identical achievement performances of black and white targets in terms of ability and effort. Consistent with predictions 2 and 3d and 3e combined, the white subjects placed greater emphasis upon the role of effort in evaluating blacks than in evaluating whites. Yet equal emphasis was given to the importance of ability for both races. Black subjects did not reveal the effect. Banks and his colleagues explain this failure to replicate with the black subjects in terms of differential racial association and familiarity of their two subject groups. The students came from a high school that had only a token enrollment of less than ten percent blacks. Hence, the black subjects were more familiar with their white peers than the white subjects were with them; and this differential familiarity may have influenced the findings. Independent measures of racial prejudice in the two groups were not gathered, but the present approach would lead one to predict that the black subjects were less anti-white than the white subjects were anti-black. But if Banks et al. (1977) are correct in their interaction and familiarity explanation, it would be consistent with prediction 6 concerning the effects of convergent boundaries.

Other studies, too, suggest that lower-status groups do not show the same effects as upper-status groups. Doise and Sinclair (1973) found that lower-status Swiss boys often gave *more* favorable outgroup than ingroup ratings even after group status had been made salient through interaction with upper-status, college-preparatory boys. By contrast, the college-bound Swiss boys typically rated their group differentially more favorable as group status became more salient. Similarly, studies on sex biases among American undergraduates often find effects that resemble the ultimate attribution error among men but not among women. On a male-oriented task, women are regarded by both sexes as succeeding relative to men less because of ability than of luck (Deaux & Emswiller, 1974). The reverse did not hold true on a female-oriented task.

Do these findings across race, social class, and sex indicate that the ultimate attribution error is limited to high-status, dominant groups? This possibility arose earlier in our discussion of the Thibaut-Riecken (1955) and Ring (1964) experiments. Future work directed to this precise point is required. But for now it seems likely that the predicted trends act in similar ways across status

groups (save for the differences specified in predictions 3c and 3d). Three related explanations for these results are tenable. First, the lower-status groups may simply not be as prejudiced as the higher-status groups. Only the Doise and Sinclair (1973) study employed an independent measure of prejudice; and they found slightly more *favorable* ratings were assigned the outgroup in an individual setting where group status was not salient. Moreover, Doise and Sinclair (1973, p. 153) discerned a sharp split within their lower-status group between those who gave higher or gave lower ratings to the higher-status outgroup. This observation suggests that identification with the more powerful outsiders and/or acceptance of their more restricted role among some lower-status members may block and even reverse the operation of the predicted trends. A second explanation, then, is that "group consciousness" may be critical. Consistent with this possibility, Banks et al. (1977) found that their black subjects revealed no effect; while the Swiss lower-status boys and American undergraduate women, presumably with their "group consciousness" less raised, revealed a derogation of their own group. Finally, it may well be that social class differences among Swiss adolescents and sex differences among American college students simply do not evoke the depth of group identification and differentiation needed to trigger the ultimate attribution error.

We conclude, then, that tests of the ultimate attribution error require independent measures of prejudice and stereotyping. This requirement raises particular problems for experimental research that attempts to investigate black-white intergroup perceptions with American college subjects. As repeated studies have demonstrated in recent years, racial climates on college campuses have changed sharply since Allport (1954) wrote *The Nature of Prejudice*. Blatant measures of racial, ethnic, and religious prejudice once served researchers well. Now unobtrusive, subtle measures are required to detect the avoidance patterns and other more complex forms of interracial interaction that characterize today's college life. A range of such indicators have been ingeniously devised by social psychologists, such as differential helping behavior (Gaertner, 1973, 1975, 1976), differential aggressive behavior (Donnerstein and Donnerstein, 1976, 1978), and a variety of other non-verbal measures (Weitz, 1972; Word, Zanna, & Cooper, 1974). The non-verbal measures particularly commend themselves for tests of the ultimate attribution error, since voice judgments of taped speech, seating patterns, interaction distance, etc., are easily and naturally included in such research designs.

In addition to the need for independent measures of prejudice, two other requirements of such tests of the present predictions are suggested by the limitations of the relevant studies discussed here. First, the full range of resolutions outlined in Table 9.1 to the conflict created by perceiving positive outgroup acts needs to be addressed. Second, the subjects in most of these experiments were removed from the behavior itself. Having behavior described to you and actually seeing it and being involved in it yourself are, of course, radically different phenomenal experiences. The fact that these results generally support the predictions is, perhaps, made more compelling by this distant stance. Nonetheless, direct tests of the ultimate attribution error require face-to-face interaction of the perceiver and actor.

A Final Word

The cognitive analysis of prejudice has traditionally centered upon the concept of stereotype. Allport (1954) expanded this analysis with his emphasis upon categorization and the biases of normal cognitive processing. Recent advances in cognitive social psychology allow further expansion of this approach. One direction for this expansion involves systematic intergroup misattributions, an example of which has been outlined in this paper. Hopefully, the ultimate attribution error and other applications of recent work to the prejudice domain will begin to receive greater attention within social psychology so as to allow specification of the linkages between these mediating cognitions and intergroup behavior.

REFERENCES

Adorno, T. W., Frenkel-Brunswik, L., Levinson, D. J., & Sanford, R. N. (1950). *The authoritarian personality*. New York: Harper & Row.

Allport, G. W. (1937). *Personality: A psychological interpretation*. New York: Holt, Rinehart & Winston.

Allport, G. W. (1954). *The nature of prejudice*. Reading, MA: Addison-Wesley.

Allport, G. W. (1958). *The nature of prejudice*. Garden City, NY: Doubleday Anchor.

Allport, G. W., & Pettigrew, T. F. (1957). Cultural influence on the perception of movement: The trapezoidal illusion among Zulus. *Journal of Abnormal and Social Psychology, 55,* 104–113.

Allport, G. W., & Postman, L. (1947). *The psychology of rumor.* New York: Holt, Rinehart & Winston.

Aronson, E. (1978, July). Reconsiderations: *The nature of prejudice. Human Nature, 1,* 92–94, 96.

Banks, W. C., McQuarter, G. V., & Pryor, J. (1977). *In consideration of a cognitive–attributional basis for stereotypy.* Unpublished manuscript.

Brewer, M. B., & Campbell, D. T. (1977). *Ethnocentrism and intergroup attitudes: East African evidence*. Beverly Hills, CA: Sage.

Bruner, J. S., & Postman, L. (1948). An approach to social perception. In W. Dennis (Ed.), *Current trends in social psychology*. Pittsburgh, PA: University of Pittsburgh Press.

Buss, A. M., & Portnoy, N. W. (1967). Pain tolerance and group identification. *Journal of Personality and Social Psychology, 6,* 106–108.

Charters, W. W., & Newcomb, T. M. (1952). Some attitudinal effects of experimentally increased salience of a membership group. In G. E. Swanson, T. M. Newcomb, & E. L. Hartley (Eds.), *Readings in social psychology*. Revised edition. New York: Holt, Rinehart & Winston.

Deaux, K., & Emswiller, T. (1974). Explanation of successful performance on sex-linked tasks: What is skill for the male is luck for the female. *Journal of Personality and Social Psychology, 29,* 80–84.

Donnerstein, M., & Donnerstein, E. (1976), Variables in interracial aggression. *Journal of Social Psychology, 100,* 111–121.

Donnerstein, M., & Donnerstein, E. (1978). Direct and vicarious censure in the control of interracial aggression. *Journal of Personality, 48,* 162–175.

Doise, W., & Sinclair, A. (1973). The categorization process in intergroup relations. *European Journal of Social Psychology, 3,* 145–157.

Duncan, B. L. (1976). Differential social perception and attribution of intergroup violence: Testing the lower limits of stereotyping of blacks. *Journal of Personality and Social Psychology, 34,* 590–598.

Gaertner, S. (1973). Helping behavior and racial discrimination among liberals and conservatives. *Journal of Personality and Social Psychology, 25,* 335–341.

Gaertner, S. (1975). The role of racial attitudes in helping behavior. *Journal of Social Psychology, 97,* 95–101.

Gaertner, S. (1976). Nonreactive measures in racial attitude research: A focus on "liberals." In P. A. Katz (Ed.), *Towards the elimination of racism*. Elmsford, NY: Pergamon.

Goffman, E. (1959). *The presentation of self in everyday life.* New York: Doubleday Anchor.

Goffman, E. (1969). *Strategic interaction*. Philadelphia: University of Pennsylvania Press.

Goffman, E. (1971). *Relations in public*. New York: Harper & Row.

Harding, J. (1977). Suggestions for revision of Allport's *The nature of prejudice*. Private communication.

Heider, F. (1944). Social perception and phenomenal causality. *Psychological Review, 51,* 358–374.

Heider, F. (1958). *The psychology of interpersonal relations*. New York: Wiley.

Jones, E. E., & Davis, K. L. (1965). From acts to dispositions: The attribution process in person perception. In L. Berkowitz (Ed.), *Advances in experimental social psychology*, vol. 2. New York: Academic Press.

Jones, E. E., & Harris, V. A. (1977). The attribution of attitudes. *Journal of Experimental Social Psychology, 3,* 1–24.

Kanter, R. M. (1977). Some effects of proportions on group life: Skewed sex ratios and responses to token women. *American Journal of Sociology, 82,* 965–990.

Kelley, H. H. (1967). Attribution theory in social psychology. In D. Levine (Ed.), *Nebraska symposium on motivation, 1967,* vol. 15. Lincoln: University of Nebraska Press.

Kelley, H. H. (1972). Attribution in social interaction. In E. E. Jones, D. E. Kanouse, H. H. Kelley, R. E. Nisbett, S. Valins, & B. Weiner, *Attribution: Perceiving the causes of behavior.* Morristown, NJ: General Learning Press.

Lambert, W. E., Lieberman, E., & Poser, E. G. (1960). The effect of increased salience of membership group on pain tolerance. *Journal of Personality, 28,* 350–357.

Langer, E. J., Blank, A., & Chanowitz, B. (1978). The mindlessness of ostensibly thoughtful action. *Journal of Personality and Social Psychology, 36,* 635–642.

Langer, E. J., & Newman, H. M. (1979). The role of mindlessness in a typical social psychological experiment. *Personality and Social Psychology Bulletin.*

Leeper, M. R., & Greene, D. (1975). Turning play into work: Effects of adult surveillance and extrinsic rewards on children's intrinsic motivation. *Journal of Personality and Social Psychology, 31,* 479–486.

McKillip, J., DiMiceli, A. J., & Luebke, J. (1977). Group salience and stereotyping. *Social Behavior and Personality, 5,* 81–85.

Monson, T. C., & Snyder, M. (1977). Actors, observers, and the attribution process. *Journal of Experimental Social Psychology, 13,* 89–111.

Pettigrew, T. F. (1971). *Racially separate or together?* New York: McGraw-Hill.

Pettigrew, T. F. (1978). Three issues in ethnicity: Boundaries, deprivations, and perceptions. In J. M. Yinger & S. J. Cutler (Eds.), *Major social issues: A multidisciplinary view.* New York: Free Press.

Pettigrew, T. F. (1979). Foreword. In G. W. Allport, *The nature of prejudice.* Reading, MA: Addison-Wesley.

Phares, E. J. (1976). *Locus of control in personality.* Morristown, NJ: General Learning Press.

Ring, K. (1964). Some determinants of interpersonal attraction in hierarchical relationships: A motivational analysis. *Journal of Personality, 32,* 651–665.

Ross, L. D. (1977). The intuitive psychologist and his shortcomings: Distortions in the attribution process. In L. Berkowitz (Ed.), *Advances in experimental social psychology,* vol. 10. New York: Academic Press.

Ross, L. D., Amabile, T. M., & Steinmetz, J. L. (1977). Social roles, social control, and biases in social-perception processes. *Journal of Personality and Social Psychology, 35,* 485–494.

Rotter, J. B. (1966). Generalized expectancies for internal versus external control of reinforcement. *Psychological Monographs, 80*(1), Whole no. 609.

Runciman, W. G. (1906). *Relative deprivation and social justice.* London: Routledge & Kegan Paul.

Smith, M. B. (1978). The psychology of prejudice. *New York University Education Quarterly, 9*(2), 29–32.

Summer, W. G. (1906). *Folkways.* New York: Ginn.

Tajfel, H. (1969). Cognitive aspects of prejudice. *Journal of Social Issues, 25,* 79–97.

Tajfel, H. (1970). Experiments in intergroup discrimination. *Scientific American, 223*(5), 96–102.

Tajfel, H. & Billig, M. (1974). Familiarity and categorization in intergroup behavior. *Journal of Experimental Social Psychology, 10,* 159–170.

Taylor, D. M., & Jaggi, V. (1974). Ethnocentrism and causal attribution in a south Indian context. *Journal of Cross-Cultural Psychology, 5,* 162–171.

Taylor, S. E. (in press). The token in the small group: Research findings and theoretical implications. In J. Sweeney (Ed.), *Psychology and politics.* New Haven, CT: Yale University Press.

Taylor, S. E., & Koivumaki, J. H. (1976). The perception of self and others: Acquaintanceship, affect, and actor-observer differences. *Journal of Personality and Social Psychology, 33,* 403–408.

Thibaut, J. W., & Riecken, M. (1955). Some determinants and consequences of the perception of social causality. *Journal of Personality, 25,* 115–129.

Tversky, A., & Kahneman, D. (1974). Judgment under uncertainty: Neuristics and biases. *Science, 185,* 1124–1131.

Vanneman, R. D., & Pettigrew, T. F. (1972). Race and relative deprivation in the urban United States. *Race, 13,* 461–486.

Wang, G., & McKillip, J. (1978). Ethnic identification and judgements of an accident. *Personality and Social Psychology Bulletin, 4,* 296–299.

Weiner, B., Frieze, I., Kukla, A., Reed, L., Rest, S., & Rosenbaum, R. M. (1972). Perceiving the causes of success and failure. In E. E. Jones, D. E. Kanouse, H. H. Kelley, R. E. Nisbett, S. Valins, & B. Weiner, *Attribution: Perceiving the causes of behavior.* Morristown, NJ: General Learning Press.

Weitz, S. (1972). Attitude, voice and behavior: A repressed affect model of interracial interaction. *Journal of Personality and Social Psychology, 24,* 14–21.

Word, C. O., Zanna, M. P., & Cooper, J. (1974). The nonverbal mediation of self-fulfilling prophecies in interracial interaction. *Journal of Experimental Social Psychology, 10,* 109–120.

Zipf, G. K. (1949). Human behavior and the principle of least effort. Reading, MA: Addison-Wesley.

Intergroup Behavior and Discrimination

In the previous section we focused on some of the attitudinal and social explanation effects of social categorization. We also discovered that there may not always be a one-to-one correspondence between intergroup attitudes and intergroup behavior. Social psychologists have long known that attitudes and behavior do not necessarily correspond closely to one another. However, it is usually behavior that we notice, and in the area of intergroup relations this behavior is often at best competitive and at worst outright hostile and discriminatory.

A substantial amount of research on intergroup relations has focused on discriminatory intergroup behavior that is biased in favor of the ingroup. Indeed, one of the classic paradigms for intergroup research, the minimal group paradigm (e.g., Tajfel et al., 1971; also see Bourhis, Sachdev & Gagnon, 1994; Diehl, 1990), was originally designed to show that the mere fact of being explicitly categorized as a group member might be sufficient to produce ingroup bias. Our first reading, by Henri Tajfel (1970), then at Bristol University, describes the minimal group paradigm and its findings. The main feature of the paradigm is that participants are explicitly categorized into two groups either randomly or on the basis of a trivial criterion (e.g., over- or underestimation of dots). The groups are minimal because they do nothing, members are anonymous, the group has no history and no future, and group membership does not mediate any personal gain or loss. The results show that merely being categorized is sufficient and necessary to produce ingroup favoritism in a subsequent point-allocation task. This paradigm, and variants of it, has become a staple methodology for subsequent research on intergroup behavior and social identity processes. By now there must be literally thousands of studies which employ this paradigm.

Although the minimal group studies robustly show discrimination on the basis of mere categorization, a rather pessimistic prognosis for humanity, other research has qualified this finding by showing that whether social categorization produces bias or not may rest on a multitude of qualifying conditions—for example, people's motivational state (e.g., uncertainty; Hogg, in press), the dimensions available for expressing ingroup affiliation (e.g., positive-negative asymmetry; Otten, Mummendey, & Blanz, 1996), concerns about whether discrimination is just or not (e.g., Tyler, DeGoey, & Smith, 1996), and of course, beliefs about the nature of the relations between the groups (the core feature of social identity theory's macrosocial analysis; e.g., Ellemers, 1993; Hogg & Abrams, 1988; Tajfel & Turner, 1979).

To illustrate these qualifying conditions we have selected two readings. The first is by Sabine Otten, at the University of Jena, and her colleagues (Otten et al., 1996), and the second is by Tom Tyler, now at New York University, and his colleagues (Tyler et al., 1996). Otten et al. discuss what they have called the positive-negative asymmetry effect—in intergroup settings people do discriminate against an outgroup when they are allocating positive stimuli (e.g., rewards, points representing money), but do not do so when they are allocating a negative stimulus (e.g., punishment). However, this differential effect for positive and negative stimuli disappears when people feel that their positive social identity is under threat by being in a minority or inferior ingroup. Under these circumstances, they discriminate in the allocation of both positive and negative stimuli.

Tyler et al. focus on an often overlooked aspect of intergroup discrimination. While people are discriminating against outgroups (treating outgroups unfairly), how should they behave towards ingroup members? Tyler's research suggests that what really seems to matter within groups is procedural justice. People don't mind having less than their fellow ingroup members (distributive inequality) but they do like to feel that they have been treated fairly within their group (procedural justice). A sense of fair procedures within a group tends to help bond people to the group.

Discussion Questions

1. Under what conditions do group members challenge outgroups?
2. Why do people leave their in-group?
3. How do people react to group outcomes they feel are unjust?
4. Is rewarding the in-group more, the same as punishing the out-group less?
5. When and why will people tolerate injustice in intergroup situations?

Suggested Readings

Brewer, M. B., & Campbell, D. T. (1976). *Ethnocentrism and intergroup attitudes: East African evidence*. New York: Sage. A very detailed naturalistic study of ethnocentrism and intergroup attitudes as they occur in real, non-laboratory, social settings.

Bourhis, R. Y., Moiese, L. C., Perreault, S., & Senecal, S. (1997). Towards an interactive acculturation model: A social psychological approach. *International Journal of Psychology, 32,* 369–386. A model of intergroup behavior in the context of relations between immigrant and non-immigrant groups, and the acculturation orientation and attitudes of the groups.

Ellemers, N. (1993). The influence of socio-structural variables on identity management strategies. *European Review of Social Psychology, 4,* 27–57. An overview of how, according to social identity theory, beliefs about the nature of intergroup relations influence the diverse forms that intergroup behavior can take—overt discrimination is not the only outcome.

Gaertner, L., & Insko, C.A. (2000). Intergroup discrimination in the minimal group paradigm: Categorization, reciprocation, or fear? *Journal of Personality and Social Psychology, 79,* 77–94. Empirical study exploring the role of interdependence in contrast to self-categorization/social identification in minimal intergroup discrimination.

Jetten, J. S., Spears, R., & Manstead, A. S. R. (1998). Defining dimensions of distinctiveness: Group variability makes a difference to differentiation. *Journal of Personality and Social Psychology, 74,* 1481–1492. Empirical study of distinctiveness and discrimination in minimal and natural groups—elaborates the idea that there may be different logics to discriminatory behavior in minimal and natural groups.

Mummendey, A., & Wenzel, M. (1999). Social discrimination and tolerance in intergroup relations: Reactions to intergroup difference. *Personality and Social Psychology Review, 3,* 158–174. A detailed theoretical analysis of the conditions under which groups do or do not engage in discrimination and conflict.

Tyler, T. R. (1997). The psychology of legitimacy: A relational perspective on voluntary deference to authorities. *Personality and Social Psychology Review, 1,* 323–345. Description of Tyler's model of how some aspects of perceptions and relations within groups may influence group atmosphere and intergroup behavior.

Experiments in Intergroup Discrimination

Henri Tajfel • University of Bristol

Can discrimination be traced to some such origin as social conflict or a history of hostility? Not necessarily. Apparently the mere fact of division into groups is enough to trigger discriminatory behavior.

Intergroup discrimination is a feature of most modern societies. The phenomenon is depressingly similar regardless of the constitution of the "ingroup" and of the "outgroup"that is perceived as being somehow different. A Slovene friend of mine once described to me the stereotypes—the common traits attributed to a large human group—that are applied in his country, the richest constituent republic of Yugoslavia, to immigrant Bosnians, who come from a poorer region. Some time later I presented this description to a group of students at the University of Oxford and asked them to guess by whom it was used and to whom it referred. The almost unanimous reply was that this was the characterization applied by native Englishmen to "colored" immigrants: people coming primarily from the West Indies, India and Pakistan.

The intensity of discrimination varies more than the nature of the phenomenon. In countries with long-standing intergroup problems—be they racial as in the U.S., religious as in Northern Ireland or linguistic-national as in Belgium—tensions reach the boiling point more easily than they do elsewhere. In spite of differing economic, cultural, historical, political and psychological backgrounds, however, the *attitudes* of prejudice toward outgroups and the *behavior* of discrimination against outgroups clearly display a set of common characteristics. Social scientists have naturally been concerned to try to identify these characteristics in an effort to understand the origins of prejudice and discrimination.

The investigative approaches to this task can be roughly classified into two categories. Some workers stress the social determinants of prejudice and discrimination. Others emphasize psychological causation. In *The Functions of Social Conflict*, published in 1958, Lewis A. Coser of Brandeis University established a related dichotomy when he distinguished between two types of intergroup conflict: the "rational" and the "irrational." The former is a means to an end: the conflict and the attitudes that go with it reflect a genuine competition between groups with divergent interests. The latter is an end in itself: it serves to release accumulated emotional tensions of various kinds. As both popular lore and the psychological literature testify, nothing is better suited for this purpose than a well-selected scapegoat.

These dichotomies have some value as analytical tools but they need not be taken too seriously. Most cases of conflict between human groups, large or small, reflect an intricate interdependence of social and psychological causation. Often it is difficult, and probably fruitless, to speculate about what were the first causes of real present-day social situations. Moreover, there is a dialectical relation between the objective and the subjective determinants of intergroup attitudes and behavior.

Once the process is set in motion they reinforce each other in a relentless spiral in which the weight of predominant causes tends to shift continuously. For example, economic or social competition can lead to discriminatory behavior; that behavior can then in a number of ways create attitudes of prejudice; those attitudes can in turn lead to new forms of discriminatory behavior that create new economic or social disparities, and so the vicious circle is continued.

The interdependence of the two types of causation does not manifest itself only in their mutual reinforcement. They actually converge because of the psychological effects on an individual of his sociocultural milieu. This convergence is often considered in terms of social learning and conformity. For instance, there is much evidence that children learn quite early the pecking order of evaluations of various groups that prevails in their society, and that the order remains fairly stable. This applies not only to the evaluation of groups that are in daily contact, such as racial groups in mixed environments, but also to ideas about foreign nations with which there is little if any personal contact.

In studies conducted at Oxford a few years ago my colleagues and I found a high consensus among children of six and seven in their preference for four foreign countries. The order was America, France, Germany and Russia, and there was a correlation of .98 between the preferences of subjects from two different schools. As for adults, studies conducted by Thomas F. Pettigrew in the late 1950s in South Africa and in the American South have shown that conformity is an important determinant of hostile attitudes toward blacks in both places (above and beyond individual tendencies toward authoritarianism, which is known to be closely related to prejudice toward outgroups).

These studies, like many others, were concerned with attitudes rather than behavior, with prejudice rather than discrimination. Discrimination, it is often said, is more directly a function of the objective social situation, which sometimes does and sometimes does not facilitate the expression of attitudes; the attitudes of prejudice may be socially learned or due to tendencies to conform, but they are not a very efficient predictor of discriminatory behavior. According to this view, psychological

considerations are best suited to explaining and predicting the genesis and functioning of attitudes; the facts of intergroup discrimination are best related to, and predicted from, objective indexes of a social, economic and demographic nature.

Although I have no quarrel with this view, I am left with a nagging feeling that it omits an important part of the story. The fact is that behavior toward outgroups shows the same monotonous similarity as attitudes do, across a diversity of socioeconomic conditions. This apparent diversity may, of course, obscure an underlying common factor of "rational" conflict, of struggle to preserve a status quo favorable to oneself or to obtain an equitable share of social opportunities and benefits. Another kind of underlying regularity is nonetheless common to a variety of social situations and is an important psychological effect of our sociocultural milieu. It is the assimilation by the individual of the various norms of conduct that prevail in his society.

For the purposes of this article I shall define social norms as being an individual's expectation of how others expect him to behave and his expectation of how others will behave in any given social situation. Whether he does or does not behave according to these expectations depends primarily on his understanding of whether or not and how a situation relates to a specific set of expectations. If a link is made between the one and the other—if an individual's understanding of a situation in which he finds himself is such that in his view certain familiar social norms are pertinent to it—he behaves accordingly.

There is nothing new to this formulation; it is inherent in most studies and discussions of intergroup prejudice and discrimination that stress the importance of conformity. The point I wish to make is broader. Conformity contributes to hostile attitudes and behavior toward specified groups of people in situations that are usually characterized by a history of intergroup tensions, conflicts of interest and early acquisition by individuals of hostile views about selected outgroups. We are dealing, however, with a process that is more general and goes deeper than the learning of value judgments about a specific group and the subsequent acting out of accepted patterns of behavior toward that group. The child learns not only whom

A

MATRIX 1

-19	-16	-13	-10	-7	-4	-1	0	1	2	3	4	5	6
6	5	4	3	2	1	0	-1	-4	-7	-10	-13	-16	-19

MATRIX 2

12	10	8	6	4	2	0	-1	-5	-9	-13	-17	-21	-25
-25	-21	-17	-13	-9	-5	-1	0	2	4	6	8	10	12

B

MATRIX 3

1	2	3	4	5	6	7	8	9	10	11	12	13	14
14	13	12	11	10	9	8	7	6	5	4	3	2	1

MATRIX 4

18	17	16	15	14	13	12	11	10	9	8	7	6	5
5	6	7	8	9	10	11	12	13	14	15	16	17	18

C

MATRIX 5

-14	-12	-10	-8	-6	-4	-2	-1	3	7	11	15	19	23
23	19	15	11	7	3	-1	-2	-4	-6	-8	-10	-12	-14

MATRIX 6

17	14	11	8	5	2	-1	-2	-3	-4	-5	-6	-7	-8
-8	-7	-6	-5	-4	-3	-2	-1	2	5	8	11	14	17

FIGURE 10.1 ■ First Experiment conducted by the author and his colleagues utilized these six matrices. The numbers represented points (later translated into awards or penalties in money) to be assigned by a subject to other individuals; by checking a box the subject assigned the number of points in the top of the box to one person and the number in the bottom of the box to another person; he did not know the identity of these people but only whether each was a member of his own group or "the other group." (The groups had been established by the experimenters on grounds that were artificial and insignificant.) Each matrix appeared three times in a test booklet with each row of numbers labeled to indicate whether the subject was choosing between two members of his own group (ingroup) other than himself, two members of the outgroup or one member of the ingroup and one member of the outgroup. Choices were scored to see if subjects chose for fairness, maximum gain to their own group or maximum difference in favor of the ingroup.

INGROUP–OUTGROUP CHOICES

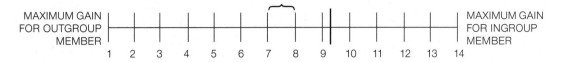

MAXIMUM GAIN FOR OUTGROUP MEMBER ... MAXIMUM GAIN FOR INGROUP MEMBER

1 2 3 4 5 6 7 8 9 10 11 12 13 14

INGROUP–OUTGROUP CHOICES

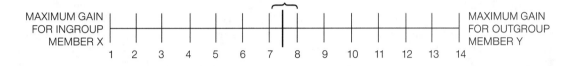

MAXIMUM GAIN FOR INGROUP MEMBER X ... MAXIMUM GAIN FOR OUTGROUP MEMBER Y

1 2 3 4 5 6 7 8 9 10 11 12 13 14

INGROUP–OUTGROUP CHOICES

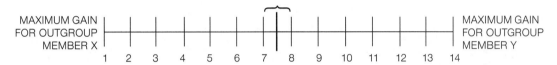

MAXIMUM GAIN FOR OUTGROUP MEMBER X ... MAXIMUM GAIN FOR OUTGROUP MEMBER Y

1 2 3 4 5 6 7 8 9 10 11 12 13 14

FIGURE 10.2 ■ Results were scored by ranking the choices from 1 to 14 depending on which box was checked. The end of the matrix at which the ingroup member got the minimum number of points (and the outgroup member the maximum) was designated 1; the other end, giving the ingroup member the maximum, was 14. The mean choices are shown here. In the intergroup situation the subjects gave significantly more points to members of their own group than to members of the other group. In the intragroup situations, however, the means of the choices fell at Rank 7.5, between the choices of maximum fairness (*brackets*).

he should like or dislike in the complex social environment to which he is exposed but also something more basic. An individual constructs his own "web of social affiliations" by applying principles of order and simplification that reduce the complexity of crisscrossing human categorizations. Perhaps the most important principle of the subjective social order we construct for ourselves is the classification of groups as "we" and "they"— as ingroups (any number of them to which we happen to belong) and outgroups. The criteria for these assignments may vary according to the situation, and their emotional impact may be high or low, but in our societies this division into groups most often implies a competitive relation between the groups. In other words, intergroup categorizations of all kinds may bring into play what seems to the individual to be the appropriate form of intergroup behavior.

What this essentially means is that the need to bring some kind of order into our "social construc-

tion of reality" (a term recently used by Peter L. Berger of the New School for Social Research and Thomas Luckmann of the University of Frankfurt) combines with the hostility inherent in many of the intergroup categorizations to which we are continually exposed to develop a "generic norm" of behavior toward outgroups. Whenever we are confronted with a situation to which some form of intergroup categorization appears directly relevant, we are likely to act in a manner that discriminates against the outgroup and favors the ingroup.

If this is true, if there exists such a generic norm of behavior toward outgroups, several important consequences should follow. The first is that there may be discrimination against an outgroup even if there is no reason for it in terms of the individual's own interests—in terms of what he can gain as a result of discriminating against the outgroup. The second consequence is that there may be such discrimination in the absence of any previously existing attitudes of hostility or dislike toward the outgroup. And the third consequence, following directly from the second, is that this generic norm may manifest itself directly in behavior toward the outgroup before any attitudes of prejudice or hostility have been formed. If this reasoning is correct, then discriminatory intergroup behavior can sometimes be expected even if the individual is not involved in actual (or even imagined) conflicts of interest and has no past history of attitudes of intergroup hostility.

At the University of Bristol, in collaboration with Claude Flament of the University of Aix-Marseille, R. P. Bundy and M. J. Billig, I have conducted experiments designed to test this prediction and others that follow from it. The main problem was to create experimental conditions that would en-

able us to assess the effects of intergroup categorization per se, uncontaminated by other variables, such as interactions among individuals or preexisting attitudes. We aimed, moreover, to look at the behavior rather than the attitudes of the subjects toward their own group and the other group, to ensure that this behavior was of some importance to them and to present them with a clear alternative to discriminating against the outgroup that would be a more "sensible" mode of behavior.

Perhaps the best means of conveying the way these criteria were met is to describe the procedure we followed in the first experiments and its variants in subsequent ones. Our subjects were 64 boys 14 and 15 years old from a state, or "comprehensive," school in a suburb of Bristol. They came to the laboratory in separate groups of eight. All the boys in each of the groups were from the

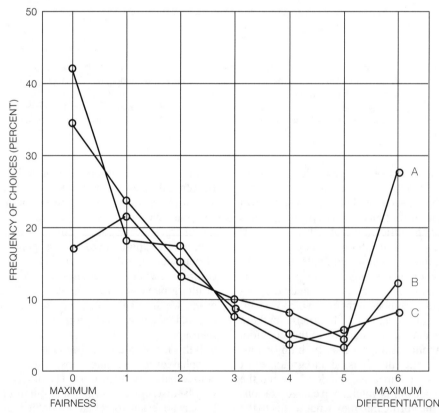

FIGURE 10.3 ■ Intergroup discrimination was a deliberate strategy in the ingroup-outgroup choices (A) and fairness a deliberate strategy in the ingroup-ingroup (B) and outgroup-outgroup (C) choices. This is indicated by the fact that the frequencies of intergroup choices differed significantly from those of the intragroup choices only at the extreme points of the distribution, the points of maximum fairness and of maximum discrimination. (For this analysis the two fairest choices in each matrix, the two middle ones, were ranked together as 0 and departures in either direction were scored from 1 to 6.)

same house in the same form at the school, so that they knew each other well before the experiment. The first part of the experiment served to establish an intergroup categorization and in the second part we assessed the effects of that categorization on intergroup behavior.

In the first part the boys were brought together in a lecture room and were told that we were interested in the study of visual judgments. Forty clusters of varying numbers of dots were flashed on a screen. The boys were asked to estimate the number of dots in each cluster and to record each estimate in succession on prepared score sheets. There were two conditions in this first part of the experiment. In one condition, after the boys had completed their estimates they were told that in judgments of this kind some people consistently overestimate the number of dots and some consistently underestimate the number, but that these tendencies are in no way related to accuracy. In the other condition the boys were told that some people are consistently more accurate than others. Four groups of eight served in each of the two conditions.

After the judgments had been made and had been ostentatiously "scored" by one of the experimenters, we told the subjects that, since we were also interested in other kinds of decision, we were going to take advantage of their presence to investigate these as well, and that for ease of coding we were going to group them on the basis of the visual judgments they had just made. In actuality the subjects were assigned to groups quite at random, half to "underestimators" and half to "overestimators" in the first condition, half to "better" and half to "worse" accuracy in the second one.

Instructions followed about the nature of the forthcoming task. The boys were told that it would consist of giving to others rewards and penalties in real money. They would not know the identity of the individuals to whom they would be assigning these rewards and penalties since everyone would have a code number. They would be taken to another room one by one and given information as to which group they were in. Once in the other room they were to work on their own in separate cubicles. In each cubicle they would find a pencil and a booklet containing 18 sets of ordered numbers, one to each page. It was stressed that on no occasion would the boys be rewarding or penalizing themselves; they would always be allot-

ting money to others. At the end of the task each boy would be brought back into the first room and would receive the amount of money the other boys had awarded him. The value of each point they were awarding was a tenth of a penny (about a tenth of a U.S. cent). After these instructions were given, the boys were led individually to their cubicles to fill out their booklets.

On each page in the booklet there was one matrix consisting of 14 boxes containing two numbers each. The numbers in the top row were the rewards and penalties to be awarded to one person and those in the bottom row were those to be awarded to another. Each row was labeled "These are rewards and penalties for member No. ___ of your group" or " . . . of the other group." The subjects had to indicate their choices by checking one box in each matrix. On the cover of each booklet and at the top of each page was written: "Booklet for member of the ___ group."

There were six matrices (Figure 10.1) and each of them appeared three times in the booklet—once for each of three types of choice. There were ingroup choices, with the top and the bottom row signifying the rewards and penalties to be awarded to two members of the subject's own group (other than himself). Then there were outgroup choices, with both rows signifying the rewards and penalties for a member of the other group. Finally there were intergroup, or "differential," choices, one row indicating the rewards and penalties to be awarded to an ingroup member (other than himself) and the other the points for an outgroup member. (The top and bottom positions of ingroup and outgroup members were varied at random.)

The results for the intergroup choices were first scored in terms of ranks of choices. In each matrix Rank 1 stood for the choice of the term that gave to the member of the ingroup the minimum possible number of points in that matrix; Rank 14, at the opposite extreme of the matrix, stood for the maximum possible number of points. Comparable (but more complex) methods of scoring were adopted for the other two kinds of choice, the ingroup choices and the outgroup ones, and for comparison of these choices with those made in the differential situation.

The results were striking. In making their intergroup choices a large majority of the subjects, in all groups in both conditions, gave more money to members of their own group than to members of

A

MATRIX 1

19	18	17	16	15	14	13	12	11	10	9	8	7
1	3	5	7	9	11	13	15	17	19	21	23	25

MIP
MD

MATRIX 2

23	22	21	20	19	18	17	16	15	14	13	12	11
5	7	9	11	13	15	17	19	21	23	25	27	29

MJP
MJP
MIP
MD

B

MATRIX 3

7	8	9	10	11	12	13	14	15	16	17	18	19
1	3	5	7	9	11	13	15	17	19	21	23	25

MD

MIP
MJP
MIP
MJP
MD

MATRIX 4

11	12	13	14	15	16	17	18	19	20	21	22	23
5	7	9	11	13	15	17	19	21	23	25	27	29

FIGURE 10.4 ■ Second Experiment involved new matrices. Each was presented in four versions labeled (as in the illustration in Figure 10.5) to indicate whether the choice was between members of different groups or between two members of the same group; the intergroup choices sometimes had the ingroup member's points in the top row and sometimes had them in the bottom row. The objective now was to analyze the influence of three variables on the subjects' choices: maximum ingroup profit (*MIP*), maximum joint profit (*MJP*) and maximum difference in favor of the ingroup member (*MD*). These varied according to different patterns in the Type *A* and Type *B* matrices and in the different versions; in some cases the maxima were together at one end of the matrix and in other cases they were at opposite ends. For example, in the ingroup-over-outgroup version of Type A matrices the maximum ingroup profit and maximum difference were at one end and the maximum joint profit at the other end; in the outgroup-over-ingroup version of the same matrices the three maxima were together at the right-hand end of the matrices. Type *B* ingroup-over-outgroup versions, on the other hand, distinguish the difference in favor of ingroup from the other two gains.

the other group. All the results were—at a very high level of statistical significance—above both Rank 7.5, which represents the point of maximum fairness, and the mean ranks of the ingroup and outgroup choices. In contrast the ingroup and outgroup choices were closely distributed about the point of fairness. Further analysis made it clear that intergroup discrimination was the deliberate strategy adopted in making intergroup choices.

Before continuing, let us review the situation. The boys, who knew each other well, were divided into groups defined by flimsy and unimportant criteria. Their own individual interests were not affected by their choices, since they always assigned points to two other people and no one could know what any other boy's choices were. The amounts of money were not trivial for them: each boy left the experiment with the equivalent of about

BOOKLET FOR GROUP PREFERRING KLEE

These numbers are rewards for:

member no. 74 of Klee group	25	23	21	19	17	15	13	11	9	7	5	3	1
member no. 44 of Kandinsky group	19	18	17	16	15	14	13	12	11	10	9	8	7

Please fill in below details of the box you have just chosen:

	Amount
Reward for member no. 74 of Klee group	21
Reward for member no. 44 of of Kandinsky group	17

FIGURE 10.5 ■ Page of Booklet, presenting a single matrix, is reproduced as a subject might have marked it. In addition to checking a box, the subject filled in the blanks below it to confirm his choice. The page heading reminded him which group he was in. The awards were made to persons identified only by number and group; the subject did not know who they were but only their group identification.

a dollar. Inasmuch as they could not know who was in their group and who was in the other group, they could have adopted either of two reasonable strategies. They could have chosen the maximum-joint-profit point of the matrices, which would mean that the boys as a total group would get the most money out of the experimenters, or they could choose the point of maximum fairness. Indeed, they did tend to choose the second alternative when their choices did not involve a distinction between ingroup and outgroup. As soon as this differentiation was involved, however, they discriminated in favor of the ingroup. The only thing we needed to do to achieve this result was to associate their judgments of numbers of dots with the use of the terms "your group" and "the other group" in the instructions and on the booklets of matrices.

The results were at a very high level of statistical significance in all eight separately tested groups of eight boys. In view of the consistency of the phenomenon we decided to analyze it further and also to validate it with a different criterion for intergroup categorization. We tested three new groups of 16 boys each, this time with aesthetic preference as the basis of the division into two groups. The boys were shown 12 slides, six of which were reproductions of paintings by Paul

Klee and six by Wassily Kandinsky, and they were asked to express their preference for one or the other of these two "foreign painters." The reproductions were presented without the painter's signature, so that half of the subjects could be assigned at random to the "Klee group" and half to the "Kandinsky group."

The matrices that confronted the boys subsequently in their individual cubicles were different from those in the first experiment. We were now interested in assessing the relative weights of some of the variables that may have pulled decisions in one direction or the other. In this experiment we looked at three variables: maximum joint profit, or the best possible joint award to both people; maximum ingroup profit, or the largest possible award to a member of the group, and maximum difference, or largest possible difference in gain between a member of the ingroup and a member of the outgroup in favor of the former.

There were four different matrices (Figure 10.4). As in the first experiment, there were three types of choice: between two members of the ingroup and a member of outgroup, between two members of ingroup and between two members the outgroup. In the outgroup-over-ingroup version of Type A matrices (that is, where the numbers in the top row represented amounts given to a member of the outgroup and in the bottom row to a member of the ingroup) the three gains—joint profit, ingroup profit and difference in favor of the ingroup— varied together; their maxima (maximum joint profit, maximum ingroup profit and maximum difference) were all at the same end of the matrix. In the ingroup-over-outgroup version, ingroup profit and difference in favor of ingroup went together in one direction and were in direct conflict with choices approaching maximum joint profit. In the Type *B* matrices outgroup-over-ingroup versions again represented a covariation of the three gains; in the ingroup-over-outgroup versions, difference in favor of ingroup varied in the direction opposite to joint profit and ingroup profit combined.

A comparison of the boys' choices in the various matrices showed that maximum joint profit exerted hardly any effect at all; the effect of maximum ingroup profit and maximum difference combined against maximum joint profit was strong and highly significant; the effect of maximum difference against maximum joint profit and maximum ingroup profit was also strong and highly significant. In other words, when the subjects had a choice between maximizing the profit for all and maximizing the profit for members of their own group, they acted on behalf of their own group. When they had a choice between profit for all and for their own group combined, as against their own group's winning *more* than the outgroup at the sacrifice of both of these utilitarian advantages, it was the maximization of *difference* that seemed more important to them.

Evidence leading in the same direction emerged from the other two types of choice, between two members of the ingroup and between two members of the outgroup: the ingroup choices were consistently and significantly nearer to the maximum joint profit than were the outgroup ones— and this was so in spite of the fact that giving as much as possible to two members of the outgroup in the choices applying solely to them presented no conflict with the ingroup's interest: It simply would have meant giving more to "the others" without giving any less to "your own." This represented, therefore, a clear case of gratuitous discrimination. We also included in the second experiment some of the original matrices used in the first one, with results much the same as before. Again all the results in this experiment were at a high level of statistical significance.

In subsequent experiments we tested the importance of fairness in making the choices, the effect on the choices of familiarity with the situation and the subjects' ideas about the choices that others were making. Fairness, we found, was an important determinant; most of the choices must be understood as being a compromise between fairness and favoring one's own group. We found that discrimination not only persisted but also increased when the entire situation became more familiar to the subjects. With familiarity there was also an increase (when the boys were asked to predict the other subjects' behavior) in their expectation that other boys were discriminating.

Much remains to be done to analyze the entire phenomenon in greater detail and to gain a fuller understanding of its determining conditions, but some clear inferences can already be made. Outgroup discrimination is extraordinarily easy to trigger off. In some previous studies of group conflict, such as one conducted by Muzafer Sherif at the University of Oklahoma, groups had to be placed in intense competition for several days for such results to occur [see "Experiments in Group Conflict," by Muzafer Sherif; *Scientific American*, November, 1956]; in other situations behavior of this kind can occur without direct conflict if it is based on previously existing hostility. Yet neither an objective conflict of interests nor hostility had any relevance whatever to what our subjects were asked to do. It was enough for them to see themselves as clearly categorized into an ingroup and an outgroup, flimsy as the criteria for this division were—even though the boys knew one another well before the experiments, their own individual gains were not involved in their decisions and their actions could have been aimed to achieve the greatest common good.

It would seem, then, that the generic norm of outgroup behavior to which I have referred does exist and that it helps to distort what might have been more reasonable conduct. This norm determines behavior—as other social norms do—when an individual finds himself in a situation to which, in his view, the norm applies. Behavior is never motiveless, but it is a crude oversimplification to think that motives in social situations include no more than calculations of self-interest or that they can be derived from a few supposedly universal human drives such as aggression toward the outsider, the need to affiliate and so on. To behave socially is a complex business. It involves a long learning process; it is based on the manipulation of symbols and abstractions; it implies the capacity for modification of conduct when the situation changes—and social situations never remain static. To behave *appropriately* is therefore a powerful social motive, and attempting to do so means to behave according to one's best understanding of the situation. Judgments of what is appropriate are determined by social norms, or sets of expectations.

It seems clear that two such norms were understood by our subjects to apply to the situation we imposed on them: "groupness" and "fairness." They managed to achieve a neat balance between the two, and one might assume that in real-life situations the same kind of balance would apply. Unfortunately it is only too easy to think of examples in real life where fairness would go out the window, since groupness is often based on criteria more weighty than either preferring a painter one has never heard of before or resembling someone else in one's way of counting dots. Socialization into "groupness" is powerful and unavoidable; it has innumerable valuable functions. It also has some odd side effects that may—and do—reinforce acute intergroup tensions whose roots lie elsewhere. Perhaps those educators in our competitive societies who from the earliest schooling are so keen on "teams" and "team spirit" could give some thought to the operation of these side effects.

Intergroup Discrimination in Positive and Negative Outcome Allocations: Impact of Stimulus Valence, Relative Group Status, and Relative Group Size

Sabine Otten, Amélie Mummendey, and Mathias Blanz
• Westfälische Wilhelms-Universität

Three studies investigated the determination of social discrimination by the valence of stimuli that are allocated between groups. The studies were based on either the minimal group paradigm or a more reality-based laboratory intergroup setting with stimulus valence, group status, and group size as factors and with pull scores on Tajfel matrices as dependent variables. In general, the results showed that group members did not discriminate against the out-group when allocating negative stimuli, whereas for positive stimuli the typical in-group bias was found. However, those participants whose positive social identity was threatened by assigning them to inferior or minority groups showed an increased willingness to favor the in-group over the out-group in the allocation of both positive and negative stimuli.

Since the first studies on the effects of mere categorization of participants into distinct laboratory groups (Rabbie & Horwitz, 1969; Tajfel, Billig, Bundy, & Flament, 1971), many experiments have demonstrated group members' willingness to favor their own group and to discriminate against members of other groups even in minimal intergroup situations (see Messick & Mackie, 1989; Tajfel, 1982). Empirical evidence from typical experiments conducted in the minimal group paradigm (MGP) seems to imply that social discrimination inevitably results from group members' striving for positive social identity. Accordingly, Brown (1988) concludes that "the mere act of allocating people into arbitrary social categories is sufficient to elicit biased judgments and discriminatory behavior" (p. 224) and assumes a "persistent tendency for people to display inter-group discrimination" (p. 240).

Discrimination can be understood as a means achieving or maintaining a positive or secure social identity (Lemyre & Smith, 1985). However, social identity theory (Tajfel, 1978, 1982; Tajfel & Turner, 1986), while providing a theoretical explanation of in-group favoritism, does not claim that the striving for positive group distinctiveness automatically results in in-group favoritism or out-group derogation. According to Hinkle and Brown (1990), it "has been clear from the start of empirical research on intergroup biases that in-group favoritism is not a universal occurrence" (p. 50). Some experiments document that under specific conditions one may find not only a lack of in-group favoritism in intergroup allocations but even out-group favoritism.

Determinants of Socially Discriminative Behavior

Meanwhile, several factors from intergroup contexts have been identified that crucially determine people's willingness to discriminate against a given out-group. Variables that turned out to have an important impact on the occurrence and degree of in-group favoritism or out-group derogation are— among others—the relative status of the groups in question (e.g., Sachdev & Bourhis, 1987, 1991; Turner & Brown, 1978), the similarity between groups (Brown, 1984; van Knippenberg & Ellemers, 1990), their structure of interdependence (Blake & Mouton, 1962; Sherif, 1966), their relative power, and their relative size (see, e.g., Mullen, Brown, & Smith, 1992; Sachdev & Bourhis, 1984, 1991).

Recently, however, Mummendey and her colleagues claimed that—besides characteristics of the intergroup relation—there are still further determinants of social discrimination that need to be investigated (Mummendey et al., 1992). They stressed that there is a deficiency in current research on discrimination between groups: Usually, the experiments are concerned with the distribution of positive resources (benefits, goods) between members of different groups. Either the allocation of negative stimuli (burdens, aversive treatments) is not taken into account, or it is assumed that results from studies in the domain of positive resources can be simply extrapolated to the negative domain. One exception is a study by Hewstone, Fincham, and Jaspars (1981) concerning the allocation of penalties, which showed a decrease in in-group-favoring behavior as compared with similar studies on the allocation of positive stimuli. Nevertheless, until the experiments by Mummendey et al. (1992), this result did not stimulate further research on the impact of stimulus valence on intergroup allocations.

Effects of Stimulus Valence

The studies by Mummendey et al. (1992) dealt with the allocation of negative stimuli (Experiment 1: duration of unpleasant noise; Experiment 2: duration of unpleasant tasks) between members of ad hoc laboratory groups in a minimal intergroup setting. Dependent variables were matrices similar to those used in typical minimal group experiments (Tajfel et al., 1971). In the first study, with no differences between groups in either status or size, participants did not show any discriminative behavior in their intergroup allocations. The only powerful allocation strategy was fairness (i.e., equal treatment of members of the two groups). In the second study, differences in group status and group size were introduced. Results of this experiment showed that only members of low-status or minority groups favored their in-group in their allocation decisions. In the other conditions—as in the first experiment—fairness was the only important strategy for distributing negative stimuli. Thus intergroup discrimination was restricted to those conditions that, by threatening their positive social identity, tended to enhance participants' striving for positive distinctiveness. For participants assigned to minority groups or low-status groups, discriminating against the out-group may have compensated their relatively weak social identity (Tajfel, 1981). On the basis of this evidence, Mummendey and coworkers advanced the hypothesis that there is a positive-negative asymmetry in social discrimination. The idea is that the valence of stimuli in intergroup allocations determines the occurrence of social discrimination. On the whole, biases in favor of the in-group should be weaker when located in the domain of negative resources.

The experiments by Mummendey et al. (1992) underline that it is not only promising but also necessary to analyze stimulus valence as a determinant of behavior in intergroup allocations. However, these studies are only a first step in this new area of research: Both experiments by Mummendey and coworkers concerned negative intergroup allocations only. They compared their findings with those from similar studies on positive outcome allocations within the minimal group paradigm. What is still missing is a systematic comparison of positive and negative outcome allocations in identical empirical settings.

Equivalence of Positive and Negative Outcomes

When trying to make such a comparison, we were inevitably confronted with the question of equivalence: We cannot be sure that positive stimuli have identical psychological weights to those of negative stimuli. Is positive distinctiveness in terms of money comparable with positive distinctiveness in terms of minutes of unpleasant noise? This is a problem already inherent in positive-negative comparisons in other psychological domains—for example, in studies on impression formation and negativity biases (Abele & Petzold,1993; Peeters & Czapinski, 1990). Nor can the problem be resolved by looking only at one kind of resource that is either given to or taken from allocation targets: Is the pleasantness of gaining $5 equivalent to the unpleasantness of losing the same amount of money? Are these two events equally relevant to the recipients? As illustrated by the literature on framing effects, one can expect that they are not (see Kahneman & Tversky, 1979; Rutte, Wilke, & Messick, 1987; Skowronski & Carlston, 1987, 1989).

Consequently, one has to be aware of the possibility that while operationalizing the two valence conditions, one also introduces differences in relevance. We at least tried to minimize this problem in the following studies: Instead of comparing the allocation of positive and negative stimuli per se, we looked only at the *differences* in the distributions for in- and out-group members (as measured by the pull scores on Tajfel matrices). Irrespective of which concrete amount of positive or negative treatment was allocated by the participants, we tested whether the pull scores significantly differed from zero. These tests were done for each kind of matrix and within each cell of the designs. Therefore, the occurrence of in-group favoritism in one condition and its absence in another cannot be explained by possible differences in the variances of either positive or negative allocation decisions. Finally, one might argue that in-group biases in minimal group settings have proved to be a robust phenomenon *in spite of* the different operationalizations of measures of intergroup behavior (see Brown, 1988). Accordingly, measures that are negatively valenced can be expected to produce similar results.

Summing up, the three studies reported below were conducted to substantiate and supplement the findings by Mummendey and coworkers (1992) by offering a direct comparison of positive and negative outcome allocations. The experiments consider not only the impact of stimulus valence per se but also its possible interaction with the two independent variables included in the 1992 study,

relative group status and relative group size. Study 1 provides a positive-negative comparison in the original experimental setting from Mummendey's study in 1992; in a different experimental setting, Study 2 analyzes the mere impact of stimulus valence in intergroup allocations, and Study 3 shows how this "pure" valence effect changes with groups' status and size.

Hypotheses

The experimental series focused on two hypotheses, which both derived mainly from the empirical evidence obtained by Mummendey et al. (1992):

1. The asymmetry hypothesis assumed that the willingness to favor the in-group in intergroup allocations would be stronger in the domain of positive than in the domain of negative resources.
2. The aggravation hypothesis claimed that under conditions threatening participants' positive social identity, in-group favoritism would increase. This effect was hypothesized for the allocation of both negative and positive stimuli.

So far, *asymmetry* has not meant that specific characteristics of the intergroup context (such as relative group status and relative group size) in principle have different effects on positive and negative outcome allocations, but only that the probability of in-group favoritism differs as a function of stimulus valence. In the present studies, we assumed that the direction of aggravation effects would be identical in positive and negative outcome allocations.

Study 1

Study 1 partly reanalyzed and partly supplemented the data already published by Mummendey et al. (1992, Experiment 2). Their experiment tested the effects size and status differences between groups on negative outcome allocations exclusively. With respect to the assumed positive-negative asymmetry in social discrimination, the findings could be interpreted only with reference to other, classical studies in the positive domain. Adding an analysis of positive outcome allocations under the same experimental conditions made it possible to realize a direct statistical test of the asymmetry hypothesis.

Whereas in the positive stimulus valence condition we expected a general willingness of group members to favor their in-group over the out-group, we assumed that in negative outcome allocations in-group biases would be restricted to what we call aggravating conditions. In the following experiments, *aggravation* refers to inferiority in group status and/or group size, providing conditions that should threaten participants' positive social identity. The aggravation hypothesis assumed that these conditions should elicit an increased motivation to establish some positive distinctiveness of one's own group. Accordingly, we expected that members of inferior groups and members of minority groups would be more prone to show social discrimination than those of superior groups and majority groups.

With respect to the hypothesized direction of the status effects, it has to be emphasized that our dependent measures (intergroup allocation matrices as typically used in the MGP) were not related to the status-constituting dimension. With status-related dependent variables, we would expect the opposite effect—namely, a reflection of the experimentally induced status differences (see Sachdev & Bourhis, 1984; Turner & Brown, 1978).

Method

Participants and design. Participants were 179 school-children from a grammar school, 97 female and 82 male, with a mean age of 14 years. The design included three between-subjects factors, each with two levels: (a) stimulus valence (positive, negative), (b) relative group status (inferior, superior) and (c) relative group size (minority, majority).

Dependent variables. The crucial dependent variables were participants' allocations of either positive stimuli (money) or negative stimuli (duration of unpleasant tasks) to members of in- and out-groups on matrices measuring the following allocation strategies: (a) maximum profit[1] for the in-group (MIP); (b) maximum difference between in- and out-group in favor of the in-group (MD); (c) maximum joint profit (MJP) for both in- and out-group members irrespective of which group gains more, and (d) fairness (F)—that is, treating in- and out-group members equally. It has to be stressed that *fairness* in this sense could be replaced

by *parity* or *equality*. The "fair" solutions are not related to any prior inputs of the group members in question (as fairness according to the equity concept would imply). Table 11.1 shows the three types of matrices used in the experiments.

Each matrix is constructed in such a way that each of its extremes represents a maximum realization of one or two of the allocation strategies mentioned above. To measure the pulls (i.e., the relative strength) of the different allocation strategies, each matrix had to be presented once with an in-group member and once with an out-group member in the top row. Additionally, all six matrices were presented with columns and rows reversed. Thus there were 12 matrices in total. Order of presentation was randomized for each subject. Pull scores were computed by contrasting the decisions on the complementary in-group/out-group and out-group/in-group matrices (for more details of the construction and statistical analysis of matrices, see, e.g., Tajfel et al., 1971; Turner, Brown, & Tajfel, 1979).

Manipulation checks. To check the salience of our social categorization, identification with the in-group was measured by the following items: On 5-point scales, participants were asked which of the two groups they would prefer (1 = *prefer clearly the other group*, 5 = *prefer clearly my own group*) and whether they liked belonging to their own group (1 = *not at all,* 5 = *very much*).

Procedure. The study was conducted in the tradition of the minimal group paradigm (Tajfel et al., 1971): There was neither intra- nor intergroup interaction. The experiment, introduced as being concerned with cognitive abilities, was run in a school setting. Participants completed a short dot-estimation test and then—allegedly on the basis of this test—were assigned to groups labeled "subestimators" and "hyperestimators." In fact, group assignment was random; care was taken that participants did not exchange information about group membership (information was given covertly to the participants). Participants in the high-status/majority position were told that in-group members could be expected to give more correct estimates than out-group members and that usually about 80% of the total population belongs to their in-group. This information was reinforced later by claiming that the results of a perceptual

---

[1]In the negative stimulus condition, *profit* means "getting less aversive stimulation."

TABLE 11.1 Matrices Used in the Experiments

Matrix and Strategies	Points Allocated												
Matrix A	19	18	17	16	15	14	13	12	11	10	9	8	7
(MJP vs. MIP + MD)	1	3	5	7	9	11	13	15	17	19	21	23	25
Matrix B	7	8	9	10	11	12	13	14	15	16	17	18	19
(MD vs. MIP + MJP)	1	3	5	7	9	11	13	15	17	19	21	23	25
Matrix C	13	14	15	16	17	18	19	20	21	22	23	24	25
(F vs. MIP + MD)	13	12	11	10	9	8	7	6	5	4	3	2	1

Note: Points stand for duration of noise (in minutes) or money (in DM). MJP, maximum joint profit; MIP, maximum in-group profit; MD maximum difference in favor of in-group; F, fairness. MIP + MD = FAV (in-group favoritism). Matrices A and B were adopted from Tajfel, Billig, Bundy, and Flament (1971), Matrix C from Billig and Tajfel (1973).

task done by the participants immediately after the dot-estimation test closely resembled the information given about relative group status and relative group size.

As already mentioned, the dependent variables were participants' allocations of negative or positive resources on matrices. In the negative stimulus condition, participants distributed lists of meaningless syllables (which ostensibly should be memorized in a later task) to anonymous in- and out-group members. In the positive resource condition, they allocated money, allegedly as a motivating stimulus in a further task (for a more detailed description, see Mummendey et al., 1992).

Results and Discussion

MANIPULATION CHECKS

We formed an overall group identification score by averaging the means from the two 5-point subscales (alpha = .63). The resulting mean was 3.52 (SD = 0.94); for a minimal intergroup situation, this score seems sufficiently high. Analysis of covariance revealed that degree of identification with the in-group did not significantly affect the other dependent measures. Therefore, low-identification participants were not excluded from further data analyses.

An analysis of variance (ANOVA) with identification as the dependent variable indicated a highly significant effect of relative group status, $F(1, 176) = 81.84, p < .001$, such that inferior group members indicated lower in-group identification than superior group members (M/inf = 3.00, SD = 0.96, n = 85; M/sup = 4.03, SD = 0.65, n = 94). This result can be interpreted as showing that relative group status was successfully operationalized: As intended, superior group members felt more

positive about their group membership than members of inferior groups (who should be faced with an aggravating condition with respect to a positive social identity).[2]

MATRICES

The data from our six types of matrices allowed us to analyze the following pulls of specific intergroup allocation strategies: (a) maximum in-group profit and maximum joint profit at the expense of maximum (positive) difference between in- and out-group (MIP + MJP on MD), (b) fairness at the expense of in-group favoritism (F on FAV), (c) maximum joint profit at the expense of in-group favoritism (MJP on FAV), (d) maximum difference in favor of the in-group at the expense of maximum in-group profit and maximum joint profit (MD on MIP + MJP), (e) in-group favoritism at the expense of maximum joint profit (FAV on MJP), and (f) in-group favoritism at the expense of parity (FAV on F). Whereas the first three pulls represent more cooperative behaviors in intergroup allocations, the latter three reflect competitive, in-group-favoring orientations. The pulls of each strategy were calculated by comparing the decisions on those matrices on which this strategy coincided with the given alternative orientation and those where these two conflicted with each other. The statistical significance of each of the six pull scores was tested by two-tailed t tests comparing the decisions from the in-group/out-group version

---

[2]However, it should be noted that our status effects on intergroup allocations cannot be treated as the result of mere differences in in-group identification. As discussed in Blanz, Mummendey, and Otten (1995a), regression analyses show that relative group status and in-group identification independently are strong predictors with respect to allocation decisions.

of a specific matrix with those of the complementary out-group/in-group version (for further details, see Turner et al., 1979). The effects of the three experimental factors were tested by $2 \times 2 \times 2$ (Stimulus Valence × Relative Group Size × Relative Group Status) ANOVAs for the six pulls.

Asymmetry effects. The mere comparison of positive and negative outcome allocations confirmed the asymmetry hypothesis (see Table 11.2). In the negative condition there was only one significant in-group-favoring pull (FAV on F), whereas in the positive condition all competitive pull scores were clearly significant. The ANOVAs reflected this result, indicating significant effects of stimulus valence on "FAV on F," $F(1,186) = 16.39$, $p < .001$, and "FAV on MJP," $F(1, 186) = 8.68$, $p < .01$. In each case the respective pull scores were stronger in the positive than in the negative stimulus valence condition. However, stimulus valence also had significant effects on fair intergroup allocation strategies. Although in any case fairness was the most pervasive strategy, the pull scores of both "MIP + MJP on MD" and "F on FAV" were higher in positive than in negative allocations: MIP + MJP on MD, $F(1, 186) = 5.49$, $p < .05$; F on FAV, $F(1, 186) = 6.91$, $p < .01$.

Additionally, there was a significant interaction between stimulus valence and relative group status: For the FAV on MJP pull, we found a stronger impact of status variation in the negative stimulus valence condition, $F(1, 165) = 3.85$, $p < .01$. Although in any case there was more favoritism by inferior group members, the difference between the inferior and superior status conditions was

TABLE 11.2. Mean Pull Scores of Participants' Allocation Strategy by Valence of Outcome Allocation, Study 1

	Valence	
Allocation Strategy	Positive	Negative
MIP + MJP on MD	5.21*** (4.84)	3.31*** (5.60)
F on FAV	4.16*** (4.90)	2.04** (5.68)
MJP on FAV	1.41*** (2.83)	0.52 (4.36)
MD on MIP + MJP	0.73** (2.68)	0.58 (3.51)
FAV on MJP	2.28*** (4.38)	0.47 (3.93)
FAV on F	3.43*** (4.43)	0.92* (354)

Note: Mean pull scores for each allocation strategy can range from – 12 to +12. MIP, maximum in-group profit; MJP, maximum joint profit; MD, maximum difference in favor of the in-group; F, fairness; FAV, in-group favoritism (MD + MIP). Cell *ns* vary from 99 to 103 for positive valence; for negative valence, cell *ns* are 74. Standard deviations are in parentheses.
*$p < .05$.   **$p < .01$.   ***$p < .001$. (two-tailed *t* tests).

TABLE 11.3. Menu Pull Scores for the FAV on MJP Strategy by Stimulus Valence and Relative Group Status, Study 1

	Valence	
Relative In-group Status	Positive	Negative
Inferior	2.71** (4.11)	2.08* (3.76)
Superior	1.19* (4.61)	−1.15a (3.45)

Note: Mean pull scores can range from –12 to + 12. FAV, in-group favoritism (MD + MIP); MJP, maximum joint profit; MD, maximum difference in favor of the in-group; MIP, maximum in-group profit. Cell *ns* vary from 37 to 56. Standard deviations are in parentheses.
a. Mean differs at $p = .05$ or better from the other means according to Scheffé test.
*$p < .01$.   **$p < .001$. (two-tailed *t* tests).

much stronger in negative outcome allocations (see Table 11.3).

Aggravation effects. The results also support the aggravation hypothesis: As can be seen from Table 11.4, in both positive and negative stimulus valence conditions, the only significant pull scores for the most competitive in-group-favoring allocation strategy, MD on MIP + MJP, were found for members of inferior minorities. A similar pattern of data—with highest positive pull scores in the inferior minority condition—was measured for the FAV on MJP pull.

ANOVA revealed that for the in-group-favoring allocation strategies, there were two significant main effects of relative group status and one significant main effect of relative group size, all in line with the aggravation assumption: The pulls for both "MD on MIP + MJP" and "FAV on MJP" were significantly stronger for inferior than for superior group members; MD on MIP + MJP: $M/\text{inf} = 1.49$, $SD = 2.97$, $n = 81$, $M/\text{sup} = -0.05$, $SD = 2.96$, $n = 92$, $F(1, 165) = 13.49$, $p < .001$; FAV on MJP: $M/\text{inf} = 2.43$, $SD = 3.95$, $n = 84$, $M/\text{sup} = 0.67$, $SD = 4.43$, $n = 93$, $F(1, 165) = 10.52$, $p < .001$. With respect to the FAV on F pull, there was a significant main effect of relative group size, $F(1, 165) = 4.20$, $p < .05$, minority members showing more in-group favoritism at the expense of fairness than majority members ($M/\text{min} = 2.95$, $SD = 4.21$, $n = 86$; $M/\text{maj} = 1.81$, $SD = 4.24$, $n = 89$). There was also a significant main effect of relative group status on the nondiscriminating strategy MIP + MJP on MD: This strategy was more strongly preferred by superior than by inferior group members.

Though not directly relevant for our two hypoth-

TABLE 11.4. Mean Pull Scores of Participants' Allocation Strategies by Stimulus Valence, Relative Group Status, and Relative Group Size, Study 1

	Inferior Status		Superior Status	
Allocation Strategy	Minority In-Group	Majority In-Group	Minority In-Group	Majority In-Group
	Positive Valence			
HIP + MJP on MD	2.48* (4.25)	6.86***(4.43)	5.93*** (4.63)	5.39*** (5.11)
F on FAV	4.16*** (5.07)	3.56** (4.95)	3.18*** (4.36)	5.64*** (5.14)
MJP on FAV	0.24 (2.19)	2.42** (3.42)	1.32* (3.18)	1.59*** (2.06)
MD on MIP + MJP	2.11*** (2.60)	0.27 (2.70)	0.79 (3.00)	–0.07 (2.02)
FAV on MJP	3.15*** (3.67)	2.29* (4.52)	1.86* (4.48)	1.98* (4.81)
FAV on F	3.37*** (4.01)	3.22*** (3.87)	3.07** (5.09)	3.21*** (4.62)
	Negative Valence			
MIP + MJP on MD	2.24 (6.48)	2.08 (6.19)	5.81 *** (4.39)	3.25** (4.59)
F on FAV	3.00 (6.89)	1.92 (5.34)	1.00 (5.97)	2.13 (4.62)
MJP on FAV	–0.80 (3.95)	0.61 (4.44)	1.36 (5.39)	0.89 (3.58)
MD on MIP + MJP	1.76*** (2.02)	1.82 (4.12)	–0.31 (2.83)	–1.08 (3.97)
FAV on MJP	3.03** (4.18)	1.18 (3.16)	–1.25* (2.44)	–1.05 (4.26)
FAV on F	2.05* (3.53)	–0.66 (3.09)	1.88* (3.24)	0.50 (3.79)

Note: Mean pull scores for each allocation strategy can range from –12 to +12. MIP, maximum in-group profit; MJP, maximum joint profit; MD, maximum difference in favor of the in-group; F, fairness; FAV, in-group favoritism (MD + MIP). Cell *n*s vary from 17 to 28. Standard deviations are in parentheses.
*$p < .05$. **$p < .01$. ***$p < .001$. (two-tailed *t* tests)

eses, two further interaction effects with respect to the nondiscriminating MIP + MJP on MD pull should be briefly outlined here. The interaction between stimulus valence and relative group size, $F(1, 165) = 4.45$, $p < .05$, was caused by the fact that majority members exhibited a relatively low pull in the negative condition ($M = 2.65$, $SD = 5.43$, $n = 37$) and an especially high pull in the positive one ($M = 6.02$, $SD = 4.83$, $n = 49$), whereas minority members were only slightly (and not significantly, according to a Scheffé test) affected by the variation of stimulus valence ($M/\text{neg} = 3.97$, $SD = 5.77$, $n = 37$; $M/\text{pos} = 4.41$, $SD = 4.75$, $n = 50$). Furthermore, there was an interaction between relative group status and relative group size, $F(1, 165) = 5.53$, $p < .05$: The very low mean of inferior minority members ($M = 2.36$, $SD = 5.43$, $n = 41$) differed, according to Scheffé test, from all three other scores, whereas no other differences were significant ($M/\text{sup}/\text{min} = 5.88$, $SD = 4.49$, $n = 46$; $M/\text{inf}/\text{maj} = 4.59$, $SD = 5.79$, $n = 40$; $M/\text{sup}/\text{maj} = 4.55$, $SD = 4.97$, $n = 46$). In accordance with the aggravation idea, those participants who were assumed to be experiencing the strongest threat to a positive social identity showed the weakest tendency (albeit still significant) to combine maximum in-group profit with some cooperation with

the out-group (as implied by the MIP + MJP strategy) instead of maximizing the positive distinctiveness for their in-group (MD).

Summing up, it can be stated that data are strongly supportive of both the asymmetry and the aggravation hypotheses. In-group-favoring behaviors were mostly restricted to the distribution of positive outcomes. For both positive and negative outcome allocations, in-group favoritism increased under conditions threatening participants' positive social identity.

Study 2

To substantiate and generalize the finding that the occurrence of in-group favoritism is determined by the valence of stimuli to be allocated, the positive-negative asymmetry was tested in a more reality based experimental setting. Reality of group categorization (Mullen et al., 1992) was enhanced by introducing face-to-face interaction within and between experimental groups. We introdated this "enriched" intergroup setting to analyze whether and how the effects of stimulus valence on intergroup allocations differ between a nonminimal and a minimal intergroup setting.

When creating the MGP, Henri Tajfel and his coworkers were looking for the most reduced intergroup situation sufficient to elicit in-group biases (Tajfel et al., 1971). In this sense, enriching the setting by allowing participants to interact within their own group (which may strengthen group boundaries and in-group identification) should increase participants' willingness to discriminate against laboratory out-groups. The same line of reasoning was advanced by Mullen et al. (1992), who pointed out that because the salience of in-groups is higher in real than in laboratory groups, the former should show higher in-group biases than the latter. This conclusion was supported by their meta-analysis integrating 137 studies on in-group bias.

Although the two studies reported below are still based on ad hoc laboratory groups, there is an increase in the reality of the group categorization: Group membership is not anonymous, and the in-group can be experienced during intragroup interaction. If a more realistic intergroup setting increases the salience of the in-group, it can be understood as an aggravating condition, raising participants' interest in a positive social identity. This assumption is supported by a study by Blanz, Mummendey, and Otten (1995b) analyzing effects of the salience of status and size differences between groups on negative intergroup evaluations. Accordingly, we might expect that the probability of ingroup-favoring behavior will be higher in our nonminimal than in our minimal experimental situation (Study 1). However, the differences between minimal and other intergroup settings are not straightforward (see, e.g., Ellemers, 1993; Spears & Oyen, 1993). Diehl (1990) even suggests that instead of being minimal, the MGP provides maximal conditions facilitating the occurrence of in-group favoritism, because participants are anonymous and not mutually responsible. Besides, there is not only the question "How minimal is the minimal intergroup setting?" (Spears & Oyen, 1993); as pointed out in a review by Messick and Mackie (1989), there is also some inconsistency in the experimental findings within the categories of both minimal and nonminimal studies on social discrimination.

In light of these considerations, we did not hypothesize specific effects due to differences between the experimental setting of Study 1, on the one hand, and those of Studies 2 and 3, on the other.

Method

Participants and design. Participants were recruited by means of small advertisements in local newspapers or by announcements in university courses. They were assigned to small groups, usually consisting of three persons. To minimize possible effects due to specific characteristics of the subgroups, one randomly chosen subject from each subgroup filled in the allocation matrices, while the remaining participants worked through another questionnaire (which will not be discussed here). The results reported below refer only to those participants whose allocation decisions on matrices were analyzed. These participants were 34 pupils and students (20 female, 14 male; mean age 22 years). Each subject received 25 DM (about $15) for participation.

The design involved only one independent variable, the valence of stimuli to be allocated.

Dependent measures. Participants allocated either a limited sum of money (0 to 12 DM) or a limited amount of negative treatment (0 to 12 min of unpleasant noise) to members of in- and out-groups. As in Study 1, we measured pull scores on three kinds of matrices adopted from Tajfel et al. (1971) and Billig and Tajfel (1973). To make the task more plausible to our participants, we limited the range of numbers on the matrices to 0 to 12 (instead of 1 to 25).

Manipulation checks. To check the salience of the social categorization introduced in our experiment, participants were asked how much they identified with their experimental in-group. The items were selected from the identification scales by Brown, Condor, Mathews, Wade, and Williams (1986) and Ellemers, van Knippenberg, de Vries, and Wilke (1988). On 7-point scales, participants indicated how much they agreed with the following statements: "I would have preferred to be a member of the other group," "My group was well matched," "I enjoyed being a member of my group," and "I would like to continue cooperating with my group." Additionally, in the negative allocation condition, we checked how distressed the participants felt when listening to the administered noise. This way we could establish whether the participants were really confronted with negative, aversive stimuli.

Procedure. The experiment, which was allegedly concerned with concentration, took place in the psychology department. Typically, six participants at a time participated, and two experimenters ran the experiment. If not enough "real" participants attended a given experimental session, the missing persons were replaced by stooges. First, all participants worked on a short concentration test ("d2"; see Brickenkamp, 1972). After that, one experimenter supposedly analyzed the test data in order to assign the participants to two groups differing in their concentration ability. We emphasized that participants' group membership would not refer to their overall concentration ability but to the way their concentration would change over time; one group, the "convexes," would show highest concentration at the beginning and the end of the task, and the other group, the "concaves," would show highest concentration in the middle of the task. In fact, group membership was determined at random (taking care that gender was balanced in the experimental conditions). Information about group membership was given overtly in the presence of all participants, so that they had a clear picture about the in- and the out-group.

After group formation, the two groups worked successively on a short task in different rooms. For 3 min they compared a detailed picture with a copy containing several mistakes. While one group was looking for mistakes, it was observed by the other through a screen. However, the task was organized in such a way that no obvious differences in groups' performances emerged: The number of mistakes in the copy was extremely high (no group could obviously fail), and when observing the out-groups, participants could not see much more than the backs of the out-group members. This procedure was chosen to create a more realistic and salient but at the same time sufficiently standardized intergroup setting.

After the group task, participants completed a short questionnaire concerning their impressions of the in- and out-group during the preceding task.[3] Next, a further task was announced, which was supposed to analyze how concentration ability and its sequential characteristics were affected by further variables. In the positive condition, we claimed that we were interested in how concentration might change because of increased motivation elicited by attractive stimuli (money). In the negative condition, participants were told that the following experiment would be concerned with the effects of aversive conditions. Matrices were introduced by arguing that participants themselves should

determine the specific experimental conditions in a task to follow. As in Study 1, experimenters claimed that this procedure for determining the treatment of specific participants had already been successfully used in many past experiments. On each of 12 matrices, participants had to decide individually about the treatment of a pair of one in- and one out-group member, whose anonymity was assured by code numbers. It was stressed that none of the participants would be confronted with his or her own code number in the questionnaire. In the negative condition, participants listened to the unpleasant noise for 30 s and rated its unpleasantness before filling in the matrices. Finally, participants answered the questions about their group identification. Participants were then fully debriefed. Before getting paid, they signed a declaration that they would not talk to other people about the experiment during the next 6 months.

Results and Discussion

MANIPULATION CHECKS

Group identification (salience of categorization). An overall identification score was computed by averaging the answers on the four 7-point subscales (alpha = .81), with scores on the first item (preference for the out-group) recoded so that on all items high numbers indicated high identification with the in-group. The resulting mean identification score was 5.07 (SD = 1.07), indicating that our social categorization was sufficiently salient.

ANOVAs using valence as a factor and group identification as a covariate did not reveal any significant effect of degree of identification on the matrix pull scores. Therefore, participants with low identification scores were not excluded from further data analysis.

Unpleasantness of negative stimulus. On a 7-point scale from 1, *not unpleasant,* to 7, *very unpleasant,* the mean was 5.20 (SD = 1.52) . Al-

---

[3]It goes beyond the scope of this article to discuss the result obtained with respect to these in- and out-group evaluations. However, we would like to underline that objective measures of the groups, performance during the task (i.e., number of mistakes identified), as intended by the experimenters, did not show crucial differences between groups. Therefore, we feel encouraged to assume that (a) we did not introduce any "hidden" status differentials by our real group interaction and (b) possible biases cannot be interpreted as simple reflections of experimental experiences.

though this manipulation check does not really solve the problem of equivalence outlined under Equivalence of Positive and Negative Outcomes, this very high mean can be interpreted as indicating that a possible decrease in in-group favoritism cannot easily be explained by the irrelevance of our negative stimulus compared with the positive stimulus (money). As all participants indicated feeling at least mildly uncomfortable when listening to the given noise (unpleasantness scores of 3 and higher), it was possible to include the whole sample in further data analyses. Additionally, the unpleasantness ratings were tested as a covariate in the statistical analysis of the matrix data. This analysis did not reveal any significant effects of this variable.

MATRICES

Asymmetry effects. Table 11.5 shows the mean pull scores for the six types of matrices differentiated according to stimulus valence. In the intergroup allocations of both positive and negative outcomes, fairness was the most influential allocation strategy. In the allocation of positive outcomes, the striving for maximum joint profit (MJP) was also important. There was a highly significant pull of MIP + MJP on MD and a marginally significant pull of MJP on FAV.

With respect to those allocation strategies representing discriminating behavior FAV and MD), significant pull scores were found only in the positive condition: The pull of in-group favoritism (FAV = MIP + MD) on the strategy of maximizing both groups' joint profit (FAV on MJP) was significant. Additionally, there was a marginally significant pull of MD on MIP + MJP.

One-way ANOVAs yielded a significant effect of stimulus valence on the allocation strategy FAV on MJP, $F(1, 31) = 4.63, p < .05$. As already mentioned, the in-group-favoring behavior occurred only in the positive outcome allocations condition.

In sum, these results show that the positive-negative asymmetry is not restricted to a minimal experimental setting: The significant main effect on "FAV on MJP" and the corresponding pattern of data for the MD pull corroborate the asymmetry hypothesis and are consistent with the asymmetry effects obtained in Study 1. Accordingly, the present study further emphasizes the need to take account of the valence of outcome allocations when investigating the phenomenon of social discrimination.

TABLE 11.5. Mean Pull Scores of Participants' Allocation Strategies by Stimulus Valence, Study 2

	Valence	
Allocation Strategy	Positive ($n = 18$)	Negative ($n = 16$)
MIP+ MJP on MD	4.61** (4.88)	2.31† (5.10)
F on FAV	7.28** (6.12)	7.53** (5.34)
MJP on FAV	0.73† (1.42)	0.06 (1.53)
MD on MIP + MJP	0.67† (1.48)	0.19 (2.24)
FAV on MJP	1.72* (2.94)	0.03 (1.23)
FAV on F	0.56 (2.22)	0.53 (2.16)

Note: Mean pull scores for each strategy can range from -12 to +12. MIP, maximum in-group profit; MJP, maximum joint profit; MD, maximum difference in favor of the in-group; F, fairness; FAV, in-group favoritism (MD + MIP). Standard deviations are in parentheses.
†$p < .10$.   *$p < .05$.   **$p < .001$. (two-tailed t tests)

Study 3

Our next concern was to test not only the asymmetry hypothesis but also the aggravation hypothesis in a more reality-based experimental setting. As in Study 1, we expected that participants assigned to an inferior and/or minority group would show more discriminating behavior than members of superior and/or majority groups.

Method

Participants and design. Participants were assigned to small groups, typically of three (exceptionally two) persons. As in Study 2, only one person in each subgroup filled in the allocation matrices. The final sample consisted of 95 participants, 63 female and 32 male, with a mean age of 22 years.)

The design included three between-subjects factors, each with two levels: stimulus valence (positive, negative), relative group status (inferior, superior), and relative group size (minority, majority).

Dependent measures and manipulation checks. Dependent variables were identical to those in Study 2 (allocation matrices). Once again, identification with the in-group and the perceived unpleasantness of the negative treatment were measured as manipulation checks. Additionally, participants rated the subjective relevance of the variable used to establish the two groups ("How important is it for you to perform well in concentration tasks?") .

Procedure. The experimental procedure was

essentially the same as in Study 2. However, some details were added to establish intergroup differences in status and size. Participants were told that the two groups usually differ in the quality of their performance in concentration tasks and that 80% of the total population belongs to one group and 20% to the other. The experimenters took care that the group labels were varied in the two size and status conditions. The information about relative group status and relative group size was reinforced by claiming that the results of the initial concentration task reflected the differences expected on the basis of prior research. To give a more vivid impression of the minority and the majority, two confederates were additionally assigned to the majority group. Usually there were three members in the minority group and five members in the majority group. On the alleged grounds that groups should have comparable working conditions, only three of the five majority members were allowed to participate in the group tasks, while the others were merely observing. Ostensibly by chance, it was decided that the two confederates were to act as observer during the task.

Results and Discussion

MANIPULATION CHECKS

Group identification (salience of categorization). As in Study 2, we computed an averaged overall identification score from the four subscales (alpha = .79). The mean for this score was 4.57 (SD = 1.08), indicating a sufficiently salient social categorization. Analysis of variance with group identification as a covariate and matrix pull scores as dependent measures did not reveal any significant effects due to degree of identification.

An ANOVA analyzing identification as a dependent variable revealed a significant main effect of relative group status, $F(1, 86) = 8.71$, $p < .01$. Members of inferior groups identified less with their in-group than members of superior groups (M/inf = 4.26, SD = 0.94, n = 48; M/sup = 4.89, SD = 1.13, n = 46). This result may be understood as showing that the operationalization of relative group status was successful. Additionally, there was a significant main effect of relative group size, $F(1, 86) = 4.69$, $p < .05$, such that minority members identified more strongly with their in-group (M = 4.83, SD = 1.13, n = 43) than majority participants (M = 4.34, SD = 0.99, n = 51). This result

TABLE 11.6. Mean Pull Scores of Participants' Allocation Strategy Stimulus Valence, Study 3

Allocation Strategy	Valence	
	Positive (n = 48)	Negative (n = 46)
MIP + MJP on MD	3.07*** (3.69)	3.87*** (3.79)
F on FAV	7.34*** (4.88)	4.32*** (5.94)
MJP on FAV	−0.28 (2.13)	−0.37 (2.70)
MD on MIP + MJP	0.86* (2.54)	−0.26 (2.94)
FAV on MJP	1.22** (2.61)	−1.20* (3.19)
FAV on F	1.36** (2.85)	0.60 (3.15)

Note: Mean pull scores for each strategy can range from −12 to +12. MIP, maximum in-group profit; MJP, maximum joint profit; MD, maximum difference in favor of the in-group; F, fairness; FAV, in-group favoritism (MD + MIP). Standard deviations are in parentheses.
*$p < .05$. **$p < .01$. ***$p < .001$. (two-tailed t tests).

is in accordance with other studies (Simon & Brown, 1987; Simon & Pettigrew, 1990) where it is argued that there is an increased feeling of entitativity and groupness within minorities.

Unpleasantness of negative stimulus. In the negative stimulus condition, we measured how unpleasant the participants found the negative stimulus (i.e., noise). Participants estimated the negative treatment as clearly unpleasant (M = 5.87, SD = 1.21). Only one subject did not meet our criterion of an unpleasantness score of at least 3 and was excluded from further data analyses.

Subjective relevance of status-constituting variable. To assess the psychological salience of the status differentials established between the two groups, participants were asked to indicate the subjective relevance of the status-constituting variable. The mean score was well above the midpoint (M = 4.91, SD = 1.56). It can therefore be assumed that being assigned to the inferior group was in fact an aggravating condition for participants.

MATRICES

Asymmetry effects. When we focus only on the positive-negative comparison, the results look quite similar to those obtained in Studies 1 and 2. Table 11.6 shows the mean pull scores differentiated according to the two levels of stimulus valence.

With negative outcome allocations, there were significant positive scores only on fair distribution strategies (MIP + MJP on MD, F on FAV) and even a significant negative pull with respect to FAV on MJP. With positive outcome allocations, there are significant pulls for all three in-group-favoring strategies (MD on MIP + MJP, FAV on MJP, FAV on F) as well as the two above-mentioned fairness strategies. This result again corresponds to the asymmetry hypothesis, showing less willingness to discriminate against out-group members in negative outcome allocations.

ANOVAs testing the impact of the three experimental factors on each of the six pulls resulted in three significant main effects of stimulus valence and one significant main effect of status. With respect to stimulus valence, the pull of fairness on in-group favoritism was significantly higher in the positive condition, $F(1, 86) = 7.50$, $p < .01$. The pulls of FAV on MJP and of MD on MIP + MJP were also stronger in the positive condition: FAV on MJP, $F(1, 86) = 15.55$, $p < .001$; MD on MIP + MJP, $F(1, 86) = 5.64$, $p < .05$.

Aggravation effects. The mean pull scores differentiated according to the additional factors relative group status and relative group size vary in accordance with the aggravation hypothesis (see Table 11.7). The only significant in-group-favoring pull (FAV on F) in the negative stimulus condition was found for members of the inferior minority (MD on MIP + MJP even received a negative pull score). A similar pattern could be identified in the positive stimulus condition, most obviously for the

FAV on F and the MD on MIP + MJP pulls.

The significant effect of relative group status was concerned with the MD on MIP + MJP pull: In line with the aggravation hypothesis, members of inferior groups showed a greater tendency to maximize the positive difference between in- and out-group than did members of superior groups.

Summing up, it can be stated that Study 3 consolidated the assumption that there is a positive-negative asymmetry in social discrimination. Stimulus valence was found to be a crucial determinant of group members' willingness to favor the in-group over the out-group. However, there was also a significant effect of stimulus valence on the FAV on F pull, showing—although the score is still highly significant—a decreased interest in fair allocations between in- and out-group in negative compared with positive outcome allocations. In line with the aggravation hypothesis, the only significant pull of in-group favoritism in the negative domain was measured for inferior minority members. Additionally, inferior group members showed the highest tendency to maximize the difference between the groups. Although there were no further significant ANOVA effects, a similar pattern of data was obtained for the two other in-group-favoring pulls.

TABLE 11.7. Mean Pull Scores of Participants' Allocation Strategies by Stimulus Valence, Relative Group Status, and Relative Group Size, Study 3

Allocation Strategy	Inferior Status		Superior Status	
	Minority In-group	Majority In-group	Minority In-group	Majority In-group
	Positive Valence			
MIP + MJP on MD	2.00† (3.14)	4.38*** (3.64)	2.75* (4.34)	2.88 (3.54)
F on FAV	6.65** (5.09)	6.96*** (5.60)	7.87*** (4.87)	7.77*** (4.44)
MJP on FAV	−0.90† (1.45)	−1.00 (2.41)	0.33 (2.64)	0.35 (1.52)
MD on MIP + MJP	1.80* (2.50)	0.61 (2.05)	0.67 (3.28)	0.58 (2.38)
FAV on MJP	1.90 (3.56)	1.08 (2.67)	1.08† (1.73)	0.96 (2.62)
FAV on F	2.55* (2.77)	1.19 (3.25)	1.04 (2.33)	0.92 (3.01)
	Negative Valence			
MIP + MJP on MD	4.10*** (2.63)	3.33* (4.85)	3.75* (4.50)	4.50*** (2.49)
F on FAV	2.80 (5.85)	5.37** (5.74)	3.15 (6.85)	5.32* (5.77)
MJP on FAV	0.25 (4.08)	−0.73 (2.12)	0.50 (1.97)	−1.23 (2.41)
MD on MIP + MJP	1.10 (3.20)	0.67 (1.96)	−2.85* (2.93)	−0.41 (2.47)
FAV on MJP	−0.05 (3.52)	−1.27 (3.59)	−1.80 (3.17)	−1.59† (2.39)
FAV on F	1.60* (2.11)	0.37 (3.64)	0.15 (3.73)	0.41 (2.91)

Note: Mean pull scores for each allocation strategy can range from −12 to +12. MIP, maximum in-group profit; MJP, maximum joint profit; MD, maximum difference in favor of the in-group; F, fairness; FAV, in-group favoritism (MD +MIP). Cell *n*s vary from 10 to 15. Standard deviations are in parentheses.
†*p* < .10. **p* < .05. ***p* < .01. ****p* < .001. (two-tailed *t* tests).

General Discussion

Positive-Negative Asymmetry in Social Discrimination

The central aim of the three studies presented in this article was to demonstrate a positive-negative asymmetry in social discrimination that could previously only be deduced from the results of Mummendey and her coworkers (1992). The empirical evidence reported above provides a consistent picture of the predicted difference in social discrimination as a function of positive or negative resources. This consistency underlines the reliability of the observed effects, as the studies were conducted in a minimal intergroup setting as well as in an experimental situation with nonanonymous group memberships and intergroup interaction. When we consider only the significance of pull scores measured in the experiments, the different studies provide very similar patterns of data. All experiments provide firm evidence that members of ad hoc groups in laboratory settings are less prone to discriminate against out-group members in negative than in positive outcome allocations. This finding is corroborated by results of studies measuring intergroup evaluations on either positive or negative attribute scales (Blanz, Mummendey & Otten, 1995c; Wenzel & Mummendey, 1995). In these studies it was also demonstrated that as soon as participants were forced to describe in- and out-groups (or their products) in negative terms, their willingness to favor the in-group decreased. In sum, the empirical evidence shows that the proposed positive-negative asymmetry is restricted neither to a single experimental setting nor to a specific dependent measure.

The stability of these effects, irrespective of the differences in the experimental intergroup situation, is noteworthy: According to the idea of the *minimal* group paradigm, one might have expected stronger discrimination effects in Study 3 than in Study 1, whereas according to Diehl (1990), who argues that the MGP maximizes participants' willingness to discriminate, the opposite difference would have been expected. The robustness of the positive-negative asymmetry is shown by the fact that even under conditions where participants need not fear being made personally responsible for their decisions, they were reluctant to make in-group-favoring allocations of negative out-

comes. With respect to the findings of Mullen et al. (1992), who showed more discriminative behavior in real than in laboratory intergroup settings, our results do not provide any serious challenge, because our distinction between "minimal" and "less minimal" laboratory conditions may not be sufficient to elicit distinct effects.

Concerning the problem of equivalence of positive and negative stimuli, we believe that the effects obtained in our study cannot simply be reduced to differences in the psychological weights of our stimuli: Nearly all significant valence effects were obtained between experimental conditions where there were significant positive pulls in one cell and either no difference or even a negative in-group/out-group difference in the other. Accordingly, we were not forced to compare differences in the absolute strength of in-group favoritism (high vs. very high in-group biases) but can state that the *direction* of differential treatments of in- and out-group members can be distinguished in the domain of either positive or negative stimuli.

Finally, it should be mentioned that we found asymmetry effects not only on in-group-favoring behavior but also with respect to the preference for fair intergroup allocations. At first glance, it seems puzzling that there are effects of stimulus valence for the strategies of fairness and in-group favoritism: In negative resource allocations, participants showed both less parity and less in-group favoritism than in positive resource allocations. However, this result becomes more plausible if one takes into account that a decrease in the relative strength of fairness can be caused by both in-group and out-group favoritism. Examination of the raw scores used to compute the pull scores shows that the weaker parity pull in the negative condition is associated with an increased willingness to favor the out-group.

Aggravating Variables

Although we consistently found less in-group-favoring behavior in the domain of negative stimuli, there is also evidence that the restraints against discrimination in negative intergroup allocations are not universal: Whereas in Study 2—without status and size differences between groups—there were no significant pulls on ingroup-favoring strategies, Studies 1 and 3 showed that under aggravating conditions that threaten participants' positive social identity, one can also find an increase in competitive intergroup behaviors in negative outcome allocations. However, because the aggravating conditions also affect the distribution of positive stimuli, the measures of social discrimination are mostly still lower in the case of negative allocations. The two interaction effects found between stimulus valence and relative group status may be interpreted in terms of a threshold explanation: There seems to be a higher normative threshold inhibiting discriminating behavior if negative rather than positive stimuli are distributed between groups. This inhibiting threshold against in-group favoritism can be overcome if participants' interest in positive distinctiveness is enhanced. Therefore, it is reasonable that the effect of placing participants in an inferior status position is stronger in the negative than in the positive stimulus valence condition.

In our experiments, we examined two possible aggravating variables, relative group status and relative group size. In Studies 1 and 3, we found only one significant main effect of relative group size on in-group favoritism but three significant effects of relative group status. Perhaps the latter variable has a more important impact on discriminating behavior in members of experimental ad hoc groups. Additionally, studies on the impact of relative group size on intergroup allocations demonstrate that the effects of minority memberships are more complex than those of (legitimate) status inferiority (see Sachdev & Bourhis, 1984, 1991).

Explaining the Positive-Negative Asymmetry

Until now, we only speculated about possible explanations for the effects of stimulus valence on intergroup outcome allocations. In the following, we will propose four accounts that seem plausible and worthwhile for further research. For the sake of clarity, these different accounts are outlined separately. Nevertheless, at least the first three of them are closely related.

1. *Normative account.* We assume that there are more strict normative constraints inhibiting social discrimination in the negative domain. In everyday life there is general consensus that negative treatments should be avoided. Because this was not possible in the present experiments, participants tried to minimize the burden for both in-group and out-group. In the positive outcome allocations, however, both groups received some additional attractive stimuli: Even if participants assigned less money to out-group members, they nevertheless gave them something positive. In other words, in-group favoritism in negative intergroup allocations may appear more antisocial than in distributions of positive stimuli. Similarly, Törnblom (1988; Törnblom, Muhlhausen, & Jonsson, 1991) has discussed the possibility that different justice principles may be relevant in positive and negative outcome allocations. Justice theories, especially those referring to multiple principles of justice (e.g., Schwinger, 1980), may provide explanations for both aggravation effects (as legitimate attempts to compensate for disadvantages in the relative position of the in-group) and the decrease in social discrimination in the negative domain.

2. *Functional account.* Related to the idea of a normative regulation of socially discriminating behavior is the assumption that positive distinctiveness between in-group and out-group is not as effective in achieving or maintaining a positive social identity if it is realized through the allocation of negative rather than positive outcomes. Social identity theory does not claim that group members favor the in-group over the out-group at any price and without taking into account the specific intergroup situation (see, e.g., Brown, 1988; Hinkle & Brown 1990; Mullen et al., 1992). Participants achieving positive distinctiveness for their in-group are striving to validate this relation by social consent (Tajfel, 1978). If there is some socially shared positive meaning attached to the in-group's positive distinctiveness, it may provide a favorable social identity. The empirical evidence from our studies suggests that this is not or not so much the case in negative compared with positive outcome allocations.

3. *Categorical account.* Another possible explanation for the asymmetry in social discrimination could be derived from self-categorization theory (Turner, Hogg, Oakes, Reicher, & Wetherell, 1987). The positive function of positive in-group distinctiveness in either positive or negative outcome allocations might also differ because of different levels of abstraction in participants' self-categorization (Oakes, Haslam, & Turner, 1994). Being inevitably

confronted with aversive conditions might have weakened the intergroup categorization and instead caused a feeling of "common fate." Accordingly, a higher-order categorization as "one group of poor participants who are facing an unpleasant experiment" might have arisen. As Gaertner, Mann, Murrell, and Dovidio (1989) showed, "The greater the extent to which the aggregates felt like one group, the lower the degree of bias" (p. 244). This idea could also account for the aggravation effects: The implementation of status and size differentials increased the salience of the original social categorization and thus inhibited a recategorization on a higher level of inclusiveness.

4. *Cognitive account.* Generalizing from studies of negativity effects in person perception and impression formation (e.g., Czapinski, 1986; Peeters & Czapinski, 1990), it is also possible to assume that different cognitive processes underlie decisions about positive and negative stimuli. If negative stimuli per se elicit more precise and elaborated information processing, then it is unlikely that participants will claim a positive distinctiveness for the in-group that cannot be justified by reality. Accordingly, in-group bias should be more likely in positive outcome allocations if these are based on a more spontaneous decision-making process and less fear of invalidity. This idea could be tested by measuring reaction times for allocation decisions or by manipulating fear of invalidity in positive outcome allocations (see, e.g., Kruglanski & Freund, 1983). The differences between the high and low fear-of-invalidity conditions may be very similar to the positive-negative asymmetry effects. However, when we try to explain differences in social discrimination, possible underlying cognitive mechanisms have to be understood within the specific social context (see Haslam, Oakes, & Turner, 1996; Turner, Oakes, Haslam, & McGarty, 1994): "Cognition reflects not only the stimulus array to be represented but also always the social context in which it takes place" (Turner et al., 1994, p. 462).

Concluding Comments

Mummendey and colleagues concluded from their studies on negative intergroup outcome allocations

that "the present piece of research should be read as a caveat against a silent generalization from the realm of positive to the realm of negative outcome allocations" (1992, p. 142). The results reported in the present article show that this caveat should be taken seriously. At the same time, the results raise many interesting questions for future research. For example, besides relative group status and relative group size, many other variables could be analyzed with respect to their aggravating effects on the positive-negative asymmetry, such as power differences (Sachdev & Bourhis, 1991), groups' history, and the presence or absence of realistic intergroup conflict or superordinate goals (Blake & Mouton, 1962; Sherif, 1966). Beyond this, we are aware that the simple positive-negative distinction needs more differentiation. Further studies are planned to analyze whether and how the degree of attractiveness/aversiveness of the treatments moderates the observed asymmetry effects. Most important, we now need to examine the processes underlying the positive-negative asymmetry in social discrimination. Here it seems worthwhile to consider both the motivational and the cognitive roots of the phenomenon.

REFERENCES

Abele, A., & Petzold, P. (1993). *Asymmetrical ingroup-outgroup differentiation effects: An information integration perspective.* Unpublished manuscript, University of Erlangen-Nurnberg.

Billig, M., & Tajfel, H. (1973). Social categorization and similarity in intergroup behavior. *European Journal of Social Psychology, 3,* 27–52.

Blake, R. R., & Mouton, J. S. (1962). Over-evaluation of own group's product in intergroup competitions. *Journal of Abnormal and Social Psychology, 64,* 237–238.

Blanz, M., Mummendey, A., & Otten, S. (1995a). *Ingroup identification and the positive-negative asymmetry in social discrimination.* Manuscript submitted for publication.

Blanz, M., Mummendey A., & Otten, S. (1995b). Perceptions of relative group size and relative group status on intergroup discrimination in negative evaluations. *European Journal of Social Psychology, 25,* 231–247.

Blanz, M., Mummendey, A., & Otten, S. (1995c). Positive-negative asymmetry in social discrimination: The impact of stimulus valence and size- and status-differentials on intergroup evaluations. *British Journal of Social Psychology, 34,* 409–419.

Brickenkamp, R. (1972). *Test d2—Aufmerksamkeits-Belastungs-Test.* Göttingen: Hofgrefe.

Brown, R. (1984). The role of similarity in intergroup relations. In H. Tajfel (Ed.), *The social dimension: European developments in social psychology.* Cambridge, UK: Cambridge University Press.

Brown, R. (1988). *Group processes: Dynamics within and between groups.* Oxford, UK: Basil Blackwell.

Brown, R., Condor, S., Mathews, A., Wade, G., & Williams, J. (1986). Explaining intergroup differentiation in an industrial organisation. *Journal of Occupational Psychology, 59,* 273–286.

Czapinski, J. (1986). Informativeness of evaluations in interpersonal communication: Effects of valence, extremity of evaluations and ego-involvement of evaluator. *Polish Psychological Bulletin, 17,* 155–164.

Diehl, M. (1990). The minimal group paradigm: Theoretical explanations and empirical findings. In W. Stroebe & M. Hewstone (Eds.), *European, review of social psychology* (Vol. 1, pp. 263–292). New York: John Wiley.

Ellemers, N. (1993, September). Opening paper. At *Social identity and intergroup differentiations.* Symposium conducted at the 10th general meeting of the European Association of Experimental Social Psychology, Lisbon.

Ellemers, N., van Knippenberg, A., de Vries, N., & Wilke, H. (1988). Social identification and permeability of group boundaries. *European Journal of Social Psychology, 18,* 497–513.

Gaertner, S. L., Mann, J., Murrell, A., & Dovidio, J. E. (1989). Reducing intergroup bias: The benefits of recategorization. *Journal of Personality and Social Psychology, 57,* 239–249.

Haslam, S. A., Oakes, P. J., & Turner, C. (1996). Social identity, self-categorization, and the perceived homogeneity of ingroups and outgroups: The interaction between social motivation and cognition. In M. Sorrentino & E. T. Higgins (Eds.), *Handbook of motivation and cognition, Vol. 3: The interpersonal context* (pp. 182–222). New York: Guilford.

Hewstone, M., Fincham, F., & Jaspars, J. (1981). Social categorization and similarity in intergroup behavior. A replication with "penalties." *European Journal of Social Psychology, 11,* 101–107.

Hinkle, S., & Brown, R. J. (1990). Intergroup comparisons and social identity: Some links and lacunae. In D. Abrams & M. A. Hogg (Eds.), *Social identity theory: Constructive and critical advances* (pp. 48–70). New York: Harvester Wheatsheaf.

Kahneman, D., & Tversky, A. (1979). Prospect theory: An analysis of decision under risk. *Econometrics, 47,* 263–291.

Kruglanski, A. W., & Freund, T. (1983). The freezing and unfreezing of lay-inferences: Effects of impressional primary, ethnic stereotyping, and numerical anchoring. *Journal of Experimmlal Social Psychology, 19,* 448–468.

Lemyre, L., & Smith, P. (1985). Intergroup discrimination and self-esteem in the minimal group paradigm. *Journal of Personality and Social Psychology, 24,* 33–41.

Messick, D. M., & Mackie, D. M. (1989). Intergroup relations. *Annual Review of Psychology, 40,* 45–81.

Mullen, B., Brown, R. Jr., & Smith, C. (1992). Ingroup bias as a function of salience, relevance, and status: An integration. *European Journal of Social Psychology, 22,* 103–122.

Mummendey, A., Simon, B., Dietze, C., Grünert, M., Haeger, G., Kessler, S., Lettgen, S., & Schiferhoff, S. (1992). Categorization is not enough: Intergroup discrimination in negative outcome allocation. *Journal of Experimental Social Psychology, 28,* 125–144.

Oakes, P. J., Haslam, S. A., & Turner, J. C. (1994). *Stereotyping and social reality.* Oxford, UK: Basil Blackwell.

Peeters, G., & Czapinski, J. (1990). Positive-negative asymmetry in evaluations: The distinction between affective and informational negativity effects. In W. Stroebe & M.

Hewstone (Eds.), *European review of social psychology* (Vol. 1, pp. 33–60) . Chichester, UK: Wiley.

Rabbit, J., & Horwitz, M. (1969). Arousal of ingroup-outgroup bias by a chance win or loss. *Journal of Personality and Social Psychology, 13,* 269–277.

Rutte, C. G., Wilke, H. A. M., & Messick, D. M. (1987). The effects of framing social dilemmas as give-some or take-some games. *British Journal of Social Psychology, 26,* 103–108.

Sachdev, I., & Bourhis, R. Y. (1984). Minimal majorities and majorities. *European Journal of Social Psychology, 14,* 35–52.

Sachdev, I., & Bourhis, R. Y. (1987). Status differentials and intergroup behaviour. *European Journal of Social Psychology, 17,* 277–293.

Sachdev, I., & Bourhis, R. Y. (1991). Power and status differentials in minority and majority group relations. *European Journal of Social Psychology, 21,* 1–24.

Schwinger, T. (1980). Gerechte Güter-Verteilungen: Entscheidungen zwischen drei Gerechtigkeitsprinzipien. In G. Mikula (Ed.), *Gerodtiglteil und soziale Interaktion* (pp. 107–136). Bern: Huber.

Sherif, M. (1966). *Group conflict and co-operation.* London: Routledge & Kegan Paul.

Simon, B., & Brown, R. (1987). Perceived intragroup homogeneity in minority-majority contexts. *Journal of Personality and Social Psychology, 48,* 863–875.

Simon, B., & Pettigrew, T. F. (1990). Social identity and perceived group homogeneity: Evidence for the ingroup homogeneity effect. *Euoropean Journal of Social Psychology, 20,* 269–286.

Skowronski, J. J., & Carlston, D. E. (1987). Social judgment and social memory: The role of cue diagnosticity in negativity, positivity, and extremity biases. *Journal of Personality and Social Psychology, 52,* 689–699.

Skowronski, J. J., & Carlston, D. E. (1989). Negativity and extreme biases in impression formation: A review of explanations. *Psychological Bulletin, 105,* 131–142.

Spears, R., & Oyen, M. (1993). *How minimal is the minimal group?* Unpublished manuscript. University of Amsterdam.

Tajfel, H. (1978). Social categorization, social identity and social comparison. In H. Tajfel (Ed.), *Differentiation between social groups* (pp. 61–76). London: Academic Press.

Tajfel, H. (1981). The social psychology of minorities. In H. Tajfel (Ed.), *Human groups and social categories* (pp. 309–343). Cambridge UK: Cambridge University Press.

Tajfel, H. (1982). *Social identity and intergroup relations.* Cambridge, UK: Cambridge University Press.

Tajfel, H., Billig, M. G., Bundy, R. E., & Flament, C. (1971). Social categorization and intergroup behaviour. *European Journal of Social Psychology, 1,* 149–178.

Tajfel, H., & Turner, J. C. (1986). The social identity theory of intergroup behavior. In S. Worchel & W. G. Austin (Eds.), *Psychology of intergroup relations* (2nd ed., pp. 7–24). Chicago: Nelson-Hall.

Törnblom, K. Y. (1988). Positive and negative allocations: A typology and a model for conflicting justice principles. *Advances in Group Processes, 5,* 141–168.

Törnblom, K. Y., Muhlhausen, S. M., & Jonsson, D. R. (1991). The allocation of positive and negative outcomes: When is the equality principle fair for both? In R. Vermunt & H. Steensma (Eds.), *Social justice in human relations* (pp. 59–100). New York: Plenum.

Turner, J. C., & Brown, R. (1978). Social status, cognitive alternatives, and intergroup relations. In H. Tajfel (Ed.), *Differentiation between social groups* (pp. 201–234). London: Academic Press.

Turner, J. C., Brown, R., & Tajfel, H. (1979). Social comparison and group interest in ingroup-favouritism. *European Journal of Social Psychology, 9,* 187–204.

Turner, J. C., Hogg, M. A., Oakes, P. J., Reicher, S. D., & Wetherell, M. S. (1987). *Rediscovering the social group: A self-categorization theory.* Oxford, UK: Basil Blackwell.

Turner, J. C., Oakes, P. J., Haslam, S. A., & McGarry, C. (1994). Self and collective: Cognition and social context. *Personality and Social Psychology Bulletin, 20,* 454–463.

van Knippenberg, A., & Ellemers, N. (1990). Social identity and intergroup identification processes. *European Review of Social Psychology, 1,* 137–169.

Wenzel, M., & Mummendey, A. (1995). *Positive-negative asymmetry of social discrimination: Differential evaluations of ingroup and outgroup on positive and negative attributes.* Manuscript submitted for publication.

Understanding Why the Justice of Group Procedures Matters: A Test of the Psychological Dynamics of the Group-Value Model

Tom Tyler, Peter Degoey, and Heather Smith • University of California, Berkeley

Procedural justice research has documented many positive consequences of fair decision-making procedures and treatment by authorities. However, it is unclear why these effects of procedural justice occur. The group-value model proposes that fair procedures matter because they communicate two symbolic messages about group membership: (a) whether individuals are respected members of a group and (b) whether they should feel pride in the group as a whole. These messages are conveyed by three relational aspects of the actions of authorities—actions that indicate neutrality, trustworthiness, and status recognition. Results from four different studies provide evidence that: (a) relational aspects of fair procedures communicate group-relevant information, and (b) this information mediates the influence of procedural judgments on group-oriented behaviors and feelings of self-esteem.

During the past two decades, research has provided widespread evidence that people's feelings and actions in social interaction are affected by the perceived justice of the decision-making procedures they experience when dealing with others (see Lind & Tyler, 1988; Tyler & Lind, 1992, for reviews). When people feel they have been fairly treated, they are more willing to accept the decisions resulting from the procedures (Greenberg, 1987; Lind, Kulik, Ambrose, & de Vera Park, 1993), more satisfied with the procedures (Thibaut & Walker, 1975), more likely to comply with general group rules and laws (Tyler, 1990; Tyler & Degoey, 1995), more willing to remain a group member (Brockner, Tyler, & Cooper-Schneider, 1992; Tansky, 1993), and more

willing to help the group, even at a cost to themselves (Tyler & Degoey, 1995).

Although this research has documented the importance of procedural justice, it is unclear *why* procedural justice influences group-oriented behaviors and attitudes. One approach is to emphasize the social contract. According to Thibaut and Walker (1975), for example, the concern with fair procedures springs ultimately from and is maintained by self-interest. Self-interest might be enlightened or broad, but it is rational. An alternative approach emphasizes the social bonds among group members and group authorities. The group-value model of procedural justice (Lind & Tyler, 1988; Tyler & Lind, 1992) suggests that fair procedures and treatment by authorities communicate identity-relevant information to the individuals affected by these procedures. In particular, the model proposes that fair procedures and treatment communicate information about: (a) the degree to which individuals are respected members of their groups and (b) the degree to which they can feel pride in their group membership. In this article, we explicitly tested whether fair procedures, in fact, communicate such identity-relevant information and whether it is this information that mediates the influence of procedural justice on general group-oriented behaviors. We also tested whether pride and respect represent identity-relevant information by investigating whether pride and respect mediate the influences of procedural justice on feelings of self-esteem (Koper, Van Knippenberg, Bouhuijs, Vermunt, & Wilke, 1993; Vermunt, Wit, van den Bos, Lind, 1993).

Procedural Justice Research

An Instrumental Model of Justice

Historically, procedural justice effects have been explained by the instrumental model proposed by Thibaut and Walker (1975). Based on social exchange theory (Thibaut & Keller, 1959), the instrumental model links evaluations of authorities to judgments of direct and indirect control over the outcome of allocation procedures. An instrumental or social exchange explanation assumes that people are motivated to maximize their self-interest when they interact with each other (Tyler, 1994). As a consequence, people are sensitive to the efforts of others to control their behavior and only reluctantly submit themselves to external control, for example, control by a third party authority. When they give up control to a third party, people seek to maintain some degree of indirect control over the decisions of those authorities, for example, through the presentation of evidence ("voice"). Hence, the instrumental model suggests that procedural fairness judgments are linked to evaluations about control because such evaluations reflect people's assessments of the likelihood that a procedure will serve their self-interest.

Studies have shown that the opportunity to have control over the decision-making process influences people's views about procedural justice. They have not, however, supported an instrumental model of the psychology of procedural justice.

On the contrary, people have been found to care about having "voice" even when they believe that their arguments have little or no influence over their outcomes (Lind, Lissak, & Conlon, 1983; Tyler, Rasinski, & Spodick, 1985). Furthermore, judgments about the quality of the social relationship between individuals and decisionmakers have been shown to have a greater influence on procedural justice judgments than instrumental judgments of control over the procedures and the favorability of outcomes resulting from the procedures (Tyler, 1989, 1994). In particular, judgments of procedural fairness are dominated by three types of relational judgments about authorities (Tyler, 1989). The first, *neutrality*, involves assessments of the degree to which decision-making procedures are unbiased, honest, and promote decisions based on evidence. The second, *trustworthiness*, involves assessments of the motives of authorities—judgments about their benevolence and concern for the needs of those with whom they deal. The third, *status recognition*, involves assessments of politeness, treatment with dignity, and respect for rights and entitlements due to every group member.

Two other recent findings also suggest that an instrumental model of procedural justice is incomplete. First, procedural justice judgments influence a wide variety of group-oriented attitudes and behaviors that are not directly linked to decision-making processes (Brockner et al., 1992; Organ, 1988; Tansky, 1993; Tyler, 1990; Tyler & Degoey, 1995). If people are most concerned with achieving desired outcomes, it is unclear why their experiences with a specific decisionmaker would be relevant to attitudes and behaviors that are not instrumentally related to the particular decision. More important, research suggests that relational judgments of procedural justice are more closely related than are instrumental judgments to people's willingness to voluntarily perform tasks that help the group but are not required (Fahr, Podsakoff, & Organ, 1990; Konovsky & Folger, 1991; Moorman, 1991).

A second difficulty for an instrumental explanation of procedural justice is the influence of procedural justice on self-esteem. Recent experimental research shows that the fairness of the procedures with which participants are treated significantly influences their self-esteem (Koper et al., 1993; Vermunt et al., 1993). Furthermore, students' self-esteem during their college years has been found to be related to how fairly they remember being treated by their parents (Joubert, 1991). An instrumental approach might suggest that unfavorable outcomes influence general self-esteem. However, this model does not hypothesize a direct relationship between self-esteem and procedural evaluations. Furthermore, an instrumental model does not explain why relational evaluations are associated with greater self-esteem.

The Group-Value Model of Procedural Justice

Lind and Tyler proposed the group-value model (Lind & Tyler, 1988; Tyler, 1989; Tyler & Lind, 1992) as an alternative explanation for procedural justice effects. Their model suggests that procedural justice is important because it informs people about their social connection to groups and group authorities. The group-value model suggests that fair treatment and fair decision making by group authorities communicates to group members two symbolic messages about group memberships. First, the model suggests that fair treatment indicates a positive, respected position within the group. Unfair treatment indicates marginality and disrespect (Tyler, 1994; Tyler & Lind, 1992). When a faculty member is treated fairly or unfairly by his or her departmental chairperson, for instance, this indicates to the faculty member whether he or she is a valued member of the department.

Second, the use of fair or unfair decision-making procedures in groups also indicates whether members can take pride in their group membership (Deutsch & Steil, 1988; Lind & Earley, 1992). For example, politicians attempt to engage in public displays of fair procedures for decision making as symbols of government to encourage the development of national pride. The group-value model suggests that fair treatment and procedures can communicate this kind of identity-relevant information because authorities act as prototypical representatives of groups, and their actions can be seen as highly salient indicators of group opinions (Hogg & Abrams, 1988; Tyler & Lind, 1992). Furthermore, in organized groups, authorities express the values and norms of the group (Calder, 1977; Meindl, Ehrlich, & Dukerich, 1985; Pfeffer, 1981; Pfeffer & Salancik, 1978).

Feelings of pride and respect that result from fair treatment, in turn, are hypothesized to lead to group-serving behaviors. This prediction reflects

social identity research, which shows that people who identify with their group and evaluate their group positively internalize the group's interests, equating them with their own self-interest (Brewer & Kramer, 1986). This provides a set of internalized group norms that guide individual behavior and encourage conformity to group rules (Turner, Hogg, Oakes, Reicher, & Wetherell, 1987). In addition, affiliation with a group leads to more commitment to remain with the group and to engage in assertive extrarole activities, such as staying late for work or volunteering to help in emergencies (O'Reilly & Chatman, 1986). On the basis of this research, we expected that group members who feel more respected and more proud of their group as a result of being treated fairly by group authorities would be more likely to comply with group rules, more likely to engage in extrarole behaviors that help the group, and more committed to remain with the group.

The group-value model also incorporates another key premise from social identity theory— that people use groups as sources of information about themselves (Hogg & Abrams, 1988, 1990; Tajfel, 1978; Tajfel & Turner, 1986). In particular, it is expected that people who feel more proud and more respected will report higher levels of self-esteem. Fair procedures communicate pride and respect to group members, which in turn increase self-esteem, suggesting one reason why procedural justice is related to self-esteem.

Although both the group-value model and social identity theory offer identity-based explanations for behavior that contrast with self-interested or resource-dependent explanations posited in earlier literatures (e.g., realistic conflict theory; Sherif, Harvey, White, Hood, & Sherif, 1961), social identity theory focuses on how identity-based explanations can illuminate *inter*group relations, whereas the group-value model offers an identity-based explanation for *intra*group relations. In other words, the group-value model focuses on individual group members' relationships to decision-making authorities and the single group or category that those authorities represent rather than relationships between different groups.

Figure 12.1 is a schematic representation of the hypotheses offered by the group-value model of procedural justice. Path c shows that the relational judgments people make about authorities are related to general compliance with group rules, extrarole behavior, commitment to the group, and

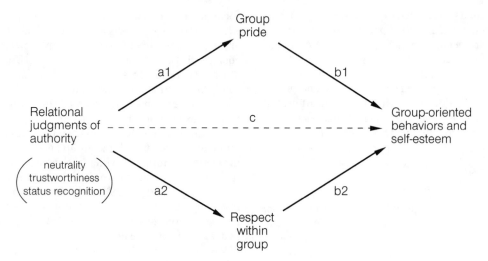

FIGURE 12.1 ■ The group-value model of procedural justice.

self-esteem, as demonstrated in previous research. The group-value model suggests, however, that the psychological dynamics of procedural justice can be better understood by considering the mediating roles that feelings of group pride (Paths a1 and b1) and feelings of respect within groups (Paths a2 and b2) play between people's relational judgments about authorities and group-oriented behaviors. Because pride and respect are identity-relevant information that are linked to people's senses of self, we expect pride and respect to mediate between relational judgments about authorities and self-esteem. The group-value model suggests that when the paths through pride and respect are included, the importance of Path c will be reduced to zero (full mediation) or significantly reduced (partial mediation). The lesser significance of Path c in the group-value model is indicated by the dotted line in Figure 12.1. Note that people's instrumental judgments about authority may or may not have a direct effect on group-oriented behaviors but are not suggested in the group-value model to be mediated by pride and respect. For the sake of clarity, instrumental judgments are not represented in Figure 12.1.

Studies 1–4

Research and Analysis Design

To analyze the hypotheses offered by the group-value model, three goals needed to be ac-

complished. The first was to determine whether people, in fact, experience group pride and respect within groups and whether they distinguish between the two constructs. Although the group-value model suggests the importance of pride and respect, these have not been directly measured in previous research. Therefore, our first purpose was to develop measures of pride and respect and subject them to exploratory factor analyses.

The second goal was to assess the mediating roles of pride and respect in procedural justice effects. Mediation is tested with a multistage regression approach (Baron & Kenny, 1986; James & Brett, 1984): First, each of the mediators is regressed on the independent variable (assessing Paths a1 and a2 in Figure 12.1); second, the dependent variables are regressed on each of the mediators (assessing Paths b1 and b2); and third, the dependent variables are regressed sequentially on the independent variable (assessing Path c), and then on both the independent variable and each of the mediators (simultaneously assessing Paths c and b1 and Paths c and b2, respectively). Mediation is indicated if the following conditions are met: (a) the independent variable explains a significant amount of the variance in the mediating variables, (b) the mediating variables explain a significant amount of variance in the dependent variables, and (c) entering the mediating variables into the third regression equation reduces the independent variable's contribution to the explained variance of the dependent variables. In all analyses reported below, the role of each of the mediators in the group-value model—pride and respect—was assessed independently. Furthermore, in all of the analyses, instrumental judgments about authority were controlled. Finally, because we expected that pride and respect are related aspects of group membership, we assessed the joint role of pride and respect by entering them both in the regression equations.

Note that the path diagram in Figure 12.1 depicts a causal chain of relationships between variables, as the group-value model hypothesizes should exist. The data reported below, however, are correlational in nature, and hence causality among the observed relationships cannot be inferred from the analyses. In other words, for the purposes of this article, Figure 12.1 can be better viewed as patterns of covariations between variables than as a set of cause-and-effect relationships. A greater degree of confidence, however, that the observed relationships might follow the causal direction proposed by the group-value model can be derived from two types of additional analyses.

First, it is helpful to show that the mediating and dependent variables are not simply highly related constructs by demonstrating that the independent variable continues to covary with each of the mediating variables when the dependent variables are controlled (i.e., Paths a1 and a2 in Figure 12.1 remain significant when Paths b1 and b2, respectively, are controlled). If entering the dependent variables into the regression equation does not significantly diminish the relationship between independent and mediator variables, this would also support the argument that the dependent variables are not really the mediators and the mediators the dependent variables (e.g., self-esteem does not mediate between relational judgments and respect, following Paths c–b2 rather than Path a2). Second, a more convincing argument for mediation in the proposed direction can be made when the relationships between the mediating and dependent variables remain unaffected when the independent variable is controlled (i.e., Paths b1 and b2 in Figure 12.1 remain unaffected when Paths a1 and a2, respectively, are controlled). In the analyses described below, these additional analyses are reported as well. Again, however, it is important to note that the data are correlational in character, so any causal inferences must be viewed as tentative.

The third goal of this research was to test the robustness of the group-value model. Procedural justice effects have been replicated in legal (Lind, Kanfer, & Earley, 1990; Lind, Kurtz, Musante, Walker, & Thibaut, 1980; Tyler, 1984), political (Tyler & Caine, 1981; Tyler & Degoey, 1995; Tyler, Rasinski, & McGraw, 1985), managerial (Alexander & Ruderman, 1987; Folger & Konovsky, 1989; Greenberg, 1990), interpersonal (Barrett-Howard & Tyler, 1986), and educational settings (Tyler & Caine, 1981). The analyses reported below reflect this diversity of contexts in that they used studies of four groups that differ widely in their composition and types of relationships that group members have with a representative authority. A discovery of the same psychological dynamics across all four studies would provide evidence for the robustness of the group-value model.

Method

In Study 1, college students at the University of California at Berkeley ($n = 335$) completed a questionnaire that asked how a recent conflict with one or both of their parents had been resolved.[1] Students completed the questionnaire as part of a course requirement and reported on their attitudes and behaviors toward their families as well as their feelings of self-esteem. Families constitute a more close-knit and affectively important group than the groups typically studied in procedural justice research. We chose the family setting, however, to examine issues of pride and respect because people's sense of identity is closely aligned with family membership and their parents. Hence, we expected that the dynamics of pride and respect outlined by the group-value model would be particularly well supported in this data set. Although the use of college students as respondents has sometimes been criticized (e.g., Sears, 1986), it seems quite appropriate within the current context. College students are still connected with their parents, both emotionally and cognitively.

Studies 2 and 3 were conducted in two research contexts typically studied in procedural justice

---

[1]A complete description of the methods and data reported for Study 1 was published in Tyler and Degoey (1996). A complete description of the methods and data reported for Study 2 will be published in Huo, Smith, Tyler, and Lind (1996). A complete description of the methods and data reported for Study 4 was published in Tyler (1994). However, none of the analyses reported in this article have been published.

research: work organizations and university settings. Both contexts represent hierarchical groups in which people have direct experiences with representative authorities. In Study 2, university employees ($n = 355$) completed a mail survey in which they described a recent conflict with their immediate work supervisor (29% response rate). Respondents reported their evaluations of the supervisor and their attitudes and behaviors toward the university. Although this response rate is typical for mail surveys (Dillman, 1978), it is low in absolute terms. However, the purpose of this study is to examine the psychological relationships between key variables, not to establish the general representativeness of particular opinions.

In Study 3, college students ($n = 228$) completed a questionnaire in which they described a recent conflict (within the last 12 months) with a faculty or staff member. Students completed the questionnaire as part of a course requirement and reported their evaluations of the relevant authority, their attitudes and behaviors toward the university community (broadly defined as including faculty, staff and students), and their feelings of self-worth.

The fourth study was a telephone survey of people's attitudes about the United States Supreme Court, an authority representative of Americans in general but rarely experienced directly by individual Americans. Recent research shows that the same procedural justice relationships observed in studies of personal experiences with work or legal authorities also occur with national-level political authorities (Tyler, 1994). Five hundred and two randomly selected San Francisco Bay Area resi-

dents participated in the survey (74% response rate). The mean age of respondents was 41.91 years ($SD = 15.95$ years). Approximately half (53%) the respondents were female, 39% of the respondents reported graduating from college, and 53% of the respondents reported annual incomes greater than $40,000. Similar patterns of relationships between variables in all four data sets would demonstrate the robustness of the group-value model.

CONSTRUCT MEASUREMENTS

All items in all data sets were assessed with Likert-type scales. Nonstudent respondents (Studies 2 and 4) were given a *don't know* response option, and those responses were treated in the analyses as missing data. Items reported below that were reverse-coded are marked (*R*). Table 12.1 contains summary information about scale reliabilities, item response ranges, means, and standard deviations for all the variables in the four data sets (the intercorrelations among constructs are shown in the Appendix). Information about the measures of pride and respect reflects the final scales that were constructed on the basis of the exploratory factor analyses reported below.

Group Pride and Respect Within Groups. Group pride and respect within groups—the proposed mediators in the group-value model—were assessed with newly developed instruments. Although items for both constructs were roughly similar across all four data sets, their exact wording was adapted for the particular group contexts.

TABLE 12.1. Descriptive Statistics For Variables

Variable	Family[a]			Work[b]			University[c]			Nation[d]		
	α	M	SD	α	M	SD	α	M	SD	α	M	SD
Group pride	.87	2.82	1.26	.77	2.05	0.66	.71	2.41	0.97	.58	2.36	1.39
Respect within groups	.86	2.43	1.09	.80	1.73	0.58	.85	2.87	1.05	.68	2.49	1.25
Instrumental judgments	.89	3.78	1.47	.88	2.40	0.86	.87	3.02	0.83	.70	3.55	1.06
Relational judgments	.92	3.32	1.31	.96	1.96	0.88	.92	2.52	0.73	.83	3.52	1.27
Compliance with rules	.74	2.40	0.82	.64	2.06	0.88	.54	1.61	0.59	.59	4.30	1.36
Extrarole behaviors	.81	2.74	0.91	.68	1.72	0.49	.69	2.29	0.54	—	—	—
Group commitment	—	—	—	.74	2.25	0.75	.75	1.74	0.64	—	—	—
Self-esteem	.80	3.09	1.07	—	—	—	.88	1.97	0.70	.71	2.40	0.95

Note. For scale reliabilities, Cronbach's alphas are shown. Dashes indicate that the variable was not assessed in a particular data set.
[a]Responses on all items could range from 1 through 7.
[b]Responses on all items could range from 1 through 4.
[c]Responses ranged from 1 to 4 for all variables except pride and respect (1 to 7) and self-esteem (1 to 5).
[d]Responses on all items could range from 1 through 7.

Group pride. Questions measuring pride were drawn from scales designed to measure the affective and evaluative aspects of identification with groups (Brown, Condor, Mathew, Wade, & Williams, 1986; Tajfel, 1978) and scales designed to measure affective evaluations of organizations (O'Reilly & Chatman, 1986). The items are shown subsequently, when we discuss the exploratory factor analyses of the pride and respect items in all four data sets. Final scale reliabilities (Cronbach's alphas) for Studies 1 , 2, 3, and 4 were .87, .77, .71, and .58, respectively.

Respect within groups. Across all four studies, three items used to measure respect began with the stem "if they knew me well." These items were designed to measure people's perceptions of where they stood in the group publicly or what they though their social reputation was, rather than whether they saw themselves as worthy of respect. Furthermore, we wanted an approach that would allow people to answer the question even for groups in which not all group members could possibly know them (e.g., "other Americans" in Study 4). To assess the validity of the "If they knew me well" approach to measuring feelings of respect in groups, additional items that were designed to capture the same concept but that did not use the "If they knew me well" stem also were included in some of the studies. The items are again reported subsequently. Final scale reliabilities for Studies 1, 2, 3, and 4 were .86, .80, .85, and .68, respectively.

Evaluations of the Behavior of Group Authorities. Relational judgments about authority—neutrality, trustworthiness, and status recognition—the independent variables in the group-value model, were assessed in all data sets. These three aspects of the relational model were not differentiated. Instead, we created a single overall index. To control for the consequences of instrumental judgments about authorities in groups, we also assessed instrumental judgments. Both types of judgments were measured with well-established scales in Studies 1–3. For Study 4, which concerned the United States Supreme Court, we developed special items that reflected the nondirect and nonpersonal context of that situation but that nevertheless were similar in content to the items in the other three studies.

Previous research has indicated that the influence of relational judgments is affected by the degree to which people draw their identity from groups (Tyler & Degoey, 1995). In this study we assessed the degree of identification with the group by asking participants how important "their family, their job, the university, or America" were to "the way they think of themselves as a person." In Study 4, participants were also asked about the similarity of their values to those of "most Americans." In all four studies the relational index was weighted by identification. This weighting increased the influence of relational judgments among those more closely identified with their group. The average correlation of compliance with relational judgments was .24, whereas the average correlation with the weighted index was .29. The average correlation of extrarole behavior with relational judgments was .11, whereas the average correlation with the weighted index was .22. The average correlation of commitment with the relational judgments was .31, whereas the average correlation with the weighted index was .46. Finally, the average correlation of relational judgments to self-esteem was .10, whereas the average correlation with the weighted index was .11.

Instrumental judgments. Instrumental judgments about group authorities reflected respondents' evaluations of the degree of control they had over the authorities' decisions as well as their evaluations of the outcome of these decisions. We assessed instrumental judgments in Studies 1–3 using the same six items: "How much influence did you have over the decisions made by [the authority]?"; "Overall, how satisfied were you with the outcome?"; "How favorable was the outcome to you?"; "Compared to what you expected before you talked to [the authority], how much better or worse was the situation after the conflict was resolved?"; "How does your outcome compare to the outcomes you have received in the past when dealing with [the authority]?"; and "In terms of your outcome, how much did you gain or lose?" The questions were adapted for the particular contexts of the studies, with the authority in the family data set being the student's parent or parents, in the work data set being the respondent's supervisor, and in the university data set being the university representative with whom students had resolved their conflicts. Cronbach's alphas of the instrumental judgment about authority scales for Studies 1, 2, and 3 were .89, .90, and .82 respectively.

For the study of the United States Supreme

Court, we developed five instrumental items: "How often do you agree with Court decisions? "How often have you agreed with recent Court decisions?"; "Do the views of average citizens influence Court decisions?"; "If you joined a group which presented its views to the Court, how likely is it that your views would influence the Court?"; "If you joined a group which presented its views to the Court, how likely is it that the Court would make a decision that you agreed with?" The reliability of the instrument judgments scale in this study was .70.

Relational judgments. In the first three studies, relational judgments about authority were also assessed similarly. The relational index—a combined assessment of neutrality, trustworthiness, and status recognition—comprised 11 items: "How politely were you treated by [the authority]?", "How much concern did [the authority] show for your rights?", "How hard did [the authority] try to bring the issues into the open so that they could be resolved?", "How much of an opportunity were you given to describe your problem before any decisions were made about how to handle it?", "How dignified was [the authority's treatment of you?", "How hard did [the authority] try to explain why he or she made the decisions they made?", "How likely do you think it is that the reasons [the authority] gave for their decisions were the real reasons for making those decisions?", "How honest was [the authority in what he or she said to you?", "How much consideration was given to your views when decisions were made about how to handle the conflict?", "How hard did [the authority] try to do the right thing by you?" and "How hard did [the authority) try to take account of your needs in the situation?" Reliabilities of the relational judgments about authority scales for Studies 1, 2, and 3 were .92, .96, and .92, respectively.

For the fourth study, we again adapted items to the particular context. Relational assessments about the Supreme Court were indexed by eight items. Respondents were asked whether they agreed or disagreed that: "The Court considers the concerns of average citizens when making decisions," "The Supreme Court gives equal consideration to the views of all of the different groups in America," "The Supreme Court is concerned about protecting the average citizen's rights," "There are ways for the average citizen to have their views presented to the Court," and "The Court gets the kind of

information it needs to make informed decisions." Respondents also were asked: "If you belonged to a group that went before the Court," would the Court "consider your views?", "try to be fair to your group?", and "genuinely care about your views?" Cronbach's alpha for this scale was .83.

Group-Oriented Attitudes and Behaviors. We assessed three types of group-oriented attitudes and behaviors that previously have been linked to evaluations of procedural justice. All items were drawn from existing scales and adapted to the different contexts of the four studies. The first type of group-oriented attitude or behavior was respondents' willingness to comply with group rules. Items were drawn from C. A. Smith, Organ, and Near's (1983) study and reflected both attitudinal responses to obedience as well as self-reports of actual compliance with group rules.

The second type of group-oriented attitude and behavior entailed measures of respondents' willingness to engage in extrarole behaviors that go beyond what is required or expected of them within their particular group contexts. Items were drawn from the Organizational Citizenship Behavior Scale (Mackenzie, Podsakoff, & Fetter, 1991) and again reflected both attitudinal measures as well as self-reports of actual extrarole behaviors. We assessed these behaviors in Studies 1–3 only.

The final type of group-oriented attitude previously linked to procedural justice effects and assessed here was group commitment. Items in this case were drawn from Mowday, Porter, and Steer's (1982) Organizational Commitment Questionnaire and focused on respondents' desire to remain a member of their particular group. Because family membership (Study 1) and nationality (Study 4) are often thought of as ascribed memberships, and also because deciding to terminate membership in these groups is an uncommon occurrence, we did not assess group commitment in these studies.

Compliance with group rules. In each of the first three studies, measures of respondents' compliance with group rules again reflected similar content, although the wording was adapted to the various contexts. For example, employee compliance with organizational rules in the worker data set was assessed with the following five items: "I always try to follow the rules of my organization, even when I think they are wrong"; "I follow work rules and instructions with extreme care"; "I come to work on time"; "I follow the policies established by my supervisor"; and "In order for an organization to function, employees should follow their supervisors' orders without question." Reliabilities of the scales in Studies 1, 2, and 3 were .74, .64, and .54, respectively.

In the fourth data set, items were again adapted for the impersonal nature of respondents' relationship with the Supreme Court. We used four items to assess general compliance with federal authorities: "I feel that I should accept the decisions made by government leaders in Washington even when I disagree with them," "People should obey the laws made by the federal government even if they go against what they think is right," "There are times when it is all right for people to disobey the government (R)," and "I can think of situations in which I would stop supporting the policies of our government (R)." Cronbach's alpha for this scale was. 59.

Extrarole behaviors. In the family, work, and university data sets, the same six questions (adapted for their contexts) assessed whether group members engaged in extrarole behaviors. Items in the family study, for instance, asked respondents "To what extent do you make suggestions to improve your family life?", "Generally, how hard do you try to keep up with the lives of your family members?", "How much effort do you put into helping your family members beyond that what is generally expected of you?", "How common is it that you give up some of your personal time for the sake of your family", "How often do you attend family events that are not required?", and "How frequently do you help other family members when they have heavy work loads or other burdens?" Reliabilities for Studies 1, 2, and 3 were .81, .68, and .69, respectively.

Group commitment. Respondents' commitment to their work organization or university community were assessed similarly as well. In the university data set, for instance, the following four items were used: "I cannot think of another university I would rather attend," "I think about transferring often" (R), "I regret the decision to come to the University of California at Berkeley" (R), and "I will probably look for an alternative university within the next year" (R). Cronbach's alphas for the group commitment scales in the work and university data sets were .74 and .75, respectively.

Self-Esteem. For the family study, we used 7 items adapted from Rosenberg's Self-Esteem Scale

(1979) to assess students' feelings of self-esteem. Students were asked to what extent they agreed or disagreed with statements of the following type: "1 am pretty sure of myself," "I generally feel satisfied with myself," "I sometimes think of myself as a failure" (R), "I am proud of what I have accomplished in my life," "I often give in too easily" (R), "There are a lot of things about myself that I would change if I could" (R), and "I often wish I were someone else" (R; $\alpha = .80$). The same 7 items were used in the nation study ($\alpha = .71$). For the university study, 10 items from the Rosenberg Self-Esteem Scale were used ($\alpha = .88$).

Note that in some cases the scale reliabilities are less than desirable, particularly for the scales of pride and respect in the study of the Supreme Court. Generally, the effects of measurement error are that the size of measures of association are attenuated. Such attenuation of effects in mediation analyses tends to underestimate the effects of the mediator and overestimate the effect of the independent variable (if all coefficients are positive; Judd & Kenny, 1981). Hence, the mediation analyses reported below are best seen as conservative estimates of the dynamics of procedural justice described by the group-value model.

Results

FACTOR ANALYSES

The first issue addressed was whether pride in group membership and feelings of respect within a group could be distinguished from each other. Principal-components factor analysis of the responses to the pride and respect items developed for all four studies indicated two factors that accounted for 58% or more of the total variance. Because we expected feelings of pride and respect to be positively correlated, we conducted a two-factor oblique rotation that resulted in the factor structure reported in Tables 12.2 and 12.3.

Pride items in all four studies assessed the degree of pride in group membership participants felt. In the family study, additional items assessed students' feelings of pride in their parent or parents; these items were included because parents are important members of the family group. As we noted previously, in all four studies respect was measured with items that asked respondents to indicate how they believed they were viewed by

TABLE 12.2. Results of Factor Analyses

| | Factor loadings | | | | | | | |
| | Family | | Work | | University | | Nation | |
Questionnaire item	I	II	I	II	I	II	I	II
Group pride								
I am proud to think of myself as a member of this group.	.85	.45	.86	.10	.81	.24	.85	.27
It would be hard to find another group I would like as much to be a part of.	.80	.41	.74	.05	.56	.23	—	—
When someone praises my group's members, I feel it is a personal compliment to me.	.76	.26	.71	.14	.74	.21	.84	.30
I talk up my group to friends as a great group to be a part of.	.77	.32	.79	.08	.75	.35	—	—
I frequently tell others how much I like my parent(s).	.83	.30	—	—	—	—	—	—
It would be hard to think of other parent(s) I would like as much.	.72	.33	—	—	—	—	—	—
When someone praises my parent(s), it feels as a personal compliment to me.	.73	.27	—	—	—	—	—	—
Respect within groups								
If they knew me well, most members of my group would respect my values.	.30	**.78**	.06	**.84**	.20	**.74**	.18	**.82**
If they knew me well, most members of my group would think highly of my accomplishments in life.	.29	**.82**	.01	**.82**	.21	**.77**	.35	**.79**
If they knew me well, most members of my group would approve of how I live my life.	.28	**.82**	.19	**.86**	.25	**.82**	.26	**.69**
My parent(s) respect my values.[a]	.65	**.72**	—	—	—	—	—	—
My parent(s) approve of my life.	.36	**.83**	—	—	—	—	—	—
My parent(s) think I have accomplished a great deal in my life.	.36	**.75**	—	—	—	—	—	—
I believe that most members of my group respect me.	—	—	—	—	.39	.77	—	—
I believe I make a good impression on other members of my group.	—	—	—	—	.42	**.83**	—	—

Note. Numbers in boldface type are primary loadings. Dashes indicate items that were not assessed in a data set.
[a]Cross-loading of item on both factors: Item was dropped from final scale.

those who "knew them well." The university study extended the range of respect items by including "I believe that most members of my group respect me" and "I believe I make a good impression on other members of my group." In addition, items in the family study assessed whether participants felt their parents, as important members of their family, respected them. For these additional items in the family data set, we did not use the "If they knew me well" stem because we assumed that students felt their parents knew them well. The factor analyses loaded the additional items in the family and university studies onto the same factor as the items starting with the "If they knew me well" stem, suggesting that both the items that used the sentence stem and those that did not use the stem

tapped a general judgment about respect in a similar fashion.

For all studies, two factors met the selection criteria of eigenvalues greater than 1.0. In addition, all items loaded on the factor they were intended to measure. We deleted one item in the family study from the final scale of respect within groups because of multiple loadings on both factors. Overall, the consistency of the items across the data sets and the magnitude of their loadings provide strong empirical support that people (a) experience group pride and respect and (b) distinguish between the two constructs. Correlations between the final scales of pride and respect in Studies 1–4 were .43, .12, .38, and .35, respectively.

Table 12.3. Summary Factor Statistics

Factor statistic	Family I	Family II	Work I	Work II	University I	University II	Nation I	Nation II
Eigenvalue	5.97	2.11	3.57	1.99	3.71	1.54	2.18	1.04
Percentage of variance explained	46	16	37	29	41	17	44	21
Cumulative percentage of variance explained	—	62	—	65	—	58	—	64

We also used factor analyses to assess whether items used to measure instrumental and relational judgments about group authorities loaded on two separate factors (because these analyses replicate previous studies, details are not reported). All items loaded on their respective factors. Furthermore, as in previous research, relational judgments were significantly related to evaluations of procedural fairness. Pearson correlations between relational judgments and a 3-item procedural justice scale (e.g., "Overall, how fair were the procedures used to resolve the conflict?") for Studies 1–4 were .85, .92, .56, and .75, respectively. Correlation coefficients for the relationships between instrumental judgments and the overall procedural justice scale also were substantial but less strong than those for the relational judgments. For Studies 1–4, the coefficients were .68, .81, .41, and .69, respectively.

STAGE 1 OF THE MEDIATION ANALYSES: ASSESSING RELATIONSHIPS BETWEEN INDEPENDENT AND MEDIATOR VARIABLES

The group-value model argues that the relational aspects of procedural judgments communicate information about pride and respect (or, in correlational terms, covary with these two constructs). These relational judgments are hypothesized to covary more strongly with pride and respect than instrumental aspects of fairness judgments are. We used multiple regression analyses to test these hypotheses. Two types of analyses were conducted. First, we regressed pride and respect on instrumental and relational judgments alone. Second, we added each of the dependent variables to the regression equations to control for the covariation between dependent and mediator variables.

Tables 12.4 and 12.5 show the regression equations, with the first type of equations reported in the top part of the tables and all subsequent analyses below them. The first type of analysis revealed significant relationships between relational judgments and both pride and respect in all four data sets except for one case. Relational judgments about the Supreme Court were only marginally linked to feelings of respect among Americans, not a surprising finding given the distant and impersonal link between members of the Supreme Court and Americans in general. Instrumental judgments were marginally related to the measures of pride in two data sets, but no significant relationships were found in any of the other analyses.

Controlling for the relationships between the dependent variables (compliance with groups' rules, extrarole behaviors, group commitment, and self-esteem) and group pride and respect did not alter these findings very much, except in a few cases. Introducing extrarole behaviors and group commitment into the regression analyses for the university data reduced the relationships between relational judgments and respect to insignificance. In the work data set, controlling for group commitment reduced the relationship between relational judgments and pride to marginal significance. Finally, introducing self-esteem to the regression equation reduced the relationship between relational judgments and respect to insignificance in the nation study. Note, however, that only a marginally significant relationship between relational judgments and respect was found in that data set when the regression analysis was conducted without any controls.

Overall, 20 of the 24 regression equations in which the dependent variables were controlled showed significant relationships between relational judgments about authorities and the mediators, pride and respect, as the group-value model predicts. These additional analyses indicated that pride, respect, and the dependent variables are not simply highly correlated constructs reflecting general positive affect toward the groups but rather are independent, yet related, aspects of group mem-

Table 12.4.   Relationships Between Evaluations of Authorities and Group Pride

Evaluations of authorities and dependent variables	Group Pride			
	Family	Work	University	Nation
Instrumental judgments	−.02	.16**	−.15**	.05
Relational judgments	.62****	.28****	.48****	.38****
R^2	.37****	.15****	.18****	.17****
Instrumental judgments	−.01	.17**	−.15**	.04
Relational judgments	.52****	.25****	.47****	.31****
Compliance with rules	.24****	.26****	.12**	.20****
R^2	.42****	.20****	.19****	.20****
Instrumental judgments	−.02	.10	−.13**	—
Relational judgments	.52****	.25****	.44****	—
Extrarole behaviors	.35****	.39****	.18****	—
R^2	.48****	.29****	.21****	—
Instrumental judgments	—	.03	−.12**	—
Relational judgments	—	.12	.32****	—
Group commitment	—	.63****	.47****	—
R^2	—	.48****	.38****	—
Instrumental judgments	−.03	—	−.15**	.07
Relational judgments	.59****	—	.46****	.36****
Self-esteem	.22****	—	.17***	.08
R^2	.42****	—	.21****	.17****

Note. Values for independent variables are beta weights. Dashes indicate dependent variables that were not included in a particular study. See Results section for details regarding the different analyses.
**$p < .05$.   ***$p < .01$.   ****$p < .001$.

bership. Possibly the only exceptions to this statement are the constructs of pride and group commitment. Even though the items used to assess these constructs differ considerably at face value, the strong relationships between commitment and pride in the two data sets in which commitment was measured suggests that these constructs may tap into similar feelings about group membership.

STAGE 2 OF THE MEDIATION ANALYSES: ASSESSING RELATIONSHIPS BETWEEN MEDIATOR AND DEPENDENT VARIABLES

In Stage 2 of the mediation analyses, we assessed the relationships among group pride, respect within groups, and group-oriented attitudes and behaviors. For each of the dependent variables, we used multiple regression analyses to test whether pride or respect were related to the target variable. Two types of analyses were conducted. In the first, the dependent variables were regressed on pride and respect, respectively. The second type of analyses controlled for the relationships between the dependent variables and instrumental and relational judgments about group authorities.

Table 12.6 shows that when compliance with group rules was the dependent variable, both pride and respect were significantly related to compliance in all four data sets. When extrarole behavior was the dependent variable, both pride and respect were significantly related to that dependent variable in all three of the studies in which it was measured (see Table 12.7). Pride dominated in the family and work studies, whereas respect was more closely related to students' willingness to engage in extrarole behaviors in the university study. Table 12.8 shows that when group commitment was the dependent variable, pride was related to commitment in both studies in which commitment was measured, whereas respect was related to group commitment in the university study. When self-esteem was the dependent variable, both pride and respect were significantly related to self-esteem in all three studies in which self-esteem was measured (see Table 12.9). However, when both pride and respect were included in the same regression equation, respect dominated the amount of variance explained in respondents' self-esteem.

The bottom portions of Tables 12.6–12.9 show that including both instrumental and relational

TABLE 12.5. Relationships Between Evaluations of Authorities and Respect Within the Group

Evaluations of authorities and dependent variables	Respect within the group			
	Family	Work	University	Nation
Instrumental judgments	.05	.15	−.10	.06
Relational judgments	.43****	.29****	.19***	.l5*
R^2	.20****	.04***	.02**	.03***
Instrumental judgments	.07	.16	−.09	.05
Relational judgments	.29****	.23***	.18***	.12*
Compliance with rules	.35****	.20***	.15**	.09
R^2	.30****	.07****	.04***	.03***
Instrumental judgments	.06	.11	−.05	—
Relational judgments	.37****	.31****	.09	—
Extrarole behaviors	.19****	.25****	.39****	—
R^2	.23	.10****	.17****	—
Instrumental judgments	—	.14	−.08	—
Relational judgments	—	.29****	.10	—
Group commitment	—	.01	.28****	—
R^2	—	.04***	.09****	—
Instrumental judgments	.05	—	−.11	.14
Relational judgments	.37****	—	.12**	.06
Self-esteem	.42****	—	.48****	.35****
R^2	.37****	—	.24****	.14

Note. Values for independent variables are beta weights. Dashes indicate dependent variables that were not included in a particular study. See Results section for details regarding the different analyses.
*$p < .10.$ **$p < .05.$ ***$p < .01.$ ****$p < .001.$

judgments about authority in the regression equations did not significantly alter the findings, except for the nation study. In that study, the relationship between respect and compliance with group rules, and between pride and self-esteem, became insignificant when instrumental and relational judgments about authorities were controlled. Again, however, out of the 32 regression equations in which the independent variables were controlled, 30 showed significant relationships be-

Table 12.6. Relationships Between Feelings About Group Membership and Compliance With Group Rules

Feelings about group membership and independent variables	Compliance with group rules			
	Family	Work	University	Nation
Group pride	.45****	.25***	.15***	.34****
R^2	.20****	.10****	.02**	.11****
Group pride	.33****	.27****	.14**	.21****
Instrumental judgments	−.04	.09	−.01	.06
Relational judgments	.21***	.32****	.03	.27****
R^2	.22****	.16****	.01*	.18****
Respect within group	.47****	.24****	.16***	.16****
R^2	.21****	.05****	.02***	.02****
Respect within group	.37****	.19***	.15**	.08
Instrumental judgments	−.06	.07	−.02	.06
Relational judgments	.26****	.25***	.07	.34****
R^2	.26****	.13****	.02**	.16****

Note. Values for independent variables and mediators are beta weights. See Results section for details regarding the different analyses.
*$p < .10.$ **$p < .05.$ ***$p < .01.$ ****$p < .001.$

Table 12.7. Relationships Between Feelings About Group Membership and Extrarole Behaviors

Feelings about group membership and independent variables	Extrarole behaviors		
	Family	Work	University
Group pride	.49****	.45****	.27****
R^2	.24****	.20****	.07****
Group pride	.50****	.44****	.21****
Instrumental judgments	.00	.08	−.09
Relational judgments	−.03	−.05	.15**
R^2	.24****	.19****	.08****
Respect within group	.30****	.22****	.41****
R^2	.09****	.04****	.17****
Respect within group	.22****	.25****	.38****
Instrumental judgments	−.02	.11	−.09
Relational judgments	.19***	.15	.18***
R^2	.11****	.09****	.18****

Note. Values for independent variables and mediators are beta weights. See Results section for details regarding the different analyses.

**p < .05.   ***p < .01.   ****p < .001.

tween each of the mediators and the dependent variables, as the group-value model predicts.

STAGE 3 OF THE MEDIATION ANALYSES: ASSESSING THE ROLES OF MEDIATORS BETWEEN INDEPENDENT AND DEPENDENT VARIABLES

The previous two stages of the mediation analyses generally showed that: (a) relational judgments about group authorities were significantly linked to feelings of pride and respect, and (b) feelings of pride and respect were each significantly linked to group-oriented behaviors and self-esteem. With few exceptions, these relationships were observed in all four data sets. In the final sets of analyses we addressed two issues. First, we attempted to replicate previous procedural justice research by assessing whether relational judgments about authorities are significantly linked to the group-oriented attitudes and behaviors measured in these studies. Replication of earlier self-esteem findings in justice research also were attempted.

Second, the analyses assessed whether the significant linkages between relational judgments,

group-oriented behaviors, and self-esteem would be reduced or made nonsignificant when the mediators (pride and respect) were introduced. To demonstrate mediation it is necessary to show that (a) the mediation influences the dependent variable and (b) the introduction of the mediation into the equation either reduces (partial mediation) or eliminates (full mediation) the significant relationship between the independent variables and the dependent variables.

The top parts of Tables 12.10–12.13 report on the relationships between the independent and dependent variables alone, and the regression equations in the remainders of the tables reflect these relationships when the mediators were included. The roles of each of the mediators—pride and respect—were assessed independently, as they were in the previous analyses, as well as simultaneously. The simultaneous analyses allowed for a test of the full group-value model, by allowing the covariation between pride and respect to affect the results. Note that the analyses in which pride and respect are controlled independently are essentially the same as the analyses reported in the bottom parts of Tables 12.6–12.9. In Tables 12.6–12.9, however, we attempt to show that the relationships between the mediators and the dependent variables remained significant when the independent variables were controlled. In contrast, in Tables 12.10–12.13 we attempt to indicate whether the relation-

TABLE 12.8. Relationships Between Feelings About Group Membership and Group Commitment

Feelings about group membership and independent variables	Group commitment	
	Work	University
Group pride	.69****	.56****
R^2	.47****	.31****
Group pride	.62****	.52****
Instrumental judgments	.11	.02
Relational judgments	.08	.09
R^2	.49****	.31****
Respect within group	−.04	.30****
R^2	.00	.09****
Respect within group	.01	.26****
Instrumental judgments	.21***	−.04
Relational judgments	.25***	.29****
R^2	.16****	.15****

Note. Values for independent variables and mediators are beta weights. See Results section for details regarding the different analyses.

*** p < .01. ****p < .001.

Table 12.9. Relationships Between Feelings About Group Membership and Self-Esteem

Feelings about group membership and independent variables	Self-esteem		
	Family	University	Nation
Group pride	.31****	.23****	.12***
R^2	.09****	.05****	.01***
Group pride	.35****	.21***	.09
Instrumental judgments	.03	.04	−.23***
Relational judgments	−.08	.04	.24****
R^2	.09****	.04****	.04****
Respect within group	.48****	.48****	.34****
R^2	.23****	.24****	.12****
Respect within group	.52****	.48****	.34****
Instrumental judgments	−.01	.06	−.25***
Relational judgments	−.08	.05	.23***
R^2	.23****	.24****	.15****

Note. Values for independent variables and mediators are beta weights. See Results section for details regarding the different analyses.
***$p < .01$.   ****$p < .001$.

ships between the independent and dependent variables would be significantly reduced when the mediators (pride and respect) were included in the regression equations. For ease of comparisons, the same analyses are reported in both sets of tables.

The findings generally replicated previous procedural justice studies in showing that relational judgments were significantly linked to compliance in three of the four studies, to extrarole behaviors in two of the three studies in which they were assessed, to group commitment in both of the studies in which it was assessed, and to self-esteem in all three studies in which it was assessed. In all, our analyses replicated previous research in 10 of 12 analyses. Furthermore, instrumental judgments were not significantly related to any of the dependent variables except in 2 of the analyses that we conducted.

Table 12.10 reports on the mediation analyses for compliance with group rules. In three of four cases relational judgments influenced compliance. Of those three cases the combined analysis (including both pride and respect) shows one case of full mediation (family), one of partial mediation

(nation), and one of no mediation (work). When extrarole behavior was the independent variable (see Table 12.11), relational judgments exerted an influence in two of three cases. Of those cases a joint analysis indicated one instance of full mediation (family) and one of partial mediation (university). In the case of commitment (Table 12.12), relational judgments influenced commitment in both cases examined. Furthermore, both showed full mediation. Finally, with self-esteem, relational judgments influenced self-esteem in three of three cases. In two of those cases full mediation was found (family, university) and in one there was partial mediation (nation). Overall, relational judgments were influential in 10 of 12 cases, and in those 10 cases 6 were fully mediated by pride or respect, and 3 were partially mediated. Only 1 was not mediated by pride and respect.

Discussion

PSYCHOLOGICAL DYNAMICS OF THE GROUP VALUE MODEL

Previous research has documented that procedural justice judgments are central to the effectiveness of authorities in groups. Existing frameworks appear ill-suited, however, to explain some of the recent, striking findings of procedural justice research—in particular, the strong effects of fairness judgments on group-oriented attitudes and behaviors. The group-value model (Lind & Tyler, 1988; Tyler, 1989, Tyler & Lind, 1992) draws on insights from social identity theory for a new theoretical framework within which to understand these findings. The model suggests that authority structures, particularly people's perceptions of their relationships to group authorities, are significantly linked to people's feelings about group membership. These feelings, in turn, are suggested to mediate between people's justice evaluations of group authorities and their attitudes and behaviors toward the group.

Across four studies, the results generally supported the group value model. First, in accordance with patterns of results shown in previous research, relational aspects of people's fairness evaluations of group authorities tended to be more strongly related to their attitudes and behaviors than did instrumental, outcome-oriented aspects of these evaluations. Second, the relational aspects of procedural fairness were significantly related to two

Table 12.10. Results of Mediated Analysis of Compliance With Group Rules

Evaluations of authorities and mediators	Compliance with group rules			
	Family	Work	University	Nation
Instrumental judgments	−.05	.05	−.03	.07
Relational judgments	.41****	.30****	.09	.35****
R^2	.15****	.10****	.00	.15****
Instrumental judgments	−.04	.09	−.01	.06
Relational judgments	.21****	.32****	.03	.27****
Group pride	.33****	.27****	.14**	.21****
R^2	.22****	.16****	.01*	.18****
Instrumental judgments	−.06	.07	−.02	.06
Relational judgments	.26****	.25***	.07	.34****
Respect within group	.37****	.19***	.15**	.08
R^2	.26****	.13****	.02**	.16****
Instrumental judgments	−.06	.11	−.01	.05
Relational judgments	.12	.33****	.02	.27****
Group pride	.25****	.24****	.10	.20***
Respect within group	.32****	.14**	.12*	.04
R^2	.29****	.17****	.02**	.18****

Note. Values for independent variables and mediators are beta weights. See Results section for details regarding the different analyses.
*$p < .10$. **$p < .05$. ***$p < .01$. ****$p < .001$.

distinct types of feelings about group membership: pride in group membership and perceived respect within groups. Third, feelings of pride and respect mediate between relational judgments about group authorities and three types of group-oriented behaviors and attitudes typically studied in recent procedural justice research: compliance with group rules, group commitment, and extrarole behavior directed at groups. In seven of nine cases, relational indicators influenced group-oriented attitudes and behaviors. Of those seven cases, four show complete mediation of the effect by pride or respect, two show partial mediation, and only one shows no evidence of mediation. Fourth, the significant relationships between relational judgments about the actions of group authorities, feelings of pride and respect, and self-esteem support the group-value model's argument that procedures communicate identity-relevant information. In all three cases studied, self-esteem was influenced by relational judgments, and in all three cases that effect is mediated by pride and respect (two cases of full mediation; one of partial mediation).

Replications of these findings across four very different group contexts—from the small intimate relationships representative of families to the impersonal symbolic nature of the relationship between citizens and the Supreme Court—attest to

the robustness of the group-value model. Of course, not all the data sets showed equally strong relationships, suggesting that contextual differences are an important question for future research. In our analyses, the family data set showed the strongest support for the group-value model, and the national data set revealed the weakest relationships. Several factors distinguish the family context from the other research contexts. First, parents are easily identifiable as an authority representing the family group. In contrast, the university authorities with whom students resolved their conflicts (in the university study), or the supervisors with whom workers resolved their grievances (in the work study), may not have been viewed as representative of the university community or work organization, respectively. For example, many students described a single interaction with the professor or staffperson. Therefore, it might be easy to dismiss the authority's treatment as nonrepresentative of the group's general attitudes.

A second important difference between these group contexts is the frequency of people's experiences with the relevant authority. In the university study, for instance, students often described a one-time interaction with a university authority during which a particular school-related conflict

Table 12.11. Results of Mediated Analysis of Extrarole Behaviors

Evaluations of authorities and mediators	Extrarole behaviors		
	Family	Work	University
Instrumental judgments	−.01	.15	−.13
Relational judgments	.29****	.07	.26****
R^2	.08****	.03***	.04****
Instrumental judgments	.00	.08	−.09
Relational judgments	−.03	−.05	.15**
Group pride	.51****	.44****	.21***
R^2	.24****	.19****	.08****
Instrumental judgments	−.02	.11	−.08
Relational judgments	.19***	.15	.18***
Respect within group	.22**	.25****	.38****
R^2	.11****	.09****	.18****
Instrumental judgments	−.01	.06	−.08
Relational judgments	−.06	.01	.15**
Group pride	.48****	.40****	.08
Respect within group	.13**	.18***	.36****
R^2	.25****	.22****	.19****

Note. Values for independent variables and mediators are beta weights. See Results section for details regarding the different analyses.
**$p < .05$.   ***$p < .01$.   ****$p < .001$.

was resolved. Respondents in the national study had no direct experiences with the U.S. Supreme Court. In contrast, students' description of a conflict with their parent(s) represents one experience in a continuous relationship. Unfair treatment by a parent may be more personally meaningful than unfair treatment by a professor or a Supreme Court judge. Furthermore, for college students, a parent's decision about family issues may be more important and influential than a professor's decision about a grade. Similarly, a supervisor's decision may mean immediate changes for an employee, whereas a Supreme Court decision may mean little change for most citizens.

Still, it is important to recognize that our results suggest that even a single interaction with an authority can shape group-oriented attitudes and opinions. If people view authorities as representative of an important group, a single experience can be emblematic of general group opinions. On the one hand, students can view an appointment with a disrespectful and rude financial aid staffperson as an unusual event. On the other hand, they can view the same interaction as yet another example of cold and unfeeling bureaucracy. Furthermore, the possibility that the same dynamics occur in evaluations of national political authorities suggests that evidence of fair or unfair relations treat-

ment does not necessarily require personal experience. It may be enough to know of others' experiences, or to expect certain types of experiences. Certainly, voters form opinions of political candidates' moral character without personal contact (Tyler & Degoey, 1996).

The evidence from these studies shows how relational evaluations—respectful, neutral, and trustworthy treatment from authorities—can facilitate group-oriented behavior. People do not have to get favorable outcomes, or feel they have control over decisions, before they will comply with group rules or do things of behalf of the group. Instead, relationally fair treatment can promote feelings of pride and respect that in turn encourage group serving behavior. This is a low-cost way for leaders and authorities to be effective. It shows how leaders can pursue long-term group interests without having to provide for individual short-term benefits. The optimistic implications of the group-value model are a stark contrast to more instrumental models of the person that suggest people's attitudes and behaviors reflect their understanding of personal costs and benefits.

However, because these data are correlational, any causal inferences should be made cautiously, if at all. Of particular concern is whether feelings of pride and respect shape procedural justice judg-

Table 12.12. Results of Mediated Analysis of Group Commitment

Evaluations of authorities and mediators	Group commitment	
	Work	University
Instrumental judgments	.21***	–.06
Relational judgments	.25***	.34****
R^2	.16****	.09****
Instrumental judgments	.11	.02
Relational judgments	.08	.09
Group pride	.62****	.52****
R^2	.49****	.31****
Instrumental judgments	.21***	–.04
Relational judgments	.25***	.29****
Respect within group	.01	.26****
R^2	.16****	.15****
Instrumental judgments	.12**	.02
Relational judgments	.04	.09
Group pride	.64****	.48****
Respect within group	–.10	.12**
R^2	.48****	.32****

Note. Values for independent variables and mediators are beta weights. See Results section for details regarding the different analyses.

**p < .05.   ***p < .01.   ****p < .001.

ments, instead of the reverse. Conversely, of concern is whether, for instance, engaging in group-serving behaviors or having high self-esteem leads people to believe they are more respected within their group or feel greater pride in group membership. Partial support for the proposed causal direction of these effects can been gleaned from longitudinal studies of procedural justice effects. For example, Brockner et al. (1992) found that the perceived fairness of an organizational layoff changed workers' commitment to their work organization. Partial support can also be derived from experimental studies of group behavior. Social identity studies have shown, for instance, that when participants are arbitrarily assigned to a group and positively evaluate that group, they generally engage in attitudes and behaviors that benefit the group (Mass & Schaller, 1991). Recent experimental research also has shown that participants reported significantly higher self-esteem when the research assistant treated them respectfully and fairly than when the research assistant treated them inconsiderately and unfairly (Koper et al., 1993). These results suggest that it is not unreasonable to argue that relationally fair treatment and respect promote feelings of self-esteem and group-oriented behavior and attitudes.

The group-value model hypothesizes that the fairness of specific interactions with authorities shapes general feelings of pride and respect, which in turn influence general group-oriented attitudes and behavior. However, in this research we have not considered the variable most widely studied in justice research—the voluntary acceptance of decisions. A replication of the analyses that focused on decision acceptance suggested that, although voluntary acceptance of decisions was strongly related to relational judgments about authorities, feelings of pride and respect did not mediate that relationship to a significant degree.

Although the pattern of findings in the case of decision acceptance differed from those reported earlier in this article, it is not necessarily contrary to the predictions of the group-value model. First, we assessed voluntary decision acceptance, as it has been in many previous studies, by asking respondents about their willingness to accept a decision within a specific dispute they had described. Quite possibly, if respondents had been asked about the degree to which they *generally* were willing to accept the decisions of a group authority, the same psychological dynamics as revealed above would have been shown. Such a general-acceptance variable would parallel more closely the general attitudes and behaviors toward groups assessed above.

Second, people's willingness to accept particular decisions by group authorities may be related to their general attitudes toward their groups, attitudes that we have shown to be linked to judgments about group authorities. To test this latter possibility, we created an overall index of workers' attitudes toward their organization (in the work study) by combining the variables of commitment, feelings of obligation to comply with work rules, and willingness to engage in extrarole behaviors. The overall index explained 20% (p < .001) of respondents' willingness to voluntarily accept a particular decision made by their supervisors. Similarly, in the family study, we created an overall attitude index by combining the variables reflecting feelings of obligation to comply with family rules and willingness to engage in extrarole behaviors. Thirteen percent (p < .001) of the variance in willingness to voluntarily accept particular parental decisions was explained by this overall index. Relational judgments about group authorities,

Table 12.13. Results of Mediated Analysis of Self-Esteem

Evaluations of authorities and mediators	Self-esteem		
	Family	University	Nation
Instrumental judgments	.02	.01	−.23***
Relational judgments	.14**	.14**	.28****
R^2	.02**	.01*	.04***
Instrumental judgments	.03	.04	−.23***
Relational judgments	−.08	.04	.24***
Group pride	.35****	.21***	.09
R^2	.09****	.04***	.04***
Instrumental judgments	−.01	.06	−.25***
Relational judgments	−.08	.05	.23***
Respect within group	.52****	.48****	.34****
R^2	.23****	.24****	.15****
Instrumental judgments	−.01	.06	−.25***
Relational judgments	−.06	.03	.22***
Group pride	.23****	.03	.01
Respect within group	.48****	.47****	.34****
R^2	.26****	.24****	.14****

Note. Values for independent variables and mediators are beta weights. See Results section for details regarding the different analyses.
*$p < .10$.   **$p < .05$.   ***$p < .01$.   ****$p < .001$.

then, may affect the willingness to accept decisions directly, and indirectly through its covariation with people's general attitudes toward their groups.

In summary, the group-value model provides an exciting new way of examining the psychological underpinnings of procedural justice effects. Although a number of issues still need to be resolved, the findings of our analyses provide the first support for the hypotheses proposed in the model. Furthermore, the findings suggest a number of fruitful avenues for future research.

IMPLICATIONS OF THE GROUP-VALUE MODEL FOR SOCIAL IDENTITY THEORY

As noted earlier in the article, the group-value model draws heavily from social identity theory, a theory that suggests that people draw a sense of identity from group membership and that such sense of identity is related to group-oriented attitudes and behaviors. As we noted, the group-value model and social identity theory differ in at least one important aspect: The group-value model is mainly concerned with explaining intragroup dynamics, whereas social identity theory is primarily concerned with explaining intergroup dynamics. In focusing on intergroup relations, social identity theorists have focused on how feelings

about a social category as a whole (in contrast to other social categories) affect people's attitudes and behaviors. An important contribution of our research, however, is the suggestion that people consider two sources of information about their social category: their position within the group (respect), and the position of the group as a whole (pride). Feelings of group pride correspond more directly to the group-level judgments that have been the focus of social identity theorists. In this section, we discuss how paying attention to issues of respect within groups, and how they are linked to authority structures in groups, can inform social identity research and theory.

Social identity theory predicts that people's senses of self-worth are affected by their evaluations of the groups to which they belong. Unfortunately, related empirical research has not consistently supported this hypothesis (for reviews see Hogg & Abrams, 1988, 1990; Maass & Schaller, 1991; Messick & Mackie, 1989). Our results, however, suggest that group membership may still be related to self evaluations but that feelings about the self are more influenced by people's perceptions of respect within groups than their evaluations of the entire group (pride). In all three studies, respect explained more of the variance in self-esteem than did pride.

These results can explain why, even when people are able to change groups, they often remain identified with marginal, stigmatized, or low-status groups (Ellemers, Van Knippenberg, de Vries, & Wilke, 1988; Pettigrew, 1978). Being a respected member of a marginal group may be better for one's sense of self than being a marginal member of a respected group. For example, much of the recent writing by minority group members about affirmative action stresses the potential subjective emptiness of the objective gains that occur through affirmative action programs (Nacoste, 1990). Such gains do not enhance minority members' senses of self if they feel that they are not gaining the respect of those in the occupations that they join.

The relationship between evaluations of respect within groups and self-esteem might also explain why out-group prejudice and discrimination, which social identity theory posits arise naturally from people's need to bolster their self-esteem, have not been consistently found in social identity research (see Hinkle & Brown, 1990). Some studies have shown that group members with low self-esteem are more likely to derogate outgroups, whereas other studies have found that group members with high self-esteem are more likely to derogate out-groups (see Crocker & Luhtanen, 1990; Long, Spears, & Manstead, 1994). One explanation for this inconsistency is that people who do not feel respected by an advantaged group may be motivated to focus on the status of their larger group compared with other groups, and not their personal place within their group, to bolster their self-esteem. In contrast, individuals who feel they are valued members of their group, even if that group is of low status, may not need to focus on intergroup comparisons and out-group derogation to raise their positive feelings about themselves.

Social identity theorists have recently begun to acknowledge the potential weaknesses of their sole focus on the categorical characteristics of groups in comparisons to other groups. Hinkle and Brown (1990), for instance, suggested that "[group] membership seems more bound up with dynamics within the group than with any relationship between that group and others" (p. 67). It is interesting to note that the recognition of intragroup dynamics parallels the empirical shift from using the minimal-group paradigm to studying the effects of social categorization in experimental settings

to natural groups and field research. An important difference between laboratory and realworld groups is that real-world groups are established groups in which ongoing social relationships are expressed in authority structures and differentiation among group members. It is precisely these types of structured and differentiated groups that have been the focus of procedural justice research (see Lind & Tyler, 1988, and Tyler & Lind, 1992, for reviews). The inclusion, then, of feelings of respect within groups, and how people's relationships to group authorities affect these feelings, in a social identity theory framework may provide a more complete picture of how people derive a sense of self-worth from group membership than does social identity theory's emphasis on evaluations of one group in comparison to others.

If, as we suggest, respect, as an evaluation of one's position within the group, can supplement the traditional focus of social identity theory on evaluations of groups as a whole (pride), a key question for future research is a clearer conceptualization of what respect is. For example, in all four of the present studies, respondents were asked whether other group members would approve of their lifestyle, respect their values, and appreciate their accomplishments, *if those group members knew them well.* Our intention was to create a series of questions that would be appropriate even in contexts (such as the nation study) in which all group members could not possibly know the respondent. By drawing attention to other group members' opinions, we hoped to learn people's views of what other group members thought, not what they thought of themselves. However, respondents may have interpreted the questions as asking whether they really deserved respect, rather than how they thought other group members viewed them. Fortunately, these questions were closely related to other questions that more directly measured people's assessments of their social reputation (e.g., "I believe that most members of the university community respect me"). However, the potential ambiguity of these questions suggests that an important goal for future research will be to determine whether respect represents people's subjective evaluations of how the group, as a whole, values them as the group-value model hypothesizes or whether respect captures the quality of a particular set of interpersonal relationships.

IMPLICATIONS OF SOCIAL IDENTITY THEORY FOR THE GROUP-VALUE MODEL

In the preceding section we discussed how the group-value model can make theoretical contributions to social identity theory and research. In this final section, the reverse—how social identity theory can further inform the group-value model—is discussed.

As we noted, social identity theory argues that people's attitudes and behaviors are affected by evaluative comparisons between groups (Hogg & Abrams, 1988; Tajfel & Turner, 1986). Interestingly, the group-value model does not address such comparative processes; only "absolute" levels of pride and respect, void of explicit comparisons between groups or individuals within groups, are considered. Moreover, only absolute levels of procedural justice judgments are considered, without paying attention to the possibility that people engage in comparative evaluations between procedures or treatment by authorities, either within groups or across groups. This points to a potential limitation of the group-value model. People could, for example, be influenced by how fairly they feel treated by group authorities relative to other individuals. If so, then many of the same invidious comparisons that social identity theory suggests occur between groups ("My group is better than your group") could also occur in terms of relative respect within groups ("I am a more valued group member than you are"). These comparative aspects of evaluations of group authorities, pride, and respect were not examined in the studies reported in this article and should be explored in future studies.

Finally, social identity theory and research remind us that individuals are members of many different groups. This could take the form of cross-cutting group memberships (e.g., being female and African American) and nested group memberships—that is, groups existing within groups. Although the research reported in this article was limited to investigations of individuals' connections to a single group and its representative authority, there are numerous social situations in which people may be members of groups included within larger social categories. This suggests more complex questions, for instance, about whether feelings that one's group is respected by the larger superordinate category and its corresponding authorities will influence people's attitudes and behavior (e.g., does the university administration respect the psychology department; Thompson, Kray, & Lind, 1994). This possibility of multiple group memberships also suggests that people's choices of the groups with which they identify may influence their judgments of procedural justice (H. J. Smith & Tyler, 1996; Huo et al., 1996) and hence the psychological dynamics proposed by the group-value model.

Conclusion

Procedural justice research documents the many positive and unexpected consequences of fair and respectful treatment. Procedural justice not only encourages people to accept unfavorable decisions, but it also promotes commitment, loyalty, and effort on behalf of the larger group. Our results show why procedural justice is related to group-oriented attitudes and behaviors. Fair and respectful treatment by authorities who represent important groups communicates feelings of respect and pride. Feelings of respect and pride, in turn, are related to self-esteem, feelings of obligation to group authorities, and the desire to help the group beyond what is required. Together, these two concepts—pride and respect—can explain several inconsistencies in previous research and outline when people will be willing to act in their group's interest, even when it conflicts with their personal desires.

REFERENCES

Alexander, S., & Ruderman, A. (1987). The role of procedural and distributive justice in organizational behavior. *Social Justice Research, 1,* 177–198.

Baron, K. M., & Kenny, D. A. (1986). The moderator-mediator variable distinction in social psychology research: Conceptual, strategic, and statistical considerations. *Journal of Personality and Social Psychology, 58,* 1173–1182.

Barrett-Howard, E., & Tyler, T. R. (1986). Procedural justice as a criterion in allocation decisions. *Journal of Personality and Social Psychology, 50,* 296–304.

Brewer, M. B., & Kramer, R. M. (1986). Choice behavior in social dilemmas: Effects of social identity, group size and decision framing. *Journal of Personality and Social Psychology, 50,* 543–549.

Brockner, J., Tyler, T. R., & Cooper-Schneider, R. (1992). The influence of prior commitment to an institution on reactions to perceived unfairness: The higher they are, the harder they fall. *Administrative Science Quarterly, 37,* 241–261.

Brown, R. J., Condor, S., Mathew, A., Wade, G., & Williams, J. A. (1986). Explaining intergroup differentiation in an industrial organization. *Journal of Occupational Psychology, 59,* 273–286.

Calder, B. J. (1977). An attribution theory of leadership. In B. M. Staw & G. R. Salancik (Eds.), *New directions in organizational behavior* (pp. 179–204). Chicago: St. Clair.

Crocker, J., & Luhtanen, R. (1990). Collective self-esteem and ingroup bias. *Journal of Personality and Social Psychology, 58,* 60–67.

Deutsch, M., & Steil, J. M. (1988). Awakening the sense of injustice. *Social Justice Research, 2,* 2–23.

Dillman, D. A. (1978). *Mail and telephone surveys: The total design approach.* New York: Wiley.

Ellemers, N., Van Knippenberg, A., de Vries, N., & Wilke, H. (1988). Social identification and permeability of group boundaries. *European Journal of Social Psychology, 18,* 497–513.

Fahr, J. L., Podsakoff, P. M., & Organ, D. W. (1990). Accounting for organizational citizenship behavior: Leader fairness and task scope versus satisfaction. *Journal of Management, 16,* 705–721.

Folger, R., & Konovsky, M. (1989). Effects of procedural and distributive justice on reactions to pay raise decisions. *Academy of Management Journal, 32,* 115–130.

Greenberg, J. (1987). Reactions to procedural injustice in payment distributions: Do the ends justify the means? *Journal of Applied Psychology, 71,* 55–61.

Greenberg, J. (1990). Organizational justice: Yesterday, today, and tomorrow. *Journal of Management, 16,* 399–432.

Hinkle, S. W., & Brown, R. J. (1990). Intergroup comparisons and social identity: Some links and lacunae. In D. Abrams & M. A. Hogg (Eds.), *Social identity theory* (pp. 48–70). New York: Springer Verlag.

Hogg, M. A., & Abrams, D. (1988). *Social identifications: A social psychology of intergroup relations and group processes.* London and New York: Routledge.

Hogg, M. A., & Abrams, D. (1990). Social motivation, self-esteem and social identity. In D. Abrams & M. A. Hogg (Eds.), *Social identity theory: Constructive and critical advances* (pp. 28–47). New York: Springer-Verlag.

Huo, Y. J., Smith, H. J., Tyler, T. R., & Lind, E. A. (1996). Superordinate identification, subgroup identification and justice concerns: Is separatism the problem, is assimilation the answer? *Psychological Science, 7*(1), 40–45.

James, L. R., & Brett, J. M. (1984). Mediators, moderators and tests for mediation. *Journal of Applied Psychology, 69,* 307–321.

Joubert, C. E. (1991). Self-esteem and social desirability in relation to college students' retrospective perceptions of parental fairness and disciplinary practices. *Psychological Reports, 69,* 115–120.

Judd, C. M., & Kenny, D. A. (1981). Process analysis: Estimating mediation in treatment evaluations. *Evaluation Review, 5,* 602–619.

Konovsky, M. A., & Folger, R. (1991). The effects of procedures, social accounts, and benefits level on victims' layoff reactions. *Journal of Applied Social Psychology, 21,* 630–650.

Koper, G., Van Knippenberg, D., Bouhuijs, F., Vermunt, R., & Wilke, H. (1993). Procedural fairness and self-esteem. *European Journal of Social Psychology, 23,* 313–325.

Lind, E. A., & Earley, P. C. (1992). Procedural justice and culture. *International Journal of Psychology, 27,* 227–242.

Lind, E. A., Kanfer, R., & Earley, P. C. (1990). Voice, control, and procedural justice: Instrumental and noninstrumental concerns in fairness judgments. *Journal of Personality and Social Psychology, 59,* 952–959.

Lind, E. A., Kulik, C. T., Ambrose, M., & de Vera Park, M. V. (1993). Individual and corporate dispute resolution: Using procedural fairness as a decision heuristic. *Administrative Science Quarterly, 38,* 224–251.

Lind, E. A., Kurtz, S., Musante, L., Walker, L., & Thibaut, J. (1980). Procedure and outcome effects on reactions to adjudicated resolutions of conflicts of interest. *Journal of Personality and Social Psychology, 39,* 643–653.

Lind, E. A., Lissak, R. E., & Conlon, A. E. (1983). Decision control and process control effects on procedural fairness judgments. *Journal of Applied Social Psychology, 4,* 338–350.

Lind, E. A., & Tyler, T. R. (1988). *The social psychology of procedural justice.* New York: Plenum.

Long, K. M., Spears, R., & Manstead, A. S. R. (1994). The influence of personal and collective self-esteem on strategies of social differentiation. *British Journal of Social Psychology, 33,* 313–329.

Maass, A., & Schaller, M. (1991). Intergroup biases and the cognitive dynamics of stereotype formation. *European Review of Social Psychology, 2,* 189–209.

Mackenzie, S. B., Podsakoff, P. M., & Fetter, R. (1991). Organizational citizenship behavior and objective productivity as determinants of managerial evaluations of salespersons' performance. *Organizational Behavior and Human Decision Processes, 50,* 123–150.

Meindl, J. R., Ehrlich, S. B., & Dukerich, J. N. (1985). The romance of leadership. *Administrative Science Quarterly, 30,* 78–102.

Messick, D. M., & Mackie, D. M. (1989). Intergroup relations. *Annual Review of Psychology, 40,* 45–81.

Moorman, R. H. (1991). Relationship between organization justice and organizational citizenship behaviors: Do fairness perceptions influence employee citizenship? *Journal of Applied Psychology, 76,* 845–855.

Mowday, R. T., Porter, L. W., & Steers, R. M. (1982). *Employee-organization linkages.* San Diego, CA: Academic Press.

Nacoste, R. W. (1990). Sources of stigma: Analyzing the psychology of affirmative action. *Law and Policy, 12,* 175–195.

O'Reilly, C. A., & Chatman, J. A. (1986). Organizational commitment and psychological attachment: The effects of compliance, identification, and internalization on prosocial behavior. *Journal of Applied Psychology, 71,* 492–499.

Organ, D. W. (1988). *Organizational citizenship behavior: The good soldier syndrome.* Lexington, MA: Lexington Books.

Pettigrew, T. F. (1978). Three issues of ethnicity: Boundaries, deprivations, and perceptions. In J. M. Yinger & S. J. Cutler (Eds.), *Major social issues: A multidisciplinary view* (pp. 25–49). New York: Free Press.

Pfeffer, J. (1981). Management as symbolic action: The creation and maintenance of organizational paradigms. In L. L. Cummings & B. M. Staw (Eds.), *Research in organizational behavior* (Vol. 3, pp. 1–52). Greenwich, CT: JAI Press.

Pfeffer, J., & Salancik, G. R. (1978). *The external control of organizations: A resource dependence perspective.* New York: Harper & Row.

Rosenberg, M. (1979). *Conceiving the self.* New York: Basic Books.

Sears, D. O. (1986). College sophomores in the laboratory: Influences of a narrow database on social psychology's view of human nature. *Journal of Personality and Social Psychology, 51,* 515–530.

Sherif, M., Harvey, O. J., White, B. J., Hood, W. R., & Sherif, C. W. (1961). *Intergroup conflict and cooperation: The Robbers Cave experiment*. Norman: University of Oklahoma Book Exchange.

Smith, C. A., Organ, D. W., & Near, J. P. (1983). Organizational citizenship behavior: Its nature and antecedents. *Journal of Applied Psychology, 68,* 653–663.

Smith, H. J., & Tyler, T. R. (1996). Justice and power: When will justice concerns encourage the advantaged to support policies which redistribute economic resources and the disadvantaged to willingly obey the law? *European Journal of Social Psychology, 26,* 171–200.

Tajfel, H. (1978). *Differentiation between social groups*. London: Academic Press.

Tajfel, H., & Turner, J. (1986). The social identity theory of intergroup behavior. In S. Worchel (Ed.), *Psychology of intergroup relations* (pp. 33–47). Chicago: Nelson-Hall.

Tansky, J. W. (1993). Justice and organizational citizenship behavior: What is the relationship? *Employee Responsibilities and Rights Journal, 6,* 195–207.

Thibaut, J., & Kelley, H. H. (1959). *The social psychology of groups*. New York: Wiley

Thibaut, J., & Walker, L. (1975). *Procedural justice: A psychological analysis*. Hillsdale, NJ: Erlbaum.

Thompson, L., Kray, L., & Lind, E. A. (1994, October). *The bright and dark side of group identity*. Paper presented at the Annual Society for Experimental Social Psychology convention, Lake Tahoe, NV.

Turner, J. C., Hogg, M. A., Oakes, P. J., Reicher, S., & Wetherell, M. S. (1987). *Rediscovering the social group: A self-categorisation theory*. Oxford, England: Basil Blackwell.

Tyler, T. R. (1984). The role of perceived injustice in defendants' evaluations of their courtroom experience. *Law and Society Review, 18,* 51–74.

Tyler, T. R. (1989). The psychology of procedural justice: A test of the group-value model. *Journal of Personality and Social Psychology, 57,* 830–838.

Tyler, T. R. (1990). *Why people obey the law: Procedural justice, legitimacy, and compliance*. New Haven, CT: Yale University Press.

Tyler, T. R. (1994). Psychological models of the justice motive: The antecedents of distributive justice and procedural justice. *Journal of Personality and Social Psychology, 67,* 850–863.

Tyler, T. R., & Caine, A. (1981). The role of distributional and procedural fairness in the endorsement of formal leaders. *Journal of Personality and Social Psychology, 41,* 642–655.

Tyler, T. R., & Degoey, P. (1995). Collective restraint in social dilemmas: Procedural justice and social identification effects on support for authorities. *Journal of Personality and Social Psychology, 69,* 482–497.

Tyler, T. R., & Degoey, P. (1996). Trust in organizational authorities: The influence of motive attributions on willingness to accept decisions. In R. Kramer & T. R. Tyler (Eds.), *Trust in organizations* (pp. 331–356). Thousand Oaks, CA: Sage.

Tyler, T. R., & Lind, E. A. (1992). A relational model of authority in groups. In M. Zanna (Ed.), *Advances in experimental social psychology* (Vol. 25, pp. 115–191). New York: Academic Press.

Tyler, T. R., Rasinski, K., & McGraw, K. (1985). The influence of perceived injustice on support for political authorities. *Journal of Applied Social Psychology, 15,* 700–725.

Tyler, T. R., Rasinski, K., & Spodick, N. (1985). The influence of voice on satisfaction with leaders: Exploring the meaning of process control. *Journal of Personality and Social Psychology, 48,* 72–81.

Vermunt, R., Wit, A., van den Bos, K. & Lind, A. (1993, July). *The effect of inaccurate procedure on protest: The mediating role of perceived unfairness and situational esteem*. Paper presented at the fourth International Conference on Social Justice, Trier, Germany.

APPENDIX

Intercorrelations Among Items in Each Study

Variable	M	SD	1	2	3	4	5	6	7	8	9
Study 1: Family											
1. Relational judgments	3.32	1.31	—								
2. Relational judgments × identification	—[a]	—[a]	.68	—							
3. Instrumental judgments	3.78	1.47	.56	.39	—						
4. Pride	2.82	1.26	.43	.61	.22	—					
5. Respect	2.43	1.09	.43	.45	.22	.43	—				
6. Compliance	2.40	0.82	.28	.39	.11	.45	.47	—			
7. Extrarole	2.74	0.91	.17	.28	.10	.49	.30	.59	—		
8. Commitment	—[a]	—[a]	—[a]	—[a]	—[a]	—[a]	—[a]	—[a]	—[a]	—	
9. Self-esteem	3.09	1.07	.16	.15	.07	.31	.48	.22	.17	—[a]	—
Study 2: Work											
1. Relational judgments	1.96	0.88	—								
2. Relational judgments × identification	6.30	3.40	.85	—							
3. Instrumental judgments	2.40	0.86	.74	.62	—						
4. Pride	2.05	0.66	.38	.38	.33	—					
5. Respect	1.73	0.58	.10	.20	.03	.11	—				
6. Compliance	2.06	0.88	.30	.33	.23	.10	.24	—			
7. Extrarole	1.72	0.49	.16	.17	.20	.45	.22	.02	—		
8. Commitment	2.25	0.75	.37	.38	.37	.69	.05	.08	.31	—	
9. Self-esteem	—[a]	—[a]	—[a]	—[a]	—[a]	—[a]	—[a]	—[a]	—[a]	—[a]	—
Study 3: University											
1. Relational judgments	2.52	0.73	—								
2. Relational judgments × identification	5.12	2.48	.68	—							
3. Instrumental judgments	3.02	0.83	.60	.47	—						
4. Pride	2.41	0.97	.17	.41	.08	—					
5. Respect	2.87	1.05	.01	.14	-.01	.37	—				
6. Compliance	1.61	0.59	.09	.08	.01	.15	.16	—			
7. Extrarole	2.29	0.54	.00	.20	.00	.27	.41	.16	—		
8. Commitment	1.74	0.64	.13	.31	.10	.56	.30	.16	.27	—	
9. Self-esteem	1.97	0.70	.08	.14	.07	.23	.49	.21	.28	.29	—
Study 4: Nation											
1. Relational judgments	3.52	1.27	—								
2. Relational judgments × identification	10.86	4.93	.80	—							
3. Instrumental judgments	3.55	1.06	.73	.69	—						
4. Pride	2.36	1.39	.33	.38	.30	—					
5. Respect	2.49	1.25	.15	.14	.16	.29	—				
6. Compliance	4.30	1.36	.30	.34	.30	.34	.16	—			
7. Extrarole	—[a]	—[a]	—[a]	—[a]	—[a]	—[a]	—[a]	—[a]	—		
8. Commitment	—[a]	—[a]	—[a]	—[a]	—[a]	—[a]	—[a]	—[a]	—[a]	—	
9. Self-esteem	2.40	0.95	.05	.03	.04	.12	.35	—[a]	—[a]	.02	—

[a] Variable was not included in the data set.

Motives for Group Membership and Intergroup Behavior

In this section we ask why people engage in intergroup behavior, and perhaps
more fundamentally why people identify with groups—what motivates intergroup
behavior? There are many answers to this question, as many answers as there are
perspectives on intergroup relations. For instance, personality approaches like
Adorno et al.'s (1950) authoritarian personality, or Rokeach's (1948, 1960)
dogmatic personality (see Part 1 of this volume) suggest that discrimination is a
consequence of people's motivation to compartmentalize their social world, and in
the case of authoritarianism, to displace negative feelings onto lower status
outgroups. Functional theories, like that of Sherif (1958, see Part 2 of this volume),
argue that goal achievement is an instrumental motivation behind most behavior
and that the nature of intergroup behavior depends on the goal relations between
groups. Theories of why people affiliate have produced a range of motives, of
which social reality testing through social comparison is an important one (e.g.,
Festinger, 1954)—people come together with similar others in order to obtain
validation from individual others for their perceptions, attitudes, and feelings.
Finally, there is a plethora of motivational accounts for why people construe
themselves in particular ways (see Sedikides & Strube, 1997).

Social categorization research tends to focus on contextual factors that cause
us to categorize ourselves and others in particular ways, and on the consequences
of categorizing in that way. Other intergroup researchers ask questions dealing
directly with what motivates intergroup behavior, self-categorization, and the
particular form taken by intergroup behavior. People may be motivated by self-
enhancement (Abrams & Hogg, 1988; Hogg & Abrams, 1990, 1993; Long &

Spears, 1997), terror management (e.g., Greenberg, Solomon, & Pyszczynski, 1997), a search for an optimally distinctive self-conceptualization (Abrams, 1994; Abrams & Hogg, 2001; Brewer, 1991), or perhaps a need to reduce subjective uncertainty (e.g., Hogg, 2000; Hogg & Mullin, 1999).

Our first reading is by Dominic Abrams, at the University of Kent, and Michael Hogg, at the University of Queensland. This article (Abrams & Hogg, 1988) carefully draws out the implications, at the individual level, of the idea that intergroup behavior is motivated by a struggle between groups for evaluatively positive distinctiveness and favorable social identity. Abrams and Hogg suggest that there are two corollaries of this idea—one being that intergroup discrimination raises self-esteem, and the other that lowered self-esteem should motivate people to socially identify and to discriminate. The article critically assesses these corollaries and suggests that self-esteem may only be one motivational dimension of intergroup relations.

Our second reading is by Marilynn Brewer, at Ohio State University, who describes her theory of optimal distinctiveness. Brewer (1991) argues that people are driven by contrasting motives for assimilation/inclusiveness (e.g., being the same as other people), and for differentiation/uniqueness (e.g., being different from other people). It is a hydraulic model insofar as over-satisfaction of one motive engages the contrasting motive to reinstate

optimal distinctiveness as an equilibrium state. Intergroup contexts in which the ingroup is not overly large satisfy optimal distinctiveness—assimilation within the ingroup and differentiation between groups. Thus, social identity and intergroup behavior are the manifestation of a psychological trade-off between motives for assimilation and differentiation.

Although it is important to understand the basic motives that may produce groups and intergroup behavior, it is also important to understand the motivations behind different types of intergroup behavior. Our third reading, by Kathleen Ethier, at Yale University, and Kay Deaux, at the City University of New York, explores the role of identity threat (Ethier & Deaux, 1994). Intergroup contexts can pose a threat to self-conceptualization, that can motivate people to respond in particular ways in order to deflect or dampen the threat. Ethier and Deaux studied Hispanic students' ethnic identity as they moved to university and thus became relatively detached from the original support system that might have anchored their identity. The idea being explored is that a threat to identity will evoke a different response depending on the subjective importance of the identity—important identities will be retained and "re-moored" in the new social context even if their valence is under threat, whereas less important identities that are under valence threat are more likely to be gradually forsaken in order to avoid the lowered self-esteem implications.

Discussion Questions

1. What are the psychological benefits and costs of group membership?
2. What is the role of self-evaluation in intergroup behavior?
3. Are people ever altruistic in intergroup situations?
4. Aside from self-enhancement and self-protection, what psychological processes motivate people's behavior as group members?

Suggested Readings

Branscombe, N. R., & Wann, D. L. (1994). Collective self-esteem consequences of outgroup derogation when a valued social identity is on trial. *European Journal of Social Psychology, 24,* 641–657. A well-cited discussion of self-esteem and intergroup relations in the context of social identity threat.

Crocker, J., & Major, B. (1989). Social stigma and self-esteem: The self-protective properties of stigma. *Psychological Review, 96,* 608–630. Detailed analysis of disadvantage as stigma.

Hogg, M. A. (2000). Subjective uncertainty reduction through self-categorization: A motivational theory of social identity processes. *European Review of Social Psychology, 11,* 223–255. A very recent article that explores the possibility that a critical reason why people join groups is to reduce uncertainty about themselves, how they relate to others, and how they and others should behave.

Luhtanen, R., & Crocker, J. (1992). A collective self-esteem scale: Self-evaluation of one's social identity. *Personality and Social Psychology Bulletin, 18,* 302–318. A well-cited example of Crocker's analysis of the relationship between self-esteem, social identity, and intergroup behavior.

Rubin, M., & Hewstone, M. (1998). Social identity theory's self-esteem hypothesis: A review and some suggestions for clarification. *Personality and Social Psychology Review, 2,* 40–62. A recent and balanced assessment of the self-esteem hypothesis—that people identify with groups and discriminate between groups in order to protect or enhance their self-esteem.

Sedikides, C., & Strube, M. J. (1997). Self-evaluation: To thine own self be good, to thine own self be sure, to thine own self be true, and to thine own self be better. In M. P. Zanna (Ed.), *Advances in experimental social psychology* (vol 29, pp. 209–296). New York: Academic Press. A detailed analysis of the diversity of motivations that can drive self-construal.

Steele, C. M., & Aronson, J. (1995). Stereotype threat and the intellectual test performance of African Americans. *Journal of Personality and Social Psychology, 69,* 797–811. An analysis of the effect of identity threat on motivation to perform specific activities.

Comments on the Motivational Status of Self-Esteem in Social Identity and Intergroup Discrimination

Dominic Abrams • The University, Dundee

Michael A. Hogg • University of Melbourne

The background and development of motivational hypotheses in social identity theory are examined, revealing two general motives for intergroup discrimination: a desire for cognitive coherence, or good structure; and a need for positive self-esteem. The latter (self-esteem hypothesis: SEH) has received most attention. Both the theoretical and empirical bases of the SEH are largely rooted in research using the minimal group paradigm. However, it remains unclear whether self-esteem is to be considered primarily as a cause or an effect of discrimination. When real social groups are considered the SEH appears to provide only a partial explanation, and a variety of more or less powerful alternative social motives may underlie discriminatory behaviour. We explore some social-structural, individual and interpersonal limits to the SEH, and we call for an awareness of these motives and a re-examination of the good-structure thesis. The SEH, as it stands, provides only a partial contribution to our understanding of the relationship between social identity and discriminatory intergroup behaviour.

Introduction

The social identity approach to intergroup relations and group processes (Tajfel, 1978, 1982; Tajfel & Turner, 1979; Turner, 1981, 1982; see Hogg & Abrams, 1988) embodies an important and far reaching proposition that intergroup discrimination is motivated by individuals' desire to achieve and maintain positive self-esteem. In making an ingroup psychologically positively distinctive from an outgroup, one's self-image as a group member is thereby enhanced. Our purpose in writing this paper is to explore the ramifications of what we shall term the "self-esteem hypothesis"

(SEH), for theory and research on social identity. Although the hypothesis has been specifically applied to the desire for positive distinctiveness, that desire is itself predicated upon a need for positive self-esteem. We intend to concentrate only on the following points (i) self-esteem is not the only motivation specified by Tajfel and Turner's (1979) theory; (ii) the SEH is unclearly stated, and is hence difficult to test; (iii) the operationalization of "self-esteem" may be of key import when conducting such tests; (iv) it may be useful to draw a distinction between minimal and real group contexts when applying the SEH; (v) that social-structural relations between groups, and group members' beliefs about these relations will determine the nature of the association between discriminatory behaviour and self-esteem; and (vi) while the SEH is possibly of use as a general explanatory concept, other social motivations can be more influential in the determination of specific intergroup behaviours.

From Tajfel's early work on social perceptions and categorization the first mention of motivation is his reference to "the emotional, or if one prefers the term, value relevance of the classification to subjects" (Tajfel, 1959, p. 20). He went on to develop this idea in his (Tajfel, 1969) conceptualization of stereotyping and prejudice as a search for coherence: The "need to preserve the integrity of the self-image is the only motivational assumption we need to make in order to understand the direction that the search for coherence will take" (Tajfel, 1969, p. 92). This line of reasoning closely resembles those of balance theorists (see Abelson, Aronson, McGuire, Newcomb, Rosenberg, & Tannenbaum, 1968) in positing a need for an integrated and coherent set of cognitions (in this case, including cognitions about self), and is clearly related to the general assumption underlying contemporary social cognition that people have a need for cognitive parsimony (see Markus & Zajonc, 1985).

When the concept of social identity was introduced (Tajfel, 1972) the "coherence" view became displaced in favour of a social self-enhancement view, derived from Festinger's (1954) theory of social comparison processes. Social comparisons in intergroup settings are designed to attain a "positively, valued distinctiveness from other groups" (Tajfel 1972, p. 3), the motive is to "achieve a satisfactory concept or image of the self" (Tajfel, 1974, p. 4) through positive social identity.[1] In a formal theoretical statement by Tajfel and Turner (1979) self-esteem was explicitly referred to as a motivation behind intergroup behaviour. In their analysis of relations between large scale social groups they suggest that where low status groups acquiesce to majority rule, "the price of this has been the subordinate group's self-esteem" (p. 37). This "price" rests on the further assumption (borrowed directly from social comparison theory) that "individuals strive to maintain or enhance their self-esteem: they strive for a positive self-concept" (p. 40). It follows that groups compete, not just

for material resources, but for anything which can enhance their self-definition; i.e. for positive social identity (Oakes & Turner, 1980; Turner, 1978a, 1980, 1981, 1982 (see p. 33); Turner, Brown, & Tajfel, 1979; Turner & Giles, 1981, Chap. 1).

We have identified two themes in the account of motivation in the literature on social identity; one for cognitive coherence (which is effectively positive), and the other for an evaluatively positive self-concept. We shall investigate the latter, since it has predominated in the literature, before widening our discussion to embrace the former.

The Oakes and Turner (1980) Experiment

The SEH was initially tested by Oakes and Turner (1980), and it is worth considering their experiment again. They adopted Tajfel, Billig, Bundy, and Flament's (1971) minimal group paradigm in which subjects are divided into two groups (merely labelled X-group and Y-group) on the basis of an ad-hoc and trivial criterion. Within this paradigm it is commonly found that subjects allocate money or points in a way that favours the ingroup over the outgroup, even if such a strategy fails to optimize absolute ingroup rewards. It is also usually the case that these rewards are allocated to anonymous ingroup and outgroup members, and not directly to self (see Tajfel, 1982). The SEH was partly invoked in order to explain this apparently irrational and antinormative behaviour (Billig & Tajfel, 1973; Turner, 1980; but cf. Bornstein, Crum, Wittenbraker, Harring, Insko, & Thibaut, 1983; Branthwaite, Doyle, & Lightbrown, 1979). In Oakes and Turner's (1980) study, half of the subjects were so categorized, and were allowed to allocate rewards, while the other half merely sat, and read a newspaper. The categorized subjects displayed discriminatory behaviour, but were also found, subsequently, to have higher self-esteem than did their newspaper-reading counterparts.

We shall consider two problems with the Oakes and Turner (1980) study, both of which have theoretical and empirical ramifications. First, the re-

---

[1]Billig (1985, p. 89) believes that the introduction of a self-*evaluative* aspect was primarily to be able to explain social change: a task originally rendered problematic by reliance on the categorization process alone.

sults, as reported, can be interpreted as reflecting the self-esteem *lowering* effects of reading a newspaper article, or differential self-esteem levels contingent on inequality of psychological significance of having participated in an experiment as against having merely waited and read a newspaper to while away the time. Certainly, the self-esteem factor scores of newspaper subjects were more strongly negative than those of the categorization subjects were positive. Any replication of this experiment should probably incorporate a categorization-non-discrimination condition in order to investigate this possibility. The problem here is that self-esteem is a *relative* state rather than an absolute one, and the question is, if discriminatory intergroup behaviour does elevate self-esteem, it elevates it relative to *what?*

A second problem concerns the indices of self-esteem and their use in the Oakes and Turner study. Three valid self-esteem scales are combined by mixing the items together (mingling the scales, rather than asking subjects to respond separately to each). The consequences of this are difficult to predict, but it is unlikely that the validity of any of the scales remained intact. Furthermore, the Rosenberg Self-Esteem Scale is designed as a measure of global self-esteem, but subjects were asked to respond in terms of "how you feel at this moment." If it is possible that subjects experienced some confusion when completing these mixed format measures, there may be legitimate doubts about the interpretation of their responses as measuring self-esteem. We shall return to the issue of measurement below.

Two Self-Esteem Hypotheses

Perhaps the key problem in Oakes and Turner's test of the SEH is that the hypothesis is cast in a way which does not entirely reflect Turner's (e.g., 1982) theoretical statements. This is because the SEH can in fact be seen to embody two unstated corollaries: (i) successful intergroup discrimination will enhance social identity, and hence self-esteem (as tested by Oakes and Turner); (ii) low or threatened self-esteem will promote intergroup discrimination because of the "need" for positive self-esteem.

In other words, self-esteem is both a dependent and an independent variable in relation to intergroup behaviour: it is a product of specific forms of intergroup behaviour, as well as a motivating force for those very behaviours.

A third possibility is that, as Oakes and Turner (1980) acknowledge, self-esteem may be elevated by intergroup behaviour independently of the positive distinctiveness of social identity. Hogg, Turner, Nascimento-Schulze, and Spriggs (1986) ruled out an explanation of Oakes and Turner's results in terms of mere salience (or positive self-stereotyping as an ingroup member; also see Lemyre and Smith, 1985). When category salience and discrimination were orthogonally manipulated only the latter led to higher self-esteem (supporting corollary 1). On the other hand, Abrams (1985) found that by changing the amount of attention paid to the categorization it was possible to increase or reduce discrimination. It therefore seems likely that salience, discrimination and self-esteem are more usually bound up together.

Corollary 1

Lemyre and Smith (1985) have recently reported findings from a relatively complex minimal groups experiment designed to investigate the relationship among these variables. Briefly, it was found that "ingroup favouritism . . . restored self-esteem for categorized subjects" (p. 668), leading Lemyre and Smith to conclude that their results are "consistent with social identity theory; given categorization, discrimination in favour of ones own group results in a relative increase in self-esteem. Categorization in itself was not sufficient, nor was cognitive differentiation of the ingroup and the outgroup" (1985, p. 668). It should be noted that, while supporting corollary 1, this study does not allow a test of the motivating aspect of self-esteem (corollary 2). Lemyre and Smith themselves allude to this: "it is difficult to avoid the conclusion that we engage in ingroup formation *in order to* promote . . . well being . . . although the issue of intention has not been explicitly addressed here . . . " (p. 669).

Vickers, Abrams, and Hogg (1988) conducted a minimal group study to investigate the relationship between social categorization, intergroup discrimination, self-esteem, and local norms of cooperation. Relevant to present discusssion is the finding that subjects for whom the local norm of cooperation was salient subsequently expressed strong intergroup discrimination but experienced *lowered* self-esteem (measured on Julian, Bishop,

& Fiedler's (1966) semantic differential). Vickers et al., argue that this lowering of self-esteem is due to violation of the norm of cooperation. Here intergroup discrimination may serve to delineate groups and social identity but does not serve to enhance (or indeed to satisfy a *need* for) positive self-esteem.

Corollary 2

Corollary 2, that low self-esteem motivates intergroup discrimination is also relatively unsupported. Abrams (1982, 1983) reported two experiments in which pretested self-esteem (on Rosenberg's scale) was positively associated (*r*'s in the mid-twenties) with ingroup bias across a variety of dependent measures, thus disconfirming the hypothesis.

In an intriguing study, designed to simulate the social relations between Turks, Italians and Germans in West Germany (see Schonbach, Gollwitzer, Stiepel, & Wagner, 1981), Wagner, Lampen, and Syllwasschy (1986) constructed a three-group minimal group experiment in which one of the groups was of higher status than the others. Subjects (in a low status group) were most discriminatory against the other low status outgroup, as Tajfel and Turner would predict (see also Brown & Abrams, 1986). However, discrimination was not associated with heightened general self-esteem relative to pretest scores using Coopersmith's (1967) semantic differential measure.

Sachdev and Bourhis provide some indirect evidence from a programme of minimal group studies charting the limits of minimal group discrimination. In one experiment (1984) they varied the relative numbers of ingroup and outgroup members and predicted directly from social identity theory that "since minority group membership confers a relatively insecure and negative social identity, minorities should show more discrimination and less fairness than majorities. Discrimination . . . serves to achieve (or maintain) a positive social identity" (p. 47). The hypothesis was, by and large, unsupported: both minorities and majorities expressed comparable degrees of discrimination. In two experiments, Sachdev and Bourhis (1985, 1987) studied the effects of power inequality and status inequality, respectively and found that the greater the stable power or status the greater the discrimination. This seems to work *against* the SEH, which would predict that the *less*

the power/status, the lower the group-identity contingent self-esteem, and thus the greater the subsequent discrimination.

In their power study Sachdev and Bourhis (1985), found that "high and equal power group members reported that they felt more comfortable, satisfied and happy than lower and no power group members about their group membership" (1985, p. 430). Of course, here we cannot know whether these measures monitor self-esteem, though presumably they are related to it, nor whether they reflect power per se or the discrimination that Sachdev and Bourhis discover to be positively correlated with it. In their status study Sachdev and Bourhis (1987) explicitly acknowledge that their (almost identical) results suggest that "status per se can contribute to group members' social identities over and above the contribution made by discrimination" (p. 289), a view supported by Wagner et al.'s (1986) finding that low status groups experienced lowered self-esteem. It appears that in these modified minimal group studies the lower power/status groups resort to different behavioural and perceptual strategies to attenuate their inferiority. Discrimination may only be the strategy of groups with already relatively positive self-esteem (but see the following, and van Knippenberg, 1984) and of groups which confront each other as equals.

Another study with data on subjects' pretest self-esteem levels is by Crocker and Schwartz (1985). Subjects were divided into high and low self-esteem, on the basis of a tertile split of pretest Rosenberg scores, and then were divided into minimal groups and rated the personality of ingroup and outgroup members. Crocker and Schwartz report that although "there was a strong tendency for low self-esteem subjects to be more prejudiced in the sense of rating outgroups negatively, there was no evidence of their greater ethnocentrism or ingroup favouritism, which requires rating the outgroup negatively relative to the ingroup" (p. 383), and go on to conclude that their results "are not consistent with a self-enhancement through social comparison interpretation of ingroup favouritism effects" (p. 384).[2] Crocker and Schwartz's

---

[2] Given this reasoning, it is rather surprising that Crocker and Schwartz made no reference to social identity, the SEH, or positive distinctiveness. It should also be remarked that Crocker and Schwartz use a global rather than specific self-esteem measure. Perhaps different results may have emerged if the latter had been used.

findings have recently been replicated by Crocker, Thompson, McGraw, and Ingerman (1987).

Crocker and McGraw (1985) report an interesting field study of the relative influence of global self-esteem and group status on prejudice and ingroup favouritism. Their results reveal that lower self-esteem appears to motivate ingroup favouritism only for subjects in higher status groups. In lower status groups it is the higher self-esteem individuals who display greater ingroup favouritism. Thus the relationship between self-esteem and intergroup behaviour is clearly not a mechanical or direct one.

Crocker et al. (1987) report a minimal group study and a field study which, taken together, show that low self-esteem engenders ingroup *and* outgroup derogation rather than ingroup enhancing intergroup discrimination. It is people with high self-esteem, particularly those whose status is under threat or at risk, who indulge in discrimination. One test of both corollaries of the SEH was conducted by Hogg et al. (1986, Experiment 2). They pre-tested self-esteem (using Oakes and Turner's composite measure) and then retested after subjects had allocated points to ingroup and outgroup. The SEH predicts that low self-esteem at pre-test should promote discrimination, and should rise to a higher level by post-test. High pre-test self-esteem should attenuate or maintain discrimination (thereby maintaining a positive self-image) but need not rise or fall, by post-test. In fact, while levels of discrimination did not differ between high and low (pre-test) self-esteem subjects, lows did show a significant rise in self-esteem, whereas highs did not.

Limits to the SEH

Not surprisingly, these data provide only moderate support for the SEH. Tests of the SEH are unlikely to yield useful interpretable results until the SEH is more completely articulated and parameters placed around it. It suffers from at least two general shortcomings. First, it over-implicates self-esteem in intergroup behaviour; self-esteem can, under some conditions, be incidental or even irrelevant. The posited "need for positive self-esteem" has no more *logical* link with manifest intergroup behaviour, than does a "need for nourishment" (people do not eat outgroup members, except in certain notable cases!). Second, the term

"self-esteem" is so general as to allow considerable variation in its operationalization. For example, many of the large scale studies adopt indices of *global* self-esteem, which may indeed be predictive of intergroup attitudes. However, Tajfel and Turner's (1979) and Turner's (1982) hypothesis refers quite clearly to the esteem in which *specific* self-images are held, that is social identity-dependent self-esteem. The salience of these self-images fluctuates across situations, and thus global self-esteem measures are largely insensitive to them (Fleming and Courtney, 1984; Fleming and Watts, 1980; Wells and Marwell, 1977).

Although, as we described above, the introduction of a motive for positive self-evaluation may have helped explain social change (see Billig, 1985) and the variability of intergroup strategies at the macro-social level of analysis, the importance of the SEH in its more specific form has been its role in explaining discrimination in *minimal* group experiments (e.g. Turner 1975, 1978a,b). In these contexts it must necessarily be a transitory self-image which is made positive. Not only is there little reason to presume the effect will overflow to bathe the entire self-concept, but there is good reason to argue for its psychological containment. The debate as to whether minimal group experiments produce both normative discrimination and fairness (e.g. Billig, 1973; Bornstein et al., 1983; Branthwaite et al., 1979; Turner, 1980, 1983) attests to the fact that multiple pressures may operate. It is entirely reasonable that a personal self-image as being "equitable" would be threatened if one engaged in discriminatory behaviour in order to enhance social identity (Vickers et al. (1988) provide data consistent with this argument). However, rather than propose continual conflict between the guilty personal, and the proud social, self-images in the arena of the self-concept (resulting in neutral self-esteem?) we propose that each self-image is a discrete entity, and is only rarely likely to be dragged into conflict with others. Global self-esteem may be a reflection of the total positivity of many self-images over time, but will provide at best an insensitive indicator of short-term variations in the positivity of specific self-images.

This view is entirely in keeping with Turner's social identification model, but has not really been reflected by the methodology employed by formal tests of the SEH. Wagner et al.'s (1986) experiment also supports this view. Although global self-esteem was unrelated to discrimination, specific self-esteem related to ingroup attributes was raised following discrimination. In addition, experiments which have reported ingroup bias in terms of trait adjective ratings, affective ratings and performance evaluation ratings (e.g. Brown & Abrams, 1986) are, in effect, directly tapping the relative esteem in which subjects hold their own group. To further access self-esteem using formal scales may be merely an additional, and ironically *indirect* approach.

Social Structural Limits on the Applicability of the SEH

The discussion above has been concerned with issues which stem quite directly from research using the minimal group paradigm. In such highly controlled laboratory situations subjects may have little else to gain but self-esteem. In real group contexts the SEH may merely by *one* of a great many possibilities concerning the motives for intergroup discrimination.

Tajfel (1981, Chapters 14, 15) points out that large, stable and psychologically legitimate status differences may exist between social groups. Under such conditions, low status (minority) group members may compete with ("social change" strategy), attempt to become assimilated into ("social mobility" strategy), or may find new dimensions on which they compare favourably with (an example of "social creativity") the high status (majority) group. All of these strategies can be seen as satisfying self-esteem based motives. However, the postulation of such a motive as fundamental does not help a great deal in predicting what specific social groups do to achieve positive social identity in particular social contexts. For example, social categorization studies by Turner (1978b) and Mummendey and Schreiber (1984) were only able to predict with any accuracy the strategies used by subjects from consideration of the perceived legitimacy and stability of the status relations between the groups. In a more naturalistic laboratory study (related to Lemaine's, 1974, field work) Mummendey and Schreiber (1983) found that positive ingroup evaluation was preferentially achieved *without* indulging in relative outgroup derogation on the same comparison dimension, and that this latter strategy was only resorted to when no other alternatives were available. These findings have clear relevance for the work by Sachdev and Bourhis, and Crocker and colleagues, discussed earlier.

Where the differences between groups are highly institutionalized, and ideologically legitimized, it may be that both groups accept the status quo (cf. Hyman & Singer, 1968; Olson, Herman & Zanna, 1986; Suls & Miller, 1977), making no moves to transcend boundaries between groups. It is likely, under such conditions, that majority discrimination against the minority is also institutionalized (e.g., doctor–nurse roles, white–black status and power differentials in South Africa). If the intergroup context involves a normative and habitual pattern of discrimination, that discrimination will bear little or no relation to prior or subsequent self-esteem. Not only is self-esteem largely irrelevant in determining majority group members' behaviour, but there may be strong social sanctions against *failing* to discriminate. The obverse situation may also exist. Social norms prescribe who may not legitimately be the object of discrimination. For example, it is unlikely that abusing a physically handicapped person would be a socially viable way for non-handicapped adults to gain self-esteem, and even considering such action may provoke feelings of shame. The argument here is very much that used by Pettigrew in his classic 1958 cross-national study of the authoritarian personality. Pettigrew provided data to support his view that prejudice and discrimination is the expression of a culture of prejudice not individual psychological needs.

Beyond these formal social limits on the relationship between discrimination and self-esteem, it also seems likely that majority group members (e.g., white Britons) may not always be aware that they belong to a distinct social group (i.e. whiteness is not an informative self-categorization, cf. McGuire & McGuire, 1982). So, as the security of a majority group increases, the self-esteem of its members becomes less susceptible to the favourability of intergroup comparisons. Other social groups largely become irrelevant. Here then, intragroup social comparisons, personal aspirations to adhere to cultural norms and the position of the individual within the society defined by the group (e.g., British) may be far more immediately relevant to the individual's self-esteem than are intergroup relations (Codol, 1975). While any social categorization *may* be rendered salient in certain contexts, and need for a positive self-image may motivate subsequent intergroup behaviour it is also plausible that certain broader socio-structural factors may effectively "fix" the level of self-categorization at the interpersonal plane and thus restrict individuals' modes of self-esteem regulation. In this analysis self-esteem does not motivate intergroup discrimination, rather it is governed by real intergroup relations, either directly due to self-evaluative consequences of social identity, or indirectly due to restrictions on effective channels for achieving or maintaining self-esteem. The notion of levels of categorization comes from self-categorization theory (Turner, 1985; Turner, Hogg, Oakes, Reicher, & Wetherell, 1987), and the emphasis on the socio-structural determination of self-esteem owes much to Tajfel's (1981) concern with the esteem of the group as a *whole*. An individual's self-esteem could be plausibly associated with the esteem in which his or her group holds itself, but that, in turn, is unlikely to be a cause of intergroup behaviour, so much as an aspect of it.

But even this is problematic. It is the thorny issue of the relationship between social status and evaluation, and self-esteem. Does low status group membership mediate low self-esteem, and if so under what circumstances? Presumably it does, otherwise self-esteem cannot be a force for social change. However, the relationship, where it has been studied, is not clear. For example, Stephan (1978), reviewing evidence concerning the effects of desegregation in the United States, concluded that desegregation had no impact on black self-esteem: a point which was confirmed by Stephan and Rosenfield's (1978a) pre–post-desegregation study, in which attitudes to both ingroup and outgroup were more hostile after desegregation, although self-esteem was unaffected.

According to Rosenberg (1977) inter-racial contact can lower self-esteem among blacks because whites are a dissonant comparison reference group. On the other hand, Krause (1983) found that contact had no such effect. There is also evidence that positive self-esteem is associated with more positive racial attitudes (Rosenfield, Sheehan, Marcus, & Stephan, 1981), and that *increases* in self-esteem are associated with increasingly positive inter-racial attitudes (Stephan & Rosenfield, 1978b). While these correlational data do not disconfirm the SEH, it is possible that some third variable (e.g., social status, income) may determine both self-esteem and racial attitudes. Research on the association

between self-esteem and delinquency (Kaplan, 1980; Rosenberg, 1979) meets with similar problems, and again conclusions are hard to draw (Bynner, O'Malley, & Bachman, 1981; McCarthy & Hoge, 1984; Stager, Chassin, & Young, 1983; Wells & Rankin 1983).

Furthermore the interpretation of findings can be difficult due to inherent problems in the accurate and appropriate measurement of self-esteem. Milner concludes, in the context of British race relations, that "low self-esteem is not an automatic consequence of being black in a racist environment" (1984, p. 103), it depends upon the wider sociohistorical milieu, the more local racial context, the specific context of testing, and the age of the respondent. "Overall self-esteem may be satisfactory, but tested in inter-racial contexts in which blacks are believed to be low achievers, for example in educational institutions, inter-racial comparisons of self-esteem may disfavour blacks. In this way, much of the disparity between different research findings can be reconciled, in particular, differences between earlier and later studies (reflecting social change in the interim), and between older and younger children (reflecting both social change and individual identity development)" (Milner, 1984, pp. 103–104). A similar analysis is provided by Louden (1978). There is empirical evidence for this contextual influence on self-esteem of members of large scale allegedly lower status (and higher status) groups in the context of sex group membership, (Hogg, 1985; Hogg & Turner, 1987) and in the context of Asians and Anglo-Saxon British adolescents (Hogg, Abrams, & Patel, 1987).

In summary, *real* intergroup behaviour seems most often to be based on factors such as the distribution of wealth and power (Ng, 1982); material resources (Caddick, 1981); the nature of goal relations between groups (Brown, 1978; Brown & Abrams, 1986; Sherif, 1967); and religious or political values. Despite this self-esteem is still an important variable to consider since it is primarily a *psychological* construct, whereas those mentioned above tend to be more sociological.

Individual and Interpersonal Limits on the SEH

Social identity theorists have largely ignored the voluminous literature on self-esteem. One major issue is what effects chronic levels of self-esteem might have on an individual's negotiation of intergroup contexts. A plausible hypothesis is that individuals with low self-esteem will be psychologically less well equipped to engage in competitive intergroup behaviour.

This hypothesis is consistent both with findings reported above and with research which indicates that lowered self-esteem, depression and learned helplessness can co-occur (Beck, 1967; Abramson, Seligman, & Teasdale, 1978; Metalsky, Halbestadt, & Abramson, 1987). It may be that without what Langer (1975) calls an "illusion of control" low self-esteem people lack the initial confidence to discriminate in self-favouring ways (Alloy & Abramson, 1982). A downward spiral could then develop in which the person becomes decreasingly confident of his or her social identity, leading to a sort of discriminatory impotence. Self-esteem may therefore become increasingly depressed.[3]

Such individuals appear to lack the functional cognitive biases of those with normal self-esteem. Normal self-esteem is associated with unwarranted optimism, and viewing oneself with a rosy glow (Lewinson, Mischel, Chaplin, & Barton, 1980; Nelson & Craighead, 1977; Rozensky, Rehm, Pry, & Roth, 1977). If such self-congratulatory biases are actually indicative of a healthily operating cognitive system, it follows that, in an intergroup setting these biases might well appear as stereotyping and discrimination. Therefore, those with high self-esteem are more likely to discriminate than those with low self-esteem. The interesting prediction can also be made that low self-esteem may render individuals cognitively unable to perceive in a self-favouring way, and this cognitive deficiency will further impede elevation of self-esteem through discrimination.

Here we are referring to extremes of self-esteem. However, consistent with the principle underlying the argument, there is recent evidence that it is high self-esteem and non-depressed individuals who are more likely to engage in self-enhancing social comparisons (e.g. Crocker & Gallo, 1985; Crocker, Kayne, & Alloy, 1985; Crocker & McGraw, 1985; Crocker & Schwartz, 1985; Crocker et al., 1987, Tabachnik, Crocker, & Alloy, 1983).

Aside from the minimal intergroup context, discriminatory behaviour is usually visible to other individuals. Self-presentational concerns (Jones & Pittman, 1982; Schlenker, 1982) may well moderate the association between discrimination and self-esteem (Baumeister, 1982; Reid & Sumiga, 1984). It may be possible to elevate self-esteem not so much by discriminating, as by eliciting favourable evaluations from others. Thus, it is not only self-enhancing social comparisons with the outgroup, but also the social approval gained from ingroup members (cf. Arkin, 1981) which elevates self-esteem. A further intriguing possibility is that a person could be overtly friendly towards an outgroup member (for example at interdepartmental meetings) while psychologically and covertly positively differentiating. This scenario was also suggested by Stephenson (1981) who noted that negotiators may operate simultaneously on two levels. It is important for them to gain *interpersonal* approval in order to "win the ear" of their counterpart, but it is also crucial to *win* at an interparty level. Success in both aims will inevitably raise the negotiator's self-image at both levels.

Meaning and Coherence as Sources of Motivation

The centrality of self-esteem in social psychological theorizing (Wylie, 1979) has given rise to an emphasis on self-enhancing processes (e.g., Tesser & Campbell, 1980, 1982; Tesser & Paulus, 1983). However, both Tajfel's early work (1969, 1972), and Festinger's (1954) social comparison theory embody another primary motive—to know oneself. That is we may have a drive for "self-evaluation" per se, in addition to a need for "self-enhancement," through social comparison.

At the most human extreme, it has been proposed that individuals aspire to a state of self-enlightenment, or self-actualization (Maslow, 1954; Rogers, 1951). Any obstacle to attaining such a goal may also threaten self-esteem and the integrity of the self (Rosenzweig, 1944; Hall, 1961). Therefore, in this conception, self-esteem is a reflection of the coherence of the self, as well as its evaluative valence.

Such formulations often suffer from being

---

[3]Another related motivation concept which is of relevance is power, perhaps best captured by Nietzsche's "will to power," but see also Ng (1980) and Codol (1984). Self-esteem might be a product of successful control or of simply achieving desired goals. As is the case for "control" (Mikula, 1984) self-esteem is probably a product of what power can achieve, or of the possession of power itself.

highly individualistic. Nevertheless, the possibility of a desire to make one's experiences and one's self meaningful, what Bartlett (1932) referred to as a search after meaning, does seem to be accepted by many (e.g. Berkowitz, 1968; Katz, 1960; Reykowski, 1982) and this notion, in different guises, is an important motivational foundation of current social psychology (e.g. research into attribution, social representations and social influence). In the same vein Tajfel (1981) highlights the broadly social explanatory functions of stereotypes attached to group membership: explanations which can be internalized by individual group members through the process of self-categorization which is now posited as being responsible for group, or social identity related activity and conduct (Turner, 1985; Turner et al., 1987; also see Hogg & Abrams, 1988).[4]

Theories have also often emphasized the need for balance between different forces and components of the self (Festinger, 1957; Freud, 1922; Heider, 1958). With respect to intergroup behaviour, it is certainly possible that discrimination is produced by making consonant the characteristics ascribed to self and ingroup (Cooper & Mackie, 1983; Horwitz & Rabble, 1982). This can be theoretically understood as part of a self-categorization process which in the context of a salient social identity renders self more similar to the ingroup norm than the outgroup (Turner, 1985).

The foregoing discussion of social comparison processes has been relatively uncritical of the assumption that self-knowledge *is* gained through social comparison. However, such approaches, along with symbolic interactionist views of the self (e.g., Cooley, 1902) have been criticized for viewing self-construction as a passive, cognitive process. In particular Gecas and Schwalbe (1983), argue that people are motivated to be efficacious (cf. Bandura, 1982; McClelland, 1975; Deci, 1975) and that only through action can we know ourselves (see also Marx, 1844/1963). Their view is

that action may boost self-esteem if it occurs in valued contexts. As such, "social structural conditions enable and constrain efficacious action, influence the meanings we give to it, and are in turn reproduced by it" (Gecas & Schwalbe, 1983, p. 87). This argument is particularly relevant to intergroup behaviour. Wars give meaning to nations (Simmel, 1955) just as industrial conflicts reinforce distinctions between management and unions. Increasing group cohesiveness and distinctiveness may lead to heightened self-esteem simply by clarifying the relevant social identification, though research reviewed earlier suggests that category salience alone may not be sufficient and that action in terms of the category is necessary. So, competing in the Olympic Games may be suffcient to elevate national pride and patriotism, without necessarily winning anything. If social comparisons are relevant here they may be comparisons with one's group in the past, or with some ideal states, just as easily as with other groups (cf. Jaspars & Warnaen, 1982).

Given that both self-evaluative and self-enhancing motives may exist, it is important to address the question of which conditions favour the predominance of each. It seems that, under conditions of fear, people are more concerned with self-evaluation, at least as regards emotions (cf. Cottrell & Epley, 1977). Generally, however, self-enhancement seems dominant since people avoid self-esteem threatening situations rather than seize the opportunity to find out more about themselves (Bramel, 1962; Pepiton, 1964). Indeed, people may often prefer to compare themselves with dissimilar (worse) others, thereby gaining self-esteem, than with similar others (Brickman & Bulman, 1977; Brown & Abrams, 1986; Tesser & Campbell, 1980), contrary to Festinger's hypothesis. As mentioned above, it is also possible that self-enhancing social comparisons can be made with similar others (ingroup members) by competing in terms of displaying *normative* beliefs and behaviours (Codol, 1975). Reykowski (1982) argues that, in fact, both self-defining and self-enhancing motives are aspects of a personal meaning system, and hence, are highly related.

---

[4]Perhaps Billig's (1985) fears that, in social identity theory, categorization is associated with stability, not change would be allayed by the greater emphasis in self-categorization theory on the cognitive process of categorization than on self-esteem. The motivation here is for maximally meaningful structure, and the cognitive process which produces it is categorization. The behavioural manifestation of this process may be intergroup discrimination, acquiescence, elevated self-esteem, depressed self-esteem, in fact virtually anything. However, a *predictable* anything: predictable from socio-cultural factors and contextual variables.

Summary and Conclusions

It has been the purpose of this paper to explore the theoretical and empirical derivation of the Self-

Esteem Hypothesis in social identity theory, and the implications of the SEH for intergroup behaviour. The minimal group context does not reveal many of the social motives which may influence the behaviour of real groups, but rather, tends to encourage self-enhancing motives. Even so, the evidence for self-esteem as either a basis for or a consequence of minimal intergroup discrimination is mixed. This may be a result of methodological problems or may be because self-esteem is only indirectly associated with discrimination. A number of other mediating motives may exist, perhaps the most central of which is a need for a coherent self-conception—an idea which is consistent with Tajfel's early understanding of intergroup discrimination. Another motive which deserves attention is the search for meaning. Perhaps it is this above all else which motivates behaviour—a view consistent with assumptions underlying much of contemporary social psychology. In the intergroup context meaning may be achieved by intergroup discrimination which may enhance self-esteem, but there are many other avenues open to the seeker after meaningful structure, and there are many outcomes for the search. While categorization may be the cognitive process which maximizes meaning, the accompanying *activity* and the self-evaluative or self-conceptual outcome depends very heavily on social context.

REFERENCES

Abelson, R. P., Aronson, E., McGuire, W. J., Newcomb, T. M., Rosenberg, M. J., & Tannenbaum, P. H. (Eds.). (1968). *Theories of cognitive consistency: A sourcebook.* Chicago: Rand-McNally.

Abrams, D. (1982). *How does identity influence behaviour?* Paper presented at the Annual Conference of the Social Psychology Section of the British Psychological Society, Edinburgh, UK.

Abrams, D. (1983). *The impact of evaluative context on intergroup behaviour.* Paper presented at the Annual Conference of the Social Psychology Section of the British Psychological Society, Sheffield, UK.

Abrams, D. (1985). Focus of attention in minimal intergroup discrimination. *British Journal of Social Psychology, 24,* 65–74.

Abramson, L. Y., Seligman, M. E. P., & Teasdale, J. D. (1978). Learned helplessness in humans: critique and reformulation. *Abnormal Psychology, 87,* 49–74.

Alloy, L. B., & Abramson, L. Y. (1982). Learned helplessness, depression, and the illusion of control. *Journal of Personality and Social Psychology, 42,* 1114–1126.

Arkin, R. M. (1981). Self-presentation styles. In J. T. Tedesch (Ed.), *Impression management theory and social psychological theory.* New York: Academic Press.

Bandura, A. (1982). Self-efficacy mechanisms in human agency. *American Psychologist, 37,* 122–147.

Bartlett, F. C. (1932). *Remembering.* Cambridge, UK: Cambridge University Press.

Baumeister, R. F. (1982). A self-presentational view of social phenomena. *Psychological Bulletin, 91,* 3–26.

Beck, A. T. (1967). *Depression: Clinical, experimental, and theoretical aspects.* New York: Harper and Row.

Berkowitz, L. (1968). Social motivation. In G. Lindzey & E. Aronson (Eds.), *The handbook of social psychology,* Vol. 20 (pp. 50–135). Reading, MA: Addison-Wesley.

Billig, M. (1973). Normative communication in a minimal intergroup situation. *European Journal of Social Psychology, 3,* 339–343.

Billig, M., & Tajfel, H. (1973). Social categorization and similarity in intergroup behaviour. *European Journal of Social Psychology, 3,* 27–52.

Billig, M. (1985). Prejudice, categorization and particularization: From a perceptual to a rhetorical approach. *European Journal of Social Psychology, 15,* 79–103.

Bornstein, A., Crum, L., Wittenbraker, J., Harring, K., Insko, C. A., & Thibaut, J. (1983). On the measurement of social orientations in the minimal group paradigm. *European Journal of Social Psychology, 13,* 321–350.

Branthwaite, A., Doyle, S., & Lightbown, N. (1979). The balance between fairness and discrimination. *European Journal of Social Psychology, 9,* 149–163.

Bramel, O. (1962). A dissonance theory approach to defensive projection. *Journal of Abnormal and Social Psychology, 64,* 121–129.

Brickman, P., & Bulman, R. J. (1977). Pleasure and pain in social comparison. In J. M. Suls & R. L. Miller (Eds.), *Social comparison processes.* Washington, DC: Hemisphere.

Brown, N. J. (1978). Divided we fall: An analysis of relations between a factory workforce. In H. Tajfel (Ed.), *Differentiation between social groups.* London: Academic Press.

Brown, R. J., & Abrams, D. (1986). The effects of intergroup similarity and goal interdependence on intergroup attitudes and task performance. *Journal of Experimental Social Psychology, 22,* 78–92.

Bynner, J. M., O'Malley, P. M., & Bachman, J. G. (1981). Self-esteem and delinquency revisited. *Journal of Youth and Adolescence, 14,* 407–441.

Caddick, B. (1981). Equity theory, social identity and intergroup relations. In L. Wheeler (Ed.), *Review of personality and social psychology,* Vol. 2. London: Sage.

Codol, J. P. (1975). On the so-called "superior conformity of the self" behaviour. 20 experimental investigations. *European Journal of Social Psychology, 5,* 457–501.

Codol, J. P. (1984). Social differentiation and non-differentiation. In H. Tajfel (Ed.), *The social dimension: European developments in social psychology*, Vol. I (pp. 314–337). Cambridge University Press, and Paris: Editions de la Maison des Sciences de l'Homme.

Cooley, C. H. (1902). *Human nature and social order.* New York: Schoken Books.

Cooper, J., & Mackie, D. (1983). Cognitive dissonance in an intergroup context. *Journal of Personality and Social Psychology, 3,* 536–544.

Coopersmith, S. (1967). *The antecedents of self-esteem.* San Francisco: Freeman.

Cottrell, N. B., & Epley, S. W. (1977). Affiliation, social comparison, and socially mediated stress reduction. In J. M.

Suls & R. L. Miller (Eds.), Social comparison processes: Theoretical and empirical perspectives. Washington: Hemisphere Publishing.

Crocker, J., & Gallo, L. (1985, August). *Prejudice against outgroups: The self-enhancing effects of downward social comparisons.* Paper presented at the annual convention of the American Psychological Association, Los Angeles, CA.

Crocker, J., Kayne, N. T., & Alloy, L. B. (1985). Comparing oneself to others in depressed and nondepressed college students: A reply to McCauley. *Journal of Personality and Social Psychology, 48,* 1579–1583.

Crocker, J., & McGraw, K. M. (1985). *Prejudice in campus sororities: The effect of self-esteem and ingroup status.* Unpublished manuscript, Northwestern University, Evanston, IL.

Crocker, J., & Schwartz, I. (1985). Prejudice and ingroup favouritism in a minimal intergroup situation: Effects of self-esteem. *Personality and Social Psychology Bulletin, 11,* 379–386.

Crocker, J., Thomson, L. J., McGraw, K. M., & Ingerman, C. (1987). Downward comparison, prejudice, and evaluations of others: Effects of self-esteem and threat. *Journal of Personality and Social Psychology, 52,* 907–916.

Deci, E. L. (1975). *Intrinsic motivation,* New York: Plenum Press.

Festinger, L. (1954). A theory of social comparison processes. *Human Relations, 7,* 117–140.

Festinger, L. (1957). *A theory of cognitive dissonance.* Stanford, CA: Stanford University Press.

Fleming, J. S., & Courtney, B. E. (1984). The dimensionality of self-esteem: II. Hierarchical facet model for revised measurement scales. *Journal of Personality and Social Psychology, 46,* 404–421.

Fleming, J. S., & Watts, W. A. (1980). The dimensionality of self-esteem: some results for a college sample. *Journal of Personality and Social Psychology, 39,* 921–929.

Freud, S. (1922). *Group psychology and the analysis of the ego.* London: Hogarth Press.

Gecas, V., & Schwalbe, M. L. (1983). Beyond the looking-glass self: social structure and efficacy-based self-esteem. *Social Psychology Quarterly, 46,* 77–88.

Hall, J. F. (1961). *Psychology of motivation.* Philadelphia: J. B. Lippincott.

Heider, F. (1958). *The psychology of interpersonal relations.* New York: Wiley.

Hogg, M. A. (1985). Masculine and feminine speech in dyads and groups: A study of speech style and gender salience. *Journal of Language and Social Psychology, 4,* 99–112.

Hogg, M. A., Abrams, D., & Patel, Y. (1987). Ethnic identity, self-esteem and occupational aspirations of Indian and Anglo-Saxon British adolescents. *Genetic, Social, and General Psychology Monographs, 113,* 487–508.

Hogg, M. A., & Abrams, D. (1988). *Social identifications: A social psychology of intergroup relations and group processes.* London: Routledge.

Hogg, M. A., & Turner, J. C. (1987). Intergroup behaviour, self-stereotyping and the salience of social categories. *British Journal of Social Psychology, 26,* 325–340.

Hogg, M. A., Turner, J. C., Nascimento-Schulze, C., & Spriggs, D. (1986). Social categorization, intergroup behaviour, and self-esteem: Two experiments. *Revista de Psicologia Social, 1,* 23–37.

Horwitz, M., & Rabbie, J. M. (1982). Individuality and membership in the intergroup system. In H. Tajfel (Ed.), *Social identity and intergroup relations.* Cambridge, UK: Cambridge University Press.

Hyman, H. H., & Singer, E. (Eds.). (1968). *Readings in reference group theory and research.* New York: Macmillan.

Jaspars, J. M. F., & Warnaen, S. (1982). Intergroup relations, ethnic identity and self-evaluation in Indonesia. In H. Tajfel (Ed.), *Social identity and intergroup relations.* Cambridge, UK: Cambridge University Press.

Jones, E. E., & Pittman, T. S. (1982). Toward a general theory of strategic self-presentation. In J. Suls (Ed.), *Psychological perspectives on the self.* Hillsdale, NJ: Erlbaum.

Julian, J. W., Bishop, D. W., & Fiedler, F. E. (1966). Quasi-therapeutic effects of intergroup competition. *Journal of Personality and Social Psychology, 3,* 321–327.

Kaplan, H. B. (1980). *Deviant behaviour in defence of self.* New York: Academic Press.

Katz, D. (1960). The functional approach to the study of attitudes. *Public Opinion Quarterly, 24,* 163–204.

Krause, N. (1983). The racial context of black self-esteem. *Social Psychology Quarterly, 46,* 98–107.

Langer, E. J. (1975). The illusion of control. *Journal of Personality and Social Psychology, 32,* 311–328.

Lemaine, G. (1974). Social differentiation and social originality. *European Journal of Social Psychology, 4,* 17–52.

Lemyre, L., & Smith, P. M. (1985). Intergroup discrimination and self-esteem in the minimal group paradigm. *Journal of Personality and Social Psychology, 29,* 660–670.

Lewinson, P. M., Mischel, W., Chaplin, W., & Barton, R. (1980). Social competence and depression: The role of illusory self perception. *Journal of Abnormal Psychology, 8–9,* 203–212.

Louden, D. (1978). Self-esteem and locus of control: Some findings on immigrant adolescents in Britain. *New Community, 6,* 218–234.

McCarthy, J. D. and Hoge, D. R. (1984). The dynamics of self-esteem and delinquency. *American Journal of Sociology, 90,* 396–410.

McClelland, D. C. (1975). *Power: The inner experience.* New York: Irvington.

McGuire, W. J. and McGuire, C. V. (1982). Significant others in the self-space: Sex differences and developmental trends in the social self. In J. Suls (Ed.), *Psychological perspectives on the self.* Hillsdale, NJ: Erlbaum.

Markus, H., & Zajonc, R. B. (1985). The cognitive perspective in social psychology. In G. Lindzey & E. Aronson (Eds), *The handbook of social psychology* (Vol. 1,3rd ed., pp. 137–229). Reading, MA: Addison-Wesley.

Marx, K. (1963). *Early writings.* Bottomore, T. B. (Ed. and Trans.). New York: McGraw-Hill. (Original work published 1844)

Maslow, A. H. (1954). *Motivation and personality.* New York: Harper.

Metalsky, G., Halbestadt, L. J., & Abramson, L. Y. (1987). Vulnerability to depressive mood reaction: Toward a more powerful test of the diathesis-stress and causal mediation component of the reformulated theory of depression. *Journal of Personality and Social Psychology, 52,* 386–393.

Mikula, G. (1984). Justice and fairness in interpersonal relations: Thoughts and suggestions. In H. Tajfel (Ed.), *The social dimension: European developments in social psychology,* Vol. 1 (pp. 204–227). Cambridge University Press and Paris: Maison des Sciences de l'Homme.

Milner, D. (1984). The development of ethnic attitudes. In H. Tajfel (Ed.), *The social dimension: European developments in social psychology*, Vol. 1 (pp. 89–110). Cambridge University Press and Paris: Maison des Sciences de l'Homme.

Mummendey, A., & Schreiber, H. J. (1983). Better or just different? Positive social identity by discrimination against or by differentiation from outgroups. *European Journal of Social Psychology, 13,* 389–397.

Mummendey, A., & Schreiber, H. J. (1984). Social comparison, similarity and ingroup favouritism: A replication. *European Journal of Social Psychology, 14,* 231–233.

Nelson, R. E., & Craighead, W. E. (1977). Selective recall of positive and negative feedback, self-control behaviours, and depression. *Journal of Abnormal Psychology, 86,* 379–388.

Ng, S. H. (1980). *The social psychology of power.* London: Academic Press.

Ng, S. H. (1982). Power and intergroup discrimination. In H. Tajfel (Ed.), *Social identity and intergroup relations.* Cambridge, UK: Cambridge University Press.

Oakes, P. J., & Turner, J. (1980). Social categorization and intergroup behaviour: Does minimal intergroup discrimination make social identity more positive. *European Journal of Social Psychology, 10,* 295–301.

Olson, J. M., Herman, C. P., & Zanna, M. P. (Eds). (1986). *Relative deprivation and social comparison: The Ontario Symposium,* Vol. 4. Hillsdale, NJ: Erlbaum.

Pepitone, A. (1964). *Attraction and hostility.* New York: Atherton.

Pettigrew, T. F. (1958). Personality and socio-cultural factors in intergroup attitudes: A cross-national comparison. *Journal of Conflict Resolution, 2,* 29–42.

Reid, F. J. M., & Sumiga, L. (1984). Attitudinal politics in intergroup behaviour: Interpersonal vs. intergroup determinants of attitude change. *British Journal of Social Psychology, 23,* 335–340.

Reykowski, J. (1982). Social motivation. *Annual Review of Psychology, 33,* 123–154.

Rogers, C. R. (1951). *Client-centered therapy.* Boston: Houghton Mifflin.

Rosenberg, M. (1977). Contextual dissonance effects: nature and causes. *Psychiatry, 40,* 205–217.

Rosenberg, M. (1979). *Conceiving the self.* New York: Basic Books.

Rosenfield, D., Sheehan, D. S., Marcus, M. M., & Stephan, W. G. (1981). Classroom structure and prejudice in desegregated school. *Journal of Educational Psychology, 73,* 17–26.

Rosenzweig, S. (1944). Frustration theory. In J. M. Hunt (Ed.), *Personality and the behaviour disorders,* Vol. 1. New York: Ronald Press.

Rozensky, R. H., Rehm, L. P., Pry, G., & Roth, D. (1977). Depression and self-reinforcement in hospitalized patients? *Journal of Behaviour Therapy and Experimental Psychiatry, 8,* 35–52.

Sachdev, I., & Bourhis, R. Y. (1984). Minimal majorities and minorities. *European Journal of Social Psychology, 14,* 35–52.

Sachdev, I., & Bourhis, R. Y. (1985). Social categorization and power differentials in group relations. *European Journal of Social Psychology, 15,* 415–434.

Sachdev, I., & Bourhis, R. Y. (1987). Status differentials and intergroup behaviour. *European Journal of Social Psychology, 17,* 277–293.

Schonbach, P., Gollwitzer, P. M., Stiepel, G., & Wagner, U.

(1981). *Education and intergroup attitudes.* New York: Academic Press.

Schlenker, B. R. (1982). Translating actions into attitudes: On identity-analytic approach to the explanation of social conduct. In L. Berkowitz (Ed.), *Advances in experimental social psychology,* Vol. 15. New York: Academic Press.

Sherif, M. (1967). *Group conflict and cooperation.* London: Routledge and Kegan Paul.

Simmel, G. (1955). *Conflict and the web of group affiliations.* London: Collier-MacMillan.

Stager, S. F., Chassin, L., & Young, R. D. (1983). Determinants of self-esteem among labelled adolescents. *Social Psychology Quarterly, 46,* 3–10.

Stephan, W. G. (1978). School desegregation: an evaluation of predictions made in Brown versus Board of Education. *Psychological Bulletin, 85,* 217–238.

Stephan, W. G., & Rosenfield, D. (1978a). The effects of desegregation on race relations and self-esteem. *Journal of Educational Psychology, 70,* 670–679.

Stephan, W. G., & Rosenfield, D. (1978b). Effects of desegregation on racial attitudes. *Journal of Personality and Social Psychology, 36,* 795–804.

Stephenson, G. M. (1981). Intergroup bargaining and negotiation. In J. C. Turner & H. Giles (Eds), *Intergroup behaviour.* Oxford, UK: Blackwell.

Suls, J. M., & Miller, R. L. (Eds). (1977). *Social comparison processes.* Washington DC: Hemisphere.

Tabachnik, N., Crocker, J., & Alloy, L. B. (1983). Depression, social comparison, and the false consensus effect. *Journal of Personality and Social Psychology, 45,* 688–699.

Tajfel, H. (1959). Quantitative judgement in social perception. *British Journal of Psychology, 50,* 16–29.

Tajfel, H. (1969). Cognitive aspects of prejudice. *Journal of Social Issues, 25,* 79–97.

Tajfel, H. (1972). Social categorization (English Ms. of "La categorisation sociale"). In S. Moscovici (Ed.) *Introduction a la psychologie sociale,* Vol. 1. Paris: Larousse.

Tajfel, H. (1974). *Intergroup behaviour, social comparison and social change.* Unpublished, Katz-Newcomb lectures at University of Michigan, Ann Arbor.

Tajfel, H. (1978). Differentiation between social groups: Studies in the social psychology of intergroup relations. *European Monographs in Social Psychology,* No. 14. London: Academic Press.

Tajfel, H. (1981). *Human groups and social categories: Studies in social psychology.* Cambridge, UK: Cambridge University Press.

Tajfel, H. (1982). Social psychology of intergroup relations. *Annual Review of Psychology, 33,* 1–39.

Tajfel, H., Billig, M., Bundy, R. P., & Flament, C. (1971). Social categorization and intergroup behaviour. *European Journal of Social Psychology, 1,* 149–178.

Tajfel, H., & Turner, J. C. (1979). An integrative theory of intergroup conflict. In W. G. Austin & S. Worchel (Eds), *The social psychology of intergroup relations.* Monterey, CA: Brooks-Cole.

Tesser, A., & Campbell, J. (1980). Self-definition: the impact of the relative performance and similarity of others. *Social Psychology Quarterly, 43,* 341–347.

Tesser, A., & Campbell, J. (1982). Self-evaluation maintenance and the perception of friends and strangers. *Journal of Personality, 50,* 261–279.

Tesser, A., & Paulus, D. (1983). The definition of self: private and public self-evaluation management strategies. *Journal of Personality and Social Psychology, 44,* 672–682.

Turner, J. C. (1975). Social comparison and social identity: Some prospects for intergroup behaviour. *European Journal of Social Psychology, 5,* 5–34.

Turner, J. C. (1978a). Social categorization and social discrimination in the minimal group paradigm. In H. Tajfel (Ed.), *Differentiation between social groups: Studies in the social psychology of intergroup relations.* London: Academic Press.

Turner, J. C. (1978b). Social comparison, similarity and ingroup favouritism. In H. Tajfel (Ed.), *Differentiation between social groups: Studies in the social psychology of intergroup relations.* London: Academic Press.

Turner, J. C. (1980). Fairness or discrimination in intergroup behaviour? A reply to Braithwaite, Doyle and Lightbown. *European Journal of Social Psychology, 10,* 131–147.

Turner, J. C. (1981). The experimental social psychology of intergroup behaviour. In J. C. Turner & H. Giles (Eds), *Intergroup behaviour.* Oxford, UK: Blackwell.

Turner, J. C. (1982). Towards a cognitive redefinition of the social group. In H. Tajfel (Ed.), *Social identity and intergroup relations.* Cambridge, UK: Cambridge University Press and Paris: Maison des Sciences de l'Hommes.

Turner, J. C. (1983). Some comments on "The measurement of social orientations in the minimal group paradigm." *European Journal of Social Psychology, 13,* 351–368.

Turner, J. C. (1985). Social categorization and the self-concept: A social cognitive theory of group behaviour. In E. J. Lawler (Ed.), *Advances in group processes: Theory and research,* Vol. 2 (pp. 77–121). Greenwich, CT: JAI Press.

Turner, J. C., Brown, R. J., & Tafel, H. (1979). Social comparison and group interest in ingroup favouritism. *European Journal of Social Psychology, 9,* 187–204.

Turner, J. C., & Giles, H. (Eds.). (1981). *Intergroup behaviour.* Oxford, UK: Blackwell.

Turner, J. C., Hogg, M. A., Oakes, P. J., Reicher, S. D., & Wetherell, M. S. (1987). *Rediscovering the social group: A self-categorization theory.* Oxford, UK and New York: Blackwell.

van Knippenberg, A. (1984). Intergroup differences in group perceptions. In H. Tajfel (Ed.), *The social dimension: European developments in social psychology,* Vol. 2 (pp. 560–578). Cambridge, UK: Cambridge University Press and Paris: Maison des Sciences de l'Homme.

Vickers, E., Abrams, D., & Hogg, M. A. (1988). *The influence of social norms on discrimination in the minimal group paradigm.* Unpublished manuscript, University of Dundee, Scotland.

Wagner, U., Lampen, L., & Syllwasschy, J. (1986). Ingroup inferiority, social identity and outgroup devaluation in a modified extended minimal group study. *British Journal of Social Psychology, 25,* 15–24.

Wells, L. E., & Marwell, G. (1977). *Self-esteem: Its conceptualization and measurement.* Beverley Hills, CA: Sage.

Wells, L. E., & Rankin, J. H. (1983). Self-concept as a mediating factor in delinquency. *Social Psychology Quarterly, 46,* 11–22

Wylie, R. (1979). *The self-concept* (vols. 1 & 2, rev. ed.). Lincoln: University of Nebraska Press.

The Social Self: On Being the Same and Different at the Same Time

Marilynn B. Brewer • University of California, Los Angeles

Most of social psychology's theories of the self fail to take into account the significance of social identification in the definition of self. Social identities are self-definitions that are more inclusive than the individuated self-concept of most American psychology. A model of *optimal distinctiveness* is proposed in which social identity is viewed as a reconciliation of opposing needs for assimilation and differentiation from others. According to this model, individuals avoid self construals that are either too personalized or too inclusive and instead define themselves in terms of distinctive category memberships. Social identity and group loyalty are hypothesized to be strongest for those self-categorizations that simultaneously provide for a sense of belonging and a sense of distinctiveness. Results from an initial laboratory experiment support the prediction that depersonalization and group size interact as determinants of the strength of social identification.

In recent years, social psychologists have become increasingly "self"-centered. The subject index of atypical introductory social psychology text contains a lengthy list of terms such as *self-schema, self-complexity, self-verification, self-focusing self-referencing, self-monitoring,* and *self-affirmation,* all suggesting something of a preoccupation with theories of the structure and function of self. The concept of self provides an important point of contact between theories of personality and theories of social behavior. Yet there is something peculiarly unsocial about the construal of self in American social psychology.[1]

The *self-* terms listed above are representative of a highly *individuated* conceptualization of the self. For the most part, our theories focus on internal structure and differentiation of the self-concept rather than connections to the external world. Particularly lacking is attention to the critical importance of group membership to individual functioning, both cognitive and emotional. The human

species is highly adapted to group living and not well equipped to survive outside a group context. Yet our theories of self show little regard for this aspect of our evolutionary history. As a consequence, most of our theories are inadequate to account for much human action in the form of collective behavior. The self-interested, egocentric view of human nature does not explain why individuals risk or sacrifice personal comfort, safety, or social position to promote group benefit (Caporael, Dawes, Orbell, & van de Kragt, 1989).

Even a casual awareness of world events reveals the power of group identity in human behavior. Names such as *Azerbaijan, Serbia, Lithuania, Latvia, Estonia, Tamil, Eritrea, Basques, Kurds,*

---

[1] Here I join many other critics who have pointed to the highly individuated conceptualization of self as an ethnocentric product of the Western worldview (e.g., Caporael, Dawes, Orbell, & van de Kragt, 1989; Sampson, 1988, 1989). My point is that such a conceptualization is not adequate to an understanding of American selves either.

Welsh, and *Quebec* are currently familiar because they represent ethnic and national identities capable of arousing intense emotional commitment and self-sacrifice on the part of individuals. Furthermore, they all involve some form of separatist action—attempts to establish or preserve distinctive group identities against unwanted political or cultural merger within a larger collective entity. People die for the sake of group distinctions, and social psychologists have little to say by way of explanation for such "irrationality" at the individual level.

Social Identity and Personal Identity

It is in this context that I have been interested in the concept of social identity as developed by European social psychologists, particularly Henri Tajfel and John Turner and their colleagues from the University of Bristol (e.g., Tajfel & Turner, 1986; Turner, Hogg, Oakes, Reicher, & Wetherell, 1987). Although social identity theory has been introduced to U.S. social psychology, as a theory of self it is often misinterpreted. Americans tend to think of social identities as *aspects* of individual self-concept—part of internal differentiation. But the European conceptualization is one involving *extension* of the self beyond the level of the individual.

A schematic representation of social identity theory is presented in Figure 14.1. The concentric circles represent definitions of the self at different levels of inclusiveness within some particular domain. *Personal identity* is the individuated self—those characteristics that differentiate one individual from others within a given social context. *Social identities* are categorizations of the self into more inclusive social units that *depersonalize* the self-concept, where *I* becomes *we*. Social identity entails "a shift towards the perception of self as an interchangeable exemplar of some social category and away from the perception of self as a unique person" (Turner et al., 1987, p. 50).

The concentric circles in Figure 14.1 also illustrate the contextual nature of social identity. At each point in the figure, the next circle outward provides the frame of reference for differentiation and social comparison. To take a concrete example, consider my own identity within the occupation domain. At the level of personal identity is me as an individual researcher and teacher of social psy-

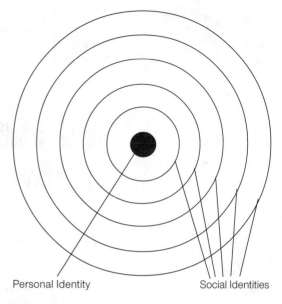

Personal Identity   Social Identities

FIGURE 14.1 ■ Personal and social identities.

chology. For this conceptualization of myself, the most immediate frame of reference for social comparison is my social psychology colleagues at UCLA. The most salient features of my self-concept in this context are those research interests, ideas, and accomplishments that distinguish me from the other social psychologists on my faculty.

My social identities, by contrast, *include* the interests and accomplishments of my colleagues. The first level of social identity is me as member of the social area within the department of psychology at UCLA.[2] Here, the department provides the relevant frame of reference, and social comparison is with other areas of psychology. At this level the most salient features of my self-concept are those which I have in common with other members of the social area and which distinguish *us* from cognitive, clinical, and developmental psychology. At this level of self-definition my social colleague and I are interchangeable parts of a common group identity—my self-worth is tied to the reputation and outcomes of the group as a whole.

A yet higher level of social identity is the De-

---

[2]The use of this particular illustration should not imply that social identity requires spatial contiguity. I also have a strong sense of identification with social psychologists all over the world who share my research specialty.

partment of Psychology within UCLA. At this level, the campus becomes the frame of reference and other departments the basis of comparison. The next level of identification is represented by UCLA as institution, with other universities providing the relevant comparison points. And, finally, there is my identification with academia as a whole, as compared with nonacademic institutions in the United States or the world.

The point to be made with this illustration is that the self-concept is *expandable and contractable* across different levels of social identity with associated *transformations* in the definition of self and the basis for self-evaluation. When the definition of self changes, the meaning of self-interest and self-serving motivation also changes accordingly.

Social Identity and Self-Esteem

In American psychology, social identity theory is associated with self-esteem. Most of the experimental research derived from the theory has focused on the consequences of being assigned to membership in a particular social group or category. Within this research tradition, category identity is imposed either by experimental instructions or by manipulation of the salience of natural group distinctions, and the emphasis is on the effect of such categorization on in-group favoritism in the service of positive self-esteem (e.g., Lemyre & Smith, 1985; Oakes & Turner, 1980). In general, social identity research has concentrated on the evaluative implications of in-group identification to the exclusion of research on why and how social identities are established in the first place (Abrams & Hogg, 1988; Doise, 1988).

Social identity should not be equated with membership in a group or social category. Membership may be voluntary or imposed, but social identities are chosen. Individuals may recognize that they belong to any number of social groups without adopting those classifications as social identities. Social identities are selected from the various bases for self-categoriation available to an individual at a particular time. And specific social identities may be activated at some times and not at others.

Available research leaves unanswered the question of the direction of causal relationship between identification and positive in-group evaluation. Do individuals select a particular social identity be-cause it has positive value or status, or does identification produce a bias toward positive in-group evaluation? In-group bias may not be a method of *achieving* self-esteem so much as an *extension* of self-esteem at the group level (Brown, Collins, & Schmidt, 1988; Crocker & Luhtanen, 1990).

Particularly problematic to self-esteem explanations of social identity are those situations in which individuals choose to identify with groups that are of low status or negatively valued by the population at large. In the real world, individuals who belong to disadvantaged minorities do not consistently reject their group identity despite its possible negative implications, nor do they suffer from excessively low self-esteem (Crocker & Major, 1989). Even though evaluative bias in favor of own-group identities may be an inevitable *consequence* of social identification, it does not fully account for the *selection* of social identities.

Optimal Distinctiveness Theory

My position is that social identity derives from a fundamental tension between human needs for validation and similarity to others (on the one hand) and a countervailing need for uniqueness and individuation (on the other). The idea that individuals need a certain level of both similarity to and differentiation from others is not novel. It is the basis of uniqueness theory, proposed by Snyder and Fromkin (1980), as well as a number of other models of individuation (e.g., Codol, 1984; Lemaine, 1974; Maslach, 1974; Ziller, 1964). In general, these models assume that individuals meet these needs by maintaining some intermediate degree of similarity between the self and relevant others.

The theory of social identity provides another perspective on how these conflicting drives are reconciled. Social identity can be viewed as a compromise between assimilation and differentiation from others, where the need for deindividuation is satisfied within in-groups, while the need for distinctiveness is met through *inter*group comparisons. Adolescent peer groups provide a prototypical case. Each cohort develops styles of appearance and behavior that allow individual teenagers to blend in with their age mates while "sticking out like a sore thumb" to their parents. Group identities allow us to be the same and different at the same time.

The model underlying this view of the function of social identity is a variant of *opposing process* models, which have proved useful in theories of emotion and acquired motivation (Solomon, 1980). Instead of a bipolar continuum of similarity-dissimilarity, needs for assimilation and differentiation are represented as opposing forces, as depicted in Figure 14.2.

As represented along the abscissa of the figure, it is assumed that within a given social context, or frame of reference, an individual can be categorized (by self or others) along a dimension of social distinctiveness-inclusiveness that ranges from uniqueness at one extreme (i.e., features that distinguish the individual from any other persons in the social context) to total submersion in the social context (deindividuation) at the other. The higher the level of inclusiveness at which self-categorization is made, the more depersonalized the self-concept becomes.[3]

Each point along the inclusiveness dimension is associated with a particular level of activation of the competing needs for assimilation and individuation. Arousal of the drive toward social assimilation is inversely related to level of inclusiveness. As self-categorization becomes more individuated or personalized, the need for collective identity becomes more intense. By contrast, arousal of self-differentiation needs is directly related to level of inclusiveness. As self-categorization becomes more depersonalized, the need for individual identity is intensified.

At either extreme along the inclusiveness dimension, the person's sense of security and self-worth is threatened. Being highly individuated leaves one vulnerable to isolation and stigmatization (even excelling on positively valued dimensions creates social distance and potential rejection). However, total deindividuation provides no basis for comparative appraisal or self-definition. As a consequence, we are uncomfortable in social contexts in which we are either too distinctive (Frable, Blackstone, & Scherbaum, 1990; Lord & Saenz, 1985) or too undistinctive (Fromkin, 1970, 1972).

In this model, equilibrium, or *optimal distinctiveness*, is achieved through identification with categories at that level of inclusiveness where the degrees of activation of the need for differentiation and of the need for assimilation are exactly equal. Association with groups that are too large or inclusive should leave residual motivation for greater differentiation of the self from that group identity, whereas too much personal distinctiveness should leave the individual seeking inclusion in a larger collective. Deviations from optimal distinctiveness in either direction—too much or too little personalization—should drive the individual to the same equilibrium, at which social identification is strongest and group loyalties most intense.

The basic tenets of the optimal distinctiveness model are represented in the following assumptions:

A1. Social identification will be strongest for social groups or categories at that level of inclusiveness which resolves the conflict between needs for differentiation of the self and assimilation with others.

A2. Optimal distinctiveness is independent of the evaluative implications of group membership, although, other things being equal, individuals will prefer positive group identities to negative identities.

A3. Distinctiveness of a given social identity is context-specifc. It depends on the frame of reference within which possible social identities are defined at a particular time, which can range from participants in a specific social gathering to the entire human race.

A4. The optimal level of category distinctiveness

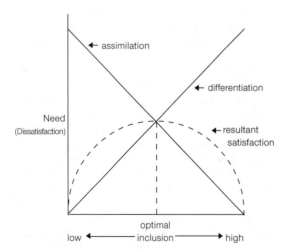

FIGURE 14.2

---

[3]In this article, the terms *deindividuation* and *depersonalization* are used more or less interchangeably, although the former refers to the identifiability of the individual to others whereas the latter refers to self-perception.

or inclusiveness is a function of the relative strength (steepness) of the opposing drives for assimilation and differentiation. For any individual, the relative strength of the two needs is determined by cultural norms, individual socialization, and recent experience.

This last assumption makes the model consistent with theories that emphasize cultural differences in definition of the self (Markus & Kitayama, 1991; Triandis, McCusker, & Hui, 1990). However, it is unlikely that any societies exist in which either the extreme of individauation or that of assimilation is optimal, except as a cultural ideal. There is a limit to the cultural shaping of fundamental human needs.

Distinctiveness and Level of Identification

The primary implication of this model of social identity is that distinctiveness per se is an extremely important characteristic of groups, independent of the status or evaluation attached to group memberships. To secure a loyalty, groups must not only satisfy members' needs for affiliation and belonging *within* the group, they must also maintain clear boundaries that differentiate them from other groups. In other words, groups must maintain distinctiveness in order to survive— effective groups cannot be too large or too heterogeneous. Groups that become overly inclusive or ill-defined lose the loyalty of their membership or break up into factions or splinter groups.

To return to the concentric circle schematic of Figure 14.1, the optimal distinctiveness model implies that there is one level of social identity that is dominant, as the primary self-concept within a domain. In contrast to theories that emphasize the prepotency of the individuated self, this model holds that in most circumstances personal identity will *not* provide the optimal level of self-definition. Instead, the prepotent self will be a collective identity at some intermediate level of inclusiveness, one that provides both shared identity with an in-group and differentiation from distinct out-groups.

Evidence for the relative potency of group identity over personal identity is available from a number of research arenas. Studies of the growth of social movements, for instance, reveal that activism is better predicted by feelings of *fraternal deprivation* (i.e., the perception that one's group is disadvantaged relative to other groups) than by feelings of personal deprivation (Dubé & Guimond, 1986; Vanneman & Pettigrew, 1972). Individual members of disadvantaged groups frequently perceive higher levels of discrimination directed against their group than they report against themselves personally (Taylor, Wright, Moghaddam, & Lalonde, 1990), but it is the former that motivates participation in collective action (Taylor, Moghaddam, Gamble, & Zellerer, 1987; Wright, Taylor, & Moghaddam, 1990).

Individuals also respond in terms of group identity when they are placed in social dilemma situations and faced with a conflict between making profit for themselves and helping to preserve a collective resource (Caporael et al., 1989). My own research in this area demonstrates that the choice subjects make is affected by the group identities available to them. If there is no collective identity, *or* if the collective is too large and amorphous, then most individuals behave selfishly, pocketing as much money as they can for themselves before the public good runs out. However, when an intermediate group identity is available, individuals are much more likely to sacrifice self-interest in behalf of collective welfare (Brewer & Schneider, 1990). When a distinctive social identity is activated, the collective self dominates the individuated self.

Recognizing the motivational properties of group distinctiveness makes sense of a number of research findings from the intergroup literature, including the seemingly paradoxical self-esteem of members of some disadvantaged minorities or deviant groups and the accentuation of small differences in intergroup stereotypes.

In a particularly relevant study, Markus and Kunda (1986) found that subjects who had been made to feel uncomfortably unique increased their self-ratings of similarity to referent in-groups but also increased their ratings of *dis*similarity to out-groups. This is exactly what would be predicted from the optimal distinctiveness model. Overindividuation should not lead to an indiscriminate preference for similarity to all other people but to a selective need for assimilation to a distinct in-group.

Effects of Group Size Versus Status

The distinctiveness of a particular social category depends in part on the clarity of the boundary that distinguishes category, membership from non-membership and in part on the number of people who qualify for inclusion. Although group size and distinctiveness are not perfectly negatively corre-lated, categories that include a vast majority of the people in a given social context are not sufficiently differentiated to constitute meaningful social groups.[4] In general, then, optimal distinctiveness theory predicts that mobilization of in-group iden-tity and loyalty will be achieved more easily for minority groups than for groups that are in the numerical majority. This prediction fits well with results of research on in-group bias and group size. In both real and laboratory groups, evaluative bi-ases in favor of the in-group tend to increase as the proportionate size of the in-group relative to the out-group decreases (Mullen, Brown, & Smith, 1990). Further, strength of identification and im-portance attached to membership in experimen-tally created groups are greater for minority than for majority categories (Simon & Brown, 1987; Simon & Pettigrew, 1990).

The effects of relative group size are more com-plicated, however, when intergroup differences in status are taken into consideration (Ng & Cram, 1988). Because minority size is often associated with disadvantages in status or power, in many contexts group distinctiveness and positive evalu-ation may be in conflict. Although membership in a high-status majority may satisfy needs for posi-tive social identity, it does not optimize distinc-tiveness. Accordingly, members of large high-status groups should seek further differentiation into subgroups, which permits greater distinctive-ness without sacrificing the positive evaluation associated with membership in the superordinate category.

Members of low-status minority groups are also faced with a conflict between positive social iden-tity and distinctiveness, but in a way that is less easily resolved than is the case for high-status majorities. On the one hand, minority individuals can dissociate themselves from their group mem-bership and seek positive identity elsewhere. This strategy, however, often violates optimal distinc-tiveness. Dissociation may be achieved either at the cost of loss of distinctiveness (e.g., "passing")

or at the cost of too much individual distinctive-ness (e.g., as a "solo" representative of a deviant group). On the other hand, minority group mem-bers can embrace their distinctive group identity, but at the cost of rejecting or defying majority cri-teria for positive evaluation (Steele, 1990). This latter strategy has particularly interesting impli-cations because once group identity has been es-tablished, disadvantage may actually enhance group loyalties rather than undermine them.

Deindividuation and Social Indentity: Initial Evidence

Data collection is just beginning on a series of re-search projects designed to test general hypoth-eses regarding the interrelationship between so-cial category distinctiveness and strength of group identification. We have already completed one laboratory experiment on the interactive effects of deindividuation and group distinctiveness as joint determinants of strength of identification with a social group or category. In this initial experiment, distinctiveness was operationalized as relative group size so that distinctive and nondistinctive groups could be studied in the same experimental context.

As in our previous research on intergroup rela-tions, we created artificial category identities in the laboratory by giving subjects a dot estimation task and then informing each of them that he or she was an "underestimator" or an "overestimator." To vary inclusiveness of the two social categories, we informed all subjects that more than and only 20% as overestimators. Thus, assignment to one of the categories meant assignment to either a majority or a minority group.

Our primary purpose in this first experiment was to determine how the preference for minority cat-egory membership is affected by loss of distinc-tiveness in the experimental context. At the outset of the experiment, we created conditions designed to alter subjects' placement on the continuum from individuated to inclusive social identity. To ma-nipulate this variable, we made use of confidenti-ality instructions that precede data collection in our experimental paradigm.

In the control condition, subjects received stan-dard assurances of confidentiality and generated an ID number that served to protect their personal identity. In the *depersonalization* condition, the

---

[4]Take as an illustration the idea of classifying persons by the number of arms they have. It is easy to imagine one-armed individuals as a meaningful social category. Having two arms, however, is not sufficiently distinctive to provide a basis for social identity, even though it is a well-defined classification.

subject was assigned an arbitrary ID number in the context of written instructions that emphasized membership in a large, impersonal category. The wording of the depersonalized instructions was as follows:

> Since in this study we are not interested in you as an individual but as a member of the college student population, we do not ask for any personal information. However, for statistical purposes we need to match up different questionnaires completed by the same person. In order to do this, we have assigned you an arbitrary code number that is to be used throughout this session. . . . We are running this study in order to assess the attitudes and perceptions of students in general. For the purposes of this study you represent an example of the average student no matter what your major is. We are only interested in the general category and not in individual differences.

By immersing the subject in the broadly inclusive category of college student, we hoped to overindulge the need for assimilation relative to the need for differentiation for most of our subjects. In accord with an opposing process model, such overindulgence should inhibit further activation of the assimilation drive and disinhibit or excite the opposing drive, resulting in devaluation of inclusive group memberships and enhanced preference for smaller, more distinctive social identities.[5]

After assignment to the overestimator and underestimator categories, subjects made a series of ratings designed to assess favoritism in their perceptions of the two social groups. In-group bias is the mean rating of the subject's own category (overestimator or underestimator) on a series of evaluative rating scales minus the rating of the out-group category on the same scales. A difference score in the positive direction constitutes one measure of strength of identification with the in-group. Figure 14.3 depicts the results for the in-group bias measure obtained from the four experimental conditions generated by the factorial combination of minority-major in-group size and initial depersonalization.

Analysis of the in-group bias measure revealed a significant interaction between the effects of depersonalization and in-group size, $F(1, 91) = 4.62$, $p < .05$. Under control conditions, subjects expressed significant ingroup bias in favor of their

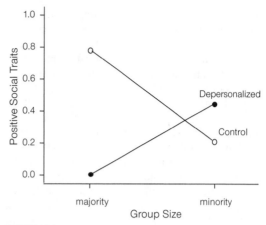

FIGURE 14.3 ■ In-group bias as a function of in-group size and depersonalization.

own group in both minority and majority conditions, but more so when the in-group was in the majority. This latter effect was somewhat surprising in light of previous research on the relationship between group size and in-group bias. Apparently in our laboratory setting, assignment to either of two mutually exclusive and distinct categories activates social identity regardless of relative group size. And in the absence of explicit information about group status, subjects may assume that majority categories are superior to minority groups.

The direction of effect of in-group size was clearly reversed, however, under conditions of deindividuation. When subjects had been exposed to depersonalizing instructions at the outset of the experiment, in-group bias was enhanced for those assigned to the minority category but virtually eliminated in the majority condition. As predicted by an opposing-process model, making subjects feel excessively depersonalized reduced valuation of identity with large social categories compared with more distinctive groups.

We are currently undertaking a series of field studies designed to parallel the laboratory experiment in a natural setting. For this purpose, we are studying student organizations at UCLA under the assumption that a large, urban university campus provides a natural deindividuated context for assessing formation of differentiated social identities. As a first step in this research, we have compiled an inventory of campus groups based on listings of student organizations registered with the

---

[5]A complete description of the full design and results of this experiment can be found in Brewer, Manzi, & Shaw, 1993.

UCLA Associated Students, which has proved to be an interesting data set in its own right. More than 425 organizations are registered, which range from social clubs (including sororities and fraternities) to interest groups based on ethnicity, religion, political positions, and sexual orientation. Both the number and the differentiation of these organizations tell an interesting story about needs for social group identification on a campus where the student body numbers more than 30,000.

The initial lab and field experiments are designed to test one side of the opposing-process model—the effects of excessive deindividuation on sensitivity to in-group size and preference for distinctive social identities. Further experiments will address the other side of the equation—the effects of too high a degree of individuation on preference for assimilation to a distinctive social category. This aspect of optimal distinctiveness theory has potential implications for the way in which people cope with being deviant or stigmatized.

The basic tenet is that excessive individuation is undesirable—having any salient feature that distinguishes oneself from everyone else in a social context (even if otherwise evaluatively neutral or positive) is at least uncomfortable and at worst devastating to self-esteem. One way to combat the nonoptimality of stigmatization is to convert the stigma from a feature of *personal identity* to a basis of *social identity*. Witness the current popularity of support groups for individuals with almost any kind of deviant characteristic or experience. Among other functions such groups serve is that of creating a categorical identity out of the shared feature. What is painful at the individual level becomes a source of pride at the group level—a badge of distinction rather than a mark of shame. Collective identities buffer the individual from many threats to self-worth, and it is time that their motivational significance is clearly recognized in social psychology's understanding of the self.

REFERENCES

Abrams. D., & Hogg, M. A. (1988). Comments on the motivational status of self-esteem in social identity and intergroup discrimination. *European Journal of Social Psychology, 18,* 317–334.

Brewer. M. B., Manzi, J., & Shaw, J. S. (1993). Ingroup identification as a function of depersonalization, distinctiveness, and status. *Psychological Science, 4,* 88–92.

Brewer, M. B., & Schneider, S. (1990). Social identity and social dilemmas: A double-edged sword. In D. Abrams & M. Hogg (Eds.), *Social identity theory: Constructive and critical advances.* London: Harvester-Wheatsheaf.

Brown, J. D., Collins, R L., & Schmidt, G. W. (1988). Self-esteem and direct versus indirect forms of self-enhancement. *Journal of Personality and Social Psychology, 55,* 445–453.

Caporael, L., Dawes, R., Orbell, J., & van de Kragt, A. (1989). Selfishness examined: Cooperation in the absence of egoistic incentives. *Behavioral and Brain Sciences, 12,* 683–699.

Codol, J-P. (1984). Social differentiation and nondifferentiation. In H. Tajfel (Ed.), *The social dimension.* Cambridge, UK: Cambridge University Press.

Crocker, J., & Luhtanen, R. (1990). Collective self-esteem and ingroup bias. *Journal of Personality and Social Psychology, 58,* 60–67.

Crocker, J., & Major, B. (1989). Social stigma and self-esteem: The self-protective properties of stigma. *Psychological Review, 96,* 608–630.

Doise, W. (1988). Individual and social identities in intergroup relations. *European Journal of Social Psychology, 18,* 99–111.

Dubé, L., & Guimond, S. (1986). Relative deprivation and social protest: The person-group issue. In J. Olson, C. P. Herman, & M. Zanna (Eds.), *Relative deprivation and social comparison: The Ontario Symposium* (Vol. 4, pp. 201–216). Hillsdale, NJ: Lawrence Erlbaum.

Frable, D., Blackstone, T., & Scherbaum, C. (1990). Marginal and mindful: Deviants in social interaction. *Journal of Personality and Social Psychology, 59,* 140–149.

Fromkin, H. L. (1970). Effects of experimentally aroused feelings of undistinctiveness upon valuation of scarce and novel experiences. *Journal of Personality and Social Psychology, 16,* 521–529.

Fromkin, H. L. (1972). Feelings of interpersonal undistinctiveness: An unpleasant affective state. *Journal of Experimental Research in Personality, 6,* 178–182.

Lemaine, G. (1974). Social differentiation and social originality. *European Journal of Social Psychology, 4,* 17–52.

Lemyre, L., & Smith, P. M. (1985). Intergroup discrimination and self-esteem in the minimal group paradigm. *Journal of Personality and Social Psychology, 49,* 660–670.

Lord, C., & Saenz, D. (1985). Memory deficits and memory surfeits: Differential cognitive consequences of tokenism for tokens and observers. *Journal of Personality and Social Psychology, 49,* 918–926.

Markus, H., & Kitayama, S. (1991). Culture and the self: Implications for cognition, emotion, and motivation. *Psychological Review, 98,* 224–253.

Markus, H., & Kunda, Z. (1986). Stability and malleability of the self-concept. *Journal of Personality and Social Psychology, 51,* 858–866.

Maslach, C. (1974). Social and personal bases of individuation. *Journal of Personality and Social Psychology, 29,* 411–425.

Mullen, B., Brown, R., & Smith, C. (1990, August). *Ingroup bias as a function of salience: The effects of proportionate ingroup size and the reality of the group.* Paper presented at the annual meeting of the American Psychological Association, Boston.

Ng, S. H., & Cram, F. (1988). Intergroup bias by defensive and offensive groups in majority and minority conditions.

Journal of Personality and Social Psychology, 55, 749–757.

Oakes, P. J., & Turner, J. C. (1980). Social categorization and intergroup behaviour: Does minimal intergroup discrimination make social identity more positive? *European Journal of Social Psychology, 10,* 295–301.

Sampson, E. E. (1988). The debate on individualism: Indigenous psychologies of the individual and their role in personal and societal functioning. *American Psychologist, 43,* 15–22.

Sampson, E. E. (1989). The challenge of social change for psychology: Globalization and psychology's theory of the person. *American Psychologist, 44,* 914–921.

Simon, B., & Brown, R. (1987). Perceived intragroup homogeneity in minority-majority contexts. *Journal of Personality and Social Psychology, 53,* 703–711.

Simon, B., & Pettigrew, T. F. (1990). Social identity and perceived group homogeneity: Evidence for the ingroup homogeneity effect. *European Journal of Social Psychology, 20,* 269–286.

Snyder, C. R., & Fromkin, H. L. (1980). *Uniqueness: The human pursuit of difference.* New York: Plenum.

Solomon, R. (1980). The opponent process theory of acquired motivation. *American Psychologist, 35,* 691–712.

Steele, C. M. (1990, August). *Protecting the self: Its role in decisions and minority involvement.* Paper presented at the annual meeting of the American Psychological Association, Boston.

Tajfel, H., & Turner, J. C. (1986). The social identity theory of intergroup behavior. In S. Worchel & W. Austin (Eds.), *Psychology of intergroup relations.* Chicago: Nelson-Hall.

Taylor, D. M., Moghaddam, F. M., Gamble, I., & Zellerer, E. (1987) Disadvantaged group responses to perceived inequality: From passive acceptance to collective action. *Journal of Social Psychology, 12,* 259–272.

Taylor, D. M., Wright, S. C., Moghaddam, E. M., & Lalonde, R. N. (1990). The personal/group discrimination discrepancy: Perceiving my group, but not myself, to be a target for discrimination. *Personality and Social Psychology Bulletin, 16,* 254–262.

Triandis, H. C., McCusker, C., & Hui, C. H. (1990). Multimethod probes of individualism and collectivism. *Journal of Personality and Social Psychology, 59,* 1006–1020.

Turner, J. C., Hogg, M., Oakes, P., Reicher, S., & Wetherell, M. (1987). *Rediscovering the social group: A self-categorization theory.* Oxford, UK: Basil Blackwell.

Vanneman, S., & Pettigrew, T. E. (1972). Race and relative deprivation in urban United States. *Race, 13,* 461–486.

Wright, S. C., Taylor, D. M., & Moghaddam, E. M. (1990). Responding to membership in a disadvantaged group: From acceptance to collective protest. *Journal of Personality and Social Psychology, 58,* 994–1003.

Ziller, R. C. (1964). Individuation and socialization. *Human Relations, 17,* 341–360.

Negotiating Social Identity When Contexts Change: Maintaining Identification and Responding to Threat

Kathleen A. Ethier • Yale University
Kay Deaux • City University of New York

The impact of change in context on identity maintenance, the implications of maintenance efforts for group identification, and the effects of perceived threats to identity on self-esteem associated with group membership are examined in a longitudinal study of Hispanic students during their lst year at predominately Anglo universities. Whereas ethnic identity is initially linked to the strength of the students' cultural background, maintenance of ethnic identity is accomplished by weakening that link and remooring the identity to the current college context. Results suggest two distinct paths by which students negotiate their ethnic identity in a new context. Students with initially strong ethnic identity become involved in cultural activities, increasing the strength of their identification. In contrast, students with initially weaker identification perceive more threat in the environment, show decreases in self-esteem associated with group membership, lowering identification with their ethnic group. The findings both support social identity theory and illustrate the need for more contextual analyses of identity processes.

Identification of oneself with other people who share common attributes is an important aspect of self-definition. Theories of social identity, developed by Tajfel (1981), Turner (1987), and others, emphasize the importance of collective membership and the significant effects that group membership can have on behavior. These behaviors include feelings of attraction toward members of the in-group, stereotypic judgments of out-group members, social influence, and preferential treatment toward the in-group (Abrams & Hogg, 1990; Hogg & Abrams, 1988; Turner, 1987).

As a number of investigators have shown, the need for and expression of social identity is not static. Brewer (1991), for example, found that the motivation to claim group membership depends on the competing needs for inclusiveness and uniqueness, whereby people seek an optimal level of distinctiveness in their choice of a collective. What particular identity is claimed can depend on situational cues that make an identity salient or that fit with one's own priorities (Deaux & Major, 1987; Oakes, 1987).

Although the presentation of self may be quite variable, it can also be argued that the self-concept is generally stable across time. Individuals not only view themselves and others in consistent terms, but they actively create social situations that support their views of themselves (Swann, 1983). Across the life span, however, there are transitions that can have significant effects on self-definition (Hormuth, 1990; Ruble, 1994). During these transitions, individuals may find it necessary to adapt in some way to changes in environmental opportunities and demands. These adaptations may involve more than momentary responses to situational pressures; rather, the new situation may elicit fundamental changes in the meaning, importance, or support that a central identity has (Deaux, 1993).

These issues of redefinition and change are particularly interesting when one considers social identity categories that are ascribed to the person, such as ethnicity or gender, and might be thought to be particularly resistant to change. The importance of ethnic identity is well documented. Within the United States, the majority of people who are demographically designated as ethnic group members subjectively claim this identity as well (Waters, 1990). Ethnic identity is embedded in a multidimensional context, related to factors such as language, cultural background, geographic region, social class, and political conflict (Christian, Gadfield, Giles, & Taylor, 1976; Giles, Llado, McKirnan, & Taylor, 1979; Giles, Taylor, & Bourhis, 1977; Giles, Taylor, Lambert, & Albert, 1976; Phinney, 1990). The importance of these links is suggested by Ethier and Deaux's (1990) finding that the strength of ethnic identity is significantly predicted by such factors as the language spoken in the home, the ethnic composition of the neighborhood, and the percentage of a student's friends who were in the same ethnic group.

If a person's group identification is supported by a particular context (Abrams, 1992; Ethier & Deaux, 1990), what happens when the person leaves that context and moves into another? According to social identity and self-categorization theories, contextual change that increases the salience of a particular identity leads to an increase in group identification (Emler & Hopkins, 1990; Oakes, 1987; Waddell & Cairns, 1986). Thus, in a study of Welsh identity, Christian et al. (1976) found that when group conflict was made salient by having subjects write essays about Welsh–English conflict, group identification was stronger.

Studies of the effect of contextual change on social identity have generally been focused on short-term situational changes (Christian et al., 1976; Haslam, Turner, Oakes, & McGarty, 1992; Waddell & Cairns, 1986). Are the issues the same for long-term contextual change? By *change in context,* we do not mean a temporary shift in situation or place (e.g., having to perform a task that has some relation to a particular social identity, or a temporary move from one environment to another). Instead, our question concerns the effects on social identity of a complete change of environment, where the former supports of an identity (e.g., contact with group members) no longer exist as the person has known them. Because we are interested in looking at long-term change, the issues may be more complex, and the predictions of social identity theory and self-categorization theory may need to be expanded.

Salience and Identity Change

Social identity theory and self-categorization theory posit that when identity is made salient, as for example by a change in context, a person will become increasingly identified with his or her group. The concept of salience can be elusive, however, particularly when dealing with long-term changes in context.

There are at least three bases on which one might make predictions about the influence of salience on group identification. First, one might posit that chronic levels of group identification would predict identity salience. Thus, those individuals who are more highly identified with their group would be more likely to experience that identity as salient, independent of situational context. In the specific context of Hispanic students entering college, we would then predict that students with a strong cultural background would be more likely to engage in activities relevant to their ethnic identification.

A second saliency prediction is based on the contrast between a student's self-definition and the current context. Thus, as the research of McGuire and his colleagues shows, people whose status (e.g., ethnicity, gender, or hair color) is a minority in their group are more likely to be aware of that characteristic than those whose status is a majority (McGuire, McGuire, Child, & Fujioka, 1978). This position would suggest that ethnicity would be equally salient for all Hispanic students entering primarily Anglo universities.

A third model of salience would consider the contrast between a student's past background and current context. If these two contexts were markedly different, salience should be greater than if there were no change. By this line of reasoning, students from primarily Hispanic neighborhoods and schools should find ethnicity more salient in the new primarily Anglo environment than students whose previous background more closely resembled their current context.

Thus, although each of these positions is consistent with the prediction from social identity theory that salience increases group identification, each proposes a different basis for determining when identity will be salient. When the change involves large-scale environments studied over an extended period of time, it must also be recognized that considerable variation exists. One specific situation within the general context (e.g., attending a relevant group meeting) may make an identity salient, whereas others (e.g., going to a history class) may not. These variations are in part dependent on individual choices and in part are a function of the opportunity structure available. Because of the possible variation in the natural environment, we would predict that individual differences in salience and identification should be particularly noticeable. As Abrams (1990) has argued, people often make choices about which course of action to follow, and social identity theory needs to take individual variation into account when considering the identitysalience relationship. Group involvement, both before the transition and in the new context, should be an important factor in determining whether an individual experiences increased salience in the new environment.

Identity Maintenance and Change

Social identity, as manifested in natural group memberships, cannot be conceptualized only as a cognitive categorization process. Rather, social identities are supported and sustained by a network of social relationships (Abrams, 1992). During times of transition, the relationship between the individual and his or her environment changes, and the person must adapt to those changes in some way (Hormuth, 1990). If a social identity is supported by a network of relationships, then one would anticipate that a change in context, for example, a change in physical location or a change in the social environment, would have some impact on identity. The ways in which the person had previously maintained the identity are no longer valid or useful in the new context, and the person must change the way in which he or she maintains the identity. Thus, in a new context, maintaining a social identity must include a process of remooring the identity to new social supports. Specifically, we hypothesize that to successfully maintain an identity in a new environment, a person must develop new bases for supporting that identity and, in the process, detach the identity from its supports in the former environment.

Because any activity expended in developing these new links implies commitment to the identity, one could also predict that the process of remooring would in turn strengthen identification with the group (Aronson & Mills, 1959). Thus, although remooring is assumed to imply a decrease in the links to previous bases of identification, it should not result in any decrease in the strength of identification itself.

Responses to Identity Threat

New environments may challenge the meaning or value of an identity. Breakwell (1986) describes a variety of situations, including the loss of employment, the loss of a spouse, and cultural conflicts, that pose threats to identity. If severe enough, threats can call into question the very existence of an identity. In other cases, the existence of the identity may not be threatened, but rather the meanings or value associated with the identity are questioned. The latter process is particularly likely when an identity is associated with membership in an ascribed category, for example, race, ethnicity, or gender. When experiencing threat to these identities, individuals are unlikely to consider abandoning the identity but may well alter the way that they feel about that identity. In other words, one's identification with the group does not change, but the self-esteem associated with that group becomes more negative. Consistent with this line of reasoning, Frable, Wortman, Joseph, Kirscht, & Kessler (1994) found that gay men who perceive more stigmatization of their group have lower self-esteem.

There has been disagreement within social identity theory concerning the consequences of lowered self-esteem. According to social identity theory, the "need for positive self-esteem" (Turner, 1982, p. 33) is a fundamental human motivation. When an identity is made salient, this need is satisfied by positive evaluation of one's own group. However, what if a positive evaluation is not possible? Tajfel (1981) would predict that, if possible, the individual would leave the group; however, a person cannot easily leave an ascribed category. Hogg and Abrams (1990) pointed out the difficulty in finding support for the self-esteem hypothesis and suggested that other self-related motives (e.g., self-consistency) might override the motive for positive self-esteem. They argued that individuals are motivated to categorize themselves in the most meaningful way as dictated by the context. This process may result in a number of behaviors, including intergroup discrimination, acquiescence, intragroup normative competition, elevated self-esteem, or depressed self-esteem, and these behaviors should be dictated by the "sociocultural and contextual factors" (p. 47). Thus, if it is not realistic to derive positive self-esteem from group membership, then other motives, such as the need to maintain a coherent and stable self-concept, could keep the individual from discarding the group membership. In other words, it might be more beneficial to live with depressed self-esteem than to lower group identification, especially if that group identification is difficult to forsake. On the other hand, if group identification is not strong, then the need for stability of the identity should also be weaker. In this case, the individual would be more likely to lower group identification to avoid further experiences of low self-esteem. In other words, the social identity theory prediction that lowered self-esteem will cause an individual to leave the group would be supported in a psychological sense, even if actual group membership could not be changed. Thus, we suggest that the relationship between self-esteem and group identification will vary depending on the importance of group membership.

In minimal group situations, like those often used in social identity research, there is probably less variation in group identification than is found in natural groups. Although individuals may respond as members of the minimal group, these reactions do not mean that their identification with the group is strong or that group membership is

central to the person. Thus, in these situations it would not be detrimental to the need for stability for the person to leave the group as a result of low self-esteem. By examining natural groups such as ethnic or racial groups in which individuals have spent their lives as group members, lived in communities with other group members, and spoken the same language as other group members, we can examine a situation in which different goals may have priority. In sum, we suggest that prior group involvement is an important factor in determining whether an individual experiences chronic salience, whether he or she becomes involved in the group in the new context, and whether he or she experiences the new context as threatening to his or her identity.

Research Questions

Ethier and Deaux (1990) explored both identity supports and perceptions of threat to ethnic identity in a study of Hispanic students who had begun their first year of university at primarily Anglo colleges. The present study extends those initial findings with a longitudinal investigation over the course of the students' first full year of college, investigating the relationships among threat, maintenance efforts, and change in a specific social identity. By interviewing the students at three times during their first year at college, we could examine the consequences for social identity in a naturally occurring situation that involves major contextual change. In so doing, we extend the range of investigation for social identity theories.

We expected these students to adapt to their new environment in several ways. First, we expected to see general trends of remooring, that is that students would change the way they supported their Hispanic identity, moving from family and home culture to group involvement at school. Second, we expected that the students would make efforts to maintain stability, so that those students who were more involved in their ethnic group would be more likely to join Hispanic groups and have Hispanic friends at the university. We also expected that group involvement would be positively related to changes in ethnic identity. Third, we considered the possibility that students would react in different ways to the new environment as a function of the strength of their ethnic identification and prior background variables and that the relationship between threat, involvement, and self-esteem would be influenced by identification and cultural background.

Method

Sample and Recruitment Procedure

Hispanic[1] first-year students at two Ivy League universities were identified through lists provided either by the Dean of Students office at the university or through the university telephone directory. Sixty-five students were telephoned and asked to participate in a study about Hispanic students in their first year of college. All students who were contacted resided on the campus. Four students declined to participate; 16 agreed but did not appear for their first scheduled interview.

Students who agreed to participate were scheduled for a first interview during late November or early December of their first semester at university. Two additional interviews were scheduled during the academic year. The second interview took place in February, shortly after students returned from the holiday break; the third was conducted in May as the students were completing their first year in college. All interviews took place in university buildings; each interview lasted approximately 45 min and was conducted in English. Students were paid $5 for their participation in each interview. Although the repeated testing necessitated keeping a record of names and questionnaires, these lists were confidential and kept separate from the data.

A total of 45 students (28 men and 17 women) participated in the first interview. Of this total, 39 students (87%) participated at both Time 1 and Time 2 and 36 students (80%) were interviewed on all three occasions. The modal age of the students was 18 years, with a range of 17 to 19 years. All of the students were of Hispanic background, but there was a mixture of nationalities. Twenty-seven of the students classified themselves as Mexican-American. Most of these students were born in the United States; however, six were born in Mexico and moved to the United States before the age of 16. Seventeen students classified themselves as Puerto Rican. Of this number, 11 were born on the mainland and six were from Puerto Rico. One student was of Spanish descent.

Measures

The key concepts measured were identity, self-esteem associated with group membership, and perceptions of threat. Each of these variables was assessed at each of the three interviews. In addition, questions concerning past and present context for ethnic identity were included at each interview.

Identity. Identity was assessed through a combination of qualitative and quantitative methods. First, to assess the pattern of identities by which individuals defined themselves, we asked each student to name all of the identities that were important to him or her. In the instructions for this task, they were given possible examples (e.g., age, gender, relationships to other people, and race or ethnicity). If any of a preestablished set of identities (Hispanic, student, son or daughter, family member, and friend) was not named voluntarily, the interviewer specifically asked the student whether he or she had these as part of the self-concept.[2] Students were then asked to list the attributes or characteristics that they associated with each identity to understand the subjective meaning that students attached to their identities. The personal significance or importance of an identity was assessed in quantitative terms with two measures. First, students were asked to rate the importance of each identity that they named on a scale of 1 (*not at all important*) to 7 (*very important*). The second measure of group identification was the identity subscale of the Collective Self-Esteem Scale (Luhtanen & Crocker, 1992), with items written to refer to Hispanic identity specifically. This scale consists of four items, including "Being Hispanic is an important reflection of who I am," and "Being Hispanic is an important part of my self-image." As reported in Ethier and Deaux (1990), coefficient alpha for this scale at Time 1 was .92. Similar alpha coefficients

---

[1] Those students who did claim this identity used a variety of terms to label themselves including *Latino, Chicana, Puerto Rican,* and *Mexican-American* in addition to *Hispanic*. Without attempting to resolve the political issues involved here, we use *Hispanic* as the more inclusive term.

[2] Although this probe increases the frequency with which a given identity is mentioned, it by no means results in universal endorsement. In our sample, 13% of the students did not claim this identity, even after being prompted.

were obtained for Times 2 and 3 (.91 and .91, respectively).

Collective self-esteem. Self-esteem can be conceptualized in terms of *personal self-esteem,* referring to a general evaluation of one's individual self, or *collective self-esteem,*[3] referring to one's membership in collective groups. In this study, we define self-esteem in collective terms, referring to one's evaluation of one's ethnic group membership. Self-esteem was assessed using the Private Acceptance subscale of Luhtanen and Crocker's (1992) Collective Self-Esteem Scale. Again, items were phrased in terms of Hispanic identity, specifically. This subscale consists of four items, including "In general, I'm glad that I'm Hispanic" and "I often regret that I am Hispanic." As reported in Ethier and Deaux (1990), coefficient alpha for this scale at Time 1 was .66. Identical alpha coefficients were obtained for Times 2 and 3.

Perceptions of threat. Perceptions of threat to one's ethnic identity were assessed by a six-item scale developed by us. This scale included items such as "I feel that my ethnicity is incompatible with the new people I am meeting and the new things I am learning" and "I can not talk to my friends at school about my family or my culture."[4] Students answered each item on a 7-point scale, indicating whether they had experienced that feeling or situation (1 = *not at all,* 7 = *a great deal*). The possible range of scores was 6 to 42; the obtained range was 6 to 41. Coefficient alpha for Times 1, 2, and 3 were .66, .82, and .72, respectively.

Ethnic involvement. At each interview, a variety of questions were asked to assess the extent of involvement with family, friends, and Hispanic culture. In the initial interview, these questions were directed at community and family background. Responses to six questions were combined to form an index termed *Strength of Cultural Background* (SCB; $\alpha = .80$). Items included in this in-

dex referred to mother's and father's birthplace, language spoken in the home, percentage of home community that was Hispanic, and percentage of Hispanic high school friends.

At the second and third interviews, questions were directed at the level of students' involvement in ethnic culture at school. At Time 2, these questions referred to involvement during the first semester, and at Time 3, they referred to involvement during the second semester. Again, composite indexes were developed. Hispanic activity consisted of two items, $rs(38) = .70$ at Time 2 and .74 at Time 3, that asked about participation in Hispanic activities at college and percentage of current friends who were Hispanic.

Results

Stability of Measures

Table 15.1 presents the means and standard deviations for each of the major variables in the study at each of the three occasions. Table 15.2 shows the correlations of each measure across the three occasions of testing. In the case of the identities, common element correlations (McNemar, 1962) were used to determine the repetition of elements across time for qualitative data. High correlations in this case indicate that students were naming a similar set of identities on the different occasions.

Table 15.1. Means and Standard Deviations of Major Variables

Variable	Time 1	Time 2	Time 3
Number of identities			
M	7.6	6.8	7.4
SD	2.4	1.8	1.6
Hispanic importance			
M	4.4	4.4	4.6
SD	2.5	2.5	2.3
Identification			
M	19.5	20.4	19.3
SD	6.4	5.6	5.5
Self-esteem			
M	24.1	23.9	23.8
SD	3.6	3.2	3.3
Perceptions of threat			
M	12.1	13.1	12.7*
SD	5.4	7.9	5.8

*$p < .06$.

---

[3]We use the term *collective self-esteem* to refer to self-esteem associated with group membership. Luhtanen and Crocker's Collective Self-Esteem Scale actually measures four different dimensions of feeling associated with group membership (membership, private acceptance, public acceptance, and identification). In the present study, we use the Private Acceptance subscale, which refers to personal feelings about the group, to index collective self-esteem.

[4]See Ethier and Deaux (1990, p. 433) for a full listing of the items of the Perceived Threat scale.

As Table 15.1 shows, there were no mean changes in the number of identities that students mentioned, the importance that they attached to their Hispanic identity, or the level of self-esteem associated with ethnic identity. Perceptions of threat to the Hispanic identity did change during the course of the year, however, $F(2, 70) = 2.91$, $p < .06$. A trend analysis shows a significant curvilinear trend in the data, $F(1, 102) = 31.25$, $p < .01$. As the means in Table 15.1 show, perceived threats were the strongest at Time 2, soon after students had returned from holiday break and were beginning the second semester, but threat did not diminish substantially over the course of the second semester.

As evident in Table 15.2, all of the measures were highly stable with the exception of self-esteem associated with group membership and, to a lesser extent, perceptions of threat. In both cases, the correlations are lowest for the longest interval of time, from early fall to late spring, as would be expected. In the case of collective self-esteem, the low correlation suggests considerable individual variation despite a constant mean level of collective self-esteem within the sample.

Characteristics of Hispanic Identity

The vast majority of the students mentioned Hispanic as one of their important identities (87%, 83%, and 86% at Times 1, 2, and 3, respectively). Although not surprising, given the explicit focus of the study, it does verify the central role that ethnicity plays for many people. Ethnicity was among the most important identities, although several others were similar in frequency of mention (e.g., student, friend, and daughter or son). In fact, both student and friend were mentioned as an identity by 100% of the students at Times 2 and 3, whereas ethnicity was still not endorsed by some

students. Furthermore, although the rated importance of Hispanic identity was stable and high, it was not as high as the rated importance of either the student identity (Ms = 5.3, 5.7, and 5.6, respectively) or the friend identity (Ms = 5.3, 5.9, and 6.0, respectively). As expected, the rated importance of Hispanic identity was significantly related to the identity subscale of the Collective Self-Esteem Scale, $r(45) = .79$, $p < .01$, at Time 1; $r(38) = .59$, $p < .01$, at Time 2; and $r(34) = .73$, $p < .01$, at Time 3.

Students used many different terms to describe their Hispanic identity. As shown in Table 15.3, at all three times, positive feelings about the group (e.g., proud, aware, and loyal) and background characteristics (e.g., culture, language, family, and tradition) were mentioned most often. Background became significantly less prominent over time (Cochran's Q = 7.05, $p < .03$), dropping from 63% and 71%, at Times 1 and 2, to 48% by the end of the year.

There is also a significant decrease (Cochran's Q = 14.0, $p < .001$) in negative feelings as well as in the use of personality attributes to characterize Hispanic identity (Cochran's Q = 18.3, $p < .001$). These qualitative changes support our view that although objective membership in the group remains stable, the subjective meaning associated with the identity is open to change.

Maintaining Identity Through Remooring

We predicted that in response to the changes in environment that the students experienced, they would change the ways in which they maintained their Hispanic identity, remooring the identity within the new context. These expectations were supported. At the beginning of the year, the importance of the student's ethnic identity was significantly related to family background, both in terms of degree of Hispanic influence, $r(43) = .42$, $p < .01$, and to the specific importance of their identity as a son or daughter, $r(43) = .30$, $p < .05$.[5] In contrast, at the second and third interviews, the link between cultural background and the strength of ethnic identification was no longer significant

Table 15.2. Stability of Variables Across Testing Occasions

Variable	Testing occasions		
	1–2	1–3	2–3
Identities named	.69	.70	.79
Hispanic importance	.75	.70	.96
Identification	.72	.82	.74
Self-esteem	.59	.42	.74
Perception of threat	.78	.58	.70

Note. N = 39 for the Occasion 1–2 comparison and N = 36 for the other comparisons.

---

[5]As reported in Ethier and Deaux (1990), the pattern of these relationships differed for men and women. General Hispanic background was the more significant predictor for men, whereas the specific parent–daughter link was more influential for women.

Table 15.3. Categories of Attributes Most Often Associated With Hispanic Identity

Category	Percentage of students		
	Time 1	Time 2	Time 3
Positive feelings about the group (e.g. proud, loyal)	57.9	51.6	51.6
Positive feelings because of membership (e.g., happy, lucky)	12.2	25.8	19.4
Others' negative reactions (e.g., prejudice)	36.8	32.3	25.8
Negative feelings (e.g., resentment, doubt)	44.7	12.9	25.8**
Active reactions (e.g., educate others)	15.8	29.0	29.0
Background (e.g., language, family)	63.2	71.0	48.4*
Personality characteristics (e.g., caring, strong)	47.4	12.9	16.1**
Identification with the group (e.g., "who I am")	21.1	38.7	32.3
Change (e.g., learning, growing)	23.7	12.9	12.9

Change over time: *p < .05.   **p < .001.

(rs = .26 and .19, respectively), suggesting that ethnic identity had been detached from its previous cultural context. The link between the importance of the identity as a son or daughter and Hispanic identity also loses its significance, although this detachment takes longer. At Time 2, ethnic identification and the importance of one's identity as a son or daughter remains important, $r(38) = .34, p < .05$. By Time 3, however, this relationship is no longer significant, $r(34) = .14, p < .25$.

Involvement with Hispanic activities on the campus appears to take the place of family background as a support for ethnic identity. At Time 2, the correlation between strength of identification and involvement in Hispanic activities during the preceding semester is significant, $r(38) = .55, p < .01$. This relation shows increased strength at Time 3, when ethnic identity is correlated with Hispanic activities during the second semester, $r(34) = .62, p < .01$.

Ethnic Involvement and Perceived Threat

Ethnic involvement played a powerful but shifting role across the students' first year at university. As a prior condition, ethnic involvement was measured by the Strength of Cultural Background

index. Initially, this background served to buffer students from perceived threats to their ethnic identity. Thus, SCB was negatively related to Perceived Threat ($r(43) = -.39, p < .01$), such that the stronger the students' cultural background, the less likely they were to perceive the new environment as threatening. Past ethnic involvement, as assessed by SCB, also predicted a student's tendency to become involved in Hispanic activities on the campus ($r(38) = .41, p < .01$). The more involved the students were in their ethnic group before the transition to college, the more likely they were to become involved in ethnic activities on campus.

The importance of these indexes of ethnic involvement to group identification is evidenced in the results of regression analyses, used to determine the influence of involvement on changes in the strength of identification. In all of the regression analyses presented here, the initial value of the dependent variable (e.g., identification at Time 2) was entered into the equation first to control for any variance in the change score that could be explained by the initial value of the variable itself. These analyses show, first, that ethnic involvement before college (as measured by SCB) was a significant predictor of changes in identification from Time 1 to Time 2 ($b = -.28, p < .05$): The stronger the students' ethnic background, the stronger the identification with the group became during the student's first semester at college. Second, ethnic involvement at the university (as measured by the Hispanic activities index) was a significant predictor of changes in identification from Time 2 to Time 3 ($b = -.65, p < .001$): The more involved the students were with their ethnic group at college, the stronger their ethnic identity became in the second semester of the year. In fact, after controlling for the initial value of identification, Hispanic activities, by itself, explained 30% of the variance in changes in identification from Time 2 to Time 3.

When ethnic involvement was not strong, the processes of identity negotiation were quite different. As suggested above, students whose ethnic involvement before college was low perceived the college environment as more threatening. Perceptions of threat, in turn, had negative effects on self-esteem. Perceived threat at Time 1 was a significant predictor of changes in self-esteem both from Time 1 to Time 2 ($b = .36, p < .01$) and from Time 2 to Time 3 ($b = .42, p < .05$). (There was no association between ethnic involvement and self-esteem.)

In support of the prediction made by social identity theory, we find that collective self-esteem at Time 2 predicts changes in identification from Time 2 to Time 3 ($b = -.32, p < .05$). Thus, if students experience low self-esteem associated with their group membership, the strength of that identification decreases. Ethnic involvement before college moderates this relationship between collective self-esteem and identification. The interaction between SCB and private acceptance significantly predicts change in identification from Time 2 to Time 3 ($b = .15, p < .05$), such that students who had lower cultural background before college and who had lower self-esteem associated with group membership showed more negative changes in identification.

Two Paths of Identity Negotiation

These results suggest that there are two quite different processes occurring as students negotiate their ethnic identity in a changed context. For students who come in with a strong ethnic background, choices are made that continue ethnic involvement and result in a strengthening of the group identification. In contrast, students with a weak ethnic background show more signs of stress with resultant lower self-esteem and negative changes in identification.

To explore this possibility further, we divided the sample into two groups, based on the initial strength of their ethnic involvement, as assessed by the SCB. Because the distribution of scores on this measure was essentially bimodal, we divided the sample at the point of separation. High ethnic involvement subjects scored between 6 and 12 on the SCB measure; low involvement subjects scored between 16 and 22.

As would be expected on the basis of the previous findings, these two groups differed significantly on their involvement in Hispanic activities at school ($t = -2.50, p < .0.1$) and in the degree of threat they perceived in the college environment ($t = 2.54, p < .01$). Students who were more ethnically involved before the transition were more likely to become involved in ethnic activities at school and were less likely to experience threats to their identity, as compared with those students who were less ethnically involved before the transition.

More interesting in terms of supporting a position that there are two distinct paths of identity

negotiation is the fact that SCB group (high vs. low) moderates the relationship between perceived threat and changes in self-esteem. The interaction between SCB group and perceived threat is a significant predictor of changes in private acceptance from Time 2 to Time 3 ($b = .20, p < .03$). Thus, those students with lower ethnic involvement before college and higher perceived threat were more likely to show negative changes in self-esteem later in the year.

Discussion

This study provides several unique insights on the process by which people negotiate a social identity when the context for enacting that identity has substantially changed. By focusing on an identity of considerable importance, that is, ethnic identity, and by tracking the students over the course of more than six months, we gained a measure of ecological validity that studies of social identity rarely attain.

One key aspect of maintaining an identity when confronted with a new environment is a process we term *remooring*. In a general sense, ethnic identity is quite stable, particularly when one considers the frequency with which the category is endorsed by the individual. (Stability is not invariant, however, as Waters [1990] has shown.) What allows this stability to be maintained, however, is the process of remooring the identity to supportive elements in the new environment. Initially, a strong ethnic identity was supported by family background, by high school friends, and by neighborhood context. With the movement to a new locale, students who wished to maintain a strong ethnic identity needed to develop a new base of support for that identity, much as Hormuth (1990) has suggested. Students in the present study did this by linking their identity to people and activities on the campus that were consistent with a Hispanic identity. It is striking that these new links did not act as a supplement to cultural background but actually replaced the earlier basis of support. We suspect that this process is particularly characteristic of identities, like ethnicity, that are not directly tied to specific role relationships.

A second important finding concerns the way in which previous group involvement shapes the individual's approach to an altered context. In this study, the students' history of ethnic involvement predicted the degree to which they made efforts to maintain their group membership. Students who came from communities with high concentrations of Hispanics, who spoke Spanish in their homes, and who had a high percentage of Hispanic friends in high school were more likely to join Hispanic organizations at college and to make friends with other Hispanic students. The students who made these efforts showed an increase in Hispanic identification; those who did not make these efforts showed a decrease in Hispanic identification.

Social identity and self-categorization theory posit that an increase in salience will lead to an increase in identification. As discussed earlier, a clear statement about salience is not easily made. One might assume that Hispanic identity would be salient for all students in this study, given their clear minority status within the college population. If so, however, not all students responded to this salience with increased group identification. Only those students for whom ethnic involvement was high initially showed the increase in identification that social identity theory would predict. The obtained pattern of results would also be consistent with an assumption of salience based on the contrast between past context and current context. From this perspective, it would again be the students from the most Hispanic backgrounds for whom ethnic identity would be most salient on the college campus.

One hesitates to infer, however, that ethnic identity was not salient for those students whose ethnic background was weaker. For these students, however, the awareness of ethnicity appears to have had negative effects, rather than the increased identification predicted by social identity theory. These findings are consistent with Abrams's (1990) contention that there may be considerable variation in people's actions once an identity is made salient. Whereas social identity theory has traditionally given little attention to individual variation, preferring to stress the common response to conditions of salience, the present results stress the need to consider more agentic possibilities by people acting in their natural environments. We have shown clearly, and indeed the finding makes a great deal of intuitive sense, that variations in the level of previous group involvement determine the effect of contextual change on ethnic identity.

A third key finding from this study involves the reaction of students to their perception that the new environment was threatening to their identity. Our results suggest that in the face of threats, evaluations associated with the identity are particularly vulnerable to negative change. Students who perceived substantial threat and ambivalence about their identity as Hispanics showed subsequent drops in self-esteem associated with that identity. Thus, perceptions of threat to ethnic identity assessed in November correlated with negative changes in collective self-esteem from early in the year to midyear and from midyear to the end of the year.

We also find strong support for Tajfel's (1981) prediction that low self-esteem associated with a particular group membership will lead the individual to move away from the group. Self-esteem associated with Hispanic identity was significantly correlated with changes in identification: Those students who evaluated their group negatively lowered their identification with the group, whereas those students who felt positively about their group showed an increase in identification.

The observation that students take one of two paths in the new environment on the basis of previous group involvement is a particularly intriguing one. As discussed earlier, these students varied in the degree to which they were involved in their ethnic group before the transition. Students with a strong cultural background were more likely to become involved in their ethnic group at college and, subsequently, to show increases in identification with that group. In contrast, students without a strong cultural background were more likely to perceive threats to their identity, to have lower self-esteem associated with that identity, and to lower their identification with the group. There could be a number of underlying reasons for this pattern. One possibility is that the students with a strong cultural background are simply continuing to manage their ethnicity in the same ways they had before. They may be responding to the upheaval of leaving home and going to college by seeking out others with similar backgrounds as a way of making themselves more comfortable. Indeed several of the students in open-ended interviews conducted at the end of the year mentioned that having a group of people who spoke the same language and had similar experiences was a benefit of being Hispanic and made adjustment to college easier for them. These highly identified students might also be more likely to use the supportive services made available by the university for minority students, such as ethnic counselors, cultural houses, and special orientations. In taking advantage of these opportunities, the highly identified students may have strengthened their identification and minimized perceptions of threat and consequent loss of self-esteem associated with group membership.

The contrasting case of students who did not come from a strong ethnic background suggests quite different events and processes. It seems quite likely that these students felt conflict about being categorized as Hispanic by the university when they themselves did not strongly identify with their ethnic group. Because they are less likely to speak the language or to come from areas densely populated by other Hispanics, they may not feel accepted by other ethnic group members, thus failing to gain the support that the group might offer. Similarly, these students might be less likely to use the ethnically oriented services that the university provides. The end result is a decrease in ethnic group identification but a drop in self-esteem associated with group membership as well. Whatever the underlying dynamics, it is quite significant that students who are more strongly identified with their ethnic group fare better during this transition than the students who are less strongly identified with the group. This finding speaks to the protective nature of group identity in situations in which the group is a numerical minority and is possibly faced with discrimination from the majority group.

Although our sample is small, the patterns are sufficiently strong to warrant confidence in the results. At the same time, we do not know how specific these phenomena are to elite private institutions in which a particular ethnic group, such as Hispanics, is such a numerical minority. When one's group is in the majority or even a substantial minority, environmental demands and opportunities could be quite different. Ethnicity might be less salient in such situations, creating fewer threats for those with weak ethnic identification and less perceived need to get involved in specific ethnic activities for those with high ethnic identification.

Beyond the specific results, this study attests to the importance of studying identity-related experience in a natural field setting over the course of time (Deaux, 1993). This approach allows us to examine the dynamics of identity work—the reinterpretation, reevaluation, and reconnection that allow identities to maintain seeming consistency over time. It also shows how theories of social identity play out with natural groups in realistic environments and how existing theories about social identity can be enriched and extended.

REFERENCES

Abrams, D. (1990). How do group members regulate their behavior? An integration of social identity and self-awareness theories. In D. Abrams & M. A. Hogg (Eds.), *Social identity theory: Constructive and critical advances* (pp. 89–112). New York: Springer-Verlag.

Abrams, D. (1992). Processes of social identification. In G. M. Breakwell (Ed.), *Social psychology of identity and the self-concept* (pp. 57–99). London: Surrey University Press.

Abrams, D., & Hogg, M. A. (1990). *Social identity theory: Constructive and critical advances.* New York: Springer-Verlag.

Aronson, E., & Mills, J. (1959). The effect of severity of initiation on liking for a group. *Journal of Personality and Social Psychology, 59,* 177–181.

Breakwell, G. (1986). *Coping with threatened identities.* London: Methuen.

Brewer, M. B. (1991). The social self. On being the same and different at the same time. *Personality and Social Psychology Bulletin, 17,* 475–482.

Christian, J., Gadfield, N. J., Giles, H., & Taylor, D. M. (1976). The multidimensional and dynamic nature of ethnic identity. *International Journal of Psychology, 11,* 281–291.

Deaux, K. (1993). Reconstructing social identity. *Personality and Social Psychology Bulletin, 19,* 4–12.

Deaux, K. (1993). Enacting social identity: Maintaining stability and dealing with change. In S. Stryker (Eds.), *Self and affect in society.*

Deaux, K., & Major, B. (1987): Putting gender into context: An interactive model of gender-related behavior. *Psychological Review, 94,* 369–389.

Emler, N., & Hopkins, N. (1990). Reputation, social identity and the self. In D. Abrams & M. A. Hogg (Eds.), *Social identity theory: Constructive and critical advances* (pp. 113–130). New York: Springer-Verlag.

Ethier, K. A., & Deaux, K. (1990). Hispanics in ivy: Assessing identity and perceived threat. *Sex Roles, 22,* 427–440.

Frable, D. E. S., Wortman, C., Joseph, J., Kirscht, J., & Kessler, R. (1994). *Predicting self-esteem, well-being, and distress in a cohort of gay men: The importance of cultural stigma and personal visibility.* Manuscript submitted for publication.

Giles, H., Llado, N., McKirnan, D. J., & Taylor, D. M. (1979). Social identity in Puerto Rico. *International Journal of Psychology, 14,* 185–201.

Giles, H., Taylor, D. M., & Bourhis, R. Y (1977). Dimensions of Welsh identity. *European Journal of Social Psychology, 7,* 165–174.

Giles, H., Taylor, D. M., Lambert, W. E., & Albert, G. (1976). Dimensions of ethnic identity: An example from northern Maine. *Journal of social Psychology, 100,* 11–19.

Haslam, S. A., Turner, J. C., Oakes, P. J., & McGarty, C. (1992). Context-dependent variation in social stereotyping: I. The effects of intergroup relations as mediated by social change and frame of reference. *European Journal of Social Psychology, 22,* 3–20.

Hogg, M. A., & Abrams, D. (1988). *Social identifications.* London: Routledge.

Hogg, M. A., & Abrams, D. (1990). Social motivation, self-esteem and social identity. In D. Abrams & M. A. Hogg (Eds.), *Social identity theory: Constructive and critical advances* (pp. 28–47). New York: Springer-Verlag.

Hormuth, S. E. (1990). *The ecology of the self: Relocation and self-concept change.* Cambridge, UK: Cambridge University Press.

Luhtanen, R., & Crocker, J. (1992). A collective self-esteem scale: Self-evaluation of one's social identity. *Personality and Social Psychology Bulletin, 18,* 302–318.

McGuire, W. J., McGuire, C. V., Child, P., & Fujioka, T. (1978). Salience of ethnicity in the spontaneous self-concept as a function of one's ethnic distinctiveness in the social environment. *Journal of Personality and Social Psychology, 36,* 511–520.

McNemar, Q. (1962). *Psychological statistics.* New York: Wiley.

Oakes, P. J. (1987). The salience of social categories. In J. C. Turner (Ed.), *Rediscovering the social group: A self-categorization theory* (pp. 117–141). Oxford, UK: Basil Blackwell.

Phinney J. S. (1990). Ethnic identity in adolescents and adults: Review of research. *Psychological Bulletin, 108,* 499–514.

Ruble, D. (1994). A phase model of transitions: Cognitive and motivational consequences. In M. Zanna (Ed.), *Advances in social psychology* (pp. 163–214). San Diego, CA: Academic Press.

Swann, W. B. (1983). Self-verification: Bringing social reality into harmony with the self. In J. Suls & A. G. Greenwald (Eds.), *Psychological perspectives on the self* (pp. 33–66). Hillsdale, NJ: Erlbaum.

Tajfel, H. (198 I). *Human groups and social categories.* Cambridge, UK: Cambridge University Press.

Turner, J. C. (1982). Towards a cognitive redefinition of the social group. In H. Tajfel (Ed.), *Social identity and intergroup relations* (pp. 1540). Cambridge, UK: Cambridge University Press.

Turner, J. C. (1987). *Rediscovering the social group: A self-categorization theory.* Oxford, UK: Basil Blackwell,

Waddell, N., & Cairns, E. (1986). Situational perspectives on social identity in Northern Ireland. *British Journal of Social Psychology, 25,* 25–31.

Waters, M. (1990). *Ethnic options: Choosing identities in America.* Berkeley: University of California Press.

Influence in Intergroup Context

Intergroup relations are marked by a struggle, not only for material resources and positive distinctiveness, but perhaps more importantly for influence. Groups try to influence one another, and intergroup contexts impact on group membership-based influence within groups. Although social influence phenomena are often viewed as occurring among individuals within a group (e.g., Asch, 1956; Sherif, 1935), they may be quite distinctly contextualized by intergroup processes and relations (e.g., Abrams, Wetherell, Cochrane, Hogg, & Turner, 1990; Turner, 1991).

For instance, intergroup comparisons can influence the context-specific defining features of ingroup membership, and thus the norm to which social influence processes cause people to conform. This idea is captured by our first reading in which Dominic Abrams, at the University of Kent, and his colleagues report a series of studies using classic social influence paradigms: Sherif's autokinetic paradigm, the Asch conformity paradigm, and the group polarization paradigm. These studies show how intergroup contexts shape the ingroup norms that people conform to through a group membership-mediated influence process (Abrams et al., 1990). People conform more to ingroup defining norms when an intergroup context is salient, and they are more influenced by fellow ingroup members than by outgroup members. In this way, intergroup relations impact on intragroup social influence processes that transform behavior.

Groups can also try to influence one another directly. Given that relations between groups are almost always marked by status and power differences, intergroup influence is often a conflict between majority and minority influence (e.g., Wood et al., 1994). Of particular interest here is how active minorities gain influence over majorities, and thus how social change can be possible (e.g., Maass & Clark, 1984; Mugny, 1982). Some research suggests that minorities that are consistent may produce deep-seated and enduring, but latent, change in majority attitudes. Inconsistent minorities are relatively ineffective, and majorities are more likely to produce surface compliance than deep-seated change. Our second reading, which is by Serge Moscovici and Bernard Personnaz (1980), at the University of Paris, tests these ideas. Moscovici and Personnaz devised an intriguing and controversial paradigm to test minority influence—a paradigm which took advantage of the fact that the chromatic afterimage of the color green (i.e., what you automatically see when the stimulus has been removed) is red/purple and of blue is yellow/orange. Participants viewed blue slides and then reported the afterimage after having been exposed to a majority that called the slide "green" or a minority that called it "green." Very generally, majority influence produced some compliance (participants called the slide green) but had no effect on the afterimage (reported as yellow/orange), whereas minority influence produced no compliance (participants called the slide blue) but did alter the afterimage (reported as red/purple). Moscovici and Personnaz present this remarkable finding as evidence for the sort of deep-seated cognitive change that minorities can have on the attitudes and perceptions of the majority, and thus their role in social change.

Discussion Questions

1. What is the relative role of majorities and minorities in bringing about social change?
2. How does intergroup context affect the influence of intragroup minorities?
3. Under what conditions are minorities influential?
4. By whom are we influenced, and when?
5. Does intragroup influence take a different form than intergroup influence?

Suggested Readings

Maass, A., & Clark, R. D. III. (1984). Hidden impact of minorities: Fifteen years of minority influence research. *Psychological Bulletin, 95,* 428–450. A detailed overview of minority influence research.

David, B., & Turner, J. C. (1999). Studies in self-categorization and minority conversion: The ingroup minority in intragroup and intergroup contexts. *British Journal of Social Psychology, 38,* 115–134. A social identity/self-categorization analysis of minority influence.

Martin, R. (1998). Majority and minority influence using the afterimage paradigm: A series of attempted replications. *Journal of Experimental Social Psychology, 34,* 1–26. A theoretical and methodological critique, and a series of studies, that question the validity of the "blue/green" minority influence paradigm.

Mackie, D. M., & Cooper, J. (1984). Attitude polarization: The effects of group membership. *Journal of Personality and Social Psychology, 46,* 575–585. An empirical study of group polarization from an intergroup perspective.

Mugny, G. (1982). *The power of minorities.* London: Academic Press. An analysis of the sorts of strategies that minorities can use to influence majorities, and the ways in which majorities may react.

Turner, J. C. (1991). *Social influence.* Buckingham, UK: Open University Press. An overview of social influence research that takes an intergroup perspective.

Wood, W., Lundgren, S., Ouellette, J. A., Busceme, S., & Blackstone, T. (1994). Minority influence: A meta-analytic review of social influence processes. *Psychological Bulletin, 115,* 323–345. Well cited meta-analysis of research on minority influence processes.

Knowing What to Think by Knowing Who You Are: Self-Categorization and the Nature of Norm Formation, Conformity and Group Polarization

Dominic Abrams • The University, Canterbury
Margaret Wetherell • The Open University
Sandra Cochrane • University of Dundee
Michael A. Hogg • University of Melbourne
John C. Turner • Macquarie University

We contrast two theoretical approaches to social influence, one stressing interpersonal dependence, conceptualized as normative and informational influence (Deutsch & Gerard, 1955), and the other stressing group membership, conceptualized as self-categorization and referent informational influence (Turner, Hogg, Oakes, Reicher, & Wetherell, 1987). We argue that both social comparisons to reduce uncertainty and the existence of normative pressure to comply depend on perceiving the source of influence as belonging to one's own category. This study tested these two approaches using three influence paradigms. First we demonstrate that, in Sherif's (1936) autokinetic effect paradigm, the impact of confederates on the formation of a norm decreases as their membership of a different category is made more salient to subjects. Second, in the Asch (1956) conformity paradigm, surveillance effectively exerts normative pressure if done by an in-group but not by an out-group. In-group influence decreases and out-group influence increases when subjects respond privately. Self-report data indicate that in-group confederates create more subjective uncertainty than out-group confederates and public responding seems to increase cohesiveness with in-group—but decrease it with out-group— sources of influence. In our third experiment we use the group polarization paradigm (e.g. Burnstein & Vinokur, 1973) to demonstrate that, when categorical differences between two subgroups within a discussion group are made salient, convergence of opinion between the subgroups is inhibited. Taken together the experiments show that self-categorization can be a crucial determining factor in social influence.

How do groups influence the decisions, beliefs and attitudes of their members? Experimental social psychology has grappled with this question for at least 50 years since Sherif (1936) first demonstrated the formation of social norms under conditions of ambiguity. We know groups constrain and direct the actions of their members, but there is considerable controversy as to how, and under what conditions, various forms of influence operate.

One approach accounts for social influence in terms of the individual's characteristics such as needs for approval and liking, to maintain individuality and for rational assessment of the social world. Social influence is presumed in this approach to result from dependence on others (Levine & Russo, 1987) for information or a positive self-image. Traditionally, social psychology has distinguished between these two kinds of dependence, providing two possible outcomes. Private acceptance of evidence about reality is contrasted with public compliance to pressure from others (Kiesler & Kiesler, 1969; but see Nail, 1986, for a more comprehensive descriptive model). People are influenced when they believe others' views to be valid and reliable, and also when they regard endorsement of those views as being socially desirable. Deutsch & Gerard (1955) have described these as informational and normative influence, respectively.

Informational influence is greatest when group members experience subjective uncertainty and objective evidence is lacking to evaluate a stimulus. In order to reduce uncertainty, individuals engage in social comparisons with other group members (Festinger, 1954; Levine & Moreland, 1986; cf. Suls & Miller, 1977). Normative influence arises when the individual's actions are open to actual (Deutsch & Gerard, 1955) or anticipated (Lewis, Langan, & Hollander, 1972) surveillance by the group. Compliance with the demands and expectations of other group members and overt agreement with their views occur because of their power to reward, punish, accept or reject individual members. Individuals who are identifiable to other group members may also feel publicly self-aware (Prentice-Dunn & Rogers, 1982), may feel pressure to conform to an explicit group norm (Froming & Carver, 1981), and may want to be accepted by the group (Fenigstein, 1979). Identifiability also increases accountability to the group, and reduces social loafing (Williams, Harkins, & Latane, 1981).

A second broad approach to social influence emphasizes the individual's self-definition as a group member (Abrams & Hogg, 1990; Hogg & Turner 1987a; Turner, 1982, 1985). It treats normative and informational influence as emanating from a single process. Accepting Moscovici (1976) and Tajfel's (1972) argument that both physical and social reality are constructed through social consensus, this perspective focuses on the psychological processes by which that consensus is understood and acted upon (Turner, 1985). When others disagree with one's opinion they exert influence by undermining the subjective validity of that opinion. But the social world is filled with dissenting voices and the question is which of these will create uncertainty? According to Turner (1985), uncertainty arises only from disagreement with those with whom one expects to agree. In particular, it is those who are regarded as members of the same category or group as oneself in respects which are relevant to judgements made in a shared stimulus situation who exert influence. Hence, social influence results from a process of self-categorization whereby the person perceives him- or herself as a group member, and thus as possessing the same characteristics and reactions as other group members. Turner (1982) terms this mode of influence, when group membership is salient, referent informational influence.

For example, individuals endorse attitudes which increase their proximity to the stereotypical group position, even in the absence of direct group pressure (Reicher, 1984), and when attention is focused on the group boundaries they strive harder to distinguish their own group from other groups (Abrams, 1985). Moreover, information is more influential when it has come from consistent in-group members than from other sources (Hogg & Turner, 1987b). This second approach stems directly from social identity theory (Tajfel & Turner, 1979; Turner, 1984; cf. Hogg & Abrams, 1988) and self-categorization theory (Turner et al., 1987).

Referent informational influence differs from normative and informational influence in the nature of the source, vehicle, enhancing conditions, and standards conformed to in influence situations (Turner, 1982). Specifically, Turner argues the source of influence rests with those who can identify criterial information concerning in-group norms (i.e. usually in-group, but occasionally out-group, members), rather than those who can reward or punish, or provide information about reality per se. The vehicle of influence is social identification (awareness of one's social identity as an in-group member) rather than group pressure or social comparison. Influence is maximized when social identity is salient rather than when behaviour is under surveillance or when the definition of physical or social reality is ambiguous. Finally, a person conforms to a *cognitive representation* of an in-group norm, based on but not necessarily synonymous with the observable behaviour of others.

The process of social categorization provides a means of dividing up the social world in a manner that renders particular groups much more influential than others (Reicher, 1984; Turner, 1982). When the self is regarded in terms of one of these social categories, a person's perception, views and feelings about the world are framed by the category. It is suggested this process underlies three phenomena which have usually attracted separate explanations in social psychology: norm formation, conformity and group polarization. In the experiments reported below we employ three classic paradigms in order to explore the contribution of referent informational influence in these domains. Since the first element in such influence is group membership, we concentrate on manipulating the salience of social categorization in all three experiments. We begin by examining Sherif's (1936) autokinetic paradigm in order to determine the minimal conditions for social influence purely in terms of group membership.

Experiment 1

Sherif demonstrated that groups spontaneously generate their own norms and frame of reference when making judgements about an ambiguous stimulus (the autokinetic illusion). Moreover, once established, this norm becomes adopted by the individual as a personal frame of reference, maintained even when the original group members are no longer present. The usual explanation is that group members need to establish the reality of their perceptions and, given the ambiguity of the stimulus, their dependence on others generates informational influence. However, Turner (1985, p. 92) has suggested it is the fact that subjects assume the illusion is objectively real, together with their expectation that they should agree—because there is usually no basis for perceivers to differ about objective reality—that lends the information its weight. Indeed, once subjects discover the autokinetic effect is merely an optical illusion, and not objectively real, mutual influence and convergence

of judgements cease (Sperling, 1946). Rather than supposing stimulus ambiguity encourages informational influence which leads to the emergence of social norms and thence group formation, Turner (1985) suggests that:

> . . . uncertainty is a social product of disagreement between people categorized as identical to self. The perception of others as an appropriate reference group for social comparison creates the shared expectations of agreement necessary for the arousal of uncertainty and mutual influence (p. 93).

Sherif's autokinetic paradigm for studying norm formation has two particular advantages. First, since it is conducted in a totally darkened room, the subjects can remain anonymous, inconspicuous and unacquainted. Under such conditions, influence on judgement is unlikely to be normative, and cannot arise through interpersonal similarity, attraction, power imbalance, self-presentation or source credibility. Second, individuals in such experiments are likely to be deindividuated (Diener, 1980). They are therefore unlikely to be concerned with their personal thoughts or feelings and will not be privately self-aware (cf. Mullen, 1983). Deindividuation in this case simply refers to a lack of behavioural regulation in terms of personal identity (Brown & Turner, 1981; Prentice-Dunn & Rogers, 1982) and does not rule out the possibility that regulation occurs at the level of self-categorized social identity (Abrams, 1984, 1985; Abrams & Brown, 1989; Reicher, 1984). Sherif's paradigm, however, cannot easily distinguish between informational and referent informational influence as it does not impose social categorization upon subjects; nor can it separate influence arising from a lack of self-regulation (i.e. the deindividuated subject merely responding to whatever cues are available) from informational influence.

In order to discover whether influence is affected by group "belongingness" we need to manipulate subjects' awareness of the judgements of other individuals in conditions where they are non-categorized compared with where they are categorized into subgroups.

Experiment 1 employed the autokinetic paradigm using sessions in which six judges observed 25 trials. Three of the judges served as confederates whose initial estimates were 5 cm greater than those of the naive subjects. There were three levels of salience of social categorization. In the control condition the difference between confederates and subjects was left implicit (by virtue of the initial behavioural divergence of the confederates). In the categorization condition subjects and confederates were given different category labels ostensibly as a part of a randomization procedure. In the grouped condition these labels were reinforced by addressing subjects and confederates entirely as members of 'H' and 'J' groups and by having them engage in a prior task as group members. Thus, the salience of social categorization increased from control to categorized to grouped conditions.

Both informational influence and deindividuation theories predict that, since norm formation is a product of mutual inter-individual informational influence, the categorization should have no effects—members of all categories should carry equal weight and contribute equally to an overall norm and frame of reference. It follows that the subjects should converge towards the confederates' estimates, irrespective of condition (as Sherif found using an uncategorized confederate and subject). In contrast, social identity and self-categorization theories predict that, if norm formation is an intragroup phenomenon based on self-categorization and referent informational influence, when category membership becomes more salient, influence will be increasingly restricted to judgements made by members of an individual's own category. Subjects should therefore establish a norm and frame of reference which contrasts with that of confederates. When the salience of social categorization is high, we should witness the simultaneous emergence of two social norms, and no convergence.

Method

DESIGN

We employed a 2 × 3 factorial design with random allocation of subjects to conditions. The first factor (role) was whether subjects served as "confederates" or as "true subjects." The second factor (salience) was the degree to which categorization was implicit (control), explicit (categorized) or reinforced (grouped).

SUBJECTS

These were 144 male and female undergraduates who were enrolled in introductory psychology at the University of Dundee and participated as a course requirement.

PROCEDURE

Subjects were randomly assigned to time slots and attended the experiment in groups of 12. On arrival at the laboratory they were told that they were to participate in an experiment on perception and, because of the nature of the apparatus, it would only be possible to conduct the experiment[1] using six people in each session. Moreover, in order to illustrate randomization procedures they would be briefed in different locations and directed at random to one of two perceptual laboratories. Following this, the "salience" of categorization manipulation was introduced. In all conditions, one experimenter escorted six of the subjects to a separate location and asked if they would act as confederates in the experiment which was to follow. There was a brief training session in which these six were divided into threes, and each three played the role of confederates and subjects. They were told that in the experiment proper the participants in each session would be given a number (1–6), and that the true subjects would be numbers 1, 2 and 3, while the confederates would be 4, 5 and 6. The task of the confederates was simply to yoke themselves to a particular subject (4 to 1, 5 to 2, and 6 to 3) and add 5 cm on to each estimate their subject gave for the first three trials, and then to maintain their estimate at ±2 cm of that for the third trial. (Thus if the subject estimated 3, 4, and 4, the confederate was to estimate 8, 9, 9 and then between 7 and 11 for all remaining trials.)[1] Meanwhile, the true subjects were simply informed about the general nature of the experiment, and were asked about the purpose of randomization procedures in research. Half of the subjects and half of the confederates were then reunited in one of the experimental laboratories, while the remainder were reunited in a second laboratory.

---

[1]Pilot research demonstrated that the apparatus and setting employed for this experiment usually result in a convergent norm of around 3–5 cm when subjects called out their estimates in groups of six. However, the range was quite large. It was therefore decided to set confederates' estimates 5 cm *greater* than true subjects so as to allow more scope for conformity and avoid a floor effect (e.g., if the initial estimates had been low). Research is currently underway employing confederates on both sides of the initial estimates of the true subjects to see if a convergence on a middle norm is obtained.

Autokinetic apparatus. Both laboratories contained six chairs numbered 1–6 in sequence. An experimenter welcomed the subjects and asked each to take a seat. It was explained that the subjects would be required to observe a point of light which would move in various directions, and to estimate the furthest distance it moved from its starting position on each trial. In order to prevent everyone calling out their estimates simultaneously, they were to call our in sequence, starting with person 1 and ending with person 6 on each trial. (At this point the salience manipulation was reinforced.) Subjects faced a large (45 × 45 cm²) black box, with a black glass screen. This was positioned on a table two metres from each chair. The box had electronic equipment mounted on top and cables extending to wall sockets. The experimenter was seated next to the box. Subjects were each provided with a pencil and a 30-page booklet, and were asked to write down their estimate for each trial on a separate page of the booklet after they had called it out. The door of the room was then closed, lights turned off, and subjects were allowed to adapt to the dark for 3 min, while the experimenter ensured that the room was completely blacked out. The front face of the box was then lowered and a pinpoint of light was turned on using a switch behind the box until all subjects confirmed that they were able to see the light. The experimenter then checked that the subjects knew what they had to do, explained there would be 25 trials of 15 s duration, and then commenced the first trial. After showing the light for 15 s, it was turned off and subjects called out their estimates in turn (true subjects, followed by confederates). On completion of the 25 trials, the laboratory lights were turned on, and the six participants were provided with a booklet of dependent measures which they completed and replaced in a sealed envelope, indicating their number and category membership (where appropriate). The true subjects were then asked whether they had any suspicions about the experiment and whether they were aware that the other three were confederates. Finally, true subjects engaged in a discussion with the confederates concerning the perceived source of influence. All subjects then returned to the main laboratory where they were debriefed on the nature of the illusion and the purpose of the experiment, and any other questions were answered.

Salience condition. The category salience manipulation was effected at three levels. In the control condition no mention was made of categories, and subjects were referred to by their personal code number (person number 1, etc.) throughout. Hence, any categorization effects in this condition were purely implicit—subjects might infer that the confederates and true subjects differed in some way because of being briefed in different locations, and might perceive them as separate because of their behavioural differentiation (cf. Doise, 1978). In the categorized condition subjects were allocated labels 'H' or 'J' in the initial briefing session (by an explicitly random procedure), supposedly as a means of determining the room in which they would participate in the experiment. In fact, H subjects were subsequently true subjects (numbers 1–3) and J subjects were confederates. Moreover, when giving their estimates of movement of the light subjects were required to preface this with their category label (e.g., H 7). Hence, categorization was explicit, was kept salient by referring to subjects only in terms of their category and by being correlated with seating position. In the grouped condition the initial allocation of subjects into categories was followed by a 1 min session of an anagram game called "Boggle." A matrix of letters was displayed on an overhead projector screen and all subjects had to make as many words out of adjacent letters as they could. The purpose of this was ostensibly to "check that there were not any differences between H group and the J group following the random division." From this point onwards subjects were only referred to as H group and J group people. Once in the experimental laboratory the procedure was similar to that in the categorized condition, except that the word "group" was used. Hence, categorization was maximally salient in that there was an explicit division into two groups, and an intergroup comparison already existed, although it was non-competitive and did not relate directly to the task at hand. At no stage in the experiment were subjects allowed to talk to one another, nor were they introduced by name. All conversation was conducted through the experimenters, and complete anonymity and confidentiality were maintained throughout.

DEPENDENT VARIABLES

The main dependent measures were the estimates provided by true subjects in each condition. However, the first three trials were excluded because the responses of true and confederate subjects were not independent. The remaining measures were obtained from responses to a booklet of questions each of which was answered using a seven-point scale (1 = very much, 7 = not at all). Subjects were asked whether they were trying to be accurate, were becoming more accurate, were trying to fit in with others' judgements, were attending to others' judgements, felt they were influenced by others' judgements, and felt confident in their own judgements. In addition, they were asked how strongly they felt a sense of belonging, felt strong ties, friendly, similar, cooperative and in agreement with members of their group (i.e., the H or J group in the categorized and group conditions, but the whole group of six in the control condition). Finally, subjects were invited to write down answers to the questions: "Did you have any ideas about the nature of the experiment? What do you think it was about?"

Results

To recap, there were three conditions, control, categorized and grouped, each containing estimates from subjects in eight sessions. Within each session there were three true subjects and three confederates. Since there were considerable differences between the *initial* estimates made in each session, it was decided to use the mean of confederates' plus true subjects' estimates for the first three trials of each session as a covariate for those subjects when inspecting effects of condition on subsequent estimates (cf. Bock, 1975, p. 495). In addition, it was decided that the middle block of trials would provide the best approximation of the estimates given, since on the initial trials (4–8) the task was somewhat unfamiliar and some of the sessions were unintentionally concluded prior to the 25th trial, and in the final trials (21–25) the experimenters reported that some subjects seemed to become slightly less involved as they were aware that the experiment was about to conclude. Therefore, the mean of estimates from trials 9–20 inclusive was taken as the main dependent measure.

These data could be analysed in two ways. On the one hand it was possible to use each subject's response as an independent item of data (yielding 144 responses on each trial, and 144 within-subject estimate means across trials 9–20). On the other hand, it seemed sensible to use the *group* in each session as the unit of analysis by averaging the estimates by true subjects on each trial, and like-

wise for the three confederates (yielding 24 responses from true subjects and 24 responses from confederates on each trial, and so on). In addition, from these group level data it was possible to compute difference scores, which indicate the degree of divergence between confederates and true subjects.

Consistent with social identity predictions true subjects converged most towards the confederates in the control condition and least in the grouped condition. Using individual level data there was a significant main effect of covariate ($F(1, 137) = 28.91, p < .0001$), and a significant effect of role (true vs. confederate) ($F(1, 137) = 113.74, p < .0001$), indicating, respectively, that different sessions began with different sizes of estimates, and that in all sessions there was a reliable difference between the estimates by confederates and by true subjects. While the effect of condition was non-significant ($F(2, 137) = 1.67$) there was a significant role × condition interaction ($F(2, 137) = 4.61, MSE = 5.12, p < .02$).

The group level analyses revealed that there were no differences between conditions for confederates' judgements ($F(2, 20) = 0.63$, n.s.) but that true subjects' estimates did differ between conditions ($F(2, 20) = 7.74, MSE = 1.85, p < .01$). Newman–Keuls analyses revealed that the control condition ($M = 4.80$) differed significantly from the grouped condition ($M = 2.44$) but neither of these differed from the categorized condition ($M = 3.67$) (see Figure 16.1). Moreover, a test of linearity on the difference scores between true subjects and confederates was also significant ($F_{lin}(2, 20) = 5.08, p < .05$), in line with predictions.[2]

Analyses of the remaining dependent measures were simply by two-way (condition × role) ANOVA. Not surprisingly, there were several significant effects of role. These all point to the fact that the confederates felt more cohesive and "groupy" than did the true subjects. Relative to the confederates, the true subjects felt that they were acting more independently of others, were not influenced by others' judgements, were trying to be accurate, and were becoming more accurate ($F(1, 137) = 38.47, 36.58, 72.03$ and 25.02, respectively; all $ps < .0001$); they felt less coopera-

---

[2] When trials 4–25 are combined the condition × role interaction remains significant ($F(1, 137) = 4.00, p < .05$), as does the linearity of true subjects' estimates ($F(1, 137) = 6.65, p < .01$).

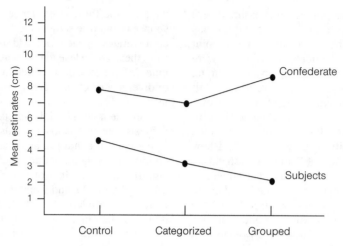

FIGURE 16.1 ■ Mean estimates by confederates and subjects as a function of salience of categorization.

tive, a weaker sense of belonging to a group, and weaker ties with the group. Surprisingly, perhaps, there were no differences between conditions in the responses of true subjects.

Discussion

The results support the hypothesis that norm formation can occur through referent informational influence which arises from social categorization. Even under conditions where the categorization was implicit, subjects perceived a discontinuity between the behaviour of two collections of individuals and may have inferred a categorical difference (see Turner's, 1985, discussion of meta-contrast ratios). When the salience of that categorization was increased by making it explicit, referent informational influence increased. Subjects resisted information purely on the basis that it was derived from a category of person to which they did not belong. There was even a slight tendency in the grouped condition to increase the difference between the two groups (i.e., to make it larger than the initial 5 cm), while the difference persisted in the categorized condition and underwent some attrition in the control condition. Thus we have demonstrated how information in a particular context can have a differential impact on perception simply through social categorization. We have illustrated the way that two norms can emerge simultaneously. Deindividuation and informational influence theories would have problems accounting for these data, since neither can

explain why social categorization per se should affect "influenceability." The pattern of results is, however, consistent with the idea that subjects conform to the norms which define them as belonging to particular categories and as not belonging to others.

In sum, this experiment demonstrated that ambiguity leads to informational influence mostly from those who are categorized as being equivalent to self. That is, self-categorization may provide the limits for informational influence. It should also provide the limits for normative influence since individuals will presumably have a stronger desire to receive rewards, approval, acceptance and so on from those who are assumed to be categorically similar to themselves. Our second experiment investigated categorization and normative influence pressures in the Asch conformity paradigm.

Experiment 2

The Asch (1952) paradigm has usually been described as inducing compliance because subjects go along with the confederates but do not privately accept their judgements (Allen, 1965, 1975). That is, influence in the Asch paradigm is normative because it seems to increase when greater numbers are present, to decrease when the confederates are divided, and to decrease when the confederates are composed of different subgroups (Mullen, 1983; Wilder, 1977). It is a direct product of surveillance by others. Yet Moscovici (1976) has pointed out that the errant confederates are actually a deviant *minority*, whose perceptions are at odds with those of most people with normal eyesight. Turner (1985) suggests that influence in the Asch paradigm might thus have an informational component: the confederates' responses disrupt the reasonable assumption that all perceivers are equivalent and interchangeable with respect to this kind of task and should perceive similarly. Indeed, subjects often experience a degree of uncertainty over their answers, even when they do not comply with the confederates. While Hogg and Turner (1987a) have investigated these issues using Crutchfield apparatus, there has been no experimental test to see whether the strength of influence in the original Asch paradigm is attributable to the informational effects associated with self-categorization (and thus to referent informational influence). It is this possibility which we explored here.

In the experiment which follows we introduced subjects to three confederates who were ostensibly either from an in-group or from an out-group. In all conditions these confederates were strangers whom the subjects would not expect to encounter again. The in-group/out-group division was not relevant to the task ("visual acuity"). Thus neither normative nor informational influence should differ in the in-group or out-group confederate conditions. Subjects were also asked to answer either publicly or privately (with responses hidden from confederates). Normative influence would mean that compliance to the confederates would be maximized when subjects' responses were public, but minimized when responses were covert (cf. Insko, Drenan, Solomon, Smith, & Wade, 1983).

The predictions from referent informational influence are quite different. There should be a main effect for in-group/out-group since subjects experience more ambiguity when disagreeing with an in-group and hence should conform more. For the private/public manipulation, private responding might individuate the subject from both the in-group and the out-group (i.e., create the potential for a self/other distinction) and hence reduce referent informational influence but leave informational influence undiminished. Public responding, in contrast, should render categorization as a group member more salient, as well as opening the way for normative influence. However, only *in-group* pressure would be influential because

normative influence pressures emerge only in relation to the members of one's own categories. Therefore, in contrast to a pure normative influence (or self-presentation) prediction, publicly responding to out-group pressure should lead to resistance and independence. We therefore predicted an interaction between group membership and publicity of responding.

Method

DESIGN

We employed a 2 × 2 factorial design with random allocation of subjects to conditions. The first factor (group) simply varied the group membership of the confederates (in-group, out-group), while the second (visibility) determined whether subjects' responses were visible to the confederates or not (public, private).

SUBJECTS

Fifty undergraduate students (23 males and 27 females) enrolled in an introductory course in psychology at the University of Dundee participated as subjects as their first course requirement for the year.

PROCEDURE

Subjects were requested to attend the laboratory to participate in an experiment on perception. The Asch (1956) procedure using three confederates was followed, adopting the standard instructions. However, at the start of the experiment, the confederates were introduced either as first year students from the psychology department of a prestigious neighbouring university (in-group condition) or as students of ancient history (out-group condition) from that university.[3] Subjects were in-

---

[3] A reviewer has suggested the categorization manipulation may be confounded with perceived credibility. While there is no a priori reason why subjects should believe the visual acuity of first year students of ancient history to be any worse than that of students of psychology, it is plausible that in-group bias might arise once an intergroup distinction is made salient, and this in turn might lead to differentiation on the dimension of credibility. The categorization enables subjects to "make sense" of the out-group's behaviour, and hence provides a highly meaningful frame of reference in the situation (cf. Boyanowski & Allen, 1973).

structed not to talk to each other. The stimulus lines were presented using ASCH, Apple II BASIC program, obtained from N. Nicholson, who originally devised the program to facilitate replications of his own (Nicholson, Cole, & Rocklin, 1985) findings. The stimulus lines were half the length of the Asch (1956) stimuli, varying in length from 1, 1.5 and 2 in to 4.5 and 6 in when displayed on a standard Apple 12 in monitor. In a pilot study nine subjects correctly identified all comparison lines. Subjects were seated 6 ft from the stimuli. A moderate error differed from the target stimulus by 0.5 in and an extreme error by 1 in. The 18-trial sequence consisted in this experiment of nine correct (C) and nine (E) error judgements by confederates, in the following order:

CCEECECECCCEECEECE

The unanimous judgements of the confederates were given in a detached and impersonal manner. The same three trained confederates served for all subjects and conditions. Each session consisted of three confederates and one naive subject who sat in a row, facing the monitor. The subject was always placed at one end of the row as a result of subtle manoeuvres on the part of the confederates. The group always gave their judgements in turn, beginning at the opposite end from the subject, and confederates behaved as if they were evaluating the line for the first time. The stimulus lines and target line remained on the screen until the subject had made his or her response. In the *public* condition all four members of the group gave their judgements aloud, and the experimenter unobtrusively recorded the real subject's responses. In the *private* condition, however, the experimenter asked if one of the subjects would note down the responses, ostensibly to leave her free to "operate the computer." The real subject, who "happened to be nearest," was asked if he or she would like to record responses. The three confederates then gave their judgements aloud in turn and the real subject recorded their responses on a score sheet along with his or her own, privately. The next trial was then displayed on the screen. The experimenter avoided giving any verbal or non-verbal reactions to the judgements.

Each experimental session of trials lasted approximately 6 min. After completing the trials subjects were required to answer a questionnaire which asked how confident they had felt, their perceptions of having been influenced, and their feelings of pride and belongingness to Dundee University. Subjects in the public condition were also asked if their answers might have been different if they had written them down rather than having to call them out, and vice versa for subjects in the private condition. These questions were answered using a seven-point scale. Subjects were debriefed on completion of the questionnaire. Only one reported any knowledge of the Asch paradigm. She had merely "heard the name before," hence her responses were retained in the analyses. However, one subject was unable to see the screen clearly due to poor eyesight, and an experimental error caused another subject to sit amongst the confederates. Both of these subjects were excluded from analyses.

Results

Preliminary analyses revealed no sex differences in conformity, self-reported reason for conformity or group identification. Hence, sex is not included in the analyses which follow.

Seventy-seven percent of all subjects conformed to the erroneous confederate judgements on at least one trial. The actual proportion of conforming responses was 138 out of a possible 432 (i.e., 32 percent). The group × visibility ANOVA on number of conforming responses for each subject revealed a significant main effect of group ($F(1, 44) = 14.0, p < .001$) which was qualified by a significant group × visibility interaction ($F(1, 44) = 7.22$, MSE = 6.03, $p < .01$). As can be seen in Figure 16.2, conformity was maximized in the in-group public condition ($M = 5.23$) and minimized in the out-group public condition ($M = 0.75$) while the in-group private and out-group private conditions did not differ significantly ($Ms = 3.00$ and 2.33, respectively). A priori contrasts revealed that the conformity increased significantly between the private in-group and public in-group conditions, but decreased significantly between the private out-group and public out-group conditions. Of the four conditions only the public out-group mean did not differ significantly from zero. Likewise, inspection of the numbers of subjects remaining independent confirmed that independence was greatest in the out-group public condition (50 percent of subjects) and least in the in-group public condition (0 percent of subjects), with the out-group private and in-group private conditions

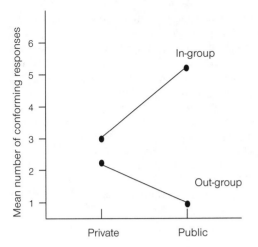

FIGURE 16.2 ■ Mean number of conforming responses as a function of subject's visibility and confederate's group membership.

TABLE 16.1. Effect of Group Manipulation on Strength of Identification with own University

| | | Confederates' group membership | |
	F	In-group	Out-group
Pride	4.64*	2.83	2.00
Ties	6.97*	3.33	2.17
Belonging	4.00**	2.88	2.00
Identification	2.64	3.21	2.42
Friendliness	3.21	3.04	2.42

*$p < .05$; **$p < .10$.
Note. 1 = strong identification, 7 = weak identification.

differing less markedly again (25 and 18 percent, respectively).

It was predicted from self-categorization theory that if the confederates were placed in a different category from self there should be an exaggeration of differences between self and confederates, and peripheral attributes of the confederates would be regarded as less attractive. While the in-group/out-group manipulation was based on study area, the fact that the confederates were from a different university could serve to differentiate the subject from the confederates, and would be predicted to do so more sharply when it was combined with their differing study area (cf. Doise, 1978). Consequently, it was predicted subjects would feel stronger identification with Dundee University relative to the other university in the out-group than in the in-group condition. This prediction was upheld. Out-group condition subjects felt greater pride, stronger ties and a greater sense of belonging to Dundee University than did in-group condition subjects (see Table 16.1).

Self-categorization theory also predicts that the basis of conformity is subjective uncertainty, and this uncertainty arises from comparison with in-group members. Consistent with this theory, subjects felt both that they had been influenced more and were less confident about their judgements in the in-group condition ($Ms = 5.23$ and 2.82) than in the out-group condition ($Ms = 6.09$ and 1.96; $Fs(1, 44) = 5.27$ and 4.63, $ps < .05$, respectively).

We also predicted that the categorization effect would be weakened in the private condition due to the behavioural differentiation of the subject from the confederates. A chi-square analysis of the proportion of subjects who perceived the situation as comprising two groups or a single group revealed that, of the 38 who responded to this item, 13 (vs. 4) saw themselves as separated from the confederates in the private condition whereas only 8 (vs. 13) saw themselves as separate in the public condition ($\chi^2(1) = 3.88, p < .05$). The analysis comparing in-group and out-group conditions also suggested that the self categorization process was at work. In the in-group condition only 6 (vs. 11) subjects saw themselves as separated from the confederates, whereas in the out-group condition 15 (vs. 6) subjects saw themselves as separated from confederates ($\chi^2(1) = 3.19, p < .05$).[4]

Overall the public out-group subjects saw themselves as most separated while public in-group subjects saw themselves as least separated from the confederates. This is confirmed by two significant group × visibility interactions on subjects' self-reported responses to influence. In-group condition subjects tried to fit in with the confederates most in the public ($M = 4.46$) and least in the private ($M = 5.55$) conditions, while the reverse was true for out-group condition subjects ($Ms = 5.42$ and 4.67, respectively; $F(1, 44) = 4.11$; MSE = 2.44, $p < .05$). A similar pattern was obtained for perceptions of being influenced: in-group public

[4]Cell sizes were too small to make it worth testing the distribution within group and within visibility cells. When subjects who perceived the categorization inappropriately are removed from the analysis, the group × visibility interaction for conforming responses remains significant ($F(1, 24) = 5.73, p < .05$) as does the main effect of group ($F(1, 24) = 14.38, p < .05$).

(4.46) was greater than private (6.00) while out-group public (6.17) was no different from private (6.00) ($F(1, 44) = 4.85$; MSE = 1.80, $p < .05$) possibly due to a ceiling effect. Although non-significant, a similar pattern was also obtained on the measure of awareness of having been influenced.

Discussion

These results converge to indicate that informational ambiguity is a product of disagreement with *in-group* members—those categorized as the same as self. The informational component in the Asch paradigm, therefore, is likely to be referent informational influence since it depends on this self-inclusive categorization of the confederates. Moreover, the normative pressure to comply is, once again, contingent on the self-definition of the complier. Our results illustrate that when the others are defined as members of a social category, this generates attraction to or repulsion from others purely as group members, and independent of their personal characteristics (see Hogg, 1987), and this could determine how far their approval and attraction to oneself are valued. An important feature of our results is that this attraction does *not* depend on public observability. Since conformity is interactively affected by group membership and visibility, it is likely that influence in this context embodies both informational and normative elements. Greater uncertainty, and hence influence, arises from a group defined as similar (and thus attractive to) self than from one which is defined as different (thus unattractive).

Another interesting aspect of our findings is that, while we demonstrated that it is still possible to observe conformity in the Asch paradigm (cf. Perrin & Spencer, 1981), public conformity exceeded the usual level (20–30 percent, cf. Nicholson et al., 1985) in the in-group condition but was far below normal in the out-group condition. The explanation for this, from self-categorization theory, is that in contrasting in-group from potential out-groups, the individual may adopt a frame of reference which accentuates the in-group's response towards one extreme of any evaluative continuum. There are two reasons for this. One is the cognitive process by which meta-contrasts arise. The other is the need to render in-groups positively distinctive from out-groups (cf. Tajfel & Turner, 1979). Both pro-

cesses make the cognitive representation of the ideal, or "prototypical" (Turner, 1985) group member—the one who best fulfils the stereotype—relatively more extreme in the already favoured direction than are the majority of the group. If the group is an out-group, its position will be perceived as over-extremitized towards the opposing pole. Thus, in our Asch paradigm experiment, in-group members may be seen as more correct, while out-group members are seen as less likely to be correct, when group membership is salient.

This analysis leads us directly to our third investigation of social influence, namely, group polarization (Wetherell, 1987).

Experiment 3

Group polarization is the tendency for group interaction and discussion to extremitize opinion. After discussion it is commonplace for group members to become even more aligned in the attitudinal direction favoured before interaction (Lamm & Myers, 1978). This effect is generally also explained in terms of normative and informational influence theories, in this case elaborated as social differentiation/social comparison models (Jellison & Arkin, 1977; Myers, Bruggink, Kersting, & Schlosser, 1980; Sanders & Baron, 1977) and persuasive arguments theory (Burnstein, 1982; Burnstein & Vinokur, 1973, 1975, 1977; Vinokur & Burnstein, 1974; 1978a, b). In the former, polarization is thought to result from the dependence of individuals on the valued opinions of others and their desire to be at least as extreme as or, preferably, even more extreme than their peers in the socially desirable or prevailing direction. In contrast, Burnstein & Vinokur argue that polarization depends on informational exchange in discussion. Group members are frequently exposed to new persuasive information which produces an opinion shift.

The self-categorization approach (Turner et al., 1987; Turner & Oakes, 1986; Wetherell, 1983, 1987; cf. also Mackie, 1986; Mackie & Cooper, 1984) claims that a precondition for polarizing opinion shifts, as for the other forms of group influence discussed in this paper, is recognition of shared category membership with respect to the items under discussion. As a baseline, polarization and mutual group influence are likely to occur when members expect to agree with other discussants, and this is most likely if those others are perceived as members of the same category (an in-group rather than an out-group) and thus seen as an appropriate reference group. Influence in polarization studies, as elsewhere, may depend on shared identity, even if this identity is minimal, induced by the experimenter's assignation of subjects to groups and the subjects' perception that all share the same relation and expertise to the items being discussed, or at least possess no salient differences.

Polarization, which at the group level represents an extremitized convergence of individual opinions (Singleton, 1978), may then, in effect, be conformity to what is perceived to be the in-group or category norm. This raises the question of how conformity to a perceived group norm can cause an *enhancement* or accentuation of opinion. The answer is that, under specific circumstances, the norm perceived by group members is not identical with the pre-discussion average of opinions but is a more extreme version of those opinions.

Self-categorization theory suggests the impact of individuals' initial opinions on group norm formation is dependent on the prototypicality or normative representativeness of those opinions. Prototypicality is defined through meta-contrast (Turner et al., 1987). In simple terms the opinions which are the most prototypical or normative for a group are the ones with (1) the greatest difference from non-category, or out-group, members and (2) the least difference from same category or in-group members. The most prototypical opinions in this sense are predicted to be the most persuasive and group discussion and interaction, all other things being equal, will produce conformity to those views. Turner, Wetherell, & Hogg (1989, and see Wetherell, 1987) have demonstrated numerically that in discussions which produce polarization the most prototypical opinions and thus perceived group norms are more extreme than the pre-discussion averages. It is therefore possible that conformity per se, in these circumstances, would be sufficient to produce accentuation of opinion.

In the third experiment reported here the aim, in line with the experiments described above, was to test the premise that polarization is open, in the first place, to categorization effects. The opinion shifts obtained in polarization experiments should be affected by subjects' perception of their category relation with other discussants just as perceptual judgements are influenced in the norm formation and conformity experiments. A demonstration of this kind would provide further support for a self-categorization theory interpretation of group polarization.

One study has been conducted (Vinokur & Burnstein, 1978a) which is directly relevant to the comparison of categorization with normative and informational effects (for evidence of the general importance of in-group identity in polarization see Doise, 1969; Mackie, 1986; Mackie & Cooper, 1984, Experiment 1; Skinner & Stephenson, 1981; Turner, Wetherell, & Hogg, 1989). Vinokur & Burnstein constructed six-person groups out of divided subgroups or opposing factions for discussions of risk-taking choice-dilemmas. Half the groups had their attention drawn to this division of opinion within the group through seating arrangements, etc., while for the remainder the difference in opinion was not made salient.

Self-categorization theory predicts that, when differences between subgroups are made salient, giving subjects an alternative basis for self-categorization in terms of subgroup rather than entire group opinion, mutual group influence should be reduced. In contrast Vinokur & Burnstein found that, despite differences in opinion and regardless of the salience of these differences, subgroups tended to converge together and polarize in the same direction, an outcome which they argue is predictable from the pattern of diffusion of novel and persuasive arguments in the discussion groups.

There are a number of problems with their study, however, which render it problematic as a test of categorization effects. First, Vinokur & Burnstein instructed subjects to reach a consensus in the group as a whole, despite differences in opinion. This instruction reinstates the higher order group identity and demands that common ground be found for successful completion of the experimental task. In addition, subgroup disagreements concerned issues of minimal importance to the subjects—the difference of opinion was not necessarily involving—and, finally, the scale used for responses presented a continuous dimension rather than the Likert type which unambiguously splits opinions into different dimensions (pro vs. anti) and thus allows clear recognition of category differences.

Our experiment followed Vinokur & Burnstein's procedure in pre-selecting discussion groups composed of recognizable subgroups with sharp divisions of opinion. There were two experimental conditions: (1) an uncategorized condition where no mention was made of, or attention drawn to the division, and thus common identity as members of the same discussion group, composed of peers, was to the fore, and (2) a categorized condition where the existence of subgroups, labelled A and B, was made salient to the subjects and emphasized by seating arrangements. Subjects discussed controversial attitude issues, using a Likert-type response scale marked into pro and anti regions with a neutral mid-point. In both conditions subjects were not required to reach a consensus.

Persuasive arguments theory predicts convergence between the subgroups and no differences between conditions, since the changes in procedure do not alter the provision of novel persuasive material. Self-categorization theory predicts a significant difference between conditions because of the inhibition of mutual influence, and convergence of one subgroup to another when an alternative basis for self-categorization is made salient.

Method

DESIGN

We employed a 2 × 2 factorial design with subjects allocated to conditions as outlined below. The first factor (pre–post) was the stage at which opinion was recorded (pre-discussion, post-discussion) while the second factor (salience) was whether intragroup divisions corresponded to a salient categorization (categorized, uncategorized).

SUBJECTS

A total of 116 male and female students, aged 16–17, attending high school in Hawkes Bay, New Zealand, participated.

MATERIALS AND PRE-TESTING

Subjects were pre-tested a week before the experiment itself on 15 controversial attitude items, supposedly as part of a nation-wide survey of attitudes. The attitude items were presented as statements in an opinion questionnaire and subjects were asked to respond on a nine-point scale running from +4 (strongly agree with the statement), through 0 (neutral with regard to the statement) to –4 (strongly disagree with the statement).

In line with the pre-testing procedure in group polarization experiments, subjects were simply asked to give their individual personal views unaware that they might later discuss these items in groups.

The five items which produced the widest spread and greatest division of opinion across the scale within the sample were then selected for the group discussions. These items were presented with the same Likert-type scale and were as follows:

1. Women are not discriminated against in New Zealand society as they now have equal opportunities for careers.
2. As cigarette smoking is bad for health, governments should protect non-smokers by banning smoking in public places.
3. Examinations for School Certificate and University Entrance penalize creative thinking.
4. Any form of censorship of material for adults is an infringement of human liberties.
5. I do not believe that parents and guardians should have control over our age group to the extent of determining friends and the time allowed out. Our age group should be free to determine its own activities.

SELECTION OF DISCUSSION GROUPS

Prior to the experimental sessions, 58 of the pre-tested subjects were randomly assigned to the uncategorized and 58 to the categorized condition. Four-person discussion groups were then pre-selected from the pool of subjects created for each condition with new groups being formed for each attitude item.

Pre-selection created groups composed of divided subgroups with two members in favour of the attitude statement and two members opposed to the statement. The gap between the two subgroups ranged from a maximum of six points on the nine-point scale to a minimum of three points with a mean gap across both conditions of 4.65. This gap always included the actual mid-point of the scale and the pre-test mean of the sample. A group with a six-point gap, for example, might be composed of members with the following pre-test scores for the attitude item: +4, +2, –4, –2; a group with a three-point gap might have these scores: +2, +2, –1, –1.

The number of divided groups which could be formed from available subjects to provide an equal N in each experimental condition varied from item to item. For items nos. 1–3, nine four-person groups were formed for each condition, for item no. 4, eight groups for each condition, and for item no. 5, twelve groups. In order that the experience of all subjects should be as consistent as possible, those who could not be allocated to a discussion group of the designated type for one of the targeted experimental items were, on each occasion, assigned to a group with a similar division of opinion but discussing another item from the 15 pre-tested. One two-person divided group of this kind was also necessary in each condition. Each subject, therefore, experienced five group discussions where there was a substantial difference in subgroup opinion but only those groups discussing the five selected experimental items were included in the analysis.

PROCEDURE AND EXPERIMENTAL CONDITIONS

The experiment was conducted in four sessions, two for each experimental condition. At the outset the experimenter explained that she would like the subjects to discuss some of the attitude items from the questionnaire completed the week before in groups and would then record their individual opinion on the issues once again. It was pointed out that there would be five discussions, with new groups being formed each time. All subjects then collected a personalized protocol which informed them who were the fellow members of their five groups and the item each group would discuss, including a response scale for recording post-discussion opinion. It was explained subjects should work from the protocol, locate their fellow members for the first discussion and sit around one of the tables provided. After a short period (5–, minutes), the experimenter would indicate that discussion time had finished for that item. They were not required to reach agreement in their group. Once discussion was over, they were instructed to separate themselves physically from the group and fill in their current individual opinion on the item on their protocol. This response would be confidential. Subjects were told they should not feel bound by their previous views as we were interested in what they felt about the issue now. The next discussion would then begin with the new set of participants and so on until all the items had been discussed. Additional instructions given varied according to experimental condition.

Uncategorized condition. Subjects in this condition were not made aware of the divided subgroups and difference of opinion within their discussion group. They were simply told that they should try and consider each item in depth in their group, go through all the pros and cons and listen carefully to what other participants had to say and the reasons for their opinions.

Categorized condition. In this condition the existence of subgroups as a basis for self-categorization was made salient. In line with Vinokur & Burnstein's instructions (1978a, p. 876) subjects were told they would find a sharp division in their group, i.e., each discussion would, in fact, involve two subgroups. They would find there were two people on one side of the issue, subgroup A, and two people supporting the other side, subgroup B. These subgroups were marked on the protocols (two names listed under the headings A and B for each item), so they should first find the other half of their subgroup and then sit around the table so that one subgroup sat on one side facing the other subgroup. (These seating arrangements were in contrast to the uncategorized condition where subjects were free to sit in any order around the table.) Like the uncategorized subjects, categorized subjects were told to consider each item in depth, to go through all the pros and cons and to listen carefully to what the other subgroup had to say and the reasons for their opinions.

In each session, once the post-discussion responses for the last item had been completed, subjects were thanked and fully debriefed about the purpose of the study.

DEPENDENT MEASURES

Following Vinokur & Burnstein, subgroup convergence was assessed. The +4 to –4 scale was first converted to a continuous 1–9 scale and analysis proceeded as follows:

> . . . in each group the mean prediscussion choice of the (pro) subgroup was subtracted from the mean prediscussion choice of the (anti) subgroup. This difference represented the initial gap. The same calculations were performed for the two subgroups after discussion using their respective final choices. The latter difference represented that postdiscussion gap. Subtracting the final gap from the initial one thus indicated whether the discrepancy between the two subgroups had decreased (with resultant positive value), remained the same,

or increased (with resultant negative value) following group discussion. (1978a, p. 877)

Vinokur & Burnstein's measure indicates the degree of mutual influence and accommodation between the subgroups in categorized and uncategorized conditions.

Attitude shift overall was also assessed. Mean pre-discussion opinion was subtracted from mean postdiscussion opinion on the unconverted +4 to –4 scale so that a negative score represented a shift in the anti or disagree with the statement direction and a positive score indicated a shift in the pro or agree with the statement direction.

Results

Table 16.2 presents the pre-discussion and post-discussion means with attitude shift scores and the mean pre-discussion and post-discussion gaps between the subgroups with subgroup convergence scores for all items and both conditions. In terms of the experimental hypothesis the subgroup convergence scores (final column) are crucial and it is clear that salience of categorization had a considerable effect on the degree of mutual influence between subgroups. Uncategorized subjects converged to a much larger extent than categorized subjects on four of the five items.

Two-way ANOVAS (salience of categorization × pre-discussion/post-discussion gaps) for each item and for all items pooled produced a significant main effect for salience of categorization for items nos. 1–3 and for all items pooled ($F(1, 16) = 5.26$, $p < .05$; $F(1, 16) = 6.70$, $p < .05$; $F(1, 16) = 13.35$, $p < .01$; and $F(1, 92) = 22.97$, $p < .0000$, respectively). Significant interactions between salience and pre/post-discussion gaps between subgroups also emerged for items nos. 1–3 and for all items pooled ($F(1, 16) = 7.54$, MSE = 1.33, $p < .01$; $F(1, 16) = 8.45$, MSE = 1.66, $p < .01$; $F(1, 16) = 43.46$, MSE = 0.38, $p < .001$; and $F(1, 92) = 21.03$, $p < .0000$), but were non-significant for items nos. 4 and 5.

Post hoc Tukey tests for the interaction effects for items nos. 1–3 and for all items pooled demonstrated a significant difference between the categorized and uncategorized subjects for the post-discussion gaps between subgroups ($q = 5.64$, $p < .005$; $q = 5.55$, $p < .006$; $q = 11.84$, $p < .0000$; $q = 10.39$; $p < .0000$, respectively). For these items and for all items pooled subgroup members converged to a significantly greater extent when the division between subgroups was not made salient. In no case was there a significant difference between categorized and uncategorized subjects for the pre-discussion gap in subgroup opinion. The interaction for all items pooled is illustrated in Figure 16.3 which clearly displays the effect of categorization salience.

As might be expected, for every item there was also a significant main effect for pre-/post-dis-

TABLE 16.2. Mean Pre-Discussion, Post-Discussion Responses and Shift Scores with Mean Gaps between Subgroups Before and After Discussion, and Difference Scores for Both Conditions for All Items

Item no.	Condition	Mean pre-discussion response	Mean post-discussion response	Shift scores[a]	Mean pre-discussion gap	Mean post-discussion gap	Pre–post difference between gaps[b]
1.	Uncategorized	+0.25	–0.72	–0.97	4.06	1.22	2.83
	Categorized	+0.11	–0.33	–0.44	4.11	3.39	0.72
2.	Uncategorized	+0.03	+0.83	+0.80	5.28	1.89	3.39
	Categorized	+0.19	–0.14	–0.33	5.17	4.28	0.89
3.	Uncategorized	+0.14	+2.53	+2.39	4.83	0.39	4.44
	Categorized	–0.06	+0.08	+0.14	4.56	2.83	1.72
4.	Uncategorized	+0.13	+2.91	+2.78	4.63	1.19	3.44
	Categorized	+0.13	+0.97	+0.84	5.13	3.19	1.94
5.	Uncategorized	–0.08	–0.15	–0.07	4.00	1.13	2.88
	Categorized	+0.02	–0.48	–0.50	4.75	1.63	3.13
All items: Uncategorized		+0.09	+1.08	–0.99	4.56	1.16	3.40
All items: Categorized		+0.08	+0.02	+.099	4.74	3.06	1.68

[a]Positive shift scores indicate a shift further in agreement with statement direction. Negative shift scores indicate a shift in disagreement with statement direction.
[b]The higher the score the greater the convergence between subgroups.

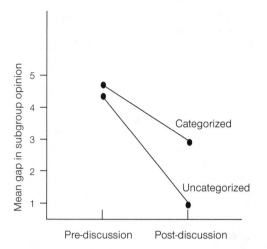

FIGURE 16.3 ■ Mean gap in subgroup opinion pre- and post-discussion as a function of categorization.

cussion gap (item no. 1, $F(1, 16) = 21.39, p < .003$; item no. 2, $F(1, 16) = 24.73, p < .001$; item no. 3, $F(1, 16) = 223.01, p < .0000$; item no. 4, $F(1, 14) = 31.15, p < .0001$; item no. 5, $F(1, 22) = 101.92, p < .0000$; all items pooled $F(1, 92) = 217.15, p < .0000$), with the post-discussion gap being smaller overall than the pre-discussion gap between subgroups.

The attitude shift scores in Table 16.2 indicate the extent and direction of opinion shift as a result of group discussion. In general, in line with the pattern for subgroup convergence, categorized subjects shifted less as a result of group discussion than uncategorized subjects. Analysis conducted for each item produced a significant interaction between salience of categorization and individual pre- and post-discussion responses on the attitude scale for items nos. 3 and 4 ($F(1, 70) = 14.81, p < .0003$ and $F(1, 62) = 8.57, p < .005$). There was a significant main effect for salience of categorization only for item no. 3 ($F(1, 70) = 8.59, p < .005$).

The attitude shift scores also demonstrate a very mixed pattern of polarizing and non-polarizing shifts. The presence and degree of attitude polarization, or enhancement of initial sample tendency as a result of group discussion, is in fact irrelevant to the experimental hypothesis since items were deliberately selected for the wide spread of opinion elicited. Thus all items had sample pre-discussion means which hovered at less than one scale point from the neutral mid-point. In this

situation it is not meaningful to talk of initial sample tendencies for items.

Discussion

The general pattern of results suggests, as in Experiments 1 and 2, that mutual influence in groups is partly dependent on self-categorization as a group member. Given a salient alternative basis for self-perception, as a member of a factional subgroup, subjects in this study were much less likely to converge and accommodate opinion within a group of their peers. People with divergent opinions became much less persuasive when seen as representative of an out-group. These results imply that Vinokur & Burnstein's failure to find a similar effect may have been due to the inadequate manipulation and thus undermining of categorization effects.

Only one of the five items departed from this outcome. The attitude shift scores for this item (no. 5) indicate it is unlikely subjects were responding, as social comparison theory might suggest, to a particular social value for this item. There is no evidence that, across the sample, one attitudinal direction exerted a strong pull on subjects and thus social comparison and social differentiation in terms of this value became a more powerful basis for influence than categorization. It seems unlikely, on the same grounds, that novel and persuasive material devolved unequally between the subgroups so that the persuasive arguments offered by one subgroup won over the other. It is also implausible that for this one item alone, but for no others, discussion threw up new arguments for both sides so that informational exchange in itself would produce convergence in both conditions.

It is possible, however, that the nature of the item undermined the intended subgroup categorization in the same manner as we suggested Vinokur & Burnstein's manipulation undermined categorization effects. This item drew attention to a common identity all group members shared, as teenagers, against parents and the older generation. Perhaps in this context each subgroup in the categorized condition found the other subgroup persuasive despite the initial difference in views. Self-categorization theory suggests that, for polarization generally, persuasion and the recognition of the novelty and cogency of arguments depend on the expectation that one will agree with fellow group members or will see them as equivalent to oneself in relation to the judgement in question. The manipulation of categorization disrupted this premise for four of the items but perhaps it was then reinstated for the fifth item. Further experimentation along these lines, systematically exploring identity cues on a within-subject basis, is required to test further the complex relationship between social values, self-categorization and persuasive arguments.

General Discussion

In Experiment 1 we demonstrated that an important basis for the formation of a social norm is common self-categorization among individuals contributing to that norm. Confederates were decreasingly influential as their membership of a different category became more apparent to true subjects. What Deutsch & Gerard (1955) describe as *informational influence* was dependent upon social identity and self-categorization.

Experiment 2 confirmed that a powerful factor in manifest social influence is, once again, the inclusion of self in the category of those attempting to exert influence. Compliance is usually attributable to *normative influence* and hence only arises under interpersonal pressure. Experiment 2 shows that when group membership is salient only an in-group seems to be effective in applying such pressure. Pressure from an out-group is publicly rejected out of hand. We conclude, therefore, that self-categorization is equally an important basis for normative influence.

Experiment 3 demonstrated that these same processes operate even when all sources of influence are free to modify their positions (i.e. there are no consistently divergent confederates). In free discussion between individuals who fall on opposite sides of a perceived mid-point, mutual influence is considerably weakened if differential category membership is superimposed. Those holding views which differ from a person's own but who are perceived as belonging to *alternative* equal status categories, are much less influential than uncategorized individuals. Results from the three experiments suggest that self-categorization can be a crucial determining factor in social influence, and that the extent of informational and normative influence may depend very largely upon

whether the source of influence is regarded as a member of a person's own category.

We asked at the outset which of the many dissenting voices in the social world would create uncertainty and potentially be influential? Our research strongly supports the idea that in-groups as defined by a process of self-categorization are most likely to inform individuals. There are numerous avenues for future research (Abrams & Hogg, in press), but perhaps the most interesting is still the question of social change (Moscovici, 1976). How do out-groups get heard, how do intersecting and overlapping self-categorizations combine to generate social influence and, following Simmel (1955), how do people deal with the problem of conflicting messages from different in-groups?

REFERENCES

Abrams, D. (1984). *Social identity, self-awareness and intergroup behaviour.* Unpublished doctoral thesis, University of Kent at Canterbury.

Abrams, D. (1985). Focus of attention in minimal intergroup discrimination. *British Journal of Social Psychology, 24,* 65–74.

Abrams, D., & Brown, R. J. (1989). Self-consciousness and social identity: Self-regulation as a group member. *Social Psychology Quarterly, 52,* 311–318.

Abrams, D., & Hogg, M. A. (1990). Social identification, self-categorization and social influence. *European Review of Social Psychology, 1,* 195–228

Allen, V. L. (1965). Situational factors in conformity. *Advances in Experimental Social Psychology, 2,* 133–175.

Allen, V. L. (1975). Social support for non-conformity. *Advances in Experimental Social Psychology, 8,* 1–43.

Asch, S. (1952). *Social psychology.* Englewood Cliffs, NJ: Prentice-Hall.

Asch, S. (1956). Studies of independence and conformity: I. A minority of one against a unanimous majority. *Psychological Monographs, 70,* 1–70.

Bock, R. D. (1975). *Multivariate statistical methods in behavioral research.* New York: McGraw-Hill.

Boyanowski, E. O., & Allen, V. L. (1973). Ingroup norms and self-identity as determinants of discriminatory behaviour. *Journal of Personality and Social Psychology, 25,* 408–418.

Brown, R. J., & Turner, J. C. (1981). Interpersonal and intergroup behaviour. In J. C. Turner & H. Giles (Eds), *Intergroup behaviour.* Oxford, UK: Blackwell.

Burnstein, E. (1982). Persuasion as argument processing. In H. Brandscatter, J. H. Davis, & G. Stocker-Kreichgauer (Eds), *Group decision making.* London: Academic Press.

Burnstein, E., & Vinokur, A. (1973). Testing two classes of theories about group indirect shifts: Individual choice. *Journal of Experimental Social Psychology, 9,* 123–137.

Burnstein, E., & Vinokur, A. (1975). What a person thinks upon learning he has chosen differently from others: Nice evidence for the persuasive-arguments explanation of choice shifts. *Journal of Experimental Psychology 11,* 412–426.

Burnstein, E., & Vinokur, A. (1977). Persuasive argumentation and social comparison as determinants of attitude polarization. *Journal of Experimental Social Psychology, 13,* 315–332.

Deutsch, M., & Gerard, H. B. (1955). A study of normative and informational social influences upon individual judgement. *Journal of Abnormal and Social Psychology, 51,* 629–636.

Diener, E. (1980). Deindividuation: The absence of self-awareness and self-regulation in group members. In P. B. Paulus (Ed.), *Psychology of group influence.* Hillsdale, NJ: Erlbaum.

Doise, W. (1969). Intergroup relations and the polarization of individual and collective judgements. *Journal of Personality and Social Psychology, 12,* 136–143.

Doise, W. (1978). *Group and individuals: Explanations in social psychology.* Cambridge: Cambridge University Press.

Fenigstein, A. (1979). Self-consciousness, self-attention and social interaction. *Journal of Personality and Social Psychology, 37,* 75–86.

Festinger, L. (1954). A theory of social comparison processes. *Human Relations, 7,* 117–140.

Froming, W. J., & Carver, C. S. (1981). Divergent influences of private and public self-consciousness in a compliance paradigm. *Journal of Research in Personality, 15,* 159–171.

Hogg, M. A. (1987). Social identity and group cohesiveness. In J. C. Turner, M. A. Hogg, P. J. Oakes, S. D. Reicher, & M. Wetherell, *Rediscovering the social group: A self-categorization theory.* Oxford, UK/New York: Blackwell.

Hogg, M. A., & Abrams, D. (1988). *Social identifications: A social psychology of intergroup relations and group processes.* London: Routledge.

Hogg, M. A., & Turner, J. C. (1987a). Social identity and conformity: A theory of referent informational influence. In W. Doise & S. Moscovici (Eds), *Current issues in European social psychology,* vol. 2. Cambridge, UK: Cambridge University Press.

Hogg, M. A., & Turner, J. C. (1987b). Intergroup behaviour, self-stereotyping and the salience of social categories. *British Journal of Social Psychology, 26,* 325–340.

Insko, C. A., Drenan, S., Solomon, M. R., Smith, R., & Wade, T. J. (1983). Conformity as a function of the consistency of positive self-evaluation with being liked and being right. *Journal of Experimental Social Psychology, 19,* 341–358.

Jellison, J., & Arkin, R. (1977). A self-presentation approach to decision-making in groups. In J. M. Sulus & R. L. Miller (Eds), *Social processes: Theoretical and empirical perspectives.* Washington, DC: Hemisphere.

Kiesler, C. A., & Kiesler, S. B. (1969). *Conformity.* Reading, MA: Addison-Wesley.

Lamm, H., & Myers, P. E. (1978). Group-induced polarization of attitudes and behavior. In L. Berkowitz (Ed.), *Advances in experimental social psychology,* vol. 11. New York: Academic Press.

Levine, J. M., & Moreland, R. L. (1986). Outcome comparisons in group contexts: Consequences for the self and others. In R. Schwarzer (Ed.), *Self-related cognitions in anxiety and motivation* (pp. 285–303). Hillsdale, NJ: Erlbaum.

Levine, J. M., & Russo, E. M. (1987). Majority and minority influence. In C. Hendrick (Ed.), *Group processes: Review of personality and social psychology,* 8 (pp. 13–54). Thousand Oaks, CA: Sage.

Lewis, S. A., Langan, C. J., & Hollander, E. P. (1972). Expec-

tations of future interaction and the choice of less desirable alternatives in conformity. *Sociometry, 35,* 440–447.

Mackie, D. M. (1986). Social identification effect in group polarization. *Journal of Personality and Social Psychology, 50,* 720–728.

Mackie, D. M., & Cooper, J. (1984). Attitude polarization: The effects of group membership. *Journal of Personality and Social Psychology, 46,* 575–586.

Moscovici, S. (1976). *Social influence and social change.* London: Academic Press.

Mullen, B. (1983). Operationalizing the effect of the group on the individual: A self-attention perspective. *Journal of Experimental Social Psychology, 19,* 295–322.

Myers, D. G., Bruggink, J. B., Kersting, R. C., & Schlosser, B. A. (1980). Does learning others' opinions change one's opinions? *Personality and Social Psychology Bulletin, 6,* 253–260.

Nail, P. R. (1986). Toward an integration of some models and theories of social responses. *Psychological Bulletin, 100,* 190–206.

Nicholson, N., Cole, S. G., & Rocklin, T. (1985). Conformity in the Asch situation: A comparison between contemporary British and U.S. university students. *British Journal of Social Psychology, 24,* 59–63.

Perrin, S., & Spencer, C. (1981). Independence or conformity in the Asch experiment as a reflection of cultural and situational factors. *British Journal of Social Psychology, 20,* 205–209.

Prentice-Dunn, S., & Rogers, R. W. (1982). Effects of public and private self-awareness on deindividuation and aggression. *Journal of Personality and Social Psychology, 43,* 503–513.

Reicher, S. D. (1984). Social influence in the crowd: Attitudinal and behavioural effects of deindividuation in conditions of high and low group salience. *British Journal of Social Psychology, 23,* 341–350.

Sanders, G. S., & Baron, R. S. (1977). Is social comparison irrelevant for producing choice shifts? *Journal of Experimental Social Psychology, 13,* 303–314.

Sherif, M. (1936). *The psychology of social norms.* New York: Harper & Row.

Skinner, M., & Stephenson, G. M. (1981). The effects of intergroup comparison on the polarization of opinions. *Current Psychological Research, 1,* 49–61.

Simmel, G. (1955). *Conflict, and the web of group affiliations.* New York: Free Press.

Singleton, R., Jr. (1979). Another look at the conformity explanation of group induced shifts in choice. *Human Relations, 32,* 37–56.

Sperling, H. G. (1946). *An experimental study of some psychological factors in judgement.* Master's thesis, New School for Social Research. Summarized in Asch (1952).

Suls, J. M., & Miller, R. L. (Eds.) (1977). *Social comparison processes: Theoretical and empirical perspectives.* Washington, DC: Hemisphere.

Tajfel, H. (1972). La categorization sociale. In S. Moscovici (Ed.), *Introduction it la psychologie sociale,* vol. 1. Paris: Larousse.

Tajfel, H., & Turner, J. C. (1979). An integrative theory of intergroup conflict. In W. G. Austin & S. Worchel (Eds), *The social psychology of intergroup relations.* Monterey, CA: Brooks/Cole.

Turner, J. C. (1982). Towards a cognitive redefinition of the social group. In H. Tajfel (Ed.), *Social identity and intergroup relations*. Paris: Maison des Sciences de l'Homme/Cambridge: Cambridge University Press. (Reprinted 1981 in *Cahiers de Plychologie Cognitive, 1,* 93–118)

Turner, J. C. (1984). Social identification and psychological group formation. In H. Tajfel (Ed.), *The social dimension: European developments in social psychology*, vol. 2. London: Cambridge University Press/Paris: Editions de la Maison des Sciences de l'Homme.

Turner, J. C. (1985). Social categorization and the self-concept: A social cognitive theory of group behaviour. In E. J. Lawler (Ed.), *Advances in group processes: Theory and research.* vol. 2. Greenwich, CT: JAI Press.

Turner, J. C., Hogg, M. A., Oakes, P. J., Reicher, S. D., & Wetherell, M. (1987). *Rediscovering the social group: A self-categorization theory.* Oxford, UK/New York: Blackwell.

Turner, J. C., & Oakes, P. J. (1986). The significance of the social identity concept for social psychology with reference to individualism, interactionism and social influence. *British Journal of Social Psychology, 25,* 237–253. (Special issue on the Individual–Society Interface)

Turner, J. C., Wetherell, M. S., & Hogg, M. A. (1989). Referent informational influence and group polarization. *British Journal of Social Psychology, 28,* 135–147.

Vinokur, A., & Burnstein, E. (1974). The effects of partially shared persuasive arguments on group-induced shifts: A problem-solving approach. *Journal of Personality and Social Psychology, 29,* 305–315.

Vinokur, A., & Burnstein, E. (1978a). Depolarization of attitudes in groups. *Journal of Personality and Social Psychology, 36,* 872–885.

Vinokur, A., & Burnstein, E. (1978b). Novel argumentation and attitude change: The case of polarization following group discussion. *European Journal of Social Psychology, 8,* 335–348.

Wetherell, M. S. (1983). *Social identification, social influence and group polarization.* Unpublished doctoral thesis, University of Bristol, UK.

Wetherell, M. S. (1987). Social identity and group polarization. In J. C. Turner, M. A. Hogg, P. J. Oakes, S. D. Reicher, & M. S. Wetherell, *Rediscovering the social group: A self-categorization theory.* Oxford, UK/ New York: Blackwell.

Wilder, D. A. (1977). Perception of groups, size of opposition, and social influence. *Journal of Experimental Social Psychology, 13,* 252–268.

Williams, K., Harkins, S., & Latane, B. (1981). Identifiability as a deterrent to social loafing: Two cheering experiments. *Journal of Personality and Social Psychology, 40,* 303–311.

Studies in Social Influence: Minority Influence and Conversion Behavior in a Perceptual Task

Serge Moscovici • Ecoles des Hautes Etudes en Sciences Sociales
Bernard Personnaz • Laboratoire de Psychologie Sociale de l'Université Paris VII associée au Centre National de Recherche Scientifique

The effects of influence attempts by a majority and by a minority, were examined on both a manifest response level and a latent perceptual level. Female subjects were exposed to a series of blue slides that were consistently labeled as green by a female confederate. The confederate was presented as a member of either a majority or a minority. On each trial, subjects were required to indicate the color of the slide presented and the color of the afterimage perceived on a white screen following removal of the slide. It was predicted that (a) the subject's judgment of the chromatic afterimage would be modified when the influence agent represented a minority, and (b) this modification will be more pronounced when the source of influence is absent than when it is present. The results supported the prediction in both the main study and its replication.

In a previous study, Moscovici, Lage, and Naffrechoux (1969) showed that if a minority consistently affirmed that it saw as green a series of slides that were objectively blue, it influenced both the public and private responses of a majority. Moreover, individuals who did not change their responses during the social interaction were even more likely than those who did conform to the minority's position to change their responses in a color discrimination task following the interaction. These results indicate "conversion" behavior, a subtle process of perceptual or cognitive modification by which a person gives up his/her usual response in order to adopt another view or response, without necessarily being aware of the change or forced to make it. In Mead's words, "there is, then, a process by means of which the individual in interaction with others inevitably becomes like them in doing the same thing, with-

out that process appearing in what we term consciousness: we become conscious of the process when we definitely take the attitude of the others, and this situation must be distinguished from the previous one" (Mead, 1970, p. 193).

Why do minorities produce such a conversion? In our opinion, there are two reasons. On one hand, the consistency of judgments by a minority shows that it has a clear view of reality, is committed to its view, and is unwilling to yield or compromise with respect to its position. This behavioral style creates a conflict both between the source and the target of influence and within the target him/herself, when he/she has to consider seriously an alternative to his/her own judgment or response. This conflict is intensified when there is no easy way to reject the source's judgement by attributing it to the source's malevolent intentions, a physical handicap, etc. On the other hand, the development of the conflict is not the same when deviant information is presented by a majority. In this case, the responses of the source appear to be legitimate and common, and to be providing accepted ("true") information about reality. When there is a divergence, an unexpected judgement, each individual *compares* his/her own judgment with that proposed to him/her by the majority, without necessarily reconsidering the object (slide, text, etc.) to which that judgment refers.

In previous experiments (Moscovici & Lage, 1976; Personnaz, 1974), we have observed that individuals, in the presence of others who call a blue slide "green" are primarily concerned with why they do not see the colored stimulus slides like the others. They attempt to resolve this problem by concentrating on what they say and on what the group says, without turning their attention to the stimulus itself. Once the social interaction is over and they are required to judge a similar stimulus privately, their subjective judgments remain undisturbed because what was said during the interaction was only loosely connected to what was seen. This method of resolving a divergence of judgment was described a long time ago in Asch's (1956) classic monograph.

In contrast, the response of a minority is immediately considered as illegitimate, wrong, or contrary to common sense or reality. Each individual is probably inclined, at first, to doubt its value. After a while, if the minority persists and appears committed and sure of its responses, members of the majority start a *validation* process by considering that the deviant response may contain some truth and by confronting the response with the corresponding object. It may be difficult, even forbidden, for the individual to agree with the minority, and he/she must have good reasons for doing so, after a careful examination of arguments or data. It follows that a conflict of responses with the minority triggers an intense intellectual or perceptual effort in order to assess the relation of the minority's judgment to reality and in order to see or think what the minority saw or thought. The consequences of this validation process are the following. During the social interaction, members of the majority avoid adopting the minority's response, bearing in mind that to do so would be to become consciously and openly deviant. Subsequently, in a private situation, when the majority individuals are in a position to evaluate the stimulus, object or event on their own, they judge or

perceive it differently from before, because during the interaction, they had tried to verify or falsify what was said. In other words, as a result of trying to see or understand what the minority saw or understood, the majority begins to see and understand as the minority would. These are the main reasons why, in our opinion, minorities generally have a greater influence on the private than on the public response.

But have our previous experiments really demonstrated a genuine perceptual change? In order to ascertain this, recall how we proceeded. As described elsewhere (Moscovici et al., 1969), groups composed of four naive subjects and two experimental confederates were asked to make a series of color perception judgments. All of the stimulus slides were blue. Subjects were asked to describe them as being either blue or green and to estimate their light intensity. Of course, on all of the trials, the confederates said that the slides were green.

Upon completing the procedure described above, subjects were asked to take part in a second, ostensibly unrelated, experiment concerning the effect of training upon vision. The subjects, who were tested, individually, were exposed to a number of disks in the blue–green zone of the Farnsworth perception test. For each disk, subjects were asked to indicate the name of the simple color they saw. The results of this second study indicated that the perceptual threshold of subjects who had previously been exposed to the consistent minority shifted. They saw as green disks which are usually perceived as being closer to blue. Furthermore, the subjects who did not change their response during the social interaction phase were more likely than those who did change their response to call the disks green.

These results might indicate a genuine change of the majority's perception, not only of its verbal response. But it must be admitted that they are not entirely convincing. It is possible that in this instance, it was not a genuine modification of color perception that occurred, but rather a generalization of a verbal response. Subjects who had heard the strange and novel response "green" on several occasions during the first experiment may have simply employed it as their own in the second experiment, without their perception of the color being altered in the slightest. In other words, these results may be evidence of a reinforcement effect on one of the verbal responses in the individual's repertory.

Given the theoretical importance of the problem, we intended to alleviate further doubt by means of a more direct experimental procedure. The subjects were again shown blue slides that a confederate described as green. However, instead of using a color test to measure modification of the perceptual scheme, we took advantage of the chromatic complementary afterimage. By this we mean that after having looked at a colored slide for a relatively short time, the subjects were requested to indicate the color they saw on a white screen. As we know, the color perceived immediately after exposure to a colored stimulus is the complementary color of that stimulus. In our case, this would be yellow–orange for a blue slide and red–purple for a green slide. If subjects merely modified their verbal responses but not their perceptual scheme, the reported complementary color would be in the yellow–orange range of the spectrum. If, on the contrary, there were a change in the perceptual scheme, with or without a related change in verbal response, subjects looking at the white screen would indicate a complementary color that is closer to red–purple.

Certainly no experiment can be free from all shortcomings, and ours is no exception. But given our objectives, one can agree that it deals rather directly with the perceptual level, since afterimages appear to have their origin in the retina (Padgham & Saunders, 1975, p. 152). At the same time, we excluded any risk of generalization of verbal responses, since the subjects knew nothing about the afterimage and had to name colors that were different from those named by the confederate. The changes observed, then, are very likely genuine.

From this analysis and previous results, we derived and tested the following hypotheses: (a) influence exerted by a consistent minority modifies the perceptual scheme of individuals, while influence exerted by a consistent majority does not necessarily have such an effect; (b) modification of the perceptual scheme is greater when the influence source is absent than when he/she is present. This second hypothesis is based upon the conjecture that once a conflict of responses has begun, the presence of the source prevents the subject from adopting the suggested response, either because the subject wants to avoid becoming openly deviant or because the source arouses reactance (Brehm, 1966). This was observed in an earlier experiment (Moscovici & Nève, 1971), and we expected to observe it here as well.

Confirmation of these hypotheses would increase our confidence in the proposition that conformity and innovation (i.e., majority and minority influence) involve two different processes, each reflecting a different way of handling the conflict of responses. At the same time, the possibility that a consistent minority can bring about a change in the perception of a majority will start to gain credence. The broad implications of this possibility lead us to consider it carefully despite the caution with which we still have to regard it. Briefly stated, the phenomenon we describe here is more suggestive than it is firmly established.

Experiment 1

Method

The experiment was presented to subjects as a study of color perception. The study was comprised of several phases, each lasting for approximately 30 min, and took place in a dark room.

Subjects

The subjects were 46 female students at the University of Paris. They had no specialized training in psychology and all of them were unaware of the complementary chromatic image effect. No data were discarded.

Materials

The stimulus consisted of a Kodak–Wratten No. 45 slide corresponding to a dominant wavelength of 486.8 nm, with a spectral transmission from 430 to 540 nm of cyanic color. The intensity of illumination was held constant across trials and conformed to the international standards of the C.I.E. (Commission Internationale de l'Eclairage). The slide was projected onto a ripple screen for 10-sec intervals. The chromatic afterimage was produced by stopping the projection for 20 sec in order to enable subjects to "perceive" a color on the screen, which (although they did not realize it) was the complement of the color perceived on the slide.

Procedure

The experiment was comprised of four phases. The first three phases were separated from one another by 30-sec intervals, and from the fourth phase by 1 min.

Phase 1. The first phase consisted of five trials: the answers were private. The subject and the female confederate wrote down their judgments of (a) the color of the slide, and (b) the color of the afterimage, on special answer sheets.

Next, the female experimenter collected the answer sheets and informed the subjects that she possessed some results, with respect to the color of the slides, that were obtained in previous studies in which a large number of people had participated. She then handed the subjects a sheet on which the percentages of people reputedly having judged the slides as blue or as green were indicated:

(a) Majority Source condition:
18.2% saw the color indicated by the naive subject (blue),
81.8% saw the color indicated by the confederate (green).
(b) Minority Source condition:
81.8% saw the color indicated by the naive subject (blue),
18.2% saw the color indicated by the confederate (green).

Phase 2. The social interaction phase was made up of 15 trials. The responses were public and related uniquely to the color of the slide. The confederate gave her responses orally and was the first to do so on each trial. Her judgment remained consistent in that she always responded "green." This response was different from the one proposed by the subject in Phase 1 of the experiment.

Phase 3. The third phase, which was similar to the first, consisted of 15 trials on which the subject and confederate noted their judgments in private with respect to (a) the color of the slide, and (b) the color of the afterimage, on special answer sheets. At the end of this phase, the confederate said she had an urgent appointment and left the room.

Phase 4. Alone now, the subject repeated the procedure of Phase 3 for another five trials.

At the end of the four phases, a postexperimental questionnaire was administered. It assessed self-perception, stimulus perception, and the way in which the source of influence was perceived by the subject. The experimenter then explained the aims of the study and debriefed the subject.

Experimental Conditions

The experimental procedure was very simple. The first independent variable was manipulated by presenting the confederate's responses as similar to those of a majority or a minority. A control condition in which the subject and confederate responded privately throughout was also run. Control subjects did not receive any information about the responses of previous subjects and, thus, were not exposed to any external influence. The second independent variable was introduced by the departure of the confederate. A manipulation of the presence/absence of the influence source has always appeared fundamental to us in discerning the effects of the conflict of responses in relation to another person and to the stimulus itself.

Dependent Measures

Manifest influence. The confederate's influence was assessed on a manifest level by the change in responses to the color of the stimulus.

Latent influence. The confederate's influence was assessed on a latent level by the reported color of the afterimage. Subjects rated the color of the afterimage on a 9-point scale, with the following values: yellow, yellow–orange, orange, orange–red, red, red–pink, pink, pink–purple, purple. Responses were scored according to the average rating of the trials for each phase. A change in the average score across phases indicated a shift in the perceptual scheme.

Postexperimental measures. The postexperimental questionnaire contained questions like: "How have you perceived your partner?" "To what extent have you complied with her judgments?" and "To what extent has she complied with your judgments?" Each item on the questionnaire was rated on a 6-point scale, e.g.:

How have you perceived your partner:

1	2	3	4	5	6

1. Not competent at all
2. Little competent
3. Just competent
4. Rather competent
5. Competent
6. Very competent

Results

Manifest Influence

During the first phase, subjects in all conditions unanimously judged the slide as blue. This indicates that at the outset, a strong consensus existed within the population and that if a different response were given during the interaction, it would provoke a particularly intense conflict. In the second phases, the number of "green" responses given by the subjects in the experimental conditions tended to increase by 5%. These responses were given by a small number of subjects, five approximately, and there was no significant difference between the conditions.

Latent Influence

Let us now turn to an examination of the results obtained on the afterimage test (see Table 17.1), which no longer represent a change in the labeling of the stimulus but rather presumably, a true modification of the subjects' perceptual scheme. This perceptual modification is measured by the change in subjects' judgments of the complementary color perceived on the white screen immediately after removal of the slide.

The subjects' afterimage judgments were indicated on 9-point scales, ranging from yellow (1) to purple (9). In order to take into account the fact that the phases were comprised of different numbers of trials, individuals' afterimage scores were standardized across conditions, separately for each phase, prior to analysis. It may be noted that the movement toward a higher score indicates a shift toward the complementary color of green (red–purple), while movement toward a lower score indicates a shift toward the complementary color of blue (yellow–orange).

The data were analyzed by means of a 3 (conditions) × 3 (phases) unweighted means analysis of variance, with repeated measures on the Phases factor. Although no main effects were found, the analysis did yield a significant conditions × phases interaction, $F(4, 86) = 2.58, p < .05$. Inspection of the means indicates that the judgments of subjects in the minority influence condition shifted toward the complement of green from the pre- to the postinfluence situations. A series of a priori comparisons revealed that this shift was marginally significant from the first to the third phase, $t(86) = 2.18, p < 0.05$, and that this shift became significant when the source of influence was absent (from the first to the fourth phase), $t(86) = 2.49, p < .02$. No such effect was obtained in the majority influence or the control conditions.

Taken together, these results confirm our hypotheses. The consistent minority tended to produce a change in perceptual responses, and this change was reliable when the minority was no longer present. The consistent majority, in comparison, produced some change only in verbal responses. Thus, conversion behavior occurred in the minority influence condition.

Postexperimental Measures

This study has two aims: (a) to evaluate influence on behavioral and perceptual levels in the differ-

TABLE 17.1. Mean Afterimage Scores: Experiment 1

Experimental condition		Phase 1 Preinfluence, presence of source	Phase 3 Postinfluence, presence of source	Phase 4 Postinfluence, absence of source
Minority source (n =18)	Mean	−.203	+.269	+.338
	SD	1.085	.948	.722
Majority source (n = 18)	Mean	+.199	−.143	−.180
	SD	.927	1.146	1.083
Control (n =10)	Mean	+.009	−.236	−.290
	SD	.990	.774	1.190

Note. These data are based on subjects' normal standard scores. A higher score represents a judgment closer to the complement of green (red–purple).

ent experimental conditions, and (b) to examine the way in which the subject perceived herself, the stimulus, and the source of influence. With regard to the latter, the postexperimental questionnaire provided us with a certain amount of useful information.

To begin with, it is interesting to note that no subject in any of the experimental conditions admitted to having been influenced. To the question "To what extent have you perceived the color indicated by your partner?" there is no difference between the subjects whatever the condition. Furthermore, when the subjects were asked, to what extent they had been influenced by their partner, they generally answered that they had not been influenced. Thus it seems that the color perceived was not green and, as usual, that the subjects had not been influenced by the confederate.

How was the source of influence perceived? The confederate was seen as pleasant, sure of herself, and consistent in her judgment, regardless of whether she represented a majority or a minority. On the other hand, the majority tended to be seen as more competent than the minority, $t(34) = 1.90$, $p < .10$, two-tailed, and the minority was judged more convincing than the majority, $t(34) = 1.78$, $p < .10$.

The first result confirms the findings of Moscovici and Lage (1976) that competence assigned to a majority is usually denied to a minority. The second result shows that despite its perceived relation with incompetence, an active minority is viewed as more forceful and its responses are considered as more persuasive.

How did the subjects perceive themselves as targets of influence? They considered their opinions equally consistent and convincing under both experimental conditions. Paradoxically, when they were faced with a majority, they felt much "surer of themselves" than when they were faced with a minority, $t(34) = 1.91$, $p < .10$, two-tailed. It should be noted that it was precisely the first category of subjects that was the least influenced on the afterimage test and when the source of influence was absent. This underlines the importance of resistance in a conformity situation. That the second category of subjects judged the deviant confederate as "sure of herself" suggests that they thought that she must be very self-confident. We have seen the same thing in other experiments. Confidence in one's opinion is seen as a type of courage—the capacity to resist publicly. The results of the post-experimental questionnaire are consistent with previous results and with the interpretations offered.

Experiment 2

In order to assess the robustness of the effect obtained in the first experiment, we replicated the two experimental conditions (e.g., majority and minority influence) in a second study. The procedure was essentially the same, except that there were five trials in each phase and the experimenter was a female student. There were 14 subjects in each condition.

The results of this replication were very similar to those obtained in the first experiment. Table 17.2 presents the means and standard deviations for the afterimage scores. An inspection of the means shows that subjects' judgments were displaced toward the chromatic afterimage of green only in the minority influence condition.

This displacement was accentuated in the absence of the influence source. Again, although no main effects were found, the repeated measures analysis of variance did yield a significant conditions × phases interaction, $F(2, 52) = 3.94$, $p < .05$. A series of a priori comparisons revealed that within the minority influence conditions, the shift in judgment from the first to the third phase was significant, $t(52) = 2.54$, $p < .02$, as was the shift from the first to the fourth phase, $t(52) = 3.03$, $p < .01$. In the fourth phase, the difference between the minority and majority influence conditions was significant, $t = 2.05$ with the critical value of t adjusted ($\alpha = .05$, two-tailed). The results of this replication are in agreement with our hypotheses, and they indicate that the effects observed are stable.

Discussion

Although the results of this study support our predictions, we consider them as provisional and as only a first step in a very difficult area to explore. The afterimage is a labile phenomenon, its mechanisms are not well understood, and genuine changes of perception have rarely been obtained. Thus, caution in this domain is necessary. Despite these limitations, our observations tend to support a new line of thought concerning influence processes. However, several points need to be clarified.

TABLE 17.2. Mean Afterimage Scores: Experiment 2[a]

Experimental condition		Phase 1 Preinfluence, presence of source	Phase 3 Postinfluence, presence of source	Phase 4 Postinfluence, absence of source
Minority source (n = 14)	Mean	5.10[a]	6.35	6.59
	SD	2.16	2.07	2.26
Majority source (n = 14)	Mean	5.06	4.85	4.71
	SD	2.73	2.44	2.87

[a]A higher score indicates a judgment closer to the complement of green (red–purple).

The first concerns our experimental procedure. In previous studies, we always used two confederates to represent the minority. This is because the response of a single confederate to a physical stimulus could have been rejected by saying that the individual was eccentric, that he/she didn't understand the task, etc. By introducing a second confederate, we eliminated the possibility of attributing the "green" response to personal factors. If two independent people make the same response, the subject is obliged to attribute it, at least partially, to the stimulus itself. In the present experiment, we tried to reach this goal by informing subjects that other people had previously given the same response as the confederate. Of course, hearing someone call a blue slide "green" was unacceptable to them. But they could not dismiss his/her judgment easily by attributing it to personal factors. Others before him/her had reputedly given the same response. So, from the point of view of social psychological processes, the procedures are similar and the results obtained may be considered comparable.

The second point concerns the presentation of the stimulus. Traditional studies of conformity have utilized different stimuli over trials. In the present experiment, subjects were asked to judge the same stimulus 40 times. We did this for obvious reasons. On one hand, we tried to reinforce the seriousness of the experiment and of the subject's responses. This could not be achieved by only verbal instructions. On the other hand, we wanted to make subjects conscious of the deviant aspects of the confederate's responses and of his/her consistency. As our interviews have shown, consistent behavior is in itself disturbing and contrary to social expectations. In other words, the demand characteristics of conformity situations are related to recognition of external pressure, of competence, and of a reality that is supposedly common to group members. In innovation situations, the demand characteristics are rather different. It is necessary that subjects be made aware that the "level of reality" on which the interaction takes place is not the usual one. Consistent responses to the same stimulus pressure the individual to undertake an "internal" deliberation, the outcome of which appears to depend on the individual him/herself. This is probably why the confederate was judged as convincing and as making one think, but not as particularly competent (Moscovici & Lage, 1976). One could say that a minority's success depends upon the internalization of alternative responses and of the decision-making process, which is not necessarily true for a majority.

The third point has to do with the chromatic afterimage. One may reasonably wonder whether it reflects a true perceptual change or simply a distortion of judgment, because the individual no longer believes in his response: The data show that belief in the response remains, because at least 90% of the time, the slides were correctly judged as blue. Moreover, what we know about color perception and afterimages, in general, suggests that an "unconscious" or "peripheral" mechanism is involved. We do not deny that cognitive elements may be involved and that they have an effect. But until some new theoretical development takes place in this area, we can assume that the observed modification is very likely of a perceptual nature. In discussions with subjects after the experiment, none of them expressed doubts about her response of awareness of having changed it. But subjects did express astonishment about the possibility that the slides were green. All of our observations indicate that the transformation of response takes place without awareness, beyond one's voluntary control. Furthermore, the change cannot be considered as an instance of response generalization given that: (a) the response to the stimulus and the response to the chromatic afterimage were different (green/blue in the first case, and a mark on a scale in the second); (b) only the response to the stimulus was given in public, the response to the afterimage was always private and, thus, the subject never heard the words yellow, orange, purple, etc., uttered; and (c) the subject was not aware of the relationship between a color and its complement.

Taken together, our observations tend to show that the conflict of responses on a verbal judgment level is transposed and may be resolved on a perceptual level. It remains, of course, to separate these different factors (social, cognitive, perceptual) and to obtain more conclusive evidence about their respective roles. To do this we do not need new experimental designs so much as new experimental techniques, enabling us to understand complex, multilevel behavior.

Our results support the notion that majority and minority influence are different processes, the former producing mostly public submissiveness without private acceptance (Festinger, 1953; Kelman, 1958), and the latter producing primarily changes in private responses. These processes, called compliance and conversion, are mutually exclusive and to a certain extent, opposite (Mugny, 1976). But this raises a problem. How does a perception or judgment that has changed on a private, latent level become public or conscious? Until now, while establishing that conformity produces overt and public compliance, social psychologists have studied how attitude change becomes covert and private. In other words, by what means is a person made to accept inwardly what he/she does outwardly? Dissonance theory provides the best known answer to this question: force a change of behavior, without much justification, and a change of mind will follow.[1] To the extent that innovation produces covert and private changes of opinion, perception, etc., we are faced with the inverse prob-

lem: By what means can a person be made to do outwardly what he accepts inwardly? This is not only a scientific problem, but also a moral and political one. Naturally, we do not propose to resolve it here. We merely wanted to present some new evidence concerning latent, or genuine, influence effects and to indicate its broader implications.

Note added in proof. In an attempt to replicate the experiment reported here, Doms and van Avermaet (1980) confirmed our findings in the minority influence condition. In the majority influence condition they observed the same tendency, but noted a chromatic aftereffect when the confederate left. Bear in mind that in our condition we manipulated two independent variables: (a) the source of influence, and (b) the withdrawal of the confederate which has an effect on influence whatever the source might be. We have illustrated this phenomenon in a purely individual situation (Moscovici & Nève, 1971), as have Brehm and Mann (1975) in a situation where an individual faced a group. The results obtained by Doms and Van Avermaet are analogous to those obtained by Brehm and Mann. There is, thus, a difference between the majority and minority influence in their experiment as well as in ours, but the withdrawal of the confederate produces a different effect that still has to be explained. But even if their findings had completely invalidated ours, one could not say, nevertheless, that conformity and innovation are identical phenomena. There are limits to what the laboratory can say against reality.

REFERENCES

Asch, S. E. (1956). Studies of independence and conformity: A minority of one against a unanimous majority. *Psychological Monographs, 70*(Whole No. 416).

Brehm, J. W. (1966). *A theory of psychological reactance.* New York: Academic Press.

Brehm, J. W., & Mann, M. (1975). Effect of importance of freedom and attraction to group members on influence produced by group pressure. *Journal of Personality and Social Psychology, 31,* 816–824.

Doms, M., & van Avermaet, E. (1980). Majority influence, minority influence, conversion behavior: A replication. *Journal of Experimental Social Psychology, 16,* 283–292.

Festinger, L. (1953). An analysis of compliant behavior. In M. Sherif & M. O. Wilson (Eds.), *Group relations at the crossroads.* New York: Harper.

Kelman, H. C. (1958). Compliance, identification, and internalization: Three processes of attitude change. *Journal of Conflict Resolution, 2,* 51–60.

Mead, G. H. (1970). *Mind, self and society.* Chicago/London: University of Chicago Press.

---

[1]One could try to explain our results in terms of dissonance theory. But to do so would require some ad hoc hypotheses concerning the existence of a forced compliance and a greater need of justification in the minority influence than in the majority influence condition. Further, the picture is complicated by the potential presence of reactance phenomena which would also have to be taken into account in a more general theory of minority influence. Before we have a more complete description of this type of influence and the changes it entails, we believe it would be premature to make a firm decision between alternative explanations. At this stage of the research, however, we feel that our hypotheses are most directly related to the phenomenon under investigation.

Moscovici, S., & Lage, E. (1976). Studies in social influence. III. Majority versus minority influence in a group. *European Journal of Social Psychology, 6,* 149–174.

Moscovici, S., Lage, E., & Naffrechoux, M. (1969). Influence of a consistent minority on the responses of a majority in a color preparation task. *Sociometry, 32,* 365–379.

Moscovici, S., & Nève, P. (1971). Studies in social influence. I. Those absent are in the right: Convergence and polarization of answers in the course of a social interaction. *European Journal of Social Psychology, 1,* 201–214.

Mugny, G. (1976). Quelle influence majoritaire? Quelle influence minoritaire? *Revue Suisse de Psychologie Pure et Appliquée, 4,* 255–268.

Padgham, C. A., & Saunders, J. E. (1975). *The perception of light and color.* London: Bell.

Personnaz, B. (1974). *La conformité minoritaire: Perte d'identité sociale ou clandestinité des référents?* Unpublished manuscript, Paris.

Personnaz, B. (1975/1976). Conformité, consensus et référents clandestins: La dépendance en tant que processus annulateur d'influence. *Bulletin de Psychologie, 29,* 230–242.

Disadvantage, Relative Deprivation, and Social Protest

Intergroup relations almost always involve inequalities of status, power, prestige, resources, and so forth. While dominant, majority groups do well out of this arrangement, subordinate, minority groups do not. Groups that lose out in the intergroup struggle for power and prestige tend to be disadvantaged, and can find that their goals and aspirations are continually frustrated relative to other groups. Although groups can sometimes acquiesce to these conditions, the sense of deprivation can sometimes be so acute that, given the right circumstances, these groups can engage in social protest or other collective behaviors including riots and demonstrations.

Explanations of collective and crowd behaviors have tended to emphasize the automatic, emotional, and impulsive aspects of such behavior—for example Berkowitz's (1972) famous "long hot summer" analysis of the 1960s urban race riots in the United States. The riots mainly occurred during heatwaves. Our first reading, by Stephen Reicher, now at the University of St. Andrews, provides a very different analysis of the crowd. Reicher (1984) argues, from a social identity perspective, that crowd behavior is much more deliberate and logical. It is tied closely to social identity and group membership and is simply intergroup behavior. In this reading, Reicher grounds his explanation in a careful analysis of a riot that occurred in Bristol in April, 1980. One of Reicher's main points is that crowd behavior has limits that are set by the social identity of the crowd. Within these limits, it is the behavior of highly prototypical members of the crowd, and/or highly group prototypical behavior itself, that is taken up by the crowd in the specific context of the event. In this way, crowd behavior can be volatile and extreme, but it is not boundless and irrational. If the intergroup context of the event pitches unemployed people against the state then the crowd may well attack the police and emblems of state "oppression" (e.g., unemployment office, bank, etc.), but it is unlikely to indulge in an orgy of destruction of private property or assaults on passers-by.

Our second reading, by Reeve Vanneman and Tom Pettigrew, both at Harvard at the time, is an analysis of relative deprivation and race relations in the United States. Vanneman and Pettigrew (1972) discuss the concept of relative deprivation to show that injustice and disadvantage are associated with a feeling that one's own group is deprived relative to relevant other groups (fraternalistic relative deprivation), rather than a feeling that oneself is deprived relative to specific other individuals (egoistic relative deprivation). Vanneman and Pettigrew use this idea to explain the substantial evidence that racist attitudes, for example in the United States and Britain, are

more extreme among skilled blue-collar people than any other group. This group is most vulnerable to competition from other (e.g., immigrant) groups, and thus feels most threatened and fraternalistically most deprived.

The final reading in this section is by Steven Wright at the University of California Santa Cruz, and his associates Don Taylor and Fathali Moghaddam. Wright and his associates (1990) draw on relative deprivation and social identity ideas to examine the different sorts of responses that people can have to being in a disadvantaged social group. When members of a disadvantaged group believe that entry to an advantaged group is open, even only marginally open (only a token percentage of people can pass), they individually pursue an upward mobility strategy. Collective action by members of a disadvantaged group is most likely to be taken when entry to the advantaged group is closed, and then only by those who believe they were closest to entry. Where collective action is taken, people only resort to extreme forms (e.g., riots, terrorism) when there are no readily available normative means (e.g., peaceful protest, lobbying) at their disposal.

Discussion Questions

1. What conditions determine whether deprived/disadvantaged groups acquiesce or rise up and protest/rebel?
2. What are the limitations of the view that crowd behavior reflects the surfacing of unconscious antisocial instincts?
3. What are the advantages of an intergroup analysis of crowd behavior?
4. What arguments would you muster to counter the view that disadvantage is of one's own making?

Suggested Readings

Branscombe, N. R., Schmitt, M. T., & Harvey, R. D. (1999). Perceiving pervasive discrimination among African Americans: Implications for group identification and well-being. *Journal of Personality and Social Psychology, 77,* 135–149. An analysis of the relationship between social identification, disadvantage, and well-being—how does it feel to be disadvantaged and how is this moderated by social identity processes?

Crosby, F. (1982). *Relative deprivation and working women.* New York: Oxford University Press. A careful analysis of the subjective perception of being disadvantaged, and its relationship to protest or acquiescence—in this case focusing upon gender.

Esses, V. M., Jackson, L. M., & Armstrong, T. L. (1998). Intergroup competition and attitudes towards immigrants and immigration: An instrumental model of group conflict. *Journal of Social Issues, 54,* 699–724. An extension and application of realistic group conflict theory to the analysis of why people protest against immigration.

Gurr, T. R. (1970). *Why men rebel.* Princeton, NJ: Princeton University Press. A heavily-cited social science analysis of relative deprivation and social action.

Klandermans, B. (1997). *The social psychology of protest.* Oxford, UK: Blackwell. A wide-ranging social psychological analysis of protest and revolt.

Postmes, T., & Spears, R. (1998). Deindividuation and antinormative behavior: A meta-analysis. *Psychological Bulletin, 123,* 238–259. A critical analysis of the idea of deindividuation in understanding collective behavior.

Reicher, S. D. (2001). The psychology of crowd dynamics. In M. A. Hogg & R. S. Tindale (Eds.), *Blackwell handbook of social psychology: Group processes* (pp. 182–208). Oxford, UK: Blackwell. Critical analysis of crowd behavior and social protest—Reicher champions a general social identity analysis that views these phenomena as intergroup behavior.

Simon, B., Lowey, M., Stuermer, S., Weber, U., Fretag, P., Habig, C., Kampmeier, C., & Spahlinger, P. (1998). Collective identification and social movement participation. *Journal of Personality and Social Psychology, 74,* 646–658. A recent analysis of social movements from the perspective of identification with the movement and/or the wider identity that spawns the movement.

Walker, I., & Pettigrew, T. F. (1984). Relative deprivation theory: An overview and conceptual critique. *British Journal of Social Psychology, 23,* 301–310. A well-cited critical and influential overview of relative deprivation theory.

READING 18

The St. Pauls' Riot: An Explanation of the Limits of Crowd Action in Terms of a Social Identity Model

Stephen D. Reicher • The University, Dundee

The paper contains a detailed study of the St. Pauls' riots of April 1980. Particular attention is paid to the limits of participation in the event and the limits of crowd action. It is argued that these limits show clear social form and cannot be explained in terms of the individualistic theories that dominate crowd psychology. Instead a model of crowd behaviour based on the social identity model is advanced to account for the observations. It is concluded that crowd behaviour is more sophisticated and creative than hitherto allowed and that the neglect of this field should be remedied.

Introduction

The fascination of crowd psychology lies in the fact that it seeks to account for behaviour that shows clear social coherence—in the sense of a large amount of people acting in the same manner—despite the lack of either pre-planning or any structured direction. The theoretical interest lies in the attempt to discover a psychological basis for this coherence. There is however a more pragmatic reason why such behaviour is of concern: it relates to the social consequence of such behaviour. Out of such concern was crowd psychology born.

The discipline emerged towards the end of last century as an establishment response to a wave of working class unrest. Faced with seemingly spontaneous protest actions involving large homogeneous masses, the establishment sought less to understand than to discredit and repress the threat. Indeed the earliest works on the crowd were written by criminologists discussing on what basis to punish crowd participants—should all be considered guilty or just a criminal core of ringleaders who incited the others? (cf. Tarde, 1890; Sighele, 1892). Moreover the most influential of all books on the crowd: Le Bon's *The Crowd—A Study of the Popular Mind* (1947) gained its repute not through any theoretical novelty (it is, if anything, an object lesson in plagiarism) but rather through its conscious attempt to advise the establishment on how to contain crowds or even use them against the socialist opposition. For his efforts Le Bon gained fulsome praise from, amongst others, Mussolini and Goebbels.

Only by bearing in mind the circumstances of its birth is it possible to understand the biases that permeate theoretical explanations of crowd behaviour. Because they were not prepared to admit that crowd action may have been a response to gross social inequality and active repression, theorists were forced to ignore the social context in which such actions occurred. This had a number of consequences, both in terms of description and of theory. On the descriptive level certain characteristics of the syndicalist crowds—as they appeared to these "gentleman" observers—were abstracted from the context of class struggle and converted into generic characteristics of the crowd: violence, irrationality, fickleness, mental inferiority. On a theoretical level there were two ways in which the social causation of crowd behaviour was denied.

The older, exemplified by Le Bon, is group mind theory. This asserts that individuals in the crowd lose their conscious personality and revert to a primitive racial unconscious which accounts for the barbarism of crowd action. Slightly more modern is the extreme individualism of Allport who asserts that the individual in the crowd is the same as the individual alone "only more so" (cf. Allport, 1924, p. 295). While these two approaches are diametrically opposed to each other, the one proposing individuality is extinguished in the crowd the other that it is accentuated, they are nonetheless united in one crucial premise. Both suggest that the only mechanism capable of directing planned or rational behaviour is a sovereign individual identity.

The principal problem with such approaches is that they systematically exclude any social basis for the coherence of crowd behaviour. Not only does this imply that crowd behaviour lacks socially meaningful form but also that it is insensitive to social context. These problems become clearer when one considers the nature of the limits of crowd events.

One can consider the question of limits in the senses. Firstly the limits of participation: that is who does and who does not take part in crowd events. Secondly the limits of content: this addresses which actions do and which do not occur during a crowd event.

Concerning the question of participation the group mind theory would suggest that all members of a given race will take part. Such an approach fails before Milgram and Toch's most basic of criteria: to explain why riot police do not get drawn in by the rhetoric of a crowd demagogue (cf. Milgram & Toch, 1969). On the other hand, the individualistic approach predicts that participation will be tied to personality type. However, despite attempts to do so, no common trait has ever been found to distinguish membership versus non-membership of a crowd (cf. McPhail, 1970).

Turning to content, both approaches are even more inadequate. The group mind theory has little to say except that whatever the situation a crowd of the same race will always act in the same way and that violence and mayhem will be involved; the crowd is only powerful for destruction says Le Bon (1947). Allportian individualism can only seek to tie behaviours to personality, but this is both empirically and theoretically insufficient. Empirically, as noted above, no common trait characterizes crowd participation, but even if it did it is unclear how personality factors could determine the precise behaviours of any crowd event.

Despite the antiquity of these theories their influence on later work has perpetuated exactly the same problems as those outlined above. (It should be noted that the focus of concern here is specifically on the psychology of crowd action. General models of social movements are of interest only insofar as they relate specifically to this question.) The group mind tradition is most directly represented in de-individuation theory, which is a translation of the Le Bonian notion of "submergence." The idea is that individuals in unstructured groups cease self-evaluation. This causes a weakening of conventional controls resulting in behaviour which is generally uncontrolled and destructive (Festinger, Pepitone, & Newcomb, 1952; Zimbardo, 1969). There is a double problem with this approach. First, the de-individuation literature ignores the context of behaviour and fails to distinguish between anonymity in a group and anonymity when isolated. There is evidence that individuals who are de-individuated in groups do not always behave anti-socially, but rather show increased adherence to group norms (Reicher, 1982a; White, 1977). Secondly, crowd members appear as anonymous only with respect to outsiders and are nearly always known to some other crowd members (McPhail, 1971).

There are two principal ways in which the individualistic tradition is represented in modern crowd-related research. The first is "social-facilitation" theory, which proposes that presence of an audience accentuates the distinctiveness of individual behaviour patterns. While there is much controversy over the theoretical basis of this relationship (cf. Geen & Gange, 1977; Sanders, 1981) there is consensus as to the effects. Thus the model is insensitive both to the nature of the audience and to the context in which the subject is acting. While it may propose that behaviours will be more extreme it cannot account for the content of social behaviours.

The second major individualistic approach is that of game theorists such as Olson (1965), taken up by sociologists such as Oberschall (1973) and developed into a psychological rational calculus by Berk (1972, 1974). The idea is that individuals act as a joint function of "payoff" and "probability of support." In the crowd the values of the second term are altered leading to more extreme behaviours. However, the model specifies neither what behaviours will be displayed nor how "payoff" or "probability of support" are to be assessed. Since understanding those behaviours which will elicit a high probability of support addresses the central questions of the basis for contagion or social influence in the crowd this approach begs the practical questions of crowd psychology. In other words it acts less as a specification of the mechanisms underlying crowd behaviour than as a metatheoretical justification of crowd action as individual rational choice.

In recent years, however, two novel approaches to the crowd have been advanced. The first is emergent norm theory (Turner & Killian, 1972). This proposes that crowd behaviour is governed by social norms. These norms emerge during an initial period of "milling" when the actions of visually prominent individuals ("keynoting activities") come to be seen as characteristic of the crowd as a whole. Thus it is implied that the homogeneity of crowds—in an initial period at least—is an illusion. Yet even an avowed supporter of the position admits that the rapidity with which norms arise does not square with this picture of extended interaction as a prerequisite for norm formation (Wright, 1978). There is, however, a more basic problem with emergent norm theory. In explaining the genesis of emergent norms, Turner and Killian relate them simply to the activities of keynoters. As such their position resolves itself into an elitist version of Allportian individualism; instead of crowd behaviour being explained in terms of the personalities of all participants it is tied to the personality of a dominant few.

The second novel approach is that taken by Moscovici (1981). Moscovici proposes that mass behavior is characterized by the persistence of mythologized perceptions of the past in the form of collective representations. These representations are based on "persons and situations with which we are identified, our parents, our nation, a war or a revolution with which especially powerful emotions are associated" (1981, p. 392). While Moscovici is above all concerned with the nature of charismatic leadership (which, he argues, resides upon the ability to reconcile the dialectic between order and equality through association with idealized images of past tyrants) and less with the details of crowd behaviour, the concept of identification and its related representations as a basis for crowd action provides a powerful conceptual tool.

The concept of identification is central to the model of crowd behaviour adopted by Reicher (1982a, b, forthcoming). This model is based on the social identity approach of Tajfel and Turner (cf. Tajfel, 1978; Turner, 1982). In essence, it is argued that a crowd is a form of social group in the sense of a set of individuals who perceive themselves as members of a common social category, or to put it another way, adopt a common *social* identification. Turner (1982) argues that social identification is a necessary and sufficient condition for a form of social influence which he calls "Referent Informational Influence" (R.I.I.). This refers to a process whereby group members seek out the stereotypic norms which define category membership and conform their behaviour to them. It is, in effect, a process of self-stereotyping. The implications of R.I.I. provide a basis for understanding the characteristics of crowd action. In order to account for the operation of R.I.I. it is necessary to consider what characterizes the crowd as a special form of group. Three criteria must obtain for a group to be considered as a crowd. The first is that group members are face to face, the second is that the situation in which the group acts is in some way novel or ambiguous and the third is that all formal means of reaching group consensus are blocked. The significance of these conditions lies in the following dilemma: how are crowd members to conform to stereotypic norms when the fact that they are in an unprecedented situation means that there are no appropriate norms? The answer is that crowd members must elaborate an appropriate situational identity which at once provides a guide for action and conforms to their common social identification. The way in which this will be done is through what Turner (1982) calls the "inductive aspect of categorization." In other words, criterial norms will be inferred from the actions of others as long as (a) they are clearly seen as ingroup members, and (b) that the action is consonant with the attributes of defining their social identification. For this to occur, however, the crowd members must be face to face. It is clear, however, that a range of behaviours will satisfy these two conditions. Since there is no formal means of validating a given behavioural norm—either by means of orders in a hierarchical system or a democratic decision-making process—then crowd norms may quickly be superceded as new behaviours come to be seen as more appropriate. This would account for the rapidly changing yet homogeneous nature of crowd action (cf. Wright, 1978).

When considering the twin problem of the limits of crowd behaviour this model has two crucial implications. Firstly, the social influence process operating in the crowd depends on social identification. Thus the basis of behavioural homogeneity is a common social identification and, conversely, only those who have identified with the relevant category will be subject to crowd influence ("contagion"). In other words, the limits of participation will be the limits of identification.

Secondly, only those behaviours which are consonant with crowd members' social identification are liable to define behavioural norms (become "contagious"). Therefore while crowds may show a range of behaviours, that range will be limited by those attributes which define the social category to which they belong. The socialist crowds of which Le Bon wrote may have done many things but they would never have attacked the poor, or crossed a picket line.

The aim of this paper is to use the data from one crowd episode in order to provide support for the above model. In particular the limits of the episode will be examined in order to demonstrate that it is impossible to explain the form of behaviours without recourse to the social conception of themselves and their world displayed by participants. The data cannot be considered as "proof" of the social identity model. Apart from anything else, events such as that described make it somewhat difficult to stop participants and measure cognitive structures such as identity. However, it is intended to show that the social identity model can account for the event in a way that previous theories cannot.

The St. Pauls' "Riots"

The events to be described occurred in Bristol on 2nd April 1980. Only a part of what happened during the so-called "St. Pauls' riots" will be considered. In particular, only the period before the police withdrew and shops were looted and various buildings set on fire will be considered. This is not because the themes to be elaborated below do not apply—although there are differences between the two periods (cf. Reicher, forthcoming), but because the data is more lengthy and detailed and adds little to the basic argument.

The data itself comes from a number of sources. The official police report was obtained as well as the statement of the Chief Fire Officer. The "St. Pauls' Riot Opinion" written by a lawyer for the Police Authority was made available to the author as well as the legal opinion for this authority and Lloyds Bank concerning insurance claims. All relevant TV and radio programmes were taped and all newspaper reports were collected. Many photographs were assembled, including photographs from public (principally newspaper files) and private sources. Twenty children (average age 11 years) were interviewed. Some 20 individuals were approached on the streets and notes were made on conversations immediately afterwards. Finally, six subjects were interviewed and interviews tape-recorded. These were simply chosen as the only six people who had taken part in the relevant events and who were prepared to be recorded. Interviews were unscheduled so as to retain maximum flexibility. Where specific quotations are used identification will include source (tape, script, conversation, radio, TV, paper) colour (white, black), sex (male, female) and age.

Before continuing with an account of the events it should be emphasized that there were considerable practical difficulties in obtaining this data. In particular black respondents were naturally suspicious of the researcher's motivations and possible uses of data. Thus, the data is open to challenge on the basis of representativeness, accuracy and so on. Such difficulties are insuperable, but it should be reiterated that, however categorical various assertions may be, the paper is not intended as absolute proof, but rather as highly suggestive, for a theoretical account of crowd behaviour.

The Events

The account to be presented below was constructed out of multiple partial accounts. The procedures used were those of methodological and data triangulation (cf. Denzin, 1970). Thus data from dif-

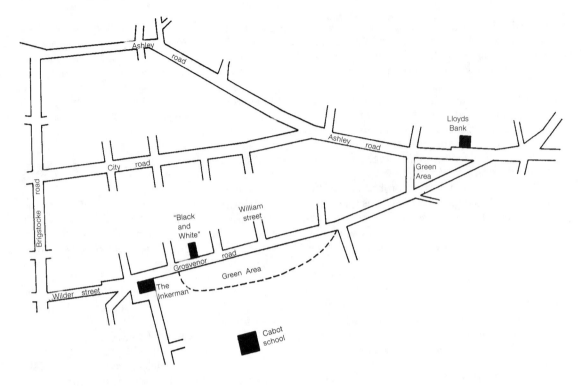

FIGURE 18.1 ■ Map of St. Pauls.

ferent types of source and from different instances of a given type was combined. Unless stated otherwise, events are only included where two or more sources confirm each other. A special problem concerned timing and sequencing of events. Subjects tended to confuse times so as to describe events as consecutive which were in fact separated by a considerable interval. Of particular help in sorting out the sequence of events were "objective" indices such as photographs, times of live radio bulletins and timings of official reports (police and fire service). Nevertheless, while the sequence seems fairly well established all timings given in the text should be taken as approximate.

(a) At approximately 3:30 p.m. on 2nd April 1980 two plain clothes policemen entered the Black and White cafe on Grosvenor Road. On the road outside were another 12 officers and more officers with dogs were held in reserve, about ¼ mile away, in Portland Square. The purpose of the raid was to execute a warrant issued to investigate allegations of illegal drinking (the B and W had lost its licence in 1979) and the sale of drugs: Shortly afterwards the 12 officers waiting outside came into the cafe. Two men, Bertram Wilkes (the

owner) and Newton Leopold Brown were arrested. The police went into the cellars and began to take out the 372 crates of beer and lager found on the premises. These were stacked outside the cafe ready to be removed.

There is little consensus as to what happened during this period. The police claim they showed a warrant and all proceeded peacefully. Several witnesses in the cafe claim no warrant was shown and that the police harassed those inside. Further rumours suggest that the two plain clothes police completed a drugs deal before calling in their colleagues (conv. BM 18) or that the police were even smoking "ganja" in the cafe (conv. BM 20). Whether true or not, these perceptions indicate a general feeling about the illegitimacy of the police action.

Just as the police initially arrived, Cabot School, behind Grosvenor Road, had broken up for Easter. As the children went home they saw the beginnings of the police action and hence the news spread very rapidly. Moreover several people who had been in the cafe during the raid were allowed to leave. They too passed on word of what was happening. Over the hour from 3:30 p.m. to 4:30

p.m. as the police stacked liquor outside the B and W a crowd gathered. It was a warm day and people just hung around watching.

(b) At about 4.30 p.m. the mood changed. It is impossible to point to one incident which sparked off the initial bout of violence. At least eight different accounts have been given of the initial flare-up. Indeed it is false to believe that there is a single "real" story of what happened. For most individuals, not at the front of the crowd, all they knew was that a commotion was going on. Accounts of what was happening filtered to the back and it was those rumours which provided a basis for their action. What is significant, therefore, is that all the accounts contained as a central theme, an unjustified and unprovoked police attack on the Black and White—seen by many as the focus for St. Pauls' inhabitants. Apart from one set of stories which centre on a man whose trousers were ripped by the police and whose requests for compensation were rudely rejected. (How a row over torn trousers led to . . . "Flashpoint," *Daily Mirror*, April 5, 1980). Most stories centre on three police who came out of the Black and White with drug exhibits. According to some they struck out calling the crowd "black bastards" (conv. BM 18); according to others they had a man with them who made a break for it and dogs were set on him (radio BM?); according to one witness the police ran after a black youth and beat him up (Guardian, April 5, 1980).

Whatever the exact cause, the three police and others in the area were pelted with bricks. The windscreen of the police car to which these three fled was smashed, as was that of a civilian who, according to one informant, "had smiled when the police hassled us" (conv. BM 24). One police motorcyclist and a police dog-handler were hit in the face by bricks.

(c) As the police came under attack a help call went out and many police vehicles flowed into the area. By about 5 o'clock, the situation had calmed down. The police began to leave again. The last of the beer was loaded into a police van. As this van drew off the police came under attack again. The van tried to get away but was stopped outside the Inkerman Pub, overturned and the beer was stolen. Several police who had been outside the Black and White fled; however, a number were trapped inside. Two police cars parked further down Grosvenor Road, opposite William Street, came under attack and were turned over. Police officers

from one turned it back over and drove off—the occupants of the other fled leaving it upside down. More help calls went out and about 30–40 police regrouped behind the Inkerman Pub.

(d) At about 5:30 p.m. the police marched up Grosvenor Road from the Inkerman in close formation, intending, according to the official report, to relieve their colleagues inside the Black and White. As they drew near to the cafe they again came under attack. This attack intensified as they reached the cafe and, according to one witness (conv. WM 30), smashed in the windows with their truncheons. Some police defended themselves with milk crates and with the help of dogs made forays into the crowd, whom they managed to disperse. At about this time the police car that was left, upside down, opposite William Street, was set on fire—a group of three or four youths (including at least one white) ran up to it and threw a match in the petrol tank.

(e) At about 5:45 p.m. the situation was calm again. Some police withdrew back to the Inkerman Pub, others patrolled the grass area opposite the Black and White with dogs. Yet others stood around in groups. A fire engine came to extinguish the burning car—it was not impeded and children helped unroll the hoses. All through this period people were coming home from work and large numbers of people lined the streets to watch what was going on. Although calm, there was a feeling of tension, of "I don't know what is going to happen next" (conv. WF 26).

(f) The police had called a removal van to tow away the burnt out car. It arrived at 6:30 p.m. and the car was hitched up to it. The police drew up in formation in front of the van with a line of police dogs in front. As they started to move the crowd withdrew, then a stone was thrown and a hail of 30–40 stones descended on the police. They began to scatter, in some disarray, up Grosvenor Road, towards the grass area at the junction with Ashley Road, all the way coming under attack from the crowds lining the streets.

At the same time as this, the police regrouped at the other end of Grosvenor Road, by the Inkerman, then marched up the road in formation. They too came under a fierce barrage of sticks, stones and bottles. By way of side streets, they retreated into City Road where, for the first time, riot shields were issued.

(g) For the next 30 minutes, from about 6:45 p.m. to 7:15 p.m. there was a running battle between police and the crowd. It had two centres, one being the junction of City Road and Ashley Road, and the other being the junction of Grosvenor Road and Ashley Road (round the grass area). The numbers involved are unclear—estimates varying from 300 to 3000. A reasonable estimate seems to be that a total of about 60 police faced two groups of 2/300 people actively attacking them with a total of 2000 in the area (cf. 'St. Pauls' Riot Opinion', Malcolm Cotterill).

As the first group of police reached the grass area there was a pause. Then an old man walked up to a parked panda car and kicked in its lights. There was a loud cheer and missiles were flung at the police. These were exposed on all sides and after a while were so fiercely pressed that they were forced to fall back towards City Road. On City Road itself the police seemed to be fairly disorganized—marching up the road in a phalanx protected by shields and then falling back as they came under attack and then, again, marching forward.

During this period two noticeable events occurred involving police cars. The first incident concerned three police cars which came in from lower Ashley Road. Outside Lloyds Bank they were blocked by the crowd. The occupants got out and fled. The crowd converged on the cars, stoned them, in so doing breaking the bank windows, turned them over and later set fire to them.

The second incident involved two cars which sped into the area from the west end of Ashley Road. According to one witness (tape WM 35) they were doing 70–80 mph; according to another (tape WF 25) 50–60 mph. The first car was met by a barrage of bricks, the windscreen shattered, the driver was hit, his face was covered in blood. (He later needed nine stitches in the head.) The car swerved wildly nearly going into the crowd, then raced on and out of the area. The second car braked hard and reversed as fast as possible away from the crowd.

Despite all this, throughout this time traffic was flowing through the area, people were coming home, some were shopping, many were watching

(h) By about 7:15 p.m. all the police were deployed on City Road. They had formed a cordon at the end, but were so badly exposed that they were forced to retreat. As they retreated the crowd surged forward flinging missiles at them. Skips along the road provided ample ammunition. As the police retreated some people came out of their houses joining in the attack, others came from the side streets to stone the police from behind. Outnumbered and outflanked the police line disintegrated and they retreated in disarray, some being chased up the side streets. Officially the police "withdrew" at 7:26 p.m.; by about 7:30 p.m. they were back at Trinity Road Police Station.

(i) After the police had left the crowd did not stray beyond the boundaries of St. Pauls. Indeed as soon as the last officer had been chased beyond the junction of City Road and Brigstock Road nobody followed after them. Moreover with the police gone the crowd then moved apart to let the traffic back through and even helped direct it in order to ease congestion.

The Limits of Behaviour: Some Problems for Explanation

In this section three themes will be drawn out from the data. The first will be to show that the "riot" was marked by uniform behaviour showing distinct social limits. The second, that the event was not pre-planned and that rather the behaviour was spontaneous. The third theme concerns the way in which both participation and the content of crowd action can be related to social definitions of themselves and their social world.

(a) In his survey of the American urban riots of the 1960s, Fogelson (1971) was moved to write "restraint and selectivity were among the most crucial features of the riots" (p. 17). The same statement holds true for the present study. Indeed, perhaps the most remarkable feature of the whole episode was the backdrop of normality on which the so-called "battle of Bristol" (*Bristol Evening Post*, April 3, 1980) was played out. As police cars were burnt and officers stoned, cars flowed through the area, people walked home, families did their shopping, neighbours watched and chatted about the events.

Apart from the police, who, without exception, seem to have been targets of attack, the only other victims of intentional violence were camera operators and photographers. This seems to have been simply a function of the fact that people in the crowd were afraid of the film being used by the police (tape WM 35, conv. WM 30). Of the 60-odd police in the area 22 were injured and 27 received minor injuries. In all, 21 police vehicles were damaged, eight by fire with six completely destroyed (these figures, from the official police report, include the period up until 11:05 p.m. when the police reentered the area; most however, occurred in the period under consideration). At the same time not a single individual was intentionally attacked on the streets nor a single private property maliciously damaged. However, it is important not to over-simplify the case. During this time ten civilians were hurt, five private vehicles were damaged and a number of windows were broken. Apart from the photographers, all the civilians seem to have been hurt either by the police or in the cross-fire between police and crowd. Similarly, some windows were broken as missiles aimed at the police or police cars missed their target. This is certainly true of the Black and White, Lloyds Bank and the Criterion Pub. The case of the damaged cars is slightly more complicated. First of all, as mentioned above, one car belonging to a man who was seen to approve of alleged police harassment was attacked. Secondly, there was a suspicion that several cars coming into the area shortly after 7:30 p.m. were unmarked police cars which were therefore attacked (tape WM 17). This may explain why one or two private cars were stoned as they drove down City Road (one such story, reported by the driver, Kathleen Lee, is reported in several papers). However, there is also an important general point to be made. What is of interest is not so much isolated individual acts as acts which became rapidly generalized and which appear normative. Thus, if a single person throws a stone it cannot be considered as crowd behaviour unless many others join in. Indeed it is only possible to see the boundaries of crowd action by seeing what acts are not followed or condemned. This is a point of theoretical importance. Turner (1982) argues that one of the main ways through which group members glean categorial norms is what Tajfel calls the "inductive aspect of categorization." This refers to norms being based on the observation of the behaviour of other members of the group—the inferred logic being that if they represent the category their behaviour will be based on categorial norms; while there may be superficial similarity, this is distinguished from Turner and Killian's (1972) "keynoting" in three ways. Firstly, the only qualification for an individual to be seen as a source of norms is that he or she is clearly an ingroup member. Secondly, it is not a matter of norm *creation* but norm *inference*, therefore the norms arise immediately—hence accounting for the rapidity with which homogeneous crowd behaviour occurs. Finally, behaviours must fall within the range per-

missible in terms of the attributes defining social identity. Those which do will become generalized; those which do not will not be seen as normative. Hence an examination of those acts which do and do not generalize provides a means for examining the contours of group identification. Thus it is possible to contrast the reaction to a number of acts involving different targets.

Take the following accounts of acts directed against the police or police related targets:

> (of the second flare up described in "The events," section c). All hell was let loose, after the first brick had gone in. This policeman dodged behind this van, was getting pelted by bricks (tape WM 30).

> (As the police drew away with the first burnt out car). A few bricks went in and then people closed in the road and everyone started doing it. It just needed that initial encouragement (tape WM 17).

> (of the same incident). As soon as one brick went a sudden shower of about 30 or 40 bricks came sailing over (tape WM 30).

> (of the police cars attacked outside Lloyds Bank cf. "The events," section g). A police car came through and someone started yelling "brick it!" All hell seemed to let loose and everyone started throwing bricks (tape WM 20).

However, when other targets were attacked there was a very different response:

> "It was definitely against the police, because nothing or nobody else got hurt, except a bus—that got one window smashed. That could have been deliberate, but I think it was probably not. Everyone went 'Ugh,' 'idiots'" (tape WF 25).

> (In reply to a question about whether private cars got stoned.) There were a few but people that had done it were told off and forcibly stopped from doing it. One boy told the object was the police, direct your antagonism that way (tape WM 35).

Apart from clear limits in terms of targets, there were also clear geographical limits to the action. As described in "The events," section i, once the police had been chased out of St. Pauls, they were not followed. The only area involved consisted of City and Grosvenor Roads and the streets backing off them. As the *Sunday Times* commented (April 6, 1980), even later during the looting, the participants did not stray a yard beyond the boundaries of St. Pauls. Not only that, but once the police were drawn out no one else was stopped from entering the area; indeed crowd members even helped organize the traffic flow.

(b) The most obvious explanation of the clearly discernible form taken by the "riot" and the concerted behaviour of crowd members is in terms of a pre-existing plan carried out by leaders. Indeed the "agitator" theory of crowds is as old as crowd action itself. Such ideas were also proposed in the present case. According to one local councillor (conv. WM 55) people were phoning each other up before the trouble started and busloads came down from Coventry and Birmingham with guns. According to a senior Police Officer the participants were a mix of "emotional psychopaths and subversive anarchists" (conv. WM 55). Furthermore, shortly after the 2nd April, a rumour was circulating in police ranks that Tariq Ali (a prominent socialist) had been present on the day of the riots—in fact Tariq Ali had been there but he arrived on the afternoon of 3rd April.

An examination of the events reveals no pre-planning or leadership. Those involved in the events stress the spontaneity of the crowd's behaviour:

"There was no organization or anything like that. It was just totally spontaneous, but it was . . . I don't know, just a feeling they were invading—bringing a hundred coppers down to St. Pauls. Obviously looking for trouble" (tape WM 17).

"Well it just got around (referring to the police raid) then the niggling started it and we just got carried away" (conv. BM 17).

"It just burst into a great big riot. It burst like a small balloon first then a gigantic one" (Script BM 11).

A similar description was given of the decision not to move out of St. Pauls and to allow traffic back in.

"Cars coming down City Road, they were getting stuck because people were blocking the road. People just moved apart and people stood there directing the cars through. It just seemed really strange, like you'd taken over control of the streets (tape WM 25). (In answer to the question 'Did you consciously decide not to go outside the limits of St. Pauls?'). No, there was just that feeling. I think it was just an assumption by everyone in the crowd—get them (the police) out" (tape WM 17).

Of course, it is possible that all those interviewed were intent on concealing some plot, but given

their openness on various other matters, that could have incriminated them, this is most unlikely. Another possibility is that although people were unaware of being led there were a number of individuals inciting violence both verbally and by example. When questioned about those individuals who initiated actions (as described in "The limits of behaviour": section a) subjects gave the following types of response:

"somebody yelled police cars, pigs or something. I saw three cars come in and pull up outside the bank. Everyone charged towards them . . ."

Q. "Those guys who had yelled, were they leaders or just anyone?"

"Anyone. Everybody down there. I saw kids and their parents out, like a family outing" (tape WF 25).

"All it needed was the catalyst of one person throwing a brick and all hell let loose" (tape WM 35).

Hence, it seems that, at least in the eyes of those involved, the initiators were simply any other local participant. Of course this does still not absolutely disprove the agent provocateur thesis. Yet, even in the unlikely eventuality that such people were present, it would still be necessary to explain why some actions were generalized and some not, given that the participants were neither aware of following a pre-arranged script, nor obeying pre-determined leaders.

Despite the lack of a formal leadership, several witnesses report a "sense of leadership":

"A lot of the older black Rastas had come in and they seemed to be looked up to by the youths and they, in a sense, took control to a certain extent. Not the extent of the whole operation but to the extent of looking at them as in a sense the leader" (tape WM 35).

"A few kids would run out to throw stones, followed by a surge. . . . It didn't seem to be planned. The leaders seemed to be the most agile and the most accurate stone throwers" (conv. WM 30).

It seems, then, that the older, more daring, black youths were looked to by other participants, but not as individuals with a directing role, rather in the sense of a respected section of the community. Moreover, their influence was clearly limited in the ways shown above.

(c) While there is no evidence to support the notion of pre-conceived planning, subjects described their actions in terms of a clear purpose.

> (Talking about the police.) "What I think they were trying to do was draw us out into the centre. They could have completely got us but it wasn't like that. We were just getting them out of St. Pauls'" (tape WM 17).

> "I think it was quite honestly a case of us against them. Us, the oppressed section of society, if you like, against the police, against authority, basically" (tape WM 25).

In other words, participants saw themselves as ridding St. Pauls of an illegitimate and alien police presence. In raiding the Black and White cafe, which was the one meeting place for the black residents, which had not been closed down by previous raids, the police were seen as making a fundamental attack on the right of this community to control its own existence (the concept of control is central to the response of all sections of the community: Time after time it was stressed that there is no point in spending money *on* St. Pauls unless it is spent *with* the residents). Moreover when Desmond Pierre was asked, on behalf of the St. Pauls defence committee, to tell a television audience why the committee was set up, he replied: "We are defending ourselves on a lot of issues, but the main one is just the right to lead a free life'" (*TV Eye*). To quote Roy de Freitus, one of the more widely respected figures in St. Pauls:

> "The message I was getting last night and this morning in the area was: 'They've closed down this, they've closed down that, and if they close this particular one (the Black and White) where do we go from here?'" (*BBC Points West*, April 3, 1980).

Or, in the words of two youths outside the Black and White:

> "Man can't take oppression, man gotta fight. Them police is bastards" (conv. BM 17(a)).

> "Man can't just sit around all day smoking ganja— we just can't take it. Police think just because you're black they can do anything" (conv. BM 17(b)).

As well as having a well-formed idea of the events as purposeful action, it is clear that crowd members participated as social actors: that is to say as members of a social category rather than as private individuals. There are three types of data that support this contention.

Firstly, subjects described their own participa-

tion and that of other crowd members in the following terms:

> "It was everybody, the whole community" (conv. BM 25).

> "It was St. Pauls, you know . . . this was just St. Pauls. You know the place and the coppers didn't" (tape WM 17).

> "Just everybody came out of their houses, just everybody local" (tape WF 25).

Or, more simply, from a large group outside the Black and White, the day after the riots:

> "Everybody" (*BBC Points West,* April 3, 1980).

Thus, participants viewed themselves as the St. Pauls' community, defined in opposition to the police as outsiders. This conclusion should be explained in two ways. Firstly, it is not meant to imply that all the community was involved (although participants did stress the breadth of involvement, exemplified by the probably apocryphal story of a woman who came home around 4 p.m. to find her daughter in bed after an all-night party. "Get out of bed and go on the streets," the mother is quoted as saying, "there's a riot going on"). Moreover, as Ken Pryce showed in his intensive study of St. Pauls (Pryce, 1979) it is probably false to speak of a single community in the area. Nonetheless, crowd members did see themselves as representing the entirety of St. Pauls in the sense of an independent community, fighting for its right to survive. That is to say, the notion of community was a real, albeit ideological, creation for participants. Secondly, there is the question of race. Over the days following the 2nd April, press and politicians conducted a debate over whether the events constituted a race riot or not. After the first day when numerous papers talked of black mobs and black riots, the tendency was to stress the multiracial composition of the crowd and to down-play racial elements. Empirically, there is no doubt that both black and white were involved in stone throwing and burning police cars, and in that sense it is true that the "riot" was multi-racial. Yet in many accounts of the riots it is specifically oppression of blacks that is seen as causing and guiding the riots. The police were seen as picking on black people, especially with reference to arrests on suspicion of possession of cannabis (smoking ganja being specifically a black cultural symbol). The Black and White itself is predominantly frequented by black people. Thus there was a certain ambiguity in the use of the concept "community"; at times it was used to denote people suffering oppression because of their blackness. This will be especially clear when the reactions of participants to the riots are examined. Several subjects refer to a new relationship with the police both as people from St. Pauls and as black people. If this is so, then it may seem difficult to reconcile the notion of a homogeneous crowd with a single social conception of themselves with the participation of whites. However, while it seems true to say that the concept of community was defined in terms of black experience this does not mean it cannot be adopted by whites either because of a direct identification with blacks or because the black experience provided a potent frame for understanding their own problems: lack of a job, poverty, problems with the police. As one witness observed of the crowd, "politically they were all black" (conv. WF 28).

The second way of showing how participants saw themselves as a community against the police comes from examining social relations within the crowd in contrast to those between crowd and police. For the press, and many outsiders, the event was marked first and foremost by aggression and fear:

"I had a bit of wartime experience but then you had a foxhole or something to get into, you were inside here" (Shopowner, *BBC Radio Bristol*, April 3, 1980).

"I am afraid I and my family are going to be killed. The youngsters, hundreds of them, are out of control. They are going wild. They are setting fire to houses and shops and damaging cars" (Publican quoted in *Guardian*, April 3, 1980).

Perhaps the best illustration of the way in which outsiders viewed the event is contained in an account of the BBC radio car. It was seen reversing furiously with a look of terror on the face of the driver, alongside a large Rastafarian was running, banging on the roof. As the car passed by my informant heard what the Rastafarian was saying: "play us a request, play us a request . . ." (conv. WM 28). Crowd members tell a very different story:

"It was good, very good—everyone felt great" (conv. BM 20).

"It was lovely, I felt free" (conv. BM 16).

"All the atmosphere was against the police. It wasn't like the papers say. This absolute mad mob.

Everyone was together. They were looking at each other the whole time. It was black and white and all ages and that was fantastic" (tape WF 25).

"People were so warm: they said, 'glad to be with you, brother,' and put their arm around you" (conv. WM 35).

"It was really joyful, that's what they (the media) all leave out, the 'joy'" (conv. WM 30).

The warmth of intra-crowd feeling, this contrasts strongly with outsiders' perception and with the violence of inter-group—that is, crowd—police interactions. What is more, the basis of this warmth was mutual membership of the "community" as described above:

"It was due to police harassment. Everyone seems to be bound together against it in some way" (tape WM 19).

"You were just grinning at everyone because everyone was from St. Pauls" (tape WM 17).

Thus, intra-group cohesion seemed to exist as a function of a common identification:

The final bit of evidence that points to a common, collective self-definition adopted by participants relates to their description of the effects of the "riot."

"We took on the police and beat them. They will never again treat us with contempt. . . . They will respect us now" (BM quoted in Sun, April 5, 1980).

"We feel great, we feel confident it was a victory and we were worthy of the victory" (BM quoted in *Socialist Challenge*, April 10, 1980).

"You go to school, you learn and then—nothing. The colour of your skin determines everything. We can't beat them in the court, but we defeated them on the streets" (BM quoted in Socialist Challenge, April 10, 1980).

One witness tells how the next day there was something akin to a victory dance on the grass opposite the Black and White. He goes on: "There were songs like *Beat down Babylon* and all this lark, they were singing. Everyone was sort of smoking, like joints and stuff, in the open air and the coppers just never coming near us."

In the light of what has been written about reggae music as a conscious cultural form of resistance to oppression (cf. Johnson, 1976) it may be significant to consider the lyrics of the song specifically highlighted—*Beat down Babylon*

(Babylon signifying the land of oppression and, sometimes, more specifically, the police)—a song once banned in Jamaica for its political effect.

"I an' I going' beat down Babylon,
I an' I going' beat down Babylon,
I an' I mus' whip them wicked men,

O what a wicked situation,
I an' I starvin' for salvation,
This might cause a revolution,
and a dangerous pollution . . . "

Thus it seems that participants viewed the events of the 2nd April as a collective statement and themselves as a collective mouthpiece. It is significant that two individuals, the local parish priest and a local CRE spokesperson reminded the media of Martin Luther King's assertion that riots are the voices of the unheard. The priest went on to explain:

"The community has stood up to say, very loudly, 'I am'" (Keith Kimber in *Daily Telegraph*, April 5, 1980).

Towards an Understanding of Crowd Process

A close examination of the events of 2nd April has revealed a picture of spontaneous social behaviour with the twin characteristics of uniformity across individuals and of clear social limits. It is difficult to see how classic theories of the crowd could deal with these. Group mind theory would have to explain limits in terms of a racial unconscious, though how such an "unconscious" could determine say geographical limits to the events is unclear. Allportian individualism has a similar problem. It is hard to see individual attributes determining that people should not go beyond the junction of City and Brigstocke Roads. Nor does emergent norm theory fare much better. Firstly, the onset of certain action sequences seems to be immediate, and to preclude the process of keynoting which, for Turner and Killian (1972) is essential for the formation of group norms. Secondly, the theory cannot explain why certain actions (stoning the police) become generalized and others (stoning private cars) do not.

One of the most striking aspects of the data that was collected concerns the correspondence between the limits of behaviour and the definition of "community" in terms of which participants described themselves. The central elements of "community" comprised a geographical basis (St. Pauls), an opposition to the police, and a desire to be in control of their own lifestyle. It is interesting to note how these themes became accentuated in accounts of how the disturbances started. Nearly all interviewees stress the unnecessarily large police presence, talking of an "invasion" of the area. In describing police conduct in the Black and White the impression given is that the police acted like "a cross between the Sweeney and Kojak" (tape WM 35), in refusing to show warrants and brutalizing the clientele. The notion of control comes through with reference to the importance of ganja (cannabis). Ganja is at once an important symbol of an independent culture and of conflict between the police and locals. Crowd members' perception of the hypocrisy of the police in suppressing that independent culture is brought out in a number of accusations: that the police regularly sell ganja in St. Pauls; that the plain clothes police made a deal in the Black and White on the 2nd April; that police were smoking ganja inside the Black and White. For present purposes the importance of all these assertions lies not in their truth or otherwise, but rather in what they reveal about the meaning of the concept of community to participants. The attributes of this concept are clearly reflected in the crowd's behaviour. The geographical basis is translated into the decision of crowd members not to move beyond St. Pauls. The opposition to the police is seen in the selection of police officers and vehicles as the sole targets of collective violence. The notion of control is reflected in the way in which participants took over the area once the police had left, directing traffic through and before they left advising traffic not to go down certain roads and checking obvious strangers in the area.

Not only is there a match between the social self-definition used by participants and their actions but also actions unrelated to this definition were those that were not generalized. Thus acts, such as attacking cars or buses, which do not represent specific outgroups for the "community," here stopped rather than spread.

These relationships, then, require an explanation. One obvious possibility is that the various descriptions of self and purpose were a post hoc construction used to explain and justify the "riot." There are, however, a number of weaknesses to this explanation. Firstly, there is evidence that a concept of community comprising the elements outlined above existed in St. Pauls *prior* to 2nd April, 1980 (cf. Pryce, 1979). Secondly, while it is almost impossible to assess a cognitive construct like identity during a crowd episode, the evidence of ingroup cohesion, as a function of perceived mutual "community" membership, seems strong enough to suggest that crowd members were reacting to each other on the basis of social rather than individual factors.

The other possibility is that the participants' social self-definition plays some part in directing their behaviour. This is the conclusion canvassed by Reddy in the study of riots over a 100 year period in Rouen. As he puts it, "The targets of these crowds thus glitter in the eye of history as signs of the labourer's conception of the nature of society" (Reddy, 1977, p. 84).

Putting together these various considerations it is possible to outline a number of criteria which any adequate account of crowd behaviour must fulfill. First of all this account must explain the genesis of spontaneous behaviour, secondly it must explain the uniformity of behaviour across crowd members and thirdly it must explain the way in which a social ideology can affect the limits of crowd behaviour. If it is to meet this last criterion, the theoretical approach must accept how social factors may mould crowd actions, and therefore, must examine the social context in which these actions occur.

These are precisely the aims of the social identity model of the crowd developed by Reicher (1982a, forthcoming). Its aim is to show how a social ideology can be internalized as a cognitive construct—a social identification—and can guide collective behaviour. Applied to the present case, the social identity of "St. Pauls' community member" adopted by crowd members provides the criteria for legitimate action. In the entirely unprecedented and rapidly evolving events, participants would seek appropriate responses by reference to these criteria—that is they would be asking what do we, as the St. Pauls community do now? Possible answers are provided in the actions of others seen clearly as ingroup members and thus certain classes of person seen to exemplify the social category, such as older black youths are looked to. However, actions can only be seen to translate social identity into specific situational norms if they are congruent with that identity. Hence, the limits of crowd behaviour.

While the data provided cannot be used to prove this model nonetheless, in a negative sense, while it excludes previous account it does not exclude the social identification approach and, in a positive sense, it explains the various characteristics of the data and relationships between those characteristics.

If the model is accepted it has two implications which are of considerable importance for an assessment of the significance of crowd behaviour. Firstly, not only is crowd behaviour moulded by social identity but conversely, crowd behaviour may mould social identity. This is clear in the new found feelings of pride expressed by many resulting from the "riot," feelings which echo the black man who said after the Watts riot of August 1965: "for the first time in Watts, people feel a real pride in being black. I remember when I first went to Whittier I worried that if I didn't make it there, if I was rejected, I wouldn't have a place to go back to. Now I can say: 'I'm from Watts'" (Milgram and Toch, 1969, p. 516). Hence, crowd behaviour may play a crucial role in developing the nature of social ideologies. The second implication is closely related to this. Not only on the right, but also on the left, there is an assumption that crowd episodes are inferior in some way. Thus the *Morning Star* referred to St. Pauls as a "primitive uprising" and *Socialist Worker* called for a "paper campaign." However, the present perspective stresses how sophisticated crowd actions are in the sense of being an accurate expression of an ideological understanding of the social world.

Since Herodotus commented that "there is nothing less understanding and more proud than the blind mass" (quoted in Giner, 1976, p. 4) the crowd has been viewed as, at best, an incoherent and hostile outburst. A close examination of the facts reveals a very different picture. Far from being a negative aberration, the crowd provides one of the few contexts in which people act, not in terms of their isolated concerns, but as pure social subjects—from a wider perspective one might even say as historical subjects. Moreover, crowd action does not simply reproduce static social identities but represents a creative interpretation of these identities in a novel situation. As such, the crowd plays a central role in the development of social ideas. Put together, these facts suggest that the crowd has been too long neglected by social psychologists and that it should move back to the rightful place of prominence it occupied a century ago.

REFERENCES

Allport, F. (1924). *Social psychology*. Boston: Houghton Mifflin.

Berk, R. A. (1972). The emergence of muted violence in crowd behaviour: a case study of an almost-race-riot. In J. F. Short & M. E. Wolfgang (Eds.), *Collective violence*. Chicago: Aldine.

Berk, R. A. (1974). A gaming approach to crowd behaviour. *American Sociological Review, 39*, 355–373.

Denzin, N. K. (1970). *The research act*. Chicago: Aldine.

Festinger, L., Pepitone, A., & Newcomb, T. (1952). Some consequences of deindividuation in a group. *Journal of Abnormal and Social Psychology, 47*, 382–389.

Fogelson, R. M. (1971). *Violence in protest*. New York: Doubleday.

Geen, R. G., & Gange, J. J. (1977). Drive theory of social facilitation: Twelve years of theory and research. *Psychological Bulletin, 84*, 1257–1288.

Giner, S. (1976). *Mass society*. London: Robertson.

Johnson, L. K. (1976). The reggae rebellion. *New Society, 36,(714)*, 589.

Le Bon, G. (1947). *The crowd: A study of the popular mind*. London: Ernest Benn.

McPhail, C. (1970). Civil disorder participation: A critical examination of recent research. *American Sociological Review, 36*, 1058–1073.

McPhail, C. (1971). The assembling process: A theoretical and empirical examination. *American Sociological Review, 38*, 721–735.

Milgram, S., & Toch, H. (1969). Collective behaviour: Crowds and social movements. In G. Linzey & E. Aronson (Eds.), *Handbook of social psychology* (Vol. 4, 2nd ed.). Reading, MA: Addison-Wesley.

Moscovici, S. (1981). *L'age des Foules*. Paris: Fayard.

Oberschall, A. (1973). *Social conflict and social movements*. Englewood Cliffs, NJ: Prentice Hall.

Olson, M. (1965). *The logic of collective action*. Cambridge, MA: Harvard University Press.

Pryce, K. (1979). *Endless pressure*. Harmondsworth, UK: Penguin.

Reddy, W. M. (1977, February). The textile trade and the language of the crowd at Rouen 1752–1871. *Past and Present, 74*, 62–89.

Reicher, S. D. (1982a). The determination of collective behaviour. In H. Tajfel (Ed.), *Social identity and intergroup relations*. Cambridge, UK: Cambridge University Press/ Paris: Maison des Sciences de l'Homme.

Reicher, S. D. (1982b). *Crowd psychology and group process*. Paper given to Annual Conference of The British Psychological Society, York, April, 1982.

Reicher, S. D. (forthcoming). *The crowd: A study in the social determination of behaviour*. Academic Press.

Sanders, G. S. (1981). Driven by distraction: an integrative review of social facilitation theory and research. *Journal of Experimental Social Psychology, 17*, 227–251.

Sighele, S. (1892). *La Foule Criminelle Essai de Psychologie Collective* (Trans. from Italian by P. Vigny). Paris: Felix Alcan.

Tarde, G. (1890). *La Philosophie Pénale*. Lyon, France: Edition Storck.

Tajfel, H. (Ed.). (1978). *Differentiation between social groups studies in the social psychology of intergroup relations*. London: Academic Press.

Turner, J. C. (1982). Towards a cognitive redefinition of the social group. In H. Tajfel (Ed.), *Social identity and intergroup relations*. Cambridge, UK: Cambridge University Press/Paris: Maison des Sciences de l'Homme.

Turner, R. H., & Killian, L. (1972). *Collective behaviour*, 2nd ed. Englewood Cliffs, NJ: Prentice Hall.

White, M. J. (1977). Counter normative behaviour as influenced by de-individuating conditions and reference group thesis. *Journal of Social Psychology, 13*, 75–90.

Wright, S. (1978). *Crowds and riots*. Beverley Hills: Sage.

Zimbardo, P. G. (1969). The human choice: individuation reason and order versus de-individuation impulse and chaos. In W. J. Arnold & D. Levine (Eds.), *Nebraska Symposium on Motivation*, Vol. 17. Lincoln: University of Nebraska Press.

Race and Relative Deprivation in the Urban United States

Reeve D. Vanneman and Thomas F. Pettigrew • Harvard University

Introduction

This study develops out of two separate literatures in social psychology—one concerned with the subjective aspects of social stratification, the other with the correlates of racial attitudes. The first of these areas has a rich history in social science, while the second is of recent vintage. We shall sketch out briefly these two literatures, followed by the presentation of our research findings relevant to both.

Subjective Aspects of Social Stratification

It has long been recognized in sociology and social anthropology as well as in social psychology that the objective features of a society's social stratification system only grossly predict individual attitudes and behaviour. Deviant cases are so numerous that popular names arise to describe them: the Tory worker, the genteel poor, the limousine liberal. Early theorists took up the issue. Cooley discussed "selective affinity" to groups outside of one's immediate environment; William James argued that our potential "social self" is developed and strengthened by thoughts of remote groups and individuals who function as normative points of reference (Hyman & Singer, 1968).

But it was not until the 1940s that modern nomenclature and theory was established. Hyman (1942) advanced the term *reference group* to ac-count for his interview and experimental data on how his subjects employed status comparisons in the process of self-appraisal. An individual, he argues, typically "refers" his behaviour and attitudes to a variety of reference groups to which he may or may not belong. The concept soon found wide favour throughout social psychology, for, as Newcomb points out (1951), it focuses upon the central problem of the discipline: the relationship of the individual to society.

Later writers have contributed a number of clarifying distinctions. Charters and Newcombe (1952) demonstrated that *negative* reference groups can be just as influential in reverse as *positive* ones. Merton (1957) noted the operation of reference *individuals* as well as reference groups. Most important, Kelley (1952) made the critical distinction between *comparative* and *normative* reference groups.[1] Reference groups can provide standards of comparison for self-evaluation and can also serve as a source for an individual's attitudes, norms, and values. In practice, it is often difficult to untangle these two functions, though our research reported here dwells on the comparative function of class and racial reference groups.

The past twenty years has witnessed widespread use of the reference group concept in research. A

---

[1]Other clarifying theoretical papers include Eisenstadt (1954), Litwak (1960), Merton and Kitt (1950), Sherif (1953), Shibutani (1955), and Turner (1956).

few studies have explored the comparative effects of reference groups, ranging from job satisfaction (Patchen, 1961; Form and Geschwender, 1962) and perceptions of class inequalities (Runciman, 1966), to the self-evaluations of the blind (Strauss, 1968) and mental illness among black Americans (Parker and Kleiner, 1966).[2] By far the greatest empirical attention, however, has been paid to normative reference groups. A number of these studies have centred upon changes among college students as a function of their adopting the college as referent; the Bennington College investigation by Newcomb (1943) is an early and famous example of this genre.[3] Other research on the normative function has often employed voting as the dependent variable (Campbell et al, 1954; Campbell et al., 1960; Eulau, 1962; Kaplan, 1968); though Hyman and Singer (1968) report that these normative studies span the globe and focus on everything from student drinking behaviour (Rogers, 1958) to the fantasies of newsmen (Pool & Schulman, 1959).

The direct link of this literature with social stratification theory was forged by Centers (1949) in his classic volume on *The Psychology of Social Classes*. He asked a national probability sample of adult white males in the United States six economic questions "designed to test conservative–radical orientations." He also determined his respondents' objective occupational status as well as their subjective status positions; he obtained the latter by asking, "If you were asked to use one of these four names for your social class, which would you say you belonged in: the middle class, lower class, working class, or upper class?"

The majority of Centers' respondents chose their objective social class; that is, their membership and reference classes were the same. Yet a significant minority of manual workers specified "the middle class," just as there were white-collar workers who listed themselves among "the working class." Not surprisingly, Centers found that the higher the objective social class of the respondent, the more likely he was to be politically conservative. But subjective social class made a discernible difference. Those manual workers who regarded themselves as middle class were on the average somewhat more conservative than other manual workers; and, likewise, those white-collar workers who regarded themselves as working class were on the average considerably less conserva-

tive than other white-collar workers. Eulau (1962) has replicated these results on American national samples in both 1952 and 1956, and Runciman (1966, p. 171) has replicated them with an English national sample. Their findings provide an excellent illustration of the "cross-pressures" phenomenon where a balance is struck in the conflict between the sociological objective class and the psychological subjective class.

Another finding of Centers' investigation suggests why there is a looseness of fit between objective and subjective class positions. He asked his national sample: "In deciding whether a person belongs to your class or not, which of these other things do you think is most important to know: Who his family is; how much money he has; what sort of education he has; or how he believes and feels about certain things?" While only about one-fifth of those respondents who answered at all cited "family" or "money" and about one-third cited "education," more than half emphasized differences in beliefs and feelings. Objective standards were not denied, but more flexible beliefs were stressed. "If you believe and feel as I do, then we are of the same social grouping" is a contention that, at least in the American context, adds importance to reference group phenomena in social stratification.[4]

The single Centers question on subjective class evokes a *judgement* of one's position, but does not tap *feelings* of true class identification. Consequently, Campbell and his colleagues (1960) began by first asking in a national voting survey: "There's quite a bit of talk these days about different social classes. Most people say they belong to the middle class or to the working class. Do you ever think of yourself as being in one of these classes?" One-third of their respondents answered "no" to this query. That this failure to indicate any

---

[2]Other examples of investigations of the comparative function of reference groups include the work of Stern and Keller (1953) in France and of Pettigrew (1964, Chap. 8; 1967) on blacks in the United States.

[3]Additional research on college students has been reported by Hartley (1960a; 1960b), Pearlin (1954), and Siegel and Siegel (1957).

[4]This interpretation of Centers's finding receives important support in the findings on "belief and value congruence" in racial prejudice reported in Rokeach, Smith, and Evans (1960), Rokeach and Mezei (1966), Stein (1966), Stein, Hardyck, and Smith (1965), and Smith, Williams, and Willis (1967).

"consciousness of class" is not mere evasion is indicated by the sharp political differences by class that emerge between those who identify with their class membership and those who do not. Among the identifiers, for example, respondents who chose the working-class designation voted 14 percent more Democratic than those who chose the middle-class designation; but this difference shrinks to only 2 percent among those who did not identify (Campbell et al., 1960, p. 343). Identifiers also evinced greater subjective class differences in party identification and attitudes on economic issues. We shall in this paper provide a replication of this phenomenon using 1968 voting for Governor George Wallace for President of the United States.

Campbell notes that class identifiers are most prevalent among the young and those who were beginning their careers during the Depression of the 1930s and among those who had been raised in and presently lived in large cities. Identifiers and non-identifiers, however, did not significantly differ on sex, education, occupation, ethnicity, or race. Campbell and his University of Michigan associates attached considerable importance to the fact that one-third of the adults of the United States had no apparent "class consciousness," for these people act as a formidable buffer against the operation of extreme status polarization in American politics.

This cursory review of reference group studies points to the close interconnection between this concept and a number of other social psychological theories and concepts. Indeed, Pettigrew (1967) has attempted to show that there is a general theory of social evaluation emerging in social psychology under an assortment of related molecular concepts and hypotheses. Thus, the comparative function of reference group analysis can be directly linked with Festinger's (1954) social comparison theory, Lenski's (1954) status inconsistency theory, Thibaut and Kelley's (1959) concept of comparison level, Homans's (1961) concept of distributive justice, Blau's (1964) concept of fair exchange, and Stouffer's concept of relative deprivation (Stouffer et al., 1949). The basic tenet of this more general theory of social evaluation is that human beings learn about themselves by comparing themselves to others. A second tenet is that the process of social evaluation results in positive, neutral, or negative self-ratings which are relative to the standards set by the individuals and groups employed

for comparison. These propositions lie at the core of early social psychological thinking, especially in the writings of Cooley (1902) and Mead (1934).

It is Stouffer's famous concept of *relative deprivation* that has proved the most useful in our analyses of American race relations. Both Alexis de Tocqueville and Karl Marx employed the idea in their writings; but it gained wide attention in social science after Stouffer invoked it to account for eleven different and surprising results in his monumental research on *The American Soldier* (Stouffer et al., 1949).

The most famous example involved army advancement. World War II promotions were rapid and widespread in the United States Air Corps, but slow and piecemeal in the Military Police. Conventional wisdom predicts that the Air Corpsmen should have been more satisfied with their chances for promotion, for the "obvious" reason that they were actually moving ahead faster in their careers. But Stouffer found that the Air Corpsmen were in fact considerably more frustrated over promotions than the Military Police. What is not so obvious is that the fliers' wide-open system of promotions led them to adopt extremely high aspirations. Most of them expected such swift elevation that even the generous promotions of their service left them *relatively* dissatisfied. By contrast, morale was reasonably high among the Military Police, for they did not expect rapid promotions and were relatively content with what few advances they did achieve. Spector (1956) replicated this result in a simulated situation in the laboratory. It is not the absolute level of attainment that made for poor morale so much as relative deprivation— the discrepancy between what one anticipates and what one attains.

In the basic case, relative deprivation or gratification occurs when an individual or class of individuals feels deprived or gratified in comparison to relevant reference individuals and groups. Thus, comparison with a non-deprived referent leads to high expectations that, if unfulfilled, lead in turn to severe feelings of deprivation and unfairness. Simple as this basic structure appears, Davis (1959, 1963) has shown how relative deprivation notions can be formalized into a network of logically consistent propositions concerning phenomena ranging from social distance towards out-groups to group solidarity and differentiation. Not only did Davis make more coherent and consistent the variety of uses of the concept by Stouffer, but he also derived general propositions that are not obvious from the original statement of relative deprivation. Thus, the Stouffer (1949, pp. 125–126) examples of older and married soldiers—both from social categories with high rates of draft deferment—feeling more deprived than younger and single soldiers turn out to be particular cases of a more general statement: "If a given social categorization is correlated with objective deprivation, relative deprivation will be more frequent among the deprived in the more favoured category . . . [and] relative gratification will be more frequent among the nondeprived in the less favoured category" (Davis, 1959, pp. 286–287).[5] Davis also derived hypotheses concerning "in-group consciousness" and "out-group distance"; in general, his derivations predict that you can increase both characteristics by rewarding subgroups differentially and keeping the reward level in the system intermediate between general deprivation and general gratification.

Blau (1964) and Homans (1961) contributed the further component of *investment* to the formulation. If a reference individual or group is viewed as making a larger investment than you or your group, then proportionately greater rewards to the referent are not likely to be seen as unfair. Perceived injustice occurs when the rewards to the referent are proportionately greater than its investment relative to you or your group.[6]

Patchen (1961) found support for this contention in his study of American oil refinery workers. He asked the workers to name the occupations of others whose earnings differed from their own; and he further asked them how satisfied they were with their earnings compared with those of the others named. His respondents proved far more satisfied, in comparing themselves with others who earn more, when the others compared were professionals than when they were blue-collar workers like themselves. Professionals are perceived to make far larger investments in their jobs than others, especially in terms of education. Consequently, Patchen's findings are consistent with Homans's notion of proportionality between rewards and investments as constituting "distributive justice."

Runciman (1966, pp. 33–34) added a further refinement that proves critical in our own research. He distinguishes between *egoistic* and *fraternalistic* deprivation. Egoistic deprivation describes *individual* deprivation sensed through comparisons made between one's self and others

within one's own in-group; there is, however, no sense of deprivation concerning the in-group's position in society. By contrast, fraternalistic deprivation describes *group* deprivation sensed through comparisons made between one's in-group and other groups in the society; there is, however, no sense of deprivation concerning one's position within the in-group itself. Runciman found in England and Wales, as had been found in France (Stern & Keller, 1953) and the United States (Form & Geschwender, 1962; Hyman, 1942), that his survey respondents typically restricted their comparisons to friends and relatives within their own social class. Cross-class comparisons were minimal, then, and limited the degree of fraternalistic deprivation. Yet Runciman maintains that it is perceived *group*, not individual, deprivation that is most conducive for the perception of injustice. Our results firmly support this contention, as we shall note following a brief review of the second relevant literature.

Correlates of Racial Attitudes

Research on this topic, most of it conducted during the past decade, has generated a set of surprisingly consistent cross-national findings. At least this consistency in results extends across English-speaking nations. We shall note only the most important of these findings from the United Kingdom and the United States, with some notice paid to the more limited research from the Republics of South Africa and Rhodesia.

Racial attitudes are not, of course, unidimensional; and these various dimensions often possess somewhat different patterns of correlates. Typically, however, these differences are not large.[7] Nor are racial attitudes among the oppressors and

---

[5]This proposition is advanced for individual comparisons made within one's in-group, but it may well be reversed when cross-group comparisons are made. Basically, this difference refers to Runciman's (1966) distinction to be discussed below between egoistic and fraternalistic deprivation. The propositions of Davis (1959, 1963) concerning relative deprivation focus largely upon egoistic deprivation.

[6]Runciman (1966, Chapters 12 and 13) disagrees with this formulation, and holds that perceived congruence of earnings with need is an even more crucial condition for the existence of "social justice."

[7]Two important dimensions of racial attitudes held by white Americans will be distinguished later in our results: "contact" and "competitive" with education a more important predictor of the former.

the oppressed directly comparable. It is a comment on the racism of both Britain and the United States that the racial attitudes of coloured minorities have been relatively ignored. The first major survey of immigrant attitudes in England did not occur until 1967 (P.E.P., 1967; Daniel, 1968). The recent and otherwise comprehensive report on British race relations, *Colour and Citizenship* (Rose, 1969), omits new survey data on coloured immigrant attitudes altogether. Similarly, the first nationwide probability survey of the racial attitudes of black Americans did not occur until 1963, and that was a commercial effort undertaken for the popular weekly magazine, *Newsweek* (Brink & Harris, 1964). Once race riots broke out in the mid- and late-1960s, however, white America became considerably more interested in black American thinking and a spate of surveys conducted exclusively on blacks was undertaken (Brink & Harris, 1964, 1967; Campbell & Schuman, 1968; Marx, 1967; Meyer, 1968a, 1968b).

We shall confine ourselves, then, to the racial attitudes of the native white English and of white Americans. Two related surveys of racial prejudice in Britain were made in 1966–1967 (Rose, 1969, Chapter 28). The first study sampled extensively five English boroughs with relatively heavy concentrations of coloured immigrants; the second drew a national sample of 2,250 adults but employed a more limited questionnaire. The initial analyses of these data and the scale of "prejudice" provided in *Colour and Citizenship* were inadequate.[8] As far as they went, however, these original analyses found racial prejudice nationally to be most intense among the skilled working class, conservatives, authoritarians, the poorly educated, those low in "socio-political potency" (called "political efficacy" in the United States), and those with little contact with coloured immigrants. A voluminous American literature over the past generation has repeatedly found virtually these same relationships for white racial prejudice in the United States (e.g., Adorno et al., 1950; Allport, 1954; Brink and Harris, 1964, 1967; Campbell, 1971; Campbell & Schuman, 1968; Cantril, 1951; Erskine, 1962, 1967, 1967–1968, 1968a, 1968b, 1968–1969; Fenton, 1960; Hyman & Sheatsley, 1956, 1964; Pettigrew, 1958, 1959, 1971b; Schwartz, 1967; Sheatsley, 1966; Williams, 1964). Still further evidence for these trends in the United States is provided by the data we are about to present.

Moreover, available data over the years suggest extremely similar correlates of racial prejudice among white South Africans and Rhodesians. From McCrone's (1937, 1949, 1953) classic initial work and that of Malherbe (1946) to later investigations of limited samples (Pettigrew, 1958, 1960; van den Berghe, 1962), the importance of occupation, education, and conservative political orientation in white racial attitudes has been repeatedly noted. And these relationships seem to hold for both English and Afrikaans-speakers.

In a 1959 national sample of whites in (then) Southern Rhodesia, Rogers and Frantz (1962) found the greatest support for blatant racial discrimination resided among the skilled working class, political conservatives, and the poorly educated—as in Great Britain and the United States. These investigators were unable to test the remaining relationships reported in *Colour and Citizenship*, though they did not find significant relationships with sex, age, urban–rural residence, and income.[9]

In the five-borough English sample, the three most persistent racial concerns again recall American findings for urban whites: the presence of coloured people is bad for the neighbourhood, their presence leads to inter-marriage, and they will become a local majority.[10] And the conclusion that there is "a guarded willingness to allow coloured

---

[8]For criticisms of Chapter 28 in Rose (1969), see: Bagley (1970, appendix), Pettigrew (1971a), and letters by John Rowan, Daniel Lawrence, and Mark Abrams in *New Society* (14 August, 21 August, and 11 September 1969). The inadequate scale of prejudice, which for some reason placed major emphasis on attitudes towards housing discrimination, gave rise to such nonsense in the popular British press as only 10 percent of the native white population was "prejudiced"— an arbitrary and far-too low estimate that was forcefully corrected by Bagley (1970).

[9]The one possible exception involves the role of contact. As Allport (1954) argued and later research supports (Pettigrew, 1971b), interracial contact can lead to either increased tolerance or intolerance depending on the particular conditions under which it takes place.

[10]A salient stereotype of coloured people that emerges in the five-borough data involves an alleged lack of cleanliness and hygiene. This was the reason most often cited for considering coloured people to be inferior (Bagley, 1970, p. 23); and "be cleaner" was the chief method mentioned by the white respondents as to how the coloureds could "improve their position" (Bagley, 1970, p. 25). This, too, is similar to American results. Thus, 60 percent in 1963 and 52 percent in 1966 of national samples of white Americans believed black Americans "smell different"—the second most pervasive stereotype tapped in these surveys (Brink & Harris, 1964, 1967).

entry into the fortress of working-class privilege" (Rose, 1969, p. 580) also appears to hold with equal force on both sides of the Atlantic—a point that will be demonstrated for American workers in the following section.

Bagley (1970) re-analysed the five-borough English data, and employed a more adequate six-item scale of prejudice. He found age, education, and occupation, in that order, to be the strongest correlates of his prejudice measure.[11] And each of these demographic factors remained significantly associated with prejudice even after the other two were dichotomously controlled. Younger, well-educated, and white-collar respondents tended to be the most accepting of coloured peoples, though the effects were neither completely additive nor were they linear.[12] Most interesting of all was the curvilinear association of occupation with prejudice. While blue-collar workers in general in the five boroughs were more intolerant of coloured minorities than white-collar workers, the *skilled* manual group exhibited appreciably more animosity than the *unskilled* manual group. Thus, skilled manuals comprised only 31 percent of the total sample but 40 percent of the most prejudiced group that answered negatively all six of the scale's questions (Bagley, 1970, p. 39). By contrast, unskilled manual respondents, as well as white-collar respondents, were *under*-represented among the most prejudiced. And it is precisely the skilled manual workers who constituted the core of support for George Wallace for President in 1968 in the northern United States (Pettigrew, 1971b; Lipset and Raab, 1970).

South Africa once again appears to replicate this trend. Ethnic membership, or course, is the dominant determinate of party voting among white South Africans. And though survey data are not available, aggregate analyses of the votes for the anti-African, Afrikaner-dominated Nationalist Party, point to the lower middle-class areas as particular centres of electoral strength. Tingsten (1955, p. 23) summarizes the trend:

... industrialization and commercialization ... [have] formed that social class now constituting the stronghold of Boer nationalism: workers, shop assistants, clerks, lower grades of civil servants. Here, as in the United States, these "poor whites"—more correctly, whites threatened with poverty—are the leading guardians of prejudice and white supremacy. The Voortrekker with his vast landed property has been transformed into a

salaried worker with a three roomed house. . . . He and people like him poll the votes which support Malan as his predecessors in the American South have been supported for a century.

A similar phenomenon appears to operate in Rhodesia as well. Rogers and Frantz (1962, pp. 124–125) found craftsmen to be by far the most willing of all occupational groups to restrict African freedoms. They write:

At the conservative end of the dimension, we find the craftsmen—the fitters, motor mechanics, menial workers, plumbers, welders, and so on—who are beginning to experience the impact of African competition. In the interviews, the craftsmen continually expressed concern for the future, as did the transport, mine, service, and sales workers. Hence, it is not difficult to forecast that, in such occupational groupings, we will find the most conservative attitudes about the problems posed by African advancement.

Helpful as these survey data are in isolating and establishing the fact, they do not shed light directly upon the *process* by which the skilled worker becomes so particularly resistant to racial change. Obviously, these individuals are reflecting in Parsonian terms special strains; but just what these strains are is by no means clear. The most immediate possibilities do not afford sufficient explanations. For example, "working class authoritarianism," the social psychological theory persuasively advanced by Lipset (1960, Chapter 4), operates in the reverse direction. That is, the unskilled and the semi-skilled tend to be considerably more authoritarian than the more racist skilled workers (Lipset, 1960, pp. 93, 95, 101–102).[13] Nor is *absolute* occupational deprivation apparently an

---

[11]As in Rhodesia and as is typical of American studies, sex did not prove to be a significant correlate (Bagley, 1970, p. 38). However, Bagley (1970, pp. 63–67) found that deprivation in housing relative to that occupied by members of the same social class to be positively related to extreme prejudice. But unlike the relative fraternalistic deprivation in income results for white urban Americans provided in the next section, this result involves only egoistic deprivation.

[12]Bagley (1970, pp. 47–52) found some evidence that status discrepancy was related positively to prejudice, a result reminiscent of Rush's (1967) results in the United States on right-wing extremism.

[13]However, Lipset (1960, Chapter 4) did propose an interesting political proposition concerning the upper and lower rungs of blue-collar workers. With data from a wide variety of countries, he attempted to demonstrate that communist parties most effectively appeal to the unskilled

adequate explanation. Inkeles (1960, p. 6) has shown that job satisfaction among skilled workers and artisans is without exception considerably greater than among the semi-skilled, the unskilled, and farm labourers in survey samples of Soviet refugees, West Germans, Italians, and Americans. Further, he showed that artisans are less dissatisfied, or at least no more dissatisfied, with how they were "getting on" than workers and farm labourers in seven out of nine national samples.[14]

Rogers and Franz (1962) provided a lead from Rhodesia in the quote above, as did Abrams in his British reference to "a guarded willingness to allow coloured entry into the fortress of working-class privilege" (Rose, 1969, p. 580). Status and economic threat seems to be involved for these skilled workers who benefit most from positions closed to competition by union and colour barriers. And Runciman's (1966) formulation of *fraternalistic* deprivation offers a way to conceptualize this possibility and link it with the developing social psychological theory of social evaluation (Pettigrew, 1967). We now turn to our empirical efforts over the past three years to follow up these leads.

Fraternal Deprivation and the Racial Attitudes of Whites in Urban America

Outline of the Research

We have conducted twelve separate surveys of blacks and whites in four American cities where competent black candidates have run for mayor: Gary, Indiana; Cleveland, Ohio; Los Angeles, California; and Newark, New Jersey. We studied Gary in October 1968, just before the Presidential elections, and again in December 1970. In the first of these studies, we drew a sample of 257 white male registered voters and concentrated on both Governor George Wallace's bid as a third-party candidate for the Presidency and Mayor Richard Hatcher's successful bid in 1967 to become Gary's first black Mayor. In the second study, we drew probability samples of 192 black and 291 white

registered voters and utilized appropriately different interview schedules for each. This time we focused on Mayor Hatcher's forthcoming race for re-election in 1971, a race that he later won handsomely.

In the late spring of 1969, we began our research in Cleveland, where Mayor Carl Stokes was beginning his successful efforts to gain re-election. His initial victory in 1967 received considerable world publicity, as he also was his city's first black head. We interviewed probability samples of 400 black and 488 white registered voters. After Stokes's triumph in early November of 1969, we returned and reinterviewed the white sample. The retrieval rate was over 80 percent—a fine result in mobile America that attests to the diligence and expertise of the University of Chicago's National Opinion Research Center to whom we subcontracted interviewing in all four cities. Also in the spring of 1969, we interviewed 300 white registered voters who together comprised probability samples of two contrasting areas of sprawling Los Angeles. Our study began after Thomas Bradley, a black city council member, had surprised observers by coming in first of a large field in the initial mayoralty election. He later lost to incumbent Mayor Samuel Yorty in a run-off election after a bitter campaign. We reinterviewed our respondents immediately following Bradley's run-off defeat. Again our retrieval rate was approximately 80 percent.[15]

Finally, our research took us to Newark in the spring of 1970 where Kenneth Gibson won easily over the entrenched incumbent to become the city's first black mayor. We interviewed probability samples of 200 black and 300 white registered voters before the first election in April of 1970. Then we interviewed a fresh sample of 200 black registered voters, and reinterviewed 80 percent of the original white sample following the first election but prior to the final run-off election.

Details of these interesting and history-making elections together with our general survey results are available elsewhere (Pettigrew, 1972). For present purposes, we wish to focus upon the data

---

and the semi-skilled when they are large and offer simple programmes; but they lose this following to large socialist parties and win their most favour among the affluent workers when they are small and offer somewhat more complex programmes.

[14]The glaring exceptions are in the British and Australian samples, in which artisans express greater dissatisfaction than

lower-ranked blue-collar respondents. The Italian and Norwegian samples revealed the greatest dissatisfaction among farm labourers with virtually identical levels among the artisans and general workers (Inkeles, 1960, p. 17).

[15]We also interviewed a small fresh sample in this second wave in order to have a control for the effects of the initial interviewing.

from these surveys relevant to the relationship between' relative deprivation and the racial attitudes and behaviour of whites in these four major American cities.

The Results

We have developed over the course of our twelve surveys an elaborate battery of measures of relative deprivation, the fullest we believe yet attempted in survey research. Eight basic questions are asked requiring forty-nine different responses; and though this sounds complex, even poorly educated respondents have typically had no trouble supplying meaningful data. In addition to the standard Cantril self-anchoring ladder items (Cantril, 1965; Cantril & Roll, 1961), we asked about the respondent's economic gains over the past five years and his satisfaction with them. More important, we obtained comparative ratings of his economic gains relative to eight critical groups: white-collar workers, blue-collar workers, Negroes, professionals, whites, unskilled labourers, people in the neighbourhood, and people in the suburbs.

Two general trends across the two races and all four cities are of interest. First, the *average* ratings assigning the economic gains of the eight groups by our respondents are quite accurate. This suggests that the social science dogma that Americans are relatively unaware of their social class structure deserves serious questioning. Second, there exists a broad resentment in these cities of the economic gains of white-collar workers in gen-

TABLE 19.1. Relative Deprivation and Wallace Support, Gary, 1968

	Wallace Supporters	Nixon Supporters	Humphrey Supporters	Total
Total Sample (245)	29.8 %	42.0 %	28.2 %	100%
'In spite of what some people say the lot of the average man is getting worse, not better.' *				
Agree (118)	41.5	33.1	25.4	100%
Disagree (122)	18.9	49.2	32.0	100%
Union Members				
Agree (76)	47.3	30.2	22.5	100%
Disagree (63)	27.0	33.3	39.7	100%
Non-Members				
Agree (40)	27.5	40.0	32.5	100%
Disagree (59)	10.2	66.1	23.7	100%
Religion				
Protestants				
Agree (53)	50.9	34.0	15.1	100%
Disagree (45)	22.2	53.7	24.1	100%
Roman Catholics				
Agree (53)	34.0	34.0	32.1	100%
Disagree (51)	17.6	43.1	39.2	100%
Social-class Identification				
Close to the working class				
Agree (49)	57.1	18.4	24.5	100%
Disagree (36)	25.0	47.2	27.8	100%
Not close to the working class				
Agree (25)	36.0	36.0	28.0	100%
Disagree (20)	30.0	20.0	50.0	100%
Close to the middle class				
Agree (27)	25.9	44.4	29.6	100%
Disagree (40)	7.5	60.0	32.5	100%
Not close to the middle class				
Agree (15)	26.7	60.0	13.3	100%
Disagree (23)	21.7	56.5	21.7	100%

* This item was originally introduced in: Leo Srole, 'Social Interaction and Certain Corollaries: An Exploratory Study,' *American Sociological Review,* (Vol. 21, 1956), pp. 709–716.

TABLE 19.2. Anti-Negro Prejudice, Relative Deprivation, and Wallace Support, Gary, 1968

	Wallace Supporters	Nixon Supporters	Humphrey Supporters	Total
Total Sample (245)	29.8%	42.0%	28.2%	100%
High anti-Negro prejudice: Agree that 'the lot of the average man is getting worse' (59)	52.5	20.3	27.1	100%
Disagree (34)	23.0	42.3	34.7	100%
Moderate anti-Negro Prejudice: Agree that 'the lot of the average man is getting worse' (38)	36.8	44.7	18.5	100%
Disagree (38)	26.3	44.7	28.9	100%
Low anti-Negro prejudice: Agree that 'the lot of the average man is getting worse' (18)	27.7	44.6	27.7	100%
Disagree (58)	12.1	55.2	32.8	100%

eral and professionals in particular. Large numbers of the respondents of varying background from Newark to Los Angeles believed, for instance, that "professionals in America today have gained more economically in the past five years than they are entitled to." And this resentment of the gains of professionals was consistently greater than resentment over the gains of black Americans.

Our interest in the role of relative deprivation in racial voting was initiated by an array of consistent relationships noted between a single relative deprivation item and support for Governor George Wallace in Gary in 1968. As previously reported (Pettigrew, 1971b, Chapter 10), Table 19.1 shows how agreement with the straightforward statement—"In spite of what some say, the lot of the average man is getting worse, not better"— predicted Wallace voting intentions within a number of relevant social controls.[16] Moreover, as Table 19.2 indicates, the item's predictive value is independent of anti-Negro prejudice despite their positive relationship.

Once we measured relative deprivation with a battery of items beginning with the Cleveland sur-

veys, we soon learned that the most effective approach was through use of the scheme shown in Table 19.3. This scheme builds on Runciman's (1966) theoretical analysis of relative deprivation discussed earlier. Table 19.3 is formed with two pieces of information: how each respondent views his own economic gains over the past five years in relation (1) to his ingroup (his class or racial category) and (2) to the relevant outgroup (e.g., white-collar workers for the blue-collar respondent, or blacks for the white respondent). Type A respondents are *doubly gratified*, for they feel they have been doing as well or better than both their ingroup and outgroup. Type B are the critical respondents, for they feel *fraternally deprived* in Runciman's sense. They feel they have kept up with or even surpassed the gains of their own group but that they have slipped behind those of their outgroup. Consequently, their deprivation is fraternal in that it is their group as a whole which is

---

[16]Relevant to the earlier discussion, note how the cell sizes in Table 19.1 reveal Wallace's special strength among union members and those highly identified with the working class.

TABLE 19.3. Four Types of Relative Deprivation and Gratification

		Personal Economic Gains Compared to Outgroup ('White-Collar Workers' or 'Negroes')	
		Equal or Greater than	Less than
Personal economic gains compared to ingroup ('blue-collar workers' or 'whites')	Equal or Greater than	A. Doubly gratified	B. Fraternally deprived
	Less than	C. Egoistically deprived	D. Doubly deprived

TABLE 19.4. Class Deprivation and 1968: Wallace Vote Percentages in Cleveland

	Class Deprivation Type			
	A. Doubly Gratified	B. Fraternally Deprived	C. Egoistically Deprived	D. Doubly Deprived
Entire Cleveland Sample*	%	%	%	%
(N= 301)	16	31	15	13
Just those who identify themselves with working class				
(N = 154)	11	41	23	15
Just those who identify themselves with middle class				
(N = 156)	21	17	12	12

*Those who did not vote in the 1968 presidential election are omitted.

seen as losing ground in comparison with the outgroup.

By contrast, Type C consists of individuals who sense their gains to have been less than those of their ingroup but at least equal to those of their outgroup; they are therefore termed, following Runciman, as the *egoistically deprived*. Finally, and least interesting, are the *doubly deprived* respondents of Type D who feel they have lost ground to both their ingroup and outgroup. These individuals are typically older and often retired; their fixed incomes probably have in fact been surpassed by younger groups generally,

Both social class and racial comparisons, using the scheme of Table 19.3, have been found to be important. The class comparisons contrast blue-collar versus white-collar workers; the racial comparisons, of course, contrast whites versus blacks in economic gains. Tables 19.4 and 19.5 demonstrate that the Wallace vote came disproportionately from respondents who felt that white-collar, but not blue-collar, workers were making greater economic gains than they. Since our respondents were largely blue-collar workers themselves, the results support the importance of fraternal depri-

vation. Nevertheless the perception that white-collar gains are greater than blue-collar gains should be interpreted as fraternal deprivation only for those respondents who subjectively identify with other blue-collar workers. In Cleveland we were able to divide the sample into working- and middle-class identifiers. As we would predict, the effect of the class comparisons is limited to working-class identifiers. In Gary we were able to measure identification with other blue-collar workers even more directly, employing a scale from 1 ("little in common with, not close at all") to 8 ("great deal in common with, very close"). Again, the class comparisons had a larger effect among those who identified more closely with blue-collar workers.

Some, but not all, of these differences, however, are traceable to background differences of the four class deprivation types. Whites who feel fraternally deprived in class terms are disproportionately concentrated among those of medium income and education who are younger, full-time, working-class members of labour unions. These respondents are precisely the ones we have isolated in other analyses as especially prone to being pro-Wallace

TABLE 19.5. Class Deprivation and 1972: Wallace Preference Percentages in Gary, 1970

	Class Deprivation Type			
	A. Doubly Gratified	B. Fraternally Deprived	C. Egoistically Deprived	D. Doubly Deprived
Entire Gary sample	%	%	%	%
(N = 288)	12	24	15	17
High (6-8) blue-collar identifiers				
(N = 132)	15	30	15	13
Low (1-5) blue-collar identifiers				
(N = 150)	9	19	15	18

TABLE 19.6. Racial Deprivation and the Reactions of Whites to Black Mayoralty Candidates

	Racial Deprivation Type			
Reactions to Black Candidates	A. Doubly Gratified %	B. Fraternally Deprived %	C. Egoistically Deprived %	D. Doubly Deprived %
Mayoralty voting				
For *Stokes* v. Perk, Cleveland 1969*	31	12	49	29
For *Bradley* v. Yorty,				
L.A. primary vote, 1969	26	17	34	30
Run-off preference, 1969	51	30	46	46
Run-off vote, 1969	35	21	52	42
For *Gibson* v. Addonizio, Newark, 1970	19	14	29	20
For *Hatcher* v. Williams, etc.,				
Gary primary, 1971	17	7	30	15
Candidate image				
(% favourable)‡				
Stokes, 1969	57	33	64	50
Bradley, 1969	65	44	71	49
Gibson, 1970	25	18	27	36
Hatcher, 1970	35	17	36	29

*For Democrats only, since this was a partisan final election.

‡The respondents were each presented a printed card with twelve adjectives from which three were chosen as the most descriptive of the black candidate. Half of the adjectives were favourable in tone (e.g., intelligent, honest) and half were unfavourable (e.g., out-for-himself, prejudiced). The favourable percentages provided here represent those whites who chose three favourable adjectives in the cases of Stokes and Gibson, and two or three favourable adjectives in the cases of Bradley and Hatcher.

and against black candidates. Yet controls for these factors, as in the earlier Gary analysis of Table 19.1, reduce but do not remove the predictive value of the relative class deprivation measures. This fact strongly implies that *fraternal class deprivation acts as a mediator of some, though not all, of the special skilled worker component of the Wallace phenomenon in the North*. In sharp contrast, fraternal race deprivations do not effectively predict Wallace leanings in either city. This suggests, together with other evidence (Pettigrew, 1971b, Chapter 10), that *the Wallace appeal had a strong economic as well as racist flavour.*

Perceived racial deprivations become important, however, for predicting white support of black mayoralty candidates. Table 19.6 provides these consistent and dramatic results across the four cities. Note that *the fraternally deprived on race report less willingness to vote for, and a more negative image of, the black candidate in every instance.* The background differences between the four racial deprivation types are similar to those between the four class deprivation types noted above, though they are less extensive. Controls for these background variables do not substantially affect the relationships shown in Table 19.6.

Table 19.7 presents additional data that thicken

the plot further. Observe that there is a tendency across cities for the fraternally deprived to not only believe that blacks have economically received more than they are entitled to (item a), but to more readily subscribe to a number of other conspiratorial and competitive statements.[17] Hence, the fraternally deprived are more likely to believe that race riots are caused by subversive elements rather than discrimination (item b), that politicians care too much about the disadvantaged (item c), and that Negroes could get along without welfare aid (item d). However, items which directly concern interracial interaction (items e, f, g, and h) do not elicit such a special reaction from the fraternally deprived.

These results suggest that we are dealing here with more than a single dimension of "prejudice." In order to understand fully the operation of relative deprivation and the racial attitudes and voting of our respondents, then, we must factor analyse our various attitude items. The results of this operation are provided in Table 19.8.

Two reasonably clear factors emerge. Factor I

---

[17]It is noteworthy that the exceptions to this trend involve Type D, the doubly deprived, who reflect as previously noted an older, more traditional sub-sample.

TABLE 19.7. Racial Deprivation and White Attitudes Towards Blacks

Attitudes toward Blacks (% Agreement)	Racial Deprivation Type			
	A. Doubly Gratified %	B. Fraternally Deprived %	C. Egoistically Deprived %	D. Doubly Deprived %
a. Negroes have gained more than they are entitled to.				
Cleveland 1969	15	37	10	19
Los Angeles 1969	6	13	2	23
Newark 1970	23	57	15	21
Gary 1970	17	46	24	32
b. Single most important cause of riots is . . . [looters/agitators/militants/communist influence/ violent instincts of Negroes].				
Cleveland 1969	66	79	63	68
Los Angeles 1969	54	73	44	79
Newark 1970	67	84	45	65
Gary 1970	76	80	55	84
c. Nowadays most politicians care too much about the disadvantaged and not enough about the average man.				
Cleveland 1969	71	87	62	77
Los Angeles 1969	53	68	65	64
Newark 1970	74	89	73	69
Gary 1970	66	80	67	80
d. . . . most Negroes who receive money from welfare . . . could get along without it if they tried. . . .				
Cleveland 1969	70	84	61	72
Los Angeles 1969	43	64	42	59
Newark 1970	58	71	48	62
Gary 1970	65	75	76	72
e. Negroes and whites can never be really comfortable with each other, even if they are close friends.				
Cleveland 1969	44	54	45	61
Los Angeles 1969	20	27	22	34
Newark 1970	49	64	69	66
Gary 1970	42	53	49	66
f. . . . white students and black students should go to . . . separate schools.				
Cleveland 1969	22	37	22	32
Los Angeles 1969	5	5	4	9
Newark 1970	12	8	13	22
Gary 1970	15	21	21	34
g. . . . would object if a member of . . . family wanted to bring a Negro home to dinner.				
Cleveland 1969	47	59	47	58
Los Angeles 1969	21	23	27	31
Newark 1970	44	56	55	66
Gary 1970	43	41	38	54
h. . . . would mind if a Negro family with about the same income and education moved next door.				
Cleveland 1969	52	66	65	63
Los Angeles 1969	31	38	33	46
Newark 1970	46	36	39	49
Gary 1970	39	50	28	56

TABLE 19.8. Rotated Factor Loadings of Eighteen Racial Items*

Racial Item	Factor I 'Contact Racism'	Factor II 'Competitive Racism'	Communality
Major contact racism items			
a. Would object if family member wanted to bring a Negro friend home to dinner.	+.754	+.081	0.575
b. Would mind if Negro family with about the same income and education moved next door.	+.718	+.013	0.516
c. Agrees that Negroes and whites can never be comfortable with each other, even if close friends.	+.615	+.276	0.454
d. Thinks white and black students should go to separate schools.	+.599	−.012	0.359
e. Would not vote for a Negro for President even if nominated by own party.	+.521	+.172	0.301
f. Has not visited socially with Negroes in home during last month.	+.401	−.030	0.162
Items loaded on both factors			
g. Believes Negroes over the past few years have got more than they deserve.	+.516	+.462	0.480
h. Agrees that Negroes should not push themselves where they are not wanted.	+.460	+.516	0.478
i. Agrees that 'hardworking people like me have not done as well as Negroes over the past few years'.	+.484	+.309	0.329
Major competitive racism items			
j. Believes race riots caused by looters, agitators, militants, violent instincts, communist influence rather than bad conditions and racial discrimination.	+.123	+.531	0.298
l. Thinks most Negroes who receive welfare aid could get along without it if they tried.	+.306	+.514	0.358
m. Believes poverty programmes promote laziness and not hard work.	+.187	+.495	0.280
n. Agrees that 'most politicians care too much about the disadvantaged and not enough about the average man'.	+.280	+.475	0.305
o. Denies that Negroes miss out on jobs or promotions in his city because of racial discrimination.	+.260	+.432	0.254
p. Believes busing elementary school children harms their education.	−.038	+.539	0.292
q. Disagrees that it is best for children to attend elementary school outside their neighbourhood.	+.090	+.415	0.181
r. Thinks race riots hurt Negro cause.	+.005	+.428	0.184
Miscellaneous additional item			
s. Believes Negroes with same education and income are 'better off' than himself.	+.029	.247	0.062
Sum of Squares	3.266	2.602	5.868

*Based on the probability samples of 1,539 white registered voters in the 1969–70 studies of Gary, Cleveland, Los Angeles, and Newark. Varimax rotations were made of the original principal components solution.

weights are heaviest on items involving interracial contact, so it seems appropriate to label it *contact racism*. The one exception is item e, concerning voting for a Negro for President. What this non-contact item appears to have in common with the contact items is a certain hypothetical quality. Just as it is highly unlikely for most of our respondents that a "family member wanted to bring a Negro friend home to dinner" (item a), it is equally unlikely that the United States will soon

TABLE 19.9. Types of Racism and Deprivation by City*

Type of Deprivation	Contact Racism Factor Scores				
	L.A. Sample	Cleveland Sample	Newark Sample	Gary Sample	Total Unweighted Means
A. Doubly gratified	−61.4	+6.1	−14.0	−14.4	−20.9
B. Fraternally deprived	−40.8	+58.1	+16.4	+23.5	+14.3
C. Egoistically deprived	−48.9	+18.8	−11.9	−13.4	−13.9
D. Doubly deprived	−25.0	+62.7	+24.3	+54.5	+29.1
Total unweighted means	−44.0	+36.4	+3.7	+12.6	+ 2.2
	Deprivation type	F = 10.1, p < .001			
	City	F = 20.7, p < .001			
	Deprivation × city	F = 0.4, not significant			

Type of Deprivation	Competitive Racism Factor Scores				
	L.A. Sample	Cleveland Sample	Newark Sample	Gary Sample	Total Unweighted Means
A. Doubly gratified	−52.0	−17.6	+ 27.1	+19.6	−5.7
B. Fraternally deprived	− 1.4	+4.7	+89.3	+73.7	+41.6
C. Egoistically deprived	−58.4	−34.2	+2.0	+34.3	−14.1
D. Doubly deprived	−32.3	−27.7	−8.3	+32.3	−9.0
Total unweighted means	−36.0	−18.7	+27.5	+40.0	+3.2
	Deprivation type	F = 12.5, p < .001			
	City	F = 24.7, p < .001			
	Deprivation x city	F = 1.2, not significant			

*The total sample of respondents for these unweighted means analyses of variance was 1,176. In order to have the Type D, the doubly deprived, more nearly approach the background characteristics of the other three types, all respondents over 65 years of age were removed from the total sample.

witness a major black candidate for President. Consistent with this interpretation of a certain hypothetical quality in Factor I is the fact that it is heavily related to education (Table 19.9). If we are right, item e's weights on Factor I should decrease and on Factor II increase over time as the probability of a Negro President increases.

Factor II is labelled *competitive racism* for its heavily weighted items include opposition to government programmes to help blacks and beliefs that racial discrimination is not an important problem.[18] Thus, "politicians care too much about the disadvantaged" (item n), Negroes do not need welfare aid (item 1), and "poverty programmes promote laziness" (item m). Items s, p, and q refer to the current euphemisms in America for opposing the racial desegregation of schools through objecting to court-ordered "busing" away from segregated "neighbourhood schools."[19] Moreover, Factor II includes denial of the role of racial discrimination (items j and o) and of the liberal interpretation of race riots (items j and r).

Three additional items (g, h, i) in our battery of eighteen contain elements of each of these factors and achieve sizeable weights on both. Another (item s) is relatively unrelated to either factor. Note

also that most of the Factor II items contain modest weights on Factor I. This indicates that there would be a small but definite positive correlation between our two racism factors if oblique rotation were utilized.

Table 19.9 employs the factor scores for each of these two factors and relates them to the four types of deprivation in each of our urban samples. Contact racism is consistently related to the doubly deprived; and competitive racism is consistently related to fraternal deprivation. Observe that deprivation type is significantly related to both types of racism as is the city variable,[20] but there is no significant interaction between deprivation type and city. In other words, while the cities vary

[18]This factor seems to tap the type of "competitive prejudice" that van den Berghe (1958) has maintained in an ideal-type analysis to be critical and characteristic of modern industrial societies.

[19]No less a figure than President Nixon has blatantly legitimated this thinly disguised opposition to racial change as a cynical component of his "southern political strategy."

[20]It is of interest to note that competitive racism is without exception inversely related to city size, with Los Angeles and Gary at the extremes. The same would be true for contact racism were it not for the sharp degree of contact racism in Cleveland.

considerably in measured racism, the deprivation effects are essentially the same across cities.

Note, too, that the fraternally deprived are the second highest group in contact racism in three of the four cities and for the total sample. Thus, both of the groups high in contact racism—the doubly deprived and the fraternally deprived—share an *individual* sense of not having done as well economically as black Americans. By contrast, the doubly deprived do not typically exhibit competitive racism; in Newark they are the lowest group, and for the total sample they are not significantly different from either the doubly gratified or the egoistically deprived. Competitive racism, then, is strongly associated with just the *group* sense of deprivation represented by fraternals alone.

Tables 19.10 and 19.11 explore these results further by controlling for both education and age—the two key background correlates in our data just as in Bagley's (1970) five-borough English data. Contact racism, shown in Table 19.10, is highly related to education but not to age. Indeed, fifteen out of the sixteen educational comparisons within the age and deprivational type controls show reduced contact racism with each increase in educational level. And while there is no education and

age interaction, the jump from high school graduate to college reflects a considerably larger reduction in contact racism among the younger respondents, and from grade school to high school graduate among the older respondents. In four of the six comparisons, the doubly deprived have higher scores. Interestingly, both exceptions occur for high school graduates—the modal educational category of the affluent worker; and this fact is reflected in the weakly significant interaction term between type of deprivation and education. Notice also that the fraternally deprived had the second highest scores in five instances and the highest in the sixth.

A contrasting pattern appears for competitive racism in Table 19.11. Education and age are both significantly related; yet the fraternally deprived achieve the highest average factor scores in all six comparisons. Unlike with contact racism, the effects of education are not consistent. While the major effect is found between the high school graduate and college groups for both age groups, the key cluster of young high school graduates tend to possess slightly *higher* scores than the 11 years-or-less group. This trend is not true for the older respondents. Age, which did not relate to

TABLE 19.10. Contact Racism Factor Scores and Types of Deprivation by Age and Education*

Type of Deprivation		Younger Respondents (21–40) Education	
	11 Yrs. or Less	High School Graduate (12)	College (13+)
A. Doubly gratified	+16.3	−7.2	−78.4
B. Fraternally deprived	+51.7	+31.2	−36.5
C. Egoistically deprived	+13.0	−16.5	−61.8
D. Doubly deprived	+69.3	+20.8	−22.7
		Older Respondents (41–65) Education	
	11 Yrs. or less	High School Graduate (12)	College (13+)
A. Doubly gratified	+2.2	−22.3	−71.4
B. Fraternally deprived	+32.6	+8.2	−18.5
C. Egoistically deprived	+28.0	+15.1	−84.9
D. Doubly deprived	+93.1	−24.2	−9.7
	Deprivation type	$F = 9.9, p < .001$	
	Age	$F = 0.1$, not significant	
	Education	$F = 46.9, p < .001$	
	Deprivation × age	$F = 0.3$, not significant	
	Deprivation × ed.	$F = 1.8, p < .11$	
	Age × education	$F = 0.5$, not significant	
	Deprivation × age × ed.	$F = 1.3$, not significant	

*As in Table 19.9, all respondents over 65 years of age were removed from this total sample, leaving a total of 1,176 for the unweighted means analysis of variance.

TABLE 19.11. Competitive Racism Factor Scores and Types of Deprivation by Age and Education*

Type of Deprivation	11 Yrs. or Less	Younger Respondents (21–40) Education High School Graduate (12)	College (13+)
A. Doubly gratified	−5.8	+3.3	−91.4
B. Fraternally deprived	+*35.7*	+*39.1*	−*8.0*
C. Egoistically deprived	−38.6	−27.4	−65.3
D. Doubly deprived	+24.6	+19.4	−92.8

	11 Yrs. or Less	Older Respondents (41–65) Education High School Graduate (12)	College (13+)
A. Doubly gratified	+32.2	+25.2	−38.8
B. Fraternally deprived	+*58.1*	+*41.6*	+*17.4*
C. Egoistically deprived	+5.0	+38.6	−27.2
D. Doubly deprived	0.0	−22.8	−8.2

Deprivation Type	$F = 8.9$, p. $< \cdot 001$
Age	$F = 12.7$, p. $< \cdot 001$
Education	$F = 21.6$, p. $< \cdot 001$
Deprivation × age	$F = 1.6$, not significant
Deprivation × ed.	$F = 1.0$, not significant
Age × education	$F = 2.3$, p. $< .11$
Deprivation × age × ed.	$F = 1.7$, p. $< .11$

* As in Tables 19.9 and 19.10, all respondents over 65 years of age were removed from the total sample leaving a total of 1,176 for the unweighted means analysis of variance.

contact racism, provides an interesting pattern. In ten out of twelve comparisons, the young reveal that they are less threatened by blacks; but the two exceptions are suggestive, since they consist of the doubly deprived young who did not obtain college training. These trends lie behind the two interaction terms which approach significance.

We can summarize the results of Tables 19.9, 19.10, and 19.11, then, by stating that: *across city, educational, and age samples, contact racism is strongest among those who individually regard their economic gains as inferior to the gains of blacks; while competitive racism is strongest among those who collectively regard white economic gains as inferior to the gains of blacks.*

It remains, however, to test the links between these relative deprivation findings and the "affluent worker phenomenon" discussed earlier. If our reasoning is correct then at least part of the greater prejudice of the affluent workers may be attributed to their greater sense of fraternal deprivation. Unlike the poorer workers below them, they have both the fraternal solidarity of doing as well as most white workers and the increased aspirations resulting from past successes. And unlike the truly affluent above them they are not doing so well as

to be free from any threat of deprivation. This should reflect itself in a curvilinear relationship of our fraternal deprivation measures with socio-economic status. Table 19.12 reports the incidence of fraternal deprivation according to income and education. In general, the results confirm our expectations although some of the relationships are not strong. For racial deprivation, only 12 percent of the low-education low-income group feels fraternally deprived. This increases to 26 percent among high school graduates making $7,500 to $10,000 a year and then decreases again to 16 percent of the college graduates making over $15,000. For class deprivation the analogous percentages are 6 percent, 29 percent and 11 percent, again showing a curvilinear trend.

Discussion

Merton and Kitt (1950), in reviewing the Air Corps and Military Police example of relative deprivation cited earlier, raise an issue that becomes critical in our own analysis.

> We note that [the dependent variable] consists in soldiers' evaluations of the institutional system of

TABLE 19.12. Fraternal Deprivation by Income and Education

	Fraternal Racial Deprivation Income				
Education	$5,000 or less	$5,000– $7,500	$7,500– $10,000	$10,000– $15,000	$15,000 or More
11 years or less	12%*	22%	24%	21%	20%
High school graduate	19%	24%	26%	19%	24%
College	10%	18%	19%	16%	16%
	Fraternal Class Deprivation ‡ Income				
Education	$5,000 or less	$5,000– $7,500	$7,500– $10,000	$10,000– $15,000	$15,000 or More
11 years or less	6%	13%	17%	13%	(7%)
High school graduate	(21 %)	9%	29%	14%	14%
College	(8%)	(25%)	22%	32%	11%

*Percentages are the percentages of the total respondents in each cell who were classified as fraternally deprived.
‡As in Tables 19.4 and 19.5 results are from Gary and Cleveland only. Parentheses indicate percentages are based on small cell sizes ($N < 20$).

promotion in the Army, and not to self evaluations of personal achievement within that system. . . . This introduces a problem, deserving attention which it has not yet received: *do the two types of evaluations, self-appraisals and appraisals of institutional arrangements, involve similar mechanisms of reference group behaviour?* [italics added].

This question finally began receiving conceptual attention years later from Runciman (1966), as we have noted, in his distinction between egoistic and fraternalistic deprivation. His answer to the query posed by Merton and Kitt was basically, *no,* in that two mechanisms of reference behaviour appear to be involved. Runciman insisted that it is only fraternal, and not egoistic, deprivation that results in movements for and against fundamental structural change in society.

This point seems almost obvious on closer analysis. Structural change involves by definition changes in the position of groups within society and not the movements of particular individuals within that structure. It seems obvious, then, that attitudes about structural change would involve group-to-group comparisons (fraternalist) and not individual-to-group comparisons (egoistic). And yet this point has been largely ignored or obscured by most of the researchers who have sought to link relative deprivation to movements for and against social change. There has been, in short, a consis-

tent and erroneous individualistic bias throughout this literature.

Perhaps the most frequent definition of relative deprivation in these studies refers to the gap between individual aspirations and satisfactions. Davies (1962), Feierabend and Feierabend (1966), and Gurr (1970), for example, all make use of such an individually focused definition.[21] And recent research based on the Cantril Self-Anchoring Scale has provided an empirical method for measuring the gap between aspirations and satisfactions (e.g., Crawford & Naditch, 1970). Defined in this way, relative deprivation is virtually divorced from its original reference group links. The hypothesized comparison is entirely within the individual, between his present or expected satisfactions and his past aspirations. Some of these investigators, for example, Gurr (1970), admit that reference groups do influence the nature of an individual's aspirations, but the *anchor* to the comparison process is still assumed to be the individual himself. "How are the blacks doing relative to *me*?"

The point is not that such individualistic comparisons are never made or are never relevant to social action. Rather the problem with this past research is that it fails to distinguish between

---

[21]Other writers have confused the two orientations, among them one of the present authors (Pettigrew, 1964). For collections of the relevant studies in this literature, see Masotti and Bowen (1968) and Davies (1971).

self-evaluations and structural evaluations and, thus, between the different comparisons which underlie these evaluations. The frustrated aspirations of whites, or their failure to keep up with the perceived gains of black Americans, has important consequences for one's self and perhaps for how one interacts with blacks. But not until this deprivation is generalized to one's entire membership group are there implications for desired institutional changes in the fundamental structure of society. Our own research demonstrates that evaluations of *structural* changes in race relations are related to fraternal comparisons, while attitudes towards *individual* intergroup behaviour (contact with blacks) is more closely associated with individualistic cross-group comparisons.

Two important differences between individual and group comparisons that relate to reference group ideas require emphasis. First, as Hyman and Singer (1968), Pettigrew (1967), and others have emphasized, the weakest link in reference group theory is the failure to explain adequately how reference groups are selected in the first place. This weakness exists especially for egoistic deprivation; but it holds with less force for fraternal deprivation, because of the tendency for reference groups to be reciprocally paired much in the manner of social roles: white–black, native–immigrant, blue collar–white collar. Thus, once an individual has identified with his in-group, the relevant group referent with which to compare the status of the in-group is largely determined.

For fraternal deprivation the nature of the question is therefore quite different. We know what the appropriate comparison group is, but what determines how the individual makes that comparison? Our data indicate that there is a curvilinear relationship between the individual's objective position and his perception of fraternal deprivation. The poor tend to feel deprived relative to their in-group as well as to the comparative referent, while the wealthy can avoid any feeling of deprivation. Those in the middle, however, can maintain fraternal solidarity with their own in-group while resenting or envying gains made by external referents.

Secondly, fraternal deprivation presents a unique solution for the tension created between mobility aspirations and the *Gemeinschaft* bonds of the in-group. As one rises in the social structure, there necessarily are created pressures for breaking old in-group ties. In essence, this tension is implicit in Durkheim's distinction between organic and mechanical solidarity; and it marks the limits, as Davis (1966) has noted, to the operation of balance theory—the currently popular social psychological version of mechanical solidarity. But fraternal aspirations skirt the problem by opting for, in essence, group mobility. If structural change succeeds in raising the status of one's group, then one achieves a type of personal mobility while maintaining—indeed strengthening—in-group bonds. This phenomenon is in marked contrast to egoistic aspirations; and it suggests that fraternal aspirations and deprivation will be most prevalent in societies where rapid mobility is perceived and cohesive subgroups exist. Put differently, fraternal deprivation is created when perceptions of rapid mobility raise aspirations while in-group solidarity channels the aspirations into group terms.

Finally, the findings presented here distinguish between two, only slightly related, dimensions of anti-black prejudice—*contact racism* and *competitive racism*. We strongly suspect that many omnibus measures of prejudice employed in previous research have confounded these and other dimensions of prejudice. This confounding in turn introduces unnecessary error and retards the progress of the field by rendering more difficult comparisons across diverse investigations.

Consequently, we believe our results point to five conclusions:

1. Runciman's (1966) distinction between egoistic and fraternalistic deprivation is vital to any use of reference group theory and the relative deprivation hypothesis for the study of social movements for or against major structural change in society. The key form of relative deprivation for producing social unrest is group-to-group, fraternalistic comparisons, even though other forms of individual comparisons are critical for self-evaluations.

2. Special resistance to racial change in urban America today is centred among the affluent workers and the fraternally deprived. Wallace support is particularly found among younger affluent workers who feel their class is relatively deprived in reference to white-collar job holders. Indeed, it appears as if fraternal *class* deprivation acts as a mediator for the affluent worker component of the "Wallace phenom-

enon." Resistance to black mayoralty candidates is particularly found among those who feel their *racial* group (whites) is deprived relative to blacks.

3. Negative individual evaluations in comparison with black Americans, as exemplified by both the doubly and the fraternally deprived, tend towards *contact racism* involving an expressed aversion to reasonably intimate interracial contact. By contrast, negative group-to-group evaluations in comparison with black Americans, as exemplified by the fraternally deprived alone, tend strongly towards *competitive racism* involving resentment of government programmes designed to help blacks and a denial of the existence of racial discrimination. These suggestive results hold up even after crude controls for city sample, education, and age are applied.

4. The incidence of fraternal deprivation is greatest at intermediate economic levels. This curvilinear relationship suggests that fraternal deprivation acts as a mediating link in the relationship between racial prejudice and working-class affluence.

5. Finally, future research in this realm would be well advised to: (a) measure perceived deprivation in a wide variety of ways; (b) draw sharp distinctions between various types of deprivation, especially fraternal and egoistic, relative to a large array of potential comparison groups; and (c) divide the dependent variable of prejudice into its several components.

REFERENCES

Adorno, T. W., Frenkel-Brunswik, E., Levinson, D. F., & Sanford, R. N. (1950). *The authoritarian personality.* New York: Harper-Row.

Allport, G. W. (1954). The nature of prejudice. Cambridge, MA: Addison-Wesley.

Bagley, C. (1970). *Social structure and prejudice in five English boroughs.* London: Institute of Race Relations.

Blau, P. M. (1964). *Exchange and power in social life.* New York: Wiley.

Brink, W. & Harris, L. (1964). *The negro revolution in America.* New York: Simon and Schuster.

Brink, W. & Harris, L. (1967). *Black and White.* New York: Simon and Schuster.

Campbell, A. (1971). *White attitudes toward Black people.* Ann Arbor, MI: Institute for Social Research.

Campbell, A., Converse, P. E., Miller, W. E., & Stokes, D. E. (1960). *The American voter.* New York: Wiley.

Campbell, A., Gurin, G., & Miller, W. E. (1954). *The voter decides.* Evanston, IL: Row, Peterson.

Campbell, A., & Schuman, H. (1968). Racial attitudes in fifteen American cities. In the National Advisory Commission on Civil Disorders, *Supplemental studies.* Washington, DC: U.S. Government Printing Office.

Cantril, H., & Roll, C. W., Jr. (1971). *Hopes and fears of the American people.* New York: Universe Books.

Cantril, H. (1951). *Public opinion, 1935–1946.* Princeton, NJ: Princeton University Press.

Cantril, H. (1965). *The pattern of human concerns.* New Brunswick, NJ: Rutgers University Press.

Centers, R. (1949). *The psychology of social classes.* Princeton, NJ: Princeton University Press.

Charters, W. W., Jr., & Newcomb, T. M. (1952). Some attitudinal effects of experimentally increased salience of a membership group. In G. E. Swanson, T. M. Newcomb, & E. L. Hartley (Eds.), *Readings in social psychology* (2nd ed.). New York: Holt, Reinhart and Winston.

Cooley, C. H. (1902). *Human nature and the social order.* New York: Scribner's.

Crawford, T. J., & Naditch, N. (1970). Relative deprivation, powerlessness, and militancy: The psychology of social protest. *Psychiatry, 33.*

Daniel, W. W. (1968). *Racial discrimination in England.* Harmondsworth, UK: Penguin.

Davies, J. C. (1962). Toward a theory of revolution. *American Sociological Review, 27,* 5–19.

Davies, J. C. (Ed.). (1971). *When men revolt and why: A reader in political violence and participation.* New York: Free Press.

Davis, J. A. (1959). A formal interpretation of the theory of relative deprivation. *Sociometry, 22,* 280–296.

Davis, J. A. (1966). Structural balance, mechanical solidarity, and interpersonal relations. *American Journal of Sociology, 72.*

Eisenstadt, S. N. (1954). Studies in reference group behaviour. *Human Relations, 7,* 191–216.

Erskine, H. G. (1962). The polls: Race relations. *Public Opinion Quarterly, 26.*

Erskine, H. G. (1967). The polls: Negro housing. *Public Opinion Quarterly, 31.*

Erskine, H. G. (1967–1968). The polls: Demonstrations and race riots. *Public Opinion Quarterly, 31.*

Erskine, H. G. (1968a). The polls: Negro employment. *Public Opinion Quarterly, 32.*

Erskine, H. G. (1968b). The polls: Speed of racial integration. *Public Opinion Quarterly, 32.*

Erskine, H. G. (1968–1969). The polls: Recent opinion on racial problems. *Public Opinion Quarterly, 32.*

Eulau, H. (1962). Class and party in the Eisenhower years. New York: Free Press.

Festinger, L. (1954). A theory of social comparison process. *Human Relations, 7,* 117–140.

Fenton, J. M. (1960). *In your opinion.* Boston: Little-Brown.

Feierabend, L., & Feierabend, R. L. (1966). Aggressive behaviors within polities, 1948–1962: A cross-national study. *Journal of Conflict Resolution, 10.*

Form, W. H., & Geschwender, J. A. (1962). Social reference basis of job satisfaction: The case of manual workers. *American Sociological Review, 27,* 228–237.

Gurr, T. R. (1970). *Why men rebel.* Princeton, NJ: Princeton University Press.

Hartley, R. E. (1960a). Relationships between perceived values and acceptance of a new reference group. *Journal of Social Psychology, 51,* 181–190.

Hartley, R. E. (1960b). Personal needs and the acceptance of a new group as a reference group. *Journal of Social Psychology, 51,* 349–358.

Homans, G. C. (1961). *Social behavior: Its elementary forms.* New York: Harcourt, Brace and World.

Hyman, H. H. (1942). The psychology of status. *Archives of Psychology, 269,* 94.

Hyman, H. H., & Sheatsley, P. B. (1956). Attitudes toward desegregation. *Scientific American, 195,* 35–39.

Hyman, H. H., & Sheatsley, P. B. (1964). Attitudes toward desegregation. *Scientific American, 211.*

Hyman, H. H., & Singer, E. (Eds.). (1968). *Readings in reference group theory and research.* New York: Free Press.

Inkeles, A. (1960). Industrial man: The relation of status to experience, perception, and value. *American Journal of Sociology, 66,* 1–31.

Kaplan, N. (1968). Reference groups and interest group theories of voting. In H. H. Hyman & E. Singer (Eds.), *Readings in reference group theory and research.* New York: Free Press.

Kelley, H. H. (1952). Two functions of reference groups. In G. E. Swanson, T. M. Newcomb, & E. L. Hartley (Eds.), *Readings in social psychology* (2nd ed.). New York: Holt, Reinhart and Winston.

Lenski, G. E. (1954). Status crystallization: A non-vertical dimension of social status. *American Sociological Review, 19,* 405–413.

Lipset, S. M. (1960). *Political man: The social bases of politics.* New York: Doubleday.

Lipset, S. M., & Raab, E. (1970). *The politics of unreason: Right-wing extremism in America, 1790–1970.* New York: Harper and Row.

Litwak, E. (1960). Reference group theory, bureaucratic career, and neighborhood primary group cohesion. *Sociometry, 23,* 72–84.

MacCrone, I. D. (1937). *Race attitudes in South Africa.* London: Oxford University Press.

MacCrone, I. D. (1949). Race attitudes. In E. Hellmann (Ed.), *Handbook of South African race relations.* New York: Oxford University Press.

MacCrone, I. D. (1953). Ethnocentric ideology and ethnocentrism. *Proceedings of the South African Psychological Association, 4,* 21–24.

Malherbe, E. G. (1946). *Race attitudes and education.* Johannesburg, SA: Institute of Race Relations.

Marx, G. T. (1967). *Protest and prejudice: A study of belief in the black community.* New York: Harper and Row.

Masotti, L. H., & Bowen, D. R. (Eds.). (1968). *Riots and rebellion: Civil violence in the urban community.* Beverly Hills, CA: Sage.

Mead, G. H. (1934). *Mind, self, and society.* Chicago: University of Chicago Press.

Merton, R. K. (1957). *Social theory and social structure* (rev. ed.). Glencoe, IL: Free Press.

Merton, K., & Kitt (Rossi), A. S. (1950). Contributions to the theory of reference group behavior. In R. K. Merton & P. F. Lazarsfeld (Eds.), *Continuities in social research: Studies in the scope and method of 'The American Soldier.'* Glencoe, IL: Free Press.

Meyer, P. (1968a). *A survey of attitudes of Detroit negroes after the riot of 1967.* Detroit, MI: Detroit Urban League.

Meyer, P. (1968b). Miami negroes: A study in depth. Miami, FL: *The Miami Herald.*

Newcomb, T. M. (1943). *Personality and social change.* New York: Holt, Reinhart, and Winston.

Newcomb, T. M. (1951). Review of continuities in social research. *American Journal of Sociology, 57.*

Parker, S. & Kleiner, R. J. (1966). *Mental illness in the urban negro community.* New York: Free Press.

Patchen, M. A. (1961). A conceptual framework and some empirical data regarding comparisons of social rewards. *Sociometry, 24.*

Pearlin, L. I. (1954). Shifting group attachments and attitudes toward negroes. *Social Forces, 33,* 47–50.

Pettigrew, T. F. (1958). Personality and socio-cultural factors in intergroup attitudes: A cross-national comparison. *Journal of Conflict Resolution, 2,* 29–42.

Pettigrew, T. F. (1959). Regional differences in anti-negro prejudice. *Journal of Abnormal and Social Psychology, 59,* 28–36.

Pettigrew, T. F. (1960). Social distance attitudes of South African sudents. *Social Forces, 38,* 246–253.

Pettigrew, T. F. (1964). *A profile of the negro American.* Princeton, NJ: Van Nostrand Reinhold.

Pettigrew, T. F. (1967). Social evaluation theory: Convergences and applications. In D. Levine (Ed.), *Nebraska Symposium on Motivation.* Lincoln: University of Nebraska Press.

Pettigrew, T. F. (1971a). Review of Rose's colour and citizenship. *Race, 12.*

Pettigrew, T. F. (1971b). *Racially separate or together?* New York: McGraw-Hill.

Pettigrew, T. F. (1958). When a Black candidate runs for mayor: Race and voting behavior. In H. Hahn (Ed.), *Urban affairs annual review.* Beverly Hills, CA: Sage.

Political and Economic Planning and Research Services Ltd. (1967). *Racial discrimination.* London: P. E. P.

de Sola Pool, I., & Shulman, I. (1959). Newsmen's fantasies, audiences, and newswritings. *Public Opinion Quarterly, 23,* 145–158.

Rogers, C. A., & Frantz, C. (1962). *Racial themes in Southern Rhodesia.* New Haven, CT: Yale University Press.

Rogers, E. M. (1958). Reference group influences on student drinking behaviour. *Quarterly Journal of Studies on Alcohol, 19,* 244–254.

Rokeach, M., & Mezei, L. (1966). Race and shared belief as factors in social choice. *Science, 151,* 167–172.

Rokeach, M., Smith, P. W., & Evans, R. I. (1960). Two kinds of prejudice or one? In M. Rokeach (Ed.), *The open and closed mind.* New York: Basic Books.

Rose, E. J. B., & Associates. (1969). *Colour and citizenship: A report on British race relations.* London: Oxford University Press for the Institute of Race Relations.

Runciman, W. G. (1966). *Relative deprivation and social justice.* London: Routledge and Kegan Paul.

Schwartz, M. A. (1967). *Trends in White attitudes towards Negroes.* Chicago: National Opinion Research Centre.

Sheatsley, P. B. (1966). White attitudes towards the negro. In T. Parsons & K. Clark (Eds.), *The Negro American.* Boston: Houghton Mifflin.

Sherif, M. (1953). The concept of reference groups in human relations. In M. Sherif & M. O. Wilson (Eds.), *Group relations at the crossroads.* New York: Harper and Row.

Shibutani, T. (1955). Reference groups as perspectives. *American Journal of Sociology, 60,* 562–569.

Siegel, A. E., & Siegel, S. (1957). Reference groups, membership groups, and attitude change. *Journal of Abnormal* and Social Psychology, 55, 360–364.

Smith, C. R., Williams, L., & Willis, R. H. (1967). Race, sex, and belief as determinants of friendship acceptance. *Journal of Personality and Social Psychology, 5.*

Spector, A. J. (1956). Expectations, fulfilment, and morale. *Journal of Abnormal and Social Psychology, 52,* 51–56.

Stein, D. D. (1966). The influence of belief systems on interpersonal preference. *Psychological Monographs, 80,* 29.

Stein, D. D., Hardyck, J. A., & Smith, M. B. (1965). Race and belief: An open and shut case. *Journal of Personality and Social Psychology, 1,* 281–289.

Stern, E., & Keller, S. (1953). Spontaneous group preference in France. *Public Opinion Quarterly, 17,* 208–217.

Stouffer, S. A., Suchman, S. A., DeVinney, L. C., Star, S. A., & Williams, R. M., Jr. (1949). *The American soldier: Vol. 1. Adjustment during army life.* Princeton, NJ: Princeton University Press.

Strauss, H. M. (1968). Reference group and social comparison processes among the totally blind. In H. H. Hyman & E. Singer (Eds.), *Readings in reference group theory and research.* New York: Free Press.

Thibaut, J. W., & Kelley, H. H. (1959). *The social psychology of groups.* New York: Wiley.

Tingsten, H. (1954). *The problem of South Africa.* London: Gollancz.

Turner, R. H. (1956). Role-taking, role standpoint, and reference group behaviour. *American Journal of Sociology, 61,* 316–328.

van den Berghe, P. L. (1958). The dynamics of racial prejudice: An ideal-type dichotomy. *Social Forces, 37,* 138–141.

van den Berghe, P. L. (1962). Race attitudes in Durban, South Africa. *Journal of Social Psychology, 57,* 55–72.

Williams, R. M., Jr. (1964). *Strangers next door.* Englewood Cliffs, NJ: Prentice-Hall.

Responding to Membership in a Disadvantaged Group: From Acceptance to Collective Protest

Stephen C. Wright, Donald M. Taylor, and Fathali M. Moghaddam
• McGill University

The question addressed is, when do disadvantaged-group members accept their situation, take individual action, or attempt to instigate collective action? Subjects attempted to move from a low-status group into an advantaged, high-status group and were asked to respond to their subsequent rejection. Subjects who believed that the high-status group was open to members of their group endorsed acceptance and individual actions. When access to the high-status group was restricted, even to the point of being almost closed (tokenism), subjects still preferred individual action. Disruptive forms of collective action were only favored by subjects who were told that the high-status group was completely closed to members of their group. Subjects who believed they were near to gaining entry into the high-status group favored individual protest, while subjects distant from entry were more likely to accept their position. The theoretical and societal implications of these findings are discussed.

The unequal distribution of resources among groups or categories arises at virtually every level of social organization: from nations, to the place of work, to the family unit. The actions taken by members of a disadvantaged group can range from apparent acceptance, to individual attempts to improve one's personal position, to episodes of collective violence.

The circumstances associated with different forms of action by disadvantaged-group members have not been systematically defined in the social psychological literature. The following three limitations to existing theory and research in intergroup relations may partially account for this deficit: (a) the tendency to focus on feelings and perceptions, not behavior, (b) the failure to study a full array of behavioral options, and (c) the reductionist nature of dominant theories of intergroup relations. The present article attempts to address each of these three limitations.

First, many theories in the area of intergroup relations attempt to predict when disadvantaged people will have strong negative feelings. The fundamental and recurring problem is the tendency of these major theories not to extend their analysis beyond feelings to the resulting behavioral consequences of membership in a disadvantaged group. The dependent measures in most research that is inspired by theories such as equity theory (K. S. Cook & Messick, 1983; Walster, Walster, & Berscheid, 1978), justice motive theory (Lerner, 1977; Lerner & Lerner, 1981), distributive justice theory (Homans, 1961), and relative deprivation theory (Crosby, 1976; Davis, 1959; Gurr, 1970; Mark, 1985; Runciman, 1966; Stouffer, Suchman, DeVinney, Starr, & Williams, 1949) have not been behavior—but feelings, attitudes, and perceptions associated with unequal treatment. Notable exceptions to this tendency exist (e.g., T. D. Cook, Crosby, & Hennigan, 1977; Guimond & Dubé, 1983; Martin & Murray, 1984; Morrison & Steeves, 1967; O'Neill & Leiter, 1986; Ross, Thibaut, & Evenbeck, 1971; Vanneman & Pettigrew, 1972; Wilensky, 1963).

However, even when behavior is the focus, a second shortcoming is frequently evidenced: Often, only one form of action is measured. The variety of specific behaviors that members of a disadvantaged group might exhibit is extensive. By focusing on only one form of behavior, these researchers offer subjects only two options: the action being studied or inaction. In these circumstances, the subject's preferred action may not be available, which may inadvertently pressure the subject to endorse the less preferred but available behavior or, alternatively, to choose inaction.

The initial challenge, then, is to develop a framework for categorizing the numerous possible behaviors that might be exhibited by disadvantaged-group members. Crosby (1976) described four categories of resultants associated with feelings of deprivation. This framework presents an initial attempt to provide a systematic structure for predicting behavior but suffers several limitations. First, one of the categories, "mental and physical stress symptoms," is not entirely a behavioral response. More important, these four categories of behavior are concerned with egoistical or personal relative deprivation. Thus, the predictors of behavior are primarily intrapersonal in nature, and a clear distinction between collective and individual behaviors is not presented. Mark and Folger (1984) also presented a "response typology" for those who are relatively deprived. This typology includes both attitudes and behavior, but again, the orientation is interpersonal, and no explicit distinction is made between collective and individual forms of action.

Most recently, Taylor, Moghaddam, Gamble, and Zeller (1987) offered the beginnings of a framework that is intergroup in orientation. First, a distinction is made between action and inaction. Second, when action does occur, a contrast is made between individual and collective forms. This distinction is not made simply on the basis of the number of group members involved. A group member engages in collective action anytime that he or she is acting as a representative of the group and the action is directed at improving the condi-

tion of the entire group. Individual action, on the other hand, is behavior that is directed at improving one's personal condition. Despite the clear social significance of these different responses to inequality, a third important distinction is necessary. Martin (1986) alludes to the distinction between action that either conforms to the norms of the existing social system, *normative,* or is outside the confines of the existing social rules and structure, *nonnormative.* From these three distinctions, five broad categories of behavior arise: (a) apparent acceptance of one's disadvantaged position, (b) attempts at individual upward mobility through normative channels made available by the system, (c) individual action outside the norms of the system, (d) instigation of collective action within the prescribed norms of the existing system, and (e) instigation of collective action outside the norms of the system.

The actions described by these five categories have dramatically different societal implications. For example, collective nonnormative action directly threatens the existing social order, whereas acceptance and individual normative actions serve to protect the status quo. These five categories of behavior, then, provide the framework for investigating behavioral responses to inequality in the present experiment.

The third shortcoming in the intergroup relations literature is that the more prominent theories of intergroup relations involve extrapolations to the intergroup context, of hypotheses formulated to explain interactions at the interpersonal level. This reductionist perspective has resulted in a tendency to focus on individualistic responses to inequality (see Taylor & Moghaddam, 1987). Thus, the major theories are incomplete in their ability to generate a complete set of predictions concerning disadvantaged-group behavior.

Equity theory and relative deprivation theory, by showing how large, objective inequalities need not lead to dissatisfaction and anger, can provide viable explanations for apparent acceptance in the face of high levels of objective inequality (K. S. Cook & Messick, 1983; Martin, 1986). However, although it is reasonable to predict no action when feelings of dissatisfaction and deprivation are absent, it does not follow that the presence of these feelings will inevitably lead to action (Tajfel, 1982). Martin (1986) discusses a variety of situations in which "inequalities may cause feelings of injustice, but these feelings may have little effect on behavior, causing a behavioral, if not emotional, tolerance of injustice" (p. 238). More directly, the presence of dissatisfaction, or even the intensity of these negative feelings, does not determine the form action will take. In short, both equity theory and relative deprivation theory fail to provide any clear insight as to when disadvantaged group members will engage in action that is individual versus collective, or if that action will be normative or nonnormative.

Runciman (1966) introduced a distinction in relative deprivation theory between personal (egoistical) and group (fraternal) relative deprivation. Personal deprivation relates to dissatisfaction with one's own treatment, whereas group deprivation results from dissatisfaction with the treatment of one's group. This distinction is an important step toward reducing the highly individualistic nature of earlier versions of relative deprivation theory. There is some evidence that feelings of group deprivation may result in collective action, whereas feelings of personal deprivation may be associated with individual action (Dubé & Guimond, 1986). However, there is substantial agreement that this personal/collective distinction is often misunderstood, poorly operationalized, or ignored in relative deprivation research (Bernstein & Crosby, 1980; T. D. Cook, Crosby & Hennigan, 1977; Isaac, Mutran, & Strykers, 1980; Martin & Murray, 1984; Walker & Pettigrew, 1984), and even when the distinction is more stringently controlled, the link to behavior remains a "troublespot" for relative deprivation theory (Martin, 1986).

The psychology of intergroup relations has recently benefited from the development of psychological theories that explicitly move away from reductionism. Prominent among these is social identity theory (Tajfel & Turner, 1979). According to social identity theory, the key determinant of how members of a disadvantaged group will respond to inequality is their perception of the intergroup structure. If the structure is perceived as illegitimate or unstable, then disadvantaged-group members will become aware of alternatives to the existing intergroup structure. Social identity theory posits that this awareness of alternatives will lead to a variety of collective responses to improve the relative status of the disadvantaged group. By contrast, the absence of perceived alternatives to the existing intergroup structure leads to either individual attempts at upward mobility or acceptance of the disadvantaged position. Social identity

theory is, however, incomplete in its predictive capacity. Beyond identifying instability and illegitimacy as the precursors to the perception of cognitive alternatives and identifying the presence of cognitive alternatives as the determinant of two possible categories of response, social identity theory provides no precise conditions that will determine which of the alternative responses will ultimately be preferred (Taylor & Moghaddam, 1987). In addition, the theory fails to indicate which variables might lead disadvantaged-group members to perceive the intergroup situation as illegitimate and unstable. It thus remains difficult to predict when the response of disadvantaged-group members will be individual or collective, normative or nonnormative.

More recently, Taylor and McKirnan (1984) developed a five-stage model of intergroup relations that builds on social identity theory and elite theory (Dye & Zeigler, 1970; Pareto, 1935). This model proposes that there are five distinct developmental stages to intergroup behavior that all intergroup relations pass through in the same sequential order. This model makes some initial predictions as to the circumstances that will lead individuals within a disadvantaged group to remain inactive, engage in individual action, and instigate collective action.

Like social identity theory, the five-stage model holds that it is their perception of the intergroup situation that determines the response of disadvantaged-group members. When group membership is perceived to be due to individual performance and when individual upward mobility is believed possible, group members attribute their advantaged or disadvantaged position to their personal characteristics. Under these conditions, members of the disadvantaged group will make interindividual comparisons and will engage in individual behaviors designed to improve their personal position. However, if their attempts at individual upward mobility are consistently blocked, the perception that social stratification is based on performance will be replaced by the belief that group membership is based on external characteristics such as race, sex, or being born into a particular socioeconomic class. This new perception of the advantaged group as closed and the resulting feelings of injustice prompt those individuals who have been denied entrance to the advantaged group to abandon interindividual comparisons in favor of intergroup comparisons. The result of intergroup comparisons is increased dis- satisfaction with their disadvantaged position, as well as an interest in collective action as a means of creating a more open system.

A key assumption underlying the five-stage model is that because intergroup comparisons are deemed inappropriate by the overriding social philosophy of stratification on the basis of indi- vidual performance, attempts at individual upward mobility—an individual normative response—are always the first strategy attempted by members of the disadvantaged group. It is only when these in- dividual attempts are blocked that the overriding social philosophy is questioned and the advantaged group is perceived as closed to the disadvantaged- group members. And it is only then that collective action will be initiated.

This model also allows for predictions about which individuals within the disadvantaged group will instigate collective action. Because the divi- sion of the two groups is initially perceived as le- gitimately based on performance, only inter- individual comparisons are viewed as appropriate. These social comparisons lead only those dis- advantaged-group members who perceive them- selves to be nearest to having the requirements necessary for entry into the advantaged group to attempt this upward social mobility. On rejection, these individuals initiate collective action.

The present experiment tests three central hy- potheses raised by the five-stage model and a fourth that arises out of other theories such as relative deprivation or the resource mobilization theory. First, the five-stage model holds that individual attempts at social mobility will be maintained as long as the advantaged group appears open and as long as entry is dependent solely on individual performance. However, when a disadvantaged- group member is prevented from gaining entry into the advantaged group and perceives the system as closed, individual social mobility will be aban- doned in favor of collective action.

Hypothesis I: (a) When entrance into an advantaged group is perceived to be completely open, individual action will ensue, and (b) when entrance into an advantaged group is perceived to be completely closed, collective action will result.

In addition to investigating the completely open and closed conditions, there is a need to investi- gate intergroup situations in which entry into the advantaged group is only partially open. In most social systems, upward mobility by members of a disadvantaged group, though not impossible, is restricted. These conditions lead to questions con- cerning the point at which restrictions on social mobility will begin to affect the responses of disadvantaged-group members.

Taylor and McKirnan (1984) made reference to situations in which a few disadvantaged-group members gained access to the advantaged group. They predicted that these individuals will serve to strengthen the belief in the openness of the social system and will serve as proof that personal abil- ity and effort lead to success. This suggests that even very limited openness in the advantaged group will lead to response patterns similar to that found in a completely open system.

Hypothesis II: Even when a mere token percent- age of the disadvantaged group is allowed access to the advantaged group, individual action will ensue, and little interest will be shown in collec- tive action.

The third hypothesis arising out of the five-stage model involves the idea that it is those members of the disadvantaged group who are led to believe that they are nearest to gaining entrance into the advantaged group who will initiate collective ac- tion. Consistent with this prediction, it is also ex- pected that those who are distant from gaining entrance (especially those faced with what appears to be an open system) will be less likely to blame the system for their failure; therefore, they will be more likely to accept their disadvantaged position.

Hypothesis III: (a) Individuals who believe themselves to be near to the level of ability neces- sary for entrance into the advantaged group will be more likely than those who feel they are far, to take collective action when the system is closed to them, and (b) individuals who believe themselves to be far from the required level of performance necessary for entrance will be more likely than those who feel they are near, to accept their disad- vantaged position.

The theoretical foundations on which to base predictions about the normative/nonnormative dis- tinction are not clearly defined. The five-stage model does not address the normative/nonnorm- ative distinction. The primary theme concerning this distinction arising from other theories (i.e., Crosby, 1976; Mark & Folger, 1984; Martin, 1986; McCarthy & Zald, 1979) seems to support the hypothesis that normative behavior is contingent mainly on the availability of a functional channel for normative responding.

Hypothesis IV: When action is taken, if there exists a normative means for action, this line of action will be preferred. However, if normative means are unavailable, or ineffective, nonnormative action will result.

Method

Subjects

The subjects were 62 male and 74 female college students from a variety of faculties and departments. All were volunteers and participated in the experiment for the chance to win $100 in a lottery. All indicated that they had never participated in a social psychology experiment.

Procedure and Materials

Subjects participated in small groups of five to nine but were required to work independently and were instructed not to interact with one another.

INSTRUCTIONS TO SUBJECTS

Initial instructions were provided through a tape-recorded message. Subjects were told that the experiment was intended to test their ability to make effective decisions about people, a skill that was characterized as one that is essential for those wishing to move up the social hierarchy and attain a position of responsibility and leadership. We designed the laboratory procedure to represent the basic elements of the North American meritocracy. Subjects were told that as in "the real world," they must begin the experiment as a member of the low-status, unsophisticated decision-making group but that there was opportunity to advance into a high-status, sophisticated decision-making group. Subjects were lead to believe that their performance on an initial decision-making task would determine if they would complete the remainder of the experiment working with members of the high- or low-status groups on a series of group decision-making tasks. In reality, there was no high-status group, and all subjects would fail in their attempt to gain access to this group. The reasons given for this failure served as the independent variables in the present experiment.

To further stimulate the subjects' interest in advancement and to make it apparent that they were, in fact, members of a disadvantaged group, the benefits of membership in the sophisticated group were clearly delineated. They were told that if accepted into the sophisticated group, they would associate with high-status others, who had already been recognized as superior decision makers. Also, consistent with most real-life organizations, the members of the high-status group set the decision-making task, evaluated the performance of unsophisticated-group members, and ultimately determined who would be allowed into their high-status group.

It was explained that a panel of three sophisticated-group members would act as judges in the evaluation of subjects' work. Finally, again consistent with the real world, there were monetary advantages to membership in the high-status group. Sophisticated-group members were to participate in the $100 lottery, whereas the unsophisticated group members would participate only in a $10 lottery. Actually, all subjects participated in the $100 lottery.

EXPERIMENTAL PROCEDURES

Following the tape-recorded instructions, participants were given 15 min to read the evidence from a criminal case and to answer three short essay-style questions, ostensibly designed to access their decision-making skills. Their answers were then collected and passed to an assistant, who was to take the answers to the panel of judges from the sophisticated group. A 12-min delay then followed, during which time the three judges presumably graded the subjects' work. During this delay period, the experimenter distributed a blank sample mark sheet and described in detail the procedure used by the judges to arrive at their mark. It was also explained that the sophisticated group collectively had set a mark of 8.5/10, or 85%, as the score required for acceptance into their group. To fill the remaining waiting time, the experimenter gave the subjects a second case with which to familiarize themselves. This case was ostensibly to be used as one of the group decision-making tasks in the second part of the experiment. In reality, this second case served only to reinforce the notion that the subjects would be participating in a second part of the experiment as a member of either the sophisticated or the unsophisticated group.

Following the prescribed delay, the completed mark sheets were returned by an assistant and distributed, one to each subject. On all mark sheets, the final decision stated that the participant was to remain in the unsophisticated group. Information provided on these mark sheets put into effect the two experimental manipulations. Because each experimental trial included five to nine subjects and the experimental manipulations were in the form of written feedback, in any given session it was possible to randomly assign subjects to the different experimental conditions. The experimenter remained blind to the experimental condition of each subject because this was determined by the assistant who returned the mark sheets.

GROUP OPENNESS MANIPULATION

This independent variable involved four conditions and was manipulated by altering the information provided in the judges' written comments on the mark sheet. In the open condition, rejection from the sophisticated group was based solely on performance (i.e., failure to reach the required mark). Subjects in this condition were lead to believe that all those who achieved the required score were accepted into the advantaged group. They were given some feedback about their work, but their total mark did not reach the required 8.5 out of 10. In the conditions that were less than open, the judges informed the subjects that the sophisticated group had decided to impose a quota on entry into their group. Subjects were informed that the 8.5 required score would be ignored and that only a specific percentage of the candidates who scored above 8.5 would be accepted. The judges gave no specific reasons to justify the change in the criterion because the manipulation was intended only to alter the apparent openness of the advantaged group and was not intended to alter the justification or legitimacy of the new restrictions. The interpretation of the additional restriction was left to the subject, but the judges' comments stated explicitly that the additional restrictions were directed at members of the unsophisticated group and that the system was no longer completely open to members of this low-status group.

The quota system allowed for easy manipulation of the degree of openness. In the extreme case, a quota of 0% was introduced, resulting in the high-status group's being completely closed. In this closed condition, subjects were told that the sophisticated group had decided not to accept any new members regardless of their performance on the task. Two partially open conditions were also introduced. In the 30% quota condition, the mark sheet indicated that the sophisticated group had decided to ignore the established cutoff of 8.5 out of 10 and was now only admitting 30% of those who had achieved 8.5 or better. The judges' comments indicated that on the basis of the performance of past unsophisticated-group members, the subject's score did not put him or her in this 30% group. In the 2% quota condition, subjects received information identical to that of the 30% quota condition, except that the comments of the judges indicated that the new restrictions were even more severe and indicated that only 2% of those achieving 8.5 or better were being admitted.

NEARNESS-TO-ENTRY MANIPULATION

The two levels of this independent variable were determined by the manipulation of the total mark given to the subject. Subjects in the far condition always received a mark of 6.0, indicating that they were substantially below the required 8.5 cutoff. Subjects in the near condition received one of two marks. Near subjects in the open group condition received a mark of 8.2, just slightly below the 8.5 cutoff. Near subjects in the other three group openness conditions (i.e., 30% quota, 2% quota, and closed) received a mark of 8.8. This mark exceeds the designated 8.5 cutoff, and had the system been completely open, this mark would have resulted in acceptance into the sophisticated group. This manipulation in the near condition resulted in a confound because the subjects in the open condition received a slightly lower mark. This confound is unavoidable because the five-stage model specifies that it is the personal experience with the injustice of a closed high-status group that leads those who are near to entry to instigate collective action. Thus, it was necessary that subjects in the closed and quota conditions be personally affected by the new restriction on entry into the advantaged group.

BEHAVIORAL OPTIONS

Subjects were given a few minutes to digest their negative feedback. The experimenter then approached the subjects individually and privately asked them if they had succeeded or failed to gain entrance into the advantaged group. Those who failed (all subjects) were given a response form.

The instructions on the top of this form informed subjects that before continuing the experiment as a member of their designated group, those who had been rejected by the judges would be given an additional opportunity to respond to the negative decision of the judges. They were then asked to rate the extent to which each of five alternative behavioral options appealed to them and were informed that they would be expected to undertake the action they rated highest.

The response alternatives were presented in the form of five statements, each accompanied by an 11-point Likert scale, anchored by *not at all* (0) and *very much* (10). Subjects rated the extent to which they were interested in the following: (a) Accepting the decision of the sophisticated group and thus agreeing to remain a member of the unsophisticated group for the remainder of the experiment. (b) Requesting an individual retest. A request for a retest was presented as an option that had been acceptable to the sophisticated group in the past. Subjects supporting this option were therefore indicating a desire to continue their attempts to gain entrance into the advantaged group through an individual normative action. (c) Making an individual protest against the decision of the sophisticated group. This option involved composing and writing of a protest demanding that the high status group reverse its decision regarding the subject. This action was described explicitly as unacceptable to the advantaged group and inconsistent with the described rules that the decision of the judges is always final. Thus, by endorsing this behavior, a subject was willing to ignore explicitly stated rules and the norms established by the high-status group, in an attempt to gain personal access to the higher status group. (d) Requesting a collective retest. This strategy involved an attempt to solicit the support of the other members of the low-status group to persuade the judges (members of the high-status group) to allow a retest for all unsuccessful members of the low-status group. Thus, this response was collective and normative in nature. (e) Attempting to instigate collective protest. Again, this option was described as unacceptable to the sophisticated group in the past. Here, subjects were to compose a written protest that urged other low-status group members to ignore the explicitly stated rule that the decision of the judges was final and to take action to force the high-status group to allow all members

of the disadvantaged group access to the advantaged group. The selection of this alternative called for action that was both collective and explicitly inconsistent with existing rules of the system and the norms established by the sophisticated group.

BEHAVIORAL CHOICE

After rating each of the five behavioral options, the subject actually carried out the action they most preferred (i.e., rated nearest to 10 on the Likert scale). Those who accepted their position in the unsophisticated group, of course, would do nothing. Subjects selecting a collective retest completed a similar request that first was to be distributed, by the experimenter, to other low-status group members in the room for their approval and then was to be given to the members of the high-status group. Those selecting either of the protest options were required to write the appropriate protest. An individual protest was to be taken to the high-status group. A collective protest was to be first distributed to the other low-status group members for their approval and then submitted to the high-status group.

MEASURES OF FEELINGS AND PERCEPTIONS

To check that the manipulations presented in the experiment were effective in producing the appropriate feelings and perceptions in the subject, the experimenter distributed a short questionnaire. Nine questions were asked. Subjects were asked to rate the following feelings and perceptions in relation to the decision and actions of the high-status group: (a) their level of frustration, (b) their level of resentment, (c) their level of hope for improvements in their personal condition, (d) their satisfaction with their personal treatment, (e) their satisfaction with their group treatment, (f) the justice of their personal treatment, (g) the justice of their group treatment, (h) their satisfaction with the distribution of power between the high- and low-status groups, and (i) their satisfaction with the distribution of money between the high- and low-status groups. All responses were rated on an 11-point Likert scale.

Following completion of this second set of questions, subjects were thoroughly debriefed and were informed that all participants were entered in the $100 lottery.

Results

Preliminary Analysis

Preliminary analysis indicated no significant gender differences across variables. In addition, no significant differences were found for the subjects' faculty or department of study.

Behavioral Options Ratings

The subject's ratings for each of the five behavioral options were analyzed using a two-way 2 × 4 multivariate analysis of variance (MANOVA) with nearness to entry (near, far), and group openness (open, 30% quota, 2% quota, closed) as between-subjects variables. The five behavioral options (acceptance, individual normative, individual nonnormative, collective normative, collective nonnormative) were the dependent measures. The mean ratings for each of the eight conditions are presented in Table 20.1.

The main effect group openness was statistically significant, $F(15, 126) = 2.67$, $p < .01$. The pattern of results for each of the five department measures is presented in Figure 20.1. The subsequent univariate analysis of variance (ANOVA) yielded a statistically significant effect of group openness, for the endorsement of collective nonnormative action, $F(3, 133) = 4.57$, $p < .01$. Subsequent post hoc, pairwise comparisons using the Newman-Keuls procedure indicated that this effect was the result of a significantly higher rating for collec-

tive nonnormative action ($\alpha = .05$) by subjects in the completely closed condition than by subjects in any of the other conditions. The equivalent test for the effect of group openness on the endorsement of individual normative action approached significance, $F(3, 133) = 2.52$, $p = .07$.

The MANOVA also revealed a significant main effect of nearness to entry, $F(5, 126) = 2.45$, $p < .05$, the pattern of the results is presented in Figure 20.2. Subsequent univariate tests showed a significant difference between the near and far conditions on the ratings of the individual nonnormative response, $F(1, 126) = 5.05$, $p < .05$, and the difference between acceptance ratings approached significance, $F(1, 126) = 3.05$, $p = .07$. Subjects in the near condition showed significantly greater interest in individual nonnormative action, and those in the far condition gave higher ratings to the acceptance option.

The Group Openness × Nearness to Entry interaction was not significant, $F(3, 126) = 1.16$, ns.

Behavioral Choice

The single behavior actually carried out by each subject yielded frequency data that were analyzed using a hierarchical log-linear modeling approach. A three-way 2 × 4 × 5 frequency table (see Table 20.2), involving the two levels of nearness to entry (N), the four levels of group openness (O), and the five behavioral responses (R), was constructed. The two manipulations (N), (O) served as independent variables because the number of subjects

TABLE 20.1. Mean Rating of Endorsement of Each of Five Behavioral Responses as a Function of Nearness to Entry and Group Openness

Behavioral response	Group openness			
	Open	30% quota	2% quota	Closed
Near-to-entry condition				
Accept	4.35	2.94	2.59	1.76
Individual normative	8.47	6.31	5.18	5.18
Individual nonnormative	5.76	5.88	7.59	6.65
Collective normative	5.00	3.75	4.88	4.29
Collective nonnormative	4.29	4.25	4.70	6.64
Far-from-entry condition				
Accept	4.30	3.44	3.94	3.69
Individual normative	5.89	6.81	6.39	5.69
Individual nonnormative	3.76	5.63	5.56	5.50
Collective normative	4.59	5.50	5.22	6.50
Collective nonnormative	3.29	3.38	4.83	6.75

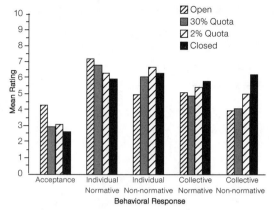

FIGURE 20.1 ■ Mean rating of endorsement of each of five behavioral responses by subjects in four group openness condtions.

in these cells was determined by the design of the experiment. For this reason, the initial model (hypothesizing independence of the behavioral response from both independent variables) included the main effects and interaction of the two independent variables, as well as the main effect of response, (NO) (R). We found that the inclusion of the Response × Nearness to Entry interaction (NR) significantly improved the fit of the model (likelihood-ratio statistic), $L^2(4) = 12.98$, $p < .01$. The subsequent inclusion of the Group Openness × Response interaction (OR) also significantly improved the fit of the model, $L^2(12) = 22.99$, $p < .05$. No other effects significantly improved the fit of the model. This model, (NO) (NR) (OR) does not differ significantly from the saturated model, $L^2(12) = 7.54$, *ns*, and was the optimal log-linear model to describe the data.

This model indicates a dependence relationship between the response chosen and the level of group openness. The pattern of this relationship is presented in Figure 20.3. Fewer subjects in the 2% quota and closed conditions accepted their situation than did those in the 30% quota and open conditions. Interest in taking individual normative action clearly declined as group openness decreased. Twice as many subjects in the open condition opted for individual normative behavior as compared to those in the closed condition. Individual nonnormative action was clearly the action of choice for those facing a 2% quota condition. The most socially disruptive behavior, collective nonnormative action, was undertaken almost exclusively by subjects in the closed condition.

The optimal log-linear model also describes a dependent relationship between the response chosen and the subject's nearness to entry into the advantaged group. This relationship is presented in Figure 20.4. Individual nonnormative action was undertaken by almost three times as many subjects in the near condition as those in the far condition. The opposite was true acceptance; this response was selected by over twice as many subjects in the far condition as subjects in the near condition.

Perceptions and Emotional Responses

We used nine measures of the subjects' perceptions and emotional responses as the dependent measures in a 2 × 4 MANOVA involving two levels of nearness to entry and four levels of group openness. A main effect of nearness to entry was statistically significant, $F(1, 126) = 3.04$, $p < .01$, and subsequent univariate tests showed that those who were far from entry indicated significantly higher feelings of justice in their personal treatment than those near to entry, $F(1, 126) = 7.92$, $p < .01$. The remaining eight univariate tests were not significant.

The MANOVA showed that neither the main effect of group openness, $F(3, 348) = 0.94$, *ns*, nor the Nearness to Entry × Group Openness interaction, $F(27, 348) = 0.93$, *ns* was significant.

Examination of the means for these responses indicates that the lack of significant effects is primarily due to the consistently low ratings of satisfaction and justice of treatment, along with

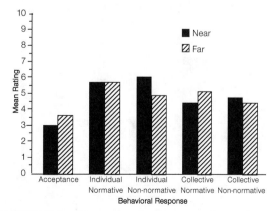

FIGURE 20.2 ■ Mean rating of endorsement of each of five behavioral responses by subjects near to and far from entry into the advantaged group.

TABLE 20.2. Frequency (Freq.) of Selection and Percentage of Subjects in Each Cell Selecting Each of the Five Behavioral Responses as a Function of Nearness to Entry and Group Openness

| Behavioral response | Group openness | | | | | | | |
| | Open | | 30% quota | | 2% quota | | Closed | |
	Freq.	%	Freq.	%	Freq.	%	Freq.	%
Near-to-entry condition								
Accept	2	11	3	18	1	6	1	6
Individual normative	10	55	5	29	4	23	3	17
Individual nonnormative	4	22	6	35	10	59	5	28
Collective normative	1	6	2	12	2	12	2	11
Collective nonnormative	1	6	1	6	0	0	7	39
Far-from-entry condition								
Accept	7	41	4	25	3	17	4	25
Individual normative	4	23	7	44	5	28	4	25
Individual nonnormative	2	12	1	6	4	22	2	13
Collective normative	3	18	4	25	4	22	1	6
Collective nonnormative	1	6	0	0	2	11	5	31

moderate-to-high levels of frustration and resentment. It seems evident that the intended feelings of injustice and dissatisfaction were present in subjects in all experimental conditions.

Discussion

The findings will be discussed in terms of their relevance to the four major hypotheses.

Hypothesis I: Responses to Open and Closed Groups

We hypothesized that subjects in the open condition would pursue individual action and that those faced with a closed group would show greater interest in collective action. Both the rating scale and frequency data (see Figures 20.1 & 20.3) yield a pattern of responding that provides some support for this hypothesis. As predicted, when entrance into the advantaged group was completely open, subjects opted for individual normative action and seldom supported collective nonnormative action. When the opportunity for upward mobility was completely closed, there was much greater support for collective nonnormative behavior and reduced interest in individual normative action.

Support for the first hypothesis, however, is qualified by the subjects' endorsement of the individual nonnormative and collective normative response options. When subjects were faced with the

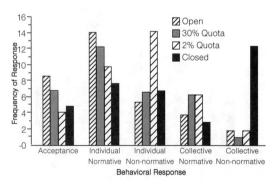

FIGURE 20.3 ■ Frequency of selection of each of five behavioral responses by subjects in four group openness conditions.

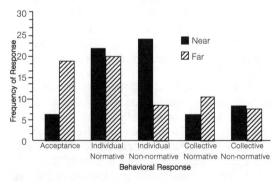

FIGURE 20.4 ■ Frequency of selection of each of five behavioral responses by subjects near to and far from entry into the advantaged group.

complete closure of the advantaged group, their interest in individual nonnormative action did not differ significantly from that of subjects in the open condition. In fact, mean ratings on this action were higher for those in the closed condition. As well, a closed advantaged group resulted in ratings of collective normative action equivalent to that of subjects in the open condition. Both Figure 20.1 and Figure 20.3 show that when individual nonnormative action and normative forms of collective action are considered, the predicted difference between open and closed advantaged groups is not found. It is only when discussions of individual action are restricted to normative forms and when discussions of collective action are restricted to nonnormative forms that the present data support the claim that individual action will be endorsed in a system that is perceived to be open and that collective action will be undertaken in a system perceived to be closed.

Although not warranted by the stringent statistical analysis performed here, an exploratory examination of the differences between those near and far from acceptance into the advantaged group points to a further qualification in the conclusions concerning the behavioral responses to open, compared to closed, advantaged groups. Table 20.2 indicates that the greater interest in individual normative action by subjects faced with an open advantaged group over subjects faced with a closed advantaged condition is exclusively found for subjects who are near to gaining entrance into the advantaged group. Subjects in the far condition are no more likely to attempt individual normative action when the advantaged group is open than when it is closed. This inspection of Table 20.2 suggests that the prediction that an open system will lead to a preference for individual normative action may only be true for individuals who are near to meeting the criterion for entrance into the advantaged group.

Hypothesis II: Responses to Partially Open Groups

The prediction that subjects faced with a partially open advantaged group will prefer to respond individually and will show little endorsement of collective action is supported. Inspection of the frequency data (see Figure 20.3) shows that a greater number of subjects in both the 30% quota and 2% quota conditions preferred individual

forms of action. The rating scale data show that the ratings for both forms of collective action by those in the two partially open groups were not significantly higher than the ratings of those in the completely open condition. In fact, inspection of both Table 20.1 and Table 20.2 appears to indicate that there were only two consistent differences between the subjects in the 30% quota condition and those in the open condition. First, subjects near to entry into the advantaged group in the 30% quota condition were much less likely to take individual normative action than were near subjects in the open condition. Second, subjects in the far/30% quota condition were less likely to accept their position than were subjects in the far/open condition. Apparently, the introduction of an arbitrary change in the criterion for entry into the advantaged group does not lead to changes in individual nonnormative action or in collective actions as long as the criterion remains adequately lenient for a perception of openness to be maintained.

Figure 20.3 indicates some differences between the 30% and 2% quota conditions. A clear shift in interest can be seen from normative forms of individual action in the 30% quota condition to nonnormative forms of individual action in the 2% quota condition. This shift casts serious doubts on the interpretation, arising from the five-stage model, that the continued endorsement of individual action is the result of a strengthened faith in the existing system. Increasing closure of the advantaged group leads to individual action that is expressly antisystem and clearly inconsistent with a strengthened faith in the system. Thus, the prediction arising from the five-stage model concerning the partially open conditions is supported, but apparently for the wrong reason.

One possible explanation for the interest in individual actions in the partially open condition could be simply a concern for personal self-interest. If a member of a disadvantaged group is primarily concerned with personal advancement, then as long as there remains even the slightest possibility for personal advancement (as is the case in the 2% quota condition), there is little appeal in improving the status of the entire disadvantaged group through collective action. If positive social identity is determined through social comparison (Tajfel & Turner, 1979), gaining personal access to a very exclusive group should be more appealing than gaining the same status along with a larger number of one's peers. Thus, even when arbitrary changes in the rules are introduced and the individual is rejected, as long as personal advancement remains a possibility, individual responding will remain the preferred form of action.

Consistent with this self-centered interpretation, the turn to collective action in the completely closed condition might not represent a shift to a more collective consciousness. The change in strategy might simply reflect the realization that when the advantaged group is completely closed, only through working in consort with one's peers can the individual have a chance to improve his or her personal position. Consequently selfish concern for personal status might be the main preoccupation even of those engaging in collective responding.

The present findings suggest that collective nonnormative action may be reserved solely for conditions in which opportunity for personal advancement is completely removed. Even the strict and arbitrary restriction on advancement evident in the 2% quota condition did not result in a significant increase in collective protest over that expressed by subjects in the open or 30% quota condition. Apparently, the introduction of a totally exclusionary criterion was so unacceptable to the subjects that it was only in this condition that they abandoned the individual meritocratic rules that they seemed to endorse in other conditions. Inspection of Table 20.1 and Table 20.2 shows that this switch to a preference for collective nonnormative action, exclusively in the closed condition, was shared by both subjects who went near to entry into the advantaged group and by those receiving a mark that put them far from the necessary criterion. In the closed condition, collective nonnormative action was endorse strongly by subjects, irrespective of their distance from the criterion for entry into the advantaged group.

This finding has important implications for the concept of tokenism. In the partially open conditions (especially the 2% quota condition), rules were instituted that allowed for minimal acceptance of disadvantaged-group members into advantaged positions but systematically kept the remainder of that group in a disadvantaged position. By definition, this is tokenism, and the present results show that this situation does not lead disadvantaged-group members to take collective nonnormative action directed at changing the system. Rather, subjects preferred the relatively benign individual action strategies. The present findings seem to indicate that the implementation of a policy of tokenism by the advantaged group could be an effective means of reducing the likelihood of change in intergroup relations or in the system itself.

Hypothesis III: Being Near to Entry Into the Advantaged Group

Two related predictions were raised in Hypothesis III. First, we hypothesized that those people who perceive themselves as near to entry into a closed advantaged group would be most likely to endorse collective action strategies. The present data provide no support for this prediction. The results presented in Figure 20.2 indicate that subjects who were near to entry into the advantaged group did not show greater interest than those who were distant from entry into the advantaged group in either form of collective action. The clearest test of this prediction would be a comparison of those people in the near and far conditions who were faced specifically with a closed advantaged group. However, the absence of a three-way (Behavioral Options × Group Openness × Nearness to Entry) interaction effect ($F < 1.0$) indicates that the lack of significant difference between the near and far conditions on interest in the collective actions was consistent across levels of the group openness variable. Therefore, interest in collective action was equally unaffected by nearness to entry in the closed condition as it was in any other group openness condition.

The present findings suggest that it is the preference for individual nonnormative action that distinguishes those who are near to entry from those who are distant. It is informative to recall that three quarters of the subjects in the near-to-entry conditions (those in the last three conditions of group openness) received a mark that by the initial rules should have qualified them for a place in the advantaged group. Subjects in the far condition were given the same information about the changing of the criterion for entrance into the advantaged group; however, they would have failed by either the new or the old criterion. Thus, subjects distant from entrance did not experience personally the consequences of the unjust and arbitrary nature of the system as did those near to entrance. The importance of the personal experience with injustice as a determinant of nonnormative action is consistent with recent work on referent cognitions theory (Folger & Martin, 1986; Folger, Rosenfield,

Rheaume, & Martin, 1983; Folger, Rosenfield, & Robinson, 1983). Folger and his colleagues found that negative attitudes toward the system are associated with the knowledge that an old procedure would have led to greater outcomes than the present procedure. In addition, present findings involving subjects' feelings and perceptions also support this interpretation. The only significant difference in these ratings was that subjects near to entry perceived their personal treatment to be less just than those far from entry.

The second prediction raised in Hypothesis III was that those distant from entry would be more likely to accept their disadvantaged position than would those near to entry into the advantaged group. Consistent with the second prediction of Hypothesis III, those distant from entrance into the advantaged group were more likely to accept their disadvantaged position. This finding has provocative social implications. It seems that by fostering the perception that disadvantaged-group members are far from the criteria necessary for entry into their group, an advantaged group could reduce the likelihood of action by disadvantaged-group members.

Hypothesis IV: Normative Versus Nonnormative Behavior

Hypothesis IV maintained that given a functional channel for normative action, disadvantaged-group members would take normative rather than nonnormative actions. The present data do not support this claim. All subjects, in all conditions, were offered normative forms of both individual and collective action as possible responses, yet many chose to ignore these options in favor of nonnormative strategies. Thus, it is not simply the absence of a normative strategy that leads to nonnormative action. A preference for nonnormative strategies was shown in the 2% quota and closed conditions. Table 20.2 indicates that this is especially true for those near to entry. Sixty percent of those in the near/2% quota condition chose individual nonnormative action, and a full two thirds of those in the near/closed condition chose a nonnormative action, either individual or collective. In these conditions, subjects were confronted with the highest levels of unfairness. This may suggest that when the actions of the advantaged group are highly inconsistent with the previously established norms

of the system, normative action will be perceived as ineffective. In these circumstances, it would seem that disadvantaged group members will respond to the advantaged group's violation of established norms with nonnormative behavior of their own.

Insights Into the Acceptance Response

Of special interest is the number of subjects in the present experiment who were faced with and perceived unfair treatment and yet chose not to act. The combination of the two dependent measures used in this experiment (rating scale and selected behavior) provides some insight into what it meant for these subjects to accept their disadvantaged position.

Subjects were required to engage in the behavior they rated highest on the rating scales; however, they did not necessarily give that option a 10 rating. So subjects who rated their most preferred option at only 6 might have engaged in that behavior with more reluctance than someone who rated his or her chosen behavior at 10. The mean rating for acceptance by those who actually chose to accept their disadvantaged position was lower than the mean rating of other subjects for their selected form of action. Subjects who accepted their situation did so with a mean rating of 7.28. Subjects who chose to undertake some form of action rated their chosen behavior as follows: For those choosing individual normative, $M = 8.85$; individual nonnormative, $M = 9.15$; collective normative, $M = 8.81$; and collective nonnormative, $M = 9.06$. A one-way ANOVA indicated significant differences between these groups, $F(4, 129) = 6.66$, $p < .001$. Subsequent Newman-Keuls comparisons showed that only the differences between the acceptance group and all four other groups were significant ($\alpha = .05$).

What these findings suggest is that subjects who actually chose to accept their disadvantaged situation did so with less commitment than those who chose to take some form of action. Consequently, although a substantial number of subjects accepted their position, they apparently did so begrudgingly. Perhaps it is this reluctant acceptance that leads to the mental stress symptoms that have been suggested as potential consequences of inaction or tolerance in the face of injustice (Crosby, 1976; Martin, 1986).

Conclusions

The present research represents an attempt to specify the conditions that are associated with specific actions taken by disadvantaged-group members in the face of inequality. The importance of the normative/nonnormative distinction is clearly demonstrated in several findings. Apparently, advantaged group openness and the individual's nearness to entry into the advantaged group both play a role in determining the likelihood of nonnormative actions over normative actions. Thus, the notion that normative action is always preferred when a functional channel for normative action exists is far too simplistic.

The results clearly demonstrate the important role of perceived openness of the advantaged group. When the advantaged group is perceived as open, individual normative action is preferred. Dramatically, interest in individual action is maintained even when the openness of the advantaged group is highly compromised by strict restrictions (2% quota condition). Collective nonnormative, the most socially disruptive action, is reserved almost exclusively for situations in which the advantaged group is perceived as completely closed to members of the disadvantaged group. These findings have disturbing implications for the discriminatory practices of tokenism. Even an explicit policy of tokenism, as in the 2% quota condition, results in subjects taking individual actions in an attempt to improve their personal position, rather than taking collective action directed at improving the condition of the group as a whole.

REFERENCES

Bernstein, M., & Crosby, E. J. (1980). An empirical examination of relative deprivation theory. *Journal of Experimental Social Psychology, 16,* 172–184.

Cook, K. S., & Messick, D. M. (1983). *Equity theory: Psychological and sociological perspectives.* New York: Praeger.

Cook, T. D., Crosby, F. J., & Hennigan, K. M. (1977). The construct validity of relative deprivation. In J. M. Suls & R. L. Miller (Eds), *Social comparison processes: Theoretical and empirical perspectives* (pp. 307–333). New York: Wiley.

Crosby, E. J. (1976). A model of egoistical relative deprivation. *Psychological Review, 83,* 85–113.

Davis, J. (1959). A formal interpretation of the theory of relative deprivation. *Sociometry, 27,* 280–296.

Dubé, L. & Guimond, S. (1986). Relative deprivation and social protest: The person-group issue. In J. M. Olson, C. P. Herman, & M. P. Zanna (Eds), *Relative deprivation and*

social comparison: The Ontario Symposium (Vol. 4, pp. 201–216). Hillsdale, NJ: Erlbaum.

Dye, T. R., & Zeigler, L. H. (1970). *The irony of democracy: An uncommon introduction to American politics.* Belmont, CA: Wadsworth.

Folger, R., & Martin, C. (1986). Relative deprivation and reference cognitions: Distributive and procedural justice effects. *Journal of Experimental Social Psychology, 12,* 531–546.

Folger, R., Rosenfield, D., Rheaume, K., & Martin, C. (1983). Relative deprivation and referent cognitions. *Journal of Experimental Social Psychology, 19,* 172–184.

Folger, R., Rosenfield, D., & Robinson, T. (1983). Relative deprivation and procedural injustice. *Journal of Personality and Social Psychology, 45,* 268–273.

Guimond, S., & Dubé-Simard, L. (1983). Relative deprivation theory and the Quebec nationalist movement: The cognitive-emotion distinction and the personal-group deprivation issue. *Journal of Personality and Social Psychology, 44,* 526–535.

Gurr, T. R. (1970). *Why men rebel.* Princeton, NJ: Princeton University Press.

Homans, G. C. (1961). *Social behavior: Its elementary forms.* New York: Harcourt, Brace & World.

Isaac, L., Mutran, E., & Strykers, S. (1980). Political protest orientation among Black and White adults. *American Sociological Review, 45,* 191–213.

Lerner, M. J. (1977). Justified self-interest and the responsibility for suffering: A replication and extension. *Journal of Human Relations, 19,* 550–559.

Lerner, M. J., & Lerner, S. C. (1981). *The justice motive in social behavior.* New York: Plenum Press.

Mark, M. M. (1985). Expectation, procedural justice and alternate reactions to being deprived of a desired outcome. *Journal of Experimental Social Psychology, 11,* 114–137.

Mark, M. M., & Folger, R. (1984). Responses to relative deprivation: A conceptual framework. In P. Shavers (Ed.), *Review of personality and social psychology* (Vol. 5, pp. 192–218). Beverly Hills, CA: Sage.

Martin, J. (1986). The tolerance of injustice. In J. M. Olson, C. P. Herman, & M. P. Zanna (Eds), *Relative deprivation and social comparison: The Ontario Symposium* (Vol. 4, pp. 217–242). Hillsdale, NJ: Erlbaum.

Martin, J., & Murray, A. (1984). Catalysts for collective violence: The importance of a psychological approach. In R. Folger (Ed.), *The sense of injustice: Social psychological perspectives* (pp. 95–139) New York: Plenum Press.

McCarthy, T. D., & Zald, M. N. (1979). Resource mobilization and social movements: A partial theory. *American Journal of Sociology, 82,* 1212–1241.

Morrison, D. E., & Steeves, A. (1967, December). Deprivation, discontent and social movement participation. *Rural Sociology,* pp. 414–435.

O'Neill, P., & Leiter, M. P. (1986). Shared assumptions: A citizen action group simulation. *Canadian Journal of Behavioural Sciences, 18,* 115–125.

Pareto, V. (1935). *The mind and society: A treatise on general sociology* (Vols. 1–4). New York: Dover.

Ross, M., Thibaut, J., & Evenbeck, S. (1971). Some determinants of the intensity of social protest. *Journal of Experimental Social Psychology, 7,* 401–418.

Runciman, W. G. (1966). *Relative deprivation and social justice: A study of attitudes to social inequity in twentieth-century England.* Berkeley, CA: University of California Press.

Stouffer, S. A., Suchman, E. A., DeVinney L. C., Starr, S. A., & Williams, R. M. (1949). *The American soldier: Adjustment to army* life (Vol. 1). Princeton, NJ: Princeton University Press.

Tajfel, H. (1982). *Social identity and intergroup relations.* London: Cardiff University Press.

Tajfel, H., & Turner, J. C. (1979). An integrative theory of intergroup conflict. In W. G. Austin & S. Worchel (Eds.), *The social psychology of intergroup relations* (pp. 33–47). Monterey, CA: Brooks/Cole.

Taylor, D. M., & McKirnan, D. J. (1984). A five stage model of intergroup relations. *British Journal of Social Psychology, 23,* 291–300.

Taylor, D. M., & Moghaddam, E. M. (1987). *Theories of intergroup relations: International social psychological perspective.* New York Praeger.

Taylor, D. M., Moghaddam, F. M., Gamble, L., & Zeller, E. (1987). Disadvantaged group responses to perceived inequity: From passive acceptance to collective action. *Journal of Social Psychology, 117,* 259–272.

Vanneman, S., & Pettigrew, T. E. (1972). Race and relative deprivation in urban United States. *Race, 13,* 461–486.

Walker, L., & Pettigrew, T. F. (1984). Relative deprivation theory: An overview and conceptual critique. *British Journal of Social Psychology, 23,* 301–310.

Walster, E., Walster, G. W., & Berscheid, E. (1978). *Equity: Theory and research.* Boston: Allyn and Bacon.

Wilensky, H. L. (1963). The moonlighter: A product of relative deprivation. *Industrial Relations, 3,* 105–124.

Intergroup Contact and Social Harmony

The goal of much intergroup relations research is to try to understand the conditions under which hostile and prejudiced intergroup behavior can be transformed into harmonious and non-prejudiced behavior that will endure. A prevalent belief is that close and pleasant interpersonal contact between people from different groups is probably the best way to achieve this—the contact hypothesis (Allport, 1954; also see Hewstone & Brown, 1986; Miller & Brewer, 1984). This idea influenced the policy that was put in place in the United States in 1954 to improve interracial attitudes by racially desegregating the school system. The practice of "busing" was partly aimed at increasing interracial contact (Schofield, 1991).

Research suggests, however, that contact is not very effective at changing negative stereotypes or improving conflictual intergroup relations. One reason is that there can be substantial anxiety associated with intergroup contact, and this renders the interaction less pleasant (e.g., Stephan & Stephan, 1985). If contact is not associated with intergroup anxiety, interaction may be quite pleasant and enduring intergroup friendships may develop. However, this may still not be enough to improve intergroup relations (but see Wright, Aron, McLaughlin-Volpe, & Ropp, 1997). Research suggests that close friendships between members of different groups often simply do not improve generalized intergroup images. People may like each other as individuals, but they still harbor negative attitudes towards the groups as a whole. Attempts to get groups to re-categorize themselves in terms of a shared superordinate identity can sometimes work, particularly in controlled settings.

Our first reading, by Sam Gaertner at the University of Delaware, and his associates Jeffrey Mann, Audrey Murrell, and Jack Dovidio, explores this idea. Gaertner and his associates (1989) proceed from the premise that distinct and sharp intergroup boundaries encourage hostile intergroup attitudes and behaviors, and suggest that this problem can be reduced by either encouraging two groups to conceive of themselves as a single group (re-categorization) or as an aggregate of individuals (de-categorization). In their research, they show that both strategies reduce intergroup discrimination, but each by different routes: re-categorization improves outgroup attitudes, whereas de-categorization worsens ingroup attitudes.

Although re-categorization may sometimes work in controlled settings, it can often backfire in the natural context of real groups in society. This is because it can threaten the distinctiveness of the groups and thus the identity of group members. At the cultural level, this addresses the question of whether assimilation or multiculturalism are most likely to produce social harmony (see Hornsey & Hogg, 2000; Prentice & Miller, 1999).

If re-categorization has a tendency to backfire, perhaps attempts to frame contact in intergroup terms may do better at producing improved generalized intergroup attitudes and relations. Our last two readings take up this challenge. It is a challenge because the intergroup nature of such contact can render the interaction unpleasant or even hostile. It can be hard to produce pleasant intergroup contact, which is a prerequisite for improved generalized images. More generally, it can be very difficult to produce enduring pluralistic contexts where people identify at the subgroup and at the superordinate group level simultaneously, and thus do not experience identity threat and do not interact in a hostile intergroup manner, but do perceive each other in group terms that enable generalization.

The reading by David Wilder, at Rutgers University, reports three studies of generalized intergroup attitudes as a result of the pleasantness and the stereotypicality of the outgroup member with whom there was contact (Wilder, 1984). These studies show that generalized improvement of intergroup attitudes occurs only when contact is pleasant and the person one has contact with is seen to be representative/stereotypical of the outgroup.

The reading by Rabiul Islam and Miles Hewstone reports a field study of contact and intergroup attitudes of Hindus and Muslims in Bangladesh (Islam & Hewstone, 1993). They examine the effect on intergroup attitudes of a range of variables, including the quantity of contact, the quality of contact, the intergroup vs. interpersonal nature of the contact, the group typicality of the outgroup member, the level of intergroup anxiety, and so forth. Through structural equation modeling techniques, a complex interactive model emerges—a model which starts to get us closer to the multi-dimensional reality of the relationship between intergroup contact and social harmony.

There are currently four candidates for ways that contact can reduce prejudice: the de-categorization model proposed by Miller and Brewer (1984), the mutual intergroup differentiation model proposed by Hewstone and Brown (1986), the common ingroup identity model (re-categorization) proposed by Gaertner and his colleagues, and the dual-identity model currently being developed and explored by many researchers (e.g., Gaertner & Dovidio, 2000; Hornsey & Hogg, 2000; Mummendey & Wenzel, 1999). Pettigrew (1998) has provided a useful integrative model that proposes where these different categorization processes should fit in sequence if intergroup contact is to have positive outcomes.

Discussion Questions

1. Can Allport's four conditions for successful reduction of prejudice through contact ever be met?
2. What are the limitations of re-categorization strategies for improving intergroup relations?
3. Can intergroup relations be improved through interpersonal relationships?
4. Whose attitudes are most likely to be affected by intergroup contact, and how?

Suggested Readings

Allport, G. W. (1954). *The nature of prejudice.* Reading, MA: Addison-Wesley. Classic book on prejudice where the contact hypothesis as an approach to improving intergroup relations is first described.

Cook, S. W. (1985). Experimenting on social issues: The case of school desegregation. *American Psychologist, 40,* 452–460. The contact hypothesis at work in a classroom setting.

Gaertner, S. L., & Dovidio, J. F. (2000). *Reducing intergroup bias: The common ingroup identity model.* Philadelphia: Psychology Press. Gaertner and Dovidio's overview, summary, and statement of their perspective on the reduction of intergroup bias—a very large body of research conducted by this prolific team and their associates over many years.

Hewstone, M. (1996). Contact and categorization: Social psychological interventions to change intergroup relations. In C. N. Macrae, C. Stangor, & M. Hewstone (Eds.), *Stereotypes and stereotyping* (pp. 323–368). New York: Guilford. A critical review of research on contact.

Hornsey, M. J., & Hogg, M. A. (2000). Assimilation and diversity: An integrative model of subgroup relations. *Personality and Social Psychology Review, 4,* 143–156. A new theoretical analysis of intergroup relations in nested multi-group social contexts, based on the social identity perspective.

Miller, D. T., & Prentice, D. A. (1999). Some consequences of a belief in group essence: The category divide hypothesis. In D. A. Prentice & D. T. Miller (Eds.), *Cultural divides: Understanding and overcoming group conflict* (pp. 213–238). New York: Russell Sage Foundation. Recognition that once you step out of the lab, some intergroup relations are so entrenched that contact, re-categorization, de-categorization, and so forth are unlikely to occur, let alone instantiate social harmony.

Miller, N., & Brewer, M. B. (Eds.). (1984). *Groups in contact: The psychology of desegregation.* New York: Academic Press. A selection of chapters from leading scholars, addressing intergroup contact as a path toward improved intergroup relations.

Pettigrew, T. F. (1998). Intergroup contact theory. *Annual Review of Psychology, 49,* 65–85. A review of recent research on contact, and description of a new model/perspective.

Reducing Intergroup Bias: The Benefits of Recategorization

Samuel L. Gaertner and Jeffrey Mann • University of Delaware
Audrey Murrell • University of Pittsburgh
John F. Dovidio • Colgate University

Three hundred sixty undergraduates participated in small groups in an experiment that tested 2 strategies, based on the social categorization approach, for reducing intergroup bias. Both strategies involved recategorizing members' conceptual representations of the aggregate compared with a control condition designed to maintain initial group boundaries. The recategorization treatments induced members of 2 3-person groups to conceive of both memberships as 1 6-person group or as 6 separate individuals. The findings revealed that the one-group and separate-individuals conditions, as compared with the control condition, reduced intergroup bias. Furthermore, these recategorized conditions reduced bias in different ways consistent with Brewer's (1979) analysis and Turner's (1985) self-categorization theory. Specifically, the 1-group representation reduced bias primarily by increasing the attractiveness of former out-group members, whereas the separate-individuals representation primarily decreased the attractiveness of former in-group members. Implications for the utility of these strategies are discussed.

Research on intergroup behavior, reviewed by Brewer (1979), Hogg and Abrams (1988), Messick and Mackie (1989), Stephan (1985), Tajfel (1978, 1982), Turner (1981), and Wilder (1986), indicates that categorization of people into distinct groups is sufficient to arouse intergroup bias. On the occurrence of social categorization, people favor in-group members in the allocation rewards (Tajfel, Billig, Bundy, & Flament, 1971), in their personal regard (Rabbie, 1982; Rabbie & Horwitz, 1969), and in the evaluation of the products of their labor (Ferguson & Kelley, 1964). Also, factors that further increase intergroup bias share the capacity to enhance the salience of the categorized representation (Abrams, 1985; Brewer, 1979;

Deschamps & Doise, 1978; Dion, 1974; Doise, 1978; Skinner & Stephenson, 1981; Turner, 1981; Worchel, 1979). The implication of these analyses is that reducing the salience of the intergroup boundary should decrease the prevalence of in-group–out-group category-based judgments and thereby reduce intergroup bias.

Within the intergroup literature, there has been some convergence of opinion (although it is not unanimous; see Rothbart & John, 1985) that degrading the salience of the categorized representation should decrease intergroup bias. Although categorization has been the common target, various strategies have been effectively used in laboratory settings, and these strategies have yielded different residual representations of the aggregate (see Wilder, 1986). For example, individuating members of the out-group by revealing variability in their opinions (Wilder, 1978, Study 1) or having out-group members respond as individuals rather than as a group (Wilder, 1978, Studies 2 and 3) renders each member more distinctive and thus potentially blurs the prior categorization scheme. Also, personalizing interactions (Brewer & Miller, 1984; Miller, Brewer, & Edwards, 1985) similarly differentiates or dehomogenizes in-group and out-group members, but perhaps on the basis of more intimate, more personally relevant information. Criss-crossing category memberships by forming new subgroups (Brewer, Ho, Lee, & Miller, 1987; Commins & Lockwood, 1978; Deschamps & Doise, 1978; Vanbeselaere, 1987), each composed of members from former subgroups, changes the pattern of who's "in" and who's "out" and can also render the earlier categorization less salient (Brown & Turner, 1979).

In the current research, we considered the benefits of two additional strategies. Specifically, members of two groups were induced to recategorize the aggregate either as one superordinate group or as separate individuals who were not members of any particular social category (i.e., decategorization). Theoretically, a one-group representation replaces the former intergroup boundary with a single, inclusive superordinate boundary. In contrast, the separate-individuals representation reduces the salience of group membership altogether. Whereas individuation (see Wilder, 1978) differentiates or dehomogenizes out-group members, a separate-individuals representation attacks the integrity of both in-group and out-group boundaries more completely and also transforms a person's salient self-identity from *we* to *me* (cf. Turner, 1982, 1985).

The rationale for the attitude-change processes underlying these strategies is based on two related conclusions from Brewer's (1979) analysis that fit nicely with social identity theory (Tajfel & Turner, 1979; Turner, 1975), as well as with self-categorization theory (Turner, 1985; Turner, Hogg, Oakes, Reicher, & Wetherell, 1987). First, intergroup bias often takes the form of in-group enhancement rather than out-group devaluation. Second, the introduction of an in-group–out-group boundary brings in-group members closer to the

self, whereas the distance between the self and out-group members remains relatively unchanged. Therefore, when the categorization process is reversed and members are left with a separate-individuals representation, intergroup bias should be reduced primarily because the distance between the self and former in-group members has increased, whereas the distance between the self and former out-group members has remained relatively unchanged. In contrast, when the salience of the categorized boundary is reduced but members are left with a superordinate or one-group representation, the cognitive and motivational processes that initially brought in-group members closer to the self could be redirected toward the establishment of more positive relations with the former out-group members. With a one-group representation, bias should be reduced primarily because the social distance with former out-group members has decreased and the social distance with former in-group members has remained relatively close. The expectation that closeness between the self and others is accentuated or reduced in relation to the salient level of self-categorization is perfectly in tune with Turner's (1985; see also Turner et al., 1987) more general theory of self-categorization on group behavior, in fact, the current predictions could have been derived from it. Specifically, Turner et al. (1987) hypothesized that "self-categories tend to be evaluated positively" (p. 57) and "that the attractiveness of an individual is not constant, but varies with the ingroup membership" (p. 60).

The potential for the one-group representation to bring out-group members closer to the self is indicated by the intergroup literature, which also suggests that a number of benefits should now be extended to these new in-group members. First, Tajfel and Turner (1979; see also Turner, 1975) proposed that a person's need for positive self-identity (i.e., self-esteem) motivates social comparisons that positively differentiate in-group members from out-group members. Whether positive differentiation is achieved by out-group devaluation (Rosenbaum & Holtz, 1985) or by in-group enhancement (which is more usual, according to Brewer, 1979), the recategorization of former out-group members as in-group members should result in more positive attitudes toward them. Second, greater belief similarity to the self is attributed to in-group members (Brown, 1984; Brown & Abrams, 1986; Hogg & Turner, 1985; Stein, Hardyck, & Smith, 1965; Wilder, 1984), and belief similarity is a powerful determinant of in-terpersonal attraction (Byrne, 1971). Third, in-group membership decreases psychological dis-tance and facilitates the arousal of promotive ten-sion, whereby a person's motivational system be-comes coordinated to the needs of another (Hornstein, 1976). Indeed, prosocial behavior is offered more readily to in-group than to out-group members (Hornstein, 1976; Piliavin, Dovidio, Gaertner, & Clark, 1981), and prosocial behavior is sensitive to interpersonal attraction (Gaertner & Dovidio, 1986). Also, people are more likely to be cooperative and to exercise more personal re-straint in their use of endangered common re-sources when they are interacting with in-group members than when interacting with others (Kramer & Brewer, 1984).

In the present study, two separate laboratory groups (of 3 persons each) were created. These groups were then provided with the opportunity for intergroup interaction under circumstances in-tended to manipulate members' conceptual repre-sentations of the aggregate. To vary whether mem-bers conceived of this aggregate as one group, two groups, or separate individuals, the specific cir-cumstances for each treatment condition were de-signed to include a set of systematically varied features that, in concert, were expected to strongly influence members' conceptual representations of the memberships. Therefore, the aim was not to determine which specific feature(s) may have con-tributed most to members' representations of the aggregate. Given the possibility that one or more of these of features, which differed across the treat-ment conditions, may influence intergroup bias through processes unrelated to members' altered representations, more typical between-treatment analyses were supplemented by within-treatment correlational analyses. Separately, within each treatment, we assessed the relation between sub-jects' conceptual representations of the aggregate and their attitudes toward in-group and out-group members unencumbered by differences across the experimental treatments.

On the basis of the social categorization ap-proach (Brewer, 1979; Hogg & Abrams, 1988; Tajfel, 1969; Tajfel & Turner, 1979; Turner, 1985), we expected that changing members' categorized representations from two groups to either recategorized representation would reduce inter-group bias. Consequently, we expected that when members of two groups were induced to conceive of themselves as either one group or as separate individuals (i.e., no groups), they would have lower degrees of bias than those encouraged to maintain the earlier two-groups representation.

Although there is no a priori reason to expect different degrees of intergroup bias between the one-group and separate-individuals conditions, there is reason to expect they would reduce bias through different processes. If the consequences of imposing a common in-group categorization involve moving in-group members closer to the self (Brewer, 1979; Turner, 1985; Turner et al., 1987), then bias in the one-group condition should be reduced primarily by increasing the attractive-ness of former out-group members because of their revised group status. Alternatively, decategori-zation to separate individuals should move former in-group members further away from the self; therefore, bias should be reduced primarily by decreasing the attractiveness of former in-group members.

Method

Subjects

Three hundred sixty undergraduates (180 men and 180 women) enrolled in the general psychology course at the University of Delaware participated in partial fulfillment of their research readings or participation requirement. Ten groups of men and 10 groups of women, run in same-sex groups of six people per session, were assigned to each of the three treatment conditions: one group, two groups, and separate individuals. Thus, each treat-ment condition was composed of 20 six-person groups.

Procedure

SUBGROUP FORMATION

In each session, two 3-person groups were assigned to two ostensibly different experiments located in separate areas within the laboratory complex. Al-though these two groups were treated identically, they were not informed of their joint participation in the experiment until just before the intergroup interaction. After being greeted by one of two experimenters, members of each group were assigned one of three different color-coded identity tags reserved for each group (purple, yellow, or brown; or green, orange, or red) as they were led to their designated laboratory. As they entered, the experimenter asked the participants to attach these identification tags to their clothing and to sit according to their color-coded identity, by matching their tag with a like-colored placemat on the group's table. Each room was also equipped with a visible video camera and microphone. Tape-recorded instructions explained that the study involved the examination of group decision-making processes and that we would be recording their group interaction as they attempted to reach a consensus concerning the winter survival problem (Johnson & Johnson, 1975). This problem is engaging and requires participants to imagine that their plane has crash-landed in the woods of northern Minnesota in mid-January and to rank-order 10 items salvaged from the plane (a gun, newspaper, can of shortening, etc.) in terms of their importance for survival. To further involve participants in the problem, a replica of each item was available for examination in the center of the table. First, each person was given 2 min to solve the problem individually. Each group then created a name for itself and was instructed to record that name on a consensus solution form placed in the center of the table, as well as on all other forms used throughout the study. We assumed that having each group create its own identifying name would contribute to the members' group awareness (see Deutsch, 1973). Each 3-person group then discussed the problem (for a maximum of 5 min) and recorded a single consensus ranking of items. Following consensus, participants made a personal record of their group's decision.

At this point, the tape-recorded instructions explained that the participants would soon discuss the problem again; however, this time they would discuss it with members of another group who had also been working on the winter survival problem, and monetary rewards for the development of the most effective solutions would be available. These instructions, as well as the circumstances of this intergroup interaction (scheduled for 10 min), were manipulated systematically so as to differentially affect members' conceptual representations of the aggregate as one group, two groups, or separate individuals (see Campbell, 1958; Zander, Stotland, & Wolfe, 1960).

EXPERIMENTAL MANIPULATIONS

One feature previously shown to influence members' representation of the aggregate involves the manner in which members of each group were positioned during the interaction (Gaertner & Dovidio, 1986; Ryen, 1974). In the one-group condition, members of each group were ushered into a larger room and seated alternately (i.e., ABABAB; facilitated by the use of color-coded placemats corresponding to subjects' color identities) around a hexagonally shaped table formed by pushing together two trapezoidal tables. Each person was thus seated between 2 members of the other group (integrated seating). In the two-groups condition, the members of each subgroup were positioned at adjacent locations on either side of the seam in the hexagonally shaped table (i.e., AAABBB; segregated seating). Thus, seating position (i.e., integrated or segregated) varied the presence or absence of a physical boundary between the two groups. In each condition, one set of the items "salvaged from the plane" was positioned along the seam in the center of the table. In the separate-individuals condition, each member was separated from the others immediately following the initial subgroup interaction and led to a separate cubicle for a short period, during which he or she composed a second personal solution to the winter survival problem. After working alone, all 6 participants were signaled simultaneously to leave their cubicles, which opened into the larger area that now had six separate square tables positioned around the room's perimeter (25 × 22 ft). Each table was color coded and positioned so that members from each group were arranged in an alternating pattern with their backs toward the center of the room. Also, each participant had available his or her own set of items salvaged from the plane.

Each participant's formal identity during the interaction was also varied systematically. In the one-group condition, the 6 participants were asked to create a new single name for themselves that did not simply combine the earlier subgroup names. Those in the two-groups condition maintained their previous group names throughout the interaction. In the separate-individuals condition, each person was asked to create a nickname for him- or herself that was to be used in place of the former group names on all subsequent experimental forms. Just before the interaction phase, the experimenter began the video recording of the interaction by announcing the name(s) of the participants. In the one-group condition, the experimenter stated,

> This will be session number _____ in which the _____ [name of 3-person Group A] has been merged with the _____ [name of 3-person Group B] and will be known as the _____ [name decided on by all 6-people].

In the two-groups and separate-individuals conditions, the experimenter announced either the 3-person group names or the individual nicknames, without mention of a merger.

We also varied the nature and purpose of the group interaction across the three treatment conditions. In the one-group condition, members freely discussed the survival problem with the purpose of arriving at the single best consensus solution. In the two-groups condition, members of each group described to each other only the rationale for their earlier 3-person group solutions. In the separate-individuals condition, each participant in turn described his or her initial personal solution to the 5 other participants. In this last condition, the video camera, which was now positioned in the center of the room, was aimed exclusively at the person who was speaking. Following the interaction, participants in the two-groups and separate-individuals conditions reconsidered their earlier solutions and prepared a final 3-person group or personal solution, respectively.

In addition, we varied the nature of the interdependence among the participants across the experimental treatments. Instructions specific to each condition explained that all participants had the opportunity to qualify to win $10 in a lottery to be conducted at the end of the semester. Qualification in each condition was dependent on the relative effectiveness of their 6-person group, 3-person group, or personal solutions, respectively. To qualify for the lottery in the one-group condition, the group's consensus solution had to be more effective than that of another 6-person group supposedly meeting concurrently in another building on campus. Hence, both 3-person groups were cooperatively interdependent with respect to one another. Qualification in the two-groups condition depended on which of the two currently participating 3-person groups developed the more effective final solution. For those in separate-individuals condition, qualification was awarded to the person whose final personal solution was most effective compared with those of the other 5 participants. Furthermore, in the one-group condition members received feedback that their solution was more effective than that of the other group; in the other conditions, feedback was only provided just before subjects left the laboratory at the conclusion of the study. The timing of this feedback was intended to further unify the members of the one-group condition and to maintain the competition and thereby the salience of the two-groups and separate-individuals representations, respectively, in the other conditions.

MEASURES

Following the intergroup interactions, the participants were given a postexperimental questionnaire containing items that asked (a) which participant they would elect as leader of these six survivors if the survival problem were real rather than hypothetical; (b) their conceptual representations of the aggregate ("During the interaction did it [the aggregate] feel like one group, two groups, or separate individuals?"), as well as to what extent (on a scale ranging from 1, *not at all* to 7, *very much*) the aggregate felt like each of these representations; (c) their evaluative ratings (1–7) of each participant (except for themselves), which involved how much they liked each of the others and their ratings of each person's honesty, cooperativeness, and value to the discussion (we calculated in-group and out-group scores separately for each subject on each rating); and (d) their 1–7 ratings of the extent to which the interaction was characterized as cooperative, friendly, quarrelsome, close, pleasant, trusting, frustrating, successful, honest, and useless.

Results

Conceptual Representations of the Aggregate

The intent of the experimental manipulations was to strongly influence subjects' conceptual representations of the aggregate. When asked to select the representation (one group, two groups, or separate individuals) that best characterized their impression of the aggregate during the interaction, sizable percentages of subjects in each treatment

TABLE 21.1. Members' Representations of the Aggregate

	Treatment condition		
	One group (20 groups)	Two groups (20 groups)	Separate individuals (20 groups)
Mean percentage of members selecting			
One group	71.67%	18.88%	15.83%
Two groups	21.67%	80.00%	16.67%
Separate individuals	6.67%	1.67%	67.50%
The extent to which it felt like (1–7)			
One group	5.37	3.72	2.95
Two groups	2.21	4.35	2.92
Separate individuals	1.94	1.77	4.94

selected the representation appropriate to their treatment condition. Because of the possible interdependence of ratings within each 6-person group, we used the group as the unit of analysis throughout ($N = 60$), unless otherwise indicated. The average percentages of subjects in each group selecting the "appropriate" representation in the one group, two-groups, and separate-individuals conditions (see Table 21.1) are 71.67%, 80.00%, and 67.5%, respectively. Between-treatment analyses indicated that, relative to the other treatment conditions, greater percentages of subjects in the one-group condition selected the one-group representation, $F(2, 54) = 51.63, p < .001$. Similarly, greater percentages of subjects in the two-groups and separate-individuals conditions most frequently, relative to each of the other treatments, selected the representation appropriate to their treatment conditions, $Fs(2, 54) = 67.32$ and 110.41, respectively, $p < .001$. In each case, there were no main effects or interactions involving subjects' sex.

In addition, subjects' ratings (1–7) of the extent to which each of these representations characterized their impressions of the aggregate (see Table 21.1) offer further support for the effectiveness of the manipulation. A $3 \times 2 \times 3$ (Treatment × Sex × Representation Measure) repeated measures multivariate analysis of variance (MANOVA) involving the mean rating (for each 6-person group) on each measure of these three representations revealed a reliable Treatment × Measures interaction effect, multivariate $F(4, 106) = 67.41 \, p < .001$.[1]

Overall, the pattern of these means (see Table 21.1), both between and within treatments, supports the efficacy of the manipulation of subjects' representations of the aggregate.

Levels of Intergroup Bias

Evaluative ratings. The primary measures of intergroup bias were subjects' ratings (1–7) of liking and how cooperative, honest, and valuable each original in-group and out-group member was during the interaction (see Table 21.2). We performed a 3 (treatment) × 2 (sex) × 2 (in-group and out-group) MANOVA, with repeated measures on the in-group–out-group variable, on the four evaluative ratings. In this overall analysis, main effects for treatment were obtained, multivariate $F(8, 106) = 4.23, p < .001$, such that evaluative ratings overall were highest in the one-group condition and lowest in the separate-individuals condition. Also, there was a main effect for group, multivariate $F(4, 54) = 22.79, p < .001$; in-group members received more favorable evaluations than did out-group members. There were no main effects or interactions involving subjects' sex; consequently, we eliminated this variable from further analyses.

The predicted Treatment × Group (In-group–Out-group) interaction supports the categorization framework, multivariate $F(8, 106) = 2.62, p < .012$. Specifically, intergroup bias varied across the treatment conditions. Figure 21.1 displays the amount of bias (i.e., the difference between in-group and out-group ratings summed across each of the evaluative measures; see Table 21.1). As expected, the one-group and separate-individuals conditions each appear to have lower degrees of bias than the two-groups condition. Planned comparisons (described in the following paragraph) using repeated measures MANOVAs that involved the in-group and out-group ratings support these observations.

Because the central hypotheses concerned changes in intergroup bias as a function of the specific residual representation, planned comparisons were performed comparing the two-groups condition first to the one-group condition and then to the separate-individuals condition. The planned comparison involving a 2 (one group vs. two groups) × 2 (in-group vs, out-group) repeated

---

[1]All multivariate tests were based on Wilk's criterion. Tests based on Pillais and Hotellings criteria yielded the same results.

Table 21.2. Evaluative Ratings of In-Group and Out-Group Members

Rating and group members	Treatment conditions		
	One group (20 groups)	Two groups (20 groups)	Separate individuals (20 groups)
Like			
In-group	5.56	5.59	5.03
Out-group	5.31	4.90	4.59
Honest			
In-group	6.04	6.13	5.78
Out-group	5.98	5.76	5.71
Cooperative			
In-group	5.80	6.00	5.51
Out-group	5.68	5.61	5.28
Valuable			
In-group	5.45	5.46	5.24
Out-group	5.20	4.99	4.91
Average[a]			
In-group	5.71	5.80	5.39
Out-group	5.54	5.31	5.12

[a]Average of like, honest, cooperative, and valuable.

measures MANOVA performed on the evaluative ratings obtained an interaction, multivariate $F(4, 35) = 3.99$, $p < .01$, that supported the prediction that the difference between in-group and out-group ratings would be lower in the one-group condition than in the two-groups condition. A similar comparison involving the separate-individuals and two groups conditions also obtained the reliable interaction between treatment conditions and the in-group-out-group ratings, multivariate $F(4, 35) = 2.60$, $p < .05$. In addition, this latter analysis revealed a reliable main effect for treatment, multivariate $F(4, 35) = 3.52$, $p < .016$, whereby the evaluative ratings overall were less favorable in the separate-individuals condition than in the two-groups condition. An additional analysis involving a 2 (one group vs. separate individuals) × 2 (in-group vs. out-group) comparison suggests that the apparent difference in bias between the one-group and separate-individuals conditions (see Figure 21.1) was not reliable, multivariate $F(4, 35)$ 0.718, $p < .59$. However, this analysis did reveal a main effect for treatment, multivariate $F(4, 35) = 11.31$, $p < .001$, indicating that the evaluative ratings, overall, were higher in the one-group condition than in the separate-individuals condition (see Table 21.2). Additional a priori comparisons (described later) bear favorably on the idea that these

recategorized treatment conditions reduce intergroup bias through different processes.

PROCESSES FOR REDUCING BIAS

Specifically, we proposed that bias would be reduced in the one-group condition largely because the attractiveness of former out-group members would be enhanced. In the separate-individuals condition, we expected reduced bias primarily because the attractiveness of former in-group members would be diminished. Converging support for these predictions was suggested first by between-treatment analyses using the two-groups condition as a baseline for the assessment of the effects of the recategorized conditions, and second by correlational analyses performed separately within each treatment condition.

We examined the process by which the one-group representation reduced bias by using two multivariate planned comparisons. The first analysis, a follow-up on the significant Treatment (One Group vs. Two Groups) × In-group–Out-group interaction, contrasted the one-group and two-groups conditions on the evaluative ratings of in-group members; the second analysis contrasted these treatments on the ratings of out-group members. First, there was no reliable difference regarding the evaluations of in-group members, multivariate $F(4, 35) = 1.96$, $p < .122$; the average in-group evaluations (presented only to illustrate the multivariate comparisons; see Table 21.2) across the four ratings in the one-group and two-groups conditions were 5.71 and 5.80, respectively. Second, the extent to which out-group members were evaluated more favorably in the one-group condition than in the two-groups condition was reliable, multivariate $F(4, 35) = 2.75$, $p < .043$; the average out-group evaluations for the one-group and two-groups conditions were 5.54 and 5.31, respectively. The aforementioned Treatment (One Group vs. Two Group) × In-group–Out-group interaction, multivariate $F(4, 35) = 3.99$, $p < .01$, not only reveals a difference in bias, but given the pattern of the ratings, also indicates that the difference between the one-group and two-groups conditions for out-group members is different than that for in-group members. These results support the idea that the induction of a one-group representation would reduce bias primarily by increasing the attractiveness of former out-group members.

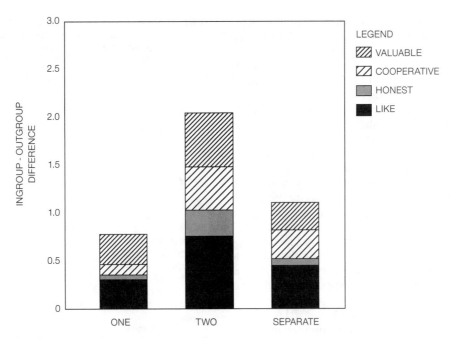

FIGURE 21.1 ■ Levels of intergroup bias among one-group, two-groups, and separate-individual conditions.

When similar comparisons involved the separate-individuals and the two-groups conditions, in-group members were evaluated less favorably among those in the separate-individuals condition (average = 5.39) relative to those in the two-groups condition (average = 5.80), multivariate $F(4, 35) = 3.44, p < .018$. Out-group members, however, were also evaluated less favorably in the separate-individuals condition (average = 5.12) than in the two-groups condition (average = 5.31), multivariate $F(4, 35) = 2.95, p < .03$. Although the reliable difference for outgroup members was unexpected, the reported Treatment (Separate Individuals vs. Two Groups) × In-group–Out-group interaction, multivariate $F(4, 35) = 2.60, p < .05$, given the pattern of the findings, indicates that the decreased attraction for in-group members was greater than the decrement for out-group members. Therefore, the pattern of these findings supports the prediction that among subjects in the separate-individuals condition bias would be reduced primarily by reducing attraction toward former in-group members.

The previous between-treatment analyses support the recategorization framework for reducing intergroup bias as well as the proposed processes by which reduced bias would be achieved within the one-group and separate-individuals conditions.

Additional within-treatment correlational analyses between subjects' ratings of the different possible representations and their average in-group and out-group ratings corroborate the between-treatment findings. We should note that statistically it is possible for individual-level and group-level correlational analyses to yield different patterns of relations. For example, at the individual level two variables could be negatively correlated within each 6-person group; however, if the group means for both variables are systematically higher for some groups than for others, the group-level analysis would indicate a positive correlation. In the current study, we hypothesized that a person's specific conceptual representation of the aggregate influences his or her evaluation of in-group and out-group members. Therefore, the individual-level analysis controlling for the mean of each person's 6-member group (by subtracting these means from each subject's representation and evaluation ratings) seems intuitively to be the most direct test of the hypothesized effects of a subject's conceptual representation. Although this individual-level analysis may not completely remove the potential dependency among the participants and also possibly overestimates the degrees of freedom, it is sensitive to the variability within each 6-person group that would otherwise be sacrificed with a group-level analysis. In any event, both analyses were conducted, but the primary focus is on the individual-level correlations.

Examination of these correlations separately within each treatment (see Table 21.3, one-tailed tests, $Ns = 120$) reveals that the intended representation for each treatment condition (in bold-face) correlates with the degree of bias (i.e., the difference between in-group and out-group members), as well as with the separate indexes for in-group and out-group members in a manner supporting the hypotheses. Specifically, within the one-group condition only, the greater the extent to which the aggregate felt like one group, the lower the degree of bias ($r = -.18$, $p < .025$) and the higher the evaluation of out-group members ($r = .25$, $p < .01$), whereas the correlation with in-group ratings ($r = .11$) was unreliable. Within the separate-individuals condition, the more the aggregate felt like separate individuals, the lower the degree of bias ($r = -.24$, $p < .01$) and the lower the evaluation of former in-group members ($r = -.25$, $p < .01$), whereas there was no reliable correlation with the ratings of out-group members ($r = -.08$).[2]

Voting for a Leader

In addition to the evaluative ratings, subjects were asked to specify which of the 6 participants they would elect as leader if the winter survival problem were real rather than hypothetical. Specifically, the dependent measure was the percentage of subjects within each 6-person group who voted for an in-group member as leader. For this measure, of course, the percentage of subjects who voted for an out-group is its complement. A 3 × 2 (Treatment × Sex) analysis of variance yielded a reliable main effect for treatment, $F(2, 54) = 6.84$, $p < .002$. The mean percentages of in-group voting (which would include a vote for oneself) by the one-group, two-groups, and separate-individuals conditions were 44%, 62%, and 65%, respectively.

Given the unexpectedly high rate of biased voting within the separate-individuals condition, in additional analyses we examined the possibility that these subjects may have more frequently voted for themselves and that this occurrence contributed to the unexpectedly high level of biased voting within the separate-individuals condition. Indeed, the extent to which participants would have elected themselves as leader increased from the

Table 21.3. Within-Treatment Correlational Analyses Between Ratings of Each Representation and the Average of the Four Evaluative Ratings for In-Group and Out-Group Members (Individual Level of Analysis Controlling for the Mean of Each Person's Six-Person Group)

Condition	In-group–out-group (bias)	In-group evaluation	Out-group evaluation
One group (N = 120)			
One group	−.18**	.11	.25***
Two groups	.07	−.12	−.18**
Separate individuals	−.06	−.15*	−.09
Two groups (N = 120)			
One group	−.22***	.03	.18**
Two groups	.20**	.01	−.18**
Separate individuals	−.04	−.18**	−.14
Separate individuals (N = 120)			
One group	−.11	.10	.21***
Two groups	.34***	−.08	−.35***
Separate individuals (1–7)	−.24***	−.25***	−.08

Note. The intended representation for each treatment appears in bold-face.
*$p < .05$, one-tailed. ** $p < .025$, one-tailed. *** $p < .01$, one-tailed.

one-group (9%) to two-groups (17%) to separate-individuals (25.6%) conditions, $\chi^2(2, N = 355) = 10.85$, $p < .001$. However, when subjects who voted for themselves are eliminated (and, therefore, bias is reflected when in-group voting exceeds 40%), both those in the separate-individuals (54%) and the two-groups (53%) conditions each continue to have higher levels of bias than

---

[2]Similar within-treatment analyses at the group level ($N = 20$ groups per condition) revealed a pattern of correlations similar to the individual-level analyses (see Table 21.3), except for the separate-individuals condition in which none of the correlations were significant. Specifically within the one-group condition, the greater the extent to which the aggregate felt like one group, the lower the degree of bias ($r = -.39$, $p < .05$) and the higher the evaluation of out-group members ($r = .43$, $p < .03$), whereas the correlation with in-group ratings ($r = .22$) was unreliable. Within the two-groups condition, the more the aggregate felt like two groups, the greater the degree of bias ($r = .46$, $p < .02$) and the lower the evaluations of out-group members ($r = -.35$, $p = .067$), whereas the relation to in-group members did not approach statistical reliability ($r = .003$). In the separate-individuals condition, the extent to which the aggregate felt like separate individuals did not correlate significantly with the degree of bias ($r = -.06$) with the evaluation of in-group members ($r = -.07$) or with out-group members ($r = -.02$).

those in the one-group (37%) condition, $F(1, 36)$ = 5.60, $p < .02$, and $F(1, 36) = 7.32$, $p < .01$, respectively.

Ratings of the Interaction

We also assessed subjects' impressions of the interaction by using an index composed of their 1–7 ratings of the extent to which the interaction was characterized as cooperative, friendly, quarrelsome, close, pleasant, trusting, frustrating, successful, honest, and useless. Cronbach's alpha was .91 for the means of each 6-person group across the 10 different response scales (.82 for individuals). A 3 × 2 (Treatment × Sex) MANOVA involving these ratings revealed a main effect for treatment, multivariate $F(20, 90) = 3.42$, $p < .001$, and subsequent comparisons indicated that the interaction was rated less favorably ($M = 4.99$) by those in the separate-individuals condition relative to those in the one-group condition ($M = 5.67$), multivariate $F(10, 29) = 5.56$, $p < .001$, and also relative to those in the two-groups condition ($M = 5.54$) multivariate $F(10, 29) = 3.75$, $p < .003$. Furthermore, there was no difference between the one-group and two-groups conditions, multivariate $F(10, 29) = 1.47$, $p < .20$.

Discussion

Our findings support the social categorization framework for understanding intergroup bias (Brewer, 1979; Tajfel, 1969; Turner, 1981; Turner et al., 1987). Members of two groups who maintained their original two-group categorization had greater levels of bias than did members whose representations were altered by the recategorization treatment conditions. Between and within-treatment analyses revealed that the one-group and separate-individuals representations were each associated with reduced bias and that these recategorized representations each had different consequences on attitudes toward former in-group and out-group members. Specifically, the one-group representation reduced bias primarily by increasing the attractiveness of former out-group members, whereas the separate-individuals representation primarily decreased the attractiveness of former in-group members. In each case, attitudes toward former in-group and out-group members became more equivalent. In addition, it

is worth noting that with a one-group representation subjects' attraction toward all participants was considerably higher than with a separate-individuals representation. Consequently, a one-group representation would perhaps be more conducive to the development of more intimate, personalized future interactions relative to a separate-individuals representation. These findings were complemented by the ratings of the intergroup interaction. In the one-group condition, the interaction was regarded as more friendly, cooperative, trusting, close, and so forth than it was in the separate-individuals condition. Therefore, whereas complete decategorization reduces intergroup bias, the various recategorization strategies may have different implications for the pattern of behavior likely to develop among the former in-group and out-group members.

The failure of the separate-individuals representation to be associated with reduced in-group bias when subjects were voting for leader was unexpected but was perhaps due to subjects in this condition not having the opportunity to observe former out-group members behave in a group context. Therefore, subjects in the separate-individuals condition may have been less capable of judging how well former out-group members (relative to former in-group members) would coordinate, initiate, or offer social support to others. Consequently, they may have felt more confident voting for former in-group members to be leader. Alternatively, these subjects may have anticipated that leaders might favor former in-group members, and therefore they voted in a manner to ensure their self-interest.

Although the experimental treatments strongly influenced subjects' representations, the treatments were compound manipulations that differed systematically on many dimensions. For example, the treatments varied the timing of the feedback about winning and whether the interactions and goal relations among the 6 participants were cooperative or competitive. These particular differences raise a question regarding the extent to which the major effects were mediated by processes implicit in reinforcement theory (see Lott & Lott, 1965) and Sherif's functional relations theory rather than by the type of social categorization. For example, on the basis of reinforcement theory, good feelings associated with successful feedback, which was provided prior to the evaluative ratings in only the one-group condition, could explain these subjects' more favorable evaluations of out-group members. Also on the basis of processes implicit in functional relations theory, the increased attraction toward former out-group members in the one-group condition and the decreased attraction for former in-group members in the separate-individuals condition could be explained by differences across conditions in the apparent helpfulness (i.e., cooperativeness) of these participants during subjects' efforts to obtain a desired goal.

Nevertheless, we believe for several reasons that intergroup bias was reduced independently and largely by changes in subjects' categorized representations. For example, if successful feedback in the one-group condition directly increased positive attitudes toward out-group members, we should have observed the development of more positive attitudes toward former in-group members as well. Although it is plausible that cooperation and competition between in-group and out-group members directly influence intergroup attitudes, we believe that these types of goal relations and interactions affect intergroup attitudes primarily by altering the salience of relevant categorized representations (see Doise, 1978; Turner, 1981; Worchel, 1979). Furthermore, evidence from the intergroup literature indicates that intergroup attitudes do not turn exclusively on the cooperative and competitive nature of the goal relations or interactions between groups per se. Rather, intergroup bias seems to be determined largely by the extent to which the situation overall emphasizes the salience of the categorized representation (Brewer, 1979; Turner, 1981; Worchel, 1979).

Although the functional relations position holds that "it is not factually true [that] prejudice against other groups . . . accompan[ies] the formation of an ingroup" (Sherif, 1966, p. 22), evidence indicates that intergroup bias does occur with categorization per se, and in the complete absence of explicit intergroup competition (Billig & Tajfel, 1973; Doise, 1969, cited in Turner, 1981; Ferguson & Kelley, 1964; Kahn & Ryen, 1972; Rabbie, 1982; Rabbie & Horwitz, 1969; Rabbie & Wilkens, 1971; Tajfel et al., 1971). Furthermore, whereas intergroup bias is often lower under cooperative conditions than under competitive conditions, it is not completely absent under cooperative circumstances (Kahn & Ryen, 1972; Rabbie & de Brey, 1971; Worchel, Axsom, Ferris, Samaha, & Schweitzer, 1978). Sometimes cooperative relations produce as much bias as competitive ones

(Brewer & Silver, 1978; Doise, Csepeli, Dann, Gouge, Larsen, & Ostell, 1971, cited in Turner, 1981; Rabbie & de Brey, 1971). In addition to whether the relations were cooperative or competitive, the degree of intergroup bias observed across these studies was largely dependent on factors that were clearly capable of influencing the salience of the categorized representation. Rabbie and de Brey (1971), for example, reported greater intergroup bias when intragroup interaction preceded either competitive or cooperative intergroup interactions. Also, according to Worchel et al. (1978), groups wearing different colored laboratory coats (i.e., Group A = red; Group B = white) during intergroup cooperative interaction had higher levels of bias compared with groups dressed in same-colored coats. Thus, whereas cooperative goal relations and interactions often contribute to reducing intergroup bias, they cannot fully account for variations in intergroup attitudes.

In research using paradigms similar to that used in this study, members' representations influenced intergroup attitudes independent of intergroup cooperative interaction. In an earlier study (Gaertner & Dovidio, 1986; see also Ryen, 1974), only the seating position (i.e., integrated or segregated) was varied while the two groups cooperatively interacted and reached consensus to the winter survival problem. In the absence of the multiplex of features characterizing the current study, subjects in the integrated condition relative to the segregated condition felt reliably more like one group, demonstrated reliably less in-group bias in their leadership votes, and tended to have lower degrees of bias toward liking in-group members more than outgroup members. Thus, without varying cooperative interaction, an additional factor that influenced the salience of the categorization also appeared to regulate the degree of intergroup bias. Furthermore, another study (Gaertner, Mann, Murrell, Pomare, & Dovidio, 1989) again varied a similar multiplex of features intended to influence members' representations as one group or two groups while members were face-to-face with each other, but without interaction or cooperative-competitive goal relations. Supporting this study's findings, subjects in the one-group condition relative to those in the two-groups condition felt reliably more like one group and had reliably lower bias in their evaluations of in-group and out-group members.

Overall, then, the literature suggests that

whereas cooperation and competition per se may influence intergroup bias, the salience of relevant categorizations is also an important factor. Sherif and Sherif (1969, pp. 268–269) recognized the capacity of intergroup cooperation to facilitate the development of a common superordinate entity, but this was conceived to be the ultimate rather than the initial consequence of cooperative activity. In view of the research we have cited, the within-treatment correlations in the current study (see Table 21.3), and the strong potential for intergroup cooperative and competitive interactions to influence the salience of members' categorized representations, we contend that the systematic variation in members' categorized representations contributed directly to the patterns of intergroup bias that we obtained in this study.

The strength of the experimental manipulations may arouse concern that our findings resulted primarily from demand characteristics. However, subjects' postexperimental self-reports of their hypotheses about the study's purposes revealed that no subject expressed a hypothesis that approximated the goals of the study. The fact that subjects were in only one condition very likely obscured the specific purpose of the research. Furthermore, the different patterns by which bias was reduced were very likely too subtle for most subjects to anticipate (e.g., the decreased attraction toward former in-group members within the separate-individuals condition) and therefore support the validity of the experimental results.

The different processes by which the one-group and separate-individuals representations reduced bias support the Brewer (1979) and Turner (1985; see also Turner et al., 1987) analyses regarding the consequences of social categorization. Apparently, in-group formation does not necessarily push out-group members or undifferentiated others further away from oneself; rather, it brings in-group members closer. Indeed, whereas some encounters would certainly arouse tendencies to denigrate out-group members (see Rosenbaum & Holtz, 1985), the fundamental dynamics of intergroup discrimination do not rely on the development of hostile, unfavorable images of out-group members. This perspective is important because it acknowledges the potential benefits of in-group formation (see Kramer & Brewer, 1984) while recognizing that it may be a fundamental instigator of intergroup conflict. The present research suggests that in-group categorization may also be used productively to bring former out-group members closer to the self and thereby reduce bias. This perspective differs from strategies that recommend that if bias is to be eliminated people must first perceive members of out-groups as individuals rather than as group members. We do not fundamentally disagree with the other perspectives, but rather believe that the one-group representation may offer an alternative to these more individuated, personalized perceptions while capitalizing on the human proclivity for categorizing the people and objects of our experience (Rosch, 1975).

In-group categorization may mobilize further changes in motivational and cognitive processes that mediate behavior toward other people. Although initially the induction of a common in-group representation may only peripherally or heuristically influence attitudes toward former out-group members, this newly formed positive bias may facilitate the occurrence of interactions that permit the development of more elaborated, individuated, and personalized impressions of former out-group members. These nonstereotypic impressions could then have important consequences for the pattern of future interpersonal and intergroup behavior. For example, Slavin and Madden's (1979) review of school practices that improve interracial attitudes revealed that participating on interracial sports teams and cooperative learning teams were the activities most related to students having positive interracial attitudes. Similarly, the "jigsaw" classroom method of reducing intergroup bias (Aronson, Blaney, Stephan, Sikes, & Snapp, 1978) may also capitalize on the benefits of an enhanced salience of a common group or team membership. From this perspective, the pursuit of superordinate goals in Sherif's robbers cave study (Sherif, Harvey, White, Hood, & Sherif, 1954) may have reduced intergroup bias because cooperation toward these goals induced the conflicting groups of summer campers to conceive of themselves as one group rather than as two groups.

We should note that the induction of a common or superordinate group representation may not necessarily require subgroups to forsake their earlier categorizations entirely. In some contexts this would be especially difficult or undesirable (Jones, 1986). Rather, this strategy may be effective even when both categorizations are salient simultaneously or alternately. For example, we may frequently categorize members of our family as *parents* and *children* without losing sight of our superordinate connection. Also, whereas coopera- tive intergroup interaction reduces bias, this ac- tivity may be at least partially instrumental, be- cause it induces participants to conceive of themselves as one group rather than as two groups. This perspective may be particularly useful in ap- plied settings because cooperation among conflict- ing groups is often difficult to implement (Worchel, 1979). However, if other factors can induce the perception of a common in-group membership, these factors could reduce bias and also potentially increase the likelihood of cooperative intergroup behavior. For example, Kramer and Brewer (1984; see also Dawes, van de Kragt, & Orbell, 1987) have shown that common in-group membership increases cooperative activity among individuals in their use of an endangered common resource. Therefore, the induction of a common in-group membership can potentially initiate a recurring se- quence of perceptions and actions that have in- creasingly positive consequences for reducing inter- group bias and conflict. In applied settings, we conceive of the strategy of increasing the salience of a superordinate or common group membership as only one of a variety of strategies to reduce inter- group conflict, but as one that has the potential to harness some of the cognitive and motivational processes that contribute to the development of in- tergroup bias and redirect them toward the establish- ment of more constructive intergroup relations.

REFERENCES

Abrams, D. (1985). Focus of attention in minimal intergroup discrimination. *British Journal of Social Psychology, 24,* 65–74.

Aronson, E., Blaney, N., Stephan, C., Sikes, J., & Snapp, M. (1978). *The jigsaw classroom.* Beverly Hills, CA: Sage.

Billig, M., & Tajfel, H. (1973). Social categorization and simi- larity in intergroup behavior. *European Journal of Social Psychology, 3,* 27–52.

Brewer, M. B. (1979). In-group bias in the minimal intergroup situation: A cognitive-motivational analysis. *Psychological Bulletin, 86,* 307–324.

Brewer, M. B., Ho, H., Lee, J., & Miller, M. (1987). Social identity and social distance among Hong Kong school chil- dren. *Personality and Social Psychology Bulletin, 13,* 156– 165.

Brewer, M. B., & Miller, N. (1984). Beyond the contact hy- pothesis: Theoretical perspectives on desegregation. In N. Miller & M. B. Brewer (Eds.), *Groups in contact: The psy- chology of desegregation* (pp. 281–302). Orlando, FL: Aca- demic Press.

Brewer, M. B., & Silver, N. (1978). Ingroup bias as a func- tion of task characteristics. *European Journal of Social Psychology, 8,* 393–400.

Brown, R. J. (1984). The effects of intergroup similarity and cooperative vs. competitive orientation on intergroup dis- crimination. *British Journal of Social Psychology, 23,* 21–33.

Brown, R. J., & Abrams, D. (1986). The effects of intergroup similarity and goal interdependence on intergroup attitudes and task performance. *Journal of Experimental Social Psy- chology, 21,* 78–92.

Brown, R. J., & Turner, J. C. (1979). The criss-cross categorisation effect in intergroup discrimination. *British Journal of Social and Clinical Psychology 18,* 371–383.

Byrne, D. (1971). *The attraction paradigm.* New York: Aca- demic Press.

Campbell, D. T. (1958). Common fate, similarity and other indices of the status of aggregates of persons as social enti- ties. *Behavioral Science, 3,* 14–25.

Commins, B., & Lockwood, J. (1978). The effects of inter- group relations of mixing Roman Catholics and Protestants: An experimental investigation. *European Journal of Social Psychology, 8,* 218–219.

Dawes, R. M., van de Kragt, & Orbell, J. M. (1987, May). *Not me or thee but we: The importance of group identity in eliciting cooperation in dilemma situations: Experimental manipulations.* Paper presented at the meeting of the Mid- western Psychological Association.

Deschamps, J. C., & Doise, W. (1978). Crossed-category membership in intergroup relations. In H. Tajfel (Ed.), *Dif- ferentiation between social groups* (pp. 141–158). London: Academic Press.

Deutsch, M. (1973). *The resolution of social conflict.* New Haven, CT: Yale University Press.

Dion, K. L. (1974). *A cognitive model of in-group–out-group bias.* Paper presented at the 82nd annual meeting of the American Psychological Association, New Orleans, LA.

Doise, W. (1978). *Groups and individuals: Explanations in social psychology.* Cambridge, England: Cambridge Uni- versity Press.

Ferguson, C. K., & Kelley H. H. (1964). Significant factors in over-evaluation of own groups' products. *Journal of Ab- normal and Social Psychology, 69,* 223–228.

Gaertner, S. L., & Dovidio, J. F. (1986). The aversive form of racism. In J. F Dovidio & S. L. Gaertner (Eds.), *Prejudice discrimination and racism.* Orlando, FL: Academic Press.

Gaertner, S. L., Mann, J., Murrell, A., Pomare, M., & Dovidio, J. F. (1989, March). *How does cooperation reduce inter- group bias?* Paper presented at the meeting of the Eastern Psychological Association, Boston.

Hogg, M. A., & Abrams, D. (1988). *Social identifications: A social psychology of intergroup relations and group pro- cesses.* London: Routledge & Kegan Paul.

Hogg, M. A., & Turner, J. C. (1985). Interpersonal attraction, social identification and psychological group formation. *European Journal of Social Psychology, 15,* 51–66.

Hornstein, H. A. (1976). *Cruelty and kindness: A new look at aggression and altruism.* Englewood Cliffs, NJ: Prentice-Hall.

Johnson, D. W., & Johnson, F. P. (1975). *Joining together: Group theory and group skills.* Englewood Cliffs, NJ: Prentice-Hall.

Jones, J. M. (1986). Racism: A cultural analysis. In J. F. Dovidio & S. L. Gaertner (Eds.), *Prejudice, discrimination and racism.* Orlando, FL: Academic Press.

Kahn, A., & Ryen, A. H. (1972). Factors influencing the bias towards one's own group. *International Journal of Group*

Tensions, 2, 33–50.

Kramer, R. M., & Brewer, M. B. (1984). Effects of group identity on resource use in a simulated commons dilemma. *Journal of Personality and Social Psychology, 46,* 1044–1057.

Lott, A. J., & Lott, B. E. (1965). Group cohesiveness as interpersonal attraction: A review of relationships with antecedent and consequent variables. *Psychological Bulletin, 64,* 259–309.

Messick, D. M., & Mackie, D. M. (1989). Intergroup relations. *Annual Review of Psychology, 40,* 45–81.

Miller, N., Brewer, M. B., & Edwards, K. (1985). Cooperative interaction in desegregated settings: A laboratory analog. *Journal of Social Issues, 41,* 63–75.

Piliavin, J. A., Dovidio, J. F., Gaertner, S. L., & Clark, R. D., III. (1981). *Emergency intervention.* New York: Academic Press.

Rabbie, J. M. (1982). The effects of intergroup competition and cooperation on intragroup and intergroup relationships. In V. J. Derlega & J. Grzelack (Eds.), *Cooperation and helping behavior: Theories and research.* New York: Academic Press.

Rabbie, J. M., & de Brey, J. H. C. (1971). The anticipation of intergroup co-operation and competition under private and public conditions. *International Journal of Group Tensions, 4,* 222–246.

Rabbie, J. M., & Horwitz, M. (1969). Arousal of ingroup-outgroup bias by a chance win or loss. *Journal of Personality and Social Psychology, 13,* 269–277.

Rabbie, J. M., & Wilkens, G. (1971). Intergroup competition and its effect on intragroup and intergroup relations. *European Journal of Social Psychology, 1,* 215–234.

Rosch, E. (1975). Cognitive representations of semantic categories. *Journal of Experimental Psychology: General, 104,* 192–233.

Rosenbaum, M. E., & Holtz, R. (1985, August). *The minimal intergroup discrimination effect: Out-group derogation, not in-group favorability.* Paper presented at the 93rd annual meeting of the American Psychological Association, Los Angeles, CA.

Rothbart, M., & John, O. P. (1985). Social categorization and behavioral episodes: A cognitive analysis of the effects of intergroup contact. *Journal of Social Issues, 41,* 81–104.

Ryen, A. (1974). *Cognitive and behavioral consequences of group membership.* Paper presented at the 82nd annual meeting of the American Psychological Association, New Orleans, LA.

Sherif, M. (1966). *In common predicament.* Boston: Houghton Mifflin.

Sherif, M., Harvey, O. J., White, B. J., Hood, W. R., & Sherif, C. (1954). *Experimental study of positive and negative intergroup attitudes between experimentally produced groups: Robbers cave experiment.* Norman: University of Oklahoma Press.

Sherif, M., & Sherif, C. W (1969). *Social psychology.* New York: Harper & Row.

Skinner, M., & Stephenson, G. M. (1981). The effects of intergroup comparisons on the polarization of opinions. *Current Psychological Research, 1,* 49–61.

Slavin, R. E., & Madden, N. A. (1979). School practices that improve social relations. *American Education Research Journal, 16,* 169–180.

Stein, D. D., Hardyck, J. A., & Smith, M. B. (1965). Race and belief. An open and shut case. *Journal of Personality and Social Psychology, 1,* 281–289.

Stephan, W. (1985). Intergroup relations. In G. Lindzey & E. Aronson (Eds.), *The handbook of social psychology* (Vol. 2, 3rd ed., pp. 599–658). New York: Random House.

Tajfel, H. (1969). Cognitive aspects of prejudice. *Journal of Social Issues, 25,* 79.

Tajfel, H. (1978). *Differentiation between social groups: Studies in the social psychology of intergroup relations.* London: Academic Press.

Tajfel, H. (1982). The social psychology of intergroup relations. *Annual Review of Psychology, 33,* 1–39.

Tajfel, H., Billig, M. G., Bundy R. P., & Flament, C. (1971). Social categorisation and intergroup behavior. *European Journal of Social Psychology, 1,* 149–177.

Tajfel, H., & Turner, J. C. (1979). An integrative theory of intergroup conflict. In W. G. Austin & S. Worchel (Eds.), *The social psychology of intergroup relations* (pp. 33–48). Monterey CA: Brooks/Cole.

Turner, J. C. (1975). Social comparison and social identity: Some prospects for intergroup behavior. *European Journal of Social Psychology, 5,* 5–34.

Turner, J. C. (1981). The experimental social psychology of intergroup behavior. In J. C. Turner & H. Giles (Eds.), *Intergroup behavior* (pp. 66–101). Chicago: University of Chicago Press.

Turner, J. C. (1982). Towards a cognitive redefinition of the social group. In H. Tajfel (Ed.), *Social identity and intergroup relations* (pp. 15–40). Cambridge, England: Cambridge University Press.

Turner, J. C. (1985). Social categorization and the self-concept: A social cognitive theory of group behavior. In E. J. Lawler (Ed.), *Advances in group processes* (Vol. 2, pp. 77–122). Greenwich, CT: JAI Press.

Turner, J. C., Hogg, M. A., Oakes, P. J., Reicher, S. D., & Wetherell, M. S. (1987). *Rediscovering the social group: A self-categorization theory.* Oxford, UK: Blackwell.

Vanbeselaere, N. (1987). The effects of dichotomous and crossed social categorization upon intergroup discrimination. *European Journal of Social Psychology, 17,* 143–156.

Wilder, D. A. (1978). Reduction of intergroup discrimination through individuation of the out-group. *Journal of Personality and Social Psychology, 36,* 1361–1374.

Wilder, D. A. (1984). Predictions of belief homogeneity and similarity following social categorization. *British Journal of Social Psychology, 23,* 323–333.

Wilder, D. A. (1986). Social categorization: Implications for creation and reduction of intergroup bias. In L. Berkowitz (Ed.), *Advances in experimental social psychology* (pp. 291–355). Orlando, FL: Academic Press.

Worchel, S. (1979). Cooperation and the reduction of intergroup conflict: Some determining factors. In W. G. Austin & S. Worchel, *The social psychology of intergroup relations* (pp. 262–273). Monterey CA: Brooks/Cole.

Worchel, S., Axsom, D., Ferris, F., Samaha, C., & Schweitzer, S. (1978). Factors determining the effect of intergroup cooperation on intergroup attraction. *Journal of Conflict Resolution, 22,* 428–439.

Zander, A., Stotland, E., & Wolfe, D. (1960). Unity of group identification with group, and self-esteem of members. *Journal of Personality, 28,* 463–478.

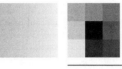

Intergroup Contact: The Typical Member and the Exception to the Rule

David A. Wilder • Rutgers, The State University of New Jersey

Three studies examined the role of the perceived typicalness of an out-group member on her effectiveness in improving evaluations of her group. Subjects were students at two adjacent colleges. In the first study they interacted with a member of the out-group college. The interaction was either pleasant or unpleasant, and the contact person either confirmed or disconfirmed several stereotypes of the out-group (typicalness manipulation). Subjects evaluated the out-group most favorably when they interacted with the typical-pleasant member of the outgroup. The second study demonstrated that contact with a highly typical member is not beneficial if her typicalness is based on stereotypes that reflect negatively on the subject's in-group. Several explanations of the typicalness findings were considered in a third study. Support was found for the hypothesis that the more typical member is perceived to be more predictive of the personality and actions of other out-group members.

S tudies of intergroup relations have demonstrated that contact between members of hostile groups can be effective in reducing bias. Conditions conducive to successful contact include cooperation in the successful pursuit of common goals, contact between equal-status group members, and contact promoted by an authority (Allport, 1954; Amir, 1976; Riordin, 1978). As reviews of the contact literature indicate, even these favorable conditions do not guarantee a lessening of bias between the groups.

For one thing, conditions that are objectively favorable, from the vantage point of someone outside the relationship, may not be interpreted as such by the participants. Much of the social perception literature suggests that our responses to others are influenced by our attributions about the causes and motivations of their actions. Surely we would not expect a contact situation to be effec-

tive if the parties are coerced to be pleasant to one another. In that situation they would simply discount each other's behavior as externally mandated and not indicative of their true feelings.

Another way of discounting positive actions of out-group members is to dissociate them from their group. If they are judged to be atypical of the out-group, an "exception to the rule" so to speak, then their pleasant behavior need not disturb our existing cognitions about the out-group (Pettigrew, 1979). Many of us can recall instances in which persons who harbor prejudices against an out-group have nevertheless interacted amicably with specific out-group members. When called upon to explain their behavior, they reason that these out-group members are not like the rest. Indeed, to the extent the "pleasant exception" is different from typical out-group members, he/she may actually reinforce the perceiver's stereotypes of the out-group, thereby making a change in evaluation of the whole out-group unlikely. The pleasant exception is "proof" that typical members are unpleasant. Success of contact depends, therefore, on the perceived relationship between the contact person and the group he/she represents.

The "typical" out-group member should match many of the stereotypes held about the out-group while the "atypical" member confirms few of them. Research on stereotype change suggests that individuals resist information contrary to their stereotypes by subtyping the discrepant information (Weber & Crocker, 1983). In other words, they partition the "exceptions" as a subset of the out-group category and, by implication, not representative of the out-group as a whole.

Social categorization theorists (Brown & Turner, 1981; Tajfel & Turner, 1979) posit that social interactions vary along an interpersonal–intergroup continuum. To be successful in changing an evaluation of an out-group, favorable contact with an out-group member must be defined as an intergroup encounter. A weak association between the contact person and the out-group (atypical member) lessens the intergroup nature of the interaction. Furthermore, persons expect differences between groups and relative homogeneity within groups (Park & Rothbart, 1982; Quattrone & Jones, 1980; Wilder, 1984). Atypical out-group members violate that expectation and may be more easily dissociated from the out-group than be the source of a change in one's evaluation of the out-group. Three hypotheses follow from the above arguments:

1. A positive interaction with an out-group member will have a favorable impact on one's evaluation of the out-group when that member is perceived to be highly typical of the out-group; in other words, when he/she corresponds closely to one's expectations about members of that group.
2. A positive interaction with an out-group member will have little impact on one's evaluation of the out-group when that member is perceived to be atypical of the out-group.
3. A negative interaction with an out-group member will have an unfavorable impact on one's evaluation of the out-group regardless of how typical he/she is of that group. Clearly, an unpleasant interaction with a typical out-group

member should be harmful to one's evaluation of the out-group. That the same should occur for unpleasant contact with an atypical member is less clear. To begin with, unpleasant behavior by any out-group member reinforces one's negative expectations of the out-group. Moreover, negative behavior by an atypical member may increase her/his perceived typicalness. Fulfillment of the negative expectations makes him/her appear to be more typical of the out-group than had events gone more favorably.

Experiment 1

To test hypotheses 1, 2, and 3, subjects were recruited from two ongoing groups that have some negative expectations about each other. Subjects were female students from two adjacent colleges. Although members of an ongoing social group, they participated in a short laboratory study. In this manner we were able to draw subjects from real social groups while retaining substantial control over their interactions. Subjects in the study interacted with a member of the out-group college over a two-day period. The out-group member was a confederate who either behaved in a positive or a negative manner, and who either appeared to be very typical or atypical of the out-group. The experimental design was a 2 (college identity of confederate: Douglass College, Rutgers College) × 2 (behavior of confederate: positive, negative) × 2 (typicalness of confederate: high, low) between subjects factorial.

Method

SUBJECTS

Subjects were 62 female undergraduates; 30 from Douglass College and 32 from Rutgers College. Eligibility was restricted to upperclasswomen who were not psychology majors. At the time of the research Douglass and Rutgers Colleges were two independent undergraduate colleges comprising a part of Rutgers, The State University of New Jersey. Rutgers and Douglass women hold a fairly complementary set of stereotypes about each other (Wilder & Thompson, 1980). For instance, Rutgers women thought Douglass women were overly concerned with their appearance and good grades while Douglass women thought Rutgers women were interested in having a good time at the expense of scholarship. In addition, Douglass women were perceived to be rather conservative while Rutgers women were considered to be liberal. Pretesting indicated that students preferred their in-group college.

PROCEDURE

The study was conducted in a classroom building a couple of miles away from the Rutgers psychology building. The confederate was blind to the hypotheses. The experimenter asked the subject and accomplice to wait in an adjacent room and introduce themselves while materials for the study were being assembled. The manipulation of typicalness occurred at this point.

Typical contact person. In half of the sessions the confederate dressed and presented herself in a manner designed to fit subjects' stereotypes of the out-group (either Douglass or Rutgers, depending, of course, on the college membership of the subject). When the confederate posed as a Douglass student, she wore a skirt and blouse and a moderate amount of makeup. She introduced herself as a junior from Douglass majoring in home economics (a major available only at Douglass). She mentioned that she hoped the experiment would be brief because she had a lot of studying to do. When the experimenter stated that subjects would have to return the next day to complete the study, she checked her appointment book to see if that conflicted with a meeting of her conservative political club. Thus, the typical Douglass student exhibited three characteristics (conservatism, neatness, studiousness) that were found in pretesting and earlier research to be attributed to Douglass women by Rutgers women (Wilder & Thompson, 1980).

When the confederate posed as a typical Rutgers student, she wore faded jeans, a plaid shirt that was too large, and no makeup. She introduced herself as a junior from Rutgers majoring in Economics (one of the more popular majors at the college). She mentioned that she hoped the experiment would be brief because she had to get ready for a party that evening. When the experimenter stated that subjects would be required to return the next day, she checked her appointment book to see if that conflicted with a meeting of her liberal political club. Thus, compared to the typical

Douglass student, the typical Rutgers woman was portrayed to be more liberal, less neat, and less studious.

Atypical contact person. The confederate identified herself as a biological science major. When she hailed from Douglass College, the confederate dressed and behaved like the typical member from Rutgers College (as described above). When ostensibly a Rutgers student, she dressed and acted like the typical student from Douglas. Thus, the atypical contact person was the antithesis of what subjects expected a typical member of the outgroup to be like.[1]

Once the introductions were completed, the experimenter led the participants to an adjacent room and asked them to sit in separate booths. He stated that he was interested in comparing the performance of groups of various sizes and member composition. The subjects were in the "two-persons-heterogeneous condition" because each was a student from a different college. He encouraged subjects to cooperate and do their best because their performance would be compared with that of other sized groups. This instruction was designed to promote cooperation between the participants because that has been shown to be an important condition for successful contact. Then the subject and confederate were given a set of problem-solving tasks that required 40 min to complete (short essays, anagrams, riddles). Each task was timed so that speed as well as accuracy affected the group's score. As they completed each task, they compared their responses by exchanging answer sheets between the booths. The pleasantness of the interaction was varied at this point.

Pleasant contact. The confederate gave the correct or most popular responses to 60% of the exercises. (From pretesting, tasks had been selected so that subjects completed 70% of them within the time constraints.) In addition, the confederate wrote brief comments of approval about the subject's performance when she succeeded or

---

[1]The atypical contact person matched stereotypes out-group members held about the subject's in-group. Perhaps subjects viewed the atypical person as similar to themselves. But remember that the stereotypes were those that each group had of the other; they were not beliefs subscribed to by subjects about their own groups. Pretesting had indicated that students at neither college shared the stereotypes each attributed to the other. Moreover, if the atypical member was more similar to the subject, that makes the hypotheses harder to confirm because they predicted the typical member would be the more effective representative of the out-group.

agreed (e.g., "I agree," "good idea") and encouraging comments in response to failure or disagreement (e.g., "We'll do better next time," "I understand your opinion but feel differently").

Unpleasant contact. The confederate succeeded on the same number of tasks. (Success was held constant so that any effect of the pleasant-unpleasant manipulation would be due solely to the affective relations between the two rather than to any differences in attributions about the confederate's competency.) But written reactions to the subject's performance were unhelpful and denigrating (e.g., "poor idea," "You blew it").

After completing the tasks, subjects were scheduled to return for a second session the following day. The tasks were similar but fewer, requiring a total of 20 min. The purpose of the second session was to reinforce the subject's initial impression of the out-group member. The accomplice's behavior was the same in both sessions, so it would be difficult for subjects to dismiss her behavior on the first day to some transitory mood or chance event. Again tasks were selected so that subjects and the confederate completed about 70% of them successfully.

At the conclusion of the second session, subjects completed a questionnaire designed to assess their impressions of the out-group member and their reactions to the study. Then the experimenter asked them if they would like to earn an extra dollar by completing a short questionnaire about college life ("Survey of College Life") for a colleague who taught at Livingston College (a third college in the Rutgers archipelago). In this manner the second questionnaire was dissociated from the subject's and confederate's colleges as well as the experimenter's study. Acting as a positive model, the confederate quickly agreed to do so, and all subjects followed suit. The second questionnaire contained items soliciting opinions about the five colleges in the Rutgers system (Cook, Douglass, Livingston, Rutgers, and University). At the top of the questionnaire there was a blank space in which the second experimenter indicated the college he was soliciting opinions about that day. He always wrote the out-group college (either Douglass or Rutgers) on each subject's questionnaire. After completing this questionnaire, subjects were debriefed and paid.

Finally, a fifth condition was included as a control or baseline. Subjects in this condition participated in the experiment individually. There was no confederate present at any time. They received the same instructions (with necessary modifications) and completed the same tasks, but there was no contact with a member of an out-group college.

DEPENDENT MEASURES

Three sets of measures were of particular interest: ratings of the contact person (confederate), evaluations of the out-group as a whole, and stereotypes of the out-group.

Three measures on the first questionnaire assessed subjects' reactions to the confederate. On 7-point bipolar scales they rated the helpfulness of the out-group person, their desire to have the out-group member as a partner again, and how typical the out-group member appeared to be of her college.

The second questionnaire, administered under the guise of a separate research project, contained three items evaluating the out-group as a whole. These were constructed as 11-point bipolar scales. (Eleven-point scales were used to make these items dissimilar in form from the seven-point items in the first questionnaire). Two questions asked subjects to rate the quality of education and the quality of students at the out-group college. End points were labeled "poor" and "excellent." For the third item subjects indicated how strongly they would recommend that a high school acquaintance attend the out-group school. No item directly asked subjects whether they liked the out-group school. A direct query would be perceived as inappropriate in the context of the survey and would be highly reactive.

Three additional measures tapped stereotypes that members of the schools held about each other. Subjects were asked to rate women at "___ College" (either Douglass or Rutgers) as a whole on the following 9-point scales: "conservative"–"liberal"; "neat"–"messy"; "studious"–"frivolous." These characteristics comprised part of the manipulation of typicalness described in the Procedure.

Results and Discussion

SUCCESS OF MANIPULATIONS: RATINGS OF THE CONTACT PERSON

Helpfulness of partner. A $2 \times 2 \times 2$ analysis of this item revealed a main effect for the pleasantness factor, $F(1, 54) = 86.72$, $p < .001$. No other effects were significant. The confederate was rated as more helpful when she was pleasant ($M = 5.41$) than when she was critical ($M = 2.73$).

Desirability of partner. Again pleasantness was the only variable that had a significant impact, $F(1, 54) = 32.87$, $p < .001$. Subjects expressed greater willingness to work with the pleasant out-group member ($M = 5.14$) than the frustrating member ($M = 3.09$) on future tasks. Neither the college affiliation nor typicalness factors affected these ratings.

Typicalness of partner. The $2 \times 2 \times 2$ analysis yielded a marginal effect for college affiliation, $F(91, 54) = 3.55$, $p < .10$, and a strong effect for typicalness, $F(1, 54) = 21.11$, $p < .001$. Subjects rated the typical contact person as more typical of her college ($M = 4.90$) than the atypical out-group member ($M = 3.25$). Douglass subjects judged the contact person (allegedly from Rutgers) to be marginally more typical of her college ($M = 4.43$) than did Rutgers subjects ($M = 3.84$).

EVALUATION OF THE OUT-GROUP

It was hypothesized that pleasant behavior by a typical member of the out-group would generalize to a more positive evaluation of the outgroup. Pleasant behavior by an atypical member or negative behavior by either a typical or atypical member would be ineffective in improving evaluations of the out-group as a whole. These hypotheses predict an interaction between the typicalness and pleasantness factors.

Quality of out-group college. Two items assessed perceived quality of the out-group college: quality of education and quality of students. Data from these measures were significantly correlated, $r = .56$, $t(77) = 5.93$, $p < .01$. Responses were combined to form a single index of quality. The $2 \times 2 \times 2$ analysis of these data revealed significant effects for the typicalness, $F(1, 54) = 4.02$, $p < .05$

and pleasantness factors, $F(1, 54) = 10.76$, $p < .001$. These effects were qualified by a significant typicalness × pleasantness interaction, $F(1, 54) = 6.80$, $p < .05$. As shown in the first line of Table 22.1, subjects rated the out-group significantly more favorably when the contact person was typical and pleasant than in any of the other conditions.

Table 22.1 also includes data from the control condition in which subjects had no contact with an out-group member. (Data were collapsed across college affiliation because there were no differences between Rutgers subjects' ratings of Douglass and Douglass subjects' ratings of Rutgers.) Comparisons with the experimental conditions yielded a significant difference between the control group and the typical-pleasant condition, $t(29) = 2.53$, $p < .01$. Subjects in the latter condition were more favorable ($M = 5.93$) in their evaluation of the out-group than those in the control condition ($M = 4.71$).

Recommendation to a friend. The main effect for pleasantness reached significance, $F(1, 54) = 9.73$, $p < .01$. Subjects recommended the out-group school more strongly when the contact person had been helpful ($M = 5.97$) than unhelpful ($M = 4.78$). The typicalness factor was marginally significant, $F(1, 54) = 3.36$, $p < .10$, but the typicalness × pleasantness interaction was not significant. Nevertheless, an examination of those means (second row of Table 22.1) clearly indicate that the most favorable evaluation of the out-group (i.e., strongest recommendation) occurred when subjects had had pleasant contact with the typical out-group member. The typical-pleasant condition ($M = 6.57$) differed significantly from the typical-unpleasant ($M = 4.86$) and atypical-unpleasant conditions ($M = 4.63$) and marginally from the atypical-pleasant condition ($M = 5.37$).

Individual comparisons between the control and the four experimental conditions revealed that only the typical-pleasant condition differed significantly

TABLE 22.1. Evaluations of the Out-Group College (Experiment 1)

Measure	Pleasant contact		Unpleasant contact		
	Typical	Atypical	Typical	Atypical	Control
Quality of college	5.93$_a$	4.60$_b$	4.24$_b$	4.31$_b$	4.71$_b$
Recommend to friend	6.57$_a$ *	5.37$_{ab}$ *	4.86$_b$	4.63$_b$	5.06$_b$

Note. Row means with completely different subscripts differed at the .05 level of significance or better (Fisher's LSD test). Means are based on 11-point scales.

*Mean values of 6.57 and 5.37 in the second row differed at the .15 level of significance (two-tailed).

from the control, $t(29) = 2.69$, $p < .01$. Subjects who interacted with the helpful, typical member gave a more positive recommendation of the out-group ($M = 6.57$) than those who had had no contact with the out-group ($M = 5.06$).

BELIEFS ABOUT THE OUT-GROUP

Conservatism. The Rutgers out-group was rated less conservative and more liberal ($M = 4.59$) than the Douglass out-group ($M = 5.63$), $F(1, 54) = 5.17$, $p < .05$. No other effects approached significance. These ratings did not differ significantly from the control means ($M = 4.75$ for ratings of Rutgers; $M = 6.11$ for ratings of Douglass). None of the contact manipulations affected subjects' beliefs about the conservatism of the out-group as a whole, even though the contact person expressed either a liberal or conservative orientation.

Neatness. Subjects attributed greater neatness to the Douglass outgroup ($M = 6.47$) than the Rutgers out-group ($M = 5.25$), $F(1, 54) = 11.01$, $p < .001$. No other effects were significant. Control subjects also attributed greater neatness to Douglass ($M = 6.78$) than Rutgers ($M = 5.38$). Again, there was no evidence that the contact experience appreciably affected this belief about the respective out-groups.

Studiousness. The college × typicalness interaction reached significance, $F(1, 54) = 4.16$, $p < .05$ (Table 22.2). Subjects thought the Douglass outgroup more studious ($M = 6.20$) than the Rutgers out-group ($M = 4.81$) when they had interacted with the typical out-group member (who did, in fact, confirm this belief). But there was no difference between means when contact occurred with the atypical member. Differences in studiousness appears to be a weak assumption; although ordered as predicted, control means did not differ significantly for the Douglass and Rutgers out-groups.

Overall, there was no evidence that the contact manipulation affected subjects' stereotypes of the out-group on two measures (conservatism, neatness). For the studiousness item, however, contact with the typical out-group member appeared to reinforce the stereotype while contact with the atypical member diminished differences between groups. But this effect was small. Thus, unlike evaluations of the out-group, beliefs about the out-group seemed to be unchanged by the contact in this study.

TABLE 22.2. Beliefs about the Out-Group: Studiousness (Experiment 1)

| | Experimental conditions | | |
| | Typical contact | Atypical contact | Control condition |
Out-group			
Douglass	6.20_a	5.40_{ab}	5.89_{ab}
Rutgers	4.81_b	5.50_{ab}	5.25_{ab}

Note. Means with completely different subscripts differ at the .05 level of significance (Fisher's LSD test). Larger means indicate stronger attributions of studiousness.

The results of Experiment 1 have several implications. First, as hypothesized, the effectiveness of favorable contact with an out-group member on evaluations of the out-group depends on how typical the person is of her/his group. Second, changes in attitudes toward an out-group may occur without changes in stereotypes of the group (Brigham, 1971; Gurwitz & Dodge, 1977; Locksley, Hepburn, & Ortiz, 1982; Weber & Crocker, 1983). Contact with the pleasant, typical member of the out-group resulted in a more favorable evaluation of the out-group but no change in stereotypes of the out-group. Indeed, contact with a typical member may reinforce the prevailing stereotypes of the out-group because the contact person matches them so well.

But something about this argument does not seem quite right. If outgroups are disliked, in part, because they are thought to possess undesirable characteristics, then typical members will likely possess some of those undesirables. The more an out-group member confirms the negative expectations, the less effective he/she should be in producing a favorable evaluation of the out-group. Intuition suggests that the successful contact person be contrary to stereotypes of the out-group (e.g., Ashmore, 1970; Deutsch & Collins, 1951). The key to this apparent contradiction may lie in the specific stereotypes the contact person displays.

Stereotypes associated with the out-group vary in their relevance to the perceiver's in-group. Some stereotypes have direct implications, usually unfavorable, for the in-group (e.g., "they despise us"; "they think themselves superior to us") while others have no direct bearing on the ingroup (e.g., "they are short"; "they are indolent"). The manipulation of typicalness in Experiment 1 employed beliefs about the out-group that had no direct references to the in-group (e.g., confederate's appearance, political orientation, studiousness, degree major). Furthermore, the contact person made no explicit comparisons between her group and the subject's in-group.

Experiment 2

A second experiment examined the effectiveness of contact with an out-group member who appeared to be very typical by confirming beliefs directly involving the subject's in-group. It was hypothesized that pleasant contact with this "typical" out-group member would be less successful than pleasant contact with the "typical" out-group member of Experiment 1. Employing the methodology of the first study, subjects had a pleasant interaction with an out-group member who confirmed stereotypes of the out-group that either involved no negative evaluation of the subject's in-group (irrelevant condition) or a negative evaluation of the in-group (relevant condition). Subjects in the irrelevant condition should generalize their positive experience with the contact person to a more positive evaluation of the out-group. But little generalization should occur in the relevant condition where the contact person, although pleasant, reinforced beliefs about the out-group that had negative implications for the in-group.

Method

SUBJECTS

Subjects were 33 female undergraduates from Rutgers College. All were juniors and seniors; none were psychology majors. Three subjects expressed suspicion about the authenticity of the confederate's actions; their data were omitted. No subjects were recruited from Douglass College. Because there were no significant interactions involving college membership in Experiment 1, replication of this factor seemed an unnecessary expense.

PROCEDURE

Typical-relevant condition. This condition was identical to the typical-pleasant condition of Experiment 1 with one qualification. In addition to displaying the "typical" characteristics described above, the contact person confirmed the belief that Douglass women thought themselves superior to Rutgers women. Pretesting had indicated that be-

cause Douglass College had maintained its original identity as a women's college, Douglass women were thought to be elitist. They were perceived to feel special and superior to those who chose to attend the coeducational colleges at Rutgers. The confederate capitalized on this belief by making some disparaging comparisons between Douglass and Rutgers. She mentioned during the introductions that she was offered a choice of attending Douglass or Rutgers. She was glad she chose Douglass because it provided women with a better opportunity to reach their potentials. She also felt that the Douglass campus was more beautiful than the Rutgers campus. Her experience taking courses at both colleges indicated that Douglass was more selective in attracting quality students and faculty. It is important to note that these comments were made at the beginning of the session, prior to participation in the tasks. The confederate was pleasant and helpful while working on the tasks.

Typical-irrelevant condition. The procedure was the same as in the preceding condition with one modification. The target of the confederate's unfavorable comparisons was Livingston College, not Rutgers College. Thus, the confederate's behavior was the same in both the relevant and irrelevant conditions. The only difference was whether the target of her elitist remarks was the in-group or another out-group.

Atypical-unpleasant-irrelevant condition (control). This condition was identical to the atypical-unpleasant condition of Experiment 1. It was included to assess the effectiveness of the typicalness and pleasantness manipulations.

Dependent measures were the same as those employed in Experiment 1. Data from the items were analyzed in a single-factor design with three conditions.

Results and Discussion

SUCCESS OF MANIPULATIONS: RATINGS OF THE CONTACT PERSON

Helpfulness. Conditions differed strongly, $F(2, 27) = 19.76$, $p < .001$. Subjects accurately reported that the partner was more helpful in the typical-relevant ($M = 5.10$) and typical-irrelevant conditions ($M = 5.50$) than in the control condition ($M = 2.60$).

Desirability. Subjects reported a greater desire to interact with the confederate when she was pleasant in the typical-irrelevant condition (M = 5.30) than when she was unpleasant in the control condition (M = 3.00), $F(2, 27) = 7.93$, $p < .01$. Although the confederate behaved pleasantly in the typical-relevant condition, she was viewed as significantly less desirable as a future partner (M = 4.10) than in the typical-irrelevant condition ($p < .05$). The typical-relevant and control conditions differed marginally ($p < .10$). Evidently the negative comments directed at the in-group poisoned the relationship between the subject and confederate somewhat, even though the latter's subsequent aid was recognized as such on the helpfulness item.

Typicalness. This manipulation was successful, $F(2, 27) = 5.24$, $p < .05$. Subjects rated the out-group member as more typical of the out-group in the typical-irrelevant (M = 4.90) and typical-relevant conditions (M = 4.70) than in the control condition (M = 3.30).

Overall, ratings of the confederate paralleled those found in the first study and indicated that the manipulations were successful.

EVALUATION OF THE OUT-GROUP

Quality of out-group college. Analysis of the combined scores for the quality of education and students measures yielded a significant effect, $F(2, 27) = 6.58$, $p < .05$ (Table 22.3). Ratings of the out-group were similar to those reported in Experiment 1 for the replicated typical-pleasant (typical-irrelevant in Experiment 2) and atypical-unpleasant (control in Experiment 2) conditions (M = 6.30 and M = 4.90, respectively). Subjects in the former condition evaluated the out-group more favorably. But evaluation of the out-group in the typical-relevant condition (M = 5.08) was no more favorable than in the control condition and significantly less positive than in the typical-irrelevant condition.

Recommendation to a friend. The same pattern of means emerged for this item, $F(2, 27) = 7.98$, $p < .01$ (Table 22.3). Subjects in the typical-irrelevant condition were more willing to recommend the out-group college (M = 6.90) than were subjects in either the typical-relevant (M = 5.50) or control conditions (M = 5.10).

Stereotypes of the out-group. There were no differences among conditions on any of the three measures. Means for the two conditions replicated from Experiment 1 were nearly the same as those reported in Experiment 1. Condition means were as follows: conservatism, typical-relevant = 5.50, typical-irrelevant = 5.80, control = 5.10; neatness, typical-relevant = 5.90, typical-irrelevant = 6.00, control = 5.40; studiousness, typical-relevant = 5.70, typical-irrelevant = 6.00, control = 5.50.

In summary, Experiment 2 demonstrated that pleasant contact with a typical out-group member can improve intergroup relations when the out-group member's typicalness is based on characteristics that do not involve negative actions directed at the in-group. Note that the typical out-group member confirmed a negative stereotype (elitism) in both the typical-relevant and irrelevant conditions. But it reduced the effectiveness of contact only when the target was the in-group. Thus, increasing the typicalness of contact persons will be counterproductive if that increase is purchased through the display of negative stereotypes involving the in-group.

Experiments 1 and 2 established the importance of the typicalness variable in contact settings. But neither study attempted to explain why the manipulation of typicalness led to the observed outcomes. A third study was designed to gather data relevant to the following explanations.

Consistency hypothesis. If the typical out-group member closely fits the perceiver's image of the out-group, then the association between the typical member and the out-group category should be

TABLE 22.3. Evaluations of the Out-Group College (Experiment 2)

	Condition		
	Typical-relevant	Typical-irrelevant	Atypical-unpleasant (control)
Quality of out-group college	5.08$_a$	6.30$_b$	4.90$_a$
Recommendation to a friend	5.50$_a$	6.90$_b$	5.10$_a$

Note. Means with different subscripts differ at the .05 level of significance (Fisher's LSD test). Larger means indicate attributions of greater quality or a more favorable recommendation.

quite strong. Relative to the atypical member, the typical member is in a stronger unit relationship with the out-group, so pressures for a consistent evaluation of both should be greater (Heider, 1958). Consequently, the out-group as a whole benefits more from positive contact with the typical than the atypical member.

Representativeness hypothesis. Because the typical out-group member possesses many of the characteristics thought to be common in the outgroup, the typical member should be highly predictive of others in the out-group. Evidence that she is a pleasant, cooperative individual carries weight in judgments about the out-group as a whole. Although the pleasant, atypical member may be appreciated for her actions, her unrepresentativeness precludes generalizations from her behavior to the group as a whole.

Contrast hypothesis. Given the existence of some intergroup animosity, pleasant contact should be less expected with the typical than the atypical out-group member. Favorable contact with the typical member may seem to be more positive than the same experience with the less typical member (analogous to contrast effects in interpersonal evaluations and judgments; e.g., Aronson & Linder, 1965; Sherif, 1967).

Status hypothesis. Because the typical out-group member confirms more stereotypes of the out-group, she may be perceived as high in status and more influential than the less typical member. A pleasant interaction with the more powerful member may be more satisfying, resulting in a more favorable evaluation.

Two additional hypotheses consider the possibility that the typicalness findings were unique to the population of Experiments 1 and 2. Perhaps the typical out-group member possessed more desirable characteristics than the less typical person (*desirability hypothesis*). Alternatively, the typical member may have been more similar than the atypical member to the perceiver (*similarity hypothesis*).

None of the six explanations is independent of the others. Nevertheless, to narrow the field somewhat, a third study was conducted partially replicating the first two experiments. Subjects interacted with a confederate who appeared to be a typical or atypical member of the out-group college. Then subjects were asked a set of questions that provided data relevant to the hypotheses outlined above.

Experiment 3

Method

SUBJECTS

Twenty female undergraduates were recruited from Rutgers College. None were psychology majors and none were freshwomen.

PROCEDURE

The purpose of Experiment 3 was to examine why the typical contact manipulation had a greater impact on evaluations of the out-group in the pleasant condition than the atypical manipulation. Subjects were randomly assigned to either of those two conditions from Experiment 1: typical-pleasant or atypical-pleasant conditions. The procedure of Experiment 1 was followed to the end of the first day's session. At that point subjects completed a questionnaire containing the dependent measures.

DEPENDENT MEASURES

The first item required subjects to list as much information about the other person (confederate) as they could remember "including what she told you, what she looked like, how she behaved, and anything else you can recall." Subjects were provided with 20 numbered blank lines to list information. No subject used more than 10 nor fewer than five lines. After completing this item, subjects turned to the second page and answered 9 questions constructed as 9-point scales. These questions were randomly ordered for each subject. At least one question was relevant to each of the interpretations of the typical/atypical finding. The number of questions was kept to a minimum to minimize potential artifacts due to demands and fatigue.

Consistency hypothesis. The open-ended recall measure was examined for references to the contact person's affiliation with her in-group (Douglass College). To the extent the typical out-group member is perceived to be in a strong unit relationship with the outgroup, that membership should be especially salient to the observer. Consequently, mention of the contact person's association with the Douglass group should occur more often and earlier in descriptions of the typical than the atypical member. This measure is a rough index of the perceived bond between the contact person and the out-group. Unfortunately, direct attempts to tap the "goodness of fit" between the typical manipulation and the outgroup category proved fruitless with pretest subjects. (For instance, when asked how closely the typical member came to their image of the "ideal" out-group member, some subjects interpreted "ideal" as what they thought the out-group member ought to be like.) The recall item always appeared first in the questionnaire to avoid contamination by other measures that directed attention to specific aspects of the confederate.

Representativeness hypothesis. Based on their interaction with the out-group member, subjects estimated the percentage of other out-group members (a) who had similar personalities and (b) who would behave like her. The 9-point scales were labeled from 10 to 90% in increments of 10.

Contrast hypothesis. On separate measures subjects rated (a) the helpfulness and (b) the extent to which they expected the contact person to behave as she did.

Status hypothesis. On 9-point scales subjects indicated (a) how influential and (b) how popular they thought the contact person was with her peers.

Desirability hypothesis. Subjects rated the extent to which the contact person possessed qualities that they would find desirable in a person.

Similarity hypothesis. Subjects rated the degree of similarity between the contact person and themselves.

Finally, subjects indicated how much they liked the out-group member based upon what they knew about her. A difference for the typical manipulation would be predicted by several of the hypotheses (Desirability, Similarity, Status, Contrast). Therefore, a significant difference would not be particularly supportive of any one interpretation, but no difference would help eliminate several hypotheses.

Results and Discussion

Consistency hypothesis. All subjects mentioned the contact person's membership in the out-group (Douglass College) as part of their open-ended description of her. Interestingly, nearly twice as many subjects in the typical condition ($n = 7$) than in the atypical condition ($n = 4$) mentioned the out-group in the first half of their lists, suggesting a stronger connection between the typical member and her group. This difference, however, was not significant, $\chi^2(1) = .89$.

Representativeness hypothesis. Subjects who interacted with the typical out-group member thought that more others in the out-group shared her personality ($M = 5.60$, approximately 56%) than did subjects who interacted with the atypical out-group member ($M = 3.50$, approximately 35%), $t(18) = 3.04$, $p < .01$. Similarly, the behavior of the typical member was judged to be more predictive of the behavior of other out-group members in the typical condition ($M = 6.80$, approximately 68%) than in the atypical condition ($M = 4.90$, approximately 49%), $t(18) = 2.90$, $p < .01$. These findings suggest that the more positive evaluation of the out-group following contact with the typical member can be interpreted in terms of the ease with which subjects generalized from that person to others in the out-group. The personality and behavior of the typical member was considered to be more indicative of what others in the out-group would be like and how they would behave in that setting.

With one exception, analysis of the other measures failed to discern any differences between the typical and atypical conditions. Subjects liked the contact person more when she was atypical ($M = 6.50$) than typical ($M = 5.50$) of her group, $t(18) = 2.07$, $p < .07$. Hence, there was no evidence to support the status, desirability, similarity, or contrast hypotheses. This does not necessarily mean that those interpretations have no impact on the success of intergroup contact; findings do suggest that they are inadequate explanations for the paradigm employed here.

General Discussion

There is consensus in the literature that face-to-face contact can be effective in improving intergroup relations if the contact occurs under cooperative conditions. The studies in this paper echoed that conclusion with pleasant, cooperative contact producing a more favorable evaluation of a rival out-group college. Moreover, the person with whom one has contact significantly affects the success of contact. Contact with a person who appeared to be highly typical of the out-group (i.e., matched several stereotypes of out-group members) led to a more favorable evaluation of the out-group than contact with a less typical member. Among the several possible interpretations of this finding, only one received support. Subjects judged the typical member's personality and behavior to be more indicative of how others in the out-group would act in the contact setting. Apparently, greater generalization of successful contact to evaluations of the out-group as a whole was due to the typical member being viewed as more predictive of the others in the out-group. Because she behaved favorably in the setting, there was a good chance that others would behave likewise.

Although contact with the out-group member affected evaluations of the out-group, contact had virtually no impact on stereotypes of the outgroup. Subjects were no less likely to endorse prevailing stereotypes when the contact person was atypical than when she was typical. Perhaps a single contact experience is insufficient to change prevailing beliefs about the out-group as a whole; beliefs that may be based on multiple confirming examples (Rothbart, 1981). Characteristics of the contact person (e.g., neatness, studiousness, conservatism) may be "averaged" in some manner with the existing store of contact experiences, thereby diluting the effect of the present interaction. Multiple exceptions may also be subtyped without affecting beliefs about the out-group as a whole (Weber & Crocker, 1983). Rather than changing stereotypes, exceptions may simply reduce the likelihood of applying stereotypes in that setting (Gurwitz & Dodge, 1977; Locksley et al., 1982).

Alternatively, the construction of the measures may have facilitated a change in evaluation while hindering a change in beliefs about the out-group. The evaluation items (quality of education and students, recommendation to a friend) required that subjects make a global judgment of the out-group college. The stereotype measures (conservatism, neatness, studiousness) refer to more specific characteristics of out-group members; characteristics for which subjects can recall specific instances. Thus, the latter measures may have been more affected by frequency; that is, subjects were more likely to use other experiences with out-group members in responding to these items as well as the contact experience in the study.

Consideration of the typicalness factor in intergroup contact may help explain the mixed results that often follow contact. To cite one example, in an early study of intergroup contact Young (1932) had a class of graduate students interact over a semester with blacks who were quite favorable models and quite different from existing racial stereotypes (e.g., a doctor, a wealthy and cultured couple, a pianist). Despite the favorable contact over an extended period of time, attitude change was mixed. Some students showed little change; some became more prejudiced; and some became less prejudiced. With perfect hindsight one may wonder if the choices of "atypical" contact persons (relative to the students' expectations) contributed to the meager success of Young's project.

On the other hand, Hamill, Wilson, and Nisbett (1980) reported a strong effect for atypical information on judgments of an out-group. They provided subjects with a description of a humane prison guard who was atypical of guards in general. Subjects given that information judged prison guards to be more humane than a control group not provided with the exception to the rule. Their finding suggests that "contact" with an atypical member can have a powerful effect on evaluations of the out-group. On reflection, however, their work does not contradict our conclusions. In the Hamill et al. research, subjects were asked to make judgments about a group with which they had had little, if any, contact. Contrast that with situations in which subjects have had many contact experiences with both in-group and out-group members (e.g., racial groups, adjacent colleges). Even the "exception to the rule" should influence attitudes toward the out-group as a whole when both knowledge of the out-group and contact experiences are minimal.

The relationship found in Experiments 1 and 2 between typicalness of a contact person and attitude change toward the out-group presents a quandry for the individual out-group member who desires to elicit both a favorable reaction to his/her group and her/himself. Benefit from positive contact will accrue to the group to the extent the person is viewed as typical of his/her group. But maximum benefit for the individual may result from being dubbed an exception to the rule, particularly if that inference implies superior abilities and more favorable attributes relative to the "typical" out-group member. In our studies the atypical member was liked somewhat better than the typical member even though contact with the typical member was more beneficial to evaluations of the out-group as a whole.

In a relevant study Linville and Jones (1980) presented whites with a description of an applicant to law school who was either white or black and either well or poorly qualified. The black applicant was rated more favorably when well qualified and more unfavorably when poorly qualified than the comparable white applicant. Assuming whites have a narrower range of expected performance for blacks than whites (which would be consistent with the assumption of homogeneity in out-groups discussed in the introduction), one interpretation is that the qualified black was viewed as an exception, deserving of praise for rising above expectations. But a comparably qualified white was more "typical" of the broader expectations about the familiar in-group.

The fact that contact situations can become self-fulfilling prophecies further complicates an out-group member's dilemma. To the extent the person is perceived to be highly typical of the out-group, expectations about the out-group may influence the manner in which information is processed (e.g., Snyder, 1981). The degree of bias will be limited by the ease with which the contact person's behavior can be distorted. Clearly positive behavior, such as that found in Experiments 1 and 2, will be difficult to distort. But motives behind actions can always be questioned. For these reasons individual out-group members may attempt to maximize a positive evaluation of themselves by behaving so as to distance themselves from their group.

From this discussion of contact, it appears that members of a negatively evaluated out-group are in a bind. On the one hand, information that strengthens their association with their group should also strengthen the favorable impact of successful contact on evaluations of their group as a whole. But to the extent they appear to be typical of the out-group, they risk confirming unfavorable stereotypes about the out-group, thereby jeopardizing evaluations of themselves as individuals. On the other hand, information that weakens their association with the out-group may encourage more favorable evaluations of themselves as individuals. But to the extent they appear to be atypical of their group, successful contact should have less impact on evaluations of their group.

REFERENCES

Allen, V. L., & Wilder, D. A. (1979). Group categorization and attribution of belief similarity. *Small Group Behavior, 10,* 73–80.

Allport, G. W. (1954). *The nature of prejudice.* Reading, MA: Addison-Wesley.

Amir, Y. (1976). The role of intergroup contact in change of prejudice and ethnic relations. In P. A. Katz (Ed.), *Towards the elimination of racism.* New York: Pergamon.

Aronson, E., & Linder, D. (1965). Gain and loss of esteem as determinants of interpersonal attractiveness. *Journal of Experimental Social Psychology, 1,* 156–171.

Ashmore, R. D. (1970). Solving the problem of prejudice. In B. E. Collins (Ed.), *Social psychology.* Reading, MA: Addison-Wesley.

Brigham, J. C. (1971). Ethnic stereotypes. *Psychological Bulletin, 76,* 15–38.

Brown, R. J., & Turner, J. C. (1981). Interpersonal and intergroup behaviour. In J. C. Turner & H. Giles (Eds.), *Intergroup behavior.* Chicago: University of Chicago Press.

Deutsch, M., & Collins, M. (1951). *Interracial housing: A psychological evaluation of a social experiment.* Minneapolis: University of Minnesota Press.

Gurwitz, S. B., & Dodge, K. A. (1977). Effects of confirmations and disconfirmations on stereotype-based attributions. *Journal of Personality and Social Psychology, 35,* 495–500.

Hamill, R., Wilson, T., & Nisbett, R. (1980). Insensitivity to sample bias: Generalizing from atypical cases. *Journal of Personality and Social Psychology, 39,* 578–589.

Heider, F. (1958). *The psychology of interpersonal relations.* New York: Wiley.

Linville, P. M., & Jones, E. E. (1980). Polarized appraisals of out-group members. *Journal of Personality and Social Psychology, 38,* 689–703.

Locksley, A., Hepburn, C., & Ortiz, V. (1982). Social stereotypes and judgments of individuals: An instance of the base-rate fallacy. *Journal of Experimental Social Psychology, 18,* 23–42.

Park, B., & Rothbart, M. (1982). Perception of out-group homogeneity and levels of social categorization: Memory for the subordinate attributes of in-group and out-group members. *Journal of Personality and Social Psychology, 42,* 1051–1068.

Pettigrew, T. F. (1979). The ultimate attribution error: Extending Allport's cognitive analysis of prejudice. *Personality and Social Psychology Bulletin, 5,* 461–476.

Quattrone, G. A., & Jones, E. E. (1980). The perception of variability within ingroups and outgroups: Implications for the law of small numbers. *Journal of Personality and Social Psychology, 38,* 141–152.

Riordin, C. (1978). Equal-status interracial contact: A review and revision of a concept. *International Journal of Intercultural Relations, 2,* 161–185.

Rothbart, M. (1981). Memory processes and social beliefs. In D. Hamilton (Ed.), *Cognitive processes in stereotyping and intergroup behavior.* Hillsdale, NJ: Erlbaum.

Sherif, M. (1967). *Group conflict and co-operation.* London: Routledge & Kegan Paul.

Snyder, M. (1981). On the self-perpetuating nature of social stereotypes. In D. L. Hamilton (Ed.), *Cognitive processes in stereotyping and intergroup behavior.* Hillsdale, NJ: Erlbaum.

Tajfel, H., & Turner, J. C. (1979). An integrative theory of intergroup conflict. In W. G. Austin & S. Worchel (Eds.), *The social psychology of intergroup relations.* Monterey, CA: Brooks Cole.

Weber, R., & Crocker, J. (1983). Cognitive processes in the revision of stereotypic beliefs. *Journal of Personality and Social Psychology, 45,* 961–977.

Wilder, D. A. (1981). Perceiving persons as a group: Categorization and intergroup relations. In D. L. Hamilton (Ed.), *Cognitive processes in stereotyping and intergroup behavior.* Hillsdale, NJ: Erlbaum.

Wilder, D. A. (1984). Predictions of belief homogeneity and similarity following social categorization. *British Journal of Social Psychology, 23,* 323–333.

Wilder, D. A., & Thompson, J. E. (1980). Intergroup contact with independent manipulation of in-group and out-group interaction. *Journal of Personality and Social Psychology, 38,* 589–603.

Young, D. (1932). *American minority peoples.* New York: Harper.

Dimensions of Contact as Predictors of Intergroup Anxiety, Perceived Out-Group Variability, and Out-Group Attitude: An Integrative Model

Mir Rabiul Işlam • University of Rajshahi
Miles Hewstone • University of Mannheim

This study tested an integrative model of how dimensions of contact (quantitative, qualitative, and intergroup) are related to intergroup anxiety, perceived out-group variability, and out-group attitude. Data were collected in a field study of minority (Hindu) and majority (Muslim) religious groups in Bangladesh. Path analysis revealed that dimensions of contact were significant victors of all three criterion variables, although different dimensions emerged as predictors in each case, and there were some interactions with subjects' religious group. All three dimensions of contact were associated with intergroup anxiety, but whereas quantitative contact had a significant impact on perceived out-group variability, qualitative contact was associated with out-group attitude. The model highlights the central role of intergroup anxiety as associated with dimensions of contact and as a predictor of perceived out-group variability and out-group attitude.

The *contact hypothesis* (Allport, 1954/1979) proposes that contact with persons from a disliked group, under appropriate conditions, leads to the growth of liking and respect for, or at least to decreased prejudice toward, that out-group (e.g., Amir, 1969; Cook, 1984). This article tests an integrative model of the effect of specific types of contact on three criterion variables derived from a review of contemporary research on intergroup relations and stereotyping.

Allport emphasized that there was no simple relationship between contact and out-group evaluations, and he outlined a taxonomy of relevant factors constituting the "nature of contact" (see Allport, 1954/1979, pp. 262–263). These factors included simple measures of the *quantity* of contact and more specific measures of its *quality* (sta-

tus and role aspects of contact, the social atmosphere surrounding contact, etc.). Later reviews of the literature highlighted the potential positive effects of qualitative contact (e.g., equal-status, voluntary, intimate, and cooperative contact; see Amir, 1969).

Recent research has centered on another dimension of contact noted by Allport, whether contact between members of two groups is *interpersonal* or *intergroup*. Brewer and Miller (1984), on the one hand, argue for contact involving the "personalization" of individual outgroup members, rather than their perception as representatives of a particular social category (e.g., Miller, Brewer, & Edwards, 1985). Hewstone and Brown (1986), on the other hand, argued that to be successful in changing the evaluation of an out-group, favorable contact with an out-group member must be defined as an intergroup, rather than an interpersonal, encounter. This means, essentially, that in-group members who have contact with out-group members must, at some level, continue to be aware of the contact person as a member of the out-group and not simply as a positive individual. If this is not the case, positive attitudes cannot generalize. Evidence supporting this claim comes from studies showing that disconfirming attributes become associated with a group stereotype only if they belong to an individual who is otherwise a good fit to the category (Johnston & Hewstone, 1992; Weber & Crocker, 1983; see Rothbart & John, 1985; Rothbart & Lewis, 1988). Wilder (1984) also showed that pleasant contact led to a generalized improvement in out-group evaluation only when contact was with a typical out-group member.

That typicality is important for generalizing from a target out-group member to the out-group as a whole makes sense. Brewer (1988) has recently acknowledged that the "decategorization" implied by personalization reduces the probability that experiences with that individual will be generalized to more inclusive social categories. Yet we can also see that intergroup encounters may overemphasize intergroup differences, accentuate the salience of social categorization, and impede positive contact. As Wilder (1986) pointed out, if stereotypes are negative, then a "typical" out-group member may need to have some negative characteristics; but then, how are we to ensure positive changes in perceptions of the out group (see also Horwitz & Rabbie, 1989)? We explored this paradox by including, among our dimensions of contact, ratings of whether contact targets were seen as individuals or group members and whether they were seen as typical out-group members.

Whereas the first phase of contact research focused on situational dimensions, more recent work has involved detailed analysis of the cognitive processes involved in stereotyping. Rothbart and John's (1985) cognitive analysis emphasizes that objects differ in the degree to which they are viewed as prototypical examples of a category. This insight is linked to a new conception of stereotypes and, we argue, a new criterion variable that should be associated with contact—perceived out-group variability (or category differentiation), as distinct from measures of central tendency (Park & Rothbart, 1982; Quattrone & Jones, 1980).

It is highly plausible that increasing contact between members of two groups should lead to increases in perceived out-group variability (Park, Judd, & Ryan, 1991). This idea is consistent with Linville, Salovey, and Fischer's (1986) contention that greater category familiarity should be associated with greater category differentiation, although there is no simple relationship between the number of group members reported known and variability estimates (Jones, Wood, & Quattrone, 1981). A number of other studies suggesting a link between familiarity and perceived variability failed to include a measure of familiarity (e.g., Linville, Fischer, & Salovey, 1989), with which internal analyses could be conducted to examine, for example, whether individual changes in familiarity were related to changes in perceived variability (see Park et al., 1991). Contact may, moreover, involve much more than familiarity, as we have argued above.

We therefore provided a further test of the association between dimensions of contact and perceived out-group variability. We selected the range measure (e.g., Jones et al., 1981) because Park and Judd (1990) identified it as one of the least errorful of the dispersion measures and therefore more likely to reveal small relationships between contact and perceived variability. We also included a global judgment of similarity (e.g., Quattrone & Jones, 1980) to provide a simple, direct measure of variability. Both these measures assess the perceived dispersion of the groups about their central tendency (Park & Judd, 1990), which captures our idea that contact may be related to the perception that group members are dispersed around a prototype.

As a complement to purely cognitive analyses of contact, Stephan and Stephan (1985) have considered the affective nature of intergroup contact. They proposed that intergroup anxiety stems mainly from the expectation of negative consequences for oneself during contact. Some of the major antecedents of intergroup anxiety may be minimal previous contact with the out-group, the existence of large status differentials, and a high ratio of out-group to in-group members. Stephan and Stephan's own study of Hispanic Americans' perceptions of Anglos showed that high voluntary contact was negatively associated, and that high believed dissimilarity and stereotyping were positively associated with intergroup anxiety. We therefore predicted that increased contact (under appropriate conditions) would be associated with decreased intergroup anxiety and that, in the context of our field study of minority and majority religious groups, intergroup anxiety would be higher for minority group members.

Stephan and Stephan also outlined some consequences of intergroup anxiety, notably information-processing biases. Anxiety is associated, first, with a narrowed focus of attention (Easterbrook, 1959; Kahneman, 1973), which led us to predict that it would have a negative effect on perceived out-group variability. It can also lead to an increase in simplified, schematic, expectancy-confirming processing. Recent research has shown how affective states may increase reliance on stereotyping and expectancy confirmation (e.g., Bodenhausen, 1993; Mackie et al., 1989; Stroessner, Hamilton, & Mackie, 1992). These biases should mitigate the impact of any stereotype-disconfirming encountered during contact, as shown by Wilder and Shapiro (1989) . Thus intergroup anxiety should be at the core of an integrative model of how dimensions of contact influence group perceptions. Our model (see Figure 23.1) highlights three kinds of effects.

First, we tested the effects of different types of contact on intergroup anxiety. We predicted that both quantitative and qualitative aspects of contact would be associated with a reduction in intergroup anxiety. In contrast, given negative intergroup relations, we acknowledged that perception of contact as "intergroup" might be associated with an increase in intergroup anxiety.

Second, we tested the direct effects of contact on both measures of intergroup perception, perceived out-group variability and out-group attitude. We predicted that quantitative contact would have the greatest effect on variability (an indication of the complexity of intergroup perception) but that qualitative contact would be a more important predictor of out-group attitude (an evaluative measure). Again, the effect of intergroup contact is more difficult to predict. It ought to facilitate the generalization of out-group attitudes, but this effect would be undermined if it were associated with increased anxiety.

Third, we focused on the impact of intergroup anxiety on both perceived out-group variability and out-group attitude. From Stephan and Stephan's (1985) work, we predicted that intergroup anxiety would be negatively associated with variability and attitudes. We treated variability and attitude as conceptually distinct, though possibly correlated, criterion measures of contact.

These general predictions may, however, be qualified by interactions with respondents' majority or minority group status. In particular, in a context where minority group members have a much greater opportunity and need for out-group contact, we would expect reported contact to be both higher and a more influential predictor of out-group perceptions for that group. If, however, minority status is associated with intergroup anxiety, then the negative link between anxiety and out-group perceptions should be stronger for minority group members. In testing our integrative model, we therefore tested for interactions between group status and the paths specified in our model.

Thus the reported study tested an integrative model, based on existing theory, of how dimensions of contact are related to intergroup anxiety, perceived out-group variability, and out-group attitude. The research was carried out in the South Asian state of Bangladesh, a country of 110 million people, with a majority of Muslims (86% of the population) and a sizable minority of Hindus (12%). In contrast to neighboring India, the Muslims have political, social, and economic advantages over Hindus, who constitute a social as well as a numerical minority (see Maniruzzaman, 1982; Mukherjee, 1973). There has, however, been less conflict between the groups in Bangladesh than in India, and there is a considerable degree of contact in everyday life (O'Connell, 1976). This country provided, then, a unique, real-life context in which to test our extensions of the contact hypothesis.

Method

Respondents

Respondents were 65 Hindu (52 males and 13 females, mean age 28.06 years) and 66 Muslim (45 males and 21 females, mean age 22.14 years) students at the University of Rajshahi, Bangladesh.

Questionnaire

A detailed, back-translated questionnaire in Bengali contained measures of the perceived dimensions of contact and three criterion variables (intergroup anxiety, perceived out-group variability, and out-group attitude) as well as a supplementary question.

Contact variable. These questions were organized around three categories of contact; all responses were measured on 7-point bipolar scales (1–7), unless otherwise noted, and the relevant out-group (Hindu or Muslim) was always specified by name, without using the term *out-group.* Subjects were asked to respond with reference to the typical contact situation, as they experienced it.

To assess *quantitative aspects of contact,* five questions asked about "amount of contact with" the out-group: (a) at college, (b) as neighbors, (c) as close friends (*none at all—a great deal*), (d) frequency of informal talks with the out-group (*not at all—very often*), and (e) frequency of visits to an out-group home (*never—very often*). Higher scores denote more quantitative contact.

Five questions assessed *qualitative aspects of contact:* whether contact was "perceived as equal" (*definitely not—definitely yes*), "involuntary or voluntary" (*definitely involuntary—definitely voluntary*), "superficial or intimate" (*very superficial—very intimate*), "experienced as pleasant" (*not at all—very*), and "competitive or cooperative" (*very competitive—very cooperative*). Higher scores denote qualitatively better contact.

To assess *intergroup aspects of contact,* two questions asked whether "when you came into contact with [members of the out-group], you felt you met as individuals or as members representing your respective religious groups" (*as individuals—as group members*) and whether "you usually saw the [out-group members] with whom you have contact as typical [out group members]" (*not at all typical—very typical*). Higher scores denote more "intergroup" contact.

Finally, one *supplementary question* concerned the relative numbers of in-group and out-group members present in intergroup contact situations (possible answers: a single out-group member and me; several out-group members and me as a sole in-group member; a single out-group member and several in-group members; several in-group and out-group members).

Criterion variables. Three criterion variables were assessed.

To measure *intergroup anxiety,* Stephan and Stephan's (1985) intergroup anxiety scale was used. Respondents were asked, "If you were the only member of your religious group and you were interacting with people from another religious [Hindu or Muslim] group (e.g., talking with them,

working on a project with them), how would you feel compared with occasions when you are interacting with people from your own religious group?" Respondents marked on 7-point scales whether they would feel more or less awkward, self-conscious, happy, accepted, confident, irritated, impatient, defensive, suspicious, and careful (*not at all—very*). One item ("certain") was dropped from the original scale because we could not translate it precisely. Higher scores denote higher intergroup anxiety.

We assessed *perceived out-group variability* by asking respondents to rate where, on average, on each of eight dimensions, the out-group fell, using 7-point scales. On the same scales, respondents indicated where the most extreme members would fall on both sides of the scale. The eight scales (aggressive, conservative, cool-headed, deceitful, hospitable, intelligent, patriotic, and selfish) were chosen because they were not assigned stereotypically to one specific religious group; scales were anchored with the endpoints *not at all—extremely.* The difference between the rated extremes (full range) was calculated on each dimension, higher scores denoting greater variability. Respondents also rated the out-group on a direct measure of intragroup similarity (*they're all completely different from one another—they're pretty much alike*). Higher scores denote greater similarity.

As an assessment of *out-group attitude,* respondents marked on a single 7-point scale their "overall attitude toward [the out-group]" (*strongly negative—strongly positive*).[1] Higher scores denote more positive attitudes.

Procedure

Questionnaires were distributed to students individually in their dormitories by a research assistant of their own religious group and were collected within the hour. We knew in advance the religious group of each subject, from the full residence list. In this culture, students' religious group can easily be identified by their names. More than 95% of Muslim students use Arabic names, whereas Hindu students use either Bengali or San-

---

[1]A pilot study had shown that this single-item criterion was significantly correlated with a highly reliable measure employing 12 evaluative adjectives; $r(50) = .374, p < .01$, for Hindus; $r(50) = .357, p < .01$, for Muslims. We used the single-item measure to shorten the questionnaire.

skrit names. All questionnaires were completed anonymously, and respondents were told that data were being collected from other universities simultaneously, so that they would not think they were the only respondents. Our pilot study had shown that Hindus, particularly, felt suspicious if they thought they had been specially selected. Five Hindu and four Muslim students from the original sample approached declined to complete the questionnaire.

Results

Overview

To provide background information about the context of Hindu-Muslim relations in Bangladesh, we first compared the mean responses of the two groups on all the variables. We then computed a factor analy-

sis to reduce the set of possible predictors, before computing a path analysis to investigate the relationship between different types of contact and our three criterion variables. There were no differences as a function of respondents' sex, and so the data are collapsed across this variable.

Hindu-Muslim Comparisons

Because, at this stage, we were interested in specific dimensions, we conducted separate univariate analyses of variance (ANOVAs), although we adopted a stricter criterion of significance ($p < .01$) to protect against Type I errors (see Huberty & Morris, 1989). Mean ratings of Hindus and Muslims were compared using one-way ANOVAs. The means, standard deviations, and ANOVA details for all contact and criterion variables are shown in Table 23.1.

TABLE 23.1. Mean Ratings on Contact and Criterion Variables for Hindu and Muslim Respondents

| | Religious Group of Respondent | | | | |
| | Hindu (Minority) | | Muslim (Majority) | | |
Variable	Mean	SD	Mean	SD	F(1, 129)
Contact variables					
Quantitative aspects of contact					
Contact in college	5.63	1.67	4.94	1.90	4.89
Contact as neighbor	4.74	2.31	3.50	2.09	10.33*
Contact as friend	4.89	2.09	3.83	2.03	8.62*
Frequency of informal talks	5.49	1.90	4.94	1.87	2.81
Frequency of family visit	4.18	1.92	3.50	1.76	4.53
Factor Score 1 (see Table 23.2)	0.33	0.99	−0.33	0.90	15.84*
Qualitative aspects of contact					
Contact perceived as equal	4.52	2.42	6.19	1.63	21.65*
Contact involuntary or voluntary	5.36	2.02	5.60	1.73	1.84
Contact superficial or intimate	4.40	2.41	4.92	1.96	1.87
Contact experienced as pleasant	4.25	2.26	5.17	1.47	7.63*
Contact competitive or cooperative	4.18	2.42	4.93	1.72	4.25
Factor score 2	−0.39	1.10	0.38	0.72	22.58*
Intergroup aspects of contact					
Contact seen in terms of individuals or group members	2.29	1.90	2.36	2.01	< 1
Out-group members seen as typical	5.03	1.72	4.36	1.96	4.26
Factor score 3	0.06	0.90	−0.05	1.09	< 1
Criterion variables					
Intergroup anxiety	4.77	1.16	3.07	1.05	30.20*
Perceived out-group variability	3.38	0.81	3.18	0.73	2.25
Perceived out-group similarity	5.40	1.79	5.00	1.26	2.27
Out-group attitude	3.38	1.79	4.07	1.25	6.55*

Note: Ratings could range from 1 to 7; higher number indicates more quantitative contact, qualitatively better contact, more intergroup contact, greater perceived typicality, higher intergroup anxiety, greater perceived out-group variability and similarity, and more positive out-group attitude.

*$p < .01$.

Contact variables. There were significant differences between the ratings of Hindu and Muslim respondents within each of the three broad categories of contact we assessed. For quantitative aspects of contact, Hindus reported significantly more contact as neighbors and as friends than Muslims. For qualitative aspects of contact, Hindus reported contact to be less equal and less pleasant than Muslims. The groups did not differ in perceived intergroup aspects of contact.

When reporting the respective numbers of in-group and out-group members present during contact, Hindus were less likely than Muslims to report contact involving "a single out-group member and me" (frequencies: 9 vs. 18) or "a single out-group member and several in-group members" (6 vs. 32) and more likely to report that contact involved "several out-group members and me as a sole in-group member" (40 vs. 4). The groups were equally likely to report contact involving "several out group and in-group members" (10 vs. 12) . A 2 × 4 chi-square analysis revealed a significant association between religious group of respondents and number of in-group and out-group members involved in contact situations, $\chi^2 (3) = 50.42, p < .0001$.

Criterion variables. Before computing comparisons, we created two composite measures to provide more reliable variables. For intergroup anxiety, we averaged scores across the 10-item scale (with items recoded so that high scores indicate high anxiety) to yield a reliable index (alphas = .858 and .774 for Hindus and Muslims, respectively). For perceived out-group variability, a factor analysis on the eight range ratings on evaluative traits revealed one unrotated factor that had a large eigenvalue for each group (4.25 and 3.85 for Hindus and Muslims, respectively) and accounted for a high percentage of variance (53% and 48%). Scores on the first factor provided an index of perceived out-group variability.

There were two significant differences between the groups on the criterion variables. As expected, Hindus reported greater intergroup anxiety than Muslims. Hindus also reported a significantly less positive attitude toward the out-group than Muslims. Neither the full-range measure of perceived out-group variability nor the direct measure of perceived out-group similarity revealed differences between the groups. We included the direct measure of similarity only in case respondents had difficulties with the range measure. As the mea-

sures were significantly correlated for both groups ($r[65] = -.533, p < .0001$, for Hindus; $r[66] = -.383, p < .01$, for Muslims), we focused on the measure of variability.[2]

Factor Analysis

Because we included such a large number of contact variables, which we had tried to group into categories we undertook some data reduction prior to path analysis. We computed a factor analysis on all 12 contact variables, using orthogonal (varimax) rotation to minimize collinearity and to highlight the contrast between factors. Table 23.2 shows the three factors that emerged, along with constituent variables and interpretive labels. A similar factor structure was found for each group separately.

The five quantitative aspects of contact load predominantly on the first factor, which accounts for 41% of the variance. The five qualitative aspects of contact load mainly on the second factor, which accounts for 16.3% of the variance. The two measures of intergroup aspects of contact load on the third factor, which account for 9% of the variance.

We computed comparisons between the two groups' scores on each of these factors, which revealed significant differences in both quantitative and qualitative aspects of contact (see Table 23.1). The Hindu minority had higher scores on quantitative aspects of contact (i.e., they reported having had more contact) and lower scores on qualitative aspects (i.e., they rated it as less equal, less pleasant, etc.) than Muslims. There were no differences in scores on the third factor. These three factor scores now served as predictor variables for three multiple regression analyses.

Path Analysis

To assess how the three dimensions of contact (quantitative, qualitative, and intergroup) related to our three criterion measures (intergroup anxiety, perceived outgroup variability, and out-group attitude), we constructed a path-analytic model.

---

[2]These significant correlations are consistent with Park and Judd's (1990) finding that the range measure of perceived out-group variability and the global measure of homogeneity tap the same underlying construct (perceived dispersion of the group about its central tendency).

TABLE 23.2. Factor Structure From Varimax-Rotated Factor Analysis on Contact Variables (N = 131)

	Factor		
Contact Variables	1 Quantitative Aspects	2 Quantitative Aspects	3 Intergroup Aspects
Contact in college	.770	.209	−.088
Contact as neighbor	.815	−.079	−.154
Contact as friend	.818	.058	−.027
Frequency of informal talks	.809	.215	−.031
Frequency of family visit	.762	.264	−.035
Contact perceived as equal	−.151	.729	−.268
Contact involuntary or voluntary	.558	.520	−.154
Contact superficial or intimate	.418	.676	−.204
Contact experienced as pleasant	.199	.789	−.101
Contact competitive or cooperative	.185	.746	.036
Contact seen in terms of individuals or group members	−.093	−.029	.883
Out-group members seen as typical	−.124	−.367	.692
Eigenvalue	4.92	1.95	1.08
Variance explained	41.0%	16.3%	9.0%

This model provides a parsimonious description of the interrelations of theoretically relevant variables but can neither confirm nor reject their hypothetical causal links (see Everitt & Dunn, 1991). We computed three separate multiple regression analyses, using the forced-entry method in SPSSX (where all relevant variables entered into the equation simultaneously). The path diagram in Figure 23.1 summarizes the results for these analyses, where the strength of each path is indicated by the size of the standardized path coefficient. This coefficient represents the direct effect of the predictor variable on the criterion variable (i.e., with the effects of all other variables partialed out). Where a predictor variable has an indirect effect, this may be evident from the fact that the simple correlation between the two measures is substantially higher than the path coefficient (see total covariance, shown in Table 23.3).

In presenting the results of these analyses, we report first the effects from a single analysis that included all respondents, collapsing across religious group. We then tested whether the reported effects depend on religious group by testing interactions between each predictor and religious group. Where these occur, they are indicated by an *x* in parentheses after the path coefficient in Figure 23.1. We then examine the effect separately for each group. It should be noted that, consistent

with our theoretical introduction (and Stephan & Stephan, 1985), we accorded a central role to intergroup anxiety in our path model. This allows it to be both potentially predicted by types of contact and a predictor of perceived out-group variability and out-group attitude (both conceived as criterion variables, which themselves can be directly affected by contact predictors).

The regression of intergroup anxiety on contact accounted for 41% of the variance. Both quantitative and, especially, qualitative aspects of contact were, as expected, negatively related to intergroup anxiety. In addition, intergroup aspects of contact were positively related to intergroup anxiety. Thus greater intergroup anxiety was associated with less contact, worse contact, and more intergroup contact.

Quantitative contact was the only type of contact that had a significant direct effect on perceived out-group variability.[3] In addition, there was a strong negative association between intergroup anxiety and perceived out group variability. These two direct effects accounted for 43% of the vari-

[3]Although there was no direct path between qualitative contact and perceived out-group variability, there was a significant interaction with respondents' group. As neither of the separate path coefficients for Hindu and Muslim samples was found to be reliably different from zero, we discuss this result no further.

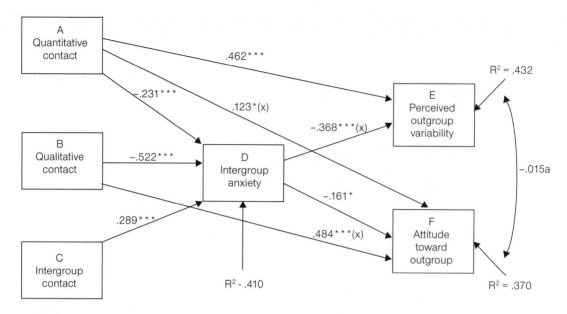

FIGURE 23.1 ■ Path diagram relating to dimensions of contact, intergroup anxiety, perceived out-group variability, and attitude toward out-group. *Note*: Significant paths only are shown. Numbers are standardized partial regression coefficients (β). *x* in parentheses denotes a significant interaction with group. Separate path coefficients for these paths are, for A–F, Hindu, .293**, Muslim, –.058; for B–F, Hindu, .604***, Muslim, .236*; and for D–E, Hindu, –.622***, Muslim, –.249*. These betas were computed separately within each sample (Hindu, *n* = 65; Muslim, *n* = 66). For zero order correlations see Table 23.3.
a. Partial correlation coefficient controlling for A, B, C, and D.
*$p < .10$;   **$p < .01$;   ***$p < .001$.

ance in perceived variability. There was, however, an interaction with respondents' religious group for the path between intergroup anxiety and perceived variability. The effect was significant for both groups but greater for Hindus than Muslims. This result is explicable in terms of the minority status of Hindu subjects, who had reported higher intergroup anxiety than majority-group Muslims.[4] Thus greater perceived out-group variability was associated with more contact and with lower intergroup anxiety.

Attitude toward the out-group also revealed direct effects of both quantitative and, especially, qualitative contact, both of which were qualified by interactions with religious group. The smaller effect of quantitative contact was significant only for the Hindus, who would have greater opportunities for contact and reported more out-group contact than Muslims. Presumably, many of the Muslims can avoid contact with Hindus, and contact is not necessary for them in the same way as it is for a small minority. The effect of qualitative contact was significant for both groups but was

greater for Hindus. Finally, intergroup anxiety had a negative effect on out-group attitude. Together, quantitative contact, qualitative contact, and intergroup anxiety accounted for 37% of the variance in out-group attitudes. Thus positive attitudes toward the out-group were associated with more contact, better contact, and lower intergroup anxiety.

Table 23.3 presents the decomposition of the total covariance (correlation) between each pair of variables in the model (except the three types of contact, variables that were created to be orthogonal). Effects are broken down into causal effects (direct path coefficients, and indirect path coefficients through the effects of other variables) and noncausal effects (or spurious components).

---

[4]We conducted an additional analysis using perceived similarity, rather than variability, as the criterion variable, which yielded very similar results. Quantitative aspects (β = –.170, $p < .046$) and intergroup anxiety (β = .221, $p < .037$) were the only significant predictors of similarity. (The different signs of the effects in these two analyses are due to the negative correlation between measures of perceived similarity and variability.)

TABLE 23.3. Correlation Decomposition for Figure 23.1

Bivariate Relationship	Total Covariance	Causal Effects		Total Effects	Noncausal Effects
		Direct	Indirect		
A–B	—	—	—	—	—
A–C	—	—	—	—	—
A–D	−.231*	−.231	—	−.231	.000
A–E	.547***	.462	−.230 × −.368 = .085	.547	.000
A–F	.160	.123	−.230 × −.161 = .037	.160	.000
B–C	—	—	—	—	—
B–D	−.522***	−.522	—	—	.000
B–E	.083	−.109	−.522 × −.368 = .192	.083	.000
B–F	.568***	.484	−.522 × −.161 = .084	.568	.000
C–D	.289*	.289	—	.289	.000
C–E	−.216*	−.110	.289 × −.368 = −.106	−.216	.000
C–F	−.079	−.032	.289 × −.161 = −.047	−.079	.000
D–E	−.449***	−.368	—	−.368	−.081
D–F	−.451***	−.161	—	−.161	−.290
E–F	.178*	—	—	—	.178

Note: A = quantitative contact; B = qualitative contact; C = intergroup contact; D = intergroup anxiety; E = perceived out-group variability; F = attitude toward out-group. Total covariance = zero-order correlation coefficient; direct effect=standardized regression coefficient (path coefficient β); indirect effect = sum of all possible products of betas of indirect paths joining the two variables in the bivariate relationship; total effects = sum of direct and indirect effects; noncausal effects = total covariance minus total causal effects. N=131.
*$p < .05$; **$p < .01$; ***$p < .001$.

All the noncausal effects are very small, with the exception of the noncausal covariance between intergroup anxiety and attitude toward the out-group. The discrepancy between the zero-order correlation (−.451) and the direct path coefficient (−.161) is due to the fact that both components are highly correlated with quantitative and qualitative contact (i.e., they share prior causes in the model).

Discussion

This research provided quite a detailed picture of intergroup contact between Hindus and Muslims in Bangladesh, which formed the background to any attempt to relate contact predictors to criterion variables. We discuss, first, the context of Hindu-Muslim contact and then the evidence for our model relating contact, intergroup anxiety, perceived out-group variability, and out-group attitude.

Contact between religious groups is clearly part of everyday life in this multicultural society. The amount and nature of contact are, however, determined by religious group membership. The Hindu minority respondents experienced more out-group contact than Muslims, but they rated contact as less pleasant and less equal and reported higher intergroup anxiety than Muslims. A dominant response to negatively experienced contact is avoidance, because it may reduce anxiety (Stephan & Stephan, 1985). Yet, in the context of Bangladesh, the Hindu minority (12% of the population) must inevitably come into contact with the Muslim majority (86%). Hindus also reported that contact tended to involve several Muslims and a sole Hindu. They also expressed less positive out-group attitudes than Muslims, a finding consistent with the trend for members of lower-status groups to show stronger in-group bias (Mullen, Brown, & Smith, 1992).

Although it is not possible, of course, to determine the direction of causality in this correlational study, there is strong evidence that differences in self-reported contact were associated with each of the three criterion variables. Although there were some interactions with respondents' religious group, the overall picture indicates that we have uncovered some general relationships. We now discuss these relationships, and the few interactions, for intergroup anxiety, perceived out-group variability, and out-group attitude.

As predicted, both quantitative and qualitative contact were associated with reduced intergroup anxiety. This effect was much stronger for qualitative contact. In contrast, the perception of contact as intergroup was associated with increased intergroup anxiety. This questions our claim that, to achieve generalized change in out-group perceptions, favorable contact must be defined as intergroup rather than interpersonal (Hewstone & Brown, 1986). In the reported study, intergroup contact means that the respondents reported viewing contact with members of the out-group in terms of their respective group memberships and that they perceived the out-group members as typical. One explanation for the positive association between intergroup contact and intergroup anxiety is that the typical out-group member was perceived in such negative terms (see Horwitz & Rabbie, 1989; Wilder, 1986). In laboratory studies we can manipulate the typicality of a contact partner and the positivity of outcomes orthogonally (e.g., Wilder, 1984) or decide when to emphasize typicality; but field studies of intergroup relations do not permit such control. Dijker (1987) also reported that increased contact with some ethnic out-groups increased anxiety and irritation. This suggested negative impact of intergroup contact highlights the need for studies of contact in both laboratory and field settings.

These results are broadly comparable with Stephan and Stephan's (1985) study, which used a different set of predictors of intergroup anxiety. Our negative associations between quantitative and qualitative contact and intergroup anxiety parallel their reported effect for voluntary contact (one of our components of qualitative contact). Our positive association between intergroup contact and intergroup anxiety mirrors their reported effects of stereotyping and believed dissimilarity on intergroup anxiety. We then went beyond their research to examine the core role of intergroup anxiety as a predictor of both perceived out-group variability and out-group attitude.

The strongest predictor of perceived out-group variability was quantitative contact. It makes intuitive sense that the more out-group members one meets, the more variable one perceives the group to be. This result appears consistent with research by Linville et al. (1986) linking perceived variability to familiarity. The same result appears inconsistent with the study by Jones et al. (1981), which found no link between familiarity and greater perceived variability. A number of qualifications to this effect should therefore be emphasized. First, quantitative contact, as measured, is not identical to "familiarity." Second, contact could

affect perceived variability, in our research, by way of its effect on other inferences (e.g., about the size of the out-group as a whole, which then affects variability; Simon & Brown, 1987) or by way of its effect on how knowledge about the out-group is organized (e.g., if the out-group is organized into a greater number of specific subgroups, this increases variability; Linville et al., 1986; Park, Ryan, & Judd, 1992). These are different relationships from that implied by the familiarity-variability hypothesis. Third, we emphasize that contact need not always be associated with variability. Particularly in cases of contact between real-life groups, there may be strong situational sample bias, such that contact occurs within a restricted range of situations (Quattrone, 1986; Wilder, 1986). Where this is the case, contact may be unrelated to perceived variability. Thus our research identified a reliable association between quantitative contact and variability but one whose process is not yet clear. This finding nonetheless provides evidence that contact can be associated with changes in the constraint values of out-group schemata (see Crocker, Fiske, & Taylor, 1984) and argues for the inclusion of variability as a criterion measure in future research on the contact hypothesis (Linville et al., 1986; Park & Judd, 1990).

The other reliable predictor of out-group variability was intergroup anxiety. The negative association between these variables is consistent with the suggestion that anxiety narrows the focus of attention (see Stephan & Stephan, 1985), because out-group members will tend to be treated less as individuals and more as equivalent members of a category. More recent research has shown that experimentally induced affective states reduced perceived out-group variability (Stroessner & Mackie, 1992, 1993) and that affect that is either integral or incidental to the intergroup situation reduces recognition of stereotype-inconsistent members, effectively reducing perceived variability (Wilder, 1993). More generally, there is evidence that induced affective states may increase stereotyping (e.g., Bodenhausen, 1993; Stroessner et al., 1992). The negative effect of anxiety on variability was reliable for both groups but was stronger for members of the Hindu minority, for whom intergroup anxiety was a more potent affect.

Out-group attitude is the standard criterion variable in contact research and serves as a measure of generalization from out-group contact partners to evaluation of the out-group as a whole. For the Hindus only, quantitative contact had a small direct effect on out-group attitude. It is interesting to note that quantitative contact had a greater impact on perceived variability than on out-group attitudes. One possibility is that changes in perceived variability open the way to changes in attitudes and stereotypes (central tendencies). However, increases in perceived variability may also be used to restrict central-tendency change, if perceivers simply accept a wider range of out-group members or organize them into subtypes, thus maintaining their stereotypes (Johnston & Hewstone, 1992; Weber & Crocker, 1983). A task for future research is to uncover the relationship between measures of perceived out-group variability and central-tendency measures of intergroup perception.

The much more reliable predictor of out-group attitude, for both groups, was qualitative contact, although this effect too was stronger for Hindus (who cannot avoid out-group contact). The stronger effect of qualitative contact is in line with the emphasis, since Allport (1954/1979), on the "nature of contact" and not just its amount (see Amir's, 1969, review).

There was also a small negative effect of intergroup anxiety on out-group attitude. This finding is again consistent with the documented relationship between negative affective states and reliance on stereotyping (as argued by Stephan & Stephan, 1985; see Bodenhausen 1993). In contrast, intergroup contact had no effect on out-group attitude, contrary to our prediction that perceptions of the contact situation in intergroup terms will enhance generalization of out-group attitudes. Again, we emphasize the difficulties associated with Hewstone and Brown's (1986) model of intergroup contact and Rothbart and John's (1985) cognitive analysis of intergroup contact. Experimental evidence has shown that disconfirming attributes will become associated with a group stereotype only if they belong to an individual who is perceived as typical (see Johnston & Hewstone, 1992). However, in cases of realistic intergroup conflict, and in the absence of experimental manipulations, it may well be that typical out-group members are primarily associated with negative attributes. Moreover, an emphasis on group memberships under these circumstances appears more likely to increase intergroup anxiety than to bring about the desired generalization of positive out-group attitudes. Thus personalized, or interpersonal contact

may be more effective in such circumstances, as argued by Brewer and Miller (1984), but we still believe that encountered members of the out-group need to be perceived as having out-group membership as an attribute, or any change of attitude will not generalize to the group as a whole.

To conclude, this study revealed that dimensions of intergroup contact were significant predictors of all three criterion variables, although different dimensions emerged as predictors in each case, and there were some interactions with respondents' religious group. Of course, the minority (Hindus) differ in terms of power, numerosity, and other characteristics from the majority (Muslims), and in a field study we cannot isolate the precise determinants of observed relationships. We did, however, report a number of general relationships between variables. In particular, we highlighted the central role of intergroup anxiety in our integrative model. On the input side, it was negatively associated with both quantitative and, especially, qualitative contact but positively associated with the intergroup nature of contact. On the outcome side, intergroup anxiety was a major negative predictor of perceived out-group variability and was negatively related to out-group attitude. These findings confirm the importance of Stephan and Stephan's (1985) notion of intergroup anxiety and support their focus on the interaction between factors within contact situations and factors within individuals.

REFERENCES

Allport, G. W. (1979). *The nature of prejudice*. Reading, MA: Addison-Wesley. (Original work published 1954)

Amir, Y. (1969). Contact hypothesis in ethnic relations. *Psychological Bulletin, 71*, 319–342.

Bodenhausen, G. V. (1993). Emotions, arousal, and stereotypic judgments: A heuristic model of affect and stereotyping. In D. M. Mackie & D. L. Hamilton (Eds.), *Affect, cognition and stereotyping: Interactive processes in group perception* (pp. 13–37). San Diego, CA: Academic Press.

Brewer, M. B. (1988). A dual process model of impression formation. In T. K. Srull & R. S. Wyer (Eds.), *Advances in social cognition* (Vol. 1, pp. 1–36). Hillsdale, NJ: Lawrence Erlbaum.

Brewer, M. B., & Miller, N. (1984). Beyond the contact hypothesis: Theoretical perspectives on desegregation. In N. Miller & M. B. Brewer (Eds.), *Groups in contact: The Psychology of desegregation* (pp. 281–302). New York: Academic Press.

Cook, S. W. (1984). Cooperative interaction in multiethnic contexts. In N. Miller & M. B. Brewer (Eds.), *Groups in contact: The psychology of desegregation* (pp. 156–186). New York: Academic Press.

Crocker, J., Fiske, S. T., & Taylor, S. E. (1984). Schematic bases of belief change. In J. R. Eiser (Ed.), *Attitudinal judgment* (pp. 197–226). New York: Springer-Verlag.

Dijker, A. J. (1987). Emotional reactions to ethnic minorities. *European Journal of Social Psychology, 17,* 305–325.

Easterbrook, J. A. (1959). The effect of emotion on cue utilization and the organization of behavior. *Psychological Review, 66,* 183–201.

Everitt, B. S., & Dunn, G. (1991). *Applied multivariate data analysis.* London: Edward Arnold.

Hewstone, M., & Brown, R. J. (1986). Contact is not enough: An intergroup perspective on the "contact hypothesis." In M. Hewstone & R. J. Brown (Eds.), *Contact and conflict in intergroup encounters* (pp. 1–14). Oxford, UK: Basil Blackwell.

Horwitz, M., & Rabbie, J. M. (1989). Stereotypes of groups, group members, and individuals in categories: A differential analysis. In D. Bar-Tal, C-F. Graumann, A. W. Kruglanski, & W. Stroebe (Eds.), *Stereotyping and prejudice: Changing conceptions* (pp. 105–129). New York: Springer-Verlag.

Huberty, C. J., & Morris, J. D. (1989). Multivariate analysis versus multiple univariate analyses. *Psychological Bulletin, 105,* 302–308.

Johnston, L., & Hewstone, M. (1992). Cognitive models of stereotype change: (3) Subtyping and the perceived typicality of disconfirming group members. *Journal of Experimental Social Psychology, 28,* 360–386.

Jones, E. E., Wood, G. C., & Quattrone, G. A. (1981). Perceived variability of personal characteristics in in-groups and out-groups: The role of knowledge and evaluation. *Personality and Social Psychology Bulletin, 7,* 523–528.

Judd, C. M., & Park, B. (1988). Outgroup homogeneity: Judgments of variability at the individual and group levels. *Journal of Personality and Social Psychology, 54,* 778–788.

Kahneman, D. (1973). *Attention and effort.* Englewood Cliffs, NJ: Prentice-Hall

Linville, P. W., Fischer, G. W., & Salovey, P. (1989). Perceived distributions of characteristics of ingroup and outgroup members: Empirical evidence and a computer simulation. *Journal of Personality and Social Psychology, 57,* 165–188.

Linville, P. W., Salovey, P., & Fischer G. W. (1986). Stereotyping and perceived distributions of social characteristics: An application to ingroup-outgroup perception. In J. Dovidio & S. L. Gaertner (Eds.), *Prejudice, discrimination and racism* (pp. 165–208). New York: Academic Press.

Mackie, D. M., Hamilton, D. L., Schroth, H. A., Carlisle, C. J., Gersho, B. F., Meneses, L. M., Nedler, B. F., & Reichel, L. D. (1989). The effects of induced mood on expectancy-based illusory correlations. *Journal of Experimental Social Psychology, 25,* 524–544.

Maniruzzaman, T. (1982). The future of Bangladesh. In A. J. Wilson & D. Dalton (Eds.), *The states of South Asia: Problems of national integration* (pp. 265–294). London: Hurst.

Miller, N., Brewer, M. B., & Edwards, R. (1985). Cooperative interaction in desegregated settings: A laboratory analogue. *Journal of Social Issues, 41,* 63–79.

Mukherjee, R. (1973). The social background of Bangladesh. In K. Cough & H. P. Sharma (Eds.), *Imperialism and revolution in South Asia* (pp. 399–418). New York: Monthly Review Press.

Mullen, B., Brown, R., & Smith, C. (1992). Ingroup bias as a

function of salience, relevance and status: An integration. *European Journal of Social Psychology, 22,* 103–122.

O'Connell, J. T. (1976). Dilemmas of secularism in Bangladesh. *Journal of Asian and African Studies, 11,* 64–81.

Park, B., & Judd, C. M. (1990). Measures and models of perceived group variability. *Journal of Personality and Social Psychology, 59,* 173–191.

Park, B., Judd, C. M., & Ryan, C. S. (1991). Social categorization and the representation of variability information. In W. Stroebe & M. Hewstone (Eds.), *European review of social psychology* (Vol. 2, pp. 211–245). Chichester, UK: John Wiley.

Park, B., & Rothbart, M. (1982). Perception of out-group homogeneity and levels of social categorization: Memory for the subordinate attributes of in-group and out-group members. *Journal of Personality and Social Psychology, 42,* 1051–1068.

Park, B., Ryan, C. S., & Judd, C. M. (1992). The role of meaningful subgroups in explaining differences in perceived variability for in-groups and out-groups. *Journal of Personality and Social Psychology, 63,* 553–567.

Quattrone, G. A. (1986). On the perception of a group's variability. In S. Worchel & W. G. Austin (Eds.), *Psychology of intergroup relations* (pp. 25–48). Chicago: Nelson-Hall.

Quattrone, G. A., & Jones, E. E. (1980). The perception of variability within in-groups and out-groups: Implications for the law of small numbers. *Journal of Personality and Social Psychology, 38,* 141–152.

Rothbart, M., & John, O. P. (1985). Social categorization and behavioral episodes: A cognitive analysis of the effects of intergroup contact. *Journal of Social Issues, 41,* 81–104.

Rothbart, M., & Lewis, S. (1988). Inferring category attributes from exemplar attributes: Geometric shapes and social categories. *Journal of Personality and Social Psychology, 55,* 861–872.

Simon, B., & Brown, R. (1987). Perceived intragroup homogeneity in minority-majority contexts. *Journal of Personality and Social Psychology, 53,* 703–711.

Stephan, W. G., & Stephan, C. W. (1985). Intergroup anxiety. *Journal of Social Issues, 41,* 157–175.

Stroessner, S. J., Hamilton, D. L., & Mackie, D. M. (1992). Affect and stereotyping: The effect of induced mood on distinctiveness-based illusory correlations. *Journal of Personality and Social Psychology, 62,* 564–576.

Stroessner, S. J., & Mackie, D. M. (1992). The impact of induced affect on the perceptions of variability in social groups. *Personality and Social Psychology Bulletin, 18,* 546–554.

Stroessner, S. J., & Mackie, D. M. (1993). Affect and perceived group variability: Implications for stereotyping and prejudice. In D. M. Mackie & D. L. Hamilton (Eds.), *Affect, cognition and stereotyping: Interactive processes in group perception* (pp. 63–86). San Diego, CA: Academic Press.

Weber, R., & Cracker, J. (1983). Cognitive processes in the revision of stereotypic beliefs. *Journal of Personality and Social Psychology, 45,* 961–977.

Wilder, D. A. (1984). Intergroup contact: The typical member and the exception to the rule. *Journal of Experimental Social Psychology, 20,* 177–194.

Wilder, D. A. (1986). Cognitive factors affecting the success of intergroup contact. In S. Worchel & W. G. Austin (Eds.), *Psychology of intergroup relations* (pp. 49–66). Chicago: Nelson-Hall.

Wilder, D. A. (1993). The role of anxiety in facilitating stereotypic judgments of out-group behavior. In D. M. Mackie & D. L. Hamilton (Eds.), *Affect, cognition and stereotyping: Interactive processes in group perception* (pp. 87–109). San Diego, CA: Academic Press.

Wilder, D. A., & Shapiro, P. N. (1989). Role of competition-induced anxiety in limiting the beneficial impact of positive behavior by an out-group member. *Journal of Personality and Social Psychology, 56,* 60–69.

References

Abrams, D. (1994). Social self-regulation. *Personality and Social Psychology Bulletin, 20,* 473–483.

Abrams, D., & Hogg, M. A. (1988). Comments on the motivational status of self-esteem in social identity and intergroup discrimination. *European Journal of Social Psychology, 18,* 317–334.

Abrams, D., & Hogg, M. A. (1998). Prospects for research in group processes and intergroup relations. *Group Processes and Intergroup Relations, 1,* 7–20.

Abrams, D., & Hogg, M. A. (Eds.). (1999). *Social identity and social cognition.* Oxford, UK: Blackwell.

Abrams, D., & Hogg, M. A. (2001). Collective identity: Group membership and self-conception. In M. A. Hogg & R. S. Tindale (Eds.), *Blackwell handbook of social psychology: Group processes* (pp. 425–460). Oxford, UK: Blackwell.

Abrams, D., Wetherell, M. S., Cochrane, S., Hogg, M. A., & Turner, J. C. (1990). Knowing what to think by knowing who you are: Self-categorization and the nature of norm formation, conformity, and group polarization. *British Journal of Social Psychology, 29,* 97–119.

Adorno, T. W., Frenkel-Brunswik, E., Levinson, D. J., & Sanford, R. M. (1950). *The authoritarian personality.* New York: Harper.

Allport, F. H. (1924). *Social psychology.* Boston: Houghton-Mifflin.

Allport, G. W. (1954). *The nature of prejudice.* Reading, MA: Addison-Wesley.

Altemeyer, B. (1994). Reducing prejudice in right-wing authoritarians. In M. P. Zanna & J. M. Olsen (Eds.), *The psychology of prejudice: The Ontario symposium* (pp. 131–148). Hillsdale, NJ: Erlbaum.

Amir, Y. (1969). Contact hypothesis in ethnic relations. *Psychological Bulletin, 71,* 319–342.

Andreyeva, G. (1984). Cognitive processes in developing groups. In L. H. Strickland (Ed.), *Directions in soviet social psychology* (pp. 67–82). New York: Springer.

Asch, S. E. (1956). Studies of independence and conformity: A minority of one against a unanimous majority. *Psychological Monographs: General and Applied, 70*(416).

Bargh, J. A. (1994). The four horsemen of automaticity: Awareness, intention, efficiency, and control in social cognition. In R. S. Wyer, Jr., & T. K. Srull (Eds.), *Handbook of social cognition* (Vol. 1, 2nd ed., pp.1–40). Hillsdale, NJ: Erlbaum.

Berkowitz, L. (1972). Frustrations, comparisons, and other sources of emotion arousal as contributors to social unrest. *Journal of Social Issues, 28,* 77–91.

Billig, M. (1976). *Social psychology and intergroup relations.* London: Academic Press.

Blake, R. R., & Mouton, J. S. (1961). Reactions to intergroup competition under win/lose conditions. *Management Science, 7,* 420–435.

Blake, R. R., Shepard, H. A., & Mouton, J. S. (1964). *Managing intergroup conflict in industry.* Texas: Gulf Publishing Company.

Blumer, H. (1958). Race prejudice as a sense of group position. *Pacific Sociological Review, 1,* 3–7.

Bobo, L. (1999). Prejudice as group position: Microfoundations of a sociological approach to racism and race relations. *Journal of Social Issues, 55,* 445–472.

Bobo, L., & Hutchings, V. L. (1996). Perceptions of racial group competition: Extending Blumer's theory of group position to a multiracial social context. *American Sociological Review, 61,* 951–972.

Bochner, S. (1982). The social psychology of cross-cultural relations. In S. Bochner (Ed.), *Cultures in contact: Studies in cross-cultural interaction.* Oxford, UK: Pergamon.

Bourhis, R. Y., Sachdev, I., & Gagnon, A. (1994). Intergroup research with the Tajfel matrices: Methodological notes. In M. Zanna & J. Olson (Eds.), *The psychology of prejudice: The Ontario symposium* (Vol. 7, pp. 209–232). Hillsdale, NJ: Erlbaum.

Brauer, M., Wasel, W., & Niedenthal, P. (2000). Implicit and explicit components of prejudice. *Review of General Psychology, 4,* 79–101.

Brewer, M. B. (1991). The social self: On being the same and different at the same time. *Personality and Social Psychology Bulletin, 17,* 475–482.

Brewer, M. B., & Campbell, D. T. (1976). *Ethnocentrism and intergroup attitudes: East African evidence.* New York: Sage.

Capozza, D., & Brown, R. J. (Eds.). (2000). *Social identity processes.* London: Sage.

Cook, S. W. (1985). Experimenting on social issues: The case of school desegregation. *American Psychologist, 40,* 452–460.

Crocker, J., & Major, B. (1989). Social stigma and self-esteem: The self-protective properties of stigma. *Psychological Review, 96,* 608–630.

Crosby, F., Bromley, S., & Saxe, L. (1980). Recent unobtrusive studies of black and white discrimination and prejudice: A literature review. *Psychological Bulletin, 87,* 546–563.

Crosby, F., Cordova, D., & Jaskar, K. (1993). On the failure to see oneself as disadvantaged: Cognitive and emotional components. In M. A. Hogg & D. Abrams (Eds.), *Group motivation: Social psychological perspectives* (pp. 87–104). London: Harvester Wheatsheaf.

Davies, J. C. (1969). The J-curve of rising and declining satisfaction as a cause of some great revolutions and a contained rebellion. In H. D. Graham & T. R. Gurr (Eds.), *The history of violence in America: Historical and comparative perspectives* (pp. 690–730). New York: Praeger.

Davis, J. A. (1959). A formal interpretation of the theory of relative deprivation. *Sociometry, 22*, 280–296.

Deutsch, M. (1949). A theory of cooperation and competition. *Human Relations, 2*, 129–152.

Deutsch, M. (1973). *The resolution of conflict*. New Haven, CT: Yale University Press.

Devine, P. G. (1989). Stereotypes and prejudice: Their automatic and controlled components. *Journal of Personality and Social Psychology, 56*, 5–18.

Diab, L. N. (1970). A study of intragroup and intergroup relations among experimentally produced small groups. *Genetic Psychology Monographs, 82*, 49–82.

Diehl, M. (1990). The minimal group paradigm: theoretical explanations and empirical findings. *European Review of Social Psychology, 1*, 263–292.

Doise, W. (1986). *Levels of explanation in social psychology*. Cambridge, UK: Cambridge University Press.

Dovidio, J. F., & Gaertner, S. L. (1996). Affirmative action, unintentional racial biases, and intergroup relations. *Journal of Social Issues, 52(4)*, 51–75.

Dovidio, J. F., & Gaertner, S. L. (1998). On the nature of contemporary prejudice: The causes, consequences, and challenges of aversive racism. In J. L. Eberhardt & S. T. Fiske (Eds.), *Confronting prejudice: The problem and the response* (pp. 3–32). Thousand Oaks, CA: Sage.

Duckitt, J. (1989). Authoritarianism and group identification: A new view of an old construct. *Political Psychology, 10*, 63–84.

Durkheim, E. (1898). Représentations individuelles et représentations collectives [Individual and collective representations]. *Revue de Metaphysique et de Morale, 6*, 273–302.

Eagly, A. H., & Chaiken, S. (1993). *The psychology of attitudes*. San Diego, CA: Harcourt Brace Jovanovich.

Ehrlich, H. J. (1973). *The social psychology of prejudice*. New York: Wiley.

Ellemers, N. (1993). The influence of socio-structural variables on identity management strategies. *European Review of Social Psychology, 4*, 27–57.

Ellemers, N., Spears, R., & Doosje, B. (Eds.). (1999). *Social identity*. Oxford, UK: Blackwell.

Emler, N., & Reicher, S. D. (1995). *Adolescence and delinquency: The collective management of reputation*. Oxford, UK: Blackwell.

Esses, V. M., Jackson, L. M., & Armstrong, T. L. (1998). Intergroup competition and attitudes toward immigrants and immigration: An instrumental model of group conflict. *Journal of Social Issues, 54*, 699–724.

Ethier, K. A., & Deaux, K. (1994). Negotiating social identity when contexts change: Maintaining identification and responding to threat. *Journal of Personality and Social Psychology, 67*, 243–251.

Farr, R. M. (1996). *The roots of modern social psychology: 1872–1954*. Oxford, UK: Blackwell.

Farr, R. M., & Moscovici, S. (Eds.). (1984). *Social representations*. Cambridge, UK: Cambridge University Press.

Fazio, R. H., Sanbonmatsu, D. M., Powell, M. C., & Kardes, F. R. (1986). On the automatic activation of attitudes. *Journal of Personality and Social Psychology, 50*, 229–238.

Festinger, L. (1954). A theory of social comparison processes. *Human Relations, 7*, 117–140.

Fisher, R. J. (1990). *The social psychology of intergroup and international conflict resolution*. New York: Springer-Verlag.

Fiske, S. T., & Taylor, S. E. (1991). *Social cognition* (2nd ed.). New York: McGraw-Hill.

Franco, F. M., & Maass, A. (1996). Implicit versus explicit strategies of outgroup discrimination: The role of intentional control in biased language use and reward allocation. *Journal of Language and Social Psychology, 15*, 335–359.

Gaertner, S. L., Dovidio, J. F., Anastasio, P. A., Bachman, B. A., & Rust, M. C. (1993). Reducing intergroup bias: The common ingroup identity model. *European Review of Social Psychology, 4*, 1–26.

Gaertner, S. L., Mann, J., Murrell, A., & Dovidio, J. F. (1989). Reducing intergroup bias: The benefits of recategorization. *Journal of Personality and Social Psychology, 57*, 239–249.

Giles, H., & Johnson, P. (1987). Ethnolinguistic identity theory: A social psychological approach to language maintenance. *International Journal of the Sociology of Language, 68*, 66–99.

Greenberg, J., Solomon, S., & Pyszczynski, T. (1997). Terror management theory of self-esteem and cultural worldviews: Empirical assessments and conceptual refinements. In M. Zanna (Ed.), *Advances in experimental social psychology* (Vol. 29, pp. 61–139). Orlando, FL: Academic Press.

Gurr, T. R. (1970). *Why men rebel*. Princeton, NJ: Princeton University Press.

Hamilton, D. L., & Sherman, S. J. (1996). Perceiving persons and groups. *Psychological Review, 103*, 336–355.

Haslam, S. A., Oakes, P. J., McGarty, C., Turner, J. C., & Onorato, S. (1995). Contextual changes in the prototypicality of extreme and moderate outgroup members. *European Journal of Social Psychology, 25*, 509–530.

Hewstone, M., & Brown, R. J. (Eds.). (1986). *Contact and conflict in intergroup encounters*. Oxford, UK: Blackwell.

Hewstone, M., & Jaspars, J. M. F. (1982). Intergroup relations and attribution processes. In H. Tajfel (Ed.), *Social identity and intergroup relations* (pp. 99–133). Cambridge, UK: Cambridge University Press.

Hewstone, M., & Ward, C. (1985). Ethnocentrism and causal attribution in Southeast Asia. *Journal of Personality and Social Psychology, 48*, 614–623.

Hogg, M. A. (2000). Subjective uncertainty reduction through self-categorization: A motivational theory of social identity processes. *European Review of Social Psychology, 11*, 223–255.

Hogg, M. A. (2001). Social categorization, depersonalization, and group behavior. In M. A. Hogg & R. S. Tindale, (Eds.), *Blackwell handbook of social psychology: Group processes* (pp. 56–85). Oxford, UK: Blackwell.

Hogg, M. A., & Abrams, D. (1988). *Social identifications: A social psychology of intergroup relations and group processes*. London: Routledge.

Hogg, M. A., & Abrams, D. (1990). Social motivation, self-esteem and social identity. In D. Abrams & M. A. Hogg (Eds.), *Social identity theory: Constructive and critical advances* (pp. 28–47). London: Harvester Wheatsheaf.

Hogg, M. A., & Abrams, D. (1993). Towards a single-process uncertainty-reduction model of social motivation in groups. In M. A. Hogg & D. Abrams (Eds.), *Group motivation:*

Social psychological perspectives (pp. 173–190). Hemel Hempstead, UK: Harvester Wheatsheaf.

Hogg, M. A., & Abrams, D. (1999). Social identity and social cognition: Historical background and current trends. In D. Abrams & M. A. Hogg (Eds). *Social identity and social cognition* (pp. 1–25). Oxford, UK: Blackwell.

Hogg, M. A., & Mullin, B.-A. (1999). Joining groups to reduce uncertainty: Subjective uncertainty reduction and group identification. In D. Abrams & M. A. Hogg (Eds.), *Social identity and social cognition* (pp. 249–279). Oxford, UK: Blackwell.

Hogg, M. A., & Williams, K. D. (2000). From I to we: Social identity and the collective self. *Group Dynamics: Theory, Research, and Practice, 4*, 81–97.

Hornsey, M. J., & Hogg, M. A. (2000). Assimilation and diversity: An integrative model of subgroup relations. *Personality and Social Psychology Review, 4*, 143–156.

Insko, C. A., Schopler, J., Kennedy, J. F., Dahl, K. R., Graetz, K. A., & Drigotas, S. M. (1992). Individual-group discontinuity from the differing perspectives of Campbell's realistic group conflict theory and Tajfel and Turner's social identity theory. *Social Psychology Quarterly, 55*, 272–291.

Islam, M., & Hewstone, M. (1993). Intergroup attributions and affective consequences in majority and minority groups. *Journal of Personality and Social Psychology, 65*, 936–950.

Jones, E. E., Wood, G. C., & Quattrone, G. A. (1981). Perceived variability of personal characteristics in ingroups and outgroups: The role of knowledge and evaluation. *Personality and Social Psychology Bulletin, 7*, 523–528.

Jost, J. T., & Banaji, M. R. (1994). The role of stereotyping in system-justification and the production of false consciousness. *British Journal of Social Psychology, 33*, 1–27.

Judd, C. M., & Park, B. (1988). Out-group homogeneity: Judgments of variability at the individual and group levels. *Journal of Personality and Social Psychology, 54*, 778–788.

LaPiere, R. T. (1934). Attitudes vs actions. *Social Forces, 13*, 230–237.

LeBon, G. (1908). *The crowd: A study of the popular mind.* London: Unwin. (Original work published 1896)

Lepore, L., & Brown, R. (1997). Category and stereotype activation: Is prejudice inevitable? *Journal of Personality and Social Psychology, 72*, 275–287.

Linville, P. W., Fischer, G. W., & Salovey, P. (1989). Perceived distributions of the characteristics of in-group and out-group members: Empirical evidence and a computer simulation. *Journal of Personality and Social Psychology, 57*, 165–188.

Long, K., & Spears, R. (1997). The self-esteem hypothesis revisited: Differentiation and the disaffected. In R. Spears, P. J. Oakes, N. Ellemers, & S. A. Haslam (Eds.), *The social psychology of stereotyping and group life* (pp. 296–317). Oxford, UK: Blackwell.

Maass, A. Castelli, L., & Arcuri, L. (2000). Measuring prejudice: Implicit versus explicit techniques. In D. Capozza & R. J. Brown (Eds.), *Social identity processes* (pp. 96–116). London: Sage.

Maass, A., & Clark, R. D. III. (1984). Hidden impact of minorities: Fifteen years of minority influence research. *Psychological Bulletin, 95*, 428–450.

Mackie, D. M. (1986). Social identification effects in group polarization. *Journal of Personality and Social Psychology, 50*, 720–728.

Macrae, N., Bodenhausen, G. V., Milne, A. B., & Jetten, J. (1994). Out of mind but back in sight: Stereotypes on the rebound. *Journal of Personality and Social Psychology, 67*, 808–817.

Marques, J. M., & Páez, D. (1994). The black sheep effect: Social categorization, rejection of ingroup deviates, and perception of group variability. *European Review of Social Psychology, 5*, 37–68.

Martin, R. (1998). Majority and minority influence using the afterimage paradigm: A series of attempted replications. *Journal of Experimental Social Psychology, 34*, 1–26.

McConahay, J. G. (1986). Modern racism, ambivalence, and the modern racism scale. In J. F. Dovidio & S. L. Gaertner (Eds.), *Prejudice, discrimination, and racism* (pp. 91–125). New York: Academic Press.

McGarty, C., Turner, J. C., Hogg, M. A., David, B., & Wetherell, M. S. (1992). Group polarization as conformity to the prototypical group member. *British Journal of Social Psychology, 31*, 1–20.

Mead, G. H. (1934). *Mind, self and society.* Chicago, IL: University of Chicago Press.

Medin, D. L., & Ortony, A. (1989). Psychological essentialism. In S. Vosnaidou & A. Ortony (Eds.), *Similarity and analogical reasoning* (pp. 179–195). Cambridge, UK: Cambridge University Press.

Miller, D. T., & Prentice, D. A. (1999). Some consequences of a belief in group essence: The category divide hypothesis. In D. A. Prentice & D. T. Miller (Eds.), *Cultural divides: Understanding and overcoming group conflict* (pp. 213–238). New York: Russell Sage Foundation.

Miller, N., & Brewer, M. B. (Eds.). (1984). *Groups in contact: The psychology of desegregation.* New York: Academic Press.

Moreland, R. L., Hogg, M. A., & Hains, S. C. (1994). Back to the future: Social psychological research on groups. *Journal of Experimental Social Psychology, 30*, 527–555.

Moscovici, S. (1976). *Social influence and social change.* London: Academic Press.

Moscovici, S. (1980). Toward a theory of conversion behavior. In L. Berkowitz (Ed.), *Advances in Experimental Social Psychology* (Vol. 13, pp. 202–239). New York: Academic Press.

Moscovici, S., & Personnaz, B. (1980). Studies in social influence: V. Minority influence and conversion behavior in a perceptual task. *Journal of Experimental Social Psychology, 16*, 270–282.

Mugny, G. (1982). *The power of minorities.* London: Academic Press.

Mummendey, A., & Wenzel, M. (1999). Social discrimination and tolerance in intergroup relations: Reactions to intergroup difference. *Personality and Social Psychology Review, 3*, 158–174.

Nemeth, C. (1986). Differential contributions of majority and minority influence. *Psychological Review, 93*, 23–32.

Oakes, P. J., Haslam, S. A., & Turner, J. C. (1994). *Stereotyping and social reality.* Oxford, UK: Blackwell.

Otten, S., Mummendey, A., & Blanz, M. (1996). Intergroup discrimination in positive and negative outcome allocations: Impact of stimulus valence, relative group status, and relative group size. *Personality and Social Psychology Bulletin, 22*, 568–581.

Pettigrew, T. F. (1958). Personality and sociocultural factors in intergroup attitudes: A cross-national comparison. *Journal of Conflict Resolution, 2*, 29–42.

Pettigrew, T. F. (1979). The ultimate attribution error: Extending Allport's cognitive analysis of prejudice. *Personality and Social Psychology Bulletin, 5*, 461–476.

Pettigrew, T. F. (1998). Intergroup contact theory. *Annual Review of Psychology, 49*, 65–85.

Pratto, F. (1999). The puzzle of continuing group inequality: Piecing together psychological, social and cultural forces in social dominance theory. In M. P. Zanna (Ed.), *Advances in experimental social psychology* (Vol. 31, pp. 191–263). New York: Academic Press.

Pratto, F., Sidanius, J., Stallworth, L. M., & Malle, B. F. (1994). Social dominance orientation: A personality variable predicting social and political attitudes. *Journal of Personality and Social Psychology, 67*, 741–763.

Prentice, D. A., & Miller, D. T. (Eds.). (1999). *Cultural divides: Understanding and overcoming group conflict.* New York: Russell Sage Foundation.

Quattrone, G. A. (1986). On the perception of a group's variability. In S. Worchel & W. Austin (Eds.), *The psychology of intergroup relations* (Vol. 2, pp. 25–48). New York: Nelson-Hall.

Rabbie, J. M., & Bekkers, F. (1978). Threatened leadership and intergroup competition. *European Journal of Social Psychology, 8*, 9–20.

Rabbie, J. M., Schot, J. C., & Visser, L. (1989). Social identity theory: A conceptual and empirical critique from the perspective of a behavioural interaction model. *European Journal of Social Psychology, 19*, 171–202

Reicher, S. D. (1984). The St Pauls' riot: An explanation of the limits of crowd action in terms of a social identity model. *European Journal of Social Psychology, 14*, 1–21.

Reicher, S. D. (2001). The psychology of crowd dynamics. In M. A. Hogg & R. S. Tindale (Eds.), *Blackwell handbook of social psychology: Group processes* (pp. 182–208). Oxford, UK: Blackwell.

Reicher, S. D., & Hopkins, N. (1986). Seeking influence through characterising self-categories: An analysis of anti-abortionist rhetoric. *British Journal of Social Psychology, 35*, 297–311.

Rokeach, M. (1948). Generalized mental rigidity as a factor in ethnocentrism. *Journal of Abnormal and Social Psychology, 43*, 259–278.

Rokeach, M. (Ed.). (1960). *The open and closed mind.* New York: Basic Books.

Ross, L. (1977). The intuitive psychologist and his shortcomings. In L. Berkowitz (Ed.), *Advances in experimental social psychology* (Vol. 10, pp. 174–220). New York: Academic Press.

Rubin, M., & Hewstone, M. (1998). Social identity theory's self-esteem hypothesis: A review and some suggestions for clarification. *Personality and Social Psychology Review, 2*, 40–62.

Runciman, W. G. (1966). *Relative deprivation and social justice.* London: Routledge and Kegan Paul.

Schofield, J. W. (1991). School desegregation and intergroup relations: A review of the literature. In G. Grant (Ed.), *Review of research in education* (Vol. 17, pp. 335–409). Washington, DC: American Education Research Association.

Sedikides, C., & Strube, M. J. (1997). Self-evaluation: To thine own self be good, to thine own self be sure, to thine own self be true, and to thine own self be better. In M. P. Zanna

(Ed.), *Advances in experimental social psychology* (Vol 29, pp. 209–296). New York: Academic Press.

Sherif, M. (1935). A study of some social factors in perception. *Archives of Psychology, 27*, 1–60.

Sherif, M. (1958). Superordinate goals in the reduction of intergroup conflicts. *American Journal of Sociology, 63*, 349–356.

Sherif, M. (Ed.). (1962). *Intergroup relations and leadership.* New York: Wiley.

Sherif, M. (1966). *In common predicament: Social psychology of intergroup conflict and cooperation.* Boston, MA: Houghton-Mifflin.

Sherif, M., Harvey, O. J., White, B. J., Hood, W., & Sherif, C. (1961). *Intergroup conflict and cooperation: The Robbers Cave experiment.* Norman, OK: University of Oklahoma Institute of Intergroup Relations.

Sherif, M., & Sherif, C. W. (1953). *Groups in harmony and tension: An integration of studies in intergroup behavior.* New York: Harper and Row.

Sidanius, J., & Pratto, F. (1999). *Social dominance: An intergroup theory of social hierarchy and oppression.* New York: Cambridge University Press.

Simon, B., & Brown, R. J. (1987). Perceived intragroup homogeneity in minority-majority contexts. *Journal of Personality and Social Psychology, 53*, 703–711.

Steele, C. M. (1988). The psychology of self-affirmation: Sustaining the integrity of the self. *Advances in Experimental Social Psychology, 21*, 261–302.

Stephan, W. G., & Stephan, C. W. (1985). Intergroup anxiety. *Journal of Social Issues, 41*, 157–175.

Sumner, W. G. (1906). *Folkways.* Boston, MA: Ginn.

Tajfel, H. (1959). Quantitative judgement in social perception. *British Journal of Psychology, 50*, 16–29.

Tajfel, H. (1970). Experiments in intergroup discrimination. *Scientific American, 223*, 96–102.

Tajfel, H. (1972). Social categorization. English manuscript of 'La catégorisation sociale'. In S. Moscovici (Ed.), *Introduction à la Psychologie Sociale* (Vol. 1, pp. 272–302). Paris: Larousse.

Tajfel, H. (1981). Social stereotypes and social groups. In J. C. Turner & H. Giles (Eds.), *Intergroup behaviour* (pp. 144–167). Oxford, UK: Blackwell.

Tajfel, H., Billig, M., Bundy R. P., & Flament, C. (1971). Social categorization and intergroup behaviour. *European Journal of Social Psychology, 1*, 149–177.

Tajfel, H., & Turner, J. C. (1979). An integrative theory of intergroup conflict. In W. G. Austin & S. Worchel (Eds.), *The social psychology of intergroup relations* (pp. 33–47). Monterey, CA: Brooks/Cole.

Taylor, D. M., & Jaggi, V. (1974). Ethnocentrism and causal attribution in a S. Indian context. *Journal of Cross-cultural Psychology, 5*, 162–171.

Taylor, D. M., & McKirnan, D. J. (1984). A five-stage model of intergroup relations. *British Journal of Social Psychology, 23*, 291–300.

Titus, H. E., & Hollander, E. P. (1957). The California F scale in psychological research (1950–1955). *Psychological Bulletin, 54*, 47–74.

Turner, J. C. (1982). Towards a cognitive redefinition of the social group. In H. Tajfel (Ed.), *Social identity and intergroup relations* (pp. 15–40). Cambridge, UK: Cambridge University Press.

Turner, J. C. (1985). Social categorization and the self-concept: A social cognitive theory of group behavior. In E. J. Lawler (Ed.), *Advances in group processes: Theory and research* (Vol. 2, pp.77–122). Greenwich, CT: JAI Press.

Turner, J. C. (1991). *Social influence*. Milton Keynes, UK: Open University Press.

Turner, J. C., & Bourhis, R. Y. (1996). Social identity, interdependence and the social group. A reply to Rabbie et al. In W. P. Robinson (Ed.), *Social groups and identities: Developing the legacy of Henri Tajfel* (pp. 25–63). Oxford, UK: Butterworth-Heinemann.

Turner, J. C., Hogg, M. A., Oakes, P. J., Reicher, S. D., & Wetherell, M. S. (1987). *Rediscovering the social group: A self-categorization theory*. Oxford, UK: Blackwell.

Tyler, T.R. (2001). Social justice. In R. Brown & S. Gaertner (Eds.), *Blackwell handbook of social psychology: Intergroup processes* (pp. 344–364). Oxford, UK: Blackwell.

Tyler, T. R., DeGoey, P., & Smith, H. (1996). Understanding why the justice of group procedures matters: A test of the psychological dynamics of the group-value model. *Journal of Personality and Social Psychology, 70*, 913–930.

van Dijk, T. A. (1987). *Communicating racism: Ethnic prejudice in thought and talk*. Newburg Park, CA: Sage.

van Dijk, T. A. (1993). *Elite discourse and racism*. Newbury Park, CA: Sage.

Vanneman, R. D., & Pettigrew, T. F. (1972). Race and relative deprivation in the urban United States. *Race, 13*, 461–486.

von Hippel, W., Sekaquaptewa, D., & Vargas, P. (1995). On the role of encoding processes in stereotype maintenance. In L. Berkowitz (Ed.), *Advances in experimental social psychology* (Vol. 27, pp. 177–254). New York: Academic Press.

Walker, I., & Mann, L. (1987). Unemployment, relative deprivation, and social protest. *Personality and Social Psychology Bulletin, 13*, 275–283.

Walker, I., & Pettigrew, T. F. (1984). Relative deprivation theory: An overview and conceptual critique. *British Journal of Social Psychology, 23*, 301–310.

Watson, J. B. (1919). *Psychology from the standpoint of a behaviorist*. Philadelphia, PA: Lippincott.

Weber, R., & Crocker, J. (1983). Cognitive processes in the revision of stereotypic beliefs. *Journal of Personality and Social Psychology, 45*, 961–977.

Wenzel, M., & Mummendey, A. (1996). Positive-negative asymmetry of social discrimination: A normative analysis of differential evaluations of ingroup and outgroup on positive and negative attributes. *British Journal of Social Psychology, 35*, 493–507.

Wilder, D. A. (1984). Intergroup contact: The typical member and the exception to the rule. *Journal of Experimental Social Psychology, 20*, 177–194.

Wood, W., Lundgren, S., Ouellette, J. A., Busceme, S., & Blackstone, T. (1994). Minority influence: A meta-analytic review of social influence processes. *Psychological Bulletin, 115*, 323–345.

Worchel, S., Morales, J. F., Páez, D., & Deschamps, J.-C. (Eds.). (1998). *Social identity: International perspectives*. London: Sage.

Wright, S. C., Aron, A., McLaughlin-Volpe, T., & Ropp, S. A. (1997). The extended contact effect: Knowledge of cross-group friendships and prejudice. *Journal of Personality and Social Psychology, 73*, 73–90.

Wright, S. C., Taylor, D. M., & Moghaddam, F. M. (1990). Responding to membership in a disadvantaged group. *Journal of Personality and Social Psychology, 58*, 994–1003.

Wundt, W. (1916). *Elements of folk psychology: Outlines of a psychological history of the development of mankind*. London: Allen & Unwin. (German original published in 1912)

Zebrowitz, L. A. (1996). Physical appearance as a basis of stereotyping. In C. N. Macrae, C. Stangor, & M. Hewstone, (Eds.), *Stereotypes and stereotyping* (pp. 79–120). New York: Guilford.

Appendix: How to Read a Journal Article in Social Psychology

Christian H. Jordan and Mark P. Zanna • University of Waterloo

How to Read a Journal Article in Social Psychology

When approaching a journal article for the first time, and often on subsequent occasions, most people try to digest it as they would any piece of prose. They start at the beginning and read word for word, until eventually they arrive at the end, perhaps a little bewildered, but with a vague sense of relief. This is not an altogether terrible strategy; journal articles do have a logical structure that lends itself to this sort of reading. There are, however, more efficient approaches–approaches that enable you, a student of social psychology, to cut through peripheral details, avoid sophisticated statistics with which you may not be familiar, and focus on the central ideas in an article. Arming yourself with a little foreknowledge of what is contained in journal articles, as well as some practical advice on how to read them, should help you read journal articles more effectively. If this sounds tempting, read on.

Journal articles offer a window into the inner workings of social psychology. They document how social psychologists formulate hypotheses, design empirical studies, analyze the observations they collect, and interpret their results. Journal articles also serve an invaluable archival function: They contain the full store of common and cumulative knowledge of social psychology. Having documentation of past research allows researchers to build on past findings and advance our understanding of social behavior, without pursuing avenues of investigation that have already been explored. Perhaps most importantly, a research study is never complete until its results have been shared with others, colleagues and students alike. Journal articles are a primary means of communicating research findings. As such, they can be genuinely exciting and interesting to read.

That last claim may have caught you off guard. For beginning readers, journal articles may seem anything but interesting and exciting. They may, on the contrary, appear daunting and esoteric, laden with jargon and obscured by menacing statistics. Recognizing this fact, we hope to arm you, through this paper, with the basic information you will need to read journal articles with a greater sense of comfort and perspective.

Social psychologists study many fascinating topics, ranging from prejudice and discrimination, to culture, persuasion, liking and love, conformity and obedience, aggres-

403

sion, and the self. In our daily lives, these are issues we often struggle to understand. Social psychologists present systematic observations of, as well as a wealth of ideas about, such issues in journal articles. It would be a shame if the fascination and intrigue these topics have were lost in their translation into journal publications. We don't think they are, and by the end of this paper, hopefully you won't either.

Journal articles come in a variety of forms, including research reports, review articles, and theoretical articles. Put briefly, a *research report* is a formal presentation of an original research study, or series of studies. A *review article* is an evaluative survey of previously published work, usually organized by a guiding theory or point of view. The author of a review article summarizes previous investigations of a circumscribed problem, comments on what progress has been made toward its resolution, and suggests areas of the problem that require further study. A *theoretical article* also evaluates past research, but focuses on the development of theories used to explain empirical findings. Here, the author may present a new theory to explain a set of findings, or may compare and contrast a set of competing theories, suggesting why one theory might be the superior one.

This paper focuses primarily on how to read research reports, for several reasons. First, the bulk of published literature in social psychology consists of research reports. Second, the summaries presented in review articles, and the ideas set forth in theoretical articles, are built on findings presented in research reports. To get a deep understanding of how research is done in social psychology, fluency in reading original research reports is essential. Moreover, theoretical articles frequently report new studies that pit one theory against another, or test a novel prediction derived from a new theory. In order to appraise the validity of such theoretical contentions, a grounded understanding of basic findings is invaluable. Finally, most research reports are written in a standard format that is likely unfamiliar to new readers. The format of review and theoretical articles is less standardized, and more like that of textbooks and other scholarly writings, with which most readers are familiar. This is not to suggest that such articles are easier to read and comprehend than research reports; they can be quite challenging indeed. It is simply the case that, because more rules apply to the writing of research reports, more guidelines can be offered on how to read them.

The Anatomy of Research Reports

Most research reports in social psychology, and in psychology in general, are written in a standard format prescribed by the American Psychological Association (1994). This is a great boon to both readers and writers. It allows writers to present their ideas and findings in a clear, systematic manner. Consequently, as a reader, once you understand this format, you will not be on completely foreign ground when you approach a new research report—regardless of its specific content. You will know where in the paper particular information is found, making it easier to locate. No matter what your reasons for reading a research report, a firm understanding of the format in which they are written will ease your task. We discuss the format of research reports next, with some practical suggestions on how to read them. Later, we discuss how this format reflects the process of scientific investigation, illustrating how research reports have a coherent narrative structure.

TITLE AND ABSTRACT

Though you can't judge a book by its cover, you can learn a lot about a research report simply by reading its title. The title presents a concise statement of the theoretical issues investigated, and/or the variables that were studied. For example, the following title was taken almost at random from a prestigious journal in social psychology: "Sad and guilty? Affective influences on the explanation of conflict in close relationships" (Forgas, 1994, p.

56). Just by reading the title, it can be inferred that the study investigated how emotional states change the way people explain conflict in close relationships. It also suggests that when feeling sad, people accept more personal blame for such conflicts (i.e., feel more guilty).

The abstract is also an invaluable source of information. It is a brief synopsis of the study, and packs a lot of information into 150 words or less. The abstract contains information about the problem that was investigated, how it was investigated, the major findings of the study, and hints at the theoretical and practical implications of the findings. Thus, the abstract is a useful summary of the research that provides the gist of the investigation. Reading this outline first can be very helpful, because it tells you where the report is going, and gives you a useful framework for organizing information contained in the article.

The title and abstract of a research report are like a movie preview. A movie preview highlights the important aspects of a movie's plot, and provides just enough information for one to decide whether to watch the whole movie. Just so with titles and abstracts; they highlight the key features of a research report to allow you to decide if you want to read the whole paper. And just as with movie previews, they do not give the whole story. Reading just the title and abstract is never enough to fully understand a research report.

INTRODUCTION

A research report has four main sections: introduction, method, results, and discussion. Though it is not explicitly labeled, the introduction begins the main body of a research report. Here, the researchers set the stage for the study. They present the problem under investigation, and state why it was important to study. By providing a brief review of past research and theory relevant to the central issue of investigation, the researchers place the study in an historical context and suggest how the study advances knowledge of the problem. Beginning with broad theoretical and practical considerations, the researchers delineate the rationale that led them to the specific set of hypotheses tested in the study. They also describe how they decided on their research strategy (e.g., why they chose an experiment or a correlational study).

The introduction generally begins with a broad consideration of the problem investigated. Here, the researchers want to illustrate that the problem they studied is a real problem about which people should care. If the researchers are studying prejudice, they may cite statistics that suggest discrimination is prevalent, or describe specific cases of discrimination. Such information helps illustrate why the research is both practically and theoretically meaningful, and why you should bother reading about it. Such discussions are often quite interesting and useful. They can help you decide for yourself if the research has merit. But they may not be essential for understanding the study at hand. Read the introduction carefully, but choose judiciously what to focus on and remember. To understand a study, what you really need to understand is what the researchers' hypotheses were, and how they were derived from theory, informal observation, or intuition. Other background information may be intriguing, but may not be critical to understand what the researchers did and why they did it.

While reading the introduction, try answering these questions: What problem was studied, and why? How does this study relate to, and go beyond, past investigations of the problem? How did the researchers derive their hypotheses? What questions do the researchers hope to answer with this study?

METHOD

In the method section, the researchers translate their hypotheses into a set of specific, testable questions. Here, the researchers introduce the main characters of the study—the subjects or participants—describing their characteristics (gender, age, etc.) and how many of them were involved. Then, they describe the materials (or apparatus), such as any questionnaires or special equipment, used in the study. Finally, they describe chronologically the procedures of the study; that is, how the study was conducted. Often, an overview of the research design will begin the method section. This overview provides a broad outline of the design, alerting you to what you should attend.

The method is presented in great detail so that other researchers can recreate the study to confirm (or question) its results. This degree of detail is normally not necessary to understand a study, so don't get bogged down trying to memorize the particulars of the procedures. Focus on how the independent variables were manipulated (or measured) and how the dependent variables were measured.

Measuring variables adequately is not always an easy matter. Many of the variables psychologists are interested in cannot be directly observed, so they must be inferred from participants' behavior. Happiness, for example, cannot be directly observed. Thus, researchers interested in how being happy influences people's judgments must infer happiness (or its absence) from their behavior—perhaps by asking people how happy they are, and judging their degree of happiness from their responses; perhaps by studying people's facial expressions for signs of happiness, such as smiling. Think about the measures researchers use while reading the method section. Do they adequately reflect or capture the concepts they are meant to measure? If a measure seems odd, consider carefully how the researchers justify its use.

Oftentimes in social psychology, getting there is half the fun. In other words, how a result is obtained can be just as interesting as the result itself. Social psychologists often strive to have participants behave in a natural, spontaneous manner, while controlling enough of their environment to pinpoint the causes of their behavior. Sometimes, the major contribution of a research report is its presentation of a novel method of investigation. When this is the case, the method will be discussed in some detail in the introduction.

Participants in social psychology studies are intelligent and inquisitive people who are responsive to what happens around them. Because of this, they are not always initially told the true purpose of a study. If they were told, they might not act naturally. Thus, researchers frequently need to be creative, presenting a credible rationale for complying with procedures, without revealing the study's purpose. This rationale is known as a *cover story,* and is often an elaborate scenario. While reading the method section, try putting yourself in the shoes of a participant in the study, and ask yourself if the instructions given to participants seem sensible, realistic, and engaging. Imagining what it was like to be in the study will also help you remember the study's procedure, and aid you in interpreting the study's results.

While reading the method section, try answering these questions: How were the hypotheses translated into testable questions? How were the variables of interest manipulated and/or measured? Did the measures used adequately reflect the variables of interest? For example, is self-reported income an adequate measure of social class? Why or why not?

RESULTS

The results section describes how the observations collected were analyzed to determine whether the original hypotheses were supported. Here, the data (observations of behavior) are described, and statistical tests are presented. Because of this, the results section is often intimidating to readers who have little or no training in statistics. Wading through complex and unfamiliar statistical analyses is understandably confusing and frustrating. As a result, many students are tempted to skip over reading this section. We advise you not to do so. Empirical findings are the foundation of any science and results sections are where such findings are presented.

Take heart. Even the most prestigious researchers were once in your shoes and sympathize with you. Though space in psychology journals is limited, researchers try to strike a balance between the need to be clear and the need to be brief in describing their results. In an influential paper on how to write good research reports, Bem (1987) offered this advice to researchers:

> No matter how technical or abstruse your article is in its particulars, intelligent nonpsychologists with no expertise in statistics or experimental design should be able to comprehend the broad outlines of what you did and why. They should understand in general terms what was learned. (p. 74)

Generally speaking, social psychologists try to practice this advice.

Most statistical analyses presented in research reports test specific hypotheses. Often, each analysis presented is preceded by a reminder of the hypothesis it is meant to test. After an analysis is presented, researchers usually provide a narrative description of the result in plain English. When the hypothesis tested by a statistical analysis is not explicitly stated, you can usually determine the hypothesis that was tested by reading this narrative description of the result, and referring back to the introduction to locate an hypothesis that corresponds to that result. After even the most complex statistical analysis, there will be a written description of what the result means conceptually. Turn your attention to these descriptions. Focus on the conceptual meaning of research findings, not on the mechanics of how they were obtained (unless you're comfortable with statistics).

Aside from statistical tests and narrative descriptions of results, results sections also frequently contain tables and graphs. These are efficient summaries of data. Even if you are not familiar with statistics, look closely at tables and graphs, and pay attention to the means or correlations presented in them. Researchers always include written descriptions of the pertinent aspects of tables and graphs. While reading these descriptions, check the tables and graphs to make sure what the researchers say accurately reflects their data. If they say there was a difference between two groups on a particular dependent measure, look at the means in the table that correspond to those two groups, and see if the means do differ as described. Occasionally, results seem to become stronger in their narrative description than an examination of the data would warrant.

Statistics *can* be misused. When they are, results are difficult to interpret. Having said this, a lack of statistical knowledge should not make you overly cautious while reading results sections. Though not a perfect antidote, journal articles undergo extensive review by professional researchers before publication. Thus, most misapplications of statistics are caught and corrected before an article is published. So, if you are unfamiliar with statistics, you can be reasonably confident that findings are accurately reported.

While reading the results section, try answering these questions: Did the researchers provide evidence that any independent variable manipulations were effective? For example, if testing for behavioral differences between happy and sad participants, did the researchers demonstrate that one group was in fact happier than the other? What were the major findings of the study? Were the researchers' original hypotheses supported by their observations? If not, look in the discussion section for how the researchers explain the findings that were obtained.

DISCUSSION

The discussion section frequently opens with a summary of what the study found, and an evaluation of whether the findings supported the original hypotheses. Here, the researchers evaluate the theoretical and practical implications of their results. This can be particularly interesting when the results did not work out exactly as the researchers anticipated. When such is the case, consider the researchers' explanations carefully, and see if they seem plausible to you. Often, researchers will also report any aspects of their study that limit their interpretation of its results, and suggest further research that could overcome these limitations to provide a better understanding of the problem under investigation.

Some readers find it useful to read the first few paragraphs of the discussion section before reading any other part of a research report. Like the abstract, these few paragraphs usually contain all of the main ideas of a research report: What the hypotheses were, the major findings and whether they supported the original hypotheses, and how the findings relate to past research and theory. Having this information before reading a research report can guide your reading, allowing you to focus on the specific details you need to complete your understanding of a study. The description of the results, for example, will alert you to the major variables that were studied. If they are unfamiliar to you, you can pay special attention to how they are defined in the introduction, and how they are operationalized in the method section.

After you have finished reading an article, it can also be helpful to reread the first few paragraphs of the discussion and the abstract. As noted, these two passages present highly distilled summaries of the major ideas in a research report. Just as they can help guide your reading of a report, they can also help you consolidate your understanding of a report once you have finished reading it. They provide a check on whether you have understood the main points of a report, and offer a succinct digest of the research in the authors' own words.

While reading the discussion section, try answering these questions: What conclusions can be drawn from the study? What new information does the study provide about the problem under investigation? Does the study help resolve the problem? What are the practical and theoretical implications of the study's findings? Did the results contradict past research findings? If so, how do the researchers explain this discrepancy?

Some Notes on Reports of Multiple Studies

Up to this point, we have implicitly assumed that a research report describes just one study. It is also quite common, however, for a research report to describe a series of studies of the same problem in a single article. When such is the case, each study reported will have the same basic structure (introduction, method, results, and discussion sections) that we have outlined, with the notable exception that sometimes the results and discussion section for each study are combined. Combined "results and discussion" sections contain the same information that separate results and discussion sections normally contain. Sometimes, the authors present all their results first, and only then discuss the implications of these results, just as they would in separate results and discussion sections. Other times, however, the authors alternate between describing results and discussing their implications, as each result is presented. In either case, you should be on the lookout for the same information, as outlined above in our consideration of separate results and discussion sections.

Reports including multiple studies also differ from single study reports in that they include more general introduction and discussion sections. The general introduction, which begins the main body of a research report, is similar in essence to the introduction of a single study report. In both cases, the researchers describe the problem investigated and its practical and theoretical significance. They also demonstrate how they derived their hypotheses, and explain how their research relates to past investigations of the problem. In contrast, the separate introductions to each individual study in reports of multiple studies are usually quite brief, and focus more specifically on the logic and rationale of each particular study presented. Such introductions generally describe the methods used in the particular study, outlining how they answer questions that have not been adequately addressed by past research, including studies reported earlier in the same article.

General discussion sections parallel discussions of single studies, except on a somewhat grander scale. They present all of the information contained in discussions of single studies, but consider the implications of all the studies presented together. A general discussion section brings the main ideas of a research program into bold relief. It typically begins with a concise summary of a research program's main findings, their relation to the original hypotheses, and their practical and theoretical implications. Thus, the summaries that begin general discussion sections are counterparts of the summaries that begin discussion sections of single study reports. Each presents a digest of the research presented in an article that can serve as both an organizing framework (when read first), and as a check on how well you have understood the main points of an article (when read last).

Research Reporting as Story Telling

A research report tells the story of how a researcher or group of researchers investigated a specific problem. Thus, a research report has a linear, narrative structure with a beginning, middle, and end. In his paper on writing research reports, Bem noted that a research report:

> . . .is shaped like an hourglass. It begins with broad general statements, progressively narrows down to the specifics of [the] study, and then broadens out again to more general considerations. (1987, p. 175)

This format roughly mirrors the process of scientific investigation, wherein researchers do the following: (1) start with a broad idea from which they formulate a narrower set of hypotheses, informed by past empirical findings (introduction); (2) design a specific set of concrete operations to test these hypotheses (method); (3) analyze the observations collected in this way, and decide if they support the original hypotheses (results); and (4) explore the broader theoretical and practical implications of the findings, and consider how they contribute to an understanding of the problem under investigation (discussion). Though these stages are somewhat arbitrary distinctions—research actually proceeds in a number of different ways—they help elucidate the inner logic of research reports.

While reading a research report, keep this linear structure in mind. Though it is difficult to remember a series of seemingly disjointed facts, when these facts are joined together in a logical, narrative structure, they become easier to comprehend and recall. Thus, always remember that a research report tells a story. It will help you to organize the information you read, and remember it later.

Describing research reports as stories is not just a convenient metaphor. Research reports are stories. Stories can be said to consist of two components: A telling of what happened, and an explanation of why it happened. It is tempting to view science as an endeavor that simply catalogues facts, but nothing is further from the truth. The goal of science, social psychology included, is to *explain* facts, to explain *why* what happened happened. Social psychology is built on the dynamic interplay of discovery and justification, the dialogue between systematic observation of relations and their theoretical explanation. Though research reports do present novel facts based on systematic observation, these facts are presented in the service of ideas. Facts in isolation are trivia. Facts tied together by an explanatory theory are science. Therein lies the story. To really understand what researchers have to say, you need consider how their explanations relate to their findings.

The Rest of the Story

> There is really no such thing as research. There is only search, more search, keep on searching. (Bowering, 1988, p. 95)

Once you have read through a research report, and understand the researchers' findings and their explanations of them, the story does not end there. There is more than one interpretation for any set of findings. Different researchers often explain the same set of facts in different ways.

Let's take a moment to dispel a nasty rumor. The rumor is this: Researchers present their studies in a dispassionate manner, intending only to inform readers of their findings and their interpretation of those findings. In truth, researchers aim not only to inform readers, but also to *persuade* them (Sternberg, 1995). Researchers want to convince you their ideas are right. There is never only one explanation for a set of findings. Certainly, some explanations are better than others; some fit the available data better, are more parsimonious, or require fewer questionable assumptions. The point here is that researchers are very passionate about their ideas, and want you to believe them. It's up to you to decide if you want to buy their ideas or not.

Let's compare social psychologists to salesclerks. Both social psychologists and salesclerks want to sell you something; either their ideas, or their wares. You need to decide if you want to buy what they're selling or not—and there are potentially negative consequences for either decision. If you let a sales clerk dazzle you with a sales pitch, without thinking about it carefully, you might end up buying a substandard product that you don't really need. After having done this a few times, people tend to become cynical, steeling themselves against any and all sales pitches. This too is dangerous. If you are overly critical of sales pitches, you could end up foregoing genuinely useful products. Thus, by analogy, when you are too critical in your reading of research reports, you might dismiss, out of hand, some genuinely useful ideas—ideas that can help shed light on why people behave the way they do.

This discussion raises the important question of how critical one should be while reading a research report. In part, this will depend on why one is reading the report. If you are reading it simply to learn what the researchers have to say about a particular issue, for example, then there is usually no need to be overly critical. If you want to use the research as a basis for planning a new study, then you should be more critical. As you develop an understanding of psychological theory and research methods, you will also develop an ability to criticize research on many different levels. And *any* piece of research can be criticized at some level. As Jacob Cohen put it, "A successful piece of research doesn't conclusively settle an issue, it just makes some theoretical proposition to some degree more likely" (1990, p. 1311). Thus, as a consumer of research reports, you have to strike a delicate balance between being overly critical and overly accepting.

While reading a research report, at least initially, try to suspend your disbelief. Try to understand the researchers' story; that is, try to understand the facts—the findings and how they were obtained—and the suggested explanation of those facts—the researchers' interpretation of the findings and what they mean. Take the research to task only after you feel you understand what the authors are trying to say.

Research reports serve not only an important archival function, documenting research and its findings, but also an invaluable stimulus function. They can excite other researchers to join the investigation of a particular issue, or to apply new methods or theory to a different, perhaps novel, issue. It is this stimulus function that Elliot Aronson, an eminent social psychologist, referred to when he admitted that, in publishing a study, he hopes his colleagues will "look at it, be stimulated by it, be provoked by it, annoyed by it, and then go ahead and do it better.... That's the exciting thing about science; it progresses by people taking off on one another's work" (1995, p. 5). Science is indeed a cumulative enterprise, and each new study builds on what has (or, sometimes, has not) gone before it. In this way, research articles keep social psychology vibrant.

A study can inspire new research in a number of different ways, such as: (1) it can lead one to conduct a better test of the hypotheses, trying to rule out alternative explanations of the findings; (2) it can lead one to explore the limits of the findings, to see how widely applicable they are, perhaps exploring situations to which they do not apply; (3) it can lead one to test the implications of the findings, furthering scientific investigation of the phenomenon; (4) it can inspire one to apply the findings, or a novel methodology, to a different area of investigation; and (5) it can provoke one to test the findings in the context of a specific real world problem, to see if they can shed light on it. All of these are excellent extensions of the original research, and there are, undoubtedly, other ways that research findings can spur new investigations.

The problem with being too critical, too soon, while reading research reports is that the only further research one may be willing to attempt is research of the first type: Redoing a study better. Sometimes this is desirable, particularly in the early stages of investigating a particular issue, when the findings are novel and perhaps unexpected. But redoing a reasonably compelling study, without extending it in any way, does little to advance our understanding of human behavior. Although the new study might be "better," it will not be "perfect," so *it* would have to be run again, and again, likely never reaching a stage where it is beyond criticism. At some point, researchers have to decide that the evidence is compelling enough to warrant investigation of the last four types. It is these types of studies that most advance our knowledge of social behavior. As you read more research reports, you will become more comfortable deciding when a study is "good enough" to move beyond it. This is a somewhat subjective judgment, and should be made carefully.

When social psychologists write up a research report for publication, it is because they believe they have something new and exciting to communicate about social behavior. Most research reports that are submitted for publication are rejected. Thus, the reports that are eventually published are deemed pertinent not only by the researchers who wrote them, but also by the reviewers and editors of the journals in which they are published. These people, at least, believe the research reports they write and publish have something important and interesting to say. Sometimes, you'll disagree; not all journal articles are created equal, after all. But we recommend that you, at least initially, give these well-meaning social psychologists the benefit of the doubt. Look for what they're excited about. Try to understand the authors' story, and see where it leads you.

Author Notes

Preparation of this paper was facilitated by a Natural Sciences and Engineering Research Council of Canada doctoral fellowship to Christian H. Jordan. Thanks to Roy Baumeister, Arie Kruglanski, Ziva Kunda, John Levine, Geoff MacDonald, Richard Moreland, Ian Newby-Clark, Steve Spencer, and Adam Zanna for their insightful comments on, and appraisals of, various drafts of this paper. Thanks also to Arie Kruglanski and four anonymous editors of volumes in the series, *Key Readings in Social Psychology* for their helpful critiques of an initial outline of this paper. Correspondence concerning this article should be addressed to Christian H. Jordan, Department of Psychology, University of Waterloo, Waterloo, Ontario, Canada N2L 3G1. Electronic mail can be sent to chjordan@watarts.uwaterloo.ca

REFERENCES

American Psychological Association (1994). *Publication manual* (4th ed.). Washington, D.C.

Aronson, E. (1995). Research in social psychology as a leap of faith. In E. Aronson (Ed.), *Readings about the social animal* (7th ed., pp. 3–9). New York: W. H. Freeman and Company.

Bem, D. J. (1987). Writing the empirical journal article. In M. P. Zanna & J. M. Darley (Eds.), *The compleat academic: A practical guide for the beginning social scientist* (pp. 171–201). New York: Random House.

Bowering, G. (1988). *Errata*. Red Deer, Alta.: Red Deer College Press.

Cohen, J. (1990). Things I have learned (so far). *American Psychologist, 45*, 1304–1312.

Forgas, J. P. (1994). Sad and guilty? Affective influences on the explanation of conflict in close relationships. *Journal of Personality and Social Psychology, 66*, 56–68.

Sternberg, R. J. (1995). *The psychologist's companion: A guide to scientific writing for students and researchers* (3rd ed.). Cambridge: Cambridge University Press.

Author Index

Abele, A., 190, 202
Abelson, R.P., 233, 241
Aboud, F.E., 133, 145
Abrams, Dominic, 1–14, 91, 93, 110, 111, 112, 127, 128, 176, 203, 207, 223, 225, 226, 229, 230, 232–244, 244, 247, 252, 254, 255, 256, 257, 263, 264, 267, 270–288, 356, 358, 368, 397, 398, 399, 127, 241, 244, 368
Abrams, Mark, 320
Abramson, L.Y., 239, 241, 242
Adorno, T.W., 2, 8, 15, 28n.1, 34, 43, 53, 54, 73, 87, 94, 108, 163, 172, 229, 320, 334, 397
Ager, J.W., 118, 126
Aikin, K.J., 148, 161
Alan, N., 33, 53
Albert, G., 255, 264
Alexander, S., 209, 225
Allen, H.M. Jr., 148, 161
Allen, V.L., 276, 277, 286, 381
Allison, P.D., 33, 53
Alloy, L.B., 239, 241, 242, 243
Allport, Floyd H., 2, 303, 315, 397
Allport, Gordon W., 10, 12, 19, 28n.2, 73, 87, 134–135, 138, 143, 144, 162–173, 172, 173, 320, 334, 353, 355, 370, 381, 383, 393, 397
Almaguer, T., 84, 87
Alper, T.G., 67
Altemeyer, B., 3, 16, 17, 36, 38, 50, 53, 397
Amabile, T.M., 164, 173
Ambrose, M., 205, 226
American Psychological Association, 412
Amir, Y., 12, 370, 383, 393, 381, 397
Anastasio, P.A., 13, 148, 159, 160, 398
Anderson, A.B., 125, 126, 154, 161
Anderson, L.R., 118, 126
Anderson, R.A., 54
Andreyeva, G., 4, 397
Anglin, J.M., 144
Annin, P., 158, 159
Apfelbaum, E., 143, 144
Apostle, R.A., 72, 87
Arcuri, L., 7, 399
Arguellas, J.A., 54
Arkin, R.M., 239, 241, 280, 287
Armstrong, T.L., 11, 301, 398
Arnold, W.J., 315
Aron, A., 12, 401
Aronson, Elliot, 126, 145, 163, 172, 233, 241, 242, 256, 264, 315, 367, 368, 369, 378, 381, 410, 412
Aronson, J., 231
Asch, S.E., 9, 267, 270, 276, 277, 286, 290, 296, 397

Ashmore, R.D., 72, 87, 375, 381
Austin, G.A., 139, 144
Austin, Q.G., 128
Austin, W.G., 56, 126, 145, 203, 243, 288, 351, 369, 394, 400
Austrin, H., 139, 145
Avery, P.G., 32, 53
Avigdor, R., 94, 108
Axsom, D., 366, 369

Bachman, B.A., 13, 160, 398
Bachman, J.G, 238, 241
Back, K., 110, 126
Bagley, C., 320, 321, 330, 334
Baldassare, M., 87
Banaji, M.R., 9, 11, 399
Bandura, A., 240, 241
Banker, B., 160
Banks, W.C., 170–171, 172
Bargh, J.A., 5, 397
Barnes, W.R., 54
Baron, K.M., 208, 225
Baron, R.S., 280, 287
Barrett-Howard, E., 209, 225
Bar-Tal, D., 394
Bartlett, F.C., 240, 241
Barton, R., 239, 242
Bass, B.M., 94, 102, 108
Baumeister, R.F., 239, 241
Baxter, G.W., 106, 108
BBC Points West, 311
BBC Radio Bristol, 312
Beck, A.T., 239, 241
Beck, R.A., 315
Bekkers, F., 8, 400
Bell, D., 86, 87
Bem, D.J., 407, 409, 412
Bendix, R., 28n.10
Benokraitis, N.V., 153, 159
Benson, P.L., 32, 37, 53
Bentler, P.M., 120, 126, 127, 128
Berger, P.L., 142, 144
Berk, R.A., 304, 315
Berkowitz, L., 11, 94, 108, 134, 144, 172, 240, 241, 243, 287, 299, 369, 397, 399, 400, 401
Bernstein, M., 339, 350
Berry, J.W., 98, 105, 108
Berscheid, E., 125, 126, 337, 351
Bettelheim, B., 28n.3

Bettencourt, B.A., 63
Bienen, L., 33, 53
Billig, M.G., 3, 4, 16, 17, 91, 95, 99, 100, 106, 108, 109, 135, 136, 141, 144, 169, 182, 188, 192t, 195, 202, 203, 233, 236, 240, 241, 243, 356, 366, 368, 369, 397, 400
Binion, G., 159
Birrell, P., 145
Bishop, D.W., 234, 242
Blackstone, T., 10, 248, 252, 269, 401
Blake, R.R., 3, 4, 62, 94, 108, 202, 397
Blalock, H.M., 86, 87
Blan, M., 399
Blanchard, F.A., 159
Blaney, N., 367, 368
Blank, A., 164, 173
Blanz, Mathias, 8, 176, 188–204
Blau, P.M., 318, 319, 334
Blauner, R.A., 84, 87
Blumer, H., 62, 72, 75, 87, 397
Bobo, Lawrence, 4, 32, 53, 55, 62, 71–90, 146, 161, 397
Bochner, S., 12, 397
Bock, R.D., 275, 286
Bodenhausen, G.V., 6, 385, 392, 393, 399
Bogardus, E.S., 66, 72, 87
Bohinstedt, G.W., 54
Borgatta, E.F., 54
Bornstein, A., 233, 236, 241
Bouhuijs, F., 206, 226
Bourhis, R.Y., 4, 62, 91, 98, 108, 112, 128, 175, 177, 189, 191, 201, 203, 235, 237, 243, 255, 264, 397, 401
Bowen, D.R., 333, 335
Bowen, John, 132
Bowering, G., 409, 412
Boyanowski, E.O., 277, 286
Braly, K., 72, 88
Bramel, O., 240, 241
Brandscatter, H., 286
Branscombe, N.R., 231, 301
Branthwaite, A., 233, 236, 241
Brauer, M., 7, 131, 397
Braugart, R.D., 160
Braun, J.R., 98, 108
Breakwell, G., 256, 264
Brehm, J.W., 291, 296
Brett, J.M., 208, 226
Brewer, Marilyn B., 2, 4, 9, 12, 14, 63, 89, 112, 126, 127, 158, 159, 160, 161, 168, 172, 177, 207, 225, 230, 245–253, 252, 254, 264, 353, 354, 355, 358, 365, 366, 367, 368, 369, 383, 384, 393, 394, 397, 399
Brickenkamp, R., 196, 202
Brickman, P., 240, 241
Brief, D., 49, 55
Brigham, J.C., 74, 87, 98, 108, 146, 159, 375, 381
Brink, W., 320, 334
Bristol Evening Post, 308
Brockner, J., 205, 206, 222, 225
Bromley, S., 7, 147, 159, 397
Brown, D.E., 32, 53
Brown, J.D., 247, 252
Brown, N.J., 238, 241
Brown, R. Jr., 189, 203, 250, 252
Brown, R.J., 5, 6, 12, 14, 17, 106, 109, 112, 115, 126, 127, 128, 188, 189, 190, 191, 195, 198, 201, 202, 203, 204, 210, 224, 225, 226, 233, 237, 238, 240, 241, 244, 250, 252, 272, 286, 353, 357, 358, 368, 371, 381, 383, 392, 393, 394, 397, 398, 399, 400
Bruggink, J.B., 280, 287
Bruner, Jerome S., 18, 29n.38, 133, 137, 139, 144, 164, 172
Bulman, R.J., 240, 241
Bundy, R.P., 4, 91, 95, 109, 182, 188, 192t, 203, 233, 243, 356, 369, 400
Burnstein, E., 270, 280, 281, 283, 286, 287, 288
Burt, M.R., 32, 37, 54
Burton, B.T., 72, 87
Busceme, S., 10, 269, 401
Buss, A.H., 38, 54
Buss, A.R., 143, 144
Buss, A.M., 168, 172
Buss, D.M., 55
Bynner, J.M., 238, 241
Byrne, D., 99, 108, 358, 368

Caddick, B., 102, 108, 238, 241
Caine, A., 209, 226
Cairns, E., 255, 265
Calder, B.J., 207, 226
Campbell, A., 317, 318, 320, 334
Campbell, D.T., 2, 4, 75, 88, 94, 108, 112, 126, 127, 168, 169, 172, 177, 359, 368, 397
Campbell, J., 239, 240, 243
Cantril, H., 320, 323, 334
Caporael, L., 245, 249, 252
Capozza, D., 5, 397, 399
Carlisle, C.J., 394
Carlston, D.E., 190, 203
Carmines, E.G., 38, 54
Carron, 110, 125, 126
Cartwright, D., 110, 126
Carver, C.S., 271, 287
Cash, W., 28n.4
Castelli, L., 7, 399
Cattin, P., 154, 161
Cederblom, D., 106, 108
Centers, R., 28n.23, 317, 334
Chaiken, S., 7, 398
Chanowitz, B., 164, 173
Chaplin, W., 239, 242
Chapman, L.J., 136. 144
Charters, W.W. Jr., 168, 172, 316, 334
Chassin, L., 238, 243
Chatman, J.A., 207, 210, 226
Chein, I., 88
Cheng, L., 74, 79, 87
Child, P., 255, 265
Chou, C.P., 126
Christian, J., 255, 264
Christie, R., 27, 28n.5
Christopher, W., 53, 54
Citrin, J., 73, 87, 148, 161
Clark, K., 335
Clark, R.D. III, 10, 158, 161, 268, 358, 369, 399
Clayton, S.D., 153, 154, 159
Cling, B.J., 32, 55
Cobas, J.A., 72, 88
Cochrane, Sandra, 10, 267, 270–288, 397

Codol, J.P., 237, 239, 240, 241, 247, 252
Coffman, T.L., 146, 160
Cohen, J., 410, 412
Cohn, Norman, 144, 141
Cole, S.G., 278, 287
Collins, B.E., 247, 375, 381
Collins, M., 28n.7, 381
Collins, R.L., 252
Commins, B., 142, 144, 357, 368
Condor, S., 112, 126, 195,.203, 210, 225
Conlon, A.E., 206, 226
Converse, P.E., 334
Cook, K.S., 337, 338, 350
Cook, S.W., 12, 29n.40, 74, 87, 355, 383, 393, 397
Cook, T.D., 338, 339, 350
Cooley, C.H., 240, 241, 318, 334
Cooper, J., 14, 150, 161, 171, 173, 240, 241, 268, 280, 281, 287
Cooper-Schneider, R., 205, 225
Cooper-Shaw, L., 111, 127
Coopersmith, S., 235, 241
Cordova, D., 11, 156, 159, 397
Cose, E., 72, 87
Coser, Lewis A., 178
Costa, P.T., 34, 54
Cotterill, Malcolm, 308
Cottrell, N.B., 240, 241
Cough, K., 394
Courtney, B.E., 236, 242
Craighead, W.E., 239, 243
Cram, F., 250, 252
Crawford, T.J., 332, 334
Croak, M.R., 63
Crocker, J., 10, 13, 52, 54, 155, 159, 160, 224, 226, 231, 235, 236, 237, 239, 242, 243, 247, 252, 258, 259, 265, 371, 375, 380, 381, 384, 392, 393, 394, 397, 401
Crosby, F.J., 7, 11, 147, 155, 156, 157, 159, 301, 337, 338, 339, 340, 349, 350, 397
Crull, S.R., 87, 72
Crum, L., 233, 241
Csepeli, G., 99, 108, 366
Culbertson, A., 159
Cummings, L.L., 226
Cutler, S.J., 173, 226
Czapinski, J., 190, 202, 203

Dahl, K.R., 4, 63, 399
Daily Mirror, 307
Dalton, D., 394
Daniel, W.W., 320, 334
Dann, H.D., 99, 108, 366
Darity, W. Jr., 54
Darley, J.M., 149, 159, 412
Dator, J.A., 51, 54
David, B., 10, 268, 399
Davidson, B., 112, 127
Davies, J.C., 11, 332, 333, 334, 397
Davis, A., 28n.6
Davis, J.A., 11, 127, 146, 159, 318, 319, 333, 334, 337, 350, 398
Davis, J.H., 286
Davis, K.E., 72, 87

Davis, K.L., 166, 168, 172
Davis, M.H., 34, 36, 37, 38, 45, 54
Dawes, R.M., 245, 252, 368, 369
de Brey, J.H.C., 366, 369
de Sola Pool, I., 317, 335
de Vera Park, M.V., 205, 226
de Vries, N., 124, 126, 203, 224, 226
Deaux, Kay, 9, 93, 171, 172, 230, 254–265, 264, 398
Deci, E.L., 240, 242
DeGoey, Peter, 8, 176, 205–228, 226, 401
Del Boca, F.K., 72, 87
Dempsey, G.R., 72, 88
Dennis, W., 172
Denno, D.W., 33, 53
Denton, N.A., 86, 88
Denzin, N.K., 305, 315
Depret, E.F., 49, 54
Derlega, V.J., 369
Deschamps, J-C., 5, 93, 128, 143, 144, 356, 357, 368, 401
Deutsch, Morton, 4, 28n.7, 62, 63, 94, 108, 158, 159, 207, 226, 270, 271, 286, 287, 359, 368, 375, 381, 398
Devereux, E., 49, 55
Devine, P.G., 5, 129, 146, 159, 398
DeVinney, L.C., 29n.39, 337, 335, 350
Diab, L.N., 4, 94, 108, 398
Diehl, M., 4, 91, 175, 195, 200, 203, 398
Diener, E., 272, 287
Diers, J., 106, 108
Dietze, C., 203
Dietz-Uhler, B.L., 154, 160
Dijker, A.J., 392, 394
Dillman, D.A., 210, 226
DiMiceli, A.J., 168, 173
Dion, K.L., 112, 126, 356, 368
Dizard, J.E., 98, 108
Dodge, K.A., 375, 380, 381
Doise, W., 99, 102, 108, 129, 134, 136, 137, 138, 144, 168, 171, 172, 247, 252, 274, 279, 281, 287, 356, 357, 366, 368, 398
Dollard, J., 28n.8, 28n.9, 73, 87
Domhoff, G.W., 72, 89
Doms, M., 296
Donahue, E., 38, 54
Donnerstein, E., 171, 172
Donnerstein, M., 171, 172
Doob, L.W., 28n.9, 87
Doosje, B., 5, 93, 398
Doty, R.M., 43, 55
Dovidio, John F., 6, 13, 14, 54, 101, 130, 131, 146–161, 159, 160, 161, 202, 203, 354, 355, 356–369, 368, 369, 394, 398, 399
Doyle, A., 17
Doyle, S., 233, 241
Drenan, S., 277, 287
Drigotas, S.M., 4, 63, 399
Drout, C., 154, 160
Dube, L., 249, 252, 338, 339, 350
Dube-Simard, L., 350
Duck, J.M., 112, 127
Duckitt, J., 3, 36, 50, 54, 73, 87, 398
Dukerich, J.N., 207, 226
Duncan, B.L., 143, 144, 169, 172
Duncan, G., 108

Dunn, A., 79, 87
Dunn, G., 389, 394
Dunteman, G., 94, 102
Dunton, B.C., 150, 160
Durkheim, E., 2, 333, 398
Duster, T., 75, 87
Dye, T.R., 339, 350
Dyer, J., 72, 87

Eagly, A.H., 7, 398
Earley, P.C., 207, 209, 226
Easterbrook, J.J.A., 385, 394
Eberhardt, J.L., 131, 398
Edwards, K., 357, 369
Edwards, R., 383, 394
Efflal, B., 112, 128
Ehrlich, H.J., 5, 398
Ehrlich, S.B., 207, 226
Eisenstadt, S.N., 316, 334
Eiser, J.R., 136, 137, 144, 394
Eisinger, N., 159
Eisler, R., 32, 45, 54
Eisner, H.C., 72, 88
Ekehammar, B., 32, 51, 54, 55
Ellemers, N., 5, 12, 14, 93, 112, 113, 124, 126, 127, 176,
    177, 189, 195, 203, 204, 224, 226, 398, 399
Ellertson, N., 110, 128
Elliot, A.J., 146, 159
Emler, N., 8, 255, 264, 398
Emswiller, T., 171, 172
Epley, S.W., 240, 241
Erskine, H.G., 320, 334
Espiritu, Y.L., 73, 74, 79, 87
Esses, V.M., 11, 301, 398
Estrada, L.F., 54
Etcoff, N.L., 145
Ethier, Kathleen A., 9, 93, 230, 254–265, 264, 398
Eulau, H., 317, 334
Evans, A., 72, 87
Evans, N.J., 110, 126
Evans, R.I., 317, 335
Evenbeck, S., 338, 350
Everitt, B.S., 389, 394
Eysenck, H.J., 32, 34, 54

Fahr, J.L., 206, 226
Farley, R., 87, 89
Farr, R.M., 2, 6, 398
Farrell, W.C. Jr., 79, 88
Fazio, R.H., 7, 150, 159, 160, 398
Feagin, C.B., 53, 54
Feagin, J.R., 53, 54, 72, 76, 84, 86, 87, 90, 153, 159
Feierabend, L., 332, 334
Feierabend, R.L., 332, 334
Feinstein, J., 155, 160
Feldman, S., 72, 74, 87, 90
Fenigstein, A., 38, 54, 271, 287
Fenton, J.M., 320, 334
Ferguson, C.K., 99, 102, 108, 356, 366, 368
Ferris, F., 366, 369
Feshbach, S., 32, 35, 54

Festinger, L., 8, 98, 105, 108, 126, 110, 125, 229, 233, 239,
    240, 242, 271, 287, 296, 303, 315, 318, 334, 398
Fetter, R., 212, 226
Fiedler, F.E., 94, 108, 234, 242
Fincham, F., 189, 203
Fine, M., 160
Firebaugh, G., 72, 87
Fischer, G.W., 6, 384, 394, 399
Fisher, R.J., 3, 112, 126, 398
Fishman, J., 101, 108
Fiske, S.T., 5, 14, 17, 49, 54, 131, 145, 392, 394, 398
Flament, Claude, 4, 91, 95, 109, 182, 188, 192t, 203, 233,
    243, 356, 369, 400
Fleming, J.S., 236, 242
Fogelson, R.M., 308, 315
Folger, R., 206, 209, 226, 338, 340, 348, 349, 350
Ford, J.K., 151, 160
Forgas, J.P., 404, 412
Form, W.H., 74, 88, 317, 334
Fossett, M.A., 72, 86, 87
Frable, D.E.S., 248, 252, 256, 264
Franco, F.M., 7, 398
Frantz, C., 320, 321, 322, 335
Fraser, C., 108, 145
Frenkel-Brunswik, E., 2, 15, 28n.1, 34, 53, 54, 87, 94, 108,
    163, 172, 334, 397
Fretag, P., 301
Freud, S., 240, 242
Freund, T., 202, 203
Friedman, N., 98, 106, 108
Frieze, I., 173
Froming, W.J., 271, 287
Fromkin, H.L., 247, 248, 252, 253
Fujioka, T., 255, 265
Fulero, S., 145
Funk, C.L., 73, 88

Gadfield, N.J., 255, 264
Gaertner, Samuel L., 6, 13, 14, 54, 93, 130, 131, 146–161,
    159, 160, 161, 171, 172, 177, 202, 203, 354, 355, 356–
    369, 368, 369, 394, 398, 399
Gagnon, A., 91, 175, 397
Gallo, L., 239, 242
Gamble, I., 249, 253
Gamble, L., 338, 351
Gamson, W.A., 153, 160
Gange, J.J., 303, 315
Gardner, B., 28n.6
Gardner, M., 28n.6
Garrett, J.B., 36, 54
Gecas, V., 240, 242
Geen, R.G., 73, 303, 315
Greenberg, J., 160
General Accounting Office, 54
Gerard, H.B., 100, 108, 134, 144, 270, 271, 286, 287
Gersho, B.F., 394
Geschwender, J.A., 317, 319, 334
Gifford, R.K., 133, 136–137, 144
Gilbert, D.T., 14
Gilbert, E., 19, 29n.34
Giles, H., 5, 14, 63, 97, 98, 101, 108, 112, 127, 128, 233,
    243, 244, 255, 264, 286, 369, 398, 400

Giles, M.W., 72, 87
Giner, S., 314, 315
Glaser, J.M., 72, 87
Glazer, N., 74, 87
Gleicher, F., 54
Glick, P., 131
Glock, C.Y., 87
Goddard, R.W., 151, 160
Goertzel, T.G., 36, 38, 54
Goffman, E., 168, 172
Gollwitzer, P.M., 235, 243
Goodnow, J.J., 139, 144
Gossop, M.R., 136, 144
Gouge, C., 99, 108, 366
Gough, H.G., 28n.12, 33, 36, 38, 54
Graetz, K.A., 4, 63, 93, 399
Graham, H.D., 398
Grant, G., 98, 108, 400
Graumann, C–F., 394
Greeley, A.M., 72, 89
Green, D.P., 87
Green, R.T., 50, 55
Greenberg, J., 8, 153, 205, 209, 230, 226, 398
Greenblum, J., 28n.10
Greene, D., 165, 173
Greenwald, A.G., 265
Greenwell, M., 77, 87
Gregor, A.J., 97, 108
Gregory, D., 110, 128
Groves, R.M., 77, 88, 89
Grunert, M., 203
Grzelack, J., 369
Guardian, 307, 312
Guimond, S., 249, 252, 338, 339, 350
Gunther, John, 69
Gurin, G., 334
Gurr, T.R., 11, 332, 337, 301, 334, 350, 398
Gurwitz, S.B., 375, 380, 381

Habig, C., 301
Haeger, G., 203
Hagendoorn, L., 74, 88, 148, 149, 160
Hahn, H., 335
Hains, Sarah C., 5, 92, 110–128, 399
Halbestadt, L.J., 239, 242
Hall, W.S., 148
Hall, J.F., 239, 242
Hall, W.S., 161
Hamill, R., 380, 381
Hamilton, D.L., 9, 87, 133, 136, 136–137, 143, 144, 148, 159, 160, 381, 385, 393, 394, 395, 398
Hardie, E.A., 111, 113, 115, 125, 127
Harding, John, 28n.11, 74, 88, 164, 172
Hardyck, J.A., 317, 335, 358, 369
Harkins, S., 271, 288
Harring, K., 233, 241
Harris, D.B., 28n.12
Harris, L., 320, 334
Harris, S., 98, 108
Harris, V.A., 164, 173
Hartley, E.L., 28n.13, 172, 334
Hartley, R.E., 317, 334, 335

Harvey, O.J., 3, 61, 66, 94, 99, 108, 109, 226, 367, 369, 400
Harvey, R.D., 301
Haslam, S.A., 5, 10, 14, 17, 111, 128, 131, 201, 202, 203, 204, 255, 264, 398, 399
Hass, R.G., 38, 41, 45, 54
Hatchett, S., 76, 88
Heaven, P.C.L., 50, 54
Heider, Fritz, 164, 165, 169, 172, 240, 242, 378, 381
Hellmann, E., 28n.14, 335
Helmreich, R., 35, 55
Hendrick, C., 287
Hennigan, K.M., 338, 339, 350
Hensler, C.P., 74, 88, 148, 161
Hepburn, C., 375, 381
Herman, C.P., 237, 243, 252, 350
Herodotus, 314
Herzlich, C., 143, 144
Hewstone, Miles, 6, 9, 12, 112, 127, 131, 135, 143, 144, 159, 160, 189, 203, 231, 286, 353, 354, 355, 383–395
Higgins, E.T., 203
Hiller, E.T., 66
Hinde, R.A., 142, 144
Hinkle, S.W., 188, 201, 203, 224, 226
Hirschman, A.O., 96, 108
Hitt, M.A., 158, 160
Ho, H., 357, 368
Hoffman, M.L., 28n.15
Hoge, D.R., 238, 242
Hogg, Michael A., 1–14, 91, 93, 110–128, 176, 201, 203, 204, 207, 223, 225, 226, 229, 230, 231, 232–244, 246, 247, 252, 253, 254, 257, 264, 267, 270–288, 354, 355, 356, 357, 358, 368, 369, 397, 398, 399, 400, 401
Hogrefe, R., 28n.11
Hollander, E.P., 2, 271, 287, 400
Holtz, R., 357, 367, 369
Holzworth, D.W., 111, 127
Homans, G.C., 318, 319, 337, 335, 350
Hood, William R., 3, 61, 65, 66, 94, 109, 207, 226, 367, 369, 400, 109, 226, 369
Hopkins, K.D., 118, 127
Hopkins, N., 8, 255, 264, 400
Hormuth, S.E., 255, 256, 262, 264
Hornsey, M.J., 13, 354, 355, 399
Hornstein, H.A., 158, 160, 358, 368
Horowitz, E.L., 66
Horowitz, L.M., 37, 38, 54
Horwitz, M., 188, 203, 240, 242, 356, 366, 369, 384, 392, 394
Hough, J.C., 148, 160
Howard, A., 159
Howard, J., 145
Howes, P.W., 74, 89
Hoyt, M.F., 100, 108
Hraba, J., 98, 108
Hu, L., 127
Huber, J., 74, 88
Huberty, C.J., 387, 394
Hui, C.H., 249, 253
Hunt, J.M., 243
Hunter, B.A., 148, 161
Huo, Y.J., 209, 225, 226
Hutchings, Vincent L., 4, 62, 71–90, 397
Hyman, H.H., 19, 28n.16, 72, 88, 108, 237, 242, 316, 317, 319, 320, 333, 335

Ingerman, C., 236, 242
Inkeles, A., 322, 335
Insko, C.A., 4, 14, 63, 177, 233, 241, 277, 287, 399
Inverarity, J., 112, 127
Irle, M., 136, 144
Isaac, L., 339, 350
Islam, Mir Rabiul, 13, 354, 383–395, 399
Israel, J., 109, 145
Iyengar, S., 55

Jackman, M.R., 72, 73, 74, 86, 88
Jackson, B.O., 89
Jackson, D.N., 34, 35, 36, 38, 54
Jackson, J.R., 150, 160
Jackson, L.M., 11, 301, 398
Jackson, T., 87
Jacobson, C.K., 153, 160
Jaggi, V., 6, 143, 145, 169, 170, 173, 400
Jahoda, G., 104, 108
Jahoda, M., 28n.5
James, L.R., 208, 226
James, William, 316
Jamieson, D.W., 147, 161
Janowitz, M., 28n.3
Jarvis, R.A., 110, 126
Jaskar, K., 11, 397
Jaspars, J.M.F., 6, 143, 144, 189, 203, 240, 242, 398
Jellison, J., 280, 287
Jensen, C., 145
Jetten, J.S., 6, 177, 399
John, O.P., 34, 37, 38, 54, 356, 369, 384, 393, 394
Johnson, B.T., 146, 159
Johnson, C., 159
Johnson, D.W., 94, 108, 359, 368
Johnson, F.P., 359, 368
Johnson, J.H. Jr., 79, 112, 87, 88
Johnson, L.K., 312, 315
Johnson, P., 5, 127, 398
Johnston, L., 112, 127, 384, 393, 394
Jones, R., 152, 160
Jones, E., 28n.17
Jones, E.E., 6, 134, 144, 164, 166, 168, 172, 173, 239, 242, 371, 380, 381, 384, 392, 394, 399
Jones, J.M., 367, 368
Jonsson, D.R., 201, 203
Jordon, Christian H., 403–412
Joseph, J., 256, 264
Jost, J.T., 9, 11, 399
Joubert, C.E., 207, 226
Judd, C.M., 6, 118, 213, 226, 384, 388, 392, 394, 399
Julian, J.W., 94, 109, 234, 242

Kahn, A., 366, 368
Kahn, R.L., 77, 88
Kahneman, D., 136, 145, 167, 169, 173, 190, 203, 385, 394
Kalin, R., 94, 98, 108, 109
Kampmeier, C., 301
Kanfer, R., 209, 226
Kano, Y., 127
Kanouse, D.E., 173
Kanter, R.M., 167, 173

Kantor, M., 54
Kaplan, B., 144
Kaplan, H.B., 238, 242
Kaplan, N., 317, 335
Kardes, F.R., 7, 398
Karlins, M., 146, 160
Katz, D., 72, 88, 240, 242
Katz, I., 38, 41, 45, 54, 73, 74, 88, 104, 109
Katz, P.A., 87, 161, 172, 381
Kayne, N.T., 239, 242
Keats, B.W., 158, 160
Keller, S., 206, 317, 319, 335
Kelley, H.H., 99, 102, 108, 134, 145, 165, 166, 169, 173, 226, 316, 318, 335, 356, 366, 368
Kelman, H.C., 296
Kennedy, J.F., 4, 63, 399
Kenny, D.A., 118, 127, 208, 213, 225, 226
Kentle, R.L., 38, 54
Kersting, R.C., 280, 287
Kessler, R., 256, 264
Kessler, S., 203
Kidder, L.H., 98, 105, 109
Kiecolt, K.J., 72, 86, 87
Kiernan, V.G., 141, 145
Kiesler, C.A., 271, 287
Kiesler, S.B., 271, 287
Killian, L., 304, 309, 315
Kimber, Keith, 313
Kinder, D.R., 73, 74, 88, 148, 153, 154, 160
Kirscht, J., 256, 264
Kitayama, S., 49, 54, 249, 252
Kitt, A.S., 316, 331, 332
Kitt (Rossi), A.S., 335
Klandermans, B., 301
Kleck, G., 33, 54
Klein, G.S., 133, 144
Kleiner, R.J., 317, 335
Kleinpenning, G., 74, 88, 148, 149, 160
Kline, B.B., 150, 160
Klineberg, O., 104, 109
Kluckhohn, C., 139, 145
Kluegel, J.R., 32, 33, 54, 72, 73, 74, 76, 87, 88, 89, 90, 152, 160
Knopke, H., 159
Knouse, S., 159
Koivumaki, J.H., 165, 173
Konovsky, M.A., 206, 209, 226
Koomen, W., 118, 127
Koper, G., 206, 222, 226
Kosterman, R., 32, 35, 54
Kovel, J., 148, 160
Kraiger, K., 151, 160
Kramer, R.M., 158, 160, 207, 225, 226, 358, 367, 368, 369
Krause, N., 238, 242
Kravitz, D.A., 110, 127, 153, 154, 160
Kray, L., 225, 226
Krieger, L.H., 155, 157, 160
Kruglanski, A.W., 202, 203, 394
Krysan, M., 87
Kukla, A., 173
Kulik, C.T., 205, 226
Kunda, Z., 249, 252
Kurtz, S., 153, 160, 209, 226
Kutner, B., 19, 28n.18, 88

La Voie, L., 118, 127
Ladwig, G., 104, 109
Lage, E., 289, 290, 294, 295, 296, 297
Lal, B.B., 75, 88
Lalonde, R.N., 112, 113, 127, 157, 161, 249, 253
Lambert, W.E., 168, 173, 255, 264
Lamm, H., 280, 287
Lampen, L., 235, 244
Langan, C.J., 271, 287
Langer, E.J., 164, 173, 239, 242
LaPiere, R.T., 7, 19, 28n.19, 399
Larsen, K., 99, 108, 366
Latane, B., 149, 159, 271, 288
Lauderdale, P., 112, 127
Lawler, E.J., 128, 244, 288, 369, 401
Lawrence, Daniel, 320
Lazarsfeld, P.F., 335
Le Bon, G., 302, 303, 305, 315, 399
Lee, J., 357, 368
Leeper, M.R., 165, 173
Lefcourt, H., 104, 109
Letter, M.E., 338
Leitner, D.W., 53, 54
Lemaine, G., 104, 109, 237, 242, 247, 252
Lemyre, L., 188, 203, 234, 242, 247, 252
Lenski, G.E., 318, 335
Lepore, L., 5, 399
Lerner, M.J., 158, 160, 337, 350
Lerner, S.C., 337, 350
Letter, M.E., 350
Lettgen, S., 203
Levin, 52
Levin, S.L., 52, 54
Levine, D., 108, 315, 335
Levine, J.M., 126, 127, 271, 287
LeVine, R.A., 75, 88, 112, 127
Levinson, D.F., 334
Levinson, D.J., 2, 15, 28n.1, 34, 51, 53, 54, 87, 94, 108, 163, 172, 397
Lewinson, P.M., 239, 242
Lewis, S.A., 271, 287, 384, 394
Leyens, J.R., 112, 127
Lieberman, E., 173
Lieberson, S., 72, 86, 88
Lightbrown, N., 233, 241
Lilli, W., 136, 145
Lind, E.A., 153, 160, 205, 206, 207, 209, 219, 224, 225, 226
Linder, D., 378, 381
Lindzey, G., 14, 88, 126, 145, 241, 242, 315, 369
Linville, P.M., 380, 381
Linville, P.W., 6, 384, 392, 394, 399
Lipset, S.M., 28n.10, 49, 54, 321, 335
Lissak, R.E., 206, 226
Litwak, E., 316, 335
Liu, J., 33, 47, 53, 55
Llado, N., 255, 264
Locksley, A., 375, 380, 381
Lockwood, J., 142, 144, 357, 368
Loevinger, J., 35, 54
Long, K.M., 9, 224, 226, 229, 399
Lord, C., 248, 252
Lott, A.J., 110, 125, 127, 365, 369
Lott, B.E., 110, 125, 127, 365, 369

Louden, D., 238, 242
Lowey, M., 301
Loye, D., 32, 45, 54
Luckmann, T., 142, 144
Luebke, J., 168, 173
Luhtanen, R., 52, 54, 224, 226, 231, 247, 252, 258, 259, 265
Lundgren, S., 10, 269, 401

Maass, A., 7, 10, 222, 223, 226, 268, 398, 399
McBride, 110
McBride, D., 128
McCarthy, J.D., 238, 242
McCarthy, T.D., 340, 350
McClelland, D.C., 240, 242
McConahay, J.B., 32, 38, 41, 148, 54, 160
McConahay, J.G., 6, 399
MacCrone, I.D., 28n.21, 28n.22, 320, 335
McCusker, C., 249, 253
McFaul, T.R., 72, 88
McGarty, C., 10, 202, 203, 204, 255, 264, 398, 399
McGrath, John E., 110, 127, 132
McGraw, K.M., 209, 226, 236, 239, 242
McGuire, C.V., 237, 242, 255, 265
McGuire, W.J., 55, 233, 237, 241, 242, 255, 265
McIver, J.D., 38, 54
Mackenzie, S.B., 212, 226
Mackie, D.M., 10, 14, 158, 159, 160, 188, 195, 203, 223, 226, 240, 241, 268, 280, 281, 287, 356, 369, 385, 392, 393, 394, 395, 399
McKillip, J., 168, 170, 173
Mackinnon, W.J., 28n.23
McKirnan, D.J., 5, 112, 128, 255, 264, 339, 340, 351, 400
McLaughlin, J.P., 150, 160
McLaughlin-Volpe, T., 12, 353, 401
McLean, H.V., 28n.20
McNemar, Q., 259, 265
McPhail, C., 303, 315
McPherson, D.A., 97, 108
McQuarter, G.V., 170–171, 172
Macrae, C.N., 355, 401
Macrae, N., 6, 159, 399
MacRae, R.R., 34, 54
Madden, N.A., 367, 369
Mahajan, H., 32, 55
Major, B., 10, 155, 160, 231, 247, 252, 254, 264, 397
Malamuth, N., 55
Malherbe, E.G., 28n.24, 320, 335
Malle, Bertram F., 3, 16, 30–59, 400
Maniruzzaman, T., 385, 394
Mann, J.A., 13, 148, 159, 202, 203, 366, 368, 398
Mann, J.F., 143, 145
Mann, Jeffrey, 354, 356–369
Mann, L., 11, 401
Mann, M., 296
Manstead, A.S.R., 177, 224, 226
Manzi, J., 251
Marcus, M.M., 238, 243
Marino, K.E., 158,. 160
Mark, M.M., 337, 338, 340, 350
Markus, H.R., 49, 54, 233, 249, 242, 252
Marlatt, G.A., 120, 128
Marlowe, D., 94, 109

Marques, J.M., 9, 112, 127, 399
Marsh, K.L., 54
Martin, Martin, C., 350
Martin, J., 338, 338–339, 339, 340, 348, 349, 350
Martin, M., 55, 30, 39, 53
Martin, R., 10, 268, 399
Martin, W.E., 28n.12
Marwell, G., 236, 244
Marx, G.T., 320, 335
Marx, K., 240, 242
Maslach, C., 247, 252
Maslow, A.H., 239, 242
Masotti, L.H., 333, 335
Massey, D., 86, 88
Massey, J.T., 77, 89
Mathews, A., 112, 126, 195, 203, 210, 225
Mayo, C., 33, 55
Mead, G.H., 2, 289, 296, 318, 335, 399
Medin, D.L., 7, 399
Meertens, R.W., 151, 161
Meindl, J.R., 158, 160, 207, 226
Meneses, L.M., 394
Merton, R.K., 316, 331, 332, 335
Messick, D.M., 158, 160, 188, 190, 203, 223, 226, 337, 338, 350, 356, 369
Metalsky, G., 239, 242
Meyer, D.E., 150, 160
Meyer, P., 320, 335
Mezei, L., 317, 335
Mikula, G., 239, 242
Milgram, S., 303, 314, 315
Miller, A.G., 88
Miller, D.T., 7, 13, 354, 355, 399, 400
Miller, F.B., 67
Miller, M., 357, 368
Miller, N., 12, 14, 28n.9, 63, 89, 102, 109, 112, 127, 161, 353, 355, 357, 368, 369, 383, 393, 394, 399
Miller, N.E., 87
Miller, R.L., 237, 241–242, 243, 271, 287, 350
Miller, W.E., 334
Mills, D.L., 53
Mills, J., 33, 256, 264
Milne, A.B., 6, 399
Milner, D., 97, 106, 109, 238, 242
Milton, O., 28n.25
Minard, R.D., 18–19, 28n.26
Mirels, H.L., 36, 54
Mischel, W., 239, 242
Mitchell, M., 33, 47, 52, 55
Mizrahi, K., 93
Modigliani, A., 153, 160
Moffat, Susan, 88, 73
Moghaddam, Fathali M., 12, 112, 157, 249, 351, 128, 161, 253, 300, 337–351, 401
Moiese, L.C., 177
Monson, T.C., 165, 173
Monteith, M., 131
Moorman, R.H., 206, 226
Morales, J.F., 5, 93, 128, 401
Moreland, R.L., 5, 126, 127, 271, 287, 399
Morland, J.K., 97, 101, 109
Morris, J.D., 387, 394
Morrison, D.E., 338, 350

Moscovici, Serge, 6, 9, 10, 109, 134, 145, 268, 271, 277, 287, 289–297, 304, 315, 398, 399, 400
Mosk, R.M., 54
Mottola, G., 160
Mouton, J.S., 3, 4, 62, 94, 108, 189, 202, 397
Mowday, R.T., 212, 226
Mowrer, O.H., 28n.9, 87
Moynihan, D.P., 32, 55
Mudrack, P.E., 110, 127
Mugny, G., 6, 10, 144, 268, 269, 296, 297, 399
Muhan, M.J., 74, 88
Muhlhausen, S.M., 201, 203
Mukherjee, R., 385, 394
Mullen, B., 189, 194, 195, 200, 201, 203, 250, 252, 272, 276, 287, 394
Mullin, B-A., 7, 230, 399
Mummendey, Amelie, 8, 176, 177, 188–204, 237, 243, 354, 399, 401
Murphy, Gardner, 66
Murray, A., 338, 339, 350
Murrell, Audrey J., 13, 152, 154, 155, 159, 160, 202, 203, 354, 356–369, 203, 398
Musante, L., 153, 160, 209, 226
Mutran, E., 339, 350
Myers, A., 112, 127
Myers, D.G., 280, 287
Myers, P.E., 280, 287
Myrdal, G., 28n.27

Nacoste, R.W., 153, 154, 161, 224, 226
Naditch, N., 332, 334
Naffrechoux, M., 289, 297
Nail, P.R., 271, 287
Nascimento-Schulze, C., 234, 242
Near, J.P., 212, 226
Nedler, B.F., 394
Nelson, R.E., 239, 243
Nemeth, C., 10, 399
Neve, P., 291, 296, 297
Nevill, D.D., 35, 37, 56
Newcomb, M.D., 120, 128
Newcomb, T.M., 168, 172, 233, 241, 303, 315, 316, 317, 334, 335
Newman, H.M., 164, 173
Ng, S.H., 238, 239, 243, 250, 252
Nicholson, N., 278, 280, 287
Nickerson, S., 33, 55
Niedenthal, P., 7, 131, 397
Nier, J., 160
Nisbett, R.E., 173, 380, 381
Nock, S., 161
Norell, J., 159
Norvell, N., 112, 128

Oaker, G., 112, 128
Oakes, P.J., 5, 10, 14, 92, 93, 110, 111, 112, 127, 128, 131, 201, 202, 203, 204, 207, 226, 233, 234, 236, 238, 243, 244, 246, 247, 253, 254, 255, 264, 265, 270, 280, 287, 288, 357, 369, 398, 399, 401
Oberschall, A., 97, 109, 304, 315
O'Connell, J.T., 385, 394

Oliver, M.L., 79, 86, 87, 88
Olsen, J.M., 17, 397
Olson, J.M., 237, 243, 252, 304, 350, 397
Olson, M., 315
Olzak, S., 71, 88
O'Malley, P.M., 238, 241
Omi, M., 72, 88
O'Neil, M.J., 77, 88
O'Neill, P., 338, 350
Onorato, S., 10, 398
Opotow, S., 158, 161
Orbell, J.M., 245, 252, 368
Ordin, A.S., 54
O'Reilly, C.A., 207, 210, 226
Organ, D.W., 206, 212, 226
Ortiz, V., 375, 381
Ortony, A., 7, 399
Ostell, A., 99, 108, 366
Otten, Sabine, 8, 176, 188–204, 399
Ouellette, J.A., 10, 269, 401
Owen, C.A., 72, 88
Oyen, M., 195, 203

P.E.P., 320, 335
Padgham, C.A., 291, 297
Paez, D., 5, 9, 93, 112, 127, 399, 401
Paicheler, H., 128
Paige, J.M., 98, 109
Papineau, D., 145
Pareto, V., 339, 350
Park, B., 6, 371, 381, 384, 388, 392, 394, 399
Parker, J., 112, 127
Parker, R.N., 72, 88
Parker, S., 317, 335
Parsons, T., 335
Patchen, M.A., 317, 319, 335
Patel, Y., 238, 242
Paternoster, R., 33, 55
Patrick, J.R., 29n.36
Patterson, J.R., 36, 56
Paulus, D., 239, 243
Paulus, P.B., 128, 287
Peabody, D., 104, 109
Pear, T.H., 65
Pearlin, L.I., 28n.10, 317, 335
Peeters, G., 190, 202, 203
Pepitone, A., 240, 243, 303, 315
Peplau, L.A., 36, 55
Perreault, S., 177
Perret-Clermont, A.N., 134, 145
Perrin, S., 280, 287
Personnaz, Bernard, 10, 268, 289–297, 399
Pervin, L.A., 54
Peterson, B.E., 43, 55
Pettigrew, Thomas F., 3, 6, 11, 12, 16, 18–29, 28n.28, 28n.29, 73, 88, 130, 151, 157, 161, 162–173, 179, 198, 203, 224, 226, 237, 243, 249, 250, 253, 300, 301, 316–336, 318, 320, 321, 322, 324, 326, 333, 335, 338, 339, 351, 354, 355, 370, 381, 399, 400, 401
Petzold, P., 190, 202
Pfeffer, J., 207, 226
Phares, E.J., 166, 173

Phinney, J.S., 255, 265
Piazza, T., 87
Pierce, G.L., 55
Piliavin, J.A., 158, 161, 358, 369
Pittman, T.S., 239, 242
Podsakoff, P.M., 206, 212, 226
Political and Economic Planning and Research Services Ltd., see P.E.P.
Pomare, M., 366, 368
Porter, L.W., 212, 226
Portes, A., 72, 88
Portnoy, N.W., 168, 172
Poser, E.G., 173
Postman, Leo, 143, 144, 164, 169, 172
Postmes, T., 301
Potter, M.C., 133, 144, 166
Powell, L., 160
Powell, M.C., 7, 398
Powesland, P.F., 97, 98, 101, 108
Powlishta, K.K., 17
Pratkanis, A.R., 155, 161
Pratto, Felicia, 3, 16, 17, 30–59, 400
Prentice, D.A., 7, 13, 354, 355, 399, 400
Prentice-Dunn, S., 271, 272, 287
Preston, M.B., 89
Price Waterhouse v. Hopkins, 161
Proshansky, H., 88
Prothro, E.T., 24, 28n.30
Prothro, J.W., 29n.37
Pry, G., 239, 243
Pryce, Ken, 311, 314
Pryor, J., 171, 172
Pyree, K., 315
Pyszczynski, T., 8, 230, 398

Quattrone, G.A., 6, 371, 384, 392, 381, 394, 399, 400

Raab, E., 321
Rabbie, Jaap M., 4, 8, 62, 63, 99, 102, 188, 203, 240, 356, 366, 384, 392, 109, 242, 369, 394, 400
Rabinowitz, J., 52, 55
Radelet, M.L., 55
Rankin, J.H., 238, 244
Rasinski, K., 206, 209, 226
Ray, J., 50, 55
Reddy, W.M., 314, 315
Reed, L., 173
Reeves, K., 87
Regents of the University of California v. Bakke, 161
Rehm, L.P., 239, 243
Reichel, L.D., 394
Reicher, Stephen D., 5, 8, 11, 92, 93, 110, 127, 128, 201, 204, 207, 226, 238, 244, 246, 253, 270, 271, 272, 287, 288, 299, 301, 302–315, 357, 369, 398, 400, 401
Reid, A., 93
Reid, F.J.M., 239, 243
Reiman, J., 55
Rest, S., 173
Reykowski, J., 240, 243
Reynolds, K.J., 17, 111, 127
Rheaume, K., 349, 350

Riecken, M., 166, 169, 171, 173
Rieder, J., 73, 88
Ring, K., 166, 169, 171, 173
Riordin, C., 370, 381
Roberts, A.E., 72, 88
Robinson, T., 349, 350
Robinson, W.P., 127, 401
Rocklin, T., 278, 287
Rodrigues, J. S., 137, 144
Roese, N.I., 147, 161
Rogers, C.A., 320, 321, 322, 335
Rogers, C.R., 239, 243
Rogers, E.M., 317, 335
Rogers, R.W., 271, 272, 287
Rogers, R., 159
Rokeach, Milton, 3, 8, 16, 17, 229, 317, 335, 400
Roll, C.W. Jr., 323, 334
Rombough, S., 32, 37, 51, 55
Roper, E., 24, 29n.31, 29n.32
Ropp, S.A., 12, 353, 401
Rosch, E., 150, 161, 367, 369
Rose, A.M., 29n.33
Rose, Arnold, 19, 24
Rose, E.J.B., 320, 321, 322, 335
Rosenbaum, M.E., 357, 367, 369
Rosenbaum, R.M., 173
Rosenberg, M.J., 36, 37, 38, 55, 104, 109, 213, 226, 233, 234, 238, 241, 243
Rosenfeld, P., 159
Rosenfield, D., 72, 88, 238, 243, 348, 349, 350
Rosenthal, R., 48, 55
Rosenzweig, S., 239, 243
Ross, G.F., 103, 109
Ross, L., 6, 400
Ross, L.D., 164, 169, 173
Ross, M., 338, 350
Rossi, P.H., 154, 161
Roth, D., 239, 243
Rothbart, M., 133, 136, 145, 356, 369, 371, 380, 381, 384, 393, 394
Rotter, J.B., 173
Rowan, John, 320
Rozensky, R.H., 239, 243
Rubin, M., 9, 231, 400
Rubin, Z., 36, 55
Ruble, D., 255, 265
Ruderman, A., 145, 209, 225
Runciman, W.G., 11, 105, 106, 109, 167, 173, 317, 319, 322, 332, 333, 335, 337, 339, 350, 400
Rush, 321
Russ, R.C., 51, 55
Russo, E.M., 271, 287
Rust, M.C., 13, 160, 398
Rutte, C.G., 190, 203
Ryan, C.S., 384, 392, 394
Ryan, M.K., 17
Ryen, A.H., 359, 366, 368, 369

Sachdev, I., 91, 112, 128, 175, 189, 191, 201, 203, 235, 237, 243, 397
Saenger, G., 19, 29n.34
Saenz, D., 248, 252
Salancik, G.R., 207, 226

Salovey, P., 6, 384, 394, 399
Samaha, C., 366, 369
Sampson, E.E., 246, 253
Samuelson, B., 39n.35
Sanbonmatsu, D.M., 7, 398
Sanders, G.S., 280, 287, 303, 315
Sanders, L.M., 154, 160
Sanford, R.N., 2, 15, 34, 53, 54, 87, 94, 108, 163, 172, 334, 397
Sanitioso, R., 148, 159
Satorra, A., 126
Saunders, J.E., 291, 297
Saxe, L., 7, 147, 159, 397
Schachter, S., 110, 126, 128
Schaller, M., 222, 223, 226
Scheier, M.F., 38, 54
Scherbaum, C., 248, 252
Schiferhoff, S., 203
Schlenker, B.R., 239, 243
Schlosser, B.A., 280, 287
Schmidt, G.W., 247, 252
Schmitt, M.T., 301
Schneider, S., 249, 252
Schofield, J.W., 12, 353, 400
Schonbach, P., 235, 243
Schopler, J., 4, 14, 63, 399
Schot, J.C., 4, 62, 63, 400
Schreiber, H.J., 237, 243
Schroth, H.A., 394
Schuman, H. 72, 74, 76, 88, 146, 161, 317, 320, 334
Schvaneveldt, R.W., 150, 160
Schwalbe, M.L., 240, 242
Schwartz, I., 242, 320
Schwartz, M.A., 235, 239, 335
Schwarzer, R., 287
Schweitzer, S., 366, 369
Schwinger, T., 201, 203
Scodel, A., 139, 145
Scott, J., 76, 88
Searrs, R., 28n.9
Sears, D.O., 32, 73, 74, 55, 88, 148, 153, 160, 161, 209, 226
Sears, R.R., 87
Sedikides, C., 8, 14, 93, 229, 231, 400
Sedlacek, W.E., 53, 54
See, K.O., 72, 88
Sekaquaptewa, D., 6, 401
Seligman, M.E.P., 239, 241
Senecal, S., 177
Serbin, L.A., 17
Shapiro, P.N., 385, 395
Shapiro, R.Y., 32, 55
Shapiro, T., 86, 88
Sharma, H.P., 394
Shavers, P., 350
Shaw, J., 33, 47, 53, 55
Sheatsley, P.B., 19, 28n.16, 72, 88, 89, 320, 335
Sheehan, D.S., 238, 243
Shepard, H.A., 4, 62, 397
Sherif, Carolyn W., 62, 63, 64, 66, 94, 109, 207, 226, 367, 369, 400
Sherif, Muzafer, 1, 3, 4, 8, 9, 12, 61, 62, 63, 64–70, 94, 95, 101, 106, 108, 109, 112, 128, 186, 189, 202, 203, 207, 226, 229, 238, 243, 267, 270, 272, 273, 287, 296, 316, 335, 366, 367, 369, 378, 381, 400

Sherman, S.J., 9, 398
Shibutani, T., 316, 335
Shoemaker, D., 28n.17
Short, J.F., 315
Shulman, I., 335
Shulman, S., 54
Sidanius, Jim, 3, 16, 17, 30–59, 400
Siegel, A.E., 317, 335
Siegel, S., 317, 335
Sigelman, L., 72, 88
Sighele, S., 302, 315
Sikes, J., 367, 368
Sikes, M.P., 73, 84, 86, 87
Silver, N., 366, 368
Simard, L.M., 145
Simmel, G., 240, 243, 287
Simmons, R.G., 104, 109
Simon, B., 6, 129, 198, 203, 252, 301, 392, 394, 400
Simon, R., 250, 253
Sims, V.M., 29n.36
Sinclair, A., 99, 108, 168, 171, 172
Singer, E., 237, 242, 316, 317, 333, 335
Singleton, R. Jr., 281, 287
Skevington, S., 112, 128
Skinner, M., 281, 287, 356, 369
Skowronski, J.J., 190, 203
Slaughter, J.B., 54
Slavin, R.E., 367, 369
Smelser, N.J., 88
Smith, A., 55
Smith, A.W., 88
Smith, Brewster, 163
Smith, C., 189, 203, 250, 252, 394
Smith, C.A., 212, 226
Smith, C.R., 317, 335
Smith, C.U., 29n.37
Smith, E., 14
Smith, E.R., 73, 74, 76, 88, 90, 152, 160
Smith, H., 8, 176, 401
Smith, Heather J., 158, 161, 205–228
Smith, M.B., 18, 29n.38, 173, 317, 335, 358, 369
Smith, P., 188, 203
Smith, P.M., 32, 33, 54, 234, 242, 247, 252
Smith, P.W., 317, 335
Smith, R., 277, 287
Smith, T.W., 72, 88, 146, 159
Smith-Cunnien, P., 112, 127
Snapp, M., 367, 368
Sniderman, P., 32, 55
Snyder, C.R., 247, 253
Snyder, M., 38, 55, 165, 173, 381
Socialist Challenge, 312
Solomon, M.R., 277, 287
Solomon, R., 230, 248, 253
Solomon, S., 8, 398
Sorrentino, M., 203
Sowell, T., 74, 88
Spahlinger, P., 301
Spears, R., 5, 9, 14, 93, 177, 195, 203, 224, 226, 230, 301, 398, 399
Spector, A.J., 318, 335
Speer, L.K., 74, 88, 148, 161
Spence, J.T., 35, 38, 55
Spencer, C., 280, 287

Sperling, H.G., 272, 287
Spodick, N., 206, 226
Spriggs, D., 234, 242
Srole, Leo, 323t
Srull, T.K., 393, 397
Stacey, B.G., 50, 55
Stacy, A.W., 120, 128
Stager, S.F., 238, 243
Stagner, R., 112, 128
Stallworth, Lisa M., 3, 16, 30–59, 400
Stallybrass, Oliver, 132, 133, 145
Stangor, C., 159, 355, 401
Stapp, J., 35, 55
Starr, P.D., 72, 88
Starr, S.A., 29n.39, 335, 337, 350
Staw, B.M., 226
Steeh, C.G., 72, 87, 88, 146, 161
Steele, C.M., 9, 231, 250, 253, 400
Steensma, H., 203
Steers, R.M., 212, 226
Steeves, A., 338, 350
Steil, J.M., 207, 226
Stein, A.A., 112, 128
Stein, D.D., 317, 335, 358, 369
Steinmetz, J.L., 164, 173
Stephan, C., 367, 368
Stephan, C.W., 88, 384, 385, 389, 392, 393, 394, 400
Stephan, I.D., 143, 145
Stephan, W., 353, 356, 369
Stephan, W.G., 12, 72, 74, 88, 238, 243, 384, 385, 389, 392, 393, 394, 400
Stephenson, G.M., 239, 243, 281, 287, 356, 369
Stern, E., 317, 319, 335
Sternberg, R.J., 410, 412
Stewart, V.M., 98, 105, 109
Stiepel, G., 235, 243
Stivers, E., 161
Stocker-Kreichgauer, G., 286
Stokes, D.E., 334
Stone, J., 72, 89
Stone, W.F., 51, 55
Stotland, E., 359, 369
Stouffer, S.A., 29n.39, 318, 319, 337, 335, 350
Strauss, H.M., 317, 335
Strickland, L.H., 145, 397
Stroebe, W., 134, 136, 137, 144, 145, 160, 203, 286, 394
Stroessner, S.J., 385, 392, 394
Strohm, M.A., 77, 87
Strube, M.J., 8, 229, 231, 400
Strykers, S., 264, 339, 350
Stuermer, S., 301
Suchman, E.A., 29n.39, 337, 350
Suchman, S.A., 335
Suelzle, M., 87
Suls, J.M., 237, 241–242, 243, 265, 271, 287, 350
Sumiga, L., 239, 243
Sumner, G.A., 141, 168, 145
Sumner, W.G., 2, 112, 128, 173, 400
Sunday Times, 309
Super, D.E., 35, 37, 56
Swann, W.B., 255, 265
Swanson, G.E., 172, 334
Swim, J.K., 148, 157, 161
Syllwasschy, J., 235, 244

Tabachnik, N., 239, 243
Tajfel, Henri, 4, 6, 7, 8, 12, 52, 56, 91, 92, 93, 94–109, 110, 111, 112, 124, 125, 126, 128, 129, 132–145, 163, 168, 169, 173, 175, 178–187, 188, 189, 190, 191, 192t, 195, 201, 202, 203, 204, 207, 210, 225, 226, 232, 233, 235, 236, 237, 238, 239, 240, 241, 242, 243, 244, 246, 252, 253, 254, 257, 263, 265, 271, 280, 287, 288, 304, 309, 315, 338, 339, 347, 350, 356, 357, 358, 365, 366, 368, 369, 371, 381, 398, 400
Tangri, S.S., 153, 154, 159
Tannenbaum, P.H., 233, 241
Tansky, J.W., 205, 206, 226
Tarde, G., 302, 315
Taylor, D.A., 87, 161
Taylor, D.G., 72, 89
Taylor, Donald M., 5, 6, 12, 98, 108, 112, 128, 143, 145, 157, 161, 169, 170, 173, 225, 249, 253, 264, 300, 337–351, 400, 401
Taylor, S.E., 133, 136, 145, 165, 167, 173, 392, 394, 398
Teahan, J.E., 53, 56
Teasdale, J.D., 239, 241
Tedesch, J.T., 241
Tesser, A., 239, 240, 243
Tetlock, P.E., 32, 55
Thibaut, J.W., 98, 109, 134, 145, 152, 153, 160, 161, 166, 169, 171, 173, 205, 206, 209, 226, 233, 241, 318, 335, 338, 350
Thomas, K., 139, 140–141, 145
Thompson, J.E., 371, 372, 382
Thompson, L., 225, 226
Thompson, L.J., 236, 242
Thornberry, O.T., 77, 89
Thrasher, F.M., 66
Tindale, R.S., 93, 397, 398, 400
Tingsten, H., 321, 335
Titus, H.E., 2, 400
Toch, H., 303, 314, 315
Tomlinson, T.M., 98, 109
Tornblom, K.Y., 201, 203
Tranquada, R.E., 54
Triandis, H.C., 249, 253
Trolier, T.K., 148, 160
Tuan, M., 75, 87
Tuch, S.A., 72, 89
Turner, John C., 4, 5, 8, 9, 10, 12, 14, 17, 56, 52, 62, 63, 91, 92, 94–109, 110, 111, 112, 125, 127, 128, 131, 141, 142, 145, 176, 188, 189, 191, 201, 202, 203, 207, 204, 225, 226, 232, 233, 234, 235, 236, 237, 238, 240, 242, 243, 244, 246, 247, 253, 254, 257, 264, 265, 267, 268, 269, 270–288, 304, 309, 315, 316, 339, 347, 351, 356, 357, 358, 365, 366, 367, 368, 369, 371, 381, 397, 398, 399, 400, 401
Turner, M.E., 155, 161
Turner, R.H., 304, 309, 313, 315, 335
Tversky, A., 136, 145, 167, 169, 173, 190, 203
Tyler, Tom R., 8, 158, 161, 176, 177, 205–228, 401, 205–228

Uhlaner, C., 72, 89

Validzic, A., 159
Valins, S., 173
van Avermaet, E., 296
van de Kragt, A., 245, 252, 368

van den Berghe, P.L., 320, 329, 335
van den Bos, K., 206, 226
Van der Berghe, P.C., 106, 109
Van der Pligt, J., 136, 144
van Dijk, T.A., 7, 401
van Knippenberg, A., 112, 113, 124, 189, 224, 235, 126, 127, 203, 204, 226, 244
van Knippenberg, D., 206, 226
van Laar, C., 148, 161
Vanbeselaere, N., 357, 369
Vanneman, Reeve D., 11, 167, 173, 249, 253, 300, 316–336, 338, 401
Vannerman, S., 351
Vargas, P., 6, 401
Vaughan, G., 98, 106, 109
Velditz, W., 72, 87
Ventimiglia, J.C., 32, 37, 51, 55
Vermunt, R., 203, 206, 226
Vickers, E., 234, 235, 236, 244
Vinacke, W.E., 94, 109
Vincent, S., 32, 37, 53
Vinokur, A., 270, 280, 281, 283, 286, 287, 288
Visser, L., 4, 62, 63, 400
von Hippel, W., 6, 401
Vosnaidou, S., 399

Waddell, N., 255, 265
Wade, G., 112, 126, 195, 203, 210, 225
Wade, T.J., 277, 287
Wagner, U., 235, 236, 243, 244
Waldinger, R., 71, 73, 89
Walker, I., 11, 301, 401
Walker, L., 152, 153, 160, 161, 205, 209, 226, 339, 351
Walkley, R.P., 29n.40
Walster, E., 337, 351
Walster, G.W., 337, 351
Walters, G., 146, 160
Wang, G., 170, 173
Wann, D.L., 231
Wapner, S., 67, 144
Ward, C., 6, 131, 160, 398
Warnaen, S., 240, 242
Wasel, W., 7, 131, 397
Waters, M.C., 72, 73, 89, 255, 262, 265
Watson, J.B., 2, 401
Watts, W.A., 236, 242
Weary, G., 54
Weber, R., 13, 371, 375, 380, 381, 384, 393, 394, 401
Weber, U., 301
Weigel, R., 74, 89
Weinberger, M., 99, 102, 108
Weiner, B., 167, 169, 173
Weis, L., 160
Weitz, S., 171, 173
Welch, S., 72, 88
Weldon, Fay, 132
Wellman, D.T., 72, 89
Wells, L.E., 236, 238, 244
Wenzel, M., 8, 177, 200, 204, 354, 399, 401
Wetherell, Margaret S., 5, 10, 92, 93, 110, 127, 128, 201, 207, 226, 238, 244, 246, 253, 267, 270–288, 357, 369, 397, 399, 401

Wheelan, S., 161
Wheeler, L., 241
White, B.J., 61, 66, 94, 109, 207, 226, 367, 369, 400
White, D.R., 3, 17
White, M.J., 303, 315
White, R.W., 18, 29n.38
Widaman, K.R., 120, 128
Wilder, David A., 13, 276, 288, 354, 356, 357, 358, 369, 370–382, 384, 385, 392, 394, 395, 401
Wilensky, H.L., 338, 351
Wilke, H., 112, 124, 126, 190, 195, 203, 206, 224, 226
Wilkens, C., 109, 366
Wilkens, G., 9, 102, 369
Wilkes, A.L., 133, 135, 137, 145
Wilkins, C., 19, 28n.18
Williams, C.J., 150, 160
Williams, J., 112, 126, 195, 203
Williams, J.A., 210, 225
Williams, K., 271, 288
Williams, K.D., 2, 399
Williams, L., 317, 335
Williams, R.M., 68, 335, 337, 350
Williams, R.M. Jr., 29n.39, 320, 335
Willis, R.H., 317, 335
Wilson, A.J., 380, 394
Wilson, G.D., 51, 56
Wilson, M.O., 296, 335
Wilson, O.D., 33, 34, 36, 54
Wilson, T., 381
Wilson, W., 102, 109
Wilson, W.J., 72, 88, 89
Winant, H., 72, 88
Winer, B.J., 118, 128
Winston, Brian, 132
Winter, D.G., 43, 55
Wit, A., 206, 226
Witte, E., 127
Wittenbraker, J., 233, 241
Wittgenstein, L., 135, 145
Wittink, D.R., 154, 161

Wolfe, D., 359, 369
Wolfgang, M.E., 315
Wong, M., 160
Wood, G.C., 384, 394, 399
Wood, W., 6, 10, 267, 269, 401
Woodmansee, J.M., 74, 87
Worchel, I., 366, 368
Worchel, S., 5, 56, 72, 87, 93, 112, 126, 128, 145, 203, 226, 243, 288, 351, 356, 366, 369, 394, 400, 401
Word, C.O., 150, 171, 161, 173
Wortman, C., 256, 264
Wright, Stephan C., 12, 112, 128, 157, 161, 249, 253, 300, 304, 305, 315, 337–351, 353, 401
Wundt, W., 2, 401
Wyer, R.S. Jr., 393, 397
Wylie, R., 239, 244

Yarrow, P., 19, 28n.18
Yinger, J.M., 173, 226
Young, D., 380, 382
Young, R.D., 238, 243
Yzerbyt, V.Y., 112, 127

Zajone, R.B., 233, 242
Zald, M.N., 340, 350
Zander, A., 126, 359, 369
Zanna, Mark P., 17, 150, 161, 171, 173, 226, 231, 237, 243, 252, 265, 350, 397, 398, 400, 403–412
Zavalloni, M., 104, 109
Zebrowitz, L.A., 5, 401
Zeigler, L.H., 339, 350
Zeller, E., 338, 351
Zellerer, E., 249, 253
Ziller, R.C., 247, 253
Zimbardo, P.G., 303, 315
Zipf, G.K., 164, 173
Zubrinsky, C.L., 82, 87, 89
Zweigenhaft, R.L., 72, 89

Subject Index

1992 Los Angeles County Social Survey (LACSS), 71–87

Ability, 167
Abrams, Dominic, 230, 256, 263, 267, 356
Abrams, Mark, 320
Accentuation of opinion, 281
Accenturation, 164
Acceptance of competence, 150–151
Active minorities, 10, 267
Adorno, T.W., 2, 15, 229
Affirmative Action, 130, 146–159, 167
Affluent worker phenomenon, 331
Aggravation, 191
  effects of, 193, 199, 202
  hypothesis, 190, 199
Aggression, 94
Agreeableness, 34, 44
Ali, Tariq, 310
Allport, Floyd, 2, 303
Allport, Gordon W., 19, 73–74, 134, 138, 162–165, 169, 171, 172, 320, 355, 383
Allportian individualism, 303, 304, 313
Altemeyer, B., 36, 38
Altruism, 30, 34, 44–45, 48
Altruism subscale, 35
Anti-African prejudice and authoritarianism, 21t
Anti-African prejudice and social conformity, 22t
Anti-Arab racism scale, 56
Anti-Black
  bias, 150
  racism, 51
    measure, 41
    scale, 38, 41, 56
Antihedonism, 51
Anti-Negro prejudice, 24
Anti-Semitism, 24, 49, 141
Apartheid, 22
Aronson, Elliot, 163
Artisans, job satisfaction among, 322
Asch, Gordon, 267, 270, 290
Asch conformity paradigm, 276, 277, 279
Aspired hierarchy role, 53
Assimilation, 13, 230, 354
Asymmetry, 190
  effects, 193, 197, 198
    positive-negative, 176, 199
  hypothesis, 190
Attitude-behavior studies, 7
Attitudes, group-oriented, 212
Attribution, situational causal, 165

Attribution error
  fundamental, 6, 164-165
  ultimate, 6, 162-172
Attribution theory, 130, 143, 164, 165
  social, 143
Attributions, 167
  causal, 169
  dispositional, 165
Austin, G.A., 139
Authoritarian bipolar adjective choices, 38
Authoritarian personality, 24, 73, 94
  syndrome, 2, 8
  theory, 15, 43
Authoritarianism, 18, 20, 23, 24, 26, 28, 30, 34, 36, 43–44, 149, 179
  anti-African prejudice and, 21t
  reconsideration of, 50
  social class and, 49–50
  veterans and, 27
  working class, 321
Autokinetic
  apparatus, 274
  paradigm, 272
Aversive racism, 148–149, 150, 151–152, 158, 159
  opposition to affirmative action, 154–155
Avoidance, 391

Bagley, C., 320, 321, 330
Balance theory, 165
Banks, W.C., 170–171, 171
Bartlett, F.C., 240
Behavior
  generic norm of, 181–182, 186
  genesis of spontaneous, 314
  group-oriented, 212
  limits of, 310
Behavioral interdependence model, 62
Belief in a Just World Scale, 36, 41
Belief similarity, 358
Belief systems, 96–97
  social change, 96
  social mobility, 96
  socially shared, 97
Belief and value congruence, 317
Berger, Peter L., 142, 181
Berk, R.A., 304
Berkowitz, L., 299
Bias
  contemporary, 152–155
  negativity, 190

Bias (*continued*)
   racial, 154
   subtle, 151–152
Big-Five Personality Inventory, 34, 38, 44
Billig, M.J., 182, 233, 240
Bipolar personality measure, 36
Black sheep effect, 112
Blanz, Mathias, 195
Blau, P.M., 318, 319
Blumer, H., 62, 71
Blumer's theory of group position, 73, 74–75, 84–86
   hypothesis for, 77
Blumer's theory of prejudice, 71, 72
Bobo, Lawrence, 62
Bogardus, E.S., 66
Bourhis, R.Y., 235, 237
Bowen, D.R., 333
Bowen, John, 132
Boys' camp paradigm, 3
Boy's camp studies, 62, 66–70, 112
Bradley, Thomas, 322
Breakwell, G., 256
Brehm, J.W., 296
Brewer, Marilynn, 168, 230, 254, 354, 356, 357, 367, 368, 384
Brown, R., 195
Brown, R.J., 354, 393
Bruner, Jerome, 137, 139, 164
Bundy, R.P., 182, 233
Burnstein, E., 270, 280, 281, 283, 285
Busing, 353
Buss, A.H., 38

California Personality Inventory (CPI) Dominance scale, 33, 34 (*see also* CPI)
Calmness, 44
Campbell, A., 317, 318
Campbell, D.T., 94, 168, 169
Cantril Self-Anchoring Scale, 323, 332
Capitalism, 32
Categorization, 134, 164, 188
   general hypothesis for, 135
   inductive aspect of, 304
   processes, 354
   salience of, 196, 198, 356
   salience of relevant, 367
   social, 137, 175, 195
      neutral, 138
      value-loaded, 138
   social group, 136
Causal attributions, 165, 169
Causality, phenomenal, 164
Centers, R., 317
Central tendency, measures of, 384
Charters, W.W. Jr., 316
Chauvinism, 32, 48
   scale, 57–58
Chauvinist policies, 41
Child, P., 255
Christian, J., 255
Christopher Commission, 53
Civil rights, 33
Class, consciousness of, 318

Class inequalities, perceptions of, 317
Clayton, S.D., 153, 154
Closed-minded personality theory, 16 (*see also* dogmatic personality theory)
Coal-mining, race relations in, 18
Codol, J.P., 239
Cognitive
alternatives, 105
coherence, 233
dissonance, 140
Coherence, as a source of motivation, 239–240
Cohesiveness, 112
Cohn, Norman, 141
Cold War, 68
Collective action, 338, 339, 340, 346, 347
   ideologizing of, 139–141
Collective representations, 304
Collective self-esteem, 259
Collective Self-Esteem Scale, 258, 259
Colorblind opportunity, 155
Colour and Citizenship, 320
Common enemy, 68–69
Common in-group identity model, 354
Communality, 30, 34, 44–45, 48
Comparative reference groups, 316
Comparison level, concept of, 318
Competitive
interdependence, 62
orientations, 15
prejudice, 329
racism, 329, 331, 333, 334
relations, 366
threat, 77, 84–86
Concepts
of community, 314
of comparison level, 318
of distributive justice, 318
of fair exchange, 318
of relative deprivation, 318
Concern for Others Subscale, 45
Condor, S., 195
Conflicts, 107–108
Conformity, 179, 270–286, 291
Conscientiousness, 34, 44
Consciousness of class, 318
Conservatism, 30, 34, 43–44, 48, 50
   social class and, 49
Consistency hypothesis, 377, 378, 379
Consistent minorities, 10, 19
Contact hypothesis, 12, 112, 353, 383, 392
Contact racism, 328, 329, 330, 331, 333, 334
Contrast hypothesis, 378, 379
Convergent validity, 44–45
Conversion behavior, 289–296
Cooley, C.H., 316, 318
Cooper, J., 150
Cooperative contact, 383
Cooperative
interdependence, 62
intergroup interaction, 368
relations, 366
Coopersmith, S., 235
Correlates of racial attitudes, 319–322

Coser, Lewis A., 178
CPI (*see also* California Personality Inventory)
 Capacity for Status subscale, 36, 50
 dominance subscale, 36, 38, 44, 48
 flexibility subscale, 36
Crocker, J., 52, 155, 235, 236, 237, 259
Crosby, F.J., 156, 338
Cross-pressures phenomenon, 317
Crowd action, limits of, 302–314
Crowd behavior, 299–300, 302, 314
 limits of, 305, 314
 social causation of, 303
 social identity and, 314
Crowd identification, 304
Crowd membership, 303
Crutchfield apparatus, 277
Cultural elitism, 32, 41, 48
Cultural elitism scale, 56

Data triangulation, 305
Davies, J.C., 332, 333
Davis, J.A., 318, 319, 333
Davis, K.L., 166
Davis, M.H., 34, 45
de Brey, J.H.C., 366
de Freitus, Roy, 311
de Tocqueville, Alexis, 318
de Vries, N., 195
Death penalty, 47
Death Penalty survey, 58
Deaux, Kay, 230, 255, 257, 258, 259
Decategorization, 354, 358, 384
DeGoey, Peter, 209
Deindividuation, 248, 272, 276, 303
 social identity and, 250
theory, 272
Denial of disadvantage, 130
Depersonalization, 248, 250
Depersonalized attraction, 125
 hypothesis, 111
Deprivation, 11, 319, 331
 relative, 300, 331
Desegregation, 19, 28
Desirability hypothesis, 378, 379
Deutsch, Morton, 62, 271, 286
Dichotomization, 164
Dietz-Uhler, B.L., 154
Differential familiarity, 171
Differentiation, 102, 140, 141
Dijker, A.J., 392
Dimensions of contact, 383–393
DiMiceli, A., 168
Disadvantage, 299
Discounting effect, 166
Discriminant validity, 31, 33–35, 43–44
Discrimination, 7–8, 15, 130, 179, 229, 326
 on the basis of categorization, 176
 behavior of, 178–179
 beliefs about, 72
 institutional, 31, 53
 institutionalized, 237
 intergroup, 99–100, 102, 176, 188, 189, 235, 257, 367
 legitimization of, 30

 normative, 236
 racial, 33, 334
 self-esteem and, 230
 self-esteem causes of, 234
 sexual, 33
 social, 188, 190, 201
  positive-negative asymmetry in, 200
 successful intergroup, 234
Discriminatory intergroup behavior, 175
Discussion questions, 17, 62, 92, 130, 176, 231, 268, 300, 355
Displacement, 94
Dispositional attributions, fundamental error of, 165
Dissonance theory, 296
Distributive inequality, 176
Distributive justice, 319
 concept of, 318
Distributive justice theory, 337
Divergence of judgment, 290
Dogmatic personality theory, 8, 16
Doise, W., 168, 171
Dominance, 44
Dominant racial group, perceptions of, 81–82
Donahue, E., 38
Doty, R.M., 43
Dovidio, John F., 130, 154, 354
Drout, C., 154
Dual-identity model, 354
Duckitt, J., 50
Duncan, B.L., 169
Dunton, B.C., 150

Economic competition, 77
Effort, 167
Egocentric assumptions, 165
Egoistic deprivation, 319, 321, 325, 332, 333
 relative, 11, 300
Eisenstadt, S.N., 316
Ellemers, N., 124, 195
Emergency helping, 149
Emergent norm theory, 304, 313
Empathy, 30, 34, 44–45, 52
Enhancement of opinion, 281
Environmental policies, 33, 42, 57
Environmental programs, 48
Equal opportunity, 48, 155
 measures, 41
 programs, 152
 scale, 56
Equal-status contact, 383
Equity theory, 337, 338
Erroneous generalization, 163
Ethier, Kathleen A., 230, 255, 257, 258, 259
Ethnic
 identification, strength of, 257
 identity, 254, 255
 involvement, 259, 261
 membership, 321
 prejudice, 32, 41
Ethnocentrism, 2, 43, 50, 51, 66, 97–98, 100, 106, 170
 campus police officers and, 53
Eulau, H., 317
Evaluative judgments, 149–150

Evans, R.I., 317
Externalization, 18
Externalization factors, authoritarianism, 27
Extrarole behaviors, 213, 215, 219
Extraversion, 34, 44, 48

Fair exchange, concept of, 318
Familiarity, 384, 392
Familiarity-variability hypothesis, 392
Farnsworth perception test, 290
Fatalism, 49
Fazio, R.H., 150
Fear of invalidity, 202
Feierabend, L., 332
Feierabend, R.L., 332
Fenigstein, A., 38
Feshbach, R., 35
Festinger, L., 233, 239, 318
Fischer, G.W., 384
Fisher z-to-r transformation, 38
Five-stage model of intergroup relations, 339–340
Flament, Claude, 182, 233
Fogelson, R.M., 308
Folger, R., 338, 349
Frable, D.E.S., 256
Frantz, C., 320, 321, 322
Fraternal deprivation, 249
Fraternalistic deprivation, 319, 321, 322–334, 324
Fraternalistic relative deprivation, 11, 300
Frenkel-Brunswik, E., 2, 15
Friedman, N., 106
Fromkin, H.L., 247
Frustration, 94
Fujioka, T., 255
Functional theory of intergroup behavior, 61
Fundamental attribution error, 6, 164–165
Fundamentalist religiosity, 51

Gaertner, Samuel, 130, 154, 354
Gamble, L., 338
Garrett, J.B., 36
Gay and lesbian rights, 33, 48, 57
Gay rights policies, 42
Gecas, V., 240
Gemeinschaft bonds, 333
Gender, 31–32
General War Attitudes scale, 43
Generic norm of behavior, 181–182, 186
Genocide, 15
Gerard, H.B., 271, 286
Gestalt, 164
theory, 163
Gibson, Kenneth, 322
Gifford, R.K., 136
Glass ceiling, 151–152
Global judgment of similarity, 384
Goal relations, 4, 61, 62, 99
intergroup, 91
nature of between groups, 238
Goals
subordinate, 62
superordinate, 62
Goddard, R.W., 152

Goebbels, 302
Goertzel, T.G., 36, 43–44
Goodnow, J.J., 139
Green, R.T., 49
Group
authorities
evaluation of behavior, 211
instrumental judgments about, 211–212, 216–219
relational judgments about, 212, 216–219, 222–223
cohesiveness, self-categorization model of, 126
commitment, 213, 215
competition, perceptions of, 85–86
consciousness, 171
definition of, 1, 65
deprivation, 319
differentiation, 318
discrimination, 53
SDO and, 52–53
dominance, 53
identification, 115, 196, 198, 254, 255, 257
level attribution, 6
membership, 270, 299
motives, 229–230
mind theory, 303, 313
polarization, 270–286
position, Blumer's theory of, 73, 74–75, 84–86
hypothesis for, 77
racial alienation, 90
pride, 210–211, 215–216, 223
salience, 168, 169, 171
size, effects of, 249–250
solidarity, 318
Group-based prejudice, 30
Group-oriented
attitudes, 212, 222
behaviors, 212, 218, 222
Group-value model, 205, 207–208
analysis of, 208
implications for social identity theory, 223–225
psychological dynamics of, 219–223
test of robustness, 209
Gunther, John, 69
Gurr, T.R., 332

Hains, Sarah, 92
Hamill, R, 380
Hamilton, D.L., 136–137
Harding, John, 164
Hardyck, J.A., 317
Harris, Robert Alton, 38, 47, 58
Hartley, R.E., 317
Hass, R.G., 41, 45
Hatcher, Mayor Richard, 322
Heaven, P.C.L., 50
Heider, Fritz, 164, 165, 168
Herodotus, 314
Hewstone, Miles, 143, 354, 393
Hierarchy-attenuating ideologies, 48, 49
Hierarchy-enhancing
attitudes, 32
behaviors, 53
ideologies, 49
institutions, 53

Hierarchy-legitimizing myths, 30–31, 48
ethnic prejudice, 41
ideologies, 40
SDO and, 40
sexism, 41
Hierarchy-relevant ideologies, 53
High motivation, 167–168
Highly individuated conceptualization of self, 245
Hill, Anita, 46–47
Hindu-Muslim comparisons, 387–388
Hirschman, A.O., 96
Hispanic identity, characteristics of, 250
Hogg, Michael, 92, 230, 234, 236, 277, 356
Homans, G.C., 318, 319
Hormuth, S.E., 262
Horowitz, L.M., 37, 38
Hostility, 163
Housing competition, 77
Humanitarian Wars, 58
Humanitarian-Egalitarian Scale, 38, 45
Huo, Y.J., 209
Hussein, Saddam, 46
Hutchings, Vincent, 62
Hyman, H.H., 316, 317, 333
Hypothesis
aggravation, 190
asymmetry, 190

Identity
change, 255–256
maintenance, 254, 256
negotiation, 262
threat
responses to, 256–257
role of, 230
Ideologies, 40
Illusory correlations, 136
Impression formation, studies on, 190
Individual
action, 338, 339, 340, 346, 347
behavior, 91
deprivation, 319
mobility, 103–104, 105, 106
poverty, 90 (*see also* stratification beliefs)
upward mobility, 338, 339
values, social stereotypes and, 137–139
Individualism, 72, 83, 89–90 (*see also* stratification beliefs)
Individuation, 357
conceptualization of self, 245
excessive, 252
extreme of, 249
models of, 247
Inductive aspect of categorization, 304
Inequalitarianism, 72, 90 (*see also* stratification beliefs)
Influence
latent, 292, 293
manifest, 292, 293
Informational influence, 271, 272, 286
referent, 271, 272
theory, 273, 276, 280
Information-processing bias, 385
Ingerman, C., 236
In-group

bias, 99–100, 175, 190, 250, 251, 277, 391
categorization, 367
classification of, 181
cohesion, 314
consciousness, 319
enhancement, 357
favoritism, 99, 103, 188, 194, 200, 201, 236, 247
pressure, 277
redefinition of, 104
salience in, 195
size, 251
solidarity of, 68
stereotypes, 141
In-group/out-group comparisons, 101
Injustice
perceived, 319
tolerance of, 339
Inkeles, A., 322
Innovation, 291
Institutional
discrimination, 31, 53
hierarchy role, 53
Instrumental
judgments, 211–212, 216–219
model, 206
Intentionality, 157
Intergroup anxiety, 383–393
definition of, 12
Intergroup attitudes, 175, 366
Intergroup avoidance, 130
Intergroup behavior, 91, 130, 175
motives for, 229–230
social context of, 95–99
Intergroup bias
reduction of, 356–368
social categorization framework, 365
Intergroup boundaries, 354
Intergroup competition, 94
Intergroup conflict
analysis of, 92
integrative theory of, 94–108
irrational, 178
rational, 178
stratified societies hypothesis, 98
superordinate goals and, 64–70
Intergroup contact, 353–354, 383, 391–392
aspects of, 386
dimensions of, 393
Intergroup differentiation, 102
Intergroup discrimination, 99–100, 188, 189, 235, 367
experiments in, 178–187
Intergroup friction, reduction of, 68–69
Intergroup goal relations, 91
Intergroup ideology approach, 86
Intergroup influence, 10, 267
Intergroup interaction, cooperative, 368
Intergroup perception, 385
Intergroup relation theories
attribution, 143, 164, 165
authoritarian personality, 2, 8, 15, 43
authoritarianism, 30
balance, 165
closed-minded personality, 16

Intergroup relation theories (*continued*)
  conservatism, 30
  deindividuation, 273 (*see also* deindividuation)
  dogmatic personality, 8, 16
  informational influence, 273, 280 (*see also* informational influence theory)
  interpersonal dominance, 30
  normative influence, 280
  optimal distinctiveness, 9, 247–248
  persuasive arguments, 280 (*see also* persuasive arguments theory)
  realistic conflict, 61
  self-affirmation, 9
  self-categorization, 5, 201, 238, 240
  self-enhancement, 9
  social dominance, 30, 31, 52, 53
  social dominance orientation, 16
  social identity, 4, 9, 11, 52, 110, 112, 142, 176, 201, 207, 223–225, 232, 234, 246, 254, 256
  social identity/social comparison, 102
Intergroup relations, 94
  characteristics of, 65
  conceptualization for, 97
  definition of, 1, 65
  deviant behavior and, 65
  ethnolinguistic, 112
  five-stage model of, 339–340
  influence on groups, 112
  research, 353
  self-esteem as a motivational dimension of, 230
Intergroup social comparison, 106
Intergroup status, 110
Interpersonal
behavior, 95
contact, 383, 393
dependence, 270
dominance, 30, 33–34
relations, 110, 115
similarity, 116
Interpersonal Reactivity Index (IRI), 36 (*see also* IRI)
Intimate contact, 383
Intragroup
cohesion, 312
cohesiveness, 112
dynamics, group-value model explanation for, 223
relations, identity-based explanation for, 207
Introversion, 44
Investment, 319
Iraq War, 45
Iraq War Attitudes survey, 43, 46
Iraq War scales, 58
IRI, 36, 37, 38, 45 (*see also* Interpersonal Reactivity Index)
Islam, Rabiul, 354

Jackman, M.R., 86
Jackson, J.R., 38, 150
Jackson Personality Inventory (JPI), 35 (*see also* JPI)
Jackson Personality Research Form (JPRF), 33, 34 (*see also* JPRF)
Jacobson, C.K., 153
Jaggi, V., 143, 169–170
James, William, 316
Jaspars, J., 143

Job
  competition, 77
  satisfaction, 317
    among skilled workers, 322
John, Oliver P., 38, 384, 393
Jones, E.E., 166, 380, 392
Joseph, J., 256
Journal articles, how to read, 403–411
JPI (*see also* Jackson Personality Inventory)
  tolerance subscale, 36, 38
JPRF (*see also* Jackson Personality Research Form)
  dominance subscale, 36, 38, 44, 48
Judd, C.M., 384
Just World, 48
Justice motive theory, 337
Justification, 140, 141

Kahneman, D., 169
Katz, I., 41, 45
Keller, S., 317
Kelley, H.H., 166, 169, 316, 318
Kentle, R.L., 38
Kessler, R., 256
Keynoting, 313
Killian, L., 304, 313
Kirscht, J, 256
Kitt (Rossi), A.S., 316, 331, 332
Kluckhohn, C., 139
Kluegel, J.R., 152
Kosterman, R., 35
Kramer, Bernard, 163
Kramer, R.M., 368
Krieger, L.H., 156, 157

LACSS, *see* 1992 Los Angeles County Social Survey
Lage, E., 289, 294
Lampen, L., 235
Language barriers, 52
LaPiere, 7, 19
Latent influence, 292, 293, 296
Law-and-order, 51
  policies, 41, 48, 57
Lawrence, Daniel, 320
Le Bon, G., 302, 303, 305
Legitimacy, 123–125
Legitimizing myths, 30–31, 34, 35, 41, 50
  belief in, 53
  conservatism and, 51
  hierarchy-attenuating, 31
  hierarchy-enhancing, 31
  meritocracy, 33
  nationalism, 32
  noblesse oblige, 33
  original, 36
  political-economic conservatism, 32–33
  racism, 32
  scales, 56
sexism, 32
Lemaine, G., 104
Lemyre, L., 234
Lenski, G.E., 318
Levin, S.L., 52
Levinson, 2, 15

Likert-type response scale, 282
Limits of behavior, 310, 313
Limits of crowd action, 302–314
Limits of crowd behavior, 305
Lind, E.A., 207, 209
Linear structural equation modeling, 120
Linville, P.W., 380, 384, 392
Lipset, S.M., 321
Litwak, E., 316
Locus of control, 166, 167
Loevinger, J., 35
"Long hot summer" analysis, 11
Luck, 167
Luckmann, Thomas, 142, 181
Luebke, J., 168
Luhtanen, R., 52, 259

McConahay, J.B., 38, 41, 148
McCrone, I.D., 320
McGrath, John, 132
McGraw, K.M., 236
McGuire, C.V., 255
McGuire, W.J., 255
Mackie, D.M., 356
McKillip, J., 168, 170
McKirnan, D.J., 339, 340
McQuarter, G.V., 170–171
Macrojustice, 153
Madden, N.A., 367
Major, B., 155
Majority influence, 291, 296
Malherbe, E.G., 320
Malle, Bertram, 37, 38
Manifest influence, 292, 293
Manipulable situational context, 168
Mann, Jeffrey, 354
Mann, M., 296
Mark, M.M., 338
Marshall, Thurgood, 46
Martin, J., 338
Marx, Karl, 318
Masotti, L.H., 333
Mass violence, 140
Mathews, A., 195
Mead, G.H., 289, 318
Meaning, as a source of motivation, 239–240
Meritocracy, 31
Meritocracy, 30
Merton, R.K., 316, 331, 332
Messick, D.M., 356
Meyer, D.E., 150
Mezei, L., 317
MGP, see minimal group paradigm
Microjustice, 153
Milgram, S., 303
Militarism, 51
Military policy, 33
Military programs, 41, 48, 57
Miller, N., 354
Minimal group
  experiments, 189, 234
  paradigm, 91, 175, 188, 195, 200, 233
  studies, 7, 176, 236

definition of, 4
Minorities
  active, 10, 267
  consistent, 10, 19
Minority influence, 289–296, 296
  research, 10
Mirels, H.L., 36
Miscegenation, 33, 42, 48
Model relating contact, 391
Modern Racism Scale, 38, 41
Modern racism theory, 148
Moghaddam, Fathali, 300, 338
Morality, strict, 51
Moscovici, Serge, 268, 271, 277, 289, 294, 304
Motivation, sources of, 239–240
Motivational
  hypotheses in social identity theory, 232
  states, 176
Mullen, B., 195, 200
Multiculturalism, 354
Multidimensional empathy scale, 34
Mummendey, Amelie, 189, 190, 195, 200, 202, 237
Murphy, Gardner, 65
Murrell, Audrey, 154, 155, 354
Mussolini, 302
Mutual group influence, 280
Mutual intergroup differentiation model, 354

Naffrechoux, M., 289
Nascimento-Schulze, C., 234
National Election Study, 35
Nationalism, 32, 41, 43–44, 48, 51
  scale, 35, 57
Nature of contact, 383
Negative affect, 89
Negative reference groups, 316
Negativity biases, 190
Neuroticism, 34, 44, 48
Neutrality, 206
Neville, D.D., 35
Newcomb, T.M., 316, 317
Ng, S.H., 239
Nietzsche, Frederic, 239
Nisbett, R., 380
Nixon, President Richard, 329
Noblesse oblige, 33, 41, 48
  scale, 57
Nonnormative action, 338, 347, 349, 350
  collective, 345, 346
Norm formation, nature of, 270–286
Normative
  action, 338, 347, 349, 350
    individual, 343, 346
  influence, 271, 286
  theory, 280
  reference groups, 316, 317

Oakes, P.J., 233–234
Oberschall, A., 304
Object-appraisal, 18
Objective
  social class, 317
  stability, 116, 118

Objective (*continued*)
  status, 116, 118
Olson, M., 304
Openness, 34
Opposition to preferential treatment, 130
Oppression, dynamics of, 52
Optimal distinctiveness, 230, 245
  model, 249
  theory, 9, 247–248, 250
Otten, Sabine, 176, 195
Out-group
  attitude, 383, 385, 391, 392–393
  atypical members, 371
  classification of, 181
  derogation, 188
  devaluation, 357
  distance, 319
  favoritism, 188
  homogeneity in, 371, 381
  hostility towards, 65, 98
  perceived variability, 383, 384, 385, 386, 389–390, 391, 392, 393
  perception of acts by members of, 164–168 (*see also* ultimate attribution theory)
  positive evaluation of, 165
  qualities of, 66
  social distance towards, 318
  stereotypes, 75, 141

PAQ, 38, 45, 50, (*see also* Personal Attribute Questionnaire)
Park, B., 384
Patchen, M.A., 319
Patriotism, 32, 41, 48
  scale, 57
Pearlin, L.I., 317
Perceived degree of stability, 167
Perceived fairness, 152–153, 154
Perceived injustice, 319
Perceived justice, 205
Perceived out-group variability, 383, 384, 385, 386, 389–390, 391, 392, 393
Perceived similarity, 390
Perceived threat, 86, 254
  ethnic involvement and, 261
  levels of, 77–79
  social location of, 79–81
Permeability, 123–125
Personal attraction, 111, 116, 125, 126
Personal attraction-similarity correlation, 125
Personal Attribute Questionnaire (PAQ) Communality scale, 35
Personal identity, 246, 252
Personality
  differentiation, 19
  dimensions, 37
    agreeableness, 34
    conscientiousness, 34
    extraversion, 34
    neuroticism, 34
    openness, 34
Personnaz, Bernard, 268
Persuasive arguments theory, 280, 282, 286
Peterson, B.E., 43

Pettigrew, Thomas F., 16, 130, 157, 179, 237, 300, 317, 318, 320, 333
Pierre, Desmond, 311
Policy attitudes, SDO and, 41
Political competition, 77
Political efficacy, 320
Political–economic conservatism, 32, 36
  vs. SDO, 50–52
Positive action, 155
Positive distinctiveness, 235
Positive reference groups, 316
Positive social identity, threats to, 200
Positive-negative asymmetry, 200, 202
  explanation of, 201
  effect, 176, 199
Postman, Leo, 164, 169
Pratto, F., 52
Predictive measures, gender differences, 39
Predictive validity, 31–32
  gender and, 31–32
Prejudice, 15, 16, 179, 233, 326
  anti-Negro, 24, 26, 324t
  attitudes of, 178–179
  authoritarian personality model of, 73
  Blumer's theory of, 71
  children, 66
  classical model of, 71, 72–74, 81, 84–85
  cognitive analysis of, 172
  cognitive correlates of, 163, 164
  cognitive process in, 138
  comparative, 32
  competitive, 329
  contemporary, 150, 157
  ethnic, 32, 163
  group, 41
  group-based, 30
  independent measures of, 171–172
  indicators of, 79
  measures of, 82
  modern forms of, 130
  negative affect, 89
  phenomenological approach to, 164
  racial, 16, 18–28, 334
    hypothesis for, 76–77
  reduction of, 354
  relation of social class to, 321
  social distance feelings, 89
  sociocultural model of, 73–74
  stereotyping, 89
  subtle, 156
  theories, 18
  white racial, 320
Prejudiced personalities, 24
Price Waterhouse v. Hopkins, 157
Pro-Black scale, 38, 41
Procedural justice, 176
  assessment of mediating roles of pride and respect, 208
  group-value model of, 205–208 (*see also* group–value model)
  influence on group behaviors and attitude, 205–225
  instrumental model of, 206
  relational judgments of, 206
Protestant Work Ethic, 33, 48

scale, 36, 38, 41
Prototype clarity, 115
Prototypes, team, 125
Protypicality, 116
Pryce, Ken, 311
Pryor, J., 171
Psychological subjective class, 317
Psychological theories
  authoritarianism, 18 (*see also* authoritarianism)
  prejudice-frustration-aggression, 18
  psychoanalytic, 18
Publishing biases, 52
Punitive policies, 33
Punitiveness, 50

Qualitative contact, 383, 385, 389–393
  aspects of, 386
Quantitative contact, 383, 385, 389–393

Rabbie, Jaap, 62, 366
Rabinowitz, J., 52
Race relations, 18–28
  structural changes in, 333
  in the United States, 300
Race-specific beliefs, 75
Racial alienation, 75–76, 81–82, 83, 86, 90
  hypothesis, 71
  measure of, 84
Racial attitudes
  contemporary, 147–149
  correlates of, 316, 319–322
of whites in urban America, 322–334
Racial bias, 154
  unintentional, 146–159
Racial deprivation, white attitudes towards blacks and, 327t
Racial desegregation, 353
Racial discrimination, 33, 320, 334
Racial distinctiveness, 82
Racial integration, 28
Racial intolerance, 28
Racial minority, group perceptions, 82–83
Racial policies, 42, 48, 57
Racial prejudice, 16, 130, 334
  belief and value congruence, 317
  hypothesis for, 76–77
Racism, 30, 32, 43–44, 104, 130, 153
  anti-Arab, 37, 56
  anti-Black, 48, 51, 56
    measure of, 41
  aversive, 148–149, 150, 156, 158, 159
    opposition to affirmative action, 154–155
  campus police officers and, 53
  competitive, 329, 331
  contact, 328, 329, 330, 331, 333
  correlation with conservatism, 51
  modern, 152
  overt, 155
  social class and, 49
  subtle, 154
  symbolic, 148–149
Racism theory
  modern, 148
  symbolic, 148

Rape Myths Scale, 37
RCT, 3, 61, 94–95, 97–98, 104, 106 (*see also* realistic group conflict theory)
Reactance phenomena, 296
Realistic competition, 102, 103
Realistic group conflict theory (RCT), 94–95 (*see also* RCT)
Recategorization, 13, 354, 357
  benefits of, 356–368
Reference group analysis, comparative function of, 318
Reference group phenomena, 317
Reference groups, 316
  comparative effects of, 317
  comparative function of, 317
  studies, 318
Referent Informational Influence, 304 (*see also* RII)
Regents of the University of California v. Bakke, 152
Reicher, Stephen, 299, 304, 314
Relational judgments, 212, 215, 216–219, 222–223
Relative competence, 151
Relative deprivation, 300, 326, 331, 332, 333, 340
  concept of, 318, 319
theory, 337, 338, 339
  Wallace support and, 323t
Relative gratification, 318, 319
Relative group size, 188
Relative group status, 188
Remooring, maintaining identity through, 260–261
Representativeness hypothesis, 378, 379
Resolution of conflict, 68
Resource mobilization theory, 340
Respect within groups, 210–211
Response latency measures of bias, 150
Richardson, L.F., 65
Riecken, M., 166, 169, 171
Right Wing Authoritarian (RWANDA) scale, 36
RII, 304 (*see also* Referent Informational Influence)
Ring, K., 166, 169, 171
Robbers cave study, 367
Rodrigues, J.S., 137
Rogers, C.A., 320, 321, 322
Rokeach, Milton, 8, 16, 229, 317
Rombough, S., 37
Rosch, E., 150
Rose, E.J.B., 320
Rosenberg, M., 36, 238
Rosenberg Self-Esteem Scale, 36, 213, 234 (*see also* RSE)
Rosenfield, D., 238
Ross, G.F., 103
Ross, L.D., 169
Rothbart, M., 136, 384, 393
Rowan, John, 320
RSE, 36, 38, 48 (*see also* Rosenberg Self–Esteem Scale)
Runciman, W.G., 317, 319, 322, 332, 333, 339
RWA, 38, 43–44
RWANDA, *see* Right Wing Authoritarian scale

S6 Conservatism scale, 35
Sachdev, I., 235, 237
St. Paul's Riots, 302, 305–314
Salience, influence of, 255–256
Salience of categorization, 196, 198
Salovey, P., 384
Sanford, 2, 15

SCB, 262
Scheier, M.F., 38
School integration, 19
Schreiber, H.J., 237
Schvaneveldt, R.W., 150
Schwalbe, M.L., 240
Schwartz, I., 235
SDO (*see also* Social dominance orientation)
   dynamics of oppression and, 52
   group discrimination and, 52–53
   hierarchy role and, 39
   hierarchy-legitimizing myths and, 40
   policy attitudes and, 41
   political-economic conservatism vs., 50–52
   reliability of the measure, 38
   scale, 35–38
   social class and, 49–50
   social role and, 53
   stability of measure over time, 39
Search after meaning, 240
Sears, D.O., 153
Segregation, 52, 148
SEH, 232, 233, 235 (*see also* self–esteem hypothesis)
   individual and interpersonal limits on, 238–239
   limits to, 236–237
   social structural limits on applicability of, 237–238
Selective affinity, 316
Selection, 164
Self-affirmation, 245
theory, 9
Self-categorization, 110, 112, 113, 229, 270–286, 280, 286
   dependence of mutual influence in groups, 285
   depersonalization due to, 111
   depersonalized attraction and, 113
   in-groups as defined by, 286
   model of group cohesiveness, 126
   personal attraction and, 113
   relation to social categorization, 129
Self-categorization theory, 5, 92, 201, 238, 240, 263, 271,
     273, 279, 281, 282, 356, 357
   predictions of, 255
Self-complexity, 245
Self-concept, evaluatively positive, 233
Self-conceptualization, optimally distinctive, 230
Self-construction, 240
Self-definition, 255
Self-enhancement, 9, 239
Self-enhancing motives, 240
Self-esteem, 44, 98, 101, 112, 205, 206–207, 209, 213, 215,
     225, 256, 357
   effects of perceived threat on, 254
   global, 236–237
   influence of identification and cultural background, 258
   loss of associated with group membership, 264
   motivational status of, 232–241
   relational judgment influence on, 219
   relationship with delinquency, 238
   Rosenberg scale, 213
   social-identity-dependent, 236
Self-esteem hypothesis, 232, 241 (*see also* SEH)
Self-evaluation, 239
Self-evaluative motives, 240
Self-interest, 205

Self-monitoring, 245
scales, 38
Self-prototypicality, 115
Self-referencing, 245
Self-regulation, lack of, 272
Self-schema, 245
Self-stereotyping, 304
Self-verification, 245
Sexism, 32, 41, 48, 148
   contemporary forms of, 151–152
Sexist Attitudes Towards Women Scale, 37
Sexual discrimination, 33
Shapiro, P.N., 385
Shared superordinate identity, 13
Sherif, Carolyn W., 367
Sherif, Muzafer, 1, 3, 61–62, 94, 95, 186, 229, 267, 270, 272,
     316, 365, 367
   boy's camp studies, 62, 66–70, 112
Shibutani, T., 316
Sidanius, Jim, 16, 52
Siegel, A.E., 317
Siegel, S., 317
Similarity hypothesis, 378, 379
Simple self-interest, 71, 79, 82, 84–85
   hypothesis for, 76
   models of, 72–73
Sinclair, A., 168, 171
Singer, E., 317, 333
Situational identity, 304
Skilled manual workers, 321
   job satisfaction among, 322
Slavin, R.E., 367
Smith, Brewster, 163
Smith, C.R., 317
Smith, E.R., 152
Smith, Heather, 158, 209
Smith, M.B., 317
Smith, P.M., 234
Smith, P.W., 317
Snyder, C.R., 247
Snyder, M., 38
Social aggression, 140
Social attraction, 110, 111, 115, 125, 126
   intergroup extension of hypothesis, 110
   prototype-based, 123
Social attraction-prototypicality correlation, 125
Social beliefs, 112, 123–124
Social bonds, 205
Social categorization, 5, 7, 9, 99–100, 106, 129, 175, 229,
     237, 272, 276, 319, 356, 371
   approach, 358
   conception of, 101
   salience of, 195, 272, 384
Social causality, 140–141
Social change, 96, 103–107
Social class
   objective, 317
   SDO and, 49–50
   subjective, 317
Social comparison theory, 318
Social competition, 102, 103, 104
Social conformity, 20
   anti-African prejudice and, 22t

Social construction of reality, 181
Social creativity, 104, 105
Social Darwinism, 31
Social discrimination, 188, 190
  normative constraints inhibiting, 201
  positive-negative asymmetry in, 200, 202
  underlying cognitive mechanisms of, 202
Social distance, 72
feelings, 89
Social Dominance Orientation, 16, 30–53, 49
scale, 56, 59
Social dominance theory, 3, 30, 31, 52, 53
Social evaluation, 318
Social groups, definitions of, 100
Social harmony, 353–354
Social hierarchy, 104
Social identification, 113, 248, 250, 304, 305
  relation to social attraction, 123
Social identification model, 236
Social identity, 101, 111, 142, 246, 252, 254, 299
  different levels of, 247
  insecurity of dominant groups, 106
  negative, 105, 235
  positive, 190, 200, 233
  reactions to negative or threatened, 103–104
  salient, 240
  secure, 188
  self-esteem in, 232–241
  self-evaluation through, 106
  threats to, 194
Social identity model, 305
of the crowd, 314
Social identity theory, 4, 9, 11, 52, 91–92, 110, 112, 201,
    207, 234, 254, 256, 263, 271, 273, 339
  consequences of lowered self-esteem, 257
  five stage model of intergroup relations, 339–340
  implications of group-value model, 223–225
  macrosocial analysis, 176
  motivational hypotheses in, 232
  predictions of, 255
  self-esteem explanations of, 247
  self-esteem hypothesis in, 241
Social identity/social comparison theory, 102
Social ideology, effect on crowd behavior, 314
Social influence, 9, 271
phenomena, 267
process, 305
  self-categorization as a determining factor in, 270
Social justice, 319
Social mobility, 96, 103, 105
Social norms, 186–187
  definition of, 179
Social policy attitudes, 33
Social protest, 299
Social psychology, 2
Social role and SDO, 53
Social self, 316
Social self-definition, 314
Social self-enhancement, 233
Social status, 97, 103
  relation to self-esteem, 238
Social stereotypes
  cognitive functions of, 134–137

individual values and, 137–139
Social stratification, 104, 105, 339
  ideal type, 106
  subjective aspects of, 316–319
theory, 317
Social value differentials, 137
Social values, 286
Social welfare, 33
programs, 42, 48, 57
Social-adjustment, 18
Social-facilitation theory, 303
Socialism, 32
Socially discriminative behavior, determinants of, 189
Sociocultural dimensions
  armed service, 26
  church attendance, 26
  education, 26
  political party identification, 26
  sex, 26
  social mobility, 26
Sociocultural expectations, 19
Sociocultural factors, relation to racial prejudice, 28
Sociocultural model of prejudice, 73–74
Sociological objective class, 317
Socio-political potency, 320
South Africa (see also Union of South Africa)
  racial prejudice in, 19–24
Southern political strategy, 329
Southern United States, 18–19
  racial prejudice in, 24–28
Special advantage, 167
Spector, A.J., 318
Spriggs, D., 234
Stability, 123–124
beliefs, 110
Stacey, B.G., 49
Stallybrass, Oliver, 132, 133
Standard personality variables, 34
Status, 123–125
Status hierarchies, 103–107
Status hypothesis, 378, 379
Status inconsistency theory, 318
Status quo, 150
Status recognition, 206
Stein, D.D., 317
Stephan, C.W., 384–385, 392
Stephan, W., 356
Stephan, W.G., 238, 384–385, 392
Stephenson, G.M., 239
Stereotypes, 5–6, 320
  behavior that challenges, 165
  cognitive research into, 136
  definition of, 132
  ethnic, 163
  formation and use of, 137
  group functions of, 138
  hostile, 166
  individual evaluation of social situations, 143
  individual functions of, 141
  intergroup attitudes and, 129
  mechanics of, 133
  negative, 353
  negative intergroup, 167

Stereotypes (*continued*)
  perceivers, 370
  research on change, 371
  social, 72, 132–144, 133, 139
    individual values and, 137–139
    shared nature of, 138
  social function of, 129–130
  social functions of, 133, 141
  theory of contents of, 140
  tout court, 133
  value differentials in social categorization, 136
  in Yugoslavia, 178
Stereotyping, 89, 164, 233
  cognitive processes involved in, 384
  independent measures of, 171
  negative, 82
  reliance on, 393
  scale, 72
  theories for, 142
Stern, E., 317
Stimulus valence, 195, 199
  conditions, 190, 191
  effects of, 189, 194, 200
  impact of, 188, 190
Stokes, Mayor Carl, 322
Stouffer, S.A., 318, 319
Stratification, social, 72
Stratification beliefs, 71, 82, 84–85
  hypothesis for, 77
  individual poverty, 90
  individualism, 89–90
  inequalitarianism, 90
  measures of, 81
  models, 73, 74
Strength of Cultural Background index, 259, 261 (*see also* SCB)
Subjective social class, 317
Subjective status, 123
Submergence, 303
Subordinate goals, 62
Suggested readings, 17, 63, 93, 130, 176, 231, 268, 301, 355
Sumner, W.G., 168
Super, D.E., 35
Superordinate goals, 62
  reduction of conflict and, 69–70
  reduction of intergroup conflict and, 64–70
Syllwasschy, J., 235
Symbolic racism, 148–149
  opposition to affirmative action, 153
theory, 148

Tajfel, Henri, 92, 112, 129–130, 163, 168, 169, 175, 188, 195, 232, 235, 236, 237, 239, 240, 241, 246, 254, 257, 263, 271, 304, 356, 357
Tajfel matrices, 190
Tangri, S.S., 153, 154
Task difficulty, 167
Taylor, D.M., 143, 169–170, 300, 338, 339, 340
Terror management, 230
The American Soldier, 318
The Crowd—A Study of the Popular Mind, 302
The Functions of Social Conflict, 178
The Nature of Prejudice, 19, 162–164, 171

The Psychology of Social Classes, 317
Thibaut, J.W., 166, 169, 171, 205, 206, 318
Thomas, Clarence, 37, 48
  nomination to the Supreme Court, 46–47
Thomas, K., 139
Thomson, L.J., 236
Thrasher, F.M., 66
Tile contention, 166
Tingsten, H., 321
Toch, H., 303
Tokenism, 348, 350
Tolerance, 30, 34, 45, 48
Tolerance of injustice, 339
Tri-Dimensional Sexism Scale, 37
Trustworthiness, 206
Turner, John C., 92, 112, 232, 233, 233–234, 234, 235, 236, 237, 246, 254, 271, 272, 277, 304, 356, 357, 367
Turner, R.H., 304, 313, 316
Tversky, A., 169
Tyler, Tom, 158, 176, 207, 209

Ultimate attribution error, 6, 130, 162–172
UNESCO, 65
Union of South Africa (*see also* South Africa)
  racial prejudice in, 19–24
United States, southern, 18–19
  racial prejudice in, 24–28
Upward mobility, 300, 340
  individual, 338, 339

Valence of stimuli, 195
Validity
  convergent, 44–45
  discriminant, 31, 33–35, 43–44
  predictive, 31–32
Value relevance, 233
Values Scale, altruism subscale, 37
van den Berghe, P.L., 329
van Knippenberg, A., 195
Vanneman, Reeve, 300
Vaughan, G., 106
Ventimiglia, J.C., 37
Vickers, E., 234, 235
Vinokur, A., 270, 280, 281, 283, 285
Violence, mass, 140
Voluntary contact, 383

Wade, G., 195
Wagner, U., 235, 236
Walker, L., 205, 206
Wallace, Governor George, 318, 321, 322, 324, 326, 333
Wallace phenomenon, 333–334
Wang, G., 170
Wars of Dominance, 58
  scale, 43
Wars for Humanitarian Reasons scale, 43
Watts riot, 314
Weiner, B., 167, 169
Weldon, Fay, 132
Wilder, David, 354, 356, 384, 385
Wilke, H., 195
Williams, C.J., 150
Williams, J., 195

Williams, L., 317
Willis, R.H., 317
Wilson, G.D., 51
Wilson, T, 380
Winston, Brian, 132
Winter, D.G., 43
Winter survival problem, 359
Witch-hunts, 139
Wittgenstein, L., 135
Women's rights, 48, 57
    policies, 42
Word, C.O., 150

Working class authoritarianism, 321
Wortman, C., 256
Wright, Steven, 300

Xenophobia, 49

Yorty, Samuel Mayor, 322
Young, D., 380

Zanna, M.P., 150
Zeller, E., 338
Zipf, G.K., 164